THE RESISTANCE IN WESTERN EUROPE, 1940–1945

European Perspectives

EUROPEAN PERSPECTIVES
A SERIES IN SOCIAL THOUGHT AND CULTURAL CRITICISM
Lawrence D. Kritzman, Editor

European Perspectives presents outstanding books by leading European thinkers. With both classic and contemporary works, the series aims to shape the major intellectual controversies of our day and to facilitate the tasks of historical understanding.

For a complete list of books in the series, see page 489.

The Resistance in
Western Europe,
1940–1945

Olivier Wieviorka

TRANSLATED BY

Jane Marie Todd

Columbia University Press
New York

Columbia University Press
Publishers Since 1893
New York   Chichester, West Sussex
cup.columbia.edu
Translation copyright © 2019 Columbia University Press
Une histoire de la resistance en Europe occidentale 1940–1945
copyright © 2017 Perrin, a department of Edi8
All rights reserved

Library of Congress Cataloging-in-Publication Data
Names: Wieviorka, Olivier, 1960- author. | Todd, Jane Marie, 1957– translator.
Title: The resistance in Western Europe, 1940-1945 / Olivier Wieviorka;
translated by Jane Marie Todd.
Other titles: Histoire de la résistance en Europe occidentale. English.
Description: Columbia University Press : New York, [2019] |
Includes bibliographical references and index.
Identifiers: LCCN 2019006017 | ISBN 9780231189965 (cloth : alk. paper) |
ISBN 9780231548649 (ebook)
Subjects: LCSH: World War, 1939-1945—Underground movements—Europe, Western. |
Guerrillas—Europe, Western—History—20th century. | Europe, Western—History,
Military—20th century.
Classification: LCC D802.E85 W5413 2019 | DDC 940.53/4—dc23
LC record available at https://lccn.loc.gov/2019006017

Columbia University Press books are printed on permanent and durable acid-free paper.
Printed in the United States of America

Cover design: Julia Kushnirsky
Cover art: French Resistance fighters deal with Nazi snipers © Bettmann/Getty Images

Columbia University Press gratefully acknowledges
the generous contribution to this book provided by the
Florence Gould Foundation Endowment Fund for French Translation.

For Pascale and Sophie

Contents

Foreword
Robert O. Paxton xi

List of Maps xvii
List of Abbreviations xix

Prelude: A Glowing Picture 1
I   Reinventing a Coalition 7
II   Set Europe Ablaze! 25
III   Internecine Struggles 48
IV   Ententes Cordiales? 58
V   Legitimacy at Stake 72
VI   The Dual Shock of 1941 and Its Consequences 91
VII   Coming of Age 107
VIII   Developments 126
IX   Compulsory Labor: An Opportunity or a Curse? 146
X   Mixed Results 164
XI   Taking Up Arms 178
XII   Propaganda 194
XIII   Cadres 203
XIV   Minor Maneuvers, Major Policies 224
XV   Italian Complexities 243

XVI   Planning for Liberation   256
XVII   Plans and Instructions   267
XVIII   Political Liberation   287
XIX   Action!   315
XX   Peripheries   334
XXI   Order or Chaos?   349
Epilogue   384

Acknowledgments   395
Notes   397
Bibliography   457
Index   467

Foreword

ROBERT O. PAXTON

G eneral Dwight D. Eisenhower, commander of the Allied Expeditionary Forces in Western Europe in 1944–1945, recalled afterward with gratitude how the French resistance had helped him in Normandy. It was the equivalent, he wrote, of fifteen divisions.[1] No doubt he was benevolently handing out postvictory laurels. It is in fact quite difficult to measure with precision how much the resistance contributed to Allied victory. This authoritative account by the French historian Olivier Wieviorka expertly sums up the matter.

Familiar images of the resistance are colored by dramatic scenes of midnight train derailments and parachute receptions, images derived from novels, films, and personal reminiscences that could be a bit inflated. I remember discovering at the age of ten my parents' copy of John Steinbeck's novel *The Moon Is Down* (1942). I devoured this tale of an indomitable town in a country that resembles Norway, where Nazi executions only provoked further acts of sabotage. A translation of Steinbeck's novel was published clandestinely in occupied France.[2] Other translations appeared throughout Europe, and even in the Soviet Union.

Olivier Wieviorka has not written that kind of adventure story. His book is the best survey we have of how citizens across Nazi-occupied Western Europe formed and ran clandestine resistance organizations, how these interacted with the Allied military staffs in London, and what they were able to accomplish together. The Allies welcomed these organizations and gave them money and weapons. But they feared unleashing premature risings that could end only in futile bloodshed. Above all they wished to avoid setting off the social revolutions desired by some resisters. Inevitably conflicts arose between London and the various national undergrounds on the Continent. Wieviorka explains how these conflicts were resolved in ways that made effective action possible.

Wieviorka's focus on the six occupied countries of Western Europe—France, Belgium, Holland, Norway, Denmark, and Italy—is a fruitful one. Most books about the opposition to Nazi occupation treat individual nations, and logically so, since resistance movements, striving for national liberation, were inherently national. A continental focus shows that the six nations faced problems common to all of occupied Western Europe but came up with distinctive national responses. Wieviorka's continental perspective also matches that of the Allied staffs in London who were planning to invade Hitler's Fortress Europe.

So this book is as richly informative about the Allies as about the resistance. It examines more fully than any previous work the complicated three-way negotiations among the Anglo-American authorities; the exiled governments of France, Holland, Belgium, and Norway in London; and the underground movements that together made it possible to plan and execute clandestine operations.

Wieviorka omits the anti-Hitler resistance within Germany, and quite reasonably so, for the unique moral and physical obstacles it faced made it a different story. Eastern Europe constitutes another different story. Occupation regimes there were harsher, and resistance movements were more closely related to the gigantic armed clashes of the Russian front.

Resistance movements probably had more impact in Eastern Europe than in the West. After the German invasion of the Soviet Union in June 1941, the Soviet military leadership actively encouraged partisan activity behind the German lines. Eventually some 250,000 irregulars harassed German supply lines and created a climate of insecurity in the German Army's rear. In the Yelnya-Dorogobash area (today in Belarus), all or parts of nine Germans divisions were involved in trying to suppress partisan activities in May-June 1942.[3] But even there the partisans could not by themselves change the course of the war. Elsewhere, the Polish Home Army's celebrated effort to liberate Warsaw, beginning on August 1, 1944, only to be crushed by the German Army as Soviet forces waited on the opposite bank of the Vistula River, showed once again that underground forces alone could not liberate territory. Similarly, a German decision on August 29, 1944, to occupy militarily the satellite country of Slovakia set off a rising by resistance forces that at first freed large sections of the country. In the absence of effective aid from nearby Russian forces, however, the Germans recaptured these areas by the end of October. Only the Yugoslav leader Josip Broz Tito succeeded in freeing some territory from German control in the absence of regular Allied armies. These immense and sanguinary sagas of partisan warfare in Eastern Europe remain offstage in this book, as does of course the whole Pacific dimension of World War II.

Nevertheless, the Western European resistance movements were important enough to engage the Nazi occupation authorities in intensive efforts to destroy them. Their role in the liberation and in postwar Europe was not limited to sabotage. Resisters performed other, no less dangerous and indispensable, functions. They collected and transmitted intelligence about Axis forces; countered Axis propaganda with clandestine publications and symbols, like chalking *V* for victory on walls (the occupation authorities erased fifty-five hundred of these in Lille, in northern France, on March 21, 1941); and smuggled downed Allied pilots to safety.

Resistance movements in occupied Western Europe were of course not homogeneous. They contained multiple, sometimes conflicting strands. Before Hitler's invasion of the Soviet Union on June 22, 1941, the Communist parties in these areas operated illegally underground, but they were not pro-Allied, in accordance with Stalin's scrupulous adherence to the Nazi-Soviet Pact of August 1939. Their entry into active anti-German resistance in June 1941 forms a major turning point in this story. Habituated to clandestinity, ready for sacrifice, Communists came to play a leading role in Western European resistance movements. A Communist revolution, however, was never in the cards. Joseph Stalin, in desperate straits, was more interested in an early Anglo-American landing in the West, to relieve the pressure on his front, than in promoting immediate social revolution in Western Europe.

Another turning point was the Nazi regime's decision in 1942 to draft young Western European men to work in German factories. According to conventional wisdom, this dreaded coercion sent masses of young men into remote resistance encampments, giving the resistance its first popular base. Wieviorka shows more realistically that about 15 to 20 percent of the young men who refused German labor service actually joined a maquis, or resistance encampment, perhaps thirty to forty thousand in all.

Some resistance veterans have legitimately asked whether the Allied military planners made adequate use of their potential. The professional soldiers were by temperament dubious about amateurs working underground. But having resisters on the ground destroy bridges, power plants, railway yards, and other strategic targets in the invasion zone might have been more effective and less costly in collateral damage than entrusting this task to inaccurate high-altitude bombers. Between sixty and seventy thousand French civilians died in Allied air raids on French cities and coastal fortifications between 1942 and the end of the war,[4] more than the forty-three thousand British civilians who died under the Nazi blitz. Further tens of thousands of Belgian, Dutch, and Italian civilians were killed by Allied aerial bombardment. Some targets, of course, such as the submarine pens at the French port city of Saint-Nazaire, were too solid and too tightly guarded for sabotage. Faced with a choice between sabotage and bombs, the Allied military staffs supported sabotage efforts up to a point but were ultimately unwilling to rely mostly on it.

On the rare occasions when resistance forces managed to liberate single-handedly an enclave within occupied Western Europe, Allied military support became an acute necessity. The most important of these enclaves, the Vercors plateau in the foothills of the French Alps, held out against German and Vichy forces for forty-three days in June and July 1944. It was eventually extinguished when the Allied military command decided not to airlift troops there. All such isolated enclaves were doomed before the arrival of regular Allied armies, though after Allied landings resistance units helped liberate important adjacent areas, notably in Brittany and the French Alps.

Another resistance tactic that did not work was the assassination of individual German servicemen. Resistance teams executed some German officers in France in the late summer and fall of 1941, setting off Nazi reprisals that cost hundreds of French civilians their lives without significantly aiding the Allied cause. These actions were soon abandoned in France, at the urging of Free French leader General Charles de Gaulle, and were not attempted elsewhere.

Despite some failures, the Western European resistance had important successes. One was the destruction of a heavy-water reactor in Norway, a major factor (though not the only one) in the German failure to develop an atomic bomb. Another success was the disruption of German reinforcements following the Allied landing in Normandy in June 1944. During the twelve months before D–Day, resisters destroyed 1,822 locomotives. They blew up the dam and lock at Gigny on the Saône River in July 1943 and again in November, closing to the Germans a vital river passage to the Mediterranean. And their information about Axis defenses was indispensable to the D–Day landing.

Wieviorka extends his study pertinently beyond the liberation, asking why the resistance movements had less impact on their countries' postwar political and socioeconomic systems than they had reason to expect. The exile governments in London intended, of course, to reestablish their authority at home, and while they might accept progressive reforms, they were adamantly opposed to the revolutionary transformations dreamed of by some in the resistance. Allied policy also reinforced a process of restoration.

Wieviorka concludes with a final balance sheet. The Western European resistance movements could not change the outcome of the war by themselves, without the presence of traditional armies, but they contributed significantly to Allied success. Their role was tactical, not strategic. They could probably have been better used. Wieviorka concludes that "without Anglo-American assistance, the Western European resistance would have been powerless; but the Allied intelligence services would have been blind without the resistance."

Maps

Map 2.1   The Shetland Islands   45
Map 2.2   The Lofoten Islands   46
Map 20.1   The Liberation of France and Belgium   336
Map 20.2   Military Operations in Italy   343

Abbreviations

ACC	Allied Control Commission
AFHQ	Allied Force Headquarters
AMG	Allied Military Government (Italy)
AMGOT	Allied Military Government in Occupied Territory
BBC	British Broadcasting Corporation
BCRA	Bureau Central de Renseignements et d'Action (France)
BI	Bureau Inlichtingen (Netherlands)
C	Stewart Menzies, head of the Intelligence Service (United Kingdom)
CCS	Combined Chiefs of Staff
CEPAG	Commission pour l'Étude des Problèmes d'Après-Guerre (Belgium)
CFLN	Comité Français de la Libération Nationale
CIA	Central Intelligence Agency (United States)
CID	Centrale Inlichtingsdienst (Netherlands)
CLNAI	Comitato di Liberazione Nazionale Alta Italia
CNF	Comité National Français
CLN	Comitato di Liberazione Nazionale (Italy)
CNR	Conseil national de la Résistance (France)
COI	Coordinator of Information (United States)
COMAC	Commission d'Action (du CNR) (France)
Comintern	Communist International (Soviet Union)

COS	Chiefs of Staff
COSSAC	Chief of Staff to Supreme Allied Commander
DKP	Danmarks Kommunistiske Parti (Denmark)
DMN	*Délégué militaire national* (national military delegate, France)
DMR	*Délégués militaires régionaux* (regional military delegates, France)
EIAR	Ente Italiano per le Audizioni Radiofoniche
EH	Electra House (United Kingdom)
FFI	Forces Françaises de l'Intérieur
FI	Front de l'Indépendance (Belgium)
FIS	Foreign Information Service (United States)
FN	Front National de l'Indépendance de la France
FO	Foreign Office (United Kingdom)
FTP	Francs-Tireurs et Partisans (France)
GPRF	Gouvernement Provisoire de la République Française
GS (R)	General Staff, Research (United Kingdom)
IS	Intelligence Service (United Kingdom)
JCS	Joint Chiefs of Staff (United States)
JIC	Joint Intelligence Committee (United Kingdom)
MG	Militair Gezag (Netherlands)
MI	Military Intelligence (United Kingdom)
MI (R)	Military Intelligence, Research (United Kingdom)
MUR	Mouvements unis de Résistance (France)
NBS	Nederlandse Binnenlandse Strijdkrachten (Netherlands)
NS	Nasjonal Samling (Norway)
OKW	Oberkommando der Wehrmacht (Germany)
OSS	Office of Strategic Services (United States)
OVRA	Organizzazione di Vigilanza e Repressione dell'Antifascismo (Italy)
OWI	Office of War Information (United States)
PCF	Parti communiste français
PID	Political Intelligence Department (United Kingdom)
PWD	Psychological Warfare Division (Allied command)
PWE	Political Warfare Executive (United Kingdom)
RAF	Royal Air Force (United Kingdom)
R&A	Research and Analysis (Branch) (United States)
RU	Radio Unit
SA	Secret Army (France)
SFHQ	Special Forces Headquarters (United Kingdom)

SHAEF	Supreme Headquarters, Allied Expeditionary Force
SI	Secret Intelligence (United States)
SIM	Servizio Informazione Militare (Italy)
SIS	Secret Intelligence Service (United Kingdom)
SO	Special Operations (United States)
SOE	Special Operations Executive (United Kingdom)
SR	Service de renseignements
STO	Service du travail obligatoire (France)
TNA	The National Archives (United Kingdom)
WO	War Office (United Kingdom)
X2	Counter-intelligence (United States)

Prelude

A Glowing Picture

I n April 1940 Nazi Germany, shattering the deceptive tranquility of the "phony war," attacked Scandinavia, before launching its panzers against Western Europe in early May. That blitzkrieg resulted in an unabashed success: by summer, all the principal European countries apart from Great Britain had laid down their weapons, and the swastika was flying from Brussels to Warsaw, Paris to Oslo, Prague to Amsterdam. Nazi barbarism imposed its law for five long years, plunging the Old Continent into deepest darkness.

From the outset, however, the majority of the people and their leaders rejected the false fatality of the defeat. In 1940 the heads of the Belgian, Norwegian, and Dutch states or governments reached London, anxious to keep their country in the war and to bear witness by their presence to their high regard for valiant England. Responding to the appeals of the Frenchman Charles de Gaulle, the Belgian Hubert Pierlot, and the Norwegian Johan Nygaardsvold, volunteers joined en masse to fill the ranks of the regular armies or to support the cohorts of the resistance forces who, under a ruthless occupier's yoke, feverishly awaited the arrival of the Allied troops. In all the countries subjected to the Nazis' iron rule, revolt was brewing, anticipating the moment of insurrections. London and later Washington, aware of the asset these rebels represented, assisted them without reservations and offered them the resources necessary to fight the Third Reich.

In 1943–1944 the Anglo-American forces successfully landed, first in Italy, then in France, breaking through the Wehrmacht's defenses. Everywhere, patriots assisted them, providing them with invaluable intelligence, performing bold acts of sabotage, engaging in merciless guerilla warfare. Victory crowned the sacrifices made by the GIs and the Tommies. But, to an equal extent, it marked the triumph of the women and men who, in the darkness of the underground and in the sunlight of liberation, had agreed, with complete disregard for their own survival, to shake off their chains, to hasten the triumph of democracy, and to reinstate the rule of human rights.

Revisions

That interpretation, it must be admitted, seems quite dated. Until the 1970s, however, it was considered gospel. True, it corresponded to a politics of remembrance launched during the glorious hours of the Liberation. From Belgium to the Netherlands and from France to Norway, every country extolled its internal resistance and its government in exile, pleased to emphasize the preeminent role these patriotic forces had played in the liberation of their nation. At the same time, they all minimized the role of the Allies—when they did not quite simply maintain a stony silence about it: "Paris! Paris outraged! Paris broken! Paris martyred! But Paris liberated! Liberated by itself, liberated by its people with the help of the French armies, with the support and the help of all France, of the France that fights, of the only France, of the real France, of the eternal France!" So declared Charles de Gaulle on August 25, 1944, merely saluting in one rather stingy interpolated line "our dear and admirable allies," even though it was they who had forced the Germans to beat a retreat from French territory.[1] De Gaulle was more the rule than the exception in Western Europe, and his biases were largely shared. As Pieter Lagrou points out, in the kaleidoscope of wartime experiences "resistance was crucial to the formation of a national epic. 'Being liberated' was too passive a mode to celebrate the recovery of national independence, and gratitude is a weak basis for national identity. For the three countries concerned [France, Belgium, and the Netherlands], glorification of the contribution of the resistance movements was the only basis available for a true national myth."[2] The politics of remembrance launched in 1945 therefore minimized the role of the United States and

Great Britain, while praising, but in a minor key, the excellent cooperation between the exiled powers and the British and American authorities. In Denmark, for example, resistance was for a long time viewed as a ceaselessly rising tide for which the British had simply "supplied the means."[3]

In short, resistance in Western Europe was long considered a national phenomenon that had made a remarkable contribution, both politically and militarily, to the Nazi defeat. In the same vein, the cooperation between the Anglo-Americans and the national forces—both the resistance and governments in exile—was judged exemplary, with only a few sour notes. That collaboration, under the auspices of entente rather than conflict, friendship rather than rivalry, respect rather than enmity, was said to have increased the effectiveness of subversive warfare launched in Fortress Europe in 1940.

That bright view hardly tallies with the facts, however, at least as historians grasp them. The glowing picture of Allies fighting harmoniously against the Third Reich conceals an iron law: Great Britain, the United States, and their allies, even while banking on the defeat of Nazi Germany, also defended their national interests. Again and again, that reality created tensions, which encourages us to qualify the view of an irenic alliance cloudlessly uniting Berlin's adversaries. Granted, the coalition placed under the Union Jack and the Star-Spangled Banner belonged to the present tense of a world war that had to be won at all cost, a fact that overshadowed past conflicts; but that coalition suffered as well from the bitter resentments of the interwar period and had diverging, if not opposing, notions of the world's future.

Toward a Pan-European Approach to the Resistance

As a general rule, both the politics of remembrance and the historians situate resistance within a national context, and not without reason.[4] Indeed, members of the resistance were engaged *for* and usually *in* their own countries, to hasten the departure of a reviled occupier and to restore the freedoms being flouted by the new order established by the brownshirts. By that measure, the development of underground forces depended in part on the dynamics created by the occupation and the regime imposed by the German authorities. But the army of shadows would never have been able to grow without the support first of London and then of Washington. The

Allies did not underestimate the contribution the resistance could make. The British especially dreamed of setting Europe ablaze, imagining that the people under the jackboot would revolt against their servitude. Later they returned to a more realistic approach, striving to support nascent resistance movements by creating networks and arming and equipping members of the underground.

That contribution was crucial. The Anglo-Americans provided the army of shadows with radio connections, weapons, and, more generally, the material resources they so cruelly lacked. Thanks to the British Broadcasting Corporation (BBC) airwaves, the rebels were able to popularize their battle and address their instructions to the civilian populations. The recognition granted to the exiled powers also contributed toward legitimizing a struggle that Vidkun Quisling and Philippe Pétain, for example, portrayed in the sinister colors of terrorism, if not gangsterism. National factors therefore played a notable role in the *birth* of the resistance; in its *growth,* however, the Anglo-Americans' role was clearly preeminent.

That support was certainly more complex than what people of the time—or of our own time—imagined. Parachute drops, for example, involved an arduous process, which slowed the delivery by air of men, weapons, and materiel to Fortress Europe. In the United Kingdom and the United States, the secret services had difficulty gaining a foothold. They ran up against the hesitations of the Ministry of Defense and the Foreign Office, the Department of Defense and the State Department, which all had scant belief in the possibilities of subversive warfare. And London and Washington, even as they cooperated, sometimes clashed.

The Anglo-Americans, moreover, despite the prestige of their radio broadcasts, the extent of their resources, and the strength of their finances, also had to compromise. To capitalize on the internal resistance and enjoy the support of civilians on the day of the landing, they had to secure the backing of the governments in exile, the internal resistance, and the native populations. And these forces were also defending their national and political interests. They meant to impose their views without submitting blindly to Uncle Sam or Perfidious Albion, especially since the rationale driving them was at odds with that of their backers. The aim of national resistance movements was often to protect the people from the ravages of Nazification; as a result, they opted for a defensive and civilian approach. London and Washington, by contrast, sought to take down Nazi Germany militarily, an objective that assigned a primarily offensive and combative role to the underground forces. The relations between the western part of the European continent and England and the United States were thus also marked through and through by conflicts that disrupted the cooperation established between them.

Great Britain and the United States constructed their battle on a European or even global scale, disregarding the constraints of borders. Even while situating their action within the context of particular countries—the British Special Operations Executive (SOE) privileged national divisions—they thought in global terms and engaged in constant arbitration, favoring now France, now Italy, sometimes at the expense of Denmark and Norway. In addition, they incorporated resistance into an overall military strategy. They therefore adapted the policy to be followed vis-à-vis the underground forces to that reality—a truth that the postwar powers kept quiet for the sake of patriotism and that historians, blinded by the national issues inherent in the history of resistance, too often set aside.

In short, we must leave behind four oversimplifications: first, the belief that omnipotent Allies pulled the strings of the internal resistance; second, the notion that these movements were able to develop effectively on their own; third, the idea that the need to destroy Nazism suddenly obliterated arguments based on self-interest; and fourth, the overestimation of the role of national factors in the common struggle.

The time has no doubt come to broaden our perspective by freeing ourselves from borders, in order to construct a European history of the resistance.

Such is the ambition of this book. My aim here is to better understand the actions of the underground forces in Western Europe: Norway, Denmark, the Netherlands, Belgium, France, and Italy. The choice of these six countries is not random. All experienced an occupation that, though it conformed to varied modalities and followed a specific chronology in each country, remained fundamentally different from the occupation faced by Eastern Europe or the Balkans. All belonged to the Anglo-American intervention zone: they would be liberated by the British or by U.S. troops and not by the Red Army, a fact that the military staffs quickly took to heart. In 1941, therefore, SOE stopped arming paramilitary groups in Czechoslovakia and Poland.[5] Conversely, the Soviet Union had little weight in the western theater of operations. Moscow, while striving to maintain links to Western Communist parties, did not have the logistical and material resources or the desire to aid the resistance in the West, where everyone,

Communists included, turned their eyes to Big Ben rather than the Kremlin. By contrast, British and American propaganda bureaus, secret services, and general staffs, sure that their countries' forces would land in Western Europe, set out rather quickly to define the military and political contributions that the underground in those nations ought to provide to hasten the Reich's defeat. The choice of that geographical zone is thus justified by all the points these countries had in common.

In all these Western territories, a homegrown resistance came into being. Yet the underground forces benefited from the support, even the supervision, of the Anglo-Americans, a support that greatly contributed to the form the movements would take. In this book, without claiming to write the exhaustive history of resistance in Western Europe, I wish to retrace a segment of it, by analyzing these interactions, which were certainly complex, and by inserting the history of the soldiers of shadow into the Allied grand strategy. Along the way, this book will provide an assessment of the uniqueness of each country, even while constructing—in its fashion—a first transnational history of the resistance.

CHAPTER I

Reinventing a Coalition

In the spring of 1940 Hitler went on the offensive in the western theater. To secure the Baltic and the North Sea, while guaranteeing the Reich's supply of iron ore from Sweden, which was sent through the Norwegian port of Narvik, he ordered an attack on Denmark and Norway. On April 9, after a brief campaign (it lasted only four hours), the Danes were defeated. The same day, the first detachments of the Wehrmacht landed on the Norwegian coasts and began the swift conquest of that country. France and Great Britain dispatched an expeditionary corps to Narvik, but to no avail. It was a lost cause: the Norwegians capitulated on June 10.

Other storms were brewing. On May 10, 1940, the Wehrmacht began fighting farther to the west. The Netherlands could not resist the onslaught, which forced General Henri Winkelman to capitulate on May 15. Belgium followed suit on May 28, attracting the harsh judgment of France. "And so, in the midst of battle,. . . without a glance, without a word to the French and English soldiers who, responding to his anguished call, had come to his country's rescue, King Léopold III of Belgium laid down his arms. That deed is unprecedented in history," inveighed Paul Reynaud, French prime minister at the time, in a speech that was broadcast over the radio.[1] The defection of both Belgium and the Netherlands, however, was only a miserable waypoint in the rout to come. On May 12 panzers broke through the Sedan Sector; they wasted no time crossing the Meuse River into

France and then entering Paris, which was declared an open city on June 14. Three days later Philippe Pétain, having succeeded Paul Reynaud, made inquiries about the conditions for an armistice, which was promptly signed in the Rethondes clearing on June 22. An aggravating circumstance: the Italians participated in the slaughter. Having at first decided to bide its time, Rome declared war on London and Paris on June 10, 1940, to reap the benefits of the German victory. The Franco-Italian armistice was signed near Rome on June 24. In exchange for that Judas kiss, Mussolini received only a handful of square miles on the French Riviera.

The end result of that blitzkrieg was devastating. In less than three months, the Reich had conquered Denmark, Norway, Belgium, the Netherlands, Luxembourg, and France. True, the United Kingdom escaped disaster. Operation Dynamo allowed the bulk of its expeditionary corps to evacuate Dunkirk between May 26 and June 3, 1940. And, under the firm authority of Winston Churchill, resident of 10 Downing Street beginning on May 10 of the same year, the United Kingdom resisted the siren call for peace with Germany, advocated by some senior figures united behind their mentor, Foreign Secretary Lord Halifax. But such consolations gave England very little advantage. Despite the cooperation offered by the Commonwealth of Nations, it suddenly found itself without major allies on the Continent.

In Quest of Allies

The abrupt collapse of France in 1940 "came as a devastating shock" for Great Britain.[2] London, counting on a long war, had in great part relied on the Entente Cordiale. Its French ally, backed by the British expeditionary corps, would resist the Wehrmacht's blows on the ground. The few weeks the United Kingdom would thereby gain would allow it to mobilize its empire's resources and deploy its two assets: its fleet and, to a lesser extent, the Royal Air Force (RAF). Germany's unexpected victory invalidated that scenario, leaving the United Kingdom alone to wage the fight. London had at all costs to rethink its system of alliances. It was a vast program. In accordance with the German-Soviet Non-Aggression Pact, the Soviet Union, for the time being, had joined its fate to that of Nazi Germany; and the United States, despite the friendship it shared with its former suzerain, still embraced a splendid isolationism, which Franklin Roosevelt did not intend to give up. American public opinion was opposed to any intervention in Europe, at a time when the ink on the Treaty of Versailles had only just dried.

In that desolate landscape, the support of allies, however modest, proved crucial. On one hand, London feared that Berlin's unabashed victories would send the neutral countries into the Axis camp. That fear was not unfounded. Francoist Spain and its very Germanophile minister of foreign affairs, Ramón Serrano Súñer, considered allying themselves with Germany—an eventuality neutralized by the glacial meeting at Hendaye between the Führer and El Caudillo on October 23, 1940. The Balkans represented a more serious risk. Bucharest, neutral and with Anglophile leanings, fell to the pressure of Moscow, which, in stripping it of Bessarabia and Northern Bukovina, sent it rushing into Berlin's arms. Romania joined the Axis in November 1940, followed in March 1941 by Bulgaria. There was a risk, therefore, that the Nazi victory would lead, in a domino effect, to the defection of the neutral countries. If recognized leaders were to come to London, Britain could contain its losses by sending a clear signal to all the capital cities: the war was continuing.

The British authorities had a lucid assessment of the risk of maintaining legitimate and legal authorities in Fortress Europe. On June 24, 1940, Winston Churchill, referring to France, described the sequence of events that would send Philippe Pétain spiraling down into collaboration. Pétain's government, Churchill concluded, was under German control, and the French "would allow all their resources to fall into the hands of the enemy and to be used against their former allies. . . . The Germans would put every form of pressure upon the French Government to act to our detriment. The French Government would be drawn more and more into making common cause with Germany."[3] The British prime minister saw things clearly: that was precisely Hitler's calculation, which the Führer unveiled to a dumbfounded Mussolini at the meeting in Munich on June 18, 1940. "One had to be sure that the partner in the negotiations was a functioning French government on national soil, an eventuality much preferable to the prospect of leaders rejecting the German proposal and going to England."[4] For the United Kingdom, then, keeping legitimate authorities in Fortress Europe posed a great risk, that of inducing countries to serve the Reich. Conversely, the imposition of puppet—hence unpopular— regimes would ill-serve the occupier's interests and might even turn civilians against their masters, swelling the ranks of the resistance.

These reflections led London to use every means possible to ensure that the heads of states and of governments would come to the British capital. That hope was very often dashed.

New Alliances?

A cursory glance might lead one to distinguish Denmark and Vichy France—the only legal states functioning in Fortress Europe—from the other nations, whose leaders supposedly went spontaneously to England to pursue the fight against Nazi Germany. Is it necessary to point out that such a rapid appraisal would not do justice to the bewildering complexity of the itineraries followed in Western Europe in 1940?

The succession of defeats led to many upheavals. In Norway, Vidkun Quisling, head of the homegrown Nazi Party, the Nasjonal Samling (NS, National Union), announced in a speech broadcast over the radio on April 9, 1940, that he was forming a government and assuming its presidency. But King Haakon VII refused to recognize that bid for power. The Germans, aware of Quisling's unpopularity, withdrew their support for him and decided to administer the country directly. They appointed Josef Terboven, a former SA (stormtrooper) renowned for his brutality, to be Reichskommissar of Norway, with the power to exercise "the rights of governance."[5] But Berlin had not entirely given up the idea of forming a legal government, a scheme that came close to being realized.

With the arrival of the German troops, King Haakon and his cabinet had left Oslo to take refuge in Hamar, north of the capital, then in Elverum, near the Swedish border, before reaching Tromsø in the northern part of the country. On June 7 His Majesty and the cabinet set off for England on the cruiser *Devonshire*. That patriotic gesture, far from being hailed by the elites and the population, was judged harshly. The people believed they had been abandoned by their rulers; the soldiers cursed the incompetence of their leaders, who had led them into battle with obsolete weapons; and, in the eyes of many Norwegians, the defeat of France seemed to confirm the ineffectiveness of democratic regimes. In unison, the modest Norwegian Communist Party, standing firm on Moscow's line, demanded peace and collaboration with Berlin and, for good measure, called for the abdication of the king and the formation of a government founded on workers, farmers, and fishers.[6] In short, the refusal to accept defeat by no means gave rise to vibrant enthusiasm, as the Germans were fully aware.

They therefore leapt into the breach. On June 13 Josef Terboven convoked Parliament (the Storting) in order to relieve Haakon VII of his duties, dismiss the government of Prime Minister Johan Nygaardsvold, and appoint a new cabinet. In exchange, the Reichskommissar promised to step aside and let the Norwegians freely govern themselves. On June 14 the Storting informed the king of that plan via the British legation to Stockholm. Noting that the executive had left the country, the Parliament suggested that a Council of State (Riksråd) exercising plenary powers be named, that the Nygaardsvold government be forced to resign, and that the impossibility of the sovereign to exercise his "constitutional functions" be duly noted.[7]

The reply was not long in coming. On July 3 Haakon VII announced in a message that he refused to sanction a resolution passed by the Storting "under such circumstances." It should be noted that this move came at great cost to him, since he greatly feared that, in committing himself so unwaveringly, he would unbind himself from the legal framework.[8] On August 26, however, he held firm, reminding listeners on BBC radio that, had he remained in Norway, the "present rulers of the country would have been able to force us to accept what they wished."[9] The Germans did not admit defeat. In August the four main parties of the kingdom accepted a truce, and in September they resumed negotiations with the Reichskommissar. The talks hit a snag: the parties refused to name a member of the Nasjonal Samling, Quisling's Nazi group, to the Ministry of Justice. The Reich broke off negotiations. On September 25 Terboven announced that a Riksråd composed of thirteen members, nine of them belonging to the NS, would govern the country under the leadership of its Kommissariat; immediately afterward, all political parties were outlawed, with the notable exception of Quisling's group.[10] By September 1940 the German authorities harbored few illusions. The military commander concluded that, "with the exception of the . . . NS all other organizations and parties, and particularly the representatives of big business and industrials remain, now as before, *pro-English* and consequently *anti-German*. . . . The Norwegian people and their former leaders are at present in no position to adapt themselves to the political situation, and to fulfil the demands of the *New Era*."[11]

Thus, in the turbulent months between April and September, Norway did not escape the fevers of the defeat. Part of the political staff coolly considered forcing Haakon VII to abdicate, as a way to find a modus vivendi with Nazi Germany. The king himself hesitated. Even while displaying a fervent patriotism, he balked at the idea of leaving his country. Granted, he believed that the Allies would ultimately win the victory; but, in view of the situation, he judged for some time that Norway had to do business with Germany. It was therefore not until June 5 that he agreed to go to England, and he did so "under strong British pressure."[12] Above all, the line between loyalty and collaboration was drawn at a late date—after September 25, 1940.[13]

The Choices Made by the Dutch

The situation in the Netherlands proved equally complex. On May 13, 1940, two days *before* the surrender, Queen Wilhelmina had set off for England on the HMS *Hereward*. Juliana, the heir presumptive, and her two daughters were sent to Canada as a precaution, to preserve the future of the dynasty in case of a British defeat. Wilhelmina's cabinet later joined her in piecemeal fashion, by air or sea. But that patriotic movement veiled tensions and ulterior motives.

The queen, who had been on the throne since 1898, was persuaded that she, more than her ministers, embodied the Netherlands. She also intended to reestablish the rights of the Crown, which, she believed, had been unjustly chipped away at since the nineteenth century. She was close to military circles and passionate about questions of national defense. The historian Louis de Jong notes that it would no doubt be going too far to "describe her in 1940 as an embittered woman, but without a doubt she was deeply frustrated." In other words, trust hardly held sway between the head of state—anxious to extend her prerogatives—and the ministers, who wished to limit them. The case should not be overstated, however. The war smoothed out prewar conflicts, in favor of a categorical imperative: defeat the Reich. And the system of governance required compromise. The queen could influence decisions, which, in the absence of Parliament, now took the form of decrees submitted for the royal countersignature; but she could not act alone, because the agreement of the government was required for such decisions.[14] In any event, the war expanded the range of possibilities, allowing for a reassessment of the place of the monarchy in the operation of Dutch institutions, a revision that Wilhelmina doubtless ardently desired.

Some leaders, moreover, far from taking a hawkish position, called for coming to terms with Nazi Germany. In May 1940 the fervent Calvinist Hendrikus Colijn, head of the Anti-Revolutionaire Partij (Anti-Revolutionary Party)—a Protestant, antiliberal group—and five-time prime minister, called on General Winkelman, commander in chief of the armed forces, to form a government that Colijn would head, in order to conclude a peace judged inevitable. Vituperating against the government from May 15, 1940, on—"such a great mistake that we cannot yet evaluate its effects"—in June Colijn published *Op de grens van twee werelden* (On the border of two worlds), a diatribe in which he demanded that his country submit to the *lex germanica* even while preserving its sovereignty and its monarch, that it take the Nazi system as its model while renouncing any independent diplomacy and accepting close economic collaboration. On July 1 the leaders of the six major Dutch parties met in The Hague to create a national bloc able to enter into dialogue with the occupier. From June 24 to 28 talks were conducted with Generalkommissar Schmidt, but they were broken off: the German victors did not agree to the claims to Dutch independence or accept the proclaimed loyalty to the House of Orange. A movement known as Nederlandse Unie (Dutch Union) was nevertheless launched; it attracted some 800,000 adherents by February 1941, undoubtedly as a result of its ambivalent program. Because its ambition was to overcome prewar divisions, and because it positioned itself against the Dutch Nazi Party, there was good reason to consider the union the instrument of Batavian patriotism. At the same time, it supported voluntary labor in Germany and excluded Jews from its ranks, even while refusing to support the crusade against Bolshevism launched on June 22, 1941. That ambivalence ultimately grew tiresome. On May 13, 1941, Reichskommissar Arthur Seyss-Inquart, an Austrian Nazi famous for having set the Anschluss in motion, ordered the union's dissolution. Nevertheless, the venture suggested that the temptation of pacifism, if not of collaboration, did not spare either senior leaders or a substantial fringe of the population.[15]

It even enticed some ministers who had taken refuge in London. Prime Minister Dirk Jan de Geer, profoundly defeatist, believed that the war was lost and proposed sounding out the Führer about the possibility of a compromise peace.[16] In August 1940 the queen abruptly remedied the situation. Informing de Geer that he no longer enjoyed her confidence, she asked him to resign and called on Pieter Sjoerds Gerbrandy, a lower-ranking leader of the Anti-Revolutionaire Partij and minister of justice at the time, to succeed him. De Geer then asked to join a mission leaving for Indonesia, but once he arrived in Portugal, he deserted and, despite his promise, returned to the Netherlands with the agreement of the Germans.[17] That was no great loss for the British, who had considered him only a "makeshift" solution.[18] In any event, despite the narrow range of her constitutional prerogatives, Wilhelmina had twice played a decisive role: by refusing to be the plaything of the Germans and by demanding De Geer's departure. By no means, however, did her alignment with Great Britain cement a consensus. As we have seen, even within the cabinet not everyone opted for that position, and many political figures who had remained in their captive nation rejected it. But at least the queen and the government in exile spoke with a single voice, which was far from the case for Belgium.

Belgian Contradictions

When German troops entered Belgian territory, King Léopold III and the government under Hubert Pierlot's leadership seemed to be working in close harmony. True to his ancestors' example, the king, as in 1914, had insisted on leading his armies in person. Very quickly, however, defeat loomed, presenting the kingdom's leaders with an impossible choice: Should the war be pursued or not? The majority of ministers leaned in favor, for both moral and strategic reasons: they did not want to break the brotherhood-in-arms that united them to France and the United Kingdom, and they believed that the Allies would win the victory. "The war is not over. Neither England nor France is resolved to capitulate, and if Germany does not have a decisive victory within a few weeks, it will be beaten," wrote Paul-Henri Spaak, minister of foreign affairs, to his king on May 26, 1940. The government therefore judged that Léopold III needed "at all cost to escape in time the danger of being taken prisoner: whatever the course of events and so long as the Allied powers continue the fight, the fact of Belgium's existence must be asserted through the preservation and activity of the state's essential organs."[19] The British went even further. On May 24 the Foreign Office (FO) sent a message to the Belgian ambassador, emphasizing that London was "deeply impressed with the necessity, from an international point of view, of maintaining the King and the Belgian Government in a place of safety."[20]

The king defended a radically different point of view. As commander in chief, he thought that "it would be desertion to abandon" his country; he therefore had to share "the fate of his soldiers" and his people. That noble-minded preoccupation veiled less altruistic calculations. Even before the outbreak of hostilities, Léopold had conducted a personal policy: adopting toward "political leaders and ministers the tone of a dissatisfied magister . . . he admonished them regarding the malfunctioning of the institutions."[21] He also relied more on his advisers, who had no political responsibilities, than on his ministers, even though they were royalists. And, by inclination, he favored a policy of strict neutrality that gave the de facto advantage to Germany.

It was not long before the conflict between the Royal Palace of Laeken and the government erupted. Between May 18 and 25, 1940, the ministers decided to leave Belgium for France. In response, the king attempted to dismiss them and to form a cabinet headed by the Socialist dissident Henri de Man, famous for having called for a rift with Marxism and the adoption of central planning in the prewar period. That maneuver failed: it required a countersignature, which the ministers refused to give. On May 28 the Belgian army surrendered, and the king was handed over to the Germans. The Council of Ministers, following Hubert Pierlot, had taken refuge in France to continue the fight with the remnants of the Belgian forces that had retreated to that country. On the day of the surrender, it adopted a legislative order that certified the king's incapacity to rule and released officers and civil servants from their loyalty oath but did not force Léopold to abdicate.[22] That legislative order invoked article 82 of the constitution, which stipulated that if the king was prevented from governing, his powers would be transmitted to the cabinet. That was a somewhat improper interpretation, in that the article in question concerned mental incapacity and not a foreign domination that turned the king into a prisoner. Nonetheless, after meeting in Limoges on May 31, senators and representatives, a significant minority of whom were present (54 out of 167 for the Senate, 89 out of 202 for the Chamber of Representatives), unanimously supported that position.

At the same time, the cabinet avoided fanning the fire of discord. On July 21, 1940 (the Belgian national holiday), a public declaration requested that the "thought prevailing among all Belgians be that of national union around the king"[23]—a line consistently defended subsequently. A year later, a proclamation broadcast over the BBC again noted that "the fight is not over. The king, a prisoner, sustains our spirit and revives our courage by virtue of his presence. He is the symbol of passive resistance, the very image of Belgium, captive but not conquered."[24]

The spirit of resistance had collapsed in June, in view of the tragic situation that France was facing. On June 18 a council met in Bordeaux, in a "wretched, smoky, dirty" room, "with a kitchen table and a few chairs. Some ministers were sitting on crates or on a window ledge. Defeat was physically present."[25] Although Marcel-Henri Jaspar, Albert De Vleeschauwer, and Camille Gutt argued for leaving for England, the majority wanted to throw in the towel. A telegram sent to the king on June 18 reflected their distraught state: "The government will resign as soon as the fate of the Belgian soldiers in France and the refugees is resolved, in order to facilitate the likely peace negotiations between Germany and Belgium."[26] In the same vein, the idea of coming to terms with the Reich was gaining strength. On June 24, 1940, Belgian minister of foreign affairs Spaak wrote to his French counterpart:

As soon as the armistice between France and Germany goes into effect, I would be most grateful if you would let the German government know that the Belgian government is anxious to be in contact with it, in order to negotiate . . . questions relative to the Belgian officers, soldiers, and civilians in France. The Belgian government is also ready to negotiate the conditions for an armistice between Germany and Belgium, but, before taking that path, it believes it is indispensable to make contact with the king in Brussels and to that end asks for safe conduct for two of its members.[27]

Spaak confessed after the fact: "I cannot and do not want to hide . . . errors. For several weeks after the French defeat we thought the war was over. We believed ourselves completely beaten and bereft of authority to pursue the struggle."[28]

That scenario fell apart, however. Hitler rejected safe conduct for the Belgian ministers, and the king, embracing his splendid isolation, ruled out any contact with men who had handed him over for trial and prevented him from making the changes in the executive power he wanted. In early

July the vast majority of Belgian government officials went to Vichy and again attempted to negotiate with the Führer, but in vain. In his instructions of July 17, 1940, the German dictator persisted: "Any attempt by Belgian authorities to enter into relations with us must therefore be rejected."[29]

Even before that obstruction, several ministers had considered going to London. On June 18 Marcel-Henri Jaspar, the young Liberal minister of public health (he was thirty-nine at the time), had set off for England, and on the 23rd he delivered a speech on the BBC that echoed General de Gaulle's famous appeal: "As a serving minister whose mandate, with which I was legally vested, no one can contest, I am pursuing the war. . . . May the Belgians of Congo hear my appeal and my voice. Officers, NCOs, soldiers, come join me. Destroy your weapons and your ammunition, if you must. . . . Captains of ships and sailors, leave the French ports and proceed to a port of the British empire. . . . It is not time for tears, but for action. . . . Death before slavery! God will protect Belgium and its Allies."[30] His colleagues, far from responding to that injunction, disapproved of it, condemning what they took for desertion of his post and a breach of ministerial solidarity, saying that he had left "for reasons of 'personal convenience.'"[31] On June 24 a decree in the form of a legislative order relieved Jaspar of his duties, but without removing him from office, since that power lay with the king.

The cabinet, by contrast, displayed a certain imagination. On June 18 a decree entrusted to Albert De Vleeschauwer the mandate of "administrator general of the colony of the Belgian Congo and Ruanda-Urundi." It was a clever maneuver: it deprived the king of his powers over Belgium's overseas possessions. The minister of colonies "became absolute master in the Congo, with no limits on his powers but with utter respect for legal formalities."[32] That placed a colony considered, because of its wealth, a "geological scandal" (in the famous expression of the geologist Jules Cornet) in the service of the United Kingdom. Courtesy of Aristides de Sousa Mendes, Portuguese consul in Bordeaux, De Vleeschauwer was able to leave France and reach England via Lisbon. His mandate, however, remained unclear. His colleagues most likely hoped he would defend the colony against British appetites—and not without reason. On June 18, 1940, an exasperated Winston Churchill had asked Alexander Cadogan, permanent undersecretary for foreign affairs, to make "the most strenuous effort . . . to rally the Belgians to their duty. There can be no question of their going out of the war. If they do, we will wash our hands of their interests altogether, and they must clearly understand that their colonies will not be allowed to form part of the German system as long as we can prevent this by sea action. Have steps been taken by the Admiralty to lay forcible hands on all Belgian shipping within our reach?"[33] Foreign Secretary Halifax, responding to that appeal and supported by Cartier de Marchienne, the shrewd Belgian ambassador to London, declared at the BBC microphone on June 20, 1940, that, should Belgium desert, His Majesty's government would no longer guarantee the independence of that country and would prevent its colonies from supporting the Reich. That was one way to oblige its cabinet to cross the Channel.

Albert De Vleeschauwer was not taken in. An ardent patriot, he intended above all to pursue the fight alongside England. He therefore became keeper of the resistance flame, even though nothing predestined that Catholic and royalist Fleming to play such a role. After obtaining a portfolio in May 1938, he had been skewered by the newspaper *Pourquoi pas*: "His trousers were falling crooked; his morning coat, already discouraged, was sagging; and above it all was a bushy head topped by an idiotic hat, which proved that, in the De Vleeschauwer family, there has been a spirit of thrift for several generations."[34]

On July 5 Marcel-Henri Jaspar, along with the Socialist Camille Huysmans, had tried to form a "Belgian government in London," but the attempt had failed because of the opposition to Jaspar and Huysmans mounted by Ambassador Cartier de Marchienne and Minister of Colonies Albert De Vleeschauwer.[35] Vleeschauwer therefore tried to prevail on his colleagues to come to the British capital and form a different government.

On July 30 Camille Gutt, minister of finance, received from the cabinet the right to leave France to assist the minister of colonies in settling the problems pending with Great Britain. But Churchill found that a rather skimpy catch. He demanded that Spaak (at Foreign Affairs) and Pierlot (the prime minister) also take the path of exile. On August 22 their colleagues gave the two men clearance. Pierlot, however, took great care to demand their resignation, to avoid the advent of a countervailing power.

Spaak and Pierlot's trip was no walk in the park. The two men left Vichy on August 24, but the French State initially rejected their request for an exit visa. Then the Spanish authorities refused to let them in. For three days they had to camp in no-man's-land, near the village of La Jonquera, drinking from a public fountain as best they could. They were subsequently allowed to go to Girona, then to Barcelona, but were placed under house arrest. They dreamed of stealing away. On October 18 they managed a narrow escape, thanks to the Belgian consul, Marc Jottard, and a van with a secret compartment, "just large enough for two people, installed behind the driver's seat." It must have been a painful ordeal, given that both men were noted for their corpulence. Spaak recounted, "Almost immediately M. Pierlot took out his rosary and, having made sure I had no objection, began to say his prayers. Not only did I readily agree but I remember that I myself, in my hearts of hearts, called upon all the gods and prophets that I could think of, including Mohammed, Confucius and Buddha. I took the view that if I was going to take out an insurance policy at all I might as well have maximum cover."[36]

Providence was watching over them. Their guards, soccer fans, were attending a match on the big day, leaving the two men unattended. The next day, which fell on a Sunday, the guards believed that Spaak and Pierlot were at Mass, taking Communion; alerted to the contrary at two o'clock in the afternoon, the police chief, absorbed in a bullfight, did not react. The alarm thus went out belatedly, which allowed the two to cross the Portuguese border without incident. On October 24 Spaak and Pierlot took off from Lisbon in a seaplane, which delivered them to Bournemouth, on the southern coast of England.

After many ups and downs, therefore, a government in exile represented Belgium at war. But it had no spark, and the British had little regard for it. "The Belgians were . . . perceived as second-rate allies, whose attitude had not been clear and who were accorded only limited confidence."[37] Above all, heavy threats loomed. The ministers who had remained in France refused to budge, including Paul-Émile Janson, though he was Paul-Henri Spaak's uncle. They remained deaf to the appeal launched by Pierlot on January 21, 1941. Perhaps they were hoping to be called back to power by the king, once a peace agreement had been reached. In any event, the government's base was narrow, to say the least: because Jaspar was excluded, it was limited to four men in all, which alarmed the British authorities: "Originally a National Government, it has lost its national character," Lord Halifax noted.[38] Increasing its numbers proved impossible. The king, moreover, represented a threat. In refusing to choose exile, he amputated a part of the legitimacy of the government in London. And in remaining with his subjects, he created a conflict of loyalty: Whom should the citizens now obey? The same cruel dilemma—other things being equal—was tearing apart France.

The Birth of Free France

France did not escape the turbulence of that portentous year. Prime Minister Paul Reynaud, realizing the disaster and overwhelmed by the events, submitted his resignation on June 16, 1940, to French president Albert Lebrun. The next day Philippe Pétain succeeded him as head of the government. Wasting no time, his plenipotentiaries signed the armistice conventions with Germany on June 22. Pétain obtained plenary powers from the National Assembly that met in Vichy on July 10, as well as the right to draft a new constitution. The Victor of Verdun baldly displayed his ambitions. Persuaded of the German victory, he set out to build, in the shadow of the swastika, an authoritarian, anti-Semitic, corporatist, and clerical regime that would break with the ideals of the French Revolution and the principles of the Republic.

One man, however, rejected the misleading self-evidence of the defeat. Charles de Gaulle, undersecretary of war, flew to London at nine o'clock in the morning on June 17. "There was nothing romantic or difficult about the departure," he would write.[39] Immediately upon his arrival, and after receiving the green light from Churchill, the Rebel, as he was known, launched his appeal on June 18, inviting "the French officers and soldiers located in British territory, or who might come to be here," as well as "engineers and specialized workers in the armaments industries," to join him and continue the fight. That visionary text, in sharp contrast to the morose resignation of Philippe Pétain, declared that the war, far from being confined to the eternal face-off between France and Germany, was global in scope. By that measure, the armistice was a crime: in withdrawing France from the conflict, it prohibited the country from sitting at the victors' table when the day came. On these premises, Charles de Gaulle constructed a two-part plan of action. He "picked up the broken sword," so that, insofar as he was able, France could participate in the Allied effort; and he built on British soil a state whose valor would ultimately allow it to seize the legitimacy in which the Vichy regime had draped itself. By contrast, the appeal did not urge the French in the metropolis to fight, a sign that, for the moment, de Gaulle was indifferent to subversive warfare. Similarly, he did not clarify his status: Was he acting as a general or as the head of a government?

De Gaulle did have lofty ambitions, however, and he was proposing to form a government, as the speech he wanted to deliver on June 19 confirmed.

The government of France, having capitulated, is in the enemy's power. It no longer represents the French Nation. All is not lost, however. A new government composed of free men, worthy representatives of the French people, was immediately constituted in London in complete independence. It will take the country's fate in hand.

People of France!

Enormous resources are still at our disposal in our North Africa and in our colonies. We have powerful allies. We will fight. We will prevail.

As soon as the new government is constituted, it will make a declaration.[40]

The Rebel was no doubt rushing things somewhat. To be sure, as a former member of the Reynaud cabinet, he retained a remnant of legitimacy. So as not to jeopardize the future, moreover, he came round to the arguments of Georges Mandel, minister of the interior at the time, who begged him not to resign. "In any case we are only at the beginning of a world war. You will have great duties to fulfil, General! But with the advantage of being, in the midst of all of us, an untarnished man. Think only of what has to be done for France, and consider that, in certain circumstances, your present position makes things easier for you."[41] On June 19, however, the situation was not stable, at least as seen from London. France had not yet initialed the armistice conventions; the *Massilia* passenger liner, which would ferry to North Africa twenty-seven members of Parliament determined to continue the fight, had not yet been fitted out—it did not lift anchor until June 21. And finally, Philippe Pétain had not yet been vested with plenary powers. On June 24 Charles Corbin, the French ambassador, warned Lord Halifax, the British foreign secretary, against constituting a French national committee. "He said that we were giving support to a National Committee which had not yet been formed. In French eyes this Committee constituted on British soil with British support would not appear any more independent than the Bordeaux Government. The establishment of a Government in North Africa would be a different matter, but one formed in Great Britain, without representative interests, would fail, and no one would pay attention to it."[42] The British authorities therefore judged General de Gaulle's request premature and denied him permission to form a government.

In fact, they were torn. On one hand, they supported the Man of June 18, whose resolve and steadfastness inspired their full confidence. On June 28

London recognized "General de Gaulle as the leader of all free Frenchmen, wherever they may be, who rally to him in support of the Allied cause."[43] On August 7, 1940, an agreement spelled out the terms of that recognition. De Gaulle received the command of the French forces and was granted the right to create the civil bodies necessary for "the organization of force." The British agreed to finance the movement, Paris being responsible for reimbursing, on the day of victory, the money spent—a debt de Gaulle honored.[44]

On the other hand, London was hesitant to break all ties with Vichy. Although Churchill harbored few illusions about Pétain, he did not want to jeopardize the future and hoped that prominent commanders—General Maxime Weygand, for example—would sooner or later join the freedom camp. The British government was also alarmed at the fate of the French fleet and would have liked to see the number of its squadrons increased. On July 3, 1940, the prime minister took things into his own hands. Via Admiral James Somerville, he proposed that the French ships rally, that they scuttle themselves or head for British, American, or French ports in the West Indies. Faced with the refusal of Admiral Marcel Gensoul, he ordered an attack on the squadron anchored at the Mers el-Kebir base in Algeria, near Oran. That grim episode caused a break in diplomatic relations between Britain and France. But Winston Churchill kept two irons in the fire. Even while supporting his "Cross of Lorraine" (that is, de Gaulle), he was treating the Victor of Verdun with consideration: a neutral France, in his view, was still preferable to a France that closely linked its own fate to the Reich's fortunes. That calculation also inspired the British strategy toward Denmark.

Danish Ambivalence

The Kingdom of Denmark, invaded on April 9, 1940, had surrendered the same day, but until 1943 its legal situation remained irregular, to say the least. War had not officially been declared—and never would be. Furthermore, Denmark held on to its institutions: its king, its government, even its army. The Reich confined itself to exerting discreet control via a plenipotentiary minister, Cecil von Renthe-Fink.[45] That state of affairs plunged the British authorities into deep perplexity. Even while indulging in unflattering comparisons with courageous Norway, they hesitated:

Should Denmark be considered an enemy or treated like an obstructed ally?[46] The latter hypothesis appeared to be validated by the pro-Ally sentiments of the ruler, Christian X—the brother, it should be noted, of King Haakon VII. These hesitations dissipated only at a late date. They attest to the complexity of the situations the British authorities had to manage.

All in all, the collapse of the United Kingdom's coalition led it to favor the rallying of legitimate authorities. It did not compromise on that principle, even as it accepted the fact that the defeated armies had surrendered. On May 15, 1940, Lord Halifax explained to Eelco Van Kleffens, Dutch minister of foreign affairs, that he understood his country's capitulation, but that it was "essential that a state of war should continue between the Netherlands and Germany; therefore the Commander-in-Chief must not negotiate or co-operate with the Germans, but merely accept their terms under protest."[47] That imperative led London to exert strong pressure on the Belgian and Dutch authorities to cross the Channel without delay.

That clear line, however, was imposed only with difficulty. A fringe of Western European leaders, persuaded that the German victory was ineluctable, threatened to give in to the Nazi siren call and negotiate their place in the New Order. Others believed that duty obliged them to share their people's suffering. Léopold III, for example, dissociated himself from his government, and the Dutch prime minister, though living in London, preferred to throw in the towel. Under these tragic circumstances, marked by extreme confusion, the standing of these leaders proved essential. Many decisions affecting the future were made by individuals, whether Queen Wilhelmina or General de Gaulle. The historical lottery was unfair, however. Although de Gaulle set out to fulfill his destiny, De Vleeschauwer remained relatively anonymous.

These contrasting attitudes caused alarm: they undermined the legitimacy of the powers in exile. Although that question was not pertinent for the Dutch and Norwegian authorities, it arose in stark terms for the Belgian leaders, reduced to a very small number and facing hostility from their king. And what is there to say about General de Gaulle, whose stars gleamed with a faint light compared to the aura possessed by Marshal Pétain?

Ultimately, the status of the governments in exile was ambiguous. Were they cobelligerents, wholeheartedly supporting the British war effort? Or did they, under painful circumstances, represent their people and serve as their interpreters? Should they sacrifice their sovereignty or defend it tooth and nail against the encroachments of the United Kingdom? These questions would punctuate the five years of war and give rise to many tensions, particularly since nothing guaranteed that the people under the jackboot would take these émigrés to be legitimate powers. For the moment, however, Great Britain faced other perils: it had to develop a military strategy to defeat the Reich.

CHAPTER II

Set Europe Ablaze!

I n 1940 the United Kingdom faced a disastrous military situation. Waging battle alone, it could not, for the time being, depend on any major ally outside its empire. France had laid down its arms; the Soviet Union favored entente with the Reich; and the United States was hewing to its neutralist line. To be sure, the Battle of Britain, between August and October 1940, had saved the kingdom. The losses inflicted on the Luftwaffe were considerable: twenty-three hundred of its aircraft had been destroyed. Berlin, unable to control air and sea, had to abandon its plans to invade England in autumn 1940, which averted the specter of a British defeat. But though the war was not lost, nothing guaranteed London's victory. The choices that presented themselves in 1940 were limited. The British general staff, unable to consider a return to continental Europe—an unrealistic option given its weak ground forces—privileged a strategy of attrition. By attacking within peripheral theaters of operation (North Africa and the Middle East, for example), it hoped to bleed the enemy while capitalizing on its own principal advantages: the Royal Air Force and the Royal Navy. That hope was cruelly dashed. Although British troops initially defeated the Italian forces in Cyrenaica, they were badly beaten in Crete (May 1941), and in Libya they came up against General Erwin Rommel, an adversary far tougher than Marshal Rodolfo Graziani.

In that context, subversive warfare was an especially promising option, given that a few pioneers had not waited for London's injunction to take action, concealing weapons here, creating modest underground news-sheets there. In urging the people under the jackboot to revolt, in carrying out multiple sabotage operations in Fortress Europe, and in instigating guerilla movements, Great Britain would produce—there was no doubt about it—the collapse of the Third Reich.

Wagering on Subversive Warfare

That optimistic assertion rested on solid precedents. The nineteenth and early twentieth centuries had shown that David sometimes prevailed over Goliath, a lesson that Hugh Dalton, minister of economic warfare, thought deeply about.

> We have got to organize movements in enemy-occupied territory comparable to the Sinn Fein movement in Ireland, to the Chinese Guerillas now operating against Japan, to the Spanish Irregulars who played a notable part in Wellington's campaign or—one might as well admit it—to the organizations which the Nazis themselves have developed so remarkably in almost every country in the world. This "democratic international" must use many different methods, including industrial and military sabotage, labour agitation and strikes, continuous propaganda, terrorist acts against traitors and German leaders, boycotts and riots.[1]

That analysis juxtaposed four historical referents. It evoked, first, the successes enjoyed by irregular combatants in recent conflicts. During the Napoleonic campaigns (1808–1813), guerillas had inflicted heavy losses on the emperor's soldiers. An identical scenario played out during the Second Boer War in South Africa (1899–1902) and during the struggle for independence waged by the Irish Republican Army (1919–1921). In the same vein, the Spanish Civil War (1936–1939) and the battle, begun in 1937, pitting the Kuomintang and the People's Liberation Army against Japanese troops confirmed that soldiers without uniforms could get the better of regular armies.

World War I had also proven that economics now played a decisive role in the conduct of operations. In 1918 the Allied blockade had precipitated the collapse of the home front and had led Berlin to lay down its arms.

Striking at the enemy's potential for industrial growth would thus bring victory; all the protagonists understood from the outset that industrial capacities would play a decisive role in that total war.[2] Such, at least, was the projection made in September 1939 by Neville Chamberlain, prime minister at the time. "But what I hope for is not a military victory—I very much doubt the feasibility of that—but a collapse of the German home front. For that, it is necessary to convince the Germans that they cannot win." The British, still living with the memory of World War I, reactivated the concept of "economic warfare." In addition to the blockade, they embraced "the air bombing of industrial targets, sabotage, and psychological warfare,"[3] three methods that had been used during the previous conflict.

The sudden collapse of France also suggested that the Germans had relied on a "fifth column" to disrupt the Allied defenses and undermine the popular resistance.[4] British strategists hoped to turn that weapon against its creators.

A part of the Left, finally, succumbed to a form of revolutionary romanticism. In their eyes, the two Russian revolutions of 1917 confirmed that a population under the yoke of oppression was able, sooner or later, to break its chains. Many leaders believed in 1941 that, "if Nazism was evil and maintained itself in power by force, and moreover, if it was also a German phenomenon, then clearly the response of the Europeans must be to reject it." "We have on our side not only the anti-Nazi elements in Germany and Austria, not only the Czechs and the Poles, but also the whole of the democratic and liberty-loving in Norway, Denmark, Belgium, France, Holland and Italy," enumerated Hugh Dalton, a member of the Labour Party, in July 1940. "Moreover, in each of these countries except Italy, there will be a nationalist appeal which can be linked with the ideals of democracy and individual liberty. I am convinced that the potentialities of this war from within are really immense."[5]

These views, far from being confined to a small circle of dreamers, were validated by fringe elements of the Establishment. Hugh Dalton, a leftist through and through, believed in the revolutionary potential of oppressed peoples. Colin Gubbins, who joined the special services in 1939, took guerilla warfare seriously, having personally witnessed its effectiveness. Appointed aide-de-camp to General Edmund Ironside, head of the expeditionary force to Arkhangelsk, for more than a year he had had a front-row view of the civilian war that, in a Russia in the grip of chaos, set the

Whites against the Reds. At the time, he observed "the potential strength of the resister who was able to choose the terrain, the target and the moment to strike."[6] Transferred to Ireland between 1919 and 1922, he had fought the Irish Republican Army there and had been struck by the success of the "armed bandits" and their leader, Michael Collins.[7] In 1939 he even wrote a report titled "Investigation of the Possibilities of Guerrilla Activities,"[8] which gave an overview of his thinking. Finally, Winston Churchill had always shown enthusiasm for unconventional warfare. Ever since his experience in the Boer War, he had had a passion for guerilla tactics and "retained a fascination for novelties, especially of the exploding variety."[9] As minister of the interior, he had given MI 5, the service responsible for counterespionage, complete latitude in the surveillance of correspondence; as First Lord of the Admiralty, he had spared no efforts to unmask German spies.[10] In short, the country of Lawrence of Arabia, far from looking down on subversive warfare, took it seriously. In July 1940 Churchill even gave it a decisive push.

Birth of the Special Operations Executive

On June 13, 1940, Winston Churchill, the new prime minister, proposed creating an organization designed to wage subversive warfare, a suggestion that received the support of his colleagues. Exactly one month later, Lord President of the Council Neville Chamberlain circulated among his peers a preliminary draft that defined its terms: the new organization would "co-ordinate all action, by way of subversion and sabotage, against the enemy overseas." That text, adopted on July 19, gave rise to the Special Operations Executive, which henceforth considered it the organization's "founding charter."[11]

SOE, far from sprouting on virgin soil, amalgamated different preexisting services. After the Reich's annexation of Austria in March 1938, the Foreign Office had created an organization in charge of propaganda, Department EH (for "Electra House," where it was housed). The Canadian press magnate Stuart Campbell became its director. Immediately thereafter, the Secret Intelligence Service (SIS), also known by the initials MI 6 (Military Intelligence, section 6), had formed a "Section D" (for "Destruction"), entrusted to Major Lawrence Grand, to consider how enemies could be attacked, "otherwise than by the usual military means."[12]

Finally, in the autumn of 1938, the minister of war developed a department of research known as GS (R) (General Staff, Research), which, under the leadership of Major John Charles Holland, devoted itself to studying guerilla warfare. It was renamed MI (R) (Military Intelligence, Research) in early 1939. These three services, however, merely scraped by and, despite sketchy efforts at coordination, overlapped. The British authorities, in creating the Special Operations Executive, which officially came into being on July 22, 1940, intended to give new impetus to subversive warfare while avoiding rivalries and duplication.[13] It was a risky wager at best, in view of the obstacles in the way.

On July 16, 1940, Winston Churchill met with Hugh Dalton and announced to him that SOE would be attached to his Ministry of Economic Warfare. He assigned it a key mission: "Set Europe ablaze." But the choice of the Labour leader was more a canny political calculation than the result of strictly strategic considerations.

Back on October 25, 1924, the conservative *Daily Mail* had published a vociferous letter from Grigory Zinoviev, president of the Comintern (Communist International), who enjoined the small Communist Party of Great Britain to perform acts of sedition. The publication of that firebrand was ill-timed. Occurring four days before the legislative elections, it ruined the chances of the Labour Party, which was accused of being either the dupe or the accomplice of the Reds. The Tories therefore won the election, which enraged Labour. Was the document authentic? Historians have doubts,[14] as did Labour Party members, who soon suspected that His Majesty's secret services had had a hand in the affair.[15] In short, the Intelligence Service was not dear to the hearts of the democratic Left. To maintain the national union within his cabinet, the Conservative Winston Churchill had to offer guarantees to his Labour partner, as Clement Attlee, Lord Privy Seal, forcefully demanded.[16] MI 6 (espionage) reported to the Foreign Office, MI 5 (counterespionage) to the Ministry of Home Security, which were both occupied by Conservatives. "If a third secret service could be created, and run by a Labour man, the political difficulty could be quickly resolved."[17]

Hugh Dalton forthrightly demanded that responsibility, based on a theory he outlined without delay. He distinguished "war from without," which the military was called on to conduct, from "war from within," which the civilians would have to wage.[18] In his mind, subversion fell primarily to the leftist organizations—parties and labor unions—an idea he would not let go of. And he managed to convince Churchill of it. As the historian David Stafford points out, "It was certainly Dalton's view that SOE would be a 'revolutionary' organisation, just as it was his opinion that SOE had as its field of operations a Europe potentially open to revolt."[19] One logical and major consequence was that SOE would be a civilian and not a military organization. Dalton reminded Attlee that "regular soldiers are not men to stir up revolution, to create social chaos, or use all those ungentlemanly means of winning the war which come so easily to the Nazis."[20]

Was he up to the task? "Doctor Dynamo," as he was nicknamed, displayed unflagging energy. At the same time, he was a target of criticism and was even labeled "Doctor Dirty" by his detractors.[21] Dalton was brought up in Windsor and attended the select Eton College, before continuing his studies at Cambridge. Many of his peers considered him a class traitor. His temperament did him no favors. Although very active, he did not have "any great sense of organization," as his friend and personal assistant Gladwyn Jebb confided, adding, "He had a rather elephantine way of endeavouring to ingratiate himself with people."[22] The Conservative minister of information, Brendan Bracken—nicknamed BB within the circles of power[23]—despised him. At a luncheon, he criticized him repeatedly, stating that "nobody would work with him, neither the Chiefs of Staff nor any of the Ministries. Dr Dalton bored people by the way in which he talked and this would be likely to prove a serious deterrent to any progress on the part of [SOE]."[24] Finally, though the minister of economic warfare declared enormous admiration for his prime minister, the reverse was not true. That posed an operational problem. Dalton, because he did not belong to the war cabinet and did not have privileged access to 10 Downing Street, had difficulty defending the interests of SOE, which in such a context faced a difficult birth at least.

A Doctrine of Action

SOE was run by three men in succession. Frank Nelson, a businessman who had joined the Conservative Party, was in charge until May 1942. "He was now aged 57 and, somewhat to our surprise, wore the uniform of a Pilot Officer in the RAF."[25] Charles Hambro, a business banker, succeeded him in May 1942; then Colin Gubbins, a career officer, replaced Hambro in September 1943. Bickham Sweet-Escott, a former member of SOE, reported that Hambro "was just over 44; he was a man of immense energy and vitality with a quick wit, and an imagination and grasp of principle rare in a professional soldier. He enjoyed life to the full; he never forgot a face or a name, and he had a gift for inspiring confidence in those working under him. He was in fact a born leader of men."[26]

Originally, the Special Operations Executive comprised three branches. SO 1, entrusted to Reginald (Rex) Leeper, oversaw propaganda, having grown out of the Foreign Office; SO 2, under the leadership of Colin Gubbins, was in charge of special operations; and SO 3 headed up research and planning. These last two branches quickly merged, and in August 1941 propaganda was assigned to a new organization, the Political Warfare Executive (PWE), whose creation was officially announced in the House of Commons on September 11.[27] Once that organization chart was drawn up, it was necessary to construct a doctrine of action.

Hugh Dalton believed so firmly in the possibility of revolution in the occupied countries that he convened a symposium on October 19, 1940, to explore channels for bringing it about. "Among the questions which he would like discussed were: What types of Revolutions were possible in the different territories? How far could we produce one type of Revolution rather than another? Had any real study [been] made of the theory and technique of Revolutions?"[28] In his view, the oppressed masses would quite logically spearhead the revolt. "Our best friends in occupied Europe are not the bourgeoisie, much less big business, or Generals, but the masses, and principally the industrial workers. Therefore, our propaganda should primarily be addressed to them."[29]

These generous but general watchwords still had to be translated into acts. The minister of economic warfare foresaw promoting action in three areas. Subversive propaganda would turn "the population of the occupied countries against the forces of occupation" and undermine their morale. Sabotage organizations would seek to "wear down the Axis morally and economically and so hasten the date when our military forces can take the offensive." In addition, secret armies would be formed but would be used only "when immediate support by regular forces is imminent, or when the German power is actually crumbling. Otherwise they will be crushed out of hand and reprisals will be so severe that there will be no chance of their resurrection."[30] Hugh Dalton was far-sighted. He anticipated dispatching enough men and materiel between September 1, 1941, and October 1, 1942, to constitute subversive groups comprising about five hundred men for

Norway, five hundred for Denmark, and three thousand for France, and to form substantial secret armies: nineteenth thousand recruits were anticipated for Norway, twenty-four thousand for France.[31]

In addition to Dalton, other leaders broke bread at the revolutionary table. And the United Kingdom had a formidable weapon at its disposal: radio. Douglas Ritchie, BBC announcer and future director of the corporation's Europe department, believed that, thanks to its broadcasts, London could easily unleash powerful insurrection movements.

> We have here, if we develop it and make use of it, a weapon of war of an entirely new kind. No such power has ever been in the hands of man before. The Germans have no such weapon. . . .
>
> At a word from London the life of German soldiers or German-controlled police in the occupied countries can be made impossible. . . . The cafes which the Germans frequent can suddenly run out of beer and all food but the most indigestible kind. . . .
>
> With the assistance of British industrial experts the BBC can give instructions on how workers can spoil their work. . . . Towards the end of the campaign millions of workers all over Europe, at a word from London, will strike and set buildings and factories on fire. . . .
>
> When the British Government gives the word the BBC will cause riots and demonstrations in every city in Europe. Individual Germans will be killed by small bodies of local patriots who have already been instructed to single out their man and deal with him. Crowds will march through the streets demanding the return of their country's independence.
>
> To turn this possibility into reality we have to do two things. We have to sharpen this unique weapon and practice its use and we have to convince the British Government by demonstration if necessary, that the weapon has all the striking power that we claim and that it must be used to bring the war to a rapid conclusion.[32]

Radio constituted a particularly effective medium, in that many households in Fortress Europe were equipped with a set. For example, Denmark had 863,400 radio sets (224 for every thousand residents), the Netherlands 1,440,600 (160 per thousand residents), and Norway 429,400 (145 per thousand residents).[33] In autumn 1939 France counted up 5 million sets, to which an additional 1.5 million undeclared receivers can probably be added (that is, 162 per thousand residents).[34] Many households, then, could receive and spread the good word, a factor unprecedented in the history of warfare.

These grandiose prospects, however, alarmed or put off certain leaders. Some suspected SOE and its supervising minister, Hugh Dalton, of laying the groundwork for the Great Revolution in Europe. In fact, "the guidance which he regularly provided for his officials usually had a strong socialist flavour which may have made some of the working propagandists less eager to follow his lead."[35] Others pointed out how unrealistic the proposed solutions were. Indeed, nothing suggested that the people under the jackboot would unite under the banner of revolt, as Gladwyn Jebb, assistant to Hugh Dalton, made clear in October 1940:

> The most astonishing feature in Europe to-day, not only in the occupied areas, but also in Germany and Italy, is the spread of apathy and indifference. People seem to be so exhausted, physically and morally, that they do not care very much what happens so long as they get enough to eat. They are, therefore, prepared to obey anybody in authority, that is to say anybody who possesses some kind of guns. . . . On the whole, however, indifference seems to hold the field. For this reason the phrases "general uprising" or "revolution" may possibly be misleading. They have romantic connotations and imply a spirit of sacrifice and devotion which appears now largely to have vanished, at any rate from Western Europe. It is conceivable that the general collapse for which we are hoping may come about rather by a withering of confidence in the Nazi leaders, involving internecine feuds of which we could take advantage, more especially in the outlying districts of the enslaved areas, than by picturesque, mass revolts of apathetic and incidentally unarmed slaves.[36]

Many feared as well that an insurrection with no connection to an Allied offensive would end in a needless bloodbath. Colin Gubbins, chief of SOE operations at the time, explained:

> In conquered and occupied territories the eventual aim is to provoke an armed rising against the invader at the appropriate moment. It cannot, however, be made too clear that in total warfare a premature rising

is not only foredoomed to failure, but that the reprisals engendered will be of such a drastic, ferocious and all-embracing nature that the backbone of the movement will probably be broken beyond healing. A national uprising against the Axis is a card which usually can only be played once. . . . It is thus essential not only that these subterranean movements should be supported by us, but also that they should be sufficiently under our control to ensure that they do not explode prematurely.[37]

Colonel F. T. Davies, director of services, went even further: "I am not sure that the chief role of SO 2 is the creation of hidden armies; more may be achieved by stealth and on a much [more] modest scale."[38]

As a result, these considerations led SOE to scale back its mission and clarify its aims. In mid–May 1941 the new organization planned not only to produce propaganda but also to form underground organizations in the occupied countries capable of conducting raids or sabotage operations and secret armies that would be able to deploy on D–Day.[39]

Propaganda

Propaganda played a decisive role in leading peoples on the road to insurrection and individuals on the path of resistance. From that standpoint, the British made use of a large range of options, working on two registers, either simultaneously or alternately.

What was known as "open" or "white" propaganda was a message whose source was clearly identifiable, whether that was the British authorities or the exiled powers. It relied primarily on BBC radio but also on leaflets or newspapers that the Royal Air Force dropped over occupied Europe. The British were still attached to the printed word, an apparently obsolete form, for several reasons. In the first place, in view of the jamming of radio signals by the Germans, the fines imposed on listeners to British programs, the possibility of radio sets being confiscated by the enemy, and the high cost and difficulty of repairing them, given the lack of spare parts, the use of the older method—already employed during World War I—was indispensable.[40] Second, the written word had many advantages. It allowed for the elaboration of facts, statistics, or complex analyses impossible in oral propaganda. And finally, by volume, a magazine corresponded to between forty and fifty five-minute bulletins, that is, three to four hours of continuous transmission, a quantitative advantage of which the British were aware. Far from standing in opposition to each other, leaflets and radio broadcasts were "separate but complementary."[41]

"Black" propaganda, by contrast, was designed to cover its tracks. For example, it availed itself of underground radio sets, called RU (for "Radio Units"). "The first essential of black propaganda is that its content should not be recognizable as British. Its source of origin has to be concealed both in the news selected and in the way the news is presented. . . . The station is supposed to operate inside the country," explained Rex Leeper, head of the Political Intelligence Department (PID) and also in charge of SO 1. To make that fable credible, "their transmissions have not the same regularity as those of the BBC for the obvious reason that they are supposed to be operating in dangerous circumstances and it is natural that they should from time to time come off the air. But in most cases the transmissions are more or less daily in order to keep their listening public."[42] Because the authorities were not officially involved, the RU could diversify the messages, transmitting the voices of supposed Fascists disgusted with the conduct of Il Duce or Pétainists revolted by the marshal's spinelessness. They could also emancipate themselves from the BBC's heavy supervision. "Just as the Church of England regards the British heaven as its established monopoly, so did the BBC, in those days before commercial television, regard the British ether as theirs."[43]

Their experts also made broad use of rumors (called "sibs," from the Latin *sibilare*, "to hiss,"[44] because they had to be hissed in people's ears).[45] Groups and individuals would spread them through diplomats or newspapers, with particular attention to the neutral countries. All in all, thanks to its propaganda, London counted on inciting the people to rise up, a grandiose prospect outlined by Douglas Ritchie in 1941:

The first weeks might be devoted to establishing a feeling of solidarity between oppressed peoples. In fact a European consciousness.

The second stage might be the direct mobilization of the European people into an Underground Army. We should point out that in the British Empire everybody and everything is mobilised to help win the war. . . . Europe must be mobilized too. There is something for everybody to do. We shall tell them what to do when the time comes. In the meantime they must listen to us.[46]

It was difficult, however, to translate that vast program into precise instructions, whatever the country targeted. For France in 1941, the propaganda services strove "to demoralize the forces of occupation both civil and military" in the occupied zone, "to build up resistance to the Vichy government and to every form of collaboration with the Axis partners" in the free zone, and finally, "to bring Northern Africa back into the war on our side." For Denmark, the idea was to "tie down larger German forces in Denmark by driving the Danes to active resistance." The aim of propaganda in the Netherlands was to keep up the morale of the Dutch people, to demoralize the German troops, and to achieve the maximum reduction of the enemy's use of human resources and of the labor force.[47]

In short, white propaganda directed at Western Europe privileged four main lines. First, it sought to boost the morale of the subjugated peoples by proclaiming the inevitability of the Allied victory. That point constituted, for example, the "first aim" of the message sent to Denmark: to convince its population that "Germany cannot win the war."[48] Second, the British were intent on limiting the occupier's pillaging. They therefore asked laborers—in the Netherlands, for example—to refuse to go work in the Reich.[49] In France, paradoxically, they supported the return to the land championed by Philippe Pétain, which, they said, would deprive the Reich of "French factory labour."[50] Third, they hoped to demoralize the German troops. Fourth, and perhaps above all, they sought to turn civilians into resistance fighters. Propaganda was supposed to "prepare the mind of every Belgian for the day when we shall call upon him *directly* for positive action. Every Belgian must be brought to see that he personally is an important element; that he personally can hasten the day of his liberation."[51] The French, for their part, had to "realize that . . . it is now no longer possible to maintain an attitude of neutrality. The BBC has regularly offered suggestions for action, and recently it has concentrated its propaganda more than ever on persuading France that 'le moment d'agir' [the moment to act] has now come."[52]

At the same time, the British authorities were aware of how complex that transformation would be. They therefore offered exercises designed to prepare civilians for the harsh demands of the resistance. "This stage," argued Ritchie,

> must culminate with an attempt to seize the imagination of our listeners by an act of "enlistment." We could ask them to take a mental

oath to fight for the freedom that Norway (or Czechoslovakia) stands for in common with the other European peoples, and follow with a moment of silence and the playing of the National Anthem. . . . These would be the preliminaries. The exercises would follow. We would try to chalk Vs on walls all over Europe, not as a vague expression of resentment but definitely to make an anniversary. . . . Other simple exercises would include remaining indoors at certain times (this has already been done fairly successfully in the case of France and Norway; we should make the whole of Europe do it), chain letters, anonymous letters containing blood-curdling threats, and many others which will be thought out.[53]

To make the transition from instilling a conviction to spurring action, the BBC recommended two major methods. It suggested that individuals, in Denmark, for example, gather together to listen to its broadcasts. "Attempts are being made to persuade listeners to form listening groups, by suggesting that people with good sets might invite their neighbours who cannot receive distant programmes, in whenever there is an interesting transmission. If such groups can be established, they may later form centres for political discussions and moral resistance."[54] It also launched the V campaign.

The V Campaign

On January 14, 1941, Victor de Laveleye, the Francophone Belgian announcer on the BBC, called on his compatriots to scrawl Vs on walls as symbols of victory and freedom (vrijheid in Dutch). That campaign was such a success that, on May 16 of the same year, the British formed a V Committee to coordinate action in the occupied territories. That committee was intended to forge among the people "the consciousness that they are all members of a vast underground army fighting for freedom against the tyranny of Nazism." It hoped to "organize some simple exercises which would have the double effect of encouraging the morale of the oppressed people and lowering the morale of the German troops, and to suggest actions which would greatly increase the effect of the British blockade."[55] In July 1941 the campaign was even adapted to local conditions in Italy, with "the suggestion that V stands for Vittoria, Vedetta, Volonta and Vita."[56]

Launched for Denmark on June 12, 1941, it was also tailored to fit that country: the announcer Leif Gundel popularized the slogan *Vi Vil Vinde!* (We will win).[57] The first graffiti were spotted two days later in the district of Lemvig, in northwestern Jutland.[58]

The Germans tried hard to turn the argument on its head, claiming that the Vs referred to their own victory. Although their efforts had a certain success in the Netherlands, it was the occasion for irony at the BBC. "In German, victory is *Sieg*. So it begins with an S. But Goebbels couldn't take S. 'S,' as you know, hightailed it to England last May 10."[59] That was a subtle allusion to the Führer's heir apparent, Rudolf Hess (pronounced "es" in French), who had parachuted into the United Kingdom to propose an accord, whose terms remain obscure even to this day. In short, the campaign's success surpassed all expectations, and Vs blossomed throughout Europe. On March 28, 1941, for example, the police counted up—and erased—fifty-five hundred Vs in the city of Lille alone.[60]

Black Propaganda

Black propaganda complemented or shadowed that white propaganda. Several RUs began broadcasting in 1940—Radio Italia, for example, went on the air on November 17, 1940. Ruggero Orlando, former correspondent for Ente Italiano per le Audizioni Radiofoniche (EIAR; Italian Agency for Radio Broadcasting) in London, was at the microphone,[61] soon to be joined by three other Italians. These four men—one Catholic, one Liberal, one Republican, and one Socialist—covered the peninsula's political spectrum, with the notable exception of the Communists. All pleaded for a new *Risorgimento* capable of shattering Fascism, establishing peace, and repelling German domination.[62] Radio-Lorraine addressed a French public and conducted "a systematic campaign against defeatism. The spirit of resistance is encouraged, while it is stressed that the time for action is not yet come."[63] Sooner or later, all countries had a Radio Unit at their disposal, which served as a complement to the other media.

In May 1941 British propaganda for Belgium ran up against three obstacles. First, the leaflets dropped by the RAF were distributed on only a modest scale—fewer than two million from July 1940 onward. Second, the BBC treated the kingdom "as a poor relation, giving it only a quarter-of-an-hour a day in each language." And finally, that propaganda was supposed to conform to "political and legal considerations" and "the dictates of diplomatic good taste." This was a severe limitation for a country where it was now necessary to "move forward from a static to a dynamic policy—from the propaganda designed to build confidence and strengthen morale which may be regarded as British propaganda in the official scene to the propaganda of subversion, which is the special province of SO1 and SO2."[64] The PWE leaders thus called for the establishment of a Radio Unit that, far from restricting itself to patriotic exhortations, would impel the Belgians to take action.

Black propaganda, while elaborating political themes, also offered practical advice to guide listeners on the road to action. Radio-Heraus, an underground radio station broadcasting to Belgium as of July 4, 1941, suggested, for example: "Sulphur, or better still, nitric acid, in a radiator is good against frost. And cement is good against leakages. Rubber, sugar and cement in the petrol tank keep the conduits clean and are perfect for the carburetor and the pump. And when you take out a spark-plug to see if it is clean, don't forget to drop a bolt or a screw or some other metal object in the cylinder. The ignition will be much better."[65] But the underground station De Flitspuit (The Insecticide Bomb) for the Netherlands, launched in July 1941—hosted primarily by Meyer Sluyser, a Dutch journalist in exile[66]—recommended against immediately sabotaging the railroad lines. "Wait with that till the right time has come. Also wait with that till the right train is there."[67]

The British authorities, finally, were banking on rumors to complement the methods by which their propaganda was transmitted. They pointed out that the enemy's control over newspapers and the airwaves was intensifying because of the repression of the underground press and the jamming of the BBC signal. As a result, "verbal propaganda and rumours are likely to be more important." Their objective was "in no sense to convey the official or semi-official view of His Majesty's Government by covert means to officials in the countries concerned. It is rather to induce alarms, despondency and bewilderment among the enemies, and hope and confidence among the friends, to whose ears it comes. If a rumour appears likely to cheer our enemies for the time, it is calculated to carry with it the germs of ultimate and grave disappointment for them." Some two thousand rumors were spread in 1941.[68] To prevent a rumor from contradicting His Majesty's foreign policy or the underground action taken by SO 2, an Underground Propaganda Committee was formed. Various representatives—of SOE, the Intelligence Service, and the Ministry of Economic Warfare—were members, and the rumors chosen were then submitted to the Foreign Office for approval. "Darlan has agreed privately with Admiral Leahy [the American ambassador to Vichy] to sail the French fleet to American ports if the Germans try to take it." The Foreign Office rejected this rumor,[69] no doubt because it contradicted a foreign policy that portrayed the admiral in the most negative light. "US Army is training parachutist ski-troops for landing in Norway." This rumor was barred because, as it turned out, it was true.[70]

SOE's mission, however, far from being restricted to propaganda, encompassed actions as well—it was to form groups that would carry out "skilled sabotage and raids," in order to reduce the military or industrial potential of the Axis.[71]

Paving the Way for Action

To that end, SOE planned to dispatch British or foreign "organizers," whose mission would be to form underground cells in occupied Europe. Over the long term, they would create "a number of focal points, or 'bridgeheads,' staffed by men whose main task is to reorganise a network of organizers and agents, systems of communications, depots for arms and explosives etc, and any underground propaganda that may be necessary to the ultimate objective of embarking on large-scale operations of securing a general rising. *Short-term*: while keeping the eventual object in view and working towards that end, it is meanwhile necessary to exploit all immediate possibilities to attack the enemy and to maintain the offensive."[72] From 1940 on, therefore, the Special Operations Executive dispatched agents—with uneven success.

In several countries, the missions sent out in 1940 and 1941 ended in fiasco. In the Netherlands, attempts at infiltration by sea in the summer of 1941 failed. Air transport had little more success. For example, two agents—Albert Homburg and Cornelis Sporre—were dropped by parachute on September 7. Homburg was arrested on October 8, and Sporre vanished on November 19, while trying to return to England by sea (he undoubtedly drowned). Homburg was luckier: after escaping on October 24, he concealed himself in a freighter and convinced its commander to make for Yarmouth, where he landed safe and sound on February 17, 1942. But rather than continue in SOE, the agent preferred to join the Royal Air Force (he died in combat in 1945).[73]

Reports from Italy were even more devastating. As the commander of SOE noted in October 1941, "We have no Italians under training; we have no lines in Italy (with the possible exception of one or two nebulous contacts from Switzerland); and we have so far entirely failed to recruit any suitable type of Italian in this country, the Middle East or Malta."[74] Granted, it was more difficult to work in enemy territory than in the occupied zones. But after the war, those responsible for the peninsula indicated that SOE had erred out of blindness. Their naïveté had led them to believe that, "because Fascism was not universally popular in Italy, anti-Fascists would betray their country." They were ignorant of the "fundamentals of clandestine work" and did not have the "necessary inflow of intelligence of an operational nature."[75]

The situation was hardly brighter in Denmark. To be sure, Ebbe Munck, a journalist who had been a war correspondent in Finland, had returned to his country after the defeat, before going to Sweden in July 1940. Thanks to the contacts he had established with officers in the Danish intelligence services, he provided the British legation of Stockholm with information from the best source.[76] The first microfilm was transmitted in October 1940.[77] But attempts at infiltration ended in failure. To "stimulate the will to resist and to form the nucleus of a sabotage organization under the control of SOE," the service parachuted two men in on the night of December 27, 1941 (Chilblain Mission).[78] But the parachute of its leader, Carl-Johann Bruhn, did not open; he was killed instantly. His assistant, Mogens Hammer, assigned to establish radio contact with London, landed safely. It was up to him to pursue a mission that began under particularly inauspicious circumstances.[79]

SOE encountered the same stumbling blocks in Belgium, because the contacts the British had had before the invasion had been swept away by the defeat.[80] Whereas SIS picked up the threads by relying on World War I veterans under the leadership of Walthère Dewé—a member of the resistance between 1914 and 1918—SOE had to build an organization from scratch. Emile Tromme, dropped by parachute into Germany on the night of May 12, 1941, landed in the middle of a prison camp, from which he managed to escape.[81] On the night of July 5, Armand Leblicq and Abbé Jourdain were also parachuted in. But the cloth of Leblicq's parachute got tangled in the aircraft's tail section, which towed the agent until it landed on Newmarket Air Base. Hardy Amies, the officer in charge of training at the time, had to identify the body, mutilated by terror and the cold— "a memory which he never forgot."[82] Abbé Jourdain continued his intelligence mission, however. In particular, he met with Archbishop Van Roey, primate of Belgium, as well as Monsignor Kerkhofs, bishop of Liège, and then attempted to return to England via Spain. Arrested by the Francoist authorities on December 29, he did not get out of Miranda de Ebro concentration camp until August 1942. In the meantime, the assurances his interlocutors had dispensed were largely out-of-date.[83] Other missions were launched. Julien Detal was sent to France to set in place a mail service and to assist Belgian escapees in finding their way to Great Britain (Grey Mission). But he was arrested on March 17, 1942.

In May 1941 the Belgian section of SOE developed a plan to provide an organizer for each of the country's nine provinces. That confidential agent would recruit locals to form cells intended to set up reception committees, sabotage operations, mail services, and escape channels; a radio would maintain contact with London.[84] Octave Fabri (Chicken Mission), for example, was entrusted with the task of developing an organization in Antwerp province focused on passive resistance and sabotage. Although seventeen agents—nine organizers and eight telegraph operators—were dispatched in 1941, SOE ultimately set them loose, exempting them from applying the plan in place: the harsh conditions of the underground required that the agents have a certain latitude. To no avail. "None of these agents registered any spectacular successes. Some succeeded in forming sabotage groups and, here and there, in carrying out an act of sabotage, but the result was greatly below expectations."[85]

A few glimmers brightened that dark landscape. In France, SOE conducted several operations in cooperation with General de Gaulle's Free France. In response to a request formulated by the minister of air, a five-man commando set out in March 1941 to destroy the bus carrying the crews of the German Fighting Squadron 100, which was bombing England from the Meucon base near Vannes. But the crews were traveling by car, not by bus, and the operation was canceled. It had not been useless, however, in that it demonstrated the possibility of striking in the occupied zone and of counting on the population's silence or even complicity. The Special Operations Executive then targeted the transformers in Pessac, in the Bordeaux region. A first team was dogged by bad luck. Half a dozen Poles flew from the base at Tangmere on April 10, but, because of electrical problems, the aircraft had to release its two containers over the Loire, before turning back. It crashed upon landing, injuring or killing passengers and crew. A new team, formed with the assistance of the Gaullist services, took its place. On the night of May 11, three men (Forman, Varnier, and Cabard) parachuted into France; after being joined by Le Tac, they blew up six of the eight transformers on the night of June 7. The repairs were not completed until early 1942, which meant that work on the submarine base at Bordeaux and at several businesses in the Gironde was interrupted for several weeks.[86]

For its "F" (French) section, which was working independently of the Gaullist services, SOE also dispatched two dozen agents into France, four of whom had a transceiver unit; by the end of the year, a third of them had been arrested. Once again, however, a few avenues turned out to be promising. Pierre de Vomécourt, an aristocrat from Lorraine, was dropped by parachute on May 10, 1941, and immediately recruited his two brothers, Philippe and Jean. Pierre undertook to set up a sabotage network, Autogiro, in the Paris region and in Nord; Philippe took charge of southern France; and Jean, living in Pontarlier, created several small networks in the eastern part of the country. Jacques de Guélis, an advertising man who had served in 1940 as an interpreter for Lord Gort, the general in command of the British expeditionary corps, was also sent to France, where he recruited several promising agents, including Virginia Hall. A thirty-five-year old American journalist, she "stood out in a crowd, with her flaming red hair, pronounced American accent, artificial leg." She was issued credentials as a correspondent for the *New York Post*, and her apartment in Lyon quickly became the base for the men sent over from London. Other agents joined these pioneers. For example, Benjamin Cowburn, Michael Trotobas, Victor Gerson, George Langellan, Jean-Paul Marie du Puy, and Georges Bloch were dropped by parachute on the night of September 6, 1941.[87] On the whole, however, it was a meager harvest. By September 1941, twenty-one agents had been sent into France. And, though a few attacks had been committed, especially against the railroads, many volunteers had been arrested. Radio communications remained unreliable, and recruitment was at a virtual standstill: only thirteen men had been enlisted in metropolitan France.[88]

Clearly, that mixed bag was the result of multiple factors. These included the "nebulous" objectives SOE had assigned to its agents, as Major R. A. Bourne-Patterson, a veteran of section F, noted in the history he compiled in 1946. "'Insaisissable' sabotage, 'discreet' bangs, 'organisation' of resistance were supremely indefinite terms. At the same time the very indefiniteness of the objective in the early period tended to defeat itself. The organizer recruited his men and found himself unaware of what to do with them."[89]

In Norway, the situation presented itself in a radically different light. In the first place, at an early date SOE had relatively reliable connections in a country with 775 miles of coastline. Already in 1940, Major Leslie H. Mitchell opened a naval base in Cat Firth, Shetland, less than ten miles from the small town of Lerwick.

That "Shetland Bus," as it was called, exfiltrated by sea Norwegians wishing to reach the United Kingdom and also brought men and materiel into the country. The first operation took place on December 22, 1940: the fishing boat *Vita* delivered an agent to Langoy, in the Gulf of Bergen. In 1940–1941, that system, run jointly by SOE and SIS, in fourteen trips picked up eighteen resistance fighters (and thirty-nine refugees) and sent in fifteen.[90] The porousness of the long border with Sweden also allowed them to mount operations from that neutral country. In April 1941, for example, Operation Barbara targeted a tunnel and the Trondheim-Storlein railroad line. The saboteurs, however, were arrested by the Swedes upon their return.[91] In the same vein, an agent named Odd Starheim, delivered to Norway by submarine in January 1941 and who ended his odyssey in a canoe, set out to organize the resistance in the region of Agder Fylkeset, southwest of Oslo. He transmitted about a hundred cables, before returning to England on June 21 of the same year.

Above all, Norway became the theater for bold raids (twelve in all) conducted from the British archipelago. Set up with the cooperation of SOE, Operation Claymore targeted the Lofoten Islands on March 4, 1941. It sought to destroy the industries that produced herring oil, which was supposedly one of the components of glycerin. That was not the case: rather, herring oil capsules provided German submarine crews with the vitamin A and B they needed to survive.[92] Along the way, hundreds of British soldiers, backed by 52 Norwegians, destroyed 17 factories, sank 8 German ships, killed 14 enemy soldiers, and captured another 213. The British struck again. In April 1941 eleven Norwegians from the Special Operations Executive were sent out to destroy a herring oil factory in Øksfjord, Finnmark.[93] And in December of the same year, two new onslaughts (known as "Operation Anklet"), once more targeting the Lofoten Islands, destroyed

THE SHETLAND ISLANDS

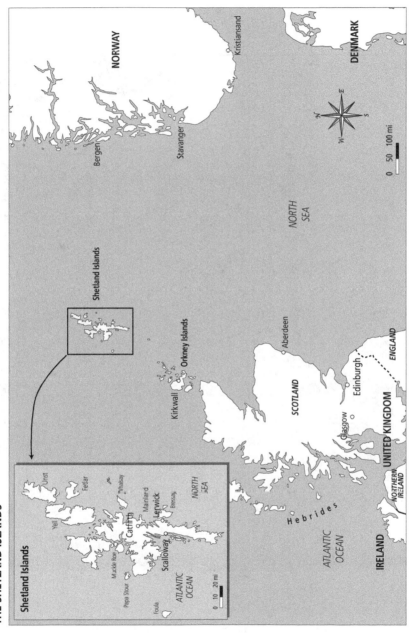

THE LOFOTEN ISLANDS

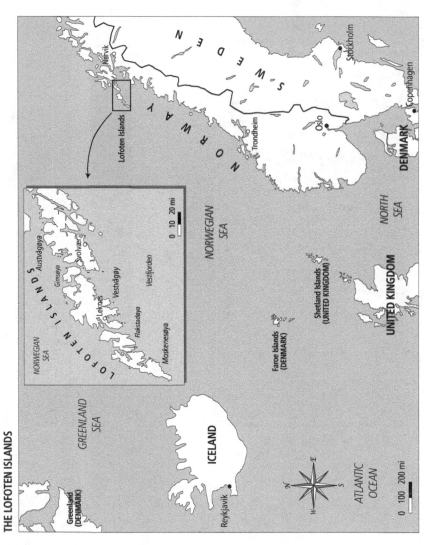

a transmitting station and allowed SOE to take German prisoners and to bring Norwegian volunteers back to the United Kingdom. Losses on the Allied side were limited. But Captain Martin Linge, the courageous leader of the seventy-seven volunteers, died during an attack on the hotels that housed the German headquarters in Vågsøy.[94]

Although these operations had little strategic interest, they showed the Norwegians that the British, far from abandoning them, were encouraging their resistance. They also offered English propaganda a few reasons for pride—a rare commodity in 1941.

Toward the end of 1941, then, the Special Operations Executive had a rather disappointing balance sheet. At the impetus of Hugh Dalton and Colin Gubbins, it had built up an organization and a doctrine of action and had developed both white and black propaganda, even while dispatching organizers to Western Europe with the assignment to "set Europe ablaze." At the same time, the hoped-for uprisings had not materialized; many agents had been arrested; and the vast majority of countries under the jackboot were still only mission fields, as yet untapped. That relative failure was partly the result of objective conditions. The harshness of the Nazi oppression and the apparent inevitability of the German victory hardly incited the people to revolt. Other factors also played a role, however. The internecine struggles that divided the British circles of power and the hesitations of the exiled governments placed formidable obstacles in the road that Hugh Dalton and his agents were taking.

CHAPTER III

Internecine Struggles

B etween 1940 and the end of 1941, ill winds fostered the birth and development of the Special Operations Executive. A number of British authorities directed a silent or a declared hostility toward that service. Far from forging a consensus in London's ruling circles, it gave rise to violent opposition. As Michael Foot points out, "Much of the energy of SOE's high command was siphoned away from its proper work by quarrels in Whitehall, at their worst during SOE's first year."[1] Gladwyn Jebb, assistant to Doctor Dynamo, observed in May 1942: "The progress of SOE was considerably impeded by the attitude of certain influential persons in the neighborhood of No. 10 [Downing Street] who had never wished Mr. Dalton to be given responsibility for subversive operations and were—no doubt quite genuinely—convinced that he could never make a success of the job."[2] Robert Bruce Lockhart, in charge of propaganda and future general director of the Political Warfare Executive, made an observation in his diary that was no less disabused: "The battle of Whitehall is far more important to civil servants than the battle of Britain," he noted in November 1940.[3]

Turf Wars

The Secret Intelligence Service was in the forefront of that opposition. The service, headed by Stewart Menzies, alias "C," might legitimately have claimed that "action" lay within its field of expertise, especially since, before the war, it had created an ad hoc branch, Service D. Its results were altogether meager, however, and the Venlo Incident had tarnished its image. In autumn 1939 German agents passing themselves off as dissidents had taken refuge in the Netherlands; they claimed they were planning to assassinate Hitler. Two members of IS, Captain Sigismund Payne Best and Major Richard Stevens, took the bait and went to Venlo, Holland, to meet the pseudo-general charged with cutting short the Führer's days. The trap set by the Germans worked like a charm. On the morning of November 9, 1939, a commando of the German secret services (SD) led by Alfred Naujocks and overseen by Walter Schellenberg (in charge of the foreign espionage section at the time) kidnapped the two men and transferred them to Germany. In that sting operation, they killed Dirk Klop, the Dutch lieutenant who was accompanying his British colleagues.[4] It was a good catch. The Reichssicherheitshauptamt, the Reich's security service, seized from Major Stevens's person a list of enemy agents operating in Europe and familiarized itself with its adversary's methods. As a direct consequence, that grim episode cast serious doubts on the operational capacities of MI 6, whose primary function since its creation in 1909 had been to collect intelligence.

Furious at having one branch of its activity amputated from it in 1940, the Intelligence Service continually proclaimed that its rival's methods were compromising its actions. The explosions set off by SOE, it said, broke the silence needed to collect information and compromised the security of spies, by attracting the attention of the agents of German repression.[5]

IS had powerful means at its disposal with which to express its rage. In particular, until 1942 it controlled the communications of all secret agents. All SOE radio traffic passed through the Whaddon Hall station in Buckinghamshire, which roused the suspicion of Hugh Dalton's men, who were quick to believe—not without reason—that their rivals were reading their most secret messages.[6] An aggravating circumstance: SOE's subordinate position vis-à-vis IS allowed Stewart Menzies to block operations of which he disapproved.[7] The Intelligence Service was also an untrustworthy colleague that withheld information: it never conveyed to the Special Operations Executive the German exchanges it had decoded via the Ultra system, thanks to the Enigma machine. Finally, though the collection of information lay by rights within the jurisdiction of the Intelligence Service and subversive action within that of SOE, turf wars were common. Denmark, for example, became the exclusive domain of SOE, which, because it had better sources than its rival, combined intelligence and subversive warfare. Although occasional cooperation was established—to operate the Shetland Bus to Norway, for example—the competition between the two services was on the whole more a hindrance than an asset. Churchill did not play favorites, however. A fatalist, he told his military assistant, General Hastings Ismay, in February 1944: "The warfare between SOE and SIS is a lamentable but perhaps inevitable feature of our affairs."[8]

War at Whitehall

Everyone in the Foreign Office viewed with suspicion the subversive warfare waged by SOE. In using the neutral countries as a rear base for its clandestine activities, its agents risked sending them into the arms of the Axis powers, provoking a German military intervention, or poisoning the relations London was maintaining with certain capitals.[9] The Foreign Office was not opposed to espionage, especially in view of the fact that the Intelligence Service reported to it. But it had misgivings about sabotage, which it attempted to restrict by imposing the principle of no explosions without its agreement.[10] Furthermore, the rather cautious temperament of the British diplomats, as well as their culture of discretion, hardly predisposed them to welcome with open arms the men of "ungentlemanly warfare," as Churchill had nicknamed them.[11] At times the diplomats made every effort to thwart them. Ronald Turnbull, having arrived in Stockholm in March 1941 to set up the SOE outpost, operated behind the discreet shield of the British legation's press service, to the great dismay of the ambassador, Victor Mallet. The cunning Mallet buried Turnbull in work, "ostensibly to support his cover, but in reality to leave less time for his SOE duties."[12] Henry Hopkinson, private secretary to the permanent undersecretary of state for foreign affairs, had to spell things out: "It is our considered opinion that SO[E] must operate from Swedish territory and that the Scandinavian activities of SO[E] are more important than any other advantages which we can obtain from Sweden. We must therefore give SO[E] the fullest possible measure of protection and co-operation, even at the risk of jeopardizing yourself and your staff. It is not pleasant for us to give this ruling to you but I know that although it will be not pleasant for you to receive it, we can count on you to do your part."[13] To be sure, Hugh Dalton avoided openly confronting Anthony Eden, who headed the Foreign Office at the time. "He was much too clever to do anything which would irritate the Foreign Secretary, if only because he knew that the goodwill of the Foreign Secretary was essential if SOE . . . was to succeed in establishing itself in the hierarchy of Whitehall."[14] But the hostility between the two ministers persisted, given that Doctor Dynamo mocked the diplomats' caution. "It is not my duty to walk about with a watering-can, but rather to light the fires and let the F.O. extinguish them if they must," he confided in his diary.[15]

Similarly, some military leaders rejected subversive warfare, which, from their point of view, contradicted the principles of the war ethos. General Charles Portal, marshal of the Royal Air Force, demanded that the agents assigned to take action against German aviators stationed in Meucon, in the department of Morbihan, wear uniforms. "I think that the dropping of men dressed in civilian clothes for the purpose of attempting to kill members of the opposing forces is not an operation with which the Royal Air Force should be associated," he explained to Gladwyn Jebb in February 1941. "I think you will agree that there is a vast difference, in ethics, between the time honoured operation of the dropping of a spy from the air and this entirely new scheme for dropping what one can only call assassins."[16] More fundamentally, the general staff questioned the value of operations it believed to be of dubious effectiveness. Portal also exclaimed: "Your work is a gamble which may give us a valuable dividend or may produce nothing. It is anybody's guess. My bombing offensive is not a gamble. Its dividend is certain; it is a gilt-edged investment. I cannot divert aircraft from a certainty to a gamble which may be a gold-mine or may be completely worthless."[17] He had forgotten that the real impact of bombing was far from certain. That view was not without consequences: because the air force, the navy, and the army controlled the resources, they could allocate or refuse to allocate them to subversive warfare. SOE, for example, because it had no bombers, could not parachute in either its agents or materiel. The three branches of the armed services, as it happened, used and abused that power, handicapping the development of the clandestine operations in which they did not believe. Although it was Dalton's ambition to have his service recognized as a "fourth arm" (that is, a fourth branch of the armed services) and treated as the equal of the other three, he had to lower his sights. "Neither he nor his successor would ever be part of the war cabinet or the defense committee, and SOE would have to confine itself to cooperating with the military coordination agencies, without being a member of them."[18] The position of the general staff thus confirmed a key state of affairs: between 1940 and 1943, the pairing of regular warfare with subversive warfare was marked by competition, especially over the resources to be allocated, since when they were granted to one area, they were necessarily denied to the other.

Tense Relations in the Field of Propaganda

In theory, until summer 1941 the Ministry of Economic Warfare controlled propaganda through SO 1. But that control came up against the opposition of the Ministry of Information, which claimed to be in charge of such activities. An agreement was reached on August 1, 1940: propaganda operations that could be debated in Parliament (radio, therefore) would be managed by the minister of information, the Conservative Duff Cooper; those that the government refused to discuss (leaflets, for example) would fall within Hugh Dalton's purview. But by no means did the tensions subside: Cooper claimed that propaganda was a single entity and should thus be assigned to him; Dalton retorted that, since it was part of an overall strategy, it belonged by rights to him.[19]

More concretely, propaganda contravened the values that the BBC was defending tooth and nail. The "Beeb" clung tightly to its credibility. While understanding that the war had completely reshuffled the cards and required flexibility, it refused to bow down to the demons of brainwashing, which, it thought, ran the risk of ruining its credit and alienating its listenership. In December 1941 Noel F. Newsome, head of the BBC's European news operation, warned: "We must give the truth as we see it, not from some bogus propaganda angle. News values are assessed by a professional estimate of what people are interested in and not by propaganda needs."[20] And he added in November 1942, "It is primarily a *news* service and not, in the first place either an experiment in pure radio or a pure 'propaganda' organ. Events and not preconceived ideas determine what it says, although events are seen against a constant background formed of certain principles and beliefs. . . . We suppress nothing of importance which we believe to be true. We give bad *news* promptly and prominently. We express no views which we do not believe to be justified by the facts."[21] That resoluteness could only cause conflicts with SOE, especially since Hugh Dalton had no means to sway an institution that held its independence so dear.

In addition, SO 1, which was in charge of propaganda, and SO 2, responsible for action, did not get along, a situation exacerbated by the fact that SO 2 claimed to be in control of SO 1. "Whereas SO1 tended to regard their colleagues as rather bungling amateur assassins, SO2 equally unjustly began to think of SO1 as half-baked terrorists, who were not to be trusted for reasons of security."[22] Moreover, Rex Leeper, head of propaganda, fell under the influence of Robert Vansittart, who, in addition to his duties as diplomatic adviser to the government, assisted SOE in international relations—at least at the beginning.[23] Propaganda thus tended to be aligned with the cautious positions the Foreign Office recommended.

Furthermore, the men charged with bringing the good word to oppressed peoples lived in Woburn Abbey, a residence generously lent to the secret services by the duke of Bedford. The ambience there was far from festive. As Bruce Lockhart told it, "I . . . rose early, made my own tea, and did most of my written work before breakfast. The rest of the day was spent in meetings, in planning and in endless discussions of the war situation. I lived frugally, took daily exercise, and kept myself reasonably fit."[24]

Above all, Woburn was located some thirty-five miles north of London, which raised obvious problems of coordination with the head office on Baker Street and with the European services of the BBC at Bush House, both of them in the capital. Between October 1940 and August 1941 the staff in charge of propaganda had 74 agents in London, compared to 458 in Woburn.[25] The distance separating them required going back and forth between the three addresses, an exhausting process that compromised the coherence of activities.

Hugh Dalton often dropped in unexpectedly at Woburn Abbey, which did not help matters, if we are to believe Thomas Barman, who was responsible for propaganda for the Scandinavian countries. The minister

> used to come down to Woburn from time to time to inspect the troops. . . . Even at breakfast time his manner was horribly hearty. He used to dress himself up in a sort of heavy white jersey, as worn by the best goal-keepers, and called for volunteers to go for a walk with him of a Sunday morning. Walkers became hard to find after a while; people tended to go to earth when they heard his voice and

that could be heard almost everywhere. . . . He was not particularly scrupulous in his methods. Many of us resented his habit of cultivating the acquaintance of very junior members of the staff in order to find out what the seniors were up [to] and what they were saying.[26]

These conflicts about assignments, stoked by personal animosities, led to a revision of the organization chart. On May 19, 1941, at a meeting of four ministers (Anderson, Dalton, Eden, and Cooper), it was suggested that white propaganda should be given to the Ministry of Information, while its secret counterpart would fall within the purview of the Ministry of Economic Warfare; any issue involving foreign policy would be submitted to the Foreign Office.[27] It was unanimously agreed that a committee consisting of the minister of information, the minister of economic warfare, and the foreign secretary would be formed to establish the main lines, which would then be applied by a technical committee.[28] The results were mixed. As Bruce Lockhart reported: "The committee of three officials [Robert Bruce Lockhart for the Foreign Office, Rex Leeper for the Ministry of Information, Dallas Brooks for the Ministry of Economic Warfare] worked reasonably well, but the committee of the three ministers was never satisfactory, and the weekly meetings, at which the three officials were present, frequently ended in a wrangle between Dr Dalton and Mr Bracken [minister of information] which might have been amusing if it had not deterred all progress so seriously."[29] And, he added, "From the beginning Dr Dalton has been on the defensive and even today when agreement has been reached, probably interprets 'joint ministerial control' in his own way. The scientific definition of daltonism is inability to distinguish between green and red, and I doubt very much if he has ever seen any danger signal to himself."[30]

But Dalton, an astute politician, knew that the imperatives of national unity obliged Winston Churchill to show him consideration. He skillfully exploited that advantage. As he commented in his memoirs: "I played the part of the wicked animal, which, when attacked, defends itself. I found these rows very futile, infuriating and time-wasting. But, in my clashes with Bracken, I had one great advantage. I had a strong position, built up over years, in the Labour Party. If it ever came to a show-down, with Labour Party loyalties aroused, I knew that I could beat him. I could raise much greater hell in the Labour Party than he could with the Tories. And I knew that others knew this too."[31] The revision of the organization chart therefore had little effect. "The main result, apart from preserving the *amour propre* of two Ministers of the Crown, was to perpetuate much of the inefficiency and frustration from which British propaganda had suffered."[32]

Birth of the Political Warfare Executive

That explosive climate led the executive branch to split off SO 1 from SO 2. In summer 1941 a new organization, the Political Warfare Executive (PWE), was formed. Its creation was officially announced in the House of Commons on September 11, 1941, in response to a timely question from an MP.[33]

PWE brought together SO 1, the Division of Foreign Affairs at the Ministry of Information, and the sections concerned with the BBC. Bruce Lockhart became the head of the new organization, while Rex Leeper was in charge of "country headquarters"—meaning black propaganda—with General Dallas Brooks, a career soldier, serving as liaison with the military staffs to align propaganda with the grand strategy.[34] In addition, seven regional management boards oversaw the speeches to be delivered to the enemy or to occupied populations.[35] Every week they submitted their directives to Ivone Kirkpatrick, controller of the European Services of the BBC, who, after approving them, sent them on to the regional editors of English radio.[36] Kirkpatrick, a member of the Foreign Office, "though a prodigious worker,. . . gave the impression of having time on his hands and possessed the gift of producing quicker than anyone else the remark which relieved the situation or the formula which resolved it."[37]

PWE seemed to inaugurate a new era, though its initials sparked sarcasm. The organization quickly acquired the nickname "the Peewees."[38] On a less trivial level, the reforms of summer 1941 were far from meeting the expectations they had raised. In fact, they did not settle the dispute between the advocates of propaganda and the proponents of information. Noel Newsome was the first to draw his sword. On December 9, 1941, the BBC man disseminated a general directive noting that the "best Political Warfare is that waged with the weapons of responsible journalism, not that carried out with the instruments of the clever advertiser." Several members of PWE had previously been employed by the J. Walter Thompson advertising agency; they therefore took that remark as a personal attack and justifiably retorted without delay.[39]

Thomas Barman, a PWE employee in charge of propaganda, noted that Kirkpatrick believed that the "BBC is first and foremost a news-disseminating organization." Barman went on to ask:

> What then of propaganda? Is the BBC a charitable organization with no other function than to provide a free news service to occupied Europe? Is our success to be measured by the frequency of our scoops? Or is the BBC a powerful propaganda weapon? Is its primary aim in occupied Europe to keep morale high so that conquered peoples may be ready to strike at the enemy on the Day? If these are our aims then news . . . becomes the handmaiden, not the mistress, of broadcasting policy. Unless Mr. Kirkpatrick can be induced to understand this, no paper solution of our difficulties, no regard for Mr. Kirkpatrick's peculiar hierarchical susceptibilities can make our present diarchy work.[40]

As a result, cooperation between the regional directors of PWE and the regional editors of the BBC hit a stumbling block. Noel Newsome urged the journalists of Bush House to resist the policy of the Political Warfare Executive, enjoining them to privilege "straight news"—or, to put it more bluntly, news selected by the central bureau of the BBC European Service, over which Newsome exerted supreme control.[41] But, complained Ivone Kirkpatrick, the regional directors of PWE had bypassed him by addressing their instructions directly to their counterparts at the Beeb.[42] This malfunctioning led to a revision of the system. Henceforth there would be meetings between the BBC editors and the PWE directors to adopt a provisional directive, which, after consultation with the Foreign Office, would be submitted to the executive committee through Kirkpatrick. The wrangling did not disappear before 1942, however, primarily because Hugh Dalton, abruptly dispossessed of SO 1, refused to give it up. He continued to interfere in an area that, in theory, was now beyond his authority. A furious Brendan Bracken, minister of information, appealed to the prime minister to intervene.

> Knowing, as I do, the weight of your burdens, I am sorry to have to ask whether you can put an end to the wasteful and harmful muddle caused by the SOE in the field of propaganda. . . .

Dr Dalton justifies his propagandist activities by a supposed distinction between the organization of overt and covert propaganda. All experience has shown that such a distinction is meaningless in practice and ought to be dropped. I suggested the setting up of PWE in the hope that it would end duplication of foreign propaganda. . . .

If Dr Dalton continues his amorphous propagandist operations, there is no case for the existence of a Ministry of Information. It would be cheaper and better to replace it by a Press and Censorship bureau under the Home Office. Dr Dalton can then add the direction of all foreign propaganda to his duties as Minister of Economic Warfare. I am quite willing to give way to him in order to end this scandalous muddle.

The alternative is that Dr Dalton should concentrate on his work as Minister of Economic Warfare and leave the direction of PWE and other propagandist authorities to the Ministry of Information. We may then be able to turn this Ministry into an organization as effective as that established by Lord Beaverbrook in the last War.[43]

But that exhortation led nowhere, because Winston Churchill, who never balked at intervening in the most varied realms, in this case preferred to play Pontius Pilate. Bruce Lockhart lamented: "Much of our teething trouble would have been modified if only the Prime Minister had been interested in political warfare. Unfortunately for us, this great man, himself our greatest war propagandist, attached at best a secondary importance to all forms of propaganda."[44] Churchill believed that "war must be won by deeds not words."[45] To be sure, in the spring of 1942 PWE was transferred from the Ministry of Economic Warfare to the Ministry of Information. The question of propaganda was far from settled. "For the rest of the war the two bodies were forced to live together, suffering all the discomforts of a close union, and enjoying none of the blessings."[46]

Rivalries, tensions, and animosities thus slowed the development of the Special Operations Executive and handicapped its activities. But the United Kingdom suffered equally from the complex relations it maintained with the powers exiled in London in the dark days of 1940.

CHAPTER IV

Ententes Cordiales?

I n fact, the exiled powers were vacillating. On one hand, they considered themselves the United Kingdom's cobelligerents and as such intended to support its war effort fully. But they also perceived themselves as the spokespersons for their suffering nations, which sometimes led them to contest the British strategy, in order to spare their compatriots the heavy tribute the god of war was demanding. For example, several voices rose up against the blockade the Royal Navy imposed on Fortress Europe. On August 3, 1940, Charles de Gaulle asked Winston Churchill to authorize the Americans to supply basic necessities to the free zone. "Behind the governments that come and go there is the French soul, the opinion of a people who, precisely because they are enlightened enough to understand that a higher interest obliges Great Britain to adopt measures from which they will suffer the harsh consequences, would appreciate only the more the gesture of friendship that would allow children and mothers especially to be spared the worst privations."[1] To no avail. The British government, with very rare exceptions, stayed the course, as Hugh Dalton explained to Paul-Henri Spaak, Belgian minister of foreign affairs, who had formulated the same request: "Hardship, is, however, part of the price to be paid for victory, and His Majesty's Government are convinced that it is a price which will gladly be paid in order to hasten the overthrow of the subjugated peoples from alien oppression at the earliest possible moment."[2] Another request, submitted by Belgian ambassador Emile-Ernest Cartier de Marchienne in July 1942, was rejected by Churchill in August in the same terms.[3] The British were afraid that the Germans would seize the food sent into Fortress Europe. That suspicion was not unfounded, given the inhumanity characteristic of the Nazi system. The Germans also took their cue from their experience in World War I; they were still haunted by the memory of the privations imposed on the population, which had led the home front to collapse in 1918.

The alliance with London left the governments in exile with an impossible choice. It obliged them to respect the injunctions of the United Kingdom, which until 1941 was solely responsible for the conduct of operations. But the leaders of the "minor allies," as the British called them—not without condescension—balked, refusing to sacrifice their sovereignty on the altar of war. Their authority had to be preserved, even if that meant accepting a few irregularities from time to time. As a result, incessant conflicts punctuated the relations Great Britain maintained with its partners. These lay primarily in three areas: raids, subversive warfare, and propaganda.

Norwegian Protests

The operations conducted by the commandos in the Lofoten Islands had sparked the enthusiasm of the British, but they provoked anger among the Norwegians. King Haakon's government deplored the brutality of the German repression, judging that the price paid for the destruction of a few herring oil factories had been too high. The government was upset that it had not been alerted in advance about the targets, believing that its knowledge of the country would have allowed it to point out more pertinent objectives. Foreign Minister Trygve Lie was thinking in particular of "the exports of mineral products such as electrolytic copper," the purity of which ensured maximum conductivity of heat and electricity. He therefore suggested that the British might make better use of intelligence provided by the Norwegians and discuss with them "more frankly than they had hitherto done the advantages and disadvantages of the various sorts of diversionary action which are now possible."[4]

That wish proved impossible to grant. Laurence Collier, British ambassador to Norway, noted that the chiefs of staff "have no doubt that, on military grounds, it is unwise to give advance information about any projected operation of war to anybody, however reliable. . . . M. Lie, however reliable he may be, should not be let into the secret about the proposed operations in Norway until they have actually started. To do so in this case would not only be unwise in itself, but would also create the most undesirable precedent." "At the same time," he added, "the Chiefs of Staff recognize that political considerations may be overriding, and that it may be thought essential in the interests of our relations with the Norwegian Government that M. Lie should be given advance information."[5] In winter 1941 the British therefore promised to attack only German installations, but the Norwegians, having been informed of a future operation north of Bergen, feared that the two herring oil factories in the city of Florø would be targeted and would lead to bloody reprisals against the populations.[6]

The British could not allow discontent to take hold, especially since the Norwegian volunteers were balking. After Operation Anklet in the Lofoten Islands, the men of Linge Company had departed for England, leaving their compatriots to face alone the chains of German repression. That situation gave rise to "murmuring."[7] The bitterness of the Norwegian ministers spread to these courageous volunteers who, left to fend for themselves in Great Britain, harbored keen resentment for the way they had been used by the English. Twelve men stated outright that they would refuse to go on if they did not receive assurances beforehand that their government approved of their actions.[8]

The British, after discussing the matter with General Wilhelm von Tangen Hansteen, commander in chief of the Norwegian forces, agreed to set up an Anglo-Norwegian collaboration committee, which met for the first time on February 16, 1942. Chaired by Charles Hambro,[9] deputy chief executive of SOE, whose Danish background made him very familiar with Scandinavia, it included equal numbers of representatives of the two countries and decided jointly on targeted objectives. Is it necessary to point this out? That cooperation was the exception rather than the rule: SOE did not intend to limit its margin for maneuvering by bringing its most modest partners into the decision-making process.

A Policy of Going It Alone?

The governments in exile, knowing that the Special Operations Executive was marginalizing them, sought to develop their own networks, in order to preserve their sovereignty and monitor the resistance emerging in Fortress Europe. Over the short term, the intelligence that their secret services were collecting was an excellent bargaining chip: the British had only a tiny number of honorable correspondents in the field to inform them directly. Over the medium term, the matter at hand was to contain a threat. If the underground forces grew in complete independence or submitted to the orders of the United Kingdom, there was a risk that, on the day of liberation, they would rise up against the émigré powers, invoking the legitimacy acquired in the struggle against the occupier.

On July 1, 1940, Charles de Gaulle therefore assigned André Dewavrin (alias Passy) to set up an intelligence service in Free France. At first it was baptized the Deuxième Bureau (Second Bureau), then the Service de Renseignements (SR; Intelligence Service), and finally the Bureau Central de Renseignement et d'Action (BCRA; Central Bureau of Intelligence and Action). Passy, born in 1911, was a professor of fortifications at the Saint-Cyr military academy. A former student at the École Polytechnique, he had participated in the Norway campaign; then, having gone to England, he immediately rallied behind the Man of June 18. Nothing predestined that novice to take on such a heavy responsibility—of which, however, he acquitted himself brilliantly. Rather than recruit professionals he did not have, Passy came up with the idea of relying on volunteers. Inexperienced but well positioned—because their windows looked out on Brest harbor or because they worked on a submarine base—they would collect intelligence, which would then be transmitted to London. Emissaries were dispatched to North Africa and metropolitan France beginning in August 1940, to recruit people of good will and set up networks.[10]

In September 1940 Jacques Mansion, a BCRA agent, brought back to France maps of the enemy's plan of action and left there a few informants. His mission had no other results. On December 22, 1940, Lieutenant-Commander Honoré d'Estienne d'Orves was delivered to Brittany to implant a network known as Nemrod. An ardent Catholic, he was betrayed by his radio operator, Alfred Gaessler. The lieutenant-commander was arrested on the night of January 21, 1941, put on trial, and executed at Mont Valérien on August 29, 1941, earning the sad privilege of becoming the first Free France agent to be shot by the occupier.

Gilbert Renault (known as Rémy) met a happier fate. A former militant in Action Française, he had set off for England on June 19, 1940. It was not long before he returned to France via Spain, to develop an organization destined for a great future, the Confrérie Notre-Dame (Our Lady Brotherhood). After recruiting Jean Fleuret, head of the pilots at the port of Bordeaux, as well as a lieutenant, Philippon, stationed in Brest, he was able rather quickly to collect intelligence, which was at first transmitted through Jacques Pigeonneau, the French consul in Madrid. Later on, the transmitting set Roméo, installed in Dordogne in the residence of a wine grower and aristocrat named Louis de La Bardonnie, performed that function. By late summer 1941 thirty-five dispatches totaling 910 pages had been sent to London via Madrid; the bulk of the effort came from Rémy's network.[11]

On the Belgian side, subversive warfare was the work of two services. Sûreté de l'État (State Security), a civilian organization created by the Pierlot government in London in November 1940 that reported to the Ministry of Justice, was entrusted to Fernand Lepage, former deputy public prosecutor to the king in Brussels.[12] By early 1943 it had come to comprise four sections. One, headed by Jean Nicodème, dealt with intelligence; another, dedicated to "political warfare," was run by Captain Georges Aronstein; an Evacuation section, rather quickly under the leadership of Commander Delloye, oversaw the exfiltration of aviators, while Idesbald Floor, in charge of the Action section and a friend of Gubbins, was responsible for the complex relations with SOE. The second organization was military in nature. Formed in December 1940, it was first called the Deuxième Section but was renamed the Deuxième Direction on November 16, 1943; it reported to the Ministry of Defense. Colonel Pierre Diepenrijckx was in charge of it from 1928 to 1934, before serving as military attaché to The Hague. Beginning in August 1941 the section was headed by an engineering officer, Jean Ducq. Far from cooperating with each other, however, Sûreté de l'État and the Deuxième Section were at each other's throats. The civilians distrusted the military personnel, whose strategy had led to their downfall during the campaign of 1940, and also suspected them of being fervent Leopoldists, or even proponents of installing an authoritarian regime.[13] That distrust explains why Sûreté had been placed under the control of civilians rather than the military.

Added to that suspicion were the never-ending power struggles, with each service attempting to get a foothold at the expense of its rival. On January 17, 1941, a meeting was convened to clarify the situation. Sûreté would be responsible for liaisons with Belgium, hence missions and contacts with the intelligence networks; the Deuxième Section would draw up questionnaires and make use of the information collected.[14] But embers smoldered under the ashes, and the quarrels never ceased. "Throughout the whole of the present war, there was constant warfare between the 2ème Direction and the Sûreté, which crystallized itself roughly into a battle between the civilians and the military. M. Lepage, an ambitious man, was constantly endeavouring to obtain control over the clandestine activities of the 2ème Direction."[15]

That battle did not prevent Sûreté from setting to work. On January 20, 1941, one of its agents, Frédéric de Selliers, arrived in Belgium to create intelligence networks. In June 1941 Pierre Vandermies (alias Dewinde) was dropped by parachute to establish escape channels and to supervise the existing networks. As it happened, several underground organizations had been formed without awaiting the arrival of emissaries from London. Zéro, founded in July 1940 by Fernand Kerkhofs, head of the Brufina information service (the financial holding company for the Banque de Bruxelles), and his assistant, Jean Moens, gathered intelligence of a military nature but especially political and economic intelligence. The Luc network, which arose within judicial circles, investigated the kingdom's political developments, a matter of interest to its founders, the civil servant Georges Leclercq and the lawyer André Cauvin, though they devoted themselves primarily to military intelligence. Then there was the Clarence network, launched in June 1940 by former members of Dame Blanche, the most important intelligence network of World War I, headed by an engineer from Liège, Walthère Dewé. On a completely different register, Comète came into being in Brussels circles that had been engaged in assisting military personnel since 1940. Under the leadership of Andrée de Jongh, a nurse and decorator, and Arnold Deppé, a radio technician, it endeavored to repatriate British soldiers abandoned after Dunkirk as well as downed RAF airmen. The first convoy left the Belgian capital on August 18, 1941.[16]

The Dutch also set up their own intelligence service (SR). In London on July 19, 1940, François van't Sant created a subbranch of the Centrale Inlichtingsdienst (CID; Central Intelligence Service), to which he had belonged before the war. On August 14, 1941, R.P.J. Derksema succeeded him, followed by Mattheus de Bruyne on February 5, 1942. On November 28, 1942, the CID was dissolved and replaced by the Bureau Inlichtingen (BI; Intelligence Bureau), entrusted to Major H. G. Broekman, a member of the resistance who had successfully reached England by crossing the North Sea. But a heart attack forced him to submit his resignation in July 1943 and to pass the torch to Jan Marginus Somer.[17]

The British, however, refused to let the governments in exile control all the intelligence services, and for obvious reasons. So long as the United Kingdom was fighting alone against Nazi Germany, it could not entrust its security to others by subordinating espionage to the good will of its "minor allies." SOE and SIS thus set up their own clandestine organizations, with uneven results. In Belgium, the Secret Intelligence Service took over Clarence and created another network, Mill; but the service's successes were less brilliant in France and Denmark.

The British secret services ran up against a major obstacle: the lack of personnel. The volunteer pool was limited. Several thousand French and Belgians already lived in England or came there, but only a few hundred Dutch crossed the Channel during World War II.[18] In addition, the job required particular abilities. A spy or saboteur had to be able to blend in, remain discreet, and have good athletic skills alongside certain intellectual gifts, which was not the case for everyone. For example, though five thousand Danes sailed under the Allied flag, few belonged to the middle class, which limited their capacity to make themselves invisible.[19] In addition, despite the spy novels, war out of uniform sometimes suffered from a sulfurous reputation, which was not enhanced by the often austere forms of combat. Colonel Passy explained to Daniel Cordier, a future BCRA agent: "You will not have the moral support that the regular army offers you, that of being surrounded at every moment by your comrades in arms. You will live alone, you will take your meals alone, etc. You are going into seclusion."[20] Few candidates applied, therefore, which obliged the secret services to fight over that scarce resource.

The British, who steered the French recruits toward the Patriotic School in Great Britain, tried to hang on to the talented, without clearly explaining to them that they could join up under the Cross of Lorraine.[21] But the harvests remained meager. "SO2 are seriously short of French personnel to operate in Occupied France and in fact De Gaulle has recruited practically all available French personnel who have the necessary courage and offensive spirit to undertake the dangerous work which is required of SO2 personnel," the British service lamented in January 1941. "We would therefore be grateful if at the interview which we trust the Prime Minister will have with General De Gaulle, he can persuade the General to cooperate by placing his subversive organisation under the direction of SOE, on a basis which will, at the same time, preserve its identity but also lend itself to full cooperation with His Majesty's Government in respect of the wider strategical and tactical issues of the war."[22] The same complaints proceeded from the Belgian section of SOE, which attempted to win recruits via the Deuxième Section. To no avail: Sûreté opposed the practice, requiring that the volunteers be screened by them. As a result, "the difficulties of recruiting . . . were to remain a constant source of trouble."[23]

The British urgently needed the governments in exile to fill the ranks of their secret services, but the reverse was also true. Indeed, logistically speaking, the foreign networks depended almost exclusively on the United Kingdom. Its authorities provided the resources necessary to deliver or exfiltrate agents and to ensure communications. For example, until late 1941 Sûreté did not have any direct liaison with Belgium, which obliged it to transmit its information via the neutral countries, Spain and Portugal in the first place.[24] In short, an entente between allies was imperative.

Negotiating Cooperation

Establishing cooperation was a particularly delicate matter, in that the rivalry between SOE and SIS was further complicated by the bitter internecine quarrels among the exiles. Initially, for example, Free France's Deuxième Bureau proposed to work with MI 6. But Stewart Menzies's men had two irons in the fire: one branch, under the leadership of Wilfred Dunderdale, was working with Vichy; another, headed by Kenneth Cohen, was cooperating with Free France. Both denied Passy the necessary resources and prevented him from gaining access to SOE, which was responsible for subversive action. SOE was just as obstructionist toward its French partner, as its executive director, Frank Nelson, bluntly admitted: "The ideal is to allow the Gestapo and the de Gaulle Staff to think that we are co-operating 100% with each other—whereas in truth, whilst I should wish you to have the friendliest day to day relationship and liaison with the de Gaulle people, I should wish you at the same time to tell them nothing of our innermost and most confidential plans." He added: "This co-operation however—to put it quite brutally—must be one sided; i.e., I should wish our F Section to be fully cognisant of every thing that the de Gaulle people are doing, but I do not wish the de Gaulle organisation to be in the least cognisant of anything that S.O.2 are doing."[25]

A détente of sorts took place in 1941, however. An RF section, assigned to cooperate with Free France, was added to section F, which worked in complete independence. Headed by Eric Piquet-Wicks, the RF section was supposed to rationalize subversive actions and plan joint operations. In actuality, the SOE leaders, "apart from any Gaullist control," took upon themselves "coordination of the paramilitary activities undertaken in France, some by section F, others by section RF."[26] It is therefore clear why General de Gaulle adopted a suspicious attitude, marked by rigidity, toward Perfidious Albion.

The situation in Belgium appeared in a different light, inasmuch as Sûreté and the Intelligence Service cooperated closely with each other. That collaboration was formalized at a meeting between Pierlot and Menzies on August 12, 1941. The accord they reached stipulated, among other things, that the intelligence networks operating in Belgium would be in the service of both countries, that British codes would be used for all wireless communications, and that the information coming from Belgium would be disseminated via IS to all the British services. A protocol, established on May 15, 1942, was formalized in a letter that the Belgian prime minister sent to the head of IS the following June 19. A harmonious collaboration therefore developed between the two services.[27] But it occurred at the expense of SOE and the Deuxième Section, since Sûreté and IS strove jointly to "monopolize intelligence activity in the country. Most of the conflicts between secret services with respect to Belgium can be analyzed from the angle of the control exerted by Sûreté/IS, which sought to be exclusive."[28] The two agencies sometimes used underhanded methods. The Intelligence Service, for example, told SOE that the unpredictable Belgian government had come to England "faute de mieux" [for lack of anything better]. It concealed the fact that it was cooperating with that government and never encouraged the Belgian authorities to work with the men from Baker Street.[29] That situation contributed toward marginalizing the Deuxième Section and hardly promoted a relationship of trust between the services collaborating in subversive warfare. That form of warfare also suffered from the ambivalence of the British authorities.

British Ambivalence

As we have seen, the United Kingdom, all alone in waging the fight against the Reich, wished to set Europe ablaze, by dispatching SOE agents charged with organizing the struggle and urging the oppressed people to revolt. At the same time, it often brushed aside that strategy in accord with imperatives where, paradoxically, opportunistic calculations and ethical principles mingled together.

For example, London sometimes preferred the reassuring certainties of the status quo to the harrowing winds of change. For many long weeks, the United Kingdom treated respectfully both Philippe Pétain and Maxime Weygand, delegate general to French Africa, hoping—like many others—that Vichy would resist German demands and that North Africa would come over to the Allied camp. Likewise, some elements in the intelligence services (SR) of the two countries cooperated with each other. SR Air, for example, under the leadership of Colonel Georges Ronin, transmitted westward a large quantity of intelligence about the aeronautics industry and the German order of battle, especially via Captain Charles Lacat and Lieutenant André Rauscher, who, from Tunis, established a liaison with Malta. Working together, Georges Ronin and Frederick Winterbotham, head of the Air Section of the Intelligence Service, were in continuous communication between 1940 and 1942; London even went so far as to supply radio sets to its French counterparts.[30] That cooperation remained limited, however. "[Vichy's] goal was not at all to work hand in hand with the British but rather to draw the maximum benefits from contacts by giving the British the minimum information required to maintain the link."[31]

To preserve these arrangements and plan for the future, London avoided provoking the French State, as Rex Leeper noted at a meeting held on November 17, 1940: "The policy of encouraging a Left revolution would come into conflict with the declared intention of HMG [His Majesty's Government] to arrive at a modus vivendi with the Petain Government. Moreover it would certainly give great offence to Weygand, with whom particularly HMG hoped to make contact."[32] The propaganda fell into line. The British did suggest, in August 1941, that the appeal to the French "to take action against Vichy government by way of manifestations or otherwise should be sharpened." But it advised against campaigns that would move "from the field of harmless agitation to that of incitement to action leading to sabotage or revolt."[33] In fact, "no premature attempts at sabotage were to be made and passive resistance was the order of the day."[34] SOE thus avoided intervening in the free zone. That line was at odds with

British public opinion, however. According to a report from the Ministry of Information, in January 1941 some 75 percent of the English were against Vichy—which did not mean, however, that they supported de Gaulle. Although 40 percent of those polled approved of him, 30 percent expressed an unfavorable opinion, and 30 percent indicated no interest.[35]

For many years, Denmark also benefited from Whitehall's indulgence. The kingdom, occupied by Nazi Germany in 1940, held on to its institutions. Its monarch, Christian X, enjoyed a glowing reputation; he was considered an ally rather than an adversary. The British authorities therefore refrained from throwing oil on the fire, believing that the benefits of neutrality took precedence over an adventurous policy. SO 1 recommended in March 1941 that "nothing should be done that might force the King to make a declaration stating that as fighting between Denmark and Germany has been called off on the orders of himself and his legally constituted Government, Danes abroad are acting illegally. . . . The King is the only national figure round whom Danish national resistance can now be rallied, and if he is compromised in any way in the eyes of free Danes by a declaration of this kind the chances of successfully organising resistance would be greatly reduced."[36] For a time the secret services had considered exfiltrating the crown prince, Knud. The Foreign Office advised against the operation. "It is important not to endanger the King's position. . . . Even if it were possible, any other action of this nature . . . might have the effect of embroiling the King with the Germans to the point where he would no longer be able to maintain his present position."[37]

That line, though it left open the full range of possibilities, ran the risk of weakening the resistance, by rewarding *attentisme* (the watch-and-wait attitude) and discouraging the underground and volunteers throughout Europe who had come to the aid of the United Kingdom in the harrowing hours of 1940. General Edward Spears, responsible for relations with Free France, warned in February 1941: "Is it realized that every encouragement given to Vichy is a blow directed at Free France?. . . We may, all unknowingly, be killing, through sheer pusillanimity the spirit of Free France. . . . The result is certain if General de Gaulle disappears and France—Occupied France the only part of the country that really counts today—will fall a victim to despair and accept its fate as a vassal of Germany."[38] Over time, British propaganda therefore adopted a harsher tone toward Vichy. Until 1943, however, it maintained a cautious attitude toward Denmark.

The Contradictions of Propaganda

That said, the peoples of Europe, far from remaining passive, were beginning to stir. At a demonstration on the Champs-Élysées on November 11, 1940, hundreds of high school and college students commemorated the French victory of 1918, which was also saluted by hundreds of Belgians in Brussels. In April 1941 regular strikes were launched in Hainaut and Ghent, and on May 10 a movement began at the Cockerill Company in Seraing, attracting some sixty thousand participants on May 19.[39] Conflicts erupted in unison on May 27, 1941, in the mines of Pas-de-Calais, suspending the work of some hundred thousand pitmen. On a completely different register, the first roundup of Jews ordered by Heinrich Himmler in the Netherlands prompted tramway workers and municipal employees to launch a strike that, having begun in Amsterdam, spread to several provincial cities (Haarlem, Zaandam, Hilversum) on February 26 and 27, 1941.[40] Above all, the Norwegians declared their rejection of the New Order with implacable determination and extraordinary courage.

Quisling, though he did not exercise power, meant to Nazify his country. On October 4, 1940, his party, the Nasjonal Samling, demanded that all civil servants sign a declaration of loyalty; in November he ordered that physicians join the party's Guild for Health and Hygiene, which the Norway Medical Association refused to do. Immediately afterward, teachers were also urged to submit. Their labor union responded by inviting its members to sign a declaration of principles: "With reference to the enquiry received, I hereby declare that I will remain true to my teaching vocation and my conscience, and that on this basis I shall in the future as in the past, carry out the decisions relating to my work which are lawfully given by my superiors." In mid-December Minister of the Interior Albert Vijam Hagelin asked—in vain—that civil servants sign a declaration of allegiance to the Nasjonal Samling and the new authorities. On April 3, 1941, twenty-two associations sent a formal protest to the Reichskommissar. On May 15 the presidents of forty-three organizations did the same and protested, also to Terboven, against the abuses of authority proliferating within the NS.[41] Finally, on September 8, 1941, the introduction of milk rationing unleashed a conflict that, in the region of Oslo alone, drew twenty to thirty thousand strikers.[42]

This (nonexhaustive) list of political and social movements confirms that the peoples of Western Europe were beginning to stand up to the intolerable German occupation. But that unrest worried the British. By their actions, the civilian populations intended to defend themselves against the subjugation that the Nazis had in store for them, without, for the time being, necessarily thinking about playing a role in their own liberation. These demonstrations, though of paramount importance ethically and politically, had only a minor strategic interest in London's eyes. At the time the United Kingdom did not possess the military resources to back the rebels by means of a landing. These efforts were therefore condemned to failure. Worse, they risked plunging the rebels into the depths of despair and destroying the trust they had in Great Britain. By that measure, the very success of the V campaign caused alarm. It had given rise to a reckless optimism. "Independent reports appear to confirm this view held by the Dutch Government that there is a danger in Holland from *over-optimism*. This over-optimism, evidenced, for example, in the recent Amsterdam riots [unleashed by anti-Semitic persecution] might result in the loss, prematurely, of the best leaders and the most outrageous fighters, and would almost certainly be followed, unless checked, by a severe reaction."[43] In addition to the risk of bloody reprisals, the campaign "provided an easy escape for those who were reluctant to undertake a more courageous stand against collaboration, they could satisfy their conscience with a 'V' act."[44]

The British authorities therefore acted with circumspection. They urged the resistance not to show itself. They explained to the Belgians and the Dutch in March 1941: "The first job we have in hand, therefore, points out, while emphasizing all the reasons for full confidence in victory which exist, that the war is not yet over, and that the fullest and most open resistance should be reserved for its latest stages, when we will give the sign."[45] Likewise, Anthony Eden told Minister of Information Brendan Bracken that "the campaign should not pass from the field of harmless agitation to that of incitement to action leading to sabotage or revolt. . . . I think it would be wise for us to do what we can to damp down in the press any suggestion that the 'V' campaign in its present stage is designed to foment violent action in the occupied territories."[46] Finally, on May 8, 1942, Bruce Lockhart, head of PWE, asked Douglas Ritchie at the BBC to suspend the V campaign.[47]

All in all, that affair revealed the ambivalence of the British, torn between the desire to urge people to revolt and the fear of hurling them downward into the abyss, for the sake of military gains that were only hypothetical. It especially illustrated the gulf between members of the resistance and the British: whereas resistance corresponded to a logic of occupation, Britain embraced the logic of war. In the end, caution prevailed, with a few minor exceptions. In March 1941 SO 1 prescribed that "the first aim of our propaganda to Norway must therefore be to persuade the Norwegians to hold their hand, and not to fritter away their energy and ingenuity on unplanned acts of sabotage. We must, however, not overlook that an apparently pointless act of sabotage may be most valuable in keeping up morale. Great care must be taken not to depress it by crude appeals for caution."[48] In September of the same year, the Belgian section of PWE also sought to draw the line between *attentisme* and premature engagement.

> The danger of driving the best and more daring elements in Belgium too quickly along the road of active resistance cannot be ignored. Meanwhile, the majority of the population, though fundamentally pro-British and anti-German, has not yet been brought to realize fully the importance of the role it can play in the war. There is far too much economic if not political collaboration with Germany.
>
> Our propaganda in this direction has not been so successful because the instructions it has issued have not been sufficiently specific and have been interpreted in too varied a sense by their recipients. The Belgian section of the BBC has begun recently to issue more specific instructions, which steer a middle course between inciting Belgians to useless acts of sabotage and allowing malingerers to remain entirely passive. This new tendency should be developed in all fields of propaganda.[49]

In short, the British authorities feared that the internal resistance would take action prematurely. For their fight to be harmonized with the Allied grand strategy, the British had to exert, directly or through the governments in exile, control over the underground forces. That control rested on one condition: the exiled powers had to be fully legitimate.

CHAPTER V

Legitimacy at Stake

I n London, the legitimacy of the exiled authorities was a key issue: the oppressed peoples and resistance groups would obey only an undisputed power. The British therefore strove to shore up the representativeness of the émigré governments, even at the risk of chipping away at the principle of noninterference in which London took such pride.

The Case of Belgium

From that standpoint, Belgium was problematic. King Léopold was at war with the government in exile, which limited the Pierlot cabinet's influence over a largely loyalist society. In addition, as we have seen, that cabinet comprised four unpopular men, which alarmed the British. "From the point of view of propaganda, the members of the Belgian Government in London mean next to nothing to the bulk of the population in the occupied territory. Three of these members—MM Pierlot, De Vleeschauwer and Gutt—never possessed any real popularity or prestige in the country. They just happened to be ministers. That of M. Spaak was shattered by the national disaster which the policy of neutrality imposed by him with tremendous assurance as a panacea, had brought upon the country or at least had been unable to avert."[1]

Downing Street therefore asked repeatedly that the Belgian cabinet be expanded. Hubert Pierlot persistently opposed the move, primarily on constitutional grounds. Because the Belgian government rested on fragile foundations, any modification could be interpreted as a violation of the mandate entrusted by the nation. The addition of new members, he believed, could lead Léopold III to form a new cabinet under pressure from the occupier, arguing that the old one no longer had any legal existence.[2] That argument left Foreign Secretary Lord Halifax unmoved. As he noted in November 1940: "This argument is unconvincing, as the Government—which has assumed the constitutional power of the Sovereign—is clearly at liberty to appoint or dismiss Cabinet Ministers. A strong Government in London, comprising the leading representatives of all parties, is less likely to be challenged by the King or by public opinion in occupied territory than the present Government which has lost so much prestige."[3]

An alternative was put forward: reincorporate the ministers who had not come to London in 1940. Pierlot brushed it aside. Because these men had resigned, they could not be automatically reincorporated, he explained in November 1941. That inflexible rule dissuaded some former ministers from crossing the Channel, because they were not assured of recovering their portfolio.[4] There were also ethical issues, as the prime minister repeated on February 16, 1943. To call back those who had resigned without due attention to legalities would amount to "giving credence to the opinion among the Allies that when the Belgian government, reduced to four members, had been installed in London, it left the largest portion of the government in France, to preserve the chances of a radically different policy from the one that was conducted here; and that, as the course of the war improves, the Belgian government may gradually shift its center of gravity by strengthening the faction in London. Nothing is more false and dangerous than such an idea."[5]

Hubert Pierlot also feared that, through the introduction of personalities he believed to be controversial, the entente within his cabinet would be threatened and he would be rejected by his fellow citizens. In a meeting with Winston Churchill in 1940, Pierlot said that the Socialist Camille Huysmann "had been burgmaster of Antwerp and had quitted his post very early because of the severities which the Germans would have used towards him. He was much criticized in Belgium, and would be a great source of disunity in the group of Belgian Ministers." Churchill added that the

Catholic Paul Van Zeeland, a prominent man who had served several times as minister, "was a controversial figure in Belgium, and his inclusion would do more harm than good. However, [Pierlot] promised to consider the representations I made, but I should not think that much would come of his reflections."[6] Finally, and perhaps above all, Pierlot, "a weak but obstinate man," according to Halifax, likely feared taking into his government "characters stronger than his own."[7]

The Belgian government, crippled by the task at hand, nonetheless decided in February 1942 to increase its numbers by adding undersecretaries. The Liberal Julius Hoste was given Public Education, the Socialist Henri Rolin National Defense, and the technocrat Gustave Joassart Refugee Assistance, Labor, and Social Planning.[8] In October of the same year, Antoine Delfosse from the Catholic Party, who had been unable to follow the government to Great Britain, became minister of justice, information, and propaganda, an office for which his knowledge of occupied Belgium had prepared him. Conversely, Henri Rolin was relieved of his duties for having been too quick to have dealings with representatives of the Légion Belge, a resistance organization, without having informed the government. In 1943 two ministers who had remained in France crossed the Channel and received portfolios—Public Works and Communications in April for the Socialist August Balthazar, Interior for the Christian Democrat August de Schryver in May.[9]

That reshuffling was intended to strengthen national unity by maintaining a balance among various political leanings and a relative parity between Francophones and Flemings. It did not come near to calming British fears, however. Until the feverish hours of the liberation, the London authorities doubted the influence of a government that, they believed, would have difficulty holding sway over its population.

Norway and the Netherlands

The situation appeared in a more favorable light for Norway and the Netherlands. In both cases, the sovereign had accompanied his or her government, each of which, united, had left the country to continue the fight alongside the United Kingdom. But the Norwegians sought to strengthen the legitimacy of their sovereigns. In August 1941 the Liberal Johan Ludwig Mowinckel, a minister without portfolio, resigned, followed in November

1941 by Colonel Birger Ljungberg, who was in charge of Defense at the time. "These changes, as M. Lie [minister of foreign affairs] admitted frankly, were intended to increase the popularity as well as the efficiency of the Government," by removing two men who were "personally unpopular" in Norway.[10] Apart from a few permutations and the creation in October 1942 of a Department of the Navy, entrusted to the Liberal Arne Sunde, the only significant change was the appointment of Paul Hartmann, former mayor of Oslo who had just escaped from Norway, to Finances on November 28, 1941. The Norwegian cabinet, displaying strong cohesion and benefiting from the high moral stature of King Haakon VII, caused no anxiety among its British counterparts. The same was true for its Dutch counterpart, once the queen, as we have seen, had obtained De Geer's resignation.

Committees and De Facto Authorities

Three countries in Western Europe did not have a government in exile, a situation that plunged the British into deep perplexity. Should they encourage the creation of de facto authorities—in other words, of powers that claimed to be "governments," without being recognized as such by the international community, and whose fragile legitimacy would limit their ability to act (to conclude treaties, for example)?[11] More than one factor pushed London in that direction. These powers, in harnessing a share of political legitimacy, would undermine the influence of the collaborationist governments, which would complicate the German occupiers' task. They would encourage the internal resistance, which, in the absence of legal support, could appear illegitimate, discouraging people of good will. Indeed, the presence of a regular authority in London "was meant to inspire hope in the people that the situation was not irreversible and to spur or reinforce their desire to fight." "In this perspective, one might suggest that the refusal of an occupied country's legitimate authorities to take part in a process of legitimizing the occupier's power is one of the key factors in the development of the people's resistance."[12] The British clearly gauged what was at stake. "The immediate provocation to action is most likely to be effective if it comes from a source felt to be openly accepting political and military responsibility," the BBC noted in 1941.[13]

France was a special case. In August 1940 Winston Churchill had bestowed legitimacy on Charles de Gaulle, and though he at first ordered the Rebel to treat Philippe Pétain with consideration, he gradually adopted a harder line. He spelled it out to Anthony Eden, the foreign secretary, in February 1941:

> We have received nothing but ill-treatment from Vichy. It would have been better to have had Laval from our point of view than Darlan who is a dangerous, bitter, ambitious man without the odium which attaches to Laval. I think it is important at the moment to be stiff with these people, and to assert the blockade whenever our ships are available. In the meantime, an end should be put to the cold-shouldering of General DG and the Free French movement, who are the only people who have done anything for us, and to whom we have made solemn engagement.[14]

At the same time, de Gaulle was only one man, and he had no eminent political supporters. He therefore had to broaden his base. An order of October 27, 1940, created the Conseil de Défense de l'Empire (Empire Defense Council), which included, in addition to de Gaulle, the governors of the territories who had rallied to the cause (Edgard de Larminat, Félix Éboué, Leclerc, Henri Sautot), military leaders (Georges Catroux and Émile Muselier), and three personalities from varied backgrounds: Father Georges Thierry d'Argenlieu, a friar and alumnus of the École Navale; René Cassin, a distinguished jurist and prominent representative of the veterans movement; and the military doctor Adolphe Sicé.[15]

Even so, the sole exercise of power on which the Man of June 18 insisted troubled some leaders of Free France, who were intent on establishing collective rule; it alarmed the British leaders, who would have liked to attract prominent personalities and had visions of keeping in check a man whose haughty inflexibility sometimes verged on intransigence. Churchill lent a hand. Without wanting to attack "General de Gaulle's stature as a champion of continued resistance to the enemy," he recommended that the movement be given "a broader basis" and that "an effective Council to shape its policy" be formed "with which His Majesty's Government could deal." The prime minister could count on Admiral Muselier, who had dreams of supplanting the Rebel. On September 18, 1941, Muselier, head of the Free French Naval Forces, demanded the creation of an "executive committee of Free France." He became its chair, leaving to de Gaulle the honorary chair and the command of the armed forces. In the storm threatening the unity of Free France, Churchill intervened, assigning Eden the mission of refereeing the dispute. On September 24, 1941, talks concluded with an order creating the Comité National Français (CNF; French National Committee). It had eight members, including René Pleven, Maurice Dejean, René Cassin, and Georges Thierry d'Argenlieu, and introduced a form of collective rule, since regulations would be adopted in common. But de Gaulle retained full and complete authority. Members of the committee answered only to him, and six of the eight were loyalists through and through.[16] Churchill admitted his disappointment: "Our intention was to compel de Gaulle to accept a suitable Council. All we have done is to compel Muselier & Co. to submit themselves to de Gaulle. . . . Our weight in the immediate future must be thrown more heavily against de Gaulle than I had hoped would be necessary."[17]

Denmark followed a radically different scenario, inasmuch as it had a regular government, which Great Britain, at least until 1942, refrained from bullying. "Great Britain did not bind herself, at the start, to any definite policy. One consolation in this, from the Danish point of view, was that the fiction of Danish neutrality was not contested."[18] But on July 26, 1940, a meeting at the Danish Club in London laid the foundations for a committee whose nature—civilian or military?—remained vague. In September two thousand copies of an appeal were printed. It invited all Danes who resided in Great Britain to unite and culminated in the creation of a "Danish Council" on October 9,[19] chaired by Michael Kroyer-Kielberg, a ship owner whose ancestors had come from the country of Hans Christian Andersen.

London, however, refused to grant the council full recognition. Roderick Gallop of the Foreign Office summed things up in November 1941: "So long as the King and government continue to rule in Denmark it would clearly be premature to recognize any London Committee as representing Denmark as a whole. But the Danish Council . . . has long since been assured of the recognition, sympathy and support of His Majesty's Government and there would now appear to be a number of cogent reasons in favour of finding some more suitable formula for according to the Free Danes the name of Allies." That indirect recognition, he continued, would augment the passive resistance of the Danes. "It would help to give these people the feeling that they are in the war on our side." Recognizing the council as a committee, or as a government, was ruled out, however.[20]

That objective concealed less noble calculations. In the first place, the committee was used primarily to encourage the Danes living in the United Kingdom to enlist under the Union Jack, while avoiding any conspicuous commitment by the London authorities, who were anxious to handle Danish patriotism gingerly.[21] In the second place, should the government in Copenhagen refuse to commit itself further in its collaboration with the Reich, it might be led to resign, leading to the monarch's abdication. Great Britain therefore had to have an alternative solution at hand, in the form, for example, of a committee set up outside Denmark that could speak in the kingdom's name and address the captive population. Furthermore, as the Foreign Office pointed out, prominent personalities would have to strengthen and consolidate Denmark's legitimacy, which was still shaky in early 1942,[22] given that Kroyer-Kielberg had become a British citizen in 1926.

As early as 1941 the British had been concerned with exfiltrating high-profile leaders. In March 1941 they had attempted to contact Christmas Møller, a Conservative minister whose resignation the Germans had demanded and obtained in October 1940. The invitation did not reach its addressee, however, or perhaps he turned a deaf ear to it, as the British legation to Stockholm suspected.[23] In June 1941 Hugh Dalton asked Hans Hedtoft Hansen, a Social Democrat whom he had run into at an international congress before the war, to rally behind Great Britain. The presence of both a leftist and a rightist was supposed to "contribute to maintaining the neutrality of the Danish council."[24] But the Social Democrat turned down that proposal after discussing it with the prime minister, Thorvald Stauning. The two men believed that the departure of an eminent Social Democrat would sow such confusion that the policy of negotiation with Germany would be compromised, and the Danish political leaders did not want such a breach.[25]

A second letter was nonetheless sent to Møller in October 1941. "With conditions in Denmark becoming daily more critical it is vitally important that at least one well-known Danish patriot should come out of Denmark to help lead the Free Danes who are at present in great need of leadership. . . . At this moment when the fate of the Stauning government, and even perhaps of the King, is in the balance there must be a representative body of Danes ready to take over the responsibility of speaking and acting for Denmark in the present great conflict."[26] SOE took charge of the operation, while the Foreign Office simply adopted a prudent reserve.

Poaching a politician would likely be met with disapproval; the Conservatives had received only 15 percent of the vote in the prewar legislative elections; and the diplomats would have preferred by far Hedtoft Hansen to Møller, whose "quick temper and awkward manner, as well as his political beliefs, inevitably raised doubts."[27] The exfiltration of the former minister was nonetheless organized. The Conservative leader secretly went to Sweden aboard a freighter transporting a load of chalk. He arrived in London on May 14, 1942, accompanied by his wife and son. The Danish Council now had a high-profile chairman—which incurred the wrath of the German occupiers. But London's tolerant policy toward Copenhagen limited its actions: the Free Danes were still not recognized as allies or as a de facto authority.

The Italian Imbroglio

In Italy, finally, Great Britain went from setback to disappointment. In 1940 Mussolini ruled his country with an iron fist, though Churchill was counting on the weariness of the population to cut short an unpopular war. He also had dreams of coming up with a political alternative to Il Duce. Even so, he needed recognized leaders.

As of 1940 the Ministry of Economic Warfare and the Ministry of Information endeavored to encourage the creation of an Italian committee, a system that had many advantages. It would "dispel the impression which appears to be prevalent that His Majesty's Government might be prepared to treat with the Fascist Government and in consequence are not going all out in the secret war effort against Italy." In addition, "such a movement would encourage anti-Fascists here and all over the world." Finally, it would impel the Italians in Italy to confront "the choice of either continuing loyal to their country or identifying themselves with a rebel movement."[28] Above all, a committee could lead the British government out of an impasse. London could not propose to Rome "a different form of government, since that would be regarded as interference and resented; nor can it offer inducements without disclosing its peace aims." By contrast, an independent Italian opposition would hold out the hope for a better regime and a brighter future, without any involvement on Great Britain's part.[29]

The Foreign Office was less enthusiastic. "The emergence in this country of a free-Italy movement, even of limited aims and ostensibly without official support, would inevitably be interpreted not only by Italian propaganda but also by Italians as a whole an artificial movement devised by His Majesty's Government."[30] In addition, it was preferable that a committee "have its roots in Italy itself," in order to shore up its legitimacy. The exiles, in fact, were either unknown or forgotten by their compatriots, be they Count Sforza, a Liberal politician, Don Sturzo, leader of the Christian Democrats, or Professor Salvemini, a historian and Socialist (all three were antifascists from day one, however).[31]

Duff Cooper and Hugh Dalton overcame Anthony Eden's resistance and saw to it that Carlo Petrone, a Christian Democratic antifascist who had taken refuge in England in 1939, would lay the foundations for a Free Italy Committee in January 1941.[32] The British authorities, without granting him full recognition, agreed that two committees should be founded, one in London, the other in Egypt.[33] But the Foreign Office balked. Petrone was totally unknown to the general public; his leadership abilities appeared perfunctory and his influence limited. What was destined to happen happened: a crisis erupted in July 1941. Some members of the committee revolted, dismissed Petrone, and named as their chairman Alessandro Magri, a radio announcer working for British propaganda. Was this crisis, as the Ministry of Information thought, "due to the latent antagonism aroused by Clerical and Left feelings among Italians in this country"? The Foreign Office did not believe so and suggested a more mundane reason: "Dr. Petrone, as we foresaw from the beginning, is an entirely unsuitable person to be a leader or Secretary of the Movement which, under pressure of Dr. Dalton and Mr Duff Cooper, we allowed to be founded." Eden's office therefore recommended that the movement no longer be supported.[34] Even so, the Free Italy Movement, formed on July 26, 1941, was authorized to follow in the footsteps of the Free Italy Committee.[35] Petrone flooded the British authorities with complaints. "Several of my friends and I are alarmed at the extreme Left tendency which seems to prevail in the Free Italy Movement. . . . I begin to see the necessity for a new, more representative organism to express the feelings of Italians who are loyal to this country and better aware of the real situation of our own," he explained to the Foreign Office. He then expressed his astonishment: "Indeed, out of a hundred members of the Free Italy Movement more than a half are Jews. It should be clear that such a movement is not representative of the Italian situation (I am, of course, not speaking of the 'racial point of view,' but from the psychological, social and religious one)."[36] The British took no account of these jeremiads, observing that "ever since he was rejected by the Free Italy Movement [Petrone] has been struggling for self-expression and he has become rather a nuisance."[37] In any event, the Free Italy Movement had little influence and was reduced to impotence during the war. In 1945 a member of SOE concluded sadly, but not without lucidity, "There were no Italian lessons to be learned from the experimental phenomenon of De Gaulle."[38]

North Africa provided a much more promising path. In January 1941 the British launched an offensive in Libya by means of which they took Bardia, then Tobruk, in Cyrenaica. On January 21 they reached the border of Tripolitania, after capturing some hundred thousand Italian soldiers. That success fired Winston Churchill's imagination. "We might even rule Cyrenaica under the Free Italian flag," he suggested to General Ismay, his closest military adviser, "and treat it in the same way as de Gaulle's colonies are being treated subject to our military control. Anyhow, I wish Cyrenaica to be petted and made extremely comfortable and prosperous, more money being spent upon them than they are intrinsically worth. . . . We might make it a model of British rule."[39] The war cabinet went even further: "The idea of a prosperous Free Italian Colony is very attractive, since, inter alia, the fact of its existence would enable us to encourage Italians to hope that the future of their country is not necessarily tied up with Germany and Fascism."[40]

But the leaders were aware of the magnitude of the task. There was a risk, the same ministers observed, that that scheme would be interpreted as a promise to return the colony to the Italians after the war, which was unthinkable. London had no intention of tying its own hands, especially since such a decision could be understood by the Arabs as a "betrayal." In addition, the United Kingdom did not wish to play mediator between the colonists and the local populations, a posture that reminded them of the unpleasant situation it faced in Palestine, where it intervened between the Jews and the Arabs. Cyrenaica, finally, was not self-sufficient, and the delivery of the goods necessary to make it prosperous was an impossible mission.[41] In any case, the incursion of the Afrikakorps troops in 1941, as well as Rommel's successes, served to shatter the wild ideas Churchill had toyed with for a time.

Then there were the prisoners. A few British leaders dreamed of tapping that unexpected source of volunteers who might join the Allied camp, on the model of the experiments conducted during World War I. They soon lowered their sights. In the first place, few volunteers responded to the call. "Generally speaking the Italian soldiers who were taken prisoners were for the most part perfectly content to remain prisoners, and showed no desire whatever, either for money or for any other reason, to return to their country in an adventurous capacity."[42] That observation was valid for both North Africa and India, where thousands of Italian prisoners had been transferred. In 1941 and 1942 several missions to separate the anti-Mussolini wheat from the Fascist chaff were carried out by SO 1, PWE, and the Mazzini Society, an antifascist group created by Gaetano Salvemini in 1939. A camp for democratic prisoners was even built in Jaipur, as the supply corps tried to respond to the captives' most urgent needs. To attract volunteers, a newspaper, *La Diana*, was launched, and it filled its columns with love and sex, two enticements believed to be attractive to men deprived of the pleasures of the flesh. Five hundred volunteers were incorporated into two battalions of pioneers—an insignificant result.[43] In fact, their selection was a complex matter. The men were surveyed about their political sentiments, but that time-consuming examination was of little use, since the British doubted the genuineness of the opinions expressed.[44] Above all, they did not take stock of the difficulty of the undertaking: many captives would not consider resuming combat against their country alongside their former enemies—a moral dilemma that surely did not arise for the Gaullists, since the French and British were allies.

Above all, that hypothetical legion would have required a prestigious leader, a matter that at first caused no anxiety: "It should not be difficult to find Italian de Gaulle."[45] Captured in Bardia, General Annibale Bergonzoli, *la barba electrica* (electric beard) as he was nicknamed, seemed to want to join the British, but he quickly disappointed his protectors. The British general Francis Davidson lashed out against him: "Considered by Bersaglieri as rather a mountebank. Rushes about paying surprise visits to units and can rarely be found in his office. . . . I consider that he would be unsuitable as a leader of any Free Italian Movement, being of an excitable and somewhat unstable temperament. He probably reached his present rank by subservience to the Fascist Party. . . . In any case he has shown speed rather than guts in fighting against us."[46] The War Office, in any case, distrusted a Free Italy movement commanded by a general. As a result, "schemes for raising a Free Italian force never reached a planning stage."[47] The mirage of Italian troops waging war alongside the Anglo-American forces vanished in the desert sands.

All in all, London considered the support of governments in exile or of de facto authorities a difficult trump card to play. Superimposed on the rigidity of partners anxious to defend their sovereignty was the ambivalence of their contradictory rationales, which reflected both the rivalry of competing institutions and hesitations about the strategy to be adopted. The confrontation between these divergent points of view, whether blunt or understated, gave rise to conflicts that, as we have seen, concerned control of the secret services. It caused equally violent clashes in the area of propaganda.

Questions of Control

Whatever the media used (leaflets, newspapers, or radio broadcasts), propaganda was destined to play a major role in the conflict. In addition to sparking the people's desire to resist, it delivered instructions to the masses and to the minority that took action, namely, resistance movements and networks. By that measure, control of propaganda was a key issue, to which the powers in exile sometimes laid claim. They meant to defend their sovereignty. And, because they knew their countries intimately, they believed they were better qualified than the British to address their fellow citizens.

The London authorities defended a diametrically opposed point of view. In their eyes, propaganda served an overall strategy, and they could not tolerate a pluralism that would undermine its coherence. Even while admitting the diversity of points of view, they also would not allow the line defended by the "minor allies" to deviate from—and even less, contradict—propaganda policy.[48] As a PWE leader pointed out, "On some of the most important issues, it is always possible that their views, inevitably influenced to some extent by thoughts of their own position after the war, will not coincide with our own."[49]

In January 1938, for the first time in its history, the BBC broadcast programs directed at foreign countries, addressing the Arab populations that the Axis was attempting to entice. After the Munich Agreement, Neville Chamberlain's speech on September 27, 1938, was retransmitted in French, German, and Italian and was soon followed by daily bulletins. Every day after that, programs were served up to France and Italy and, beginning on April 9, 1940, to Denmark and Norway as well. The Netherlands (April 11, 1940) and then Belgium (September 28, 1940) were later added to the list.[50]

These programs broadcast the United Kingdom's official line. It was not long, therefore, before the powers in exile demanded time slots on the BBC airwaves. On June 6, 1940, Queen Wilhelmina's government asked for the right to airtime, which resulted in the creation of Radio Oranje,[51] described on July 28 as a "programme in Dutch under the auspices of the Dutch Government."[52] That favor was not granted lightly, since it partly exempted the station from British control. On July 9, 1940, Ivone Kirkpatrick, controller of the European services of the BBC at the time, reasonably noted that, though that liberality had been granted to the Dutch, it should in no case be "considered a precedent which would allow for similar facilities being granted to other Refugee Governments."[53] Belgium was thus denied the privilege. In the wake of the attack on Mers el-Kebir, however, Winston Churchill offered Charles de Gaulle five minutes a day, between 8:25 and 8:30 p.m. The Man of June 18 therefore assigned Maurice Schumann, a young reporter from the Havas news agency, to spread the word from Free France. The program, which began on July 18, 1940, acquired the name "Honneur et Patrie" (Honor and Nation) in late August of the same year.[54]

Two types of programs coexisted on the BBC airwaves: some were the responsibility of the British authorities, others of the powers in exile. Each camp, of course, lay claim to a right of inspection of the other's words, but the power relation obviously served His Majesty's government.

Winston Churchill had allowed the exiled authorities to determine what propaganda was directed at their fellow citizens. "In all questions of propaganda in Belgium whether by broadcast or by the dropping of leaflets, the view of the recognized Belgian Government should normally prevail. It is only when there is a clash between the approved policy of the Cabinet and the Belgian view that any question of restraint should arise. In such an event, the Foreign secretary will decide. . . . The principles thus enunciated . . . should be made applicable . . . to the other countries who have recognized Governments now resident in Great Britain."[55] "After all," he explained to a doubtful Duff Cooper, "they must know more about their own countries than we do, and it is our interest to give them the best possible chance of keeping alive under increasingly difficult circumstances."[56]

But that principle could be seriously infringed upon. In the first place, all broadcasts were screened by the censor. The programs for Italy therefore had to be rehearsed on the morning of the day they would be broadcast.[57] All the scripts for Radio Oranje were transmitted to the Ministry of Information and to the BBC forty-eight hours in advance, although, in emergency situations, the rule could be relaxed.[58] That requirement did not especially offend the Dutch, who before the war had had their radio broadcasts censored by a council headed by Pieter Gerbrandy himself. Free France did not escape the iron law of censorship. The tensions in the Levant, for example, led the British authorities to take away the Rebel's microphone in September 1941. All in all, the "minor allies" were indeed subject to censorship—political censorship in the first place, since it was exercised in the last instance by a government service and not by the Beeb.[59] The British authorities did not intend to see their political line contradicted by remarks they deemed iconoclastic. An editorial by Maurice Schumann evoking the "unconstitutionality" of the French State, for example, was blocked on October 30, 1940, which was hardly surprising, given that, as late as September 1941, PWE demanded that any "direct attack on the person of Pétain" be avoided.[60]

The British government, far from being omnipotent, at times had difficulty imposing its views. Furthermore, it did not treat all its allies equally. The Norwegians, for instance, had a privileged status. In the turmoil of 1940 Winston Churchill ordered Frederick Ogilvie, president of the BBC at the time, to approve the requests of the Nygaardsvold government.[61] Immediately thereafter, on August 28, the British authorities reached an accord that was particularly disadvantageous to them: BBC broadcasts would be delivered in part by Norwegian announcers appointed and remunerated by their government, and editorial control would be in the hands of a Norwegian official, who owed no allegiance to His Majesty's services. An aggravating circumstance: the anchorman, Toralv Øksnevad, was uncooperative and frequently threatened to report to his minister the obstacles that the BBC officials were erecting in his path. In view of the excellent relations maintained between Trygvie Lie and Anthony Eden, the Norwegians enjoyed a favorable power relation. That drove Thomas Barman, head of propaganda for Scandinavia, to despair. "No person can be approached direct by a BBC official with the invitation to do a talk in Norwegian. All such invitations must pass through the hands of Mr Øksnevad who also reserves the right to brief the speaker. When there is a conflict between the British and the Norwegian view in news bulletin[s], the British view prevails only after conflict and after time-wasting appeals to high BBC authority." Barman therefore suggested entrusting to Mr. Winther, the subeditor of BBC Norway, "full control over *all* Norwegian bulletins, news and talks under the instructions of PWE."[62] The Norwegian authorities made a pretense of paying careful attention to these complaints. "Mr Lie is well aware of Mr Øksnevad's character and has admitted it again and again both to people in the Norwegian Government and to Mr Rowland Kenney while he was at the Ministry of Information. When he told me today that Øksnevad was returning there was a note of despair in his voice. His chief reaction seemed to be 'What on earth can we do with him!'"[63] But they refrained from alienating such a precious asset, especially since Øksnevad sometimes helped his prime minister write his speeches.

The British government had less difficulty imposing its views on the Belgian ministers. The BBC directly controlled Radio Belgique; its editor in chief, Victor de Laveleye, was believed to be loyal to British interests, even though he had been a minister.[64] It will come as no surprise that this situation greatly displeased the Pierlot cabinet, particularly because Laveleye sometimes transmitted texts written by personalities who did not belong to the cabinet. In April 1941 Paul-Henri Spaak therefore proposed a deal:

> The government's great desire would naturally be to have at its disposal, in complete freedom, the radio broadcasts for Belgium and to control them itself.
>
> It knows that it comes up against a question of principle in that regard, and it prefers, rather than waste its time in discussions that would undoubtedly lead nowhere, to propose a practical solution of a nature to give it satisfaction and also—at least it hopes so—to meet with the approval of the English Authorities.
>
> This solution is, in fact, very simple. The Belgian government should be authorized to hire at its own cost all the collaborators whose work it judges necessary to produce the broadcast it wishes.
>
> That team would be headed by M. De Laveleye who, while keeping his position at the BBC, would thus also report to the Belgian government. . . . That solution, because it creates a closer collaboration between the BBC Services and the Belgian Government, would at the same time have the advantage of settling the question of the general policy directives that the BBC asked the Belgian government to provide.[65]

The British turned down that proposal, while allowing the Belgian government to give instructions to the announcers. Spaak gave in, to the great satisfaction of the Ministry of Information, which was delighted by his "amenable" attitude.[66] The Belgian government nevertheless created an Office de Radiodiffusion Nationale Belge (Belgian National Office of Radio Broadcasting), which enjoyed all the more independence in that, beginning in 1943, it had the use of a powerful transmitter installed in the Congo.

Finally, though clashes with Free France abounded, the British ruled with a velvet glove. "From spring 1941 to autumn 1942, de Gaulle and Schumann, despite frequent recriminations (or because of these recriminations), were in the end free to say what they wanted at the BBC microphone, in return for a rare correction of a few words."[67] That did not prevent de Gaulle from creating Radio Brazzaville in 1942, to free himself from the submission London imposed on him.

Grievances

There were ample grounds for opposition, however. Grafted onto the political disputes were other kinds of grievances. For example, the United Kingdom doubted the eagerness to fight of some of its allies, at times not without reason. De Geer, the Dutch prime minister until September 1940, himself withdrew scripts that risked appearing too offensive to the Germans.[68] As a result, Radio Oranje tended to be "submissive," and, "although there is clear evidence that the organizers are aware of the existence of war, they adopt a policy which is in perfect continuity with the Dutch Government's pre-invasion policy."[69] Similarly, the Ministry of Information considered the Belgian cabinet, which was anxious to treat the king with consideration, "the most defeatist of the allied governments." Oliver Harvey thundered: "Though they are paying lip-service to the allied cause here, in reality their sympathy lies in Belgium with King Léopold."[70]

The British also criticized the amateurism of certain programs. To be sure, "Les Français parlent aux Français" (French speaking to the French), the flagship broadcast for the French Hexagon, was regularly praised to the skies,[71] to the point of being considered, from the time of its launch, "a first-class-programme of high artistic merit, and passionately sincere."[72] By contrast, the radio offerings of other nationalities incurred the wrath of the critics. The men at PWE noted: "Our fundamental trouble is that we are dealing with men [Belgian politicians] who are accustomed to the oratory of the political meeting and the Chambre des Députés, and not to radio. The tendency to hollowness and grandiloquence is very hard to eradicate in old political dogs who have been successful for many years with the help of this technique in other media and fail to grasp the essential differences of the radio medium."[73]

The BBC was just as harsh toward the Dutch, whose programs were never a "glamour service," to borrow the expression of a report written in 1950.[74] The English authorities intervened. They asked that dialogue be introduced,[75] that speeches be shortened, and that musical interludes be inserted.[76] That suggestion disgusted one of the announcers, Louis de Jong, who considered war an affair too grave to lend itself to jokes. He claimed that, if the Dutch thought the music was being introduced for "its emotional appeal, they might be distrustful of the talks that followed." The BBC tempered these alarms, pointing out that everything depended on the kind of music and the way it was used.[77] Radio Oranje had a broad listenership, but it was far from being well regarded by everyone. It was accused of being out of touch with reality and of viewing the situation through "rose-coloured glasses."[78] By ending all its broadcasts with the catchphrase "Keep courage, we are coming," it also provoked sarcasm among members of the resistance, who waited for the landing year after year.[79] The Dutch authorities, displaying an altogether Calvinist austerity, did not allow the leaflets that would be dropped over their country to pass through the expert hands of Harold Keeble, a veteran of the *Daily Express*, whose "flair for reinforcing sensational news by striking devices in lay-out" upset them. Rejecting these devices, they imposed their own printing standards, "which Mr Keeble regarded as dreary and old-fashioned."[80] The British, proud of their professionalism, clearly kept a close eye on things. They asked that bad news—from the Italian point of view—be announced whenever possible by an English voice[81] and formulated a request that was mere wishful thinking: that the members of the Italian section "arrive more punctually for meetings."[82]

The "minor allies" also expressed their discontent. Beyond political disagreements, they fought to obtain longer time slots on the British airwaves. The Belgian Camille Huysmans observed that "the Dutch have twice as much time as we have—which allows them to distribute their material better, especially since they have only one language to speak in. We must therefore gain some time. What to do? Quite simply, eliminate the daily commentary, which is already given in French by the French and in Dutch by the Dutch. And may I add that these programs are at least as good as our own. We need only refer listeners to these broadcasts every day."[83] On a completely different level, the powers in exile did not compromise on national honor. After the raid on the Lofoten Islands, Haakon complained of a reference to "Norwegian 'patriots.'" "With the exception of 2%, His Majesty said, all Norwegians were patriots. The word might suit other people, but he would prefer that we should merely say 'Norwegians' which implied that they were loyalists."[84] Ivone Kirkpatrick of the BBC sighed: "Our most difficult task was to satisfy the demands of the allied Governments in exile. As they had 'very little work' . . . they became interested in broadcasting. . . . It would have been wrong to replace too many meaty news broadcasts by the amiable exhortations and generalisations concocted in the Allied Governments' offices."[85]

All in all, conflicts of legitimacy, political differences, and mutual suspicion interfered with the relations the British were maintaining with their partners. But we must not exaggerate. On the whole, the exiled governments were well treated. London respected their sovereignty and granted them fairly broad freedom in the area of propaganda. Once again, the tensions revealed the ambivalence of the war objectives the United Kingdom was pursuing: Was it defending its national interests and British values, or was it leading an international coalition founded on universalist principles? Even in 1942 that question was far from settled. In May of that year, Douglas Ritchie reaffirmed "Britain's right to speak." In his view, the BBC ought to assist the British government "to impose their will on all countries and to win the peace, that is, to bring about an ordered civilization which is in accordance with British ideas, British values and British needs."[86] That ambition was not hollow. The "minor allies" were never invited to form a collective capable of speaking in a single voice; they signed no appeals or manifestoes.[87] Nevertheless, Noel Newsome of the BBC noted in November 1942 that he was in charge of

a *European* service, the only one of its kind in existence. . . . That is to say the Service endeavours to speak with a European voice to a European audience about European ideas. . . . The voice is at the same time predominantly British but no less European for that. The [BBC European] Service believes in Europe as a political and cultural entity not exclusive of, but contributory to, a wider world organization, just as it believes in Britain, France, Germany etc., as political and cultural entities, not exclusive of but contributory to a wider European organization.[88]

These antagonistic approaches confirmed the complexity of an alliance whose members were pursuing a common goal—the defeat of the Axis—even while developing different points of view as to their national and international future. On that level, the entry of the Soviet Union and then of the United States into the war in 1941 provided some answers but also further complicated the situation.

CHAPTER VI

The Dual Shock of 1941 and Its Consequences

T wo convulsions occurred in 1941. On June 22 German panzers, in contravention of the German-Soviet Pact, launched an assault on the Russian steppe; and on December 7 Japanese aircraft, violating American neutrality, bombed the U.S. Navy ships lying at anchor in Pearl Harbor, Hawaii. Until then, the United Kingdom had had to face the Reich alone. It now received the support of two powerful allies, the Soviet Union and the United States of America.

Soviet Support, Communist Threat

When the USSR entered the war, it turned the strategic situation on its head. Until 1941 Great Britain, because of its meager resources, had been fighting in peripheral theaters of operation, which meant it could not bring pressure to bear on Europe. The brutal confrontation between the Wehrmacht and the Red Army reshuffled the cards. London now could—and had to—return to a more classic strategy and consider going back to the Continent, which would oblige the Reich to battle on two fronts. Operation Barbarossa therefore rendered obsolete the alternatives considered in 1940, particularly the dream of inciting revolutions. That situation, as we will see, obliged SOE and the British Chiefs of Staff (COS) to revise their plans. From the start, Winston Churchill understood the magnitude of the turn of events. On July 12, 1941, he established an alliance with Joseph Stalin, despite the British prime minister's loathing for the Bolshevik regime.

That accord, though indispensable in military terms, alarmed the countries that feared their powerful neighbor. The fear was particularly keen in Danish and Norwegian ruling circles, inasmuch as the Russo-Finnish War in 1939–1940 had taken place at their doorstep. At the time, it had revealed the expansionist orientation of Moscow, which tormented Copenhagen in particular. On November 25, 1941, the Thorvald Stauning government had joined the Anti-Comintern Pact under strong pressure from Berlin, a move that offered the Reich the kingdom's support, at least ideologically speaking. PWE therefore adopted a cautious line. "In our propaganda to Denmark we must take great care not to fall in the German trap: we must in no circumstances describe Russia as an ally. Our line should be (subject to the general FO directive) that Russo-German conflict is merely another case of thieves falling out."[1] At a time when the Soviets were energetically defending from despair both Moscow, their capital, and Leningrad, the birthplace of the October Revolution, these fears appeared unfounded. They would become starkly real in 1943, when, after the Battle of Stalingrad, the fortunes of war would come to serve the Soviet Union, obliging the Scandinavian countries to rethink their diplomatic stance, which before the war had been earnestly neutralist.

Conversely, the opening of the eastern front revived Hitler's interest in Scandinavia. The raids launched on the Lofoten Islands and the convoys through the icy waters of the Barents Sea to assist the USSR increased the Führer's fears of seeing the United Kingdom go on the offensive in Norway. He therefore dispatched the battleship *Tirpitz* to Trondheim in January 1942 and hastened to fortify defenses on the Norwegian coast, further increasing the burden that oppressed the population with an ever more brutal occupation.[2]

German aggression, finally, complicated the political scene of the Western European countries. On one hand, the crusade against Bolshevism sparked enthusiasm in collaborationist ranks, even impelling volunteers to fight under the Nazi banner. For example, thirteen to fifteen thousand men from Scandinavia enlisted in the German forces during World War II.[3] Similarly, France created a Légion des Volontaires Français contre le Bolchevisme (Legion of French Volunteers Against Bolshevism); the Netherlands constituted the Nederland brigade; and the Belgians formed units destined to turn into SS divisions, Langemarck for the Flemings, Wallonie for the Francophones.

Furthermore—and this is essential—the Communists suddenly surged up on the resistance scene, where they had previously not been particularly brilliant. Until June 22, 1941, all the Red parties were faithful to Moscow and supported the German-Soviet Pact, concluded on August 23, 1939. For many months, that loyalty prevented them from moving toward a resolute opposition to the Nazi invader. Not all leaders embraced the same line, however. In Belgium, the struggle against the occupier was "incorporated into the Party's thinking as self-evident" by January 1940,[4] and in the Netherlands the Communists played a major role in the strike launched in February 1941. But their French comrades were less decisive. They confronted the Pétainist regime with determination but were respectful toward the Germans and passionately denounced the British and Gaullists: "The aim of the de Gaulle and Larminat movement, which is fundamentally reactionary and antidemocratic, is nothing other than to deprive our country of every freedom in the event of an English victory," wrote their leaders, Maurice Thorez and Jacques Duclos, in March 1941.[5]

The German attack against the Soviet Union, in turning the Communists into allies, expanded the range of possibilities, as the British leaders immediately realized. In fact, it secured "the complete unity of the Left by bringing into line the communists who are active in the unoccupied area, particularly in Marseilles, as well as in the industrial areas of the North."[6] It also brought to the resistance experienced militants reputed for their courage, their sense of organization, and their abnegation—three weighty assets in the fight against the Nazi occupier.

Operation Barbarossa also obliged the French Communists to rethink their alliances, both internal and external, as well as their modes of action. Maurice Thorez, Raymond Guyot, and André Marty, three of their leaders who had taken refuge in the Soviet Union, though continuing to vituperate against England and Free France, suddenly discovered their appeal as well. In July 1941, via Stafford Cripps, His Majesty's ambassador to Moscow, they sounded out the Foreign Office about going to the United Kingdom. They wished to meet with Charles de Gaulle and then go to metropolitan France or the colonies. That proposal was curtly rebuffed. "The behavior of the French communists was sub-human," noted Winston Churchill in the margin of the document. He was not inclined to compromise with such unpatriotic men.[7] In any event, the question was raised as to the relations between the Communist parties and the governments in exile—though its resolution came only in the years that followed.

The place that the Communist organizations were to occupy within the internal resistance also tormented their leaders. Should they go into battle alone, ally themselves with leftist forces in the manner of the Front Populaire, or promote a broad national union? The Communist International, which met on June 24 and 25, 1941, settled the matter. In a July 7 directive sent to the parties installed in the capitalist countries, it enjoined them "to achieve the greatest unity by immediately organizing a single National Front. To realize that objective, contact is to be established with all forces, independent of their political leanings and character, so long as these forces are opposed to Fascist Germany." The Comintern therefore gave up on revolution and privileged national struggle within the broadest alliances possible.[8]

In the places where they were relatively strong, the Communist Parties had anticipated the issuance of that instruction several weeks earlier, showing Nazi Germany—engaged in a trial of strength with the USSR to control Bulgaria and Romania—that it had to reckon with them. In mid-May the underground leadership of the Parti Communiste Français (PCF; French Communist Party) had launched a Front National de l'Indépendance de la France (FN; National Front for France's Independence), while the Belgians were also developing a Front de l'Indépendance (FI; Independence Front). In the minds of their promoters, however, it was the Communists who had to control these coalitions. Although they advocated union at the base, they reserved the top spots for themselves. In certain countries, by contrast, Lenin's disciples were too weak to lay claim to the leading roles. In Denmark, they had received only 2.4 percent of the vote in the legislative elections of 1939, and in Norway, they had not surpassed 0.3 percent in 1936,[9] which ruled out any Front National arrangement. But the question of whether they could fit into a system of that type was still open and remained so for many months.

Finally, the methods to be employed to shake off the Nazi yoke raised many questions. Until June 22, 1941, the Communists had primarily favored social struggle and demonstrations, both to show the Reich's allies their unpopularity and to obtain raises or other material benefits—an increase in rations or the distribution of soap to miners, for example. But at a time when the Wehrmacht's troops were surging into Russia, these battles seemed inadequate. Granted, the Comintern strategists had imagined that the people, upon learning of the assault on the citadel of socialism, would rebel, a distant echo of Hugh Dalton's own pipe dream. But the masses did not budge, plunging the leaders of the International—the Italian Giulio

Ceretti, for example—into disillusionment, if not bitterness.[10] To support the Soviet Union, it was now necessary to adopt a more aggressive line and move from the civilian realm to the military.

That metamorphosis was particularly problematic, inasmuch as Moscow only feebly supported the Communists operating in Western Europe. To be sure, between 1942 and 1944 the Allies agreed to parachute twenty-five Soviet agents into the Netherlands, France, Belgium, Germany, and Austria.[11] But that contribution was minor, and the powers in exile were wary of these operations. In June 1943 IS opposed a demand formulated by the People's Commissariat for Internal Affairs (the Soviet secret services), arguing that General Giraud would certainly be furious if he learned that any British organization had facilitated the Russians' entry into France without consulting him.[12] In the same vein, even supposing it had wanted to, the USSR would have had difficulty dropping materiel in the West, for logistical reasons alone. The distance that separated the Soviet Union from that theater of operations prohibited parachute drops, because flying over a Germany defended by formidable antiaircraft guns and by a no less formidable Luftwaffe represented a major risk for the Soviet air force. In short, the Western Communists, at least at first, had to count on their own forces.

By that measure, attacks on German soldiers were in appearance a promising approach. On August 21, 1941, the Frenchman Pierre Georges assassinated Alfons Moser, a midshipman in the Kriegsmarine, at the Barbès-Rochechouart metro station. On the following October 20, a commando executed Lieutenant-Colonel Hotz, head of the Feld-Kommandantur of Nantes. The next day, Hans Gottried Reimers, legal adviser to the military administration, was taken down in Bordeaux. Communist leaders were hoping thereby to relieve, if only on a modest scale, the pressure weighing on a Red Army in dire straits. But above all, in engaging in a cycle of attacks and reprisals, they counted on winning the support of public opinion, by revealing the hideous face of an occupier often praised for its good behavior until that time.[13]

That strategy was far from meeting with unanimous approval, however. It violated Marxist-Leninist doctrine, which preferred to put its money on the actions of the masses rather than on individual acts. It also contradicted proletarian internationalism. As Albert Ouzoulias, future leader of the Francs-Tireurs et Partisans, confided in retrospect: "Comrades would refuse to execute a German soldier, who could be a comrade from Hamburg, a worker from Berlin. An officer could be an anti-Hitler professor."[14]

Above all, that strategy met with the disapproval of public opinion, which was repulsed by the bloody reprisals the Nazis ordered. As a result, the Western Communist parties rarely followed that path. For example, the Parti Communiste Belge (Belgian Communist Party) avoided attacks on persons until March 1942. Similarly, the Danish Communists did not embark on sabotage operations—a less contested form of action, however—until April 1942, since the overwhelming majority of their fellow citizens were opposed to them until winter 1942–1943 or even 1944.[15] One sign of that uneasiness in France was that the PCF's underground press refrained from calling for such heroic deeds. Its regional newspaper in Nord even attributed the assassinations that were committed to account settling among the Germans.[16] And the Danish Communists waited until spring 1943 to mention sabotage in the columns of their newspapers.[17]

Furthermore, that tactic worried the governments in exile. They believed that the reprisals were too serious when weighed against the military gains, which were in reality minimal. On October 23, 1941, Charles de Gaulle explicitly condemned the tactic: "The war of the French people must be waged by those to whom that responsibility falls, namely, myself and the Comité National. . . . And at present, the instructions I have given for the occupied territory are not to kill Germans openly. There is one very good reason for that: at this moment, it is too easy for the enemy to retaliate by massacring our momentarily disarmed combatants."[18] The émigré leaders, whether Belgian or Norwegian, embraced the same line,[19] irritated by an activism whose consequences fell heavily on civilians. "Both the Norwegian government and the leaders on the home front believe that such acts of terrorism have no military value for the moment and that, from the political standpoint, they may lead to great calamities." The Norwegian authorities therefore requested in September 1942 "that the Soviet government for its part contribute as far as possible to seeing that such plans are abandoned."[20] The British line, by contrast, was less clear-cut.

British Conundrums

Although the English authorities believed that the attacks committed against occupation troops had no military importance, they refrained from disavowing them. Officially, they adhered to a cardinal principle: because that question originated in the internal affairs of each country, they should not intervene. In November 1941 Anthony Eden sent a note to the exiled powers clarifying his government's position:

> I should at once say that His Majesty's Government, for their part, while at the present time and in present circumstances . . . do not incite the populations of occupied territories to such individual acts of violence, would equally not give express advice in discouragement of such acts. His Majesty's Government realize, however, that the allied Governments and authorities have special responsibilities towards the populations of occupied territories, and His Majesty's Government would not therefore claim to determine what advice should be given by allied Governments and [de facto] authorities to those populations in this matter over the broadcasting system of the BBC.[21]

PWE held to its position. "Our policy remains unchanged on the question of killing German troops. We do not either encourage or discourage this; the French people themselves must judge of the expediency of such acts," it noted in January 1942.[22] But a different rationale also lay behind that rule: the United Kingdom could not denounce actions that undermined the occupier's morale, inasmuch as a condemnation would have put out the combatants' flame, which day after day the BBC strove to fan. The British thus vacillated between the desire to maintain the ardor of the resistance fighters and the wish to avoid reprisals, without making up their minds on the matter, especially since they were irritated by the reticence of certain émigré powers—the Belgian government in the first place—to advocate active resistance.

The British refused to give in to a brutal cynicism, however. To the best of their abilities, they endeavored to protect the civilian populations. Without condemning the attacks, they pointed out their dangers. In 1941 the BBC warned the French "*against unnecessary risks and isolated acts of terrorism.* . . . The line taken is that killing Germans will only entail reprisals, and that violence is therefore for the time being better directed against collaborating Frenchmen."[23]

Likewise, the London authorities did not encourage Norwegian civilians to conduct sabotage operations. They entrusted such actions to commandos trained in the United Kingdom, sent to Norway, and then exfiltrated once the task was completed. In addition, these saboteurs were supposed to "leave small signs behind them which will indicate to the German experts that the job has been done by personnel sent into the country specially for the purpose. These methods have in the past proved convincing to the Germans who have normally refrained from reprisals against the local population. . . . We are as much concerned as [the internal resistance] to put a stop to irresponsible acts of terrorism."[24]

But assassination attempts and sabotage were only the tip of the iceberg. The sudden appearance of both the Communists and the Soviet Union in the World War II arena also undermined the foundations of British propaganda.

The energy and courage of the Communists' resistance, which was widely extolled in their underground press, tended to discredit the other clandestine groups, whether they were *attentistes* or simply less skillful at lauding their own merits. That reality plunged the British into deep perplexity: Should they remain silent about these exploits, even at the risk of discouraging people of good will, or celebrate them and risk augmenting Moscow's prestige? That contradiction dogged PWE.

We are somewhat concerned by reports that Communists are now acquiring the reputation of being the boldest and the best of the patriots. The Belgian Government has in the past tended to discourage active resistance in any form and told their compatriots to reserve their strength for the "right moment." At the same time the German propaganda has attributed every act of violence committed in Belgium to Communists. Consequently it is natural that the Communists should begin to acquire a monopoly of patriotism in the eyes of certain Belgians, especially the manual worker.

With this danger in mind, we have tried fostering the impression, which already exists in the minds of our listeners, that deliverance is coming from Britain, and, moreover, that when victory is won Britain will be prepared with an effective peace programme. We have also been paying homage to those who have been punished for active resistance. We have discredited the German myth that all patriots are Communists and have thanked the Belgians for the help they have so frequently given to escaped British prisoners and members of the RAF who have had to land on Belgian soil.

It is of great importance that these themes should be constantly repeated in our programmes. Although it is unlikely that Belgium will go Communist, yet there is a danger that Communism will spread so long as the Belgian Government, in its recommendation to resistance, confines itself to exhorting the Belgian population to hide all metal objects from German collectors.[25]

The Red Army's successes, moreover, put British propaganda in a tough spot. In the name of the alliance, London was duty-bound to celebrate the Soviet troops' heroism and the successes they achieved in the snow of the eastern front. But in so doing, it promoted a flattering image of the Stalinist regime that indirectly diminished the battle of the democracies. Bruce Lockhart, director general of PWE, pointed out that "enthusiasm for Russia as the one successful combatant increased enormously, and to some extent her military success was attributed to the Russian system of government. Popular opinion about our own war effort was sullen, and there was a marked slump in the stock of the Conservatives whom the public regarded as mainly responsible for the conduct of the war." A typical example of British humor captured that state of mind: "Two Englishmen were sitting opposite each other in a railway carriage; both were reading newspapers. After a time one laid down his paper, smiled and said to the stranger opposite, 'Well, we're not doing so badly.' The other looked up in surprise and replied politely, 'You talk remarkably good English for a Russian.'"[26]

Russia's entry into the war therefore held as many questions as promises. It offered the United Kingdom a Continental ally and swelled the ranks of the resistance with ardent Communist volunteers. But it also reintroduced the Red specter on the domestic scene and put the Soviet bear back in the ring of international relations. In addition, it obliged London to rethink its strategy, to define the links that the underground movement was to maintain with its new brothers-in-arms, and finally, to reformulate its propaganda. Worrisome clouds were threatening; the sudden appearance of powerful America partly dispersed them.

The United States' Arrival on the Scene

When the United States entered the war, it opened the path of victory to Great Britain. The arsenal of democracy guaranteed that the British forces would enjoy the benefits of the American horn of plenty and the millions of men Uncle Sam would mobilize. Cooperation between the two countries could also support the resistance on the Old Continent and sustain the oppressed populations through appropriate propaganda. In short, grandiose prospects came into view. Yet the United States needed to possess the tools required to wage subversive warfare, a reality that was not obvious in 1941.

Indeed, on the eve of Pearl Harbor, America did not have any structure to speak of dedicated to that ungentlemanly war. A few intelligence services did exist—the Office of Naval Intelligence, the Military Intelligence Division, the Military Intelligence Service[27]—but no agency centralized or coordinated their efforts. William J. Donovan set out to remedy that deficiency. As one of his former agents, Robert Hayden Alcorn, reported, Donovan, a World War I veteran, "an Irish-American and a Catholic; by profession . . . a lawyer, by inclination a politician,"[28] very often sparked enthusiasm. "He was tough and soft. He was hard and gentle. He was dominating and considerate. He was direct and devious. He was a vain ladies' man and he was a rough man's man. He was all of these contradictions but only one side of his character had no opposite. That was his courage."[29] Although a Republican, Donovan, a jurist versed in politics, was also fairly close to the Democrat Franklin D. Roosevelt. In July 1940 Frank Knox, publisher of the *Chicago Daily News* and secretary of the navy, assigned Donovan to investigate the fifth column in Europe and to assess the capacity of the British to resist the Germans. Having returned to the United States in August, he made every effort to alert the authorities to the peril represented by the infiltration of enemy agents, to plead for an alliance with Great Britain, and to call for the creation of a service to take charge of subversive warfare. On June 10, 1941, he sent a memorandum to the White House in which he spelled out his views.[30] He suggested the formation of a structure capable of assembling and analyzing intelligence by the most modern methods and of disseminating them to services that would make use of them, primarily in radio propaganda.[31] His plan, however, lacked clarity, inasmuch as it did not specify the missions of the future agency (to collect intelligence? to develop propaganda?) and did not mention subversive warfare, on which SOE was so keen. Despite these gaps, the plan was approved by Roosevelt, who, on July 11, 1941, named Donovan coordinator of information (COI), despite the opposition of the chief of staff, George C. Marshall, and the hostility directed at Donovan by Robert E. Sherwood, a playwright and close adviser to the president at the time, who was also considered an expert in propaganda.

"Donovan, accustomed to command, was quick, extremely energetic, and ambitious. Sherwood, a playwright completely inexperienced in working with, under, or over other people, was slow, unpunctual, and moody," noted James Warburg, a banker and Roosevelt's financial adviser.[32] The office of the COI, having only just been launched, thus ran up against strong opposition. Added to that was the hostility of the Federal Bureau of Investigation, which, being in charge of domestic security, fumed to see a rival emerge, and that of the State Department, disturbed by the idea that propaganda over which it had no control might contradict its line. Donovan had to put his cards on the table: his bureau would remain civilian and would not encroach on the duties of the navy and army when it came to intelligence.[33]

"Wild Bill"—for that was his nickname—divided the office of the COI into two branches. The Foreign Information Service (FIS), entrusted to his enemy Robert Sherwood, elaborated pro-Allied and anti-German radio directives. The Research and Analysis Branch (R&A), headed by James P. Baxter III, a professor of history at Harvard University, collected the information available and composed reports on diverse subjects—the food situation in Europe, for example. The R&A, in recruiting distinguished academics (economist Edward Mason, political scientist Joseph Hayden, historian William Langer), became an organization that gathered as many facts as possible and then sought out "clients" likely to exploit them.[34]

After Pearl Harbor, Wild Bill flooded the White House with reports, often using information from British sources. February 25, 1942, marked a turning point: the office of the COI received the right "to organize and conduct secret subversive operations in hostile areas," which broadened its sphere of operations.[35] Conversely, the disastrous relationship between Donovan and Sherwood culminated in the split between action and propaganda. As of June 13, 1942, the two domains were overseen by twin organizations. The Office of Strategic Services (OSS), run by Donovan, was responsible for four areas: Research and Analysis (R&A), Secret Intelligence (SI), Special Operations (SO), and Counter-intelligence (X2). The Office of War Information (OWI), overseen by a radio reporter named Elmer Davis, saw to propaganda, with Robert Sherwood heading its "overseas" branch, that is, all the zones except the American continent. Finally, on June 23, 1942, a directive placed the OSS under the direct control of the Joint Chiefs of Staff (JCS).[36]

The OSS therefore combined information collection with the conduct of subversive warfare, two areas that, in the United Kingdom, belonged to

SIS and SOE, respectively; in addition, the OSS reported to the military and not to civilians. In each country, however, the war of words lay within the jurisdiction of a single service: OWI or PWE. Despite that dissymmetry, transatlantic cooperation—albeit chaotic at times—was established.

Cooperation or Rivalry?

Even before the creation of the OSS, the British and the Americans had reached an agreement on the matter of subversive warfare. In May 1940 a close friend of Winston Churchill's, the Canadian millionaire William Stephenson—nicknamed "Little Bill" to distinguish him from his senior colleague "Wild Bill"—had been dispatched to New York to serve as British security coordinator. He represented SOE, MI 5, and MI 6 on the American continent and, at the same time, developed propaganda favorable to the United Kingdom. At a time when the United States had not yet entered the war and sometimes yielded to the siren call of isolationism, this was no sinecure. In a sign of British good will, as early as 1941 the intelligence collected by SIS or SOE was transmitted through Stephenson to the COI.[37] In the interest of reciprocity, an American mission was established in London in October 1941, to learn how the British were proceeding and, along the way, to glean a few pieces of intelligence. It fell far short of success. R.M.J. Felner, charged with maintaining contact between SIS and the COI, was considered an amateur; and William Philips, assistant to the leader of the mission, was suspected of Anglophobic sentiments.[38] In February 1943 the appointment in London of David Bruce, a lawyer by training reputed for his talents as a diplomat, eased the situation. "Colonel Bruce . . . is a tall, handsome, urbane individual with grey hair, grey eyes and an easy smile. A person of almost mannered and meticulous thoughtfulness, he was an excellent counter to the Donovan impulsiveness."[39] Some British persisted in their opposition to Donovan, however: "Intense personal ambition . . . bad strategist: crystallizes opposition and underrates political enemies. Indiscreet. Inclination to flashy work." That was the opinion Dick Ellis at MI 6 formed of him.[40]

All in all, cooperation remained limited until mid-June 1942, at which time the OSS negotiated with SOE. The agreement reached on June 24 stipulated that the two services would faithfully collaborate. The accord had two flaws, however. It broke with the American conception of an entity that would cover the entire field of subversive warfare, from the collection of intelligence to sabotage operations. In fact, the division of labor between SIS and SOE obliged the Americans to deal with both of their British partners,[41] which complicated relations and opened the door to Byzantine disputes. Above all, the agreement disadvantaged the United States, since the Americans were granted the right to conduct independent operations only in a few zones: China, Finland, the South West Pacific, and Northwest Africa. The OSS thus found itself reduced to a bare-bones organization, but the apportionment was at the time neither unfair nor unjustified, given the service's weakness and inexperience.[42]

The Americans admitted their inferiority. In the words of Malcolm Muggeridge, a writer working for MI 6 at the time, they were "like innocent girls from a finishing-school anxious to learn the seasoned demimondaine ways of the old-practitioners—in this case the legendary British Secret Service."[43] The teachers were not always satisfied with their pupils, however. Bickham Sweet-Escott, who went to the United States in July 1942 to shore up the British delegation, reported with the same sort of humor: "It used to be said at the time that liaison with Americans was like having an affair with an elephant; it is extremely difficult, you are apt to get badly trampled on, and you get no result for eight years." The Americans, moreover, did not always listen to the advice of their elders, suspecting that the "Machiavellian British had . . . had some ulterior and probably sinister motives."[44]

That impugning of motives was not purely a product of the imagination. Indeed, England was intent on protecting its mysteries. Stewart Menzies, chief of IS, was afraid to expose his methods, an obsession he shared with SOE.[45] In January 1943 its director noted that "SOE must reserve certain of its most intimate secrets even from our Allies, in fact from anybody who has no sworn allegiance to the British Sovereign and Commonwealth. Although our American Allies are in a very special position and, therefore, can be treated on a more equal basis than anybody else, there is still need for discrimination with regard to the documents which should be shown to them."[46] An SOE leader commented: "It is, of course, galling for us to realize that the Americans, who watched us fighting for nearly 2 1/2 years should now come in and claim to run the war." At the same time, he continued, America's power ultimately conferred the greater role on them. "We must therefore be prepared to regard them as the senior partner and adjust our organization in Western Europe and North Africa as time goes by to satisfy their legitimate requirements."[47]

The war among the secret services also complicated the entente between partners, since each ally played on the internecine rivalries that undermined its counterpart.[48] Although OWI cooperated harmoniously with PWE,[49] that was not the case for the OSS, which, under the jurisdiction of the Joint Chief of Staffs, displayed "an acute sense of security and a tendency to put lots of documents into the secret category of 'burn after reading' in contrast to the OWI boys who as newsmen and anarchists regarded nothing as sacred or non-communicable to us."[50] As a result, the first mission of the American newcomers was to "find their way through the labyrinthine 'intelligence brothel' known as the British Secret Service," a "herculean task."[51]

In short, differences in culture and experience hindered the entente between the two allies. Sweet-Escott liked to recall the precept inculcated in him before his departure for the New World: "The Americans and the British were two nations separated by a common language."[52] Above all, the cooperation between London and Washington had trouble countering the growing appeal exerted by the Soviet Union.

Propaganda at an Impasse?

The heroic resistance of the Red Army on Moscow's doorstep roused the people and revived hopes of a German defeat. But these feats put the British leaders in an awkward position. "The Epic of Britain in 1940 has been eclipsed by the Epic of Russia in 1941–2. We now want another kind of Epic of Britain which will prove more attractive," recommended Rex Leeper.[53] But that exhortation did not solve the problem: What message could the United Kingdom send to oppressed Europe? For though England had been a model to be followed in the seventeenth century, three hundred years later it fell far short of rivaling the messianic promises of Red Russia or the universalist hopes embodied by America, land of the free.

A few British leaders reassured themselves. "We have an immense amount of freedom and democracy in England; there might be more, but at least there is enough in evidence in our every-day lives to astonish and hearten those who are living under German occupation or even (as in Vichy

France) under a form of local fascist rule. It is by producing these evidences, and not by high phrases, that those people can be induced not to hope—since hope is about all they have left—but to feel that they are justified in identifying their hopes with our victory."[54] The argument seemed a bit thin, however, as the regional leaders of PWE admitted in January 1942: "All projections of Great Britain in terms of existing democratic institutions and projected social development should be amplified as far as possible. . . . We do not however feel that this projection of Great Britain alone would serve to 'compete' with the pull of Russia as a symbol of redemption and hope."[55]

The Atlantic Charter seemed to provide a miracle solution. Announced well before Pearl Harbor, on August 14, 1941, that document set out, but in very vague terms, the main principles that guided Great Britain and the United States: it merely recalled the right of the people to choose their own form of government and made a plea for universal peace and prosperity. As a means to instill dreams in the people, it was rather meager, as those responsible for British propaganda admitted. "The Atlantic Charter was necessarily of a very general character. It was used to the utmost at the time in our propaganda to Europe, but there is no evidence that it was effective."[56] The only detail at odds with that pessimistic observation: the Atlantic Charter demonstrated that the United States, now involved in the war, was assuming its global responsibilities.[57] In any event, British propaganda had to confine itself to convincing "the European countries that we can both free them and keep them free."[58] In the realm of ideas, the Anglo-Americans therefore proved less agile than the Soviets, whose war exploits fired people's imaginations and strengthened the idea of the Stalinist system's superiority over the timeworn forms of the old democracies—a handicap for which the men of PWE and OWI struggled to compensate.

A Strategic Aggiornamento

When the USSR entered the war, the British were also led to modify the objectives of their subversive warfare. In mid-August 1941 their Chiefs of Staff Committee agreed that subversion and sabotage would be supported, but it challenged the idea of encouraging revolution and building secret armies. With Operation Barbarossa, as we have seen, the strategists returned to a more classic conception of operations. Above all, the cost of subversive warfare far surpassed the limited capacities of the United Kingdom. A plan proposed in May 1942 estimated that the organization of underground forces capable of committing sabotage and then of inciting rebellion would require the use of four hundred aircraft full-time, a largesse that exceeded the resources of the Royal Air Force. Furthermore, in the view of the British leaders, it was not worth the gamble. The United States adopted the same line. During discussions in Washington in December 1941, the two Allied general staffs agreed that the "secret armies might well have an important role to play in assisting landings, but they would not form the 'corpus of the liberating offensive,' and if necessary, landings could take place without them."[59] That consensus came at an opportune moment, inasmuch as the United States was a powerful ally that had to be heeded.

In 1941, therefore, the new state of affairs required wrenching revisions, which, on May 12, 1942, the COS conveyed as a directive. He assigned two large sets of objectives to SOE. First, in the zones of operations where the Allies would land, the service would create and equip paramilitary organizations, which on D-Day would warn of the arrival of reinforcements, disrupt the enemy's communications and its rear, and protect vital installations. Second, these volunteers would guide the Allied troops, guard the vital locations, and form commandos able to cross the German lines.[60] In awaiting the return of the Anglo-American troops to the Continent, the populations were invited to do their work as slowly as possible, to intensify invisible sabotage operations, and, as the case may be, to show their opposition by holding national demonstrations or by standing at attention. They would avoid taking risks, however, and especially refrain from launching premature movements—a less than rousing line for members of the resistance, who wanted to get in on the fight.

In other words, SOE was called on to scale back its activities from the high ambitions Hugh Dalton had entertained in the tragic hours of 1940. At the same time, it gained respectability, having been integrated into the Allied grand strategy, of which it was now a pillar—albeit a modest one, when compared to the air force, the navy, and the land army. The logistics still had to be worked out, however, and the internal resistance had to be organized.

CHAPTER VII

―――――――

Coming of Age

W hen the Soviet Union and the United States entered the war, Great Britain realigned its strategy and substantially modified the role it assigned to the resistance. The army of shadows had to prepare to support the regular troops at the dawn of liberation, by identifying, mobilizing, and training the secret troops who would act on D-Day. That plan, however, was not supposed to encourage the oppressed peoples to adopt a rigid watch-and-wait posture. To assist the Allies, the networks would collect useful intelligence and sabotage the enemy's military or industrial installations; the populations would undermine the power of the occupier and of the puppet regimes that served it, by registering their opposition through demonstrations; and the workers would engage in slowdowns to put the brakes on production that supported the Nazi war effort.

That plan resulted in a division of labor. On one hand, a battle-hardened elite would conduct raids and sabotage operations while gathering information on the enemy's plan of action, tasks that fell to the networks. On the other, the masses, guided by the good word spread by the Allies, would engage in more spontaneous forms of struggle (demonstrations, invisible sabotage, civil disobedience) that did not require resources or organizations and whose principles every individual could easily put into practice. Whereas dynamiting a train or executing a collaborator required a minimal level of expertise, staying home on a national holiday or working-to-rule was within everyone's reach and involved only limited risks. That division of labor, however, omitted one reality: the societies held captive sometimes refused to bow to the Nazi Order's dictates and invented original forms of opposition to combat the Germans.

In what has become a canonical definition, the French resistance fighter Claude Bourdet proposed the following distinction:

> A *network* was an organization created in view of a precise military task, primarily intelligence, secondarily sabotage, and frequently as well the provision of avenues of escape for prisoners of war, and especially, for pilots who fell into enemy hands. . . . By definition, a network was in close contact with a representative of the military staff, for which it worked: it had to pass on intelligence, receive precise instructions about actions to be undertaken, then report on them. It had to be able to pick up the aviators, verify their identities, and entrust them to a cooperating service when they left the country.
>
> The primary objective of a *movement,* by contrast, was to sensitize and organize the population in the broadest manner possible. It also had concrete objectives, of course. The vaster it was, the better able to gather and transmit intelligence. It too organized punitive actions and sabotage operations. . . . But on the whole, it was almost as if it performed these tasks *as a sideline,* because it would have been absurd not to use such resources that way, and because each of its members needed to feel engaged on a concrete level. It was above all *in relation to the population* that a movement undertook these tasks; *the population was its objective and its principal concern.*[1]

Resistance movements developed in all the countries of Western Europe, with the notable exception of Italy, where the Fascist yoke, imposed in 1922, complicated the advent of such organizations until 1943, despite the presence of antifascists in exile in Europe and the United States.

These various underground groups took different paths of development.

Parties and Trade Unions

From the first, parties and trade unions were able to play a role in forming resistance organizations. Accustomed to political wrangling, in possession of a pool of experienced militants, they had solid structures that they could place in the service of the cause. Such was the case in Norway, where they positioned themselves in the forefront of the fight. For example, the Landsorganisasjonen i Norge (Norwegian Confederation of Trade Unions) was a prominent actor in the civilian opposition movements, which, beginning in 1941, reacted against both the privations brought on by the German occupation and the Nazification of the country introduced by Quisling.[2] The Communist parties, moreover, launched a plethora of underground groups, over which they exerted greater or lesser control. In France, the Front National, behind an ecumenical façade, faithfully followed the party line. In Belgium, the Front de l'Indépendance was more open. Observing that the so-called bourgeois parties were more motivated than their Socialist brothers, the Communists, adopting a "pragmatic" attitude, accepted "all forms of allegiances" and endorsed "the absolute disparity of the structures composing the Front de l'Indépendance."[3] That said, national front configurations were far from the rule in Western Europe. Although the Danish Communist Party launched its underground newspaper, *Land og Folk* (Land and people) on June 29, 1941, before creating a sabotage group, the Kommunist-Partisans (KO-PA) in February 1942, it did not immediately create a united front.[4] The Soviet Union showed no interest in a configuration that, in its eyes, was inapplicable in a country it judged too conservative;[5] and the major parties preferred to play the legality card by participating in the government rather than setting out on the path of resistance. In France, meanwhile, the defeat had totally discredited the political groups in the eyes of citizens.

That vacuum prompted a few pioneers to take action while ignoring the traditional political or union structures. Noting the failure of politicians, Frode Jakobsen, a young writer close to the Socialist far left, decided in autumn 1941 to launch a resistance movement, the Ringen (Circle).[6] He set out to disseminate quality news and to defend democracy and Danish values, while criticizing the policy of accommodation the parties were conducting.[7] In the same vein, Christian Pineau, even though he was a union leader, preferred in December 1940 to found a resistance movement, Libération-Nord, rather than depend on his former organization, the Confédération Générale du Travail (General Confederation of Labor). Nevertheless, on November 15 of the same year, he had taken the initiative to remind people of the cardinal principles of trade unionism, in a manifesto cosigned by eleven other leaders. With rare exceptions, then, neither the parties nor the unions became the driving force of underground action.

The Underground Press

By contrast, the underground press played a preeminent role in structuring the internal resistance in Western European countries. The populations under the jackboot suffered from a hunger for information, which the servile press, quick to praise the feats of the Wehrmacht and the promises of the New Order, was far from satisfying. Awash in lies, the societies held captive wished to know the facts; reeling from the defeat and a cruel occupation, they also hoped to transcend the tragedy they were facing by giving it a meaning. To be sure, the BBC offered one avenue, disseminating reliable news and sometimes entertaining programs that offered an escape from the torments of everyday life. But not all Western Europeans could listen to British radio, because of the jamming of the broadcasts, the risks involved, and the lack of receivers, particularly when the German authorities decided to confiscate them, as they did in Norway in autumn 1941. Many underground fighters, moreover, believed it necessary to provide homegrown, patriotic, and partisan words: they set out to express their points of view without relying on the British leadership and to restore a form of democratic pluralism that the order of the brownshirts was negating.

The relationship between the underground press and the resistance groups took many forms. Sometimes the launch of a newspaper led to the creation of a movement. For example, Philippe Viannay, Hélène Mordkovitch, and Robert Salmon, three young Parisian students anxious to "do something," decided at the beginning of the school year of 1940 to launch a news-sheet, *Défense de la France*, which was funded by a wealthy industrialist named Marcel Lebon. The modest tract, reproduced on a Roneo machine, gave birth to a powerful resistance movement that lasted until liberation. Christian Pineau took exactly the same path, but with fewer resources: on his own, he composed the first sixty-one issues of *Libération*. Only seven copies of the first issue were produced: typed up on a portable typewriter on December 1, 1940, it was sent through the mail to friends who, he hoped, would Roneo it on their own machines. Nonetheless, Libération-Nord later became one of the major underground forces in occupied France.

Conversely, movements sometimes established a press organ that would state their views. The Communists, more than others no doubt, realized the impact of propaganda, to which they attached particular importance.

For example, the Communist Party of Belgium distributed in all 97 different newspapers, and 248 publications were more or less connected to the Front de l'Indépendance.[8] Similarly, the modest Danmarks Kommunistiske Parti (DKP; Danish Communist Party) at first dominated the underground press: of forty-seven publications identified in August 1942, forty of them were in its orbit, directly or indirectly.[9] Finally, a few publications, including three Danish newspapers, went it alone. Two non-Communist periodicals—*De Frie Danske* (The Free Danes) and *Frihedsstøtten* (Liberty column)—began appearing in December 1941, followed, on April 9, 1942, by *Frit Danmark* (Free Denmark), a publication of the DKP whose circulation rather quickly reached 150,000.[10] Like the extremely famous periodical *Libre Belgique* (Free Belgium), these three titles did not depend on any movement or network. Founded in summer 1940 by two lawyers, Robert Logelain and Paul Struye, *Libre Belgique* revived its glorious predecessor of the same name. That high-quality newspaper had been published between 1915 and 1918, under the nose of the occupying forces. Possessing a rather Catholic and conservative sensibility, "La Libre," as it was called, was not attached to any movement during the dark years, though William Ugeux, head of the intelligence network Zéro, briefly became its editor in chief in 1942.[11]

That said, the underground press was not merely a medium for conveying news and information. It could also be used to provide the populations with instructions for action, assigning them precise objectives: to demonstrate on the national holiday; to conceal metals, which the occupying forces were scooping up; to resist being conscripted to work in the Reich; and so on. The newspaper also served as a recruitment tool. By facilitating contacts, "it was the instrument that could measure the sentiments of someone you were hoping to make a sympathizer; it was also the first mode of action and, for many militants, the only likely means of practical action for many long months."[12] In displaying tangible evidence of opposition, it showed there was an alternative to morose resignation and opened the possibility of resistance.

Finally, and perhaps above all, the underground press created a dynamic. It required that logistics be set in place to print, store, and distribute its output. That led to the formation of irregular corps to guard the warehouses and printing works, groups to which the movement could later assign other missions—coups de main, for example. The organization, moreover, having provided its militants with false identity papers, could consider extending that benefit to other groups: Jews, escaped prisoners, evaders of forced labor. Philippe Viannay, founder of the Défense de la France movement, commented in retrospect: "Hence a logic was set in motion that carried us along, or rather, carried us away, and obliged us to respond to the many questions that the very development of that logic raised. The newspaper was no longer an end in itself but rather a support."[13] As a result, the underground press played a preeminent role in structuring the internal resistance. Such was not the case for the army.

Military Mirages

In a subjugated Western Europe, the armies might appear to have been predestined to play the leading roles in the underground. Claiming to be above party politics, they prided themselves on embodying the quintessence of the nation, devoting themselves body and soul to the defense of its sacred soil. Above all, they had men who had mastered the art of war and possessed the weapons necessary to wage it. Both moral and material factors, therefore, made them a force likely to contribute to the rise of the underground groups. And in two countries, France and Denmark, the occupier had in fact allowed modest armed forces to survive.

By the terms of the armistice conventions, Vichy possessed an army of 100,000 men, including some generals who barely concealed their Germanophobia: Maxime Weygand and Jean de Lattre de Tassigny, for instance. With the greatest discretion, moreover, a military fringe was planning the Revanche. General Louis Colson, minister of war in July 1940, General Odilon Picquendar, the chief of staff, and General Aubert Frère, in command of the military region of Lyon, ordered the concealment of weapons. Colonel André Zeller, head of the First Bureau of the army general staff, assigned one of his subordinates, Major Amédée Mollard, to gather together and maintain armaments and materiel in secret warehouses. In 1941 the Camouflage du Materiel (Materiel Concealment Office), supervised by that career officer, is believed to have stockpiled a total of sixty-five thousand individual weapons and four hundred cannons, as well as ammunition and transmission equipment. In the same vein, officers earnestly made plans to mobilize in support of the Allied troops on the day of the landing. Colonel Georges Revers, General Édouard Réquin's chief of staff in command of the second group of divisions, "drew up a list of favorably disposed reservists" and began to study "the possibility of doubling our four small divisions thanks to the concealed materiel, so that, instead of having four small divisions, we will have eight, no less small, granted, but eight nonetheless."[14] Similarly, General Jean-Édouard Verneau, second-in-command and later chief of staff, contemplated how to raise 150,000 men. Comptroller General René Carmille, named to head a national bureau of statistics in the Ministry of Finances, invented a system of perforated cards that made it possible to identify trained reservists and those assigned to the war industries, as well as former members of Chantiers de la Jeunesse (Youth Work Camps), the civil service for which the young could be called up in the free zone. Part of the French army was thus preparing to let weapons do the talking when the time came.

The same was true in Denmark, which, though occupied, held on to its institutions and army. A small group of military officers, including Lieutenant-Colonel Einar Nordentoft, Major H. Lunding, and Captains V. Gyth and P. Winkel, formed a resistance cell called, in all modesty, "The Princes." In Stockholm, it established a liaison with the British in March 1942 and reached an accord with SOE in April. Known as "Plan P," this agreement had two components. Under its terms, Danish officers would transmit to the men of Baker Street information coming from the best source, since they served in the intelligence services; later, upon the retreat of the German troops, the kingdom's armed forces would maintain order and protect installations, which the Nazis' foreseeable scorched-earth policy was in danger of obliterating.[15] All in all, in both France and Denmark, the army provided a solid base for underground action, or so it seemed. But the fruit often did not fulfill the promise of the blossoms.

Although the armed forces envisioned resuming combat upon a landing or a German retreat, they in no case imagined engaging in subversive warfare before D-Day. In reality, the officers' military culture did not incline them to embrace that incendiary prospect, for which, in any case, they were in no way prepared. They also feared that, were they to encourage guerilla warfare or sedition, they would be promoting Communist intrigues, an eventuality that terrified them. Furthermore, a large proportion of French officers worshipped Marshal Pétain. Although they despised his policy of collaboration, they shared many of his domestic policy choices and believed, quite naïvely, that the Victor of Verdun was playing a subtle double game with the German authorities, publicly displaying his support for the Reich only to better back the Allies surreptitiously. These officers, certainly patriotic, did not understand the indissoluble bond between the French State's domestic agenda and its diplomacy: only the alliance with Berlin would allow for the continued existence of the Vichy regime, which, to survive, had to satisfy its master whatever the cost.[16] This it did fully, until its forced departure for Sigmaringen in summer 1944. As a result, the subtle maneuvers of the armistice army were detrimental, in that they portrayed both the resistance and Charles de Gaulle as divisive factors: "In holding up the shield of the Revanche, the Vichy army denied its rival across the Channel all reason for existence and deprived it of a great part of its power of attraction."[17]

A similar statement can be made about Denmark. Although The Princes agreed to provide SOE (and not SIS) with their intelligence, they energetically refused to undertake sabotage operations on their own soil. An active policy, they claimed, ran the risk of impairing relations with the Reich and of culminating in the dissolution of their army, an eventuality that would dry up the source of the information they were offering the British.[18] London bowed to their way of seeing things. In a letter to The Princes on April 11, 1942, Ronald Turnbull, head of the SOE subbranch established in Stockholm, pledged that London would "modify its radio-propaganda in order to avoid upsetting the status quo inside your country and steps are being taken to bring American propaganda into line. In future all unnecessary incitement to sabotage will be avoided and unnecessary attacks will not be made upon the present government."[19] But that surprising agreement was by no means met with unanimous approval. On one hand, the anti–scorched earth policy foreseen by Plan P was remote and unreal, and it contradicted SOE's offensive policy, the aim of which was to take action immediately.[20] On the other hand, that plan was marked by virulent anticommunism. "Supposedly for reasons of security, they placed great stress on the fact that the organisation was primarily intended to resist communist elements which might gain the upper hand in the event of the country being liberated."[21] In addition, the pusillanimity of the Danish officers caused discord. It disgusted the resistance movements, whose activism, conversely, put off the military command, terrified by a possible rift with Berlin.[22]

As a result, the attitude of the French and Danish armed forces could not fail to spark legitimate doubts in the Allies. Skeptical of the assistance these forces could offer, London and Washington were cautious about soliciting their cooperation. Although, as we have seen, a few leaders in the Vichy intelligence services established connections with their British counterparts, London did not seek to ally itself with the meager tricolor troops. And in Denmark, SOE acted with the greatest circumspection. It refused to bind itself too closely to The Princes, a position approved by Christmas Møller,[23] who had no confidence in them.[24] The Special Operations Executive decreed that it would bypass them by sending its own teams, but with one qualification: in view of the shortage of recruits, it decided that resistance leaders and supporters would originate on Danish soil. London would confine itself to providing instructors, radio operators, and liaison officers.[25]

Later events confirmed the validity of the Allies' distrust of the armies. On November 11, 1942, when the German forces invaded the free zone controlled by Vichy, they met with almost no resistance. Rather than go to North Africa, all but a few units of the fleet scuttled themselves; and the vast majority of depots of lovingly concealed arms were handed over to the enemy. "At that moment, great fear took hold throughout the southern zone," reported Colonel Mollard. "It was a race to see who could get rid of the weapons and materiel the fastest. . . . Even those who didn't dare declare their depots shouted out in cafes: 'I have a depot, and I will not declare it,' so that their neighbors would spread the word and discharge them of all responsibility."[26] The reality may have been less dire: according to Paul Paillole, who was in charge of counterespionage at the time, "the Wehrmacht and the Abwehr in the free zone would seize a third of the arms depots. Another third would be destroyed. Another third would be recovered in various ways by the resistance organizations."[27] But that outcome was still very modest, compared to the lofty ambitions of the officers who aspired to "pick up the broken sword."

Results in Denmark were even more disastrous. When the Germans—we shall return to this point—decided to take over the country's domestic policy, on August 29, 1943, the fleet scuttled itself, the army was dissolved, and The Princes, far from participating actively in the internal resistance, fled to Sweden—with the notable exception of Hans Lunding, an officer in the intelligence services.[28] The British and the Americans could only aver that the resistance was obviously a matter too serious to be entrusted to the military.

The situation appeared in a different light in the countries where adverse historical events had led to the breakdown of the armed forces.

In Belgium, career officers disgusted by the defeat wanted to prepare for the resumption of the fighting and to guarantee the maintenance of law and order, if by chance the Reich were to collapse. Some formed a movement, the Légion Belge, under the leadership of an officer named Charles Claser; others reconstituted the Belgian army around Colonel Robert Lentz. The two organizations merged in July 1941, retaining the name "Légion Belge." Passionately royalist, somewhat hostile to the Hubert Pierlot government, and resolutely anticommunist, these men were as obsessed with the fear of a new October Revolution upon liberation as they were with the desire to contribute militarily to the Reich's defeat.[29] Yet the Légion Belge remained a powerful partner, which neither the Allies nor the government in exile could disregard.

Similarly, the Dutch army formed one of the earliest resistance cells in the Netherlands. Upon the capitulation in May 1940, officers concealed weapons, engaged in a few sabotage operations, and attempted to set up escape channels. But "amateurism, innocence and unfamiliarity with illegal activity meant that these first attempts at organized resistance were quickly countered by the German security apparatus."[30] There was one exception: Captain Pieter Jacob Six founded a movement, the Orde Dienst (Order of Service), that engaged in sabotage and intelligence gathering as of 1941–1942. He was obsessed "with the exercise of military authority after the Germans' departure,"[31] certainly a widespread orientation in such circles.

In Norway, finally, several officers became involved in the fight as early as 1940. Some formed small cells, while others succeeded in creating two organizations. The first of these, XU, was dedicated to intelligence, which, once it was sent to the Norwegian legation to Stockholm, was transmitted to the British Intelligence Service. In spring 1941 several military personnel laid the foundations for the second organization, known as Milorg, whose underground headquarters was in Oslo. It set out to "contact all military resistance groups in southern Norway and form a military organization that covers the entire region."[32] That approach elicited doubt and perplexity. Some wondered whether a secret military organization could be created within Norway. Was it not wiser to go to Great Britain? Others feared the reprisals that sabotage might provoke. In rejecting that mode of action, they were not defending an ideological orientation; rather, they were making a realistic assessment of the movement's warfare potential at the time.[33] Milorg, finally, had doubts about its own legitimacy and what line it should take. These hesitations disappeared in summer 1941, as indicated by a letter sent to the king. In it the group stated that it was earnestly forming a secret army that would act at the opportune moment. In the meantime, it would refrain from committing sabotage. It therefore did not want any weapons handed over to it.[34]

The armed forces, whether or not they were dissolved, thus represented an asset, in that they could mobilize battle-hardened men ready to take action. At the same time, the place they occupied in the underground proved problematic. Prepared to do battle in the sunlight of liberation, the military refused to become engaged beforehand in subversive warfare, a stance that contradicted the offensive position that both SOE and some resistance movements were advocating. Military milieus, often conservative, shared a virulent anticommunism, which elicited distrust from progressive groups. In short, the inclusion of the armed forces on the domestic front, far from favoring the unification of the underground, held it back. All in all, they were more a restraint than a help.

Some movements, finally, did not originate either with the army or with a newspaper but set out from the start to cover the whole spectrum of underground action. In France, Combat, founded by Captain Henri Frenay in the wake of the defeat, combined irregular corps with its eponymous newspaper and prepared to mobilize a secret army ready to intervene on D-Day. The Mouvement National Belge, a rather "centrist" organization created in December 1940 by a hairdresser named Aimé Dandoy, assisted by his brother Georges and two friends—Jules Vilain and Vilain's sister Azéma[35]—created a network to help Allied pilots escape and, at the same time, engaged in intelligence gathering in association with the British network Mill. In July 1941 Aimé Dandoy and Camille-Jean Joset founded an underground newspaper, *La Voix des Belges*, whose circulation quickly reached twenty-six thousand.[36] Along the same lines, the underground Communist organizations, as a general rule, combined a paramilitary group, a newspaper, and a civilian organization. To be sure, the rate of growth of the movements was uneven—intense in France and Belgium but weaker in Denmark (where the authorities were vigilant about protecting the society from Nazification), in Norway, and in the Netherlands, where other structures (the trade unions, for example) assumed a role.

These homegrown groups were also called on to work with the underground, a mission that sooner or later raised the question of their relations with both the Allies and the governments in exile.

Splendid Isolation?

Could the internal resistance develop without foreign assistance? At first, the movements, unlike the networks, had little need of it; the pioneers developed their organizations by relying on their own forces. For example, the first two issues of the newspaper *Valmy*, created by Raymond Burgard, who taught German at the Lycée Buffon in Paris, were reproduced on a children's printing press. Above all, the underground newspapers depended in large part on a network of complicit individuals. The first issue of *La Libre Belgique* was printed on the rotary presses of the Brufina holding company, at the headquarters of the Banque de Bruxelles. In the same vein, Tor Skjønsberg, a lawyer by training but a banker by profession, organized financial support for the Norwegian resistance in 1941.[37] To begin with, then, the underground groups could rely on their own resourcefulness and on a network of courageous printers or devoted sponsors. As they developed, however, they were obliged to find regular and continuous sources of funding, which their internal resources could not provide. By December 1942 Combat was remunerating 102 employees. Although in late 1941 it had made do with 20,000 to 30,000 francs, in 1942 it devoured 200,000 francs a month. Likewise, in 1943 the cost to produce 130,000 copies of the newspaper *Libération-Sud* was 100,000 to 300,000 francs, not counting the wages of members of the resistance.[38] To grow, therefore, it was imperative that the movements be able to rely on outside funding, whether it came from the Allies or from their governments in exile.

Communication was also a major obstacle. As a general rule, the resistance groups depended on liaison officers, who transmitted instructions orally or in written form. They also used "mailboxes," installed anonymously in buildings or provided by complicit shopkeepers, who received and delivered correspondence. But that was a drawn-out and tedious process. The messages were sometimes coded, which required endless encoding or decrypting. And the couriers exhausted themselves on interminable trips on foot, by bicycle, or in crowded trains. When Lieutenant-Colonel Aage Højland Christensen, head of region III (southern Jutland), was summoned to a meeting in the center of the Danish peninsula in winter 1944–1945, the return trip took sixty hours,[39] an enormous waste of time that many underground fighters resented. From that standpoint, too, the Allies offered a solution. In providing the underground groups with transceivers or sending messages over the BBC airwaves, they made it possible to authenticate an individual's identity; in addition, they allowed instructions to be sent to a group or even the entire country, something the movements were unable to do.

The transition from resistance to armed struggle also required the means—weapons or explosives—to commit sabotage, execute Germans and collaborators, or carry out a guerilla action. But resources were scarce. Here and there, underground fighters could steal dynamite, rob a Wehrmacht soldier, or resort to weapons hidden after the defeat. On the whole, however, the materiel remained inadequate: though revolvers, rifles, and submachine guns were sometimes available, ammunition was sorely lacking.

Finally, once underground fighters undertook immediate action, they had to coordinate with the grand strategy to improve their effectiveness. The destruction of a bridge or the sabotage of a factory was useful only if it was incorporated into a general plan. But only the Allies were in possession of the big picture that would allow them to assign pertinent objectives to the shadow forces.

In short, material, political, and strategic factors joined together to push the internal resistance closer to London or Washington, especially since the powers in exile were able to play a legitimizing role. Such aid was not considered improper: the Spanish Civil War of 1936–1939 had created a precedent, demonstrating that foreign powers could support armed movements without tarnishing the partisans' patriotism.

Entente, however, was no simple matter. Many in the resistance, sometimes with their roots in civil society or, in the case of the Communists, hostile to the former government authorities, distrusted the émigré powers, whom they deemed responsible for the defeat or illegitimate as representatives of the people. A portion of the Norwegian population contested the Nygaardsvold government, whose neutralist policy before the war had led to disaster.[40] Many Belgians were loyal to the king and had little respect for the Pierlot government. French members of the resistance, even while blaming the defunct Third Republic and the harm done by the parties, had questions about General de Gaulle's program, particularly since the Constable of Free France was not forthcoming on the subject. Taking note of the bankruptcy of the old groups, some movements in France and Norway also dreamed of reforming the political domain upon liberation, an ambition that made them, if not adversaries, then at least rivals of the authorities who had taken refuge in London. Similarly, members of the internal resistance wanted to fight for their country, without necessarily doing battle under the Union Jack or the Star-Spangled Banner. Although ready to support the Allied war effort, they did not intend to become British or American agents. As a result, though entente between the movements and the Allies was imperative, it was littered with obstacles and tensions.

First Contacts with the Governments in Exile

Some movements, however, were concerned at a fairly early date with making contact with their government in exile. Such was the case for the Norwegians. Milorg had doubts about the action it needed to take and was therefore looking for an undisputed authority to establish the foundations on which to build its strategy. At first its staff hoped to find in Norway itself a civil body that, with the king's approval, would determine the principles to be followed. That was a futile quest, however, and in a letter of June 1941 the movement appealed directly to Haakon VII. An agreement was reached on November 20 of the same year: the Norwegian authorities recognized Milorg as part of the armed forces and placed it under their command.[41] But entente met with resistance from the British. SOE disputed the centralizing principle Milorg had adopted, because, if the Germans captured its top advisers, the organization would collapse like a house of cards. In addition, in refusing to bear arms and, as a result, to consider the prospect of immediate action, Milorg contradicted the very principle of subversive warfare that Hugh Dalton's men were defending.[42] These obstacles were ultimately removed through the creation of the Anglo-Norwegian Collaboration Committee, which, as we have seen, oversaw military cooperation between the two countries beginning in February 1942.

The situation was even more complicated in France. De Gaulle, as is well known, manifested "little interest in the active resistance and even in political action in France. The collection of intelligence took precedence, along with radio propaganda."[43] But in October 1941 Jean Moulin came to London. Bearing a report with a full list of resistance forces in both the North and the South, that former Front Populaire prefect, whom the French

State had removed from office in November 1940, was able to convince de Gaulle of the political and military interest represented by the movements. De Gaulle immediately assigned Moulin a mission. On the night of January 1, 1942, he was parachuted into France to promote, notably, the unity of the three major movements in the free zone: Combat, Franc-Tireur, and Libération-Sud. Without actually merging, they were supposed to coordinate their actions and their propaganda, separate the military from the political, and, above all, recognize the general's authority. The envoy from London had major assets with which to realize these aims. Provided with a budget of 3 million francs, he could financially support the southern groups—which he did. He also introduced emissaries into the resistance groups to facilitate their liaison with Free France. Passionate discussions followed in London and metropolitan France; in October 1942 they culminated in an accord. The three major organizations agreed that their paramilitary forces would become part of a secret army, whose command was entrusted to Charles Delestraint, a retired general, and not to Henri Frenay, as he had hoped; they ratified the creation of a coordination committee that would synchronize action and apply the directives received from London. All in all, then, the cause of unification had made progress, though not in the absence of reservations and ulterior motives. The separation of the political from the military occasioned skepticism: Henri Frenay considered that division illusory, inasmuch as the rank-and-file militants were performing indiscriminately tasks belonging to both registers. Likewise, the decision to rally behind the Cross of Lorraine raised some alarm, as the head of Combat explained to the leader of Free France on November 16, 1942.

> I said, "We are resisters, free to think and do what we choose. Our freedom of choice is an inalienable right. It is up to us to decide whether, in the political domain, we shall carry out our orders or not."
>
> The general remained silent for a few moments. Evidently he found my words unseemly.
>
> "Well then, 'Charvet,' it seems that France must choose between you and me."[44]

Finally, and perhaps above all, the process of unification in the southern zone had no effect in the northern zone, despite the advances made by the Pineau mission.

Christian Pineau, the founder of Libération-Nord, set out to understand the intentions of the Man of June 18, whose opacity limited his influence. Even the British observed that "whereas General De Gaulle is admired as a symbol of active resistance to the Germans, his post-war aims have not been sufficiently defined to allow him to be adopted as a leader by any particular section of the French people."[45] Pineau meant to eliminate the ambiguity. Having consulted the principal leaders of the internal resistance beforehand, in March 1942 he managed to reach London. De Gaulle agreed at the time to compose a manifesto for the underground forces, but not before setting his own conditions. "I really do want to entrust a letter to you for your friends, but don't ask me to approve what I have condemned many times, a Republic without authority, a regime of party rule."[46] As a result, the first version of the text was blunt, to say the least. It stated: "A moral, social, political, and economic regime abdicated in defeat. Another was born of capitulation. The French people condemn both of them." In a second version, however, de Gaulle softened his tone.

For the first time, then, the Rebel spelled out his war aims. Swearing to restore the fundamental freedoms, he promised that, "once the enemy is driven from the territory, all Frenchmen and all Frenchwomen will elect the National Assembly, which will decide with sovereign authority the country's fate." "Domestically," he added, "practical guarantees must be set in place against the tyranny of perpetual abuse, guarantees that will ensure freedom and dignity to all, in their work and their lives. For us, national security and social security are imperative and joint aims."[47] In short, Charles de Gaulle did not see liberation as a return to business as usual; he promised wide-ranging reforms, a French-style New Deal.

Even as the French internal resistance and the Gaullist authority worked out a modus vivendi, the Pierlot government lapsed into confrontation. As we have seen, several movements, such as the Légion Belge, remained passionately royalist, serenely ignoring their national authorities. On July 18, 1942, Charles Claser, one of the legion's founders, went to London to discuss the terms of his cooperation with SOE. The talks resulted in a plan of action: during the Allied landing, the movement would engage in a military intervention on the coast and would conduct obstruction operations in the rear. Henri Rolin, undersecretary for defense, confirmed that arrangement with orders submitted to Claser on August 5, 1942.

Despite its patriotism, the Légion Belge emitted a sulfurous odor. Displaying a clear penchant for authoritarianism, it seemed obsessed with the idea of preventing the "extremists"—by which we should understand the Communists and the Flemish nationalists—from taking power after the Germans had gone. For that reason, the Belgian government wished to specify, in a second order, that the legion would in no case be involved in maintaining order upon liberation. Claser turned a deaf ear. He avoided meeting with the ministers of his country and left for Brussels on August 8, with carte blanche only from Rolin, who had not confided in his colleagues. That power grab set off a storm: the Belgian government believed that, because he had not accepted its orders, Claser was leaving without its approval.[48]

There were two dimensions to the conflict, two opposing notions of subversive warfare: the one defended by the Deuxième Section with the support of SOE, and the one promoted by Sûreté with the backing of IS and the Belgian authorities. Politically, that conflict divided the partisans of traditional parliamentary democracy from its adversaries,[49] though the case should not be overstated. Fernand Lepage, the head of Sûreté, "was a leftist liberal, a staunch believer, secretive and a loner by temperament, but civic-minded and courageous,"[50] while the men of the Deuxième Section, though somewhat monarchist, were not fanatics and enjoyed the support of the Socialist Henri Rolin. Nevertheless, the dispute was so violent that Major Claude Knight, head of the Belgian section of SOE, came to believe that men employed by Sûreté and the Intelligence Service had deliberately provoked the arrest of several of his agents. To be sure, that judgment was baseless. But "some of the SOE agents came into contact with agents employed jointly by the 'C' [IS] organisation and the Sûreté and were refused help from them, presumably on 'C' instructions. These actions can, of course, be defended on security grounds."[51] In short, these conflicts cannot be reduced to an ordinary power struggle. Above all, the two camps harbored opposing notions of action. The Pierlot government rejected direct action,[52] which provoked SOE's ire[53] but pleased the Intelligence Service: in preventing SOE from setting Belgium ablaze, the Belgian cabinet maintained calm, even though the population, as Charles Hambro observed, was pleading for a more active policy.[54] Because the British did not present a united front, the Belgians astutely instrumentalized the rivalries dividing His Majesty's services. "The divisions and the lack of contact which exist between our British services are very well understood by the Belgians—so well, indeed, that they have a term normally used in referring to them—le cloisonnement des services anglais [the compartmentalization of the English services].[55] "Thus the Belgians . . . find themselves able to play off C against SOE, PWE against SOE, C against PWE and so forth."[56] That situation could not go on forever. The threatening storm was about to hit.

Colin Gubbins made the first move. To limit Lepage's influence and to defend his own service, he told Paul-Henri Spaak that henceforth SOE would cooperate only with the Deuxième Service. The Belgian government retaliated by announcing, on August 14, 1942, that it was breaking off all relations with Baker Street. Immediately afterward, Henri Rolin and Henri Bernard were relieved of their duties; Hubert Pierlot seized hold of National Defense; and the Deuxième Section was entrusted to Lieutenant-Colonel Jean Marissal, who had just escaped from Belgium. On October 30, 1942, the Belgian prime minister defined the respective duties of Sûreté and the Deuxième Section. The collection of intelligence, the organization of industrial sabotage, and political action would fall to Sûreté, while the Deuxième Section would have more modest duties: the exploitation of the information collected and the design of missions involving military action. Connections with SOE were reestablished in November 1942, but the Belgians set their own conditions. Henceforth, missions would be planned and directed jointly by SOE and Sûreté, except for those of a strictly military nature, which would fall within the purview of the Deuxième Section. Outraged by these measures, which greatly reduced his sphere of operation, Marissal submitted his resignation on November 16 and again on December 7; both times, Pierlot refused to accept it.[57] Ultimately, the Claser affair ended in a threefold victory: for Sûreté, for the government in exile, and for the Intelligence Service. But it did not improve the efficiency of subversive warfare or establish the authority of the Pierlot government over certain movements, though the government did finally manage to impose its law.

The Belgian authorities, aware of the situation, rearranged the organization chart. In June 1943 a Direction Générale du Renseignement et de l'Action (General Directorate for Intelligence and Action) was created within Sûreté to collect and transmit intelligence and to organize the active and passive resistance (except for paramilitary groups). A former head of the Zéro network, William Ugeux, who had been close to Hubert Pierlot before the war, took charge of the directorate, allowing the Belgian prime minister to form a "counterweight to Lepage, who had become too closely linked to SIS and, as a result, too independent from the government." Above all, a high commissioner for state security was named in July 1943, to oversee Sûreté and the Deuxième Direction.[58] That task was entrusted to a magistrate, the auditor general Walter Ganshof Van der Meersch, who had been involved in intelligence, had spent time in Nazi prisons on two occasions, and had just been exfiltrated from Belgium.

In the other countries, the situation appeared in a different light, for obvious reasons. Neither the Danish internal resistance nor its Italian counterpart had had to negotiate its unification with a government in exile, which was nonexistent in both cases. In the Netherlands, relations were established primarily with SOE and not with the Pieter Gerbrandy government—to the great misfortune of the Dutch resistance.

CHAPTER VIII

─────────────

Developments

The evolution of SOE's doctrine was accompanied in 1942 by a reshuffling of the service's organization. On February 22 Hugh Dalton was given the Ministry of Commerce—a promotion that gracefully ousted a man who had maintained stormy relations with Anthony Eden, head of the Foreign Office, and Brendan Bracken, minister of information. "He could not be kicked out but he could be kicked upstairs," commented Harold Balfour, a Conservative MP.[1] Lord Selborne then took over the Ministry of Economic Warfare. Politically conservative, a member of the House of Lords, he was "a small, slight, stooping-man, a great deal less insignificant than he looked."[2]

That passing of the baton was not without its consequences. Selborne proved to be significantly less interventionist than his predecessor, rarely meddling in SOE's daily affairs,[3] and his personal friendship with Winston Churchill eased the heretofore complicated relations between Baker Street and 10 Downing Street. Furthermore, Dalton's departure prompted his personal assistant, Gladwyn Jebb, to return to the Foreign Office. Selborne gave him to understand rather quickly "that he no longer wanted a Foreign Office man as his principal adviser on SOE matters."[4] That change in personnel reduced the influence Anthony Eden exerted, but it had the perverse effect of depriving the SOE leaders of direct access to the man in charge of British diplomacy.[5] Finally, in May 1942, Frank Nelson, "a most capable organiser and a tireless worker,"[6] tendered his resignation, officially for health reasons but in fact because he had wearied of the job. Worn down by SOE's internecine war with the Intelligence Service, exasperated by his Belgian partners, steamrolled by the battle that had led to the creation of the Political Warfare Executive,[7] SOE's executive director yielded his place to Charles Hambro. The Danish Hambro, a banker by profession who lived by "bluff and charm,"[8] had supervised the Belgian, German, French, and Dutch sections of SOE before becoming its deputy leader in November 1941. When Hambro assumed its leadership, Colin Gubbins became his righthand man, in charge of operations over Western Europe. Gubbins was not promoted, however: despite Selborne's urging, Alan Brooke, the chief of staff, refused to allow the brigadier general to become a major general to reflect his new duties.[9]

Hugh Dalton's ouster and Colin Gubbins's rise to power nonetheless allowed the Special Operations Executive to assert itself within the state apparatus. In becoming militarized, SOE renounced the revolutionary messianism of its early days and began to play a more martial tune. Over the medium term, as Lord Selborne noted, it would prepare for the landing through the "formation of new resistance groups and the maintenance and reinforcement of existing secret organizations." But over the short term, he added, "a rising tide of sabotage is increasingly impeding the enemy."[10] His services would therefore encourage it, both by launching raids against Fortress Europe and by supporting or creating underground groups.

The Pursuit of Raids

Some sites, deemed crucial, were beyond the range of the Royal Air Force. To destroy them, the British services sent in commandos, which, once their mission was accomplished, returned to the United Kingdom. These one-off operations targeted either general categories of objectives—communications systems and power grids in the first place—or more precise marks, for example, a factory manufacturing a particular component. SOE participated in that campaign under two auspices: it mounted operations for which it assumed full responsibility, and it provided services other than its own with logistical support.

From that standpoint, Norway was a mission field, entirely open. Its distance from the British Isles prevented the RAF from intervening, particularly since the harsh Scandinavian climate handicapped air operations.

Conversely, the sympathy the population displayed toward the Allies and the proximity of the Swedish border facilitated the actions of commandos. Several expeditions were therefore launched in 1942 and 1943 to strike the iron mines, which the Germans were shamelessly exploiting. For instance, on April 21, 1942, three men transported via fishing boat on the Shetland Bus destroyed the transformer of Baardshaug, not far from Trondheim, which fed electricity to the train in the Orkla mines, whose pyrite was used in the manufacture of sulfuric acid.[11] Likewise, on the night of January 23, 1943, a raid conducted by an SOE commando destroyed the installations in the Litlabø mines, south of Bergen, which deprived the German economy of twenty-two thousand short tons a month of highly concentrated iron and fifty-five hundred tons of pyrite.[12] But the attacks against the installations that manufactured heavy water were considered—not without reason—the jewels of SOE's accomplishments in World War II.

In July 1942 the War Office approached Combined Operations Headquarters about striking the Vemork plants of Norsk Hydro, west of Oslo, which were manufacturing heavy water, a component indispensable in the manufacture of atomic weapons. Although the objective was clear, its realization was at first marked by a terrible failure. On October 18 an advance party was parachuted in (Operation Grouse) to receive a thirty-man commando, which was to be transported to the zone in gliders. The aircraft took off on November 19, but the tow plane and two gliders crashed 125 miles south of their objective. A third glider did manage to land; the few survivors were immediately captured, interrogated by the Germans, then shot on the Führer's orders. The five men in the advance party survived, however, spending a glacial winter in a hut. Another operation was mounted. Six parachutists were dropped on February 16, 1943 (Operation Gunnerside). Having rendezvoused with the men of Operation Grouse on February 24, they went on the offensive four days later.[13] Taking the Germans by surprise, they succeeded in destroying the installations and the four months of stock held by the Nazis. They then retreated, with no losses and in orderly fashion. One group remained behind in Norway to assist the local resistance organizations; another, composed of six men, skied nearly 250 miles in subzero temperatures to reach Sweden. Before crossing the border, they removed their uniforms and passed themselves off as refugees; they then returned safe and sound to the United Kingdom.[14] That was not the end of the affair, however, which unfolded in several episodes. In November 1943 the production of heavy water resumed, though at a slower pace. Quite prudently, the Germans decided to send the stock they possessed to the mother country. Knut Haukelid, a veteran of Operation Gunnerside, proposed to blow up the boat conveying the precious cargo. "At 11 am on Sunday, 20th February, the ferry-steamer Hydro went down after an explosion, and the railway wagons on board, some of which contained the stocks sank in 400 metres in the deepest part of the lake."[15] Fourteen civilians perished in the attack, but the Germans, for lack of heavy water, had to give up the nuclear arms race.

In other cases, SOE played supporting roles. Operation Biting, for example, targeted the Würzburg radar installed in Bruneval. The British wanted not to destroy it but rather to seize certain parts of it, in order to assess the progress the Germans had made in that area. On February 27, 1942, some 120 men were parachuted onto the Norman coast. Although they dismantled part of the installation in ten minutes, they could not get hold of a cathode ray tube, which can detect the presence of an airplane. Despite the losses (six parachutists killed, six missing),[16] the raid ended in success. SOE had made a modest contribution, providing tools and special explosives.[17] The attack against the dry docks of Saint-Nazaire on the night of March 28, 1942 (Operation Chariot), also benefited from the expertise of the men of Baker Street, who manufactured the explosive charge. As a result, the commando was able to destroy "the only dry-dock in France big enough to hold the *Tirpitz*," as well as a shipyard of the utmost importance.[18]

These raids, whatever their value, represented only a minuscule part of the efforts expended. Indeed, SOE was primarily concerned with forging the tools of subversive warfare in Western Europe. In dispatching its agents there, it had three distinct but complementary objectives: to support, by its experts and materiel, the underground groups that had arisen spontaneously in the occupied territories; to create its own "action" networks; and finally, to assist the underground groups in forming secret armies that would be able to act on the day of the Allied landing.

Support

Having emerged spontaneously from the defeat, movements and networks struggled to develop, in the absence of experienced cadres and also for lack of weapons and money. SOE endeavored to remedy that dual deficiency by sending organizers capable of assisting these underground groups, while at the same time providing them with the necessary resources.

The organization therefore sought to back the Norwegian resistance, despite early measures that were discouraging to say the least. In December 1941 a plan had been developed to promote guerilla warfare in the event of an Allied offensive. Three groups were dispatched to an area near Mosjøen, not far from the Arctic Circle, where they would be ready to divide the country in two if the British managed to land in the northern part of the kingdom. But on September 6, 1942, the Gestapo arrested a radio operator.[19] An ambush mounted by SOE agents freed him; in response, the Germans launched violent reprisals, shooting more than thirty hostages in all. Despite that bloodbath, General Wilhelm von Tangen Hansteen, commander in chief of the Norwegian forces, and Minister of Defense Oscar Torp decided that joint activities by SOE and the Norwegian resistance would continue.[20]

And that is what happened. On November 29, 1942, two instructors were dropped by parachute. Before returning to England in late February 1943, they held eleven classes for Milorg cadres and trained fifty-nine men in guerilla techniques, light weapons, and close combat, shoring up the internal resistance's trust in the United Kingdom. In the same vein, a propaganda agent, Petrel, arrived in the Bergen Region on December 2, 1942, to organize the receipt of materiel and new teams, while establishing liaisons between the internal resistance and the Norwegian government.[21] The Political Warfare Executive was less fortunate: in February 1942 the Norwegians refused to allow it to dispatch new envoys to develop propaganda, because the authorities considered that task among their own duties,[22] and the internal resistance deemed it pointless to take such major risks to spread the good word when morale was already "excellent."[23]

But that snag should not conceal the essential. Unlike many of the countries of Western Europe, Norway provided the United Kingdom with a partner, Milorg, reliable enough to spare SOE the need to set up its own networks. It is true that sending emissaries to form underground groups ex nihilo entailed serious risks, because it elicited "unwonted activity in a small community. Sooner or later this causes a natural curiosity amongst otherwise well-meaning people. If the man has previously been known in the locality his return is bruited abroad; if he is a stranger he is open to suspicion. There is conclusive evidence to show that agents from the UK have been regarded as agents provocateurs." Charles Hambro's services drew the logical conclusions: they decided "to stop forthwith any further attempts to set up any SOE organization as distinct from, or even parallel to, Milorg," except when no local organization existed.[24] Rather than create competing groups, they confined themselves to supporting the Norwegian internal resistance, becoming, in short, a resource provider.[25] The results obtained were not exceptional, however: in mid-1943 Milorg remained above all "an army without the means of warfare."[26]

SOE also supported the organizations of the Belgian internal resistance. For example, a liaison officer was assigned to the Légion Belge to intensify sabotage operations. For the period running from summer to November 1942, the British recommended targeting primarily the railroads leading into France, which could be used by German reinforcements. They also prescribed developing an "insaisissable" sabotage, one that the enemy's repressive services could not detect, against the transport facilities and establishments working for the enemy, with particular attention to rolling stock and canals.[27] But these instructions were rarely followed. They came up against the declared hostility of Hubert Pierlot. He rejected that form of action and, at least according to SOE, went so far as to inform saboteurs working in his country that he disapproved of their actions. With one accord, the government in exile fought to get the Special Operations Executive to inform it when it was sending agents and to have industrial sabotage remain in the hands of Sûreté and not the Deuxième Section. Antoine Delfosse, minister of justice, was of the opinion that industrial targets, because of their political and technical dimensions, lay within the jurisdiction of civilians and not the military. That quibble surprised Charles Hambro, who asked with false naïveté how to distinguish between the two spheres. In any event, in November 1942 the British authorities gave in, as we have seen: all actions would be undertaken after an agreement of the two countries, which would jointly initial the orders.[28]

That modus vivendi, however, fizzled out. In fact, relations between SOE and Sûreté were so tense that, in late 1942, no planning had occurred. In 1943 the British tried again, but Colonel Marissal, head of the Deuxième Section, turned a deaf ear, preferring to plan the paramilitary action that was to occur upon liberation rather than engage in sabotage. The British, unable to spur action in Belgium, also suffered heavy losses in that country. By the eve of 1943, almost all their agents and radio operators had fallen into enemy hands.[29] There was a modest consolation: the propaganda services had managed to send men and materiel to strengthen the underground press. Between November 1942 and September 1943 London sent out eleven propagandists,[30] along with a few prints intended for the press, some of which were reproduced by *La Libre Belgique* on July 21, 1942.[31]

In France, finally, SOE unwisely relied on the Carte network.

The Carte Disaster

In 1940 the painter André Girard, a set decorator, caricaturist, and adman all at once, had set up a network known as Carte.[32] Girard, the off-screen father of the actress Danièle Delorme, despised propaganda, which he found pointless and too politicized for his taste, and focused on military action. Upon the defeat, he had formed an organization in Antibes, which Maurice Diamant-Berger (alias André Gillois), Joseph Kessel and his nephew, Maurice Druon, along with Jean Nohain and Claude Dauphin had joined. Girard had also canvassed officers in the armistice army, well aware of their state of mind, since he had done his military service at Saint-Cyr during the interwar period. The military, in return, was drawn to a man who claimed to be apolitical, defended Pétain while vilifying Laval, and condemned in a single stroke the meeting at Montoire, de Gaulle, and Communism. In 1942 Carte probably had about a hundred agents, attracted by a very simple program: intelligence and preparations for D-Day.

Contact with SOE was established fairly quickly through Lieutenant Francis Basin (alias Olive) of F Section. Girard proved to be extremely shrewd. Far from begging for funds from the British, he turned them down, haughtily declaring: "No one, not you and not us, can ensure funds sufficient to pay the costs of all our men."[33] That bluff impressed Basin, who sent favorable reports about that supposedly powerful organization. A new SOE envoy, Peter Churchill (no relation to the prime minister), arrived on the night of January 9, 1942, carrying 700,000 francs intended in part for that promising group. His report was so laudatory that, following his second mission, between April 1 and April 20, 1942, two radio operators were placed in the service of the network, an unheard-of privilege given the scarcity of such personnel. SOE remained wary, however, and demanded that an officer be sent to Great Britain to provide information. Henri Frager, Girard's second-in-command, flew to London. Painting in glowing terms an enormous organization ready to deploy on the day of the invasion, he also asked for five minutes on the BBC to counter or nuance Gaullist propaganda. That proposal could not fail to appeal to the English, who were exasperated by de Gaulle. In late July Henri Frager returned to France, with Nicholas Bodington by his side. Dazzled by Carte, which demanded fifty thousand Sten submachine guns and fifty transceivers, the man from SOE could not praise it enough. He wrote to his superiors: "The Carte organization must be considered both civilian and military. [It] was constituted with the greatest care by specialists, under conditions of extreme secrecy. Carte has nothing in common with a group of amateurs."[34]

In fact, Carte seemed to meet fully the expectations of the British. Thanks to that network, they believed, the United Kingdom would have at its disposal an army ready to go, one that would disregard political questions. London thus hoped to circumvent de Gaulle and "counterbalance, from France, the influence of the Gaullist Resistance, which accounted for a large share of the general's legitimacy."[35]

Under such conditions, SOE could not fail to increase its support. In August 1942 it sent more than 2 tons of weapons, followed in 1943 by 116 more tons.[36] Also beginning in August 1942, Baker Street deposited a million francs with Baring Brothers, which credited the accounts of Lombard Odier Darier Hentsch et Cie. The Genevan bank ultimately turned the funds over to French establishments. Last but not least, SOE dispatched instructors. On October 2, 1942, the felucca *Seadog* delivered Major John Gilbert Goldsmith (alias Valentin and Jean Delannoy) to the Mediterranean coast. The officer introduced his recruits to the art of explosives, before taking a tour of the region.

The organization then increased the number of its subbranches along the Côte d'Azur, in Provence, and in Isère, and recruited prominent personalities, Pierre Bénouville (known as Guillain de Bénouville) in particular. The arrival on the scene of Bénouville, a former member of Action Française, a tough Pétainist who had gone to North Africa to assist the Allies (he was arrested, then acquitted),[37] confirms the attraction the network exerted over a certain far-right milieu, Vichyist but Germanophobic, patriotic but hostile to de Gaulle. In late August 1942 Carte likely had three thousand agents, three hundred of them remunerated. Above all, it had a radio station, Radio-Patrie, whose status was at the very least dubious.

In order not to involve His Majesty's Government and to circumvent the accords that bound the United Kingdom to Free France, the transmitter was a Radio Unit that was supposed to be spreading black propaganda. The station did not report to the BBC and took advantage of that freedom to broadcast, beginning on October 4, 1942, patriotic addresses delivered by André Gillois and Claude Dauphin. But in invoking General de Gaulle's patronage without his agreement, they sowed confusion and provoked anger. As de Gaulle indicated to Anthony Eden on December 30, 1942: "Just as it is not the role of a foreign, albeit Allied, authority—and which, moreover, in this instance remains anonymous and by the same token avoids responsibilities—to assign war missions to French citizens, the act of swathing those supposed 'instructions' in the ambiguous term 'Gaullist' and creating the illusion of my approval is a procedure that I am sure Your Excellency will look on with the utmost severity, as I do."[38] Called on to respond, Colonel Nigel Sutton, head of the French section of PWE, which had partnered with SOE to oversee Radio-Patrie, got bogged down in niggling denials. He conceded:

> I agreed that the phrase complained of: "tous les Français de l'Armée secrete sont par définition gaullistes" [All Frenchmen in the secret army are by definition Gaullists] is a sticky one. For the purposes of the listeners in France I maintained that it was perfectly reasonable because "gaullisme" in relation to French resistance generally has got itself into the same sort of position as the trade mark "Kodak" in relation to any camera. In other words, in current French at the present "gaullisme" transcends "de Gaullisme." I agreed, however, that it was a mistake to use the expression gaullisme.[39]

This was pettifoggery, inasmuch as Carte was the linchpin of SOE's anti-Gaullist strategy. The material support the British promised was supposed to ensure them control "of a hub of resistance with both military and political importance. As such, the absence of relations with de Gaulle constitut[ed] an indispensable precondition."[40] The network, possessing substantial resources, was also able to poach militants from the movements by promising them the moon (money) and the stars (weapons). In fact, some men in Cannes abandoned Combat for Carte, unleashing Frenay's fury. As he pointed out in February 1943, "In acting in that way, [Radio-Patrie] slowly destroyed an achievement that, however imperfect, required long and patient efforts and sometimes costly sacrifices. . . . I can only deplore and condemn such behavior. It bears the mark of a spirit we have fought to banish from the resistance. Making greed an essential recruitment method will end up perverting those who, just yesterday, were working selflessly and will take from the resistance the moral value wherein a great deal of its strength lies."[41]

Nevertheless, a gulf lay between the network's weakness and the bluff of its leader, who suggested that part of the armistice army would resume combat at his call.[42] The conclusions were finally drawn, if somewhat belatedly. The London authorities, worried at seeing no results forthcoming, demanded that André Girard give an accounting. After putting them off for a time, he flew to England on February 21, 1943. His interlocutors then discovered that the Carte network was only the most modest of organizations. In early April the British told Girard that they refused to work with him any further and barred him from returning to metropolitan France. His assistant, Henri Frager, picked up the pieces, and the English and the French assumed joint oversight of Radio-Patrie on January 21, 1943. SOE had been blinded by its anti-Gaullism; the Carte affair hardly boosted its image in the eyes of the Free French services.

All told, that disappointing outcome confirmed that SOE could in no case confine itself to supporting the underground groups that were blossoming in Western Europe. Granted, that support intensified resistance to the Nazi occupying forces and sometimes dealt them a few blows. But nothing guaranteed that the homegrown movements or networks would carry out London's instructions. The Special Operations Executive thus strove to create its own organizations, counting on them to obey without a second thought.

Building in Denmark and Belgium

Following that logic, in July 1942 SOE had dispatched two radio operators and five agents to Denmark. One of the agents, Captain Christian Rottbøll, was supposed to create a sabotage organization in that country, a difficult task to say the least. The resistance at the time "was by no means the broad popular movement that it became later. It was rather the fight of lonely men, whose motives were not understood, and it was restricted, in a great number of trivial respects, by lack of support and understanding among the mass of the population, on whom it could later rely."[43] In opting for a politics of presence, the major political parties condemned the

resistance to a marginal space limited to the far right and the far left. Rottbøll thus established contacts with The Princes, the Danish Communist
Party, and the Danish Unity Party. He was later killed by the Danish police
while it was attempting to arrest him, on September 26, 1942.[44] SOE then
decided to send Mogens Hammer, a radio operator who had just been exfiltrated to Sweden. Ralph C. Hollingworth, head of the Danish section of
SOE, assumed the risks of that operation. He explained after the fact (in
1947, to be precise): "I calculated that the Germans, once [Hammer] had
left the country, would think that the last thing he would do would be to
come back, and come back at once."[45] On the night of October 18, 1942,
the agent was thus dropped by parachute off the coast of Tisvilde, north of
Copenhagen, in an inflatable, waterproof rubber suit specially designed to
withstand the rigors of the North Sea.[46]

His mission, however, was not crowned with success. In addition to
forming a sabotage organization, Hammer was supposed to exfiltrate to
Sweden Hedtoft Hansen, the Social Democratic leader, as well as two SOE
agents, Max Mikkelsen and Vilfred Petersen. But the three men were discovered and arrested. That failure tarnished the prestige of SOE, whose
actions, in the eyes of the Danish resistance, could be summed up as
"unmitigated disappointments, vain hopes, half promises which were not
fulfilled, and confused and confusing decisions."[47] In fact, of ten agents
sent out before March 1943, four had been killed and four others captured.[48] Meanwhile, Hammer returned to London via Sweden without
having fulfilled his objectives. Rather than pursue subversive warfare, he
joined the regular army. He was killed in an accident in Hamburg in 1945.

The British had not given up on developing sabotage in Denmark, a
country whose declared neutrality exasperated some ruling circles. As of
July 30, 1942, Colin Gubbins, a proponent of the offensive, demanded that
the underground activities "support and be of immediate benefit to regular military operations,"[49] an order that included the Scandinavian kingdom. To drive the point home, London decided on January 27, 1943, to
bomb the Burmeister & Wain shipyards in Copenhagen. "This was to
remind Danish workers of the warlike character of the production, and the
advantages it gave the Germans; next, to demonstrate for the Danish population, that Denmark was also on the war map and that independent Danish sabotage . . . would protect us from further bombing." So commented
Ebbe Munck, the Danish journalist who, working from Stockholm, was
partly responsible for liaisons between the internal resistance and the British

services.[50] "It was a grim choice of Sabotage or Bombs," confirmed the head of the Danish section to the chief of operations.[51] London was indicating that the time for action had come. In February 1943 SOE, moving into high gear, dispatched a group of four men, followed on the night of March 11, 1943, by a second team, led by Flemming Muus.

He proved equal to the task. A businessman who had lived in Liberia for more than ten years, Muus had decided to return to England in support of his country. But the ship taking him from Cape Palmas to Monrovia was torpedoed. He did not give up but continued the journey in the company of two African houseboys. The three men spent the 250 miles that separated them from Monrovia bailing out the water that threatened their frail skiff.[52] Intelligent and ruthless, SOE's chief organizer for Denmark used and abused his powers of persuasion, had "a liking for bluff," and shrewdly understood how to "flatter, bribe, cajole and drive the Danes to greater activity."[53] It was therefore quite natural that he should become "the man who was to realize the British Resistance plans in Denmark."[54] Relying in part on the Communists, Flemming Muus succeeded in intensifying sabotage operations, which, at a rate of ten a month for April and May 1943, struck businesses working for the occupier, such as Lyngby, whose batteries were used on the U–Boats.[55]

SOE also developed underground groups (networks or movements) in Belgium. André Wendelen, a former law student at the Université Libre de Bruxelles, was parachuted into the country on January 28, 1942. He quickly reestablished contact with his old classmates Robert Leclercq, Henri Neuman, and Richard Altenhoff, who formed sabotage teams. Jean Burgers was the leader of "group G" (for Gérard, his pseudonym). His men, having received a parachute delivery of materiel in April of the same year, immediately took action, attacking the houses of collaborators in Namur and hitting industrial sites and railroad networks in Liège. In spring 1943 group G set out to cause maximum damage to the occupier while avoiding pointless destruction and reprisals. It therefore gave precedence to transport facilities and energy supplies, which also corresponded to London's instructions. The British did not hesitate to fund group G—they paid it 100,000 francs a month—but they were stingier about sending materiel: the movement received only two containers in 1943, which limited its capacity for action.[56]

The British also created networks that depended only on themselves. Captain Albert Toussaint, arriving by parachute on the night of August 24,

1942, launched an organization capable of providing the United Kingdom with the meteorological data it lacked, a challenge taken on by the Beagle network. Its forty agents and auxiliaries sent out 1,848 bulletins during World War II.[57] Mill, at the impetus of the Intelligence Service and later of the IS/Sûreté team, specialized in the collection of intelligence, which came both from its agents and from the men of the Mouvement National Belge. Other efforts failed, however. In 1943 SOE sought to set up an escape channel operating with Lysander aircraft or feluccas from southern France, but the plan was aborted because the organizer, C. J. Lord, had a nervous breakdown and vanished without a trace.[58]

In France, a Policy of Going It Alone

Apart from the Carte network, SOE preferred to provide its own structures in France rather than support the underground groups that had developed in the metropolis. That logic was not without foundation: the stormy relations Winston Churchill maintained with Charles de Gaulle impelled the prime minister to avoid as much as possible tying his hands through the use of a partner who was as determined as he was unpredictable. The historian Michael Foot, with typically British understatement, commented: "Resolute intransigence was the only attitude [de Gaulle's] keen sense of honour allowed him to adopt, but it did not make for any sort of smooth working."[59] The United Kingdom thus went into battle on its own.

SOE, as we have seen, had two sections, one of which—F section—acted in complete independence from the BCRA, the secret services of Free France. But it ran into serious difficulties in both the northern and the southern zone. Pierre de Vomécourt, founder of the Autogiro network, which set out to conceal weapons and develop sabotage operations, was sent to London, then parachuted into France on April 1, 1942. He was picked up by the Gestapo on April 25 but managed to convince his judges to treat him as a prisoner of war. With his comrades, he was interned in Colditz Castle, from which he returned after the war ended. A team composed of Denis Rake, Edouard Wilkinson, and Richard Heslop also formed in summer 1942; but on August 15 Rake and Wilkinson were arrested in Limoges, in the unoccupied zone, during a routine identity check. Two stupid details gave them away. Although they claimed to have met for the first time that same day, they were "each carrying plenty of brand new unpinned thousand-franc notes, numbered in a single consecutive series; and their identity cards, ostensibly issued in different towns, were made out in the same handwriting." They would finally be released by the prison warden, whose heart was with the Allies. A fourth agent, Benjamin Cowburn, had parachuted into France on the night of June 1. But unable to establish contacts, he could do no more than ask a few friends to introduce abrasives into the machines at an airplane engine factory and oversee an attack on several electrical lines extending out from Éguzon, in the Indre department. He subsequently decided to return to England.[60] In the Bordeaux region, by contrast, Claude de Baissac, a Mauritian who had been parachuted in near Nîmes on July 30, laid the foundations for the Scientist network, which was destined for a bright future.

In the free zone, SOE managed to organize the escape of agents who had been arrested the previous autumn in Marseilles. Having gathered in the Mauzac prison camp, about ten men—including Pierre Bloch, Georges Bégué, and Michael Trotobas—escaped at dawn on July 16 and resumed service. Trotobas was again dropped by parachute on November 18, 1942, and established himself in Lille to create the Farmer sabotage network. Another agent, Victor Hazan, having arrived in France on the night of May 1, taught a few men to handle British weapons and explosives—especially plastics, which were not widespread at the time. In autumn–winter 1942–1943, he trained more than ninety instructors to teach the basic use of submachine guns, pistols, and explosives.[61] That balance sheet suggests that, apart from planting a few seeds that had only to sprout, SOE's F section had mixed success, which obliged the British service to turn to the BCRA.

SOE, RF Section

To conduct their activities in metropolitan France, the British, in the absence of agents, were obliged to face the facts: they had to cooperate with the Free French services. That new situation opened up welcome prospects and led to the creation, in May–June 1941, of a liaison section within both organizations. In theory, French and British officers elaborated plans jointly. These were submitted to SOE and validated by General de Gaulle's chief of staff, General Petit. They would be carried out by preexisting local groups, with the technical assistance of two men—one of them a radio operator—detached for two months. But these principles ran up against the imbalance in power relations. As the historian Sébastien Albertelli observes, "Not only did the SOE leaders possess a right of veto over the missions proposed by the Intelligence Service, but they alone took on, outside Gaullist control, the coordination of the paramilitary activities undertaken in France, some by F section, others by RF section. In their desire to obtain the resources needed to act, the Free French leaders had no choice but to accept such conditions, which, however, would quickly become intolerable."[62]

On April 3, 1942, a meeting took place between Harry Sporborg of SOE and André Dewavrin, head of the BCRA. The two men

> agreed to undertake this year the maximum number of coups-de-main against permanent or transient enemy objectives, to be nominated, through SOE, by the British or Russian General Staffs. The attacks were to be undertaken by Action Groups, to be formed at once for this sole purpose in France, or by parachutists sent from England. . . . The BCRA hoped to form within 3 months' time a certain number of Action groups, who would receive their instructions from agents already parachuted, or who were to be sent to France at a later date.[63]

Immediately afterward, in September 1942, a senior committee was formed to debate general policy options, which a junior committee would translate into concrete terms.[64] On the French side, the senior committee was composed of André Philip, commissioner for the interior; Pierre Billotte, General de Gaulle's chief of staff; and André Dewavrin. The British side brought together Colin Gubbins and Major David Keswick. But these committees played only a minor role, inasmuch as SOE was hardly eager to facilitate its rival's enterprises. Thus, in June 1942, when de Gaulle demanded that Free France be included in the Allied plans, even as preparations for the landing in Europe were being outlined, Alan Brooke, British chief of staff, curtly replied that the coordination of subversive action in Europe was solely the responsibility of SOE. That amounted to depriving the Gaullist secret services of any access to the Anglo-American high command.[65]

In mid-1943, then, SOE faced a dual dilemma. If it set up its own organizations, it was assured of their obedience but had to deal with the scarcity of volunteers and the lack of results. If it supported existing groups, it benefited from roots in the community and potentially broader mobiliza-tion but ran the risk of having its instructions for action ignored, in favor of other objectives—political ones, for example. To cut that Gordian knot, SOE explored the two possibilities side by side, except, notably, in Norway, where it relied exclusively on Milorg. The fundamental issue was not which targets to assign to the underground forces: more or less respecting the priorities established by London, these forces struck indus-tries working for the occupier, plus electricity networks, communication routes, and even quislings who were prospering under the jackboot. At stake in the first place was the chain of command: Whom, ultimately, should the internal resistance obey? The Allied staff seemed foreordained to assume its leadership, given that that staff was defining the overall global strategy to bring down the Reich; but the governments in exile could also legitimately lay claim to the leading role, in the name of the national sovereignty they embodied. That claim was sometimes contested by members of the internal resistance, which, operating within the occu-pied countries, believed they were often better placed than the émigré powers to come up with plans for action. In short, the question of who was in command was crucial, even more so given the ardently hoped-for prospect of the landing. By that measure, the constitution of the secret armies (SA), which were supposed to act on D-Day, represented a key issue. That explains why they gave rise to debates, tensions, and clashes.

Form Your Battalions?

The letter that established the SAs circulated on May 15, 1942. It prescribed that SOE "should endeavour to build up and equip paramilitary organiza-tions in the area of the projected operations."[66] In spite of everything, the military staffs did not have overly high expectations regarding the role these underground troops might assume on D-Day. They hoped the secret armies would succeed in slowing the advance of the German reinforcements and break up their lines of communication, weaken the Luftwaffe, and finally, harass the enemy forces through guerilla warfare that would weaken their morale. Conversely, the Allies did not intend to arm the insurrectional movements that, they said, would not fail to emerge. They hoped, more-over, that the partisans would be able to channel these uprisings, to keep them from degenerating into rioting and looting.[67]

The mission assigned to the Special Operations Executive, though relatively clear in its objectives, turned out to be complicated to implement. Charles Hambro's men had to create a military instrument that would obey unquestioningly the orders of the Allied generals; but to identify people of good will and then mobilize them, the support of the government in exile proved necessary, as Colin Gubbins frankly admitted. He wrote to his superior, Frank Nelson, on April 18, 1942: "It must be accepted as strictly axiomatic that without the goodwill and assistance of the émigré governments, SOE can do little. . . . My present energies are therefore largely devoted to persuading certain reluctant governments to change their attitude and cooperate fully with us. I am not unhopeful."[68] To favor the emergence of these secret armies, several missions were dispatched to Western Europe. They all pursued a dual objective: construct an organization adapted to their aims and set up secret arms depots.

In 1942 the Lemur mission, assigned to Louis Angelo Livio (Lemur) and J. M. Pans, was supposed to form a reception committee in the region of Tournai and figure out how to store the weapons London promised to send.[69] Subsequently, five teams were parachuted into France between November 17, 1942, and May 22, 1943, to receive delivery of dropped containers (sixteen in all).[70] An organization plan also had to be devised. In summer 1942 Colonel Henri Bernard took advantage of a stay in London by Captain Charles Claser, head of the Légion Belge, to elaborate a plan to divide Belgium into five zones, each with a regional command.[71] That principle was adopted, and it prevailed until liberation. It was not so easy to appoint a leader, however. Claser would have fit the bill, but he was arrested. In November 1942 the Belgian government therefore recognized Colonel Jules Bastin as head of the underground military groups. That former chief of staff of the cavalry was arrested in November 1943 and was replaced by Colonel Ivan Gérard. He, however, feeling threatened, went to London on March 15, 1944, entrusting his command to General Jules Pire.[72]

SOE stood apart from these negotiations, wishing to judge on the basis of the evidence the viability of the ambitious plans hatched by the Belgian government. It especially wondered "how they could be fully implemented with the restricted number of men available from both the Secret Army and SOE."[73] SOE therefore decided to dispatch Adelin Marissal, who, like his brother Jean, belonged to the Deuxième Section, an organization in which Gubbins had full confidence. Delivered by airplane on July 23, 1943, the captain met with the principal leaders of the secret army and spelled out their missions. Over the short term, the underground troops were sup-posed to engage in sabotage, even while preparing for the liberation. To do so, they would receive a budget of five million francs.[74] On his return to London on October 18, 1943, Marissal brought comforting news. The SA and its regional commands were being set in place; they were close to military circles and had a team of competent cadres.[75]

The same plan was applied in Norway. Despite the blows dealt by the German repression in 1942, Milorg strengthened its central command, while accepting a form of decentralization based on the creation of fourteen districts. The British authorities and the Norwegian government, preoccu-pied with the bloody repression being waged by the occupier, recommended the greatest caution. At a meeting in Stockholm in February 1942, the Norwegian high command asked the internal resistance to prepare for the liberation but advised against exposing itself overly much. Its fears were so strong that it repeated the request at the end of the same year, again raising the question of confidence: did Milorg prefer to accelerate the liberation by joining the struggle, at the risk of reprisals, or did it recommend a more passive attitude, even if that meant a delay in the Germans' departure? In January 1943 the military organization settled the matter: it opted for struggle, believing it was important that the population "find strength and self-respect in the knowledge that the liberation was not only a gift from others but also a result of their own efforts." In May 1943, again at a meet-ing in Stockholm, it was therefore decided that the resistance would form and train units to assist the Allied troops during their offensive, before then aiding them in maintaining order.[76] But London avoided exerting too much pressure on its ally. "It was therefore tacitly decided that the steps to build solid ground on which a Secret Army could stand should be continued, but that no attempt should be made to force the pace. In other words, a more natural and less forced growth of military organization was required."[77] Humanitarian scruples and strategic imperatives combined to shape that attitude. The Allies took the measure of what the Norwegian population, subjected to a barbaric occupation, was enduring and refused to make their chains any heavier; but they also knew that, for the moment, the plans for invasion excluded Norway. They doubted the military value of the partisans, who in their eyes were incapable of taking "effective action in attacking enemy positions, although they may be of value for carrying out sabotage of communications."[78] That judgment, quite obvi-ously, did not apply to France.

Whereas the British favored a strategy of attrition, whose aim was to weaken the Reich around its periphery before dealing it a death blow, the Americans defended a diametrically opposed stance. True to their military heritage, they wanted to attack Germany where it was strongest, to ensure a more rapid victory. From that standpoint, France was becoming a linchpin. The proximity of England, the accessibility of the French coast, and the quality of its communication networks, which were key for logistics, represented assets favorable for a landing. That explains why the strategists decided in 1942 that the invasion would take place on the coasts of France. That prospect gave the French resistance a major role: on D-Day, its troops would be supporting the Allied contingent. But first they had to be in order of battle.

As early as 1940, as we have seen, Henri Frenay, head of Combat at the time, had envisioned building up a secret army capable of participating in the liberation of the country. After bitter negotiations, Franc-Tireur and Libération-Sud agreed in 1942 to contribute their forces to that army. At the time, General Charles Delestraint received the command of the SA, an assignment that was expanded to the northern zone in February 1943. This plan generally satisfied the Gaullist camp, but it upset the British. In fact, the SA had grown out of the movements, which provided it with men and cadres. SOE had no direct contact with these groups, and it had misgivings about them. It suspected them of favoring political action over "the physical sabotage of the German war effort," and of viewing themselves as General de Gaulle's loyal supporters. Far from dissipating these fears, the BCRA fueled them. In March 1942 André Dewavrin, still skeptical about the army of shadow's amateurism, claimed that Vichy and the Gestapo had infiltrated the movements and that their personnel was not up to the demands of the moment. "We should modify the conception of military action in France and instead of asking the existing organization to recruit a clandestine military force, to devise a constructive plan realizable in steps," he suggested.[79] Embracing a Jacobinist orientation, Fighting France also favored a centralized organization, which sparked London's anxiety. SOE, claiming that the SA would collapse if General Delestraint were to be taken down, pleaded for decentralization, which would have placed each region in direct contact with the Allied staff. Finally, the chain of command, exclusively French, was in no way integrated into the Allies' organization charts. The French SA was thus not included in an overall strategy, and nothing suggested that it would carry out the orders given by the Anglo-American command.

These flaws could have been corrected if SOE had dispatched envoys to the major French movements, an arrangement it had applied in Norway and Belgium. Frenay made the case for this measure: "I am renewing my request from London: to receive an SOE officer here to serve as liaison between the English organizations and our own. It is urgent that he be named," he wrote in February 1943.[80] But there was no chance that his plea would be heard: de Gaulle wanted to lead the internal resistance, which, had it benefited from direct contact with London, would have slipped from his grasp. He therefore placed emissaries within the major underground groups and bestowed broad powers—financial in particular—on Jean Moulin, in order to bypass the British services by presenting himself as the one and only interlocutor of the internal resistance.

In the eyes of the Anglo-Americans, the formation of the secret armies was therefore moving in the right direction. In mid-1943, however, the battle was far from over. The underground troops remained autonomous; their centralized organization made them vulnerable; and their command, as a general rule, was in the hands of the governments in exile and not in those of the American and British authorities. In that regard, Norway was an exception. By incorporating Milorg into its military forces, themselves headed by the Anglo-Norwegian Collaboration Committee, it had designed a setup that respected the group's sovereignty even while following the imperatives dictated by the Allied strategy. France, Belgium, Denmark, and the Netherlands, by contrast, would have to forge the terms of a compromise that, in mid-1943, had not yet been conceived. Italy, finally, was considered an enemy and was excluded from the plan of action.

A sense of urgency reigned, however: Nazi Germany, by imposing forced labor in most of the countries it ruled, was creating a flood of evaders, some of whom headed for the secret armies. The internal resistance would have to make the most of that opportunity and that challenge.

━━━━━━━━━━━━━━━

CHAPTER IX

Compulsory Labor

An Opportunity or a Curse?

B y winter 1941–1942 the labor supply had become a crucial issue for the Reich, which between June 1941 and May 1944 lost on average nearly sixty thousand men a month in the icy steppes of the Russian front.[1] To replace the men mobilized in its armed forces, Nazi Germany, after trying various makeshift solutions, decided to resort to forced labor. On March 21, 1942, Adolf Hitler named Fritz Sauckel, a Nazi from day one, "plenipotentiary general for labor deployment" and assigned him the task of recruiting throughout Europe the men and women so sorely lacking in the German economy. By summer 1943 nearly five million civilians were working in the Reich's factories or fields.[2] The countries of Eastern Europe were subjected to that severe exploitation early on, but Western Europe was not spared either.

Servitude

In February 1941 a decree stipulated that any Dutch citizen, on the order of his or her employment bureau, could be sent to Germany temporarily. Although the measure was at first applied half-heartedly, on March 23, 1942, the occupying forces instituted compulsory labor in Germany and enforced it through a series of roundups ordered by Sauckel.[3] By September 5, 1944, the Netherlands, with a population of nine million at the time, had witnessed the departure of 286,610 conscripts, a number slightly fewer, however, than that of volunteers: 430,000 civilian exiles,[4] 387,900 of whom were still in Germany at the end of the war.[5]

These departures gave rise to a vast civil disobedience movement. In late April 1943 the occupier sought to call up and exile the 300,000 former prisoners of war who had been released in 1940. A total of 500,000 workers fought back, launching a powerful strike movement. Unusually, the revolt begin in the rural areas and was carried out by residents there (who began by suspending obligatory milk deliveries) more than by city dwellers. On May 9 that *Melkstaking* (milk strike) was broken, at a cost of three hundred wounded and ninety-five dead, eighty of them summarily executed. The country was placed under martial law, radios were seized, and all men between eighteen and thirty-five were theoretically subject to compulsory labor. But by the first months of 1943—earlier than in Belgium or France[6]—the rate of compliance had begun to fall off from its original level, and resistance organizations had set out to assist the evaders. In particular, the Landelijke Organisatie voor Hulp aan Onderduikers (National Organization to Assist Evaders) provided false papers, fresh supplies, and moral support, before organizing in August 1943 the Landelijke Knokploegen (National Irregular Forces), who took on the task of burning draft registration records. The Allies, however, did not seem to be paying them any attention, or at least did not provide them with any special aid.

In Belgium, on October 6, 1942, the occupying forces, after using various methods to compel workers to go into exile (high-handedly closing businesses and construction sites judged useless, increasing work hours, prohibiting workers from changing jobs without the authorization of the National Labor Office), imposed a stint of compulsory labor in Germany, which in theory targeted men aged eighteen to fifty and women between twenty-one and thirty-five. In March 1943, however, pressure from the general secretaries who administered the country (replacements for the ministers who had left for London), from Cardinal Van Roey with the support of a bishopric that was of the same mind, and from Senator Maria Baers led the Germans to exempt the so-called weaker sex. But in June 1943 two age cohorts (men born in 1920 and 1921) were called up. In all, 189,542 Belgians were forced to leave for the factories of the Reich between November 1, 1942, and July 31, 1944. They were added to the 224,301 more or less voluntary departees. In all, 413,843 workers were tapped and exiled, a heavy tribute for a country whose population at the time was only slightly over eight million.[7]

In France, where the per capita rate of voluntary service was the lowest—200,000 to 250,000 workers agreed to leave the country over the course of four years, with never more than 70,000 of them in Germany at the same time[8]—the conscription of labor occurred in two phases. On September 4, 1942, the Vichyist regime, facing German pressure, promulgated a law "on the use and orientation of the labor force," which obliged all young men aged twenty-one to thirty-five to perform work the government judged necessary for the "higher interest of the nation." Without explicitly involving labor in Germany, the wording of the law did not rule it out. In fact, some 300,000 people—that is, nearly half the total number of conscripts under the Service du Travail Obligatoire (STO; Compulsory Work Service)—left France to fulfill that obligation.[9] On February 16, 1943, Vichy crossed another threshold, forcing males born between 1920 and 1922 (three age cohorts) to work in Germany, which brought the total number of conscripts to about 600,000 men. In Norway, finally, all able-bodied men were obliged to register by February 22, 1943, to create a labor pool.

These measures left London and the underground groups with a threefold challenge. The internal and external resistance had to protect the populations, by sparing them a difficult stay in the Reich. Otherwise, it risked being severely discredited in the eyes of the masses, whom it was relentlessly urging to disobey orders. In encouraging the workers to shirk their obligations, the movements would also be obstructing the German war effort, an objective they had in common with the British authorities. And, in impelling the evaders to go underground, they would swell the ranks of the resistance and, if need be, turn these civilians into combatants. In short, humanitarian imperatives, economic logic, and military prospects joined together to make the fight against compulsory labor an ardent obligation. But the details still had to be worked out. Geographical and historical realities dictated the course of things. Norwegians, for example, could easily reach a neutral country, Sweden, a possibility not available in either the Netherlands or Belgium. The French could hide in the mountains, an advantage the Low Countries did not have, though the terrain did not prevent 330,000 Dutchmen—evaders, Jews, and members of the resistance (the *onderduiken*)—from hiding in town, whether in attics, cellars, or rooms with hidden entrances, until the end of the war.[10] As a function of these factors, the responses to compulsory labor varied from one country to another. Generalizations are therefore not possible.

Socrate

For once, the Belgian and British authorities were on the same page: both believed that the fight against compulsory labor was imperative, particularly since it was a reminder of the horrible precedent of World War I, when 120,000 Belgian workers were rounded up and deported for forced labor. During the Civet mission in 1943, Adelin Marissal insisted that evaders be supported. In his eyes, their refusal to go to Germany had a powerful moral impact. Their existence, moreover, required that the Germans expend considerable resources and time-consuming efforts to track them down. Above all, abandoning evaders to their fate entailed considerable risks, since, to survive, they might well turn to robbery. "They were already stealing ration cards and money in the towns and attacking isolated farms, particularly in the Ardennes, where Osric [head of the SA] had already sent several officers to get them in hand and organize them as secret troops."[11]

By 1942 businesses and underground groups were doing their best to assist the evaders, but their aid was not always effective because of a lack of coordination and resources. In summer 1943, therefore, SOE parachuted in Philippe de Liedekerke (alias Claudius) and André Wendelen (Tybalt), each accompanied by his radio operator, to rationalize and intensify that activity. With that aim in mind, Tybalt expected to rely on the Front de l'Indépendance (FI). Funding from the Belgian government was to come to him via Raymond Scheyven, a manager at the Josse Allard bank and nephew of Albert-Édouard Janssen. Janssen had once been the head the Banque Nationale de Belgique and was also a former minister of finances.

Although the supposed proximity between the FI and the proletariat explained the choice of the emissaries from London, negotiations proved arduous. In fact, the leaders of the front sought to get hold of part of the funds to support all victims of repression. Above all, they believed that evaders needed to become soldiers in the national uprising, both to hasten the liberation of their country and to curb the tendency on the public's part to lump together bandits and patriots.[12] Wendelen, a loyal interpreter for the Hubert Pierlot government, did not share that view. In his eyes, Socrate—the organization in charge of fighting against compulsory labor—was supposed to prevent skilled workers from supporting the Nazi machine, not turn them into members of the resistance.[13] "The government's motivation . . . is primarily to weaken the German war effort by depriving it of the labor it needs. This aid, therefore, is not dictated by humanitarian concerns. That principle ought to influence the organization from the standpoint of its choice of rescued evaders, giving priority to skilled workers," the Belgian authorities noted.[14] The FI did not concur with that view, but, after bitter discussions, an agreement was finally reached. Through factory welfare officers, the Belgian government's budget allocation would be paid to provincial delegates chosen by the FI and approved by Tybalt or no. 17 (Scheyven). The role of the welfare officers "consisted of seeking out skilled workers who met all the requisite conditions to receive aid. If the investigation produced favorable results, the names of the parties in question were communicated to the provincial delegate and the local committee with which it was collaborating; in other cases, monthly payments were made directly to the interested parties by the Social Welfare Office."[15]

The system limited the FI's power, but it broke down in mid-September 1943. The recruitment of delegates and welfare officers came to a standstill, and some local committees attempted to bypass them. In addition, information on evaders was difficult to obtain because of distrust on the part of families. Finally, and perhaps above all, there was a shortage of money.[16]

Wendelen and Scheyven wanted to loosen the control of the FI, which, at the regional level, coupled welfare assistance with the constitution of a reserve army, forming "volontaires de la Liberté" (Freedom volunteer) groups and other shock troops. The two men, observing the blockage in the system and fearing the front's hegemony, took advantage of a wave of arrests to submit a new plan to London in November 1943. In Brabant, Hainaut, and the Liège region, the Communist group would retain control of welfare assistance. In the other provinces, assistance would be paid by local personalities, in cooperation with the front, of course, but also with the participation of other underground groups, which would prevent an organization deemed too Red from being entrusted with the monopoly on support to the rebels.[17]

The question of funding was left hanging, however. On November 23, 1943, the Belgian government approved a monthly budget of ten million francs, which was to assist between five thousand and twenty thousand evaders. In principle, therefore, every individual received five to six hundred francs a month, to which one hundred to two hundred francs were added if the person was married, plus one hundred to two hundred francs for every dependent child.[18] But the funds still had to cross the Channel. Scheyven had considered asking large companies to fund Socrate, with the Belgian authorities responsible for reimbursing them: half of the subscribed loan would be deposited in an account in London, the other half "payable in Belgian francs within a month after the government's return to Belgium."[19] But that system had only mixed success, as a telegram noted: "Industrialists demand paper with government signature do not trust radio message." For a time the leaders of Socrate considered turning to black marketeers, who promised "large capital investment in exchange for certificates bearing government's signature. . . . Some also demand anonymity of these certificates for purposes of tax immunity."[20] That prospect sparked indignation, and Socrate noted that the source of the money borrowed was obviously the object "of all its attention."[21] For the most part, executives balked. Many believed that the underground fighters could survive by doing business on the black market or hiring themselves out to farms. As a result, funds were in short supply until April 1944: at that time, they came to just 2.3 million francs a month.

The Dingo mission, sent into Belgium in 1943, was able to rescue five hundred workers. But, as a report of January 1944 concluded:

In early October, there were still 212 whose situation was disastrous. On the whole, these men were dependable and "tough." Most have not received subsidies for three, four, five, or six months. All are skilled workers and, on the strength of promises from DINGO, they went into "the maquis," at a time when such an attitude was held by only a minority. They are now literally revolted by their abandonment. They are active in sabotage and the elimination of traitors, and also transmit military intelligence through the B.B. line.

The leaders are of unequal worth. A good number of them frittered away part of the funds received (on mistresses, cars, drinking binges, and so on). Several have ended up in prison. With their funds exhausted, they turn to "coups de main" to procure more money. That is particularly the case of ONE, who spent most of the "collected" sums on himself. He escaped an assassination attempt by his former comrades and is now said to be in prison after being denounced by them. A very decisive, courageous, and intelligent man, but totally lacking in scruples and selflessness.

Another leader, TWO, seems to have been the group's accountant, and his books show a "deficit" of ninety thousand francs.

The "sound" part of the organization includes THREE, an intelligent and educated worker, extremely bold, who has all the qualities of a leader.

FOUR, very honest, selfless, but overly generous and trusting, is now a prisoner in Germany. We are assuming that this is an individual who was assigned by FIVE to distribute financial aid to a group of railroad workers we had contacted by another means: SIX. He is said to have been replaced in that position by SEVEN, but once again, there is a shortage of funds. Several payments of 100,000 francs were made on behalf of the railroad workers, thanks to the generosity of EIGHT. The advances provided by him amount to about a million, covered in part by letters of credit.[22]

In short, the situation was not always the most auspicious, though it did tend to improve in spring 1944.

On the night of April 10, 1944, Major Idesbald Floor, a Belgian industrialist responsible for liaisons between SOE and Sûreté, was parachuted in, carrying a document that confirmed Scheyven's mission and specified the conditions for paying back loans. The horizon suddenly brightened—another reason being that the Allied victory was taking shape. The director of the Josse Allard bank was able without difficulty to underwrite 126 loans, for a total of 176 million francs, and to invest 7.5 million francs in Treasury bonds.[23]

Overall, Socrate assisted thousands of evaders, though the numbers are difficult to come by. The Belgian historian Étienne Verhoeyen estimates that forty to fifty thousand men were aided, while José Gotovitch notes that the term "evaders" was applied to twenty-seven hundred people.[24] These brilliant results must not omit one fact: between October 1942 and March 6, 1943, 67,775 Belgians—which is to say, 85 percent of those called up—registered for compulsory labor; only a minority, 4,947 Belgians, refused from the start to be coerced.[25] Furthermore, the Belgian and British authorities, in breaking up the FI's monopoly on assistance to the rebels, fractured national unity while sparking "competition between the various groups. The support now given by London offered each of them an equal right to existence and the potential resources for poaching members."[26] The non-Communists' position was defensible, however: Why should they have agreed to entrust the FI with a monopoly on aid to the workers and with the privilege of embodying the union of patriots, when they were facing the same risks in the darkness of the underground night?

Socrate was a success, therefore, since it helped thousands of men avoid compulsory labor in Germany. Even so, it did not always turn them into members of the resistance, a goal on which the leaders of the French resistance set their sights.

French Responses to the STO

In France, the Service du Travail Obligatoire was a crucial issue for society in general and for the resistance in particular. The STO affected hundreds of thousands of French people, who, moreover, were handed over by their own regime to the Nazi Moloch, a phenomenon unique in Europe. In addition, its primary impact was on the working class, which, since the interwar period, had occupied a central place in French society. The growth of the Communist Party and the advent of the Front Populaire suggested that a revolution was not impossible, which led the French to keep a close eye on the proletariat, whether to suppress it or to encourage it.

The French resistance immediately seized on the issue. Thanks to the STO, it could defy Vichy while attacking it on the grounds that collaboration was openly disdainful of French patriotism. The STO gave rise to a flood of volunteers anxious to escape forced labor, and it allowed thousands of ordinary men and women to become involved in the fight. Until that time, by contrast, the movements had struggled to provide society with instructions for action, apart from patriotic exhortations to respond to the occupier with the "silence of the sea." Everyone could now participate in the fight without taking foolish risks: a town clerk could produce false identity papers, a farmer could hide a fugitive, a doctor could provide accommodating certificates. The army of shadows, in the minority until late 1942, could thus aspire to become a mass phenomenon and bring the common people over to its side.

At the same time, the conversion of evaders into members of the resistance was no simple matter. Even without considering how to arm or control them, how would the underground feed, clothe, and provide shelter for thousands of volunteers? If the movements did not meet the expectations that the French had for them, they ran the risk of being discredited as powerless. By that measure, the Service du Travail Obligatoire was a burden as well as an opportunity. As it happened, the movements mobilized immediately, especially those in the southern zone. As early as 1942, in their newspapers and leaflets they called on the people to throw off the yoke imposed by the masters from the Reich and organized or supported strikes and demonstrations, some of them large in scope. In addition, they worked earnestly to supply the rebels with false papers. Their engagement sometimes took more martial forms. On the night of March 12, 1943, Georges Guingouin's men dynamited the railway viaduct near Bussy-Varache, in Limousin, to prevent a trainload of conscripts from departing.[27] And, in late December, a few men, fleeing the STO, "went over to the maquis" (*prirent le maquis*), a turn of phrase introduced by a Combat leader named Michel Brault. Taking refuge in the mountains, usually in Haute-Savoie, they struggled to survive, for lack of being able to fight. It was not long before that trickle swelled into a stream. By January 1943 the internal resistance faced heavy responsibilities because these maquis, created spontaneously, very often placed themselves under the orders of the underground's regional leaders, whom they counted on for weapons, fresh supplies, and munitions, all riches sorely lacking within the movements.

The leaders of the southern resistance instantly understood that new, unprecedented prospects were opening up and considered how to turn the evaders into combatants. In January 1943 Henri Frenay outlined a plan for "the creation of a certain number of 'redoubts' in the Alps, the Jura, The Massif Central and the Pyrénées. These redoubts could be supplied by parachute with arms, equipment and food. Thus they could support highly mobile units of about thirty men each. Their role in the period before the Allied landing would be limited to hit-and-run operations. They would avoid participating in anything resembling a drawn battle." And he concluded, "obviously it would be impossible for us to create such redoubts without the necessary supplies."[28] In April of the same year the leader of Combat drew up directives for the Comité Directeur des Mouvements Unis de Résistance (Steering Committee for the United Resistance Movements), distinguishing between "two categories of evaders, those who want to hide, who will be assisted, and those who want to fight, who will be integrated into small mobile groups receiving assistance from the population."[29]

The maquis were therefore assigned a dual mission. They had to aid the bulk of the evaders to conceal themselves and, at the same time, select an elite prepared to engage in guerilla warfare. The maquis, combining civilian and military dimensions, thus served as both a refuge and a base for action. By contrast, there was no question of forming mobilizable maquis in which thousands of men, assembled in an impregnable bastion, would conduct attacks before launching the offensive against the enemy once the Allied troops had landed. "Fluidity, rapidity and mobility were my three basic principles," wrote Frenay.[30] That plan stipulated one condition, however: London had to give the rebels the necessary logistical support. But Jean Moulin, General de Gaulle's delegate in the French metropolis, was far from sharing the enthusiasm of the movements.

From March 1943 onward the leaders of the movements, watching as volunteers rushed to the Alps, sent telegram after telegram to alert Fighting France of the gravity of the situation. For example, the steering committee of the Mouvements Unis de Résistance (MUR) cabled General de Gaulle on March 3: "Deported French believe abandoned by Allies. . . . Payments foreseen financial resources absurd. . . . Without means action resist deportation organization will pass Communist hands your authority French opinion as whole will be quickly undermined if you do not demonstrate through us in struggle liberation begun we ask English government to understand. . . . If our appeals in vain will order desperate extreme action."[31] Moulin, who was in London at the time, refused to provide the financial aid the movements were hoping for. The March budget was identical to the allocations made in January and February and did not take into account the new dimensions of the situation. The open conflict between de Gaulle, who was making a bid for power, and Henri Giraud—supported by the Anglo-Americans in North Africa—who had no intention of relinquishing it, had increased tensions between Free France and the British government. De Gaulle's delegate was therefore cautious. Fearing that London would cut off food supplies for the Comité National Français, he preferred to use his reserves carefully. On March 11, however, in view of the new situation, he changed his mind and ordered his secretary, Daniel Cordier, to "provide all funds" for the fight against forced labor by drawing from his reserves. Nevertheless, part of the funds were handed over to trade union organizations that were fighting to keep called-up workers from departing for Germany but were not seeking to turn them into resistance fighters.[32]

Even so, the technical obstacles and the desire to hold on to Fighting France's war chest are not enough to explain Jean Moulin's reservations. He undoubtedly believed that, for lack of British support, the venture was headed for disaster. What is even more certain is that he feared that Frenay, benefiting from that windfall of evaders, would form a parallel secret army and assume its leadership via a Service National Maquis (National Maquis Service). That, at least, was the fear he expressed in a report sent to his minister, the Socialist André Philip, on June 4, 1943:

> I believe I ought to call your attention to the fact that the leaders of the movements, seeing that the SA is escaping their control to a certain extent, are trying to piece together a different SA with the maquis. In my opinion, there is no contraindication to that, provided that:
>
> 1. certain maquis, which are of geographical or strategic interest for the D-Day action, be under the control of the SA;
>
> 2. the receipt and distribution of weapons continue to be compulsorily and fully carried out by the SA. It is important, in fact, to avoid the recurrence of certain very regrettable incidents, attributable to the fact that some maquis, having appropriated weapons unbeknownst to the SA, made use of them in a reckless manner, causing very grave reprisals and prematurely exposing the organization.[33]

The head of Combat, then, was not blinded by paranoia when he claimed that the delegate of Fighting France suspected him of putting together, in a roundabout manner, a rival secret army. He was also not just picking a fight with London when he declared that, in targeting his funding, Fighting France was trying to weaken him.[34] It is true that Daniel Cordier had released small amounts of money as of March 11, 1943; but, from January to May 1943, the SA received only seven million francs, compared to the four million obtained by the Service des Opérations Aériennes et Maritimes (Air and Sea Operations Service), a mere technical organization that oversaw the transfer of agents or materiel across the Channel—not to mention the "tidy sums" received by the networks.[35] In any event, neither Moulin nor Free France displayed an unbridled enthusiasm for the maquis. As Claude Bourdet, Frenay's deputy in the Combat movement, confirmed, "If there is one area in which the incomprehension of General de Gaulle's services, both in London and in France, has been characteristic, it is in that of the maquis."[36]

Unlike Belgium, then, Fighting France refused to provide extensive funding for the fight against compulsory labor, and for obvious reasons. The Pierlot government, as we have seen, did not want to involve civilians prematurely in the struggle. But, haunted by the precedent of World War I, it was anxious to protect them, which explains why it devoted considerable resources to Socrate. Conversely, the Gaullist authorities' first priority was to keep France in the war; from that standpoint, sparing the French the rigors of the occupation was hardly an ardent obligation. The two countries therefore took different paths, which reflected in the first place the divergent objectives they set for themselves. But the Gaullists were even less inclined to commit themselves, inasmuch as the British were reluctant to support the fight against "deportation," as it was called at the time.

British Reservations

In reality, the question had two aspects. In addition to providing support for the evaders, a humanitarian concern, the question of the maquis's military potential arose.

By late 1942 the first maquis had formed. In the Vercors on December 18 of that year, Simon Samuel, a French-Romanian resistance fighter, and Louis Brun, a woodturner, reconnoitered the Ambel farm. Both men were associated with the Socialist Party and were members of Franc-Tireur, a southern zone movement. On January 6, 1943, a first contingent of evaders was established on the farm. Later on, several camps spread out across the plateau, which turned into a refuge. Their management and administration were in the hands of Socialist militants.[37] Other groups emerged in Haute-Lozère[38] and even in Brittany, where Daniel Trellu, the Front National–FTP leader from Finistère, decided on Easter Sunday 1943 to create a small maquis in Châteauneuf-du-Faou, in the Montagne Noire. But by October of the same year it had attracted only eight men. In reality, the Communists only half-heartedly supported the maquis, which they suspected of "serving as harbingers of the watch-and-wait attitude and of emptying the cities of their active elements, uselessly immobilizing them in the mountains."[39]

These few examples confirm that the maquis were at first a spontaneous phenomenon, involving only a handful of evaders. Only 5 percent of them joined the maquis in Doubs, 10 percent in Isère, 17.4 percent in Ariège, 19 percent in Tarn, 20 percent in Jura, and 20.3 percent in Alpes-Maritimes. Overall, 15 to 20 percent of the evaders headed for the mountains, for a relatively large total of thirty to forty thousand people.[40]

Accommodating them put an enormous strain on the supply system. A maquis of sixty men required eighty-eight pounds of food a day.[41] The question of armaments also arose, even though most of the maquis were more intent on concealing the evaders than on turning them into combatants. The Vercors was a notable exception.

In 1941 the resistance fighter Pierre Dalloz, an architect and site inspector, had had an intuition that the plateau offered great strategic possibilities. In December 1942 he devised a plan in two parts. In the first stage, the zone would become a base defended by irregular forces. In the second, the Allies would be able to send troops into that bastion and create, on the enemy's rear lines, "a powerful fortress from which raids could be launched under excellent conditions, on industrial regions and major communication routes."[42] In January 1943 that plan was conveyed to Yves Farge, a member of the resistance, who transmitted it to Jean Moulin. General de Gaulle's delegate accepted it and handed over an envelope containing twenty-five thousand francs. Above all, General Delestraint, head of the secret army, was persuaded by the project, now called the "Plan Montagnards" (Mountaineers' Plan). He submitted it to de Gaulle and to the BCRA, who gave their consent. On February 25 the BBC broadcast the message "The mountaineers must continue to climb the peaks." A small team that included, notably, Alain Le Ray, an officer in the mountain infantry and son-in-law of the writer François Mauriac, ascended the plateau,[43] and a "combat committee" of five members formed between early March and early April 1943.

The Gaullist authorities were thus quick to accept a plan whose viability appeared uncertain at best. The small number of men concerned, the overtly military character of the operation, and the synergy with the Allied strategy it promised no doubt explain that haste, especially since Dalloz from the outset agreed to London's supervision as a way to skirt the authority of the movements. The maquis of the Vercors was exceptionally well funded: within four months it received 4,609,750 francs, while the SA as a whole was paid only 6,166,000 francs—which suffices to show where Fighting France's priorities lay. The results fell far short of expectations: hammered by the Italian repression, the first committee dispersed in late

May 1943; it was succeeded in late June by a second, which included, among others, Alain Le Ray, Eugène Chavant, and Jean Prévost.

To survive and develop, the maquis had above all to receive London's support. On March 3, 1943, Charles de Gaulle sounded out Winston Churchill:

> In any event, it seems essential to maintain, as far as possible, the best elements of the secret army organized on French territory by Fighting France. It is possible to estimate at fifty thousand the number of men belonging to that army who possess in abundance the qualities of great fighters, who are targeted by current deportation measures, and whom the Comité National expects to advise to hide away there at all cost, in order to be on the ready to execute the combat missions assigned to them.
>
> For such an arrangement to have merit, however, it is indispensable to guarantee the subsistence of these forces concealed from the searches of the enemy and of collaborators. It is also necessary to equip them without delay with adequate weapons and equipment, so that these men, constantly under threat, have the capacity to defend themselves at any moment.

He went on to ask for aid from the United Kingdom,[44] which Lord Selborne, in charge of the Ministry of Economic Warfare, refused. Granted, the cost of such support threw Selborne into a panic. "The FFC [French Fighting Forces] had calculated that in order to sustain evaders 1000 francs per man per month was required. The requirement for August would therefore be in the neighbourhood of 50 000 000 fr." That was a considerable sum, equivalent to ten million euros. Above all, in June, following the Anglo-American landing in North Africa, France had at its disposal a Comité Français de Libération Nationale (CFLN; French National Liberation Committee) in Algiers. "It was the view of His Majesty's Government that as soon as the Committee of Liberation was functioning all these payments and all resistance work should be in the name of the Committee of Liberation." Finally, the British authorities feared a scission—which was always possible—between the committee and the Gaullist French Fighting Forces. "If this disaster occurred it would be impossible for them to be put into the position of backing the FFC against the Committee of Liberation."[45] Finally and perhaps above all, British strategists had no intention of supporting the maquis, whose military value in early 1943 appeared negligible to them. They would undoubtedly have supported these maquis had they been incorporated into the major offensive to destroy Nazi Germany. But the landing was not yet the order of the day: it became an option only after the Tehran Conference in December 1943. London drew the logical conclusions: "It is the considered opinion of the British government that maintaining an army of forty to fifty thousand men, for an indeterminable span of time, is impossible, since that permanent support would entail scaling back the operations of a very large number of [aircraft]."[46] The development of the maquis was by no means part of London's plans. On the contrary, widespread insecurity could lead the Germans to increase the number of their divisions to the west, which would weaken the chances for the landing.[47] As Colonel Passy commented in his memoirs: "The calls for open revolt, for the constitution of 'armed bastions,' could be interpreted by our Allies only as a folly of inconceivable recklessness or as intolerable pressure to force them to carry out operations without concern for the plans of the military staff."[48]

The British, waging war on a European scale, were not considering an assault on the French beaches before 1944. They therefore opposed the launch of guerilla warfare by the internal resistance, judging it premature, even as they appealed to the French via the BBC to throw off the burden of the occupation. Logically, they refused to back militarily the maquis, which therefore had to rely on the support of the internal resistance, half-heartedly shored up by Fighting France.

The fight against the STO must be put into perspective. Fritz Sauckel, nicknamed "the slave driver of Europe," had every reason to be satisfied with the French contribution. The first STO action he spearheaded (June 1–December 31, 1942) fulfilled 99 percent of its objectives, the second (January 1–March 1, 1943), 100.1 percent, and the third (April 1–December 31, 1943) 76.98 percent. In all, the first three actions had a compliance rate of 91.58 percent.[49] It was only in summer 1943 that a "real collapse in the number of departures" began to occur, "despite all the means implemented by the Germans and the Vichy regime."[50] The last action (January 1–June 23, 1944) had a 95.05 percent *non*compliance rate.

But that does not mean that all the evaders of the STO went over to the resistance. The French often took other measures to loosen its grip. In the first place, many individuals were legally exempted. With the adoption of the law of February 16, 1943, 418,000 people in the targeted cohorts received an exemption, which is to say, more than half of those on the lists in March 1943. A good share of those who were not exempted obtained false medical certificates from obliging physicians or from practitioners committed to the resistance. Others enrolled in college, returned to the land, or joined protected professions: mining, police work, the armistice army before it was dissolved, even the Milice or Nazi organizations.[51] Still others agreed to work for the Reich, but in France, a solution ratified by the accords concluded in September 1943 between Albert Speer, German minister of armaments, and Jean Bichelonne, French minister of industrial production. On the eve of the Allied landing, more than fourteen thousand protected businesses (*Sperrbetrieben*) employed nearly a million wage workers. These *refusants*, to borrow the term used by the historian Raphaël Spina, remained in France without breaking the law. Evaders in the strict sense thus comprised only a minority of the targeted men, probably between 200,000 and 250,000. Of that minority, perhaps a quarter joined the resistance, while three-quarters preferred to hide in their own homes or in those of loved ones, or especially on farms, to which they were often led by channels created or taken over by the resistance.[52]

In 1943, then, the results of the fight against the STO were mixed. It had contributed greatly to the popularity of the resistance, which was suddenly turned into a protector of the population. Thanks to labor conscription, the movements broadened their base and opened prospects for concrete and accessible action to thousands of French citizens. Assigned to spearhead that plan of action, they struggled to control the process and to prove their ability to protect civilians, while at the same time mobilizing them. Simultaneously, the resistance, which had been quite urban, tended to become ruralized (the countryside and the mountains became the natural refuge for evaders) and nationalized, since the movement affected large swaths of southern France, aided, to be sure, by its mountains. Finally, the resistance discredited the French State, which was ultimately reduced to powerlessness, and infiltrated its administration: in the second half of 1943 its members were in charge of—and sabotaged—the STO services in twenty-five administrative departments, even as the irregular corps set spectacular fires everywhere to destroy the registration files.[53] The maquis even took control of entire districts, imposing their rules and their laws, barring law enforcement agents from entering when not benefiting from their complicity.

At the same time, the great majority of evaders, rather than join the resistance, preferred to find legal escape routes to avoid exile. Fighting France did not by any means throw all its forces into the battle. And London remained skeptical at best regarding the military prospects that the maquis opened up, refusing, most notably, to arm them. It is true that France did not carry much weight. In SOE's strategic priorities for 1943, the country was ranked third, well ahead of Norway and the Netherlands (fourth), but behind the Italian islands of Corsica and Crete (first) and the Balkans (second).[54]

Mobilization in Norway

In Norway, finally, the resistance mobilized to fight against forced labor, imposed by the occupying forces on February 22, 1943, and targeting men aged eighteen to fifty-five and women between twenty-one and forty. Unlike in many countries of Western Europe, however, Berlin did not plan to send these recruits to work in the Reich. Registration for the compulsory labor service began in March 1943, without at first encountering any strong opposition. In fact, 200,000 Norwegians worked for the occupier in their own country, and it was difficult to convince them to defect, a reality acknowledged by the internal resistance. But after some shillyshallying, the resistance finally took on the challenge. In April it gave orders to refuse both conscription and forced labor;[55] then it set to work. On April 21 an attack was made on the labor registration bureaus in Oslo. In addition, a campaign was launched to prevent the mobilization of the working population, which, beginning on May 17, targeted three age cohorts (1921, 1922, and 1923). In the same vein, the machines used to register the workforce were sabotaged, and an appeal launched on May 17 encouraged the population to avoid forced labor. Many young Norwegians, nicknamed "the boys of the forest," responded: three thousand went into hiding in the Oslo region; fifteen hundred in Lower Telemark, southwest of the capital; a few hundred in the eastern part of the country. The outlawed trade unions and the internal resistance then endeavored to assist and feed them, even as, from 1944 on, the Communists advocated the formation of detachments of partisans, to whom they unwisely promised weapons and equipment.[56]

Food shortages quickly became a nagging problem, especially since, in August 1944, the collaborationist authorities decided to revoke the ration cards for those who had shirked their duty.[57] On the morning of August 9, the resistance dealt a major blow. A three-man team led by Gunnar Søn-steby hijacked the truck that was transporting more than seventy thousand ration cards. This was not in fact Sønsteby's first glorious deed. A member of Milorg, he had crossed the Swedish border several times to communicate with SOE, before traveling to England in 1943 to pursue military training. He had then returned to head up the "Oslo gang," which specialized in daring coups de main.[58] In response to the raid on their truck, the authorities negotiated. They promised, in exchange for the return of the cards, to no longer deny the evaders their rations.[59]

Despite a few initial successes, compulsory labor in Norway was thus an overall failure for the occupying powers, though thousands of civilians worked for them during the dark years. The great majority of the working population avoided spending time in the Reich: only two thousand men in all had to go there. But that was primarily the achievement of the internal resistance. Until 1944 at least, London confined itself to supporting over the airwaves that civil disobedience movement,[60] which did not receive funding comparable to the money paid by the Socrate organization in Belgium or the support—albeit moderate—that Fighting France provided the movements.

All in all, the issue of compulsory labor calls for a balanced analysis. It generally served the interests of the Reich, providing it, in autumn 1944, with more than 20 percent of its workforce. In addition, the productivity of these conscripts was relatively satisfactory—in the French case, it met 80 to 90 percent of German benchmarks.[61] But forced labor also favored the development of the internal resistance throughout Western Europe. Because it affected all strata of the population, either directly or indirectly, that conscription solidified a common front against the occupier, one that disregarded class barriers. It provided the movements with a reason to act, while allowing them to direct concrete and easily realizable watchwords toward the population. Especially in France, it opened up military prospects. Finally, it discredited the collaborating powers, by demonstrating their submission to Nazi orders, and enhanced the prestige of the governments in exile, which became the natural protectors of their compatriots. Despite their reservations and the circumspection of the British, the fight against obligatory labor was in the end a powerful—albeit uneven—factor of mobilization, which, far from responding to injunctions from London and Washington, was in the first place reliant on the captive societies.

CHAPTER X

Mixed Results

S OE, in dispatching agents to support its networks or underground groups, conducting multiple raids and sabotage operations, and preparing for the creation of secret armies able to deploy on D-Day, had spared no effort in promoting the resistance in Western Europe. In France and Belgium, in Norway and Denmark, its fortunes had been uneven, with some splendid successes compensating for resounding failures. That balanced picture did not exist in Italy or the Netherlands, two countries that experienced total disaster.

A Dutch Fiasco

SOE had followed the same plan in the Netherlands as in the other countries of Western Europe, supporting the existing groups, creating sabotage networks, and encouraging the development of a secret army. In August 1942 it had five organizers in charge of that threefold mission. Immediate action was encouraged, and in the second half of 1942 it was supposed to strike German communications as well as the Luftwaffe.[1] Beginning in May 1943 submarines, gasoline depots, canals and railway lines, shipyards, and establishments working for the Germans were preferred targets. Resistance members, while remaining active, were nevertheless supposed to avoid

threatening the Allied plans for D-Day and refrain from pointlessly exposing civilians.[2]

In addition, from November 1942 on, SOE set out to form a secret army
of ten thousand men who, on the day of liberation, would harry the enemy
while preserving communications networks from its destructive fury.[3] In
April 1943 a plan was also launched to protect the port facilities of Rot-
terdam.[4] In May the Dutch section surveyed the road traveled, not without pride. Its sabotage organization comprised five groups of sixty-two cells
for a total of 420 men, ready to take action.[5]

There was only one drawback to that laudatory stock taking: it was
completely wrong. On the night of November 7, 1941, two SOE agents,
Thijs Taconis and his radio operator, Huub Lauwers, were parachuted into
the Netherlands to track down their two predecessors, Albert Homburg
and Cornelis Sporre, who had vanished. They were also supposed to set up
an underground sabotage group. Upon his arrival, Taconis asked one of his
acquaintances to procure a truck for him, to transport the weapons that the
RAF would drop for him in short order. That friend turned to George
Ridderhof, not knowing he actually worked for Hermann Giskes, head of
the counterespionage section of the Abwehr, the German military intelligence service. On March 6 Lauwers was arrested as he was preparing to
transmit; Taconis was taken a few days later. The Germans issued an ultimatum to the two men: either collaborate or be executed. Taconis refused,
which resulted in his being taken to the hellish Mauthausen concentration
camp. But Lauwers, wrongly persuaded that the enemy had broken his
codes, agreed to participate in Operation North Pole (also called *Englandspiel*, "the England game") and to transmit messages under the enemy's
dictation. Far from being a traitor, he then peppered these messages with
warning signals, which his British correspondents ignored.

The Abwehr, by controlling the SOE's transmitters, killed two birds with
one stone. It adulterated the British services by transmitting false information, and it learned when men and material were to be sent. For example,
Arnoldus Baatsen (Watercress) parachuted in near Steenwijk on the night of
March 27, 1942, and was captured on the spot. His interrogators claimed that
he had been betrayed by an agent operating in England, which enraged him;
he therefore gave them all the information he had. Baatsen was only the first
on a very long list: nearly all SOE's men were subsequently intercepted by
the Germans, who picked them up as soon as they landed.

Finally, in June 1943, Baker Street was assailed by a few doubts. Rarely used terms in Dutch seemed to point to an awkward translation, and the information transmitted was of mediocre quality. In addition, the Royal Air Force was alarmed at the surprisingly high losses it met with when it flew over the Netherlands: they were pegged at 18 percent for winter 1942–1943, a noticeably higher proportion than for the other countries. Wisely, the RAF decided in late May 1943 to suspend its flights, a moratorium that lasted until late May 1944.

On the night of August 29, 1943, two SOE agents, Pieter Dourlein and Ben Ubbink, succeeded in escaping Haaren, a former seminary turned prison, where all the victims of Operation North Pole had been brought. Traveling through Belgium and then France, they managed to reach England via Gibraltar on February 1, 1944—only to be arrested on May 2, 1944, and interned in HM Prison Brixton, on the grounds they had committed treason! But the British authorities had the good sense to release them on June 22, 1944.[6]

Giskes, knowing that *Englandspiel* had been uncovered, sent an ironic telegram to his British counterparts on April 1, 1944:

> Messrs Blunt, Bingham and succs ltd. London. In the last times you are trying to make business in Netherlands without our assistance. Stop. We think this rather unfair in view our long and successful cooperation as your sole agents. Stop. But never mind whenever you will come to pay a visit to the continent you may be assured that you will be received with same care and result as all those you sent us before. Stop. So long.[7]

That flash of wit seems to give credence to the image of lords honorably waging a chivalrous war, very remote from the atrocities committed by the SS. The reality was more brutal. Although Lauwers got out of the Nazi penal colony alive, the few survivors of Operation North Pole—a handful of French agents and the commandos who had been captured during their raid on Saint-Nazaire—were brutalized before being coldly liquidated in Mauthausen on the morning of September 6, 1944, or the next day. Hans Gogl, the noncommissioned officer in charge of that dirty job, was tracked down by Simon Wiesenthal, then tried in Linz in 1964 but acquitted. Summoned a second time before the judges a few years later, he was treated with the same leniency in Vienna.[8]

All in all, of fifty-six agents sent by SOE, forty-three had fallen into the enemy's hands, and thirty-six were ultimately executed.[9] In addition, 3,000 Sten submachine guns, 300 Bren machine guns, and 355,500 guilders had been seized.[10] Above all, SOE had not fulfilled its mission at all, as its leaders acknowledged after the war, not without lucidity. The balance sheet, they concluded, was "one of unrelieved failure. From the end of 1942 to the spring of 1944, when the 'AS' [secret army] which was to come into action on D-Day should have been steadily gaining in strength, the whole of our organisation in Holland was not only completely penetrated but controlled and directed by the Germans."[11] That failure reined in the development of the Dutch internal resistance; it also put a brake on plans to prepare for the liberation of the country by civilians. Above all, it revealed the flaws from which the secret service was suffering.

Several factors explain that disaster. In wishing to obtain results at all cost, Hugh Dalton had no doubt exerted too much pressure on the Dutch section of SOE, which in turn prepared the missions too hastily. In addition, the Gerbrandy government did not encourage its best volunteers to join SOE, an approach that compromised the quality of recruitment efforts. And several blunders took a heavy toll. Furthermore, the British services decided that reception committees should welcome men and materiel; had they decided to parachute them in blindly, the agents would have been left to fend for themselves, but they could not have been betrayed. SOE also treated the crucial question of transmissions in a cavalier manner—as they emphasized after the war, this had been the primary cause of the failure.[12] For example, they had required agents to communicate in English. As a result, linguistic errors, sometimes made on purpose by agents who had been "turned," did not surprise the controllers. They simply attributed the mistakes to a lack of ease in the language of Shakespeare, which was in reality a legitimate assumption.[13] But they did so to such an extent that they overlooked the many signals with which Lauwers peppered his telegrams. That fact has fueled suspicion: Did SOE intentionally sacrifice its Dutch agents to confuse the Germans?

That, at least, is the thesis defended by the historian Jo Wolters.[14] Astonished not that the errors went undiscovered but that the contamination lasted for fifteen long months, he believes that *Englandspiel* was set in place deliberately, and that the tragic course it would follow was not perceived at the time. In his view, the British, in revealing to the enemy their intention to form a secret army in the Netherlands, waved the threat of invasion at the Nazis and contributed to the establishment of German divisions in the West, in order to relieve the pressure being exerted on the Red Army in the East. By spring 1943 that bluff was no longer necessary: the invasion of Normandy was in the planning stage. As a result, the disinformation campaign could be suspended without risk.

Should credence be given to that thesis? Because the SOE archives relating to that affair have disappeared, it is difficult to form a substantiated opinion, though Wolters's arguments are at the very least credible. At a minimum, the British were guilty of being remiss and perhaps cynical, and their procedures were certainly flawed. For example, because they did not identify operators by the style of their transmitted messages (slow or staccato, for instance)—a technique that would be introduced in the second half of 1943[15]—SOE was unable to identify its "pianists," as they were called, and was easily misled by imposters.

All in all, that catastrophic outcome limited the possibilities for action of the Dutch resistance, which was deprived of the support the British were supposed to provide. And SOE was no more successful in Italy—at least until July 1943.

Italian Impasses

SOE, as we recall, had attempted to spark the Italian resistance by recruiting volunteers from among prisoners of war captured in North Africa, and by supporting a Free Italy Committee. But these efforts had fallen short. The British service was not to be discouraged, however, and strove to act through its Swiss subbranch, established in Bern as of February 1941.

It is true that the proximity of the Italian border and the presence of a small community of refugees in the Italian-speaking canton of Ticino allowed its leader, Jock McCaffery, under the discreet cover of a press attaché, to nurture some hope, however weak. In fact, that lucid man had few illusions. He was in contact with antifascist groups and realized that they were "neither strong nor capable and appeared for the most part to consist of 'salon conspirators'" who had "a great faith in pamphlets, 'manifesti' and wall-scrawls." In connection with PWE, SOE helped them in spite of everything, favoring the smuggling of pamphlets and offering them materiel that would allow them to print up their propaganda.[16] It also allocated

500,000 lire to establish lines of communication or escape channels and to form reception committees.[17]

But the reality was even worse than what that already unflattering picture suggests. Through Piero Pellegrini, director of the socialist newspaper *La Libera Stampa*, based in Lugano, SOE was in contact with antifascist groups "bearing such ferocious pseudonyms as Tigers, Cubs etc. . . . The exploits of these desperadoes were reported to us from time to time and duly signaled to London." After the signing of the armistice concluded between Italy and the Allies in September 1943, the terrible truth emerged: "The Tigers, Cubs and Co were ingenious fabrications born of the brain of one Dr Ugo."[18] To be more precise, the Cubs had been invented by the Servizio Informazione Militare (SIM), the Italian counterespionage agency, and the Wolves by the regime's political police, the Organizzazione di Vigilanza e Repressione dell'Antifascismo (OVRA).[19] Another contact, Eligio Klein, alias Almerigotti, proved even more disastrous. Introduced by the U.S. Air Attaché Office, for which he had worked in Rome, he was given the green light in April 1942. "Not only did he prove to be a 'plant' working for SIM but he played his part so well that we put him in touch with other contacts who were thereby compromised and lost to us."[20]

It was not long, however, before a glimmer of hope appeared on the horizon, in the person of Emilio Lussu. A veteran of World War I, Lussu had written a masterpiece, *Un anno sull'Altipiano* (A Soldier on the Southern Front), in which he denounced the absurdity of that war. In 1921 he had founded the Sardian Action Party, which set out to fight vigorously against Mussolinian Fascism. Because his activism exposed him to condemnation by the regime, he left Italy in 1929 and, alongside Gaetanao Salvemini and Carlo Rosselli, founded the antifascist movement Guistizia e Libertà (Justice and Liberty).[21] He then made contact with the British services to propose a plan. He suggested that they incite an insurgency in Sardinia, which he proposed to lead, supported by "an Italian 'liberty division.'" Immediately thereafter, he promised, several insurrectional movements would break out in Sicily, Friuli-Venezia Giulia, and Piedmont. The unrealistic nature of a plan that would have required large-scale resources (aircraft and ships), the impossibility of levying a division of volunteers, as well as the demands made by Lussu, who wanted guarantees regarding his country's diplomatic future,[22] doomed that initiative: the Allies rejected it.[23]

The Allied landing in North Africa on November 8, 1942, reshuffled the cards. Because the Allies were now stationed a few miles from Italy, liaisons with the peninsula were greatly facilitated. An SOE mission called "Massingham" was assigned to conduct the operations from North Africa and therefore from Italy. It was set in place in Algiers in early 1943. Once more, the results were disappointing. "Attempts to find suitable recruits in North Africa gave as little results as previous efforts in this country. Interned and imprisoned Italians in French territory were interviewed and a few ardent souls were discovered who were ready to make speeches and write pamphlets, but saw little reason to risk their skins when, anyhow, the Allies would shortly 'liberate' their country."[24]

Italy was therefore a particularly difficult mission field to evangelize, and not without reason. Over the course of twenty years, Mussolini had decapitated the parties and groups hostile to his authority, which might have formed the core of the internal resistance. That political pall and the deadly and frustrating war dissuaded volunteers from engaging in a battle whose outcome appeared uncertain, at least between 1940 and 1942. But London and Washington also bore a share of the responsibility. In refusing to commit themselves for the postwar period, they discouraged people of good will. And because Italy was not offered a place at the victors' table before the fall of Mussolini in July 1943, resistance fighters could only look like traitors engaging in speculation to profit from their country's defeat. Negotiations thus became a dialogue of the deaf. "In the case of their political contacts SOE were constantly faced with the difficulty of reconciling His Majesty's Government's policy of unconditional surrender with the desire of the opposition elements in Italy to obtain an assurance that the Allies would soften their peace terms if an internal coup d'état had disorganized the fighting resistance of Italy and thus shortened the war."[25]

The Anglo-Americans refused to take that path, preferring to maintain a free hand by arguing that no representative leader had emerged. "The methods of assurances and promises can only be effective when it is a question of building up some dissident movement or leader who is ready to challenge the established government. . . . At present, there is no such leader or movement in Italy," Anthony Eden noted bluntly in November 1942.[26] That strategy prevailed in 1943. As Eden explained to Winston Churchill on February 17 of that year:

Our present line is to make no promise whatsoever, but merely to offer Italians (through our propaganda) the alternative of sinking or surviving. . . . We hope that this tough line, supplemented by heavy raids and the threat of invasion, will suffice to frighten the Italians out of the war. But if we want to go further and get some group in Italy to co-operate with us on that basis, I realize that we shall have to hold out at least some hope in regard to the future of Italy, in order to secure their co-operation. But there is nothing very definite we could promise the Italians. We can give them no comfort about their overseas possessions. We cannot guarantee the territorial restoration of metropolitan Italy, owing to the pledge we have given to the Yugoslavs to espouse their claim to Istria after the war.[27]

William Deakin, an SOE leader, summed it up: "Until we invade Italian territory, or are embarked on negotiations with a serious anti-Fascist group in Italy, Anglo-American policy should be based on a purely 'tough' line."[28]

Some members of the secret services regretted that London was cutting off all hope. For example, in October 1942 Major Cecil Roseberry, head of the Italian section, lamented that "the inability of the British Government to make a pronouncement on its attitude towards Italy made it impossible to secure the active support of potential Italian leaders."[29] Charles Hambro, taking note of that dilemma, put forward an alternative. In early 1943 he suggested that an "unofficial policy" ought to shadow the official one, which in reality was sketchy; it amounted simply to showing the Italians the desperate situation facing their country. SOE could thus "make clandestine offers" and promise that, if the Italians "would play their part," Italy would not be steamrolled in the peace treaty. "If they could be reassured the Italians would not feel that action against their government was treacherous," he concluded.[30] Inasmuch as the Foreign Office was intent on keeping the upper hand in foreign policy and had the utmost distrust of SOE's diplomatic initiatives, that proposal could not fail to be rejected—as in fact, it was. But it showed the deadlock that the Anglo-Americans were approaching. Having failed to specify whether they intended to treat Italy as an ally or an enemy, they discouraged a political and military resistance, which they greatly needed in the months after Il Duce was deposed, and they encouraged the fanaticism of the Fascist Republic of Salò.

Although different in nature, the disasters suffered in the Netherlands and Italy should not make us lose sight of the big picture. Indeed, the results in mid-May 1943 must be evaluated in terms of the distinct but complementary objectives SOE had pursued since 1940. As we have seen, the organization had to find its bearings in the jungle of the British services, impel the peoples of Fortress Europe to revolt, constitute its own networks, support the existing underground groups, and prepare for D-Day by creating a secret army, even while increasing as much as possible the number of sabotage operations. By the middle of 1943 that program was in part realized.

New Threats to SOE

As early as 1940 the Special Operations Executive had faced the combined hostility of the Intelligence Service, the Foreign Office, the Political Warfare Executive, and the Ministries of Information and of the Army—not to mention the persistent reservations of the governments in exile. These dark clouds did not dissipate until late 1943, having in the meantime subjected the Baker Street services to violent squalls.

In February 1942 General Władysław Sikorski, leader of the Polish government in exile, had suggested that a joint agency plan the strategy to be followed on the European continent. An Allied general staff, responsible for insurrections and other uprisings, would also take over liaisons with the secret armies, while overseeing the delivery of arms and materiel to them. That initiative, because it proposed to delegate SOE duties to a European structure, would have marked the death of the British service.[31] Colin Gubbins therefore immediately spoke out against it. Pointing out that the heterogeneous composition of an Allied general staff would make decision making impossible and would raise insoluble security problems, he added that an accord among the "minor allies," however hypothetical, would lead them to exert "very heavy pressure" on the British government and would therefore reduce its margin for maneuvering. Unsurprisingly, Winston Churchill endorsed that point of view; the plan that had been floated by the Polish authorities was therefore officially rejected on May 6. It nevertheless conveyed the frustration of the émigré powers, which believed that the United Kingdom was providing insufficient aid to their internal resistance, as Gubbins readily acknowledged.[32] "We are in a position to give some reasonable support for the projects of these Allied nations without really prejudicing our own war effort to any material degree—but the fact remains that we are virtually doing nothing at all," he noted. "If we continue in this way . . . we shall forfeit entirely the confidence of these junior and minor Allies and may find that they are linking themselves in a postwar world either with Russia or America to our immediate detriment."[33]

On an entirely different level, the contentious relations between the Special Operations Executive and the Intelligence Service led the Joint Intelligence Committee (JIC) to draw up a report for the British chiefs of staff on May 1, 1942. While suggesting that the two services and the joint operations cooperate more closely, the report gave the preeminent role to IS in zones where the landing was supposed to take place—Western Europe, therefore.[34] To resolve disputes between the two services, two men—John Hanbury-Williams, a businessman, and Edward Playfair, from the treasury administration—were ordered to compose a report. Submitted on June 18, 1942, it ended with a moderate defense of SOE and recommended keeping it on. Recalling that that secret service was indispensable because it was supposed to "provide an integral part of the military machine of invasion," it enumerated the wrongs committed by the Secret Intelligence Service. "We cannot escape the conclusion that SIS do not put all their cards on the table and that they are not as keen as they should be to see that, in so far as it rests with them, SOE should succeed in their enterprises," it concluded.[35] The Special Operations Executive thus escaped dissolution—at least for a while.

In fact, the disastrous *Englandspiel* affair was a new jolt. The RAF, after suspending its flights over the Netherlands, on December 1, 1943, asked the Joint Intelligence Committee to investigate the German infiltration of SOE networks in Europe. The report, presented to the chiefs of staff on January 3, 1944, far from confining itself to questions of security, sifted through all the secret service's actions and organization. Lambasting the flaws that had produced the Dutch catastrophe, the report did acknowledge that the necessary precautions had been taken in the other countries. This amounted to faint praise, and, after ridiculing the operations set in place by Baker Street, the report called for draconian changes. In addition to closer control over SOE, it pleaded for a unification of action and intelligence, and, more explicitly, the merger of the Secret Intelligence Service and the Special Operations Executive.

Lord Selborne, minister of economic warfare, wrote a response that went on for more than thirty pages. Recalling that the losses suffered lay within

an acceptable range—14 percent of the agents sent out in 1943—he enumerated the successes achieved throughout Europe as a whole and, true to
the founding principle set out in 1940, pleaded for IS and SOE to remain
separate. In a letter to his friend Churchill, moreover, he expressed astonishment at the process, finding it "highly disturbing that the JIC [Joint
Intelligence Committee] could put their signature to a series of statements
on matters of which they have no firsthand knowledge, and on which they
have taken no evidence from SOE. I fear mushrooms are not always popular among oaks. I delivered my reply yesterday and I understand that a
copy has been sent to you. It is terribly long, but criticisms take longer to
rebut than to make, and 'cet animal est très méchant' [this animal is very
vicious]."[36] On January 14, 1944, the Defense Committee agreed that air
operations would resume over Holland and asked that supplementary
resources be allocated to SOE, a sign that the British government preferred
not to dissolve the organization. The risk, however, was only just averted,
given the harsh criticism by the Intelligence Service.[37]

Revolts?

Although SOE had for a time dreamed of "setting Europe ablaze," it rather
quickly lowered its sights. In fact, the unrest in Western Europe tended to
decline over time, before flaring up again upon liberation. Although strikes
had caused upheaval in France and Belgium in 1941, and wide-ranging civil
protest movements had set fire to Norway between 1941 and 1942, forms
of open dissidence became rarer, with a few exceptions. In France, major
demonstrations celebrated May Day 1942 in the southern zone; and, the
same year, enormous processions took place in unison on Bastille Day. In
the single city of Lyon, a crowd of more than 100,000 marched in the streets,
according to the prefect of Rhône.[38] In both cases, the BBC—Charles de
Gaulle in the lead—played an important role, calling on the French to
mobilize.

In addition, a large-scale strike was launched in the Netherlands in late
April 1943, to protest a measure believed to be iniquitous. In 1940 the Reich
authorities had released all Dutch prisoners of war. But on April 29, 1943,
General Friedrich Christiansen, head of the German military administration, called them back into service to bolster the Nazi economy.[39] Immediately, the country went up in flames. Without having been encouraged

by British radio, 500,000 to 1 million Dutch spontaneously went on strike, giving rise to harsh reprisals. Anxious to prevent compulsory labor but wishing to avoid a premature uprising or acts of violence that would give the Germans a pretext to execute hostages, Pieter Gerbrandy suggested that the RAF bomb communication networks, to keep the Germans from transporting Dutch veterans to the Reich.[40] The British authorities refused. Based on its experience, SOE did not believe in "the efficacy of threats of reprisals or attempts to interfere by means of aerial bombardment."[41] In any event, the occupying forces decreed a state of emergency and sentenced eight people to death, after which they murdered sixty people.[42] Regardless, the movement continued until early May in Friesland and North Brabant, without receiving any foreign aid. The consequences of that conflict were significant: "The rift between opinion and the regime seemed definitive from then on. . . . More and more people assisted and protected the labor conscripts throughout the country."[43]

Despite that unrest, open protests decreased over time, for one obvious reason: the repression was now so violent that civilians would not risk their lives, as Bruce Lockhart, head of PWE, had noted in May 1942. "Another most important factor in gauging potential strength of resistance is change brought about by technical improvement in weapons. In Russian revolution of 1905–6 workers with rifles could still get behind barricades and put up show against troops. Today no chance against a few tanks and a dive-bomber or two."[44] The British authorities drew the logical conclusions. After the invasion of the free zone on November 11, 1942, the BBC refrained from calling on the French to demonstrate.[45] And SOE continually warned against the "danger of premature outbreaks in France owing to the repressive measures taken by the Germans in connection with the relève [the program to repatriate French POWs in exchange for workers who volunteered to go to the Reich]. . . . We are doing our best to persuade the Fighting French to damp down these movements as far as possible."[46]

Action and Organization

SOE also concerned itself with creating networks and supporting the existing underground groups. To achieve that objective, it followed a tried-and-true method—sending emissaries—and was generous with its resources. Between March and June 1942, 138 men were dispatched to Europe.[47]

Fifty-two followed between July and September 1942,[48] joined between October and December by 139 volunteers.[49] Between April and June 1943 a quantitative leap occurred, with 247 agents being sent to the Old Continent. In July 1943 Lord Selborne announced to Winston Churchill—not without pride—that 650 people were operating in Europe.[50] In addition to the "organizers" and "sub-organizers," there were wireless operators equipped with transmitters: 137 for the period between July and September 1942,[51] 211 for April to June 1943.[52] In giving the networks and movements transceivers, SOE established a rapid communication system (though one subject to the risks of repression), which resolved the nagging question of the connection between decision makers and their agents.

The results of that proactive policy were uneven, as we have seen. In Norway, SOE was able to depend on a sufficiently powerful movement, Milorg, which spared it having to set up its own networks. In France and Belgium, it opted for a combination of measures. Even while developing its own networks, it supported homegrown underground groups, with varying success. Although it succeeded in establishing a direct connection to the movements in Belgium, it accepted the fact that, in France, the Gaullists would maintain direct relations with the major organizations: Combat, Libération-Sud, and Franc-Tireur, to name only a few.[53] In Denmark, SOE developed an independent structure that, while cooperating with local groups, acted in complete autonomy. In Italy and the Netherlands, finally, the disasters the organization suffered led to the collapse of its undertakings.

The underground groups pursued a dual objective. Over the short term, they were supposed to increase the number of sabotage operations; over a longer time span, they were to train secret armies that would be able to act on D-Day. From that standpoint, the results were once again uneven.

Members of the resistance did gradually take action. For the six months between July and December 1942, SOE recorded, for all of Europe, 524 assaults on persons (Germans or collaborators), 176 attacks against railroads or shipyards, and 115 sabotage operations of factories or public utilities, figures that do not include the actions conducted by groups that escaped SOE's control.[54] The first half of 1943 was characterized by an increasing number of shows of force: there were 599 assaults against persons, 309 attacks against railroad networks and ports, and 206 cases of industrial sabotage. Several daring coups struck at the enemy's infrastructure, whether the raid against the Vermork factory in Norway or the operation in Denmark targeting Lyngby, whose batteries were used in the U-boats. On a completely different level, the resistance sometimes managed to protect civilians from the rigors of the occupation. Socrate in Belgium, backed by the British services, had, for example, proved its effectiveness in the fight against compulsory labor.

These heroic deeds must not be overestimated, however. Despite the courage of resistance fighters, the blows dealt the Nazi war machine were limited in scope. Economically, German war production was increasing, thanks to the brutal exploitation of the occupied countries and the mobilization of forced labor. Militarily, the game was being played in the African sands, the ruins of Stalingrad, or the icy waters of the Atlantic Ocean, and not on the Wehrmacht's home front, which the resistance could merely disrupt once in a while.

It was therefore imperative that the resistance, to contribute effectively to the Reich's defeat, couple its action with the Allied grand strategy. The constitution of secret armies was part of that objective, but the results, once again, were uneven. In the first half of 1943 Selborne's services estimated that these troops mobilized thirty thousand men in France, twenty thousand in Norway, ten thousand in the Netherlands, and five thousand in Belgium,[55] respectable numbers to be sure, but obviously falling short of those needed to make a significant contribution to the Old Continent's liberation— especially since, in the Dutch case, the numbers were erroneous.

The incorporation of the underground forces into a general plan was therefore required. But that objective ran up against difficult obstacles. SOE and OSS had to prove to the military staffs that the resistance could play a significant role during the landing. They had to overcome the reservations of the wavering exiled powers, which wanted to participate in the deliverance of their country while keeping their populations from being exposed to overly harsh ordeals. They had to invent the terms of action that would allow civilians unversed in the art of war to join the struggle. Finally, they had to provide the internal resistance with the means to go on the attack, obviously an imperative, but one that gave rise to fierce battles.

CHAPTER XI

Taking Up Arms

D uring and after the war, the internal resistance in many of the countries of Western Europe complained of a lack of weapons, readily accusing the Allies—the United Kingdom, in the first place—of having refused to equip it. The destitution of the underground forces thus fueled a dark legend, especially in France: the British, the Americans, and even the Gaullists, through their parsimony, deliberately torpedoed the movements for basely political reasons. "They laugh at us in Algiers—unless it's a deliberate policy. As if they'd decided not to arm us and to save the parachute drops for the trustworthy maquis. . . . Maybe they're afraid the Resistance will play too great a role in the liberation of the country?" pondered Jean-Pierre Vernant, a militant in the Libération-Sud movement, in 1944.[1] "Why didn't we get weapons from London? I was to wonder about this for a long time to come, and all the Resistance would be wondering with me," added Henri Frenay.[2] That view misjudges one essential fact: strategic choices and logistical constraints dictated the rules of the game.

An Ardent Obligation

To send out their agents and drop the materiel necessary for the underground forces, SOE and OSS had to have means of transportation at their disposal. But shortages were the rule, at least until 1944. They affected in the first place the secret services, which, for lack of airplanes or ships, could not dispatch their men to Fortress Europe. "Some 1600 men have been trained in all the arts of sabotage and subversion and W/T [wireless transmission]," explained Lord Selborne to Winston Churchill in April 1942, "while 350 are awaiting transport abroad. . . . The principal bottleneck today is the provision of transport. Many more 'agents' have been trained than it has been found possible to transport to enemy occupied territories."[3] But that deficiency also had an impact on the internal resistance, which was deprived of the weapons it was frantically awaiting.

Even so, British and American leaders understood the urgent necessity of equipping the resistance. In August 1943 General Lowell Rooks of the Anglo-American general staff in North Africa noted: "Should OSS be successful in organizing and equipping considerable numbers of resistance groups in southern France, as seems likely, their activities in destroying signal communications, interrupting rail and road communications, destroying supply dumps, providing concealed landing strips and the like, should be of inestimable value in connection with an amphibious assault." Political arguments also carried weight. General Rooks pointed out, "France has been our traditional friend. But will this bond not be weakened, and hence our postwar position, if we fail to extend to her such help as is possible—at least equal to that extended by others of the United Nations?"[4]

Granted, strategic considerations tempered that theoretical position: the Allies feared that sending arms would lead to premature unrest.

Up to September [1943], however, London answered the more and more numerous requests from the [French] Maquis with extreme meagerness. First because of the lack of planes, but also because the High Command did not wish to encourage the creation of armed groups not under some sort of control, and liable to carry out premature guerilla operations on their own initiative. London preferred to send a minimum of help to well-disciplined [French] Maquis and only when these were attacked by "miliciens" or by Germans. This [is] why in April [1943], for instance, sorties to Haute-Savoie were limited to 8.[5]

All in all, SOE and OSS agreed to arm the resistance in Western Europe, but they had to cope with the reservations of the chiefs of staff, who were inclined to play for time. For intentions to become acts, moreover, the logistics had to be worked out, and that was far from the case before 1944.

A Shortage of Airplanes

The British Bomber Command, persuaded that its bombing campaign over Germany would result in victory, allocated only a limited number of aircraft to SOE, which Charles Portal, marshal of the Royal Air Force, candidly justified in July 1943.

> The issue is a plain one. As we cannot provide aircraft for the transport of arms and materials to Resistance Groups except at the direct cost of the bomber offensive, what is the exact price we are prepared to pay? . . .
> We are unquestionably obtaining great and immediate value from the bomber offensive. . . . I have no doubt about the value of what is being done by SOE in the Balkans, or about the need to do as much more if it is possible. These activities accord with our general strategic plan, they exploit our present successes and should give us good and immediate results.
> The same, however, cannot be said about the rest of Europe, where the efforts of Resistance Groups cannot be really profitable until next year. The real value which we shall obtain from these Groups will be an up-rising. If such an up-rising is to be successful—and it can only succeed once—it will demand conditions in which German resistance in the West is reaching the point of disintegration. We are not in position to begin to apply the necessary pressure for another nine or twelve months unless the German war machine cracks seriously in the meantime. The most likely cause of this accelerated collapse is the bomber offensive which must not be handicapped by diversions to an operation whose value is obviously secondary. . . .
> I feel that it would be a serious mistake to divert any more aircraft to supply Resistance Groups in Western Europe which will only be of *potential* value next year when these aircraft could be of *immediate and actual* value in accelerating the defeat of Germany by direct attack.[6]

Two squadrons, no. 138 and no. 161—known as the "Moonlight Squadrons" because they operated only when the moon was full—served the special services.[7] But Charles Portal recommended limiting the number of bombers allocated to SOE to fifty-eight, a figure to which the Defense Committee agreed. The majority of them—thirty-two—served the Balkans. In comparison, Western Europe (sixteen), Italy and southern France (four), and Central Europe (six) were treated like poor relations.[8] The situation improved in February 1944. At that time, the special services had at their disposal twenty-two Halifaxes, thirty-two Stirlings, and twelve B-24 Liberators, in addition to four Halifaxes, three B-17 Flying Fortresses, and two Mitchells, all based in North Africa. In March twelve Liberators and thirty-three Stirlings completed the lineup, bringing the total to 120 planes, not counting the flights occasionally made by other aircraft on behalf of SOE and OSS.[9]

It should be pointed out, however, that the RAF kept the best models for its own bombing raids. SOE could not get near a Lancaster, which outperformed similar aircraft.[10] In addition, the two squadrons were based in Tempsford, Bedfordshire, north of London, a site that Bomber Command had rejected "because of the frequent fogs which descended on it, and because of a range of low hills which was dangerously near the point of take-off."[11] On that inhospitable base, SIS and SOE shared a lone, dilapidated barn: Gibraltar Farm.[12] Other bases later took part in these operations—Harrington, Laken Heath, and Alconbury—though Harris, head of Bomber Command, never gave up fighting against them. As the historian Richard Overy summed it up, Harris constantly protested, "often bitterly, any attempt to divert the forces under his command to other purposes, and when compelled to do so, he fought to have his bombers returned to what he saw as their only rational function as soon as possible."[13] Indeed, arming the resistance would have required considerable effort on the part of the RAF. To equip five thousand men a month, 280 tons of materiel had to be dropped, which is to say, a total of 24 shipping containers during 300 sorties by 24 aircraft.[14] And if, as OSS suggested in May 1943, a target of 1,650 tons was set, the RAF had to mobilize 275 aircraft during the full-moon phase,[15] the period most propitious for the flights. Although Bomber Command agreed to divert a few dozen aircraft in 1943, it refused to allocate hundreds at the expense of bombing raids on the Reich. As a result, support for the army of shadows could be only occasional and not massive.

In spite of everything, SOE's resources grew over time. That quantitative progress must not mislead us, however: the planes made only a limited number of flights, even as requests from the resistance were increasing. Estimates vary here. The British were reckoning on an average of 8 monthly missions in 1943,[16] whereas the Americans aspired to 12.5 missions per month.[17] In reality, everything depended on the aircraft and the route to be taken. In any event, one thing is clear: the Royal Air Force was very stingy in its pursuit of subversive warfare. In 1941 the 41 sorties for SOE represented only 0.13 percent of the missions that took off from England; that proportion rose to 0.68 percent (248 sorties out of 36,425) in 1942, then increased in 1943 to 2.48 percent (1,649 flights out of 66,308), still an absurdly low figure. Granted, 5,566 missions worked on behalf of Lord Selborne's service in 1944, but they had little weight (3.3 percent) compared to the total (166,844). It should be pointed out, however, that 24,654 additional sorties were made between 1941 and 1945, departing either from North Africa (21,507) or from the United Kingdom itself, but piloted by the U.S. Air Force (3,147).[18]

The amount of materiel delivered to the internal resistance in the countries of Western Europe also depended on the volume each plane was transporting. At first, a bomber carried six shipping containers. Over time, advances in aeronautics made increases in that load possible. Although the performance of the Hudson (four containers) and the Albermale (six) remained modest, the B-17 Flying Fortress (twelve), the Halifax (fifteen), and the Stirling (eleven to twenty-four)[19] increased the range of possibilities. These averages conceal a disparity, since the tonnage transported was inversely proportionate to the distance traveled. A Halifax cruising at 168 miles per hour dropped fifteen containers 620 miles from its base but only twelve containers at 683 miles of distance. Similarly, the Stirling carried a load of twenty-four containers for 480 miles but transported only eleven for a trip of 620 miles.[20] It was also necessary to prepare and pack thousands of shipping containers intended for the underground forces, a colossal task.

Standardization

Preparing the containers required considerable energy. Faced with that Sisyphean labor, the British and American authorities opted to rationalize the processes, which involved, in the first place, standardizing the materiel destined for the underground forces. Choices were limited to two models of containers: type C, long and hollow, measured about 14 by 70 inches and, when fully loaded, weighed 220 pounds; type H was composed of five cells.[21] Customized materiel, by contrast, was placed in packages.[22] A standard delivery to a maquis generally comprised fifteen containers: one filled with explosives, the other fourteen with weapons and ammunition.[23] When only twelve containers were dropped, they contained four Bren machine guns, eighteen rifles, seventy Sten submachine guns, fifty pistols, and explosives, as well as eighty Mills grenades and twenty-four Gammon grenades.[24] Movements and networks received a greater variety: their fifteen containers generally contained explosives (four containers), sabotage materiel (three), and arms and ammunition (eight).

Preparation stations were established to fill containers and packages, so that reserves would be in place before every full-moon phase.[25] Five teams, composed of a supervisor and fourteen men, busied themselves with the task. Twelve men were in charge of packing in the strict sense, while one brought the materiel to his coworkers, and the fourteenth man cleared the tables once the packing was completed.[26] In February 1944 SOE mobilized two hundred men to fill about a thousand containers a month. OSS, by contrast, had only three officers and nine men to fill 175 containers.[27]

In addition to the crucial question of packing, the British supply corps had to cope with a persistent shortage of parachutes. As early as summer 1943 Lord Selborne became worried[28]—not without reason, since the United Kingdom's production capacity proved inadequate. The British planned to manufacture 10,000 parachutes in August 1943 and 12,500 in September, before increasing the quota to 14,000 a month for October, November, and December. But the airborne forces were asking for 11,000 units a month, while SOE demanded 8,000 a month for 1943 and 10,000 a month for 1944.[29] As was often the case, salvation came from mighty America. In May 1944 Washington proudly announced that 5,000 parachutes would be supplied in March and in April, before promising 21,000 for May—as preparations for the Normandy landing required.[30]

The standardization introduced by the British and American services allowed them to respond to the growing demands of the internal resistance. It explains, for example, why the average number of container drops over France every full-moon phase rose from 4.2 to 8 per aircraft between April and August 1943.[31] That effort was flawed, however: containers of American manufacture could not be transported by British planes, which led OSS to demand that it be allocated aircraft made in the United States, either B-17s or B-24s.[32] In addition, some services refused to cooperate. It was not until September 1943 that SOE's F section agreed to participate, and even so, it covered only 85 percent of the parachute drops at the time. In fact, a certain proportion of "specials"—to meet precise requests—was "inevitable," though their number declined over time.[33]

Above all, standardization had two perverse effects. It resulted in the Allies being entrusted with control over underground operations, since, in choosing the materiel to be dropped, they determined the forms of action. Delivering arms encouraged guerilla warfare; providing explosives favored sabotage. For example, the British and the Americans decided that, beginning with the "July Moon" of 1943, for each operation launched in the regions of Lille, Amiens, Rennes, and Bordeaux, two containers out of five "would contain Mark 5 AT mines, until a total of 50 mines had been received in each locality."[34] They were thereby preparing for Plan Tortue (Tortoise Plan), which, on D-Day, was supposed to prevent the Germans from moving their reinforcements along the highways. The French resistance had no other choice but to accept that option. Like its comrades elsewhere in Western Europe, it had no way to sway its powerful suppliers.

Rationalization, moreover, made it impossible to respond to the specific needs formulated by the underground forces. When the partisans demanded more weapons than explosives, there was no chance of their being heard, since their demands risked interfering with the standardized system designed by the Allies. It should be added that, in favoring transport via containers, OSS and SOE ruled out delivering heavy weapons, which did not fit into the cylinders. All in all, the system adopted had the advantage of speeding things up, but it by no means guaranteed that the resources would correspond to the requirements of underground combat, even supposing that the weapons arrived safe and sound.

Air Drops

The containers transported from the departure airfield were subsequently equipped with parachutes and loaded onto the bombers. Sometimes the aircraft were modified to fulfill their mission. To reduce weight, the submachine guns mounted on the B-24s were removed, except for those placed in the top and rear turrets. Because the flights occurred at night, the fuselage was painted black; to avoid being spotted, the guns were equipped with bullet deflectors, and fire dampeners were placed on the engine exhaust.[35] Once the aircraft was ready to go, it took off and headed toward its objective.

Members of the resistance had selected in advance sites to receive the air drops, and the coordinates were transmitted to London. Every site, after it was approved, received a code name (in Creuse, for example, these included "Delco," "Gaëlle," and "Chance"), and a reconnaissance letter. A message over the BBC, directed at the reception team, announced the imminence of the operation. Sites labeled *homo* could receive men, while the others, called *arma*, accepted only weapons. Alerted by British radio, groups on the ground would then light fires or use flashlights to guide the airplanes. The pilot, after flying at high altitudes to avoid enemy antiair-craft defense systems, reduced speed to about 125 miles an hour, then descended to about 2,000 feet in altitude or even less—500 feet in Denmark.[36] The more the speed and altitude were reduced, the greater the precision and security of the drop. There was a risk, in fact, that a container released at great speed and from a high altitude would break apart.[37]

For the crew, that procedure raised serious risks, which SOS made every effort to avert. In early 1944 it attempted to make parachute drops over the Alps at high altitude, above the clouds. But the containers scattered and were seized by the Germans or the Milice, putting an end to the experiment.[38] The planes therefore returned to low-altitude drops, which did not always augur success. Containers sometimes opened in the air, especially when novices had prepared them;[39] many packed by the Americans broke when carrying weapons or ammunition;[40] and, in a strong wind, containers sometimes drifted more than two and a half miles from the designated site.[41] Mortars were rarely dropped because shells exploded on the way down.[42]

In addition, parachutes were not always altogether reliable. Some, poorly secured, came loose; others ripped or caught fire.[43] SOE leaders therefore had misgivings about air deliveries, especially when they were sending money. As Maurice Buckmaster, head of F section, noted with false naïveté: "It always seemed to be the money package which, by ill-luck, was wafted away into the next parish or got stuck on the top of an unclimbable tree."[44] But the case should not be overstated. Although the failure rate of parachutes was high at the beginning of the war (five out of a thousand), it had become minimal by the end of the conflict (one per hundred thousand).[45] Hence the two French sections of SOE lost only six men during parachute jumps over the course of the war. The success of an operation was never guaranteed, however: the materiel parachuted in had to be received by teams on the ground, a process too often impeded by the lack of accuracy of the drops.

Eureka!

To solve that problem, the British and Americans adopted two procedures. The first, Rebecca/Eureka, was a short-range radar composed of two elements: the Rebecca transmitter, installed aboard the airplane, emitted a signal, to which the Eureka transponder responded from the ground. In calculating the force of the signal and how long it took to arrive, the crew could measure the distance remaining and locate the site it was targeting. In addition, the S-Phone, a wireless telephone system, allowed for direct conversation between the ground and the sky. On the whole, these devices facilitated the approach of airplanes, which had previously operated by sight. They therefore made it possible to conduct operations at times other than full-moon phases, since, thanks to the navigation with instruments, bright nights were no longer indispensable for the pilots.

The British and the Americans therefore supplied the resistance with these two instruments. In France, the first liaison was established near Tarbes on July 25, 1943.[46] In the first quarter of 1944, 104 Eurekas were sent to France and 6 to Belgium; of that total, 57 went into operation in the first country, 4 in the second. At the same time, 241 S-Phones were dropped into France, 22 into Belgium—156 would be in active service in one case, 5 in the other, with good results.[47] In Norway, members of the resistance were "enthusiastic," believing that the use of the Eureka system increased the success of operations by 50 percent.[48]

Of course, these instruments did not solve all the problems. Their range was limited: fifty miles for the Rebecca/Eureka system, thirty for the S-Phone. In addition, for telephone contact to be established, a bomber had to cruise at under ten thousand feet, which placed it at the mercy of German antiaircraft devices.[49] Furthermore, the sets were dropped in packages and, though they were packed in kapok fiber, sometimes broke in contact with the ground. They also had to be handled by an experienced team, on the ground and in the air, which explains why RAF crews had a real aversion to using them.[50]

S-Phones and Eurekas did not eliminate the use of flashlights or fires, which caused a few mishaps. In Denmark, six planes sometimes appeared above a site, and the reception committee did not always succeed in signaling to the right pilot when it was his turn, fearing they would be spotted if they flashed the light at intervals too close together. Therefore the cargo was sometimes dropped at the wrong signal: a team once received forty-two containers when it was expecting only twelve, which raised a few problems when it came to transporting the materiel.[51] Language was also a barrier since members of the resistance often did not know English, or the crews were unwilling to speak it. The first S-Phone, for example, was used in Denmark on May 17, 1943, but one connection was broken off on July 25. As the organizer, Muus, reported to Hollingworth, head of the Danish section, "the pilot . . . refused to speak anything but Polish and although we are quite willing to operate the S-Phones in Danish, Swedish, Norwegian, German, French, English and two or three African dialects none of us understand Polish which we regret."[52] SOE got around the problem by placing interpreters aboard the planes, a resource envied by the Americans, who did not have access to it.[53]

But the most serious problems were how to transport the devices (Eureka weighed over sixteen pounds, the S-Phone fifteen) and where they should be set up. At first the Norwegians placed the Eurekas in cavities, which interfered with transmissions. They then chose sites out in the open, exploiting mountains and hilltops, which greatly improved the situation, with one exception: in the icy Scandinavian winters, the operators were freezing cold. It was impossible to build shelters, and, when tents were erected, they were invariably carried off by the wind.[54]

Missions Accomplished?

The flights made by the bombers were low-risk—all other things being equal—and the losses caused by the Flak antiaircraft guns or the Luftwaffe during parachuting missions were limited, on the order of 1.5 to 3 percent per year.[55] In his long report of 1943, Lord Selborne noted, for example, that the losses the enemy inflicted on the bombers working on his behalf amounted to 1.56 percent a year,[56] a very low proportion compared to that of American aircraft lost over Germany in spring 1943 (between 9 and

15 percent) or planes downed in July of the same year above Hamburg and Kiel (8.7 percent).[57]

By contrast, the reception of parachute drops was a problem so acute that it fueled strong resentment. The British and American authorities ranted about the amateurism of the partisans, who were supposedly incapable of ensuring reception of materiel dropped at great risk. In the Netherlands, the SOE leaders observed, "the Reception Committee personnel lacked discipline. The guards would leave their posts to greet the new arrivals and there was much talking and smoking, especially when the 'plane was late in arriving.'"[58] Desmond Morton, adviser to Winston Churchill, pointed out in April 1944 that the failure rate recorded in France had to be acknowledged. "It is wrong to risk the lives of British air crews on hazardous operations doomed to failure from the outset through lack of efficiency in reception arrangements at the other end," he declared.[59] Conversely, members of the resistance criticized the incompetence of their allies, saying they did not drop the promised weapons in a timely manner. However bitter these debates, the real differences were less stark than they appeared.

On average, airborne missions dedicated to subversive warfare succeeded two-thirds of the time over the war as a whole.[60] That proportion was close to the American estimate, which, in October 1943, reckoned on a success rate of 62 percent.[61] The remaining third of operations failed for various reasons. It is true that members of the resistance did not always rise to the occasion. In February 1944, 24 percent of the failures recorded in France were imputed to the absence of reception groups, a proportion that climbed to 37 percent in March and April, then leapt to 41 percent in May. But other factors figured in to a lesser degree. Errors in navigation (6–13 percent), mechanical problems (4–9 percent), and enemy antiaircraft systems or fighter planes (5–20 percent) also took a heavy toll.[62] In short, the breakdown of reception committees did not explain in and of itself the failure of operations, as the British authorities were sporting enough to acknowledge. "Neither the RAF nor SOE consider the non-reception percentage of 37% (16% of total sorties) to be unduly high," Lord Selborne noted in May 1944. "The evidence of non-reception is based largely on pilot's reports, and in many cases no evidence confirmatory or otherwise is received from the Field. Since the pilots can be interrogated and the Committees cannot, the percentage of failure due to the absence of Reception Committees is probably less than appears and accounted for to some extent by faulty navigation." He added that "63% of the failures are admitted by the RAF to be due to causes beyond the control of the reception committee, and there must therefore be many occasions where reception committees wait in vain hour after hour on cold winter nights unable to warm themselves by fire or by moving, or to solace themselves by smoking. This must have a depressing effect, and it is remarkable that we have only two cases on record where the reception committees had gone home too early."[63]

It is important to specify that France was not much different from the other nations on that score. Selborne also pointed out that "the percentage of failures is pretty constant and much the same in all countries in northern Europe. Therefore the French, who are greatly inferior in other fields of SO technique (eg security) to say the Danes, cannot be held to make a particularly bad showing in this respect."[64] The results recorded for Europe confirm that diagnosis. Out of 39,897 sorties carried out between 1941 and 1945, 26,906 (that is, 67 percent) succeeded. France fell right in the middle (10,488 successes for 16,460 flights, or 64 percent), a rate comparable to Denmark (284 missions accomplished out of 413, or 68 percent),[65] but sharply higher than Italy (2,654 successful flights out of 5,282, a failure rate of 50 percent) or Norway (619 successes for 1,042 missions, a 59 percent success rate).[66]

The committees, which played a decisive role in welcoming parachuted agents and in receiving weapons, were often distinguished by their efficiency. In Denmark, they had as a rule only thirty minutes to load the materiel onto the trucks before the Germans arrived on the scene. On one occasion they even managed to process twenty-four shipping containers in eleven minutes, a remarkable feat.[67] Sometimes, by contrast, the operation came to a tragic end. The repressive forces, alerted by double agents or by feverish activity that disturbed the nocturnal tranquility of the countryside, showed up and grabbed the weapons that had just touched down, if not the men as well. This tragedy occurred five times in France and resulted in the capture of eighteen agents—not to mention what happened in the Netherlands.[68] In all, the British calculated the losses at 20 percent on average, a proportion that included both the damage suffered by the containers during their fall and seizures of them by the enemy.[69]

Expedients

SOE and OSS privileged air transport when supplying weapons and materiel to members of the resistance, but that mode proved difficult in the case of Norway. The flights were long, given the distance, and perilous due to the climate. The terrain, moreover, provided few drop zones. The British therefore decided to rely on sea transport via the Shetland Bus. They had some success. In fact, the round trips between the archipelago and the coasts of Norway increased over time. Seventy-one operations were conducted between 1942 and 1944, for example, compared to fifty-seven between 1941 and 1942.[70] In the early days of heroic deeds, fishing boats transported men and materiel; but, beginning in 1943, the Germans imposed restrictions on fishing, which hindered the movements of craft that had suddenly become suspect. At the request of Charles Hambro, the Americans agreed to hand over three submarine chasers to SOE. Served by Norwegian crews, the *Hitra*, the *Hessa*, and the *Vigra*[71] proved perfectly well adapted to their new functions, given their speed, range, and seaworthiness,[72] three factors that explain the upswing in the number of trips.

That said, the sea was no more reliable than the sky. Indeed, storms and the actions of the German air force and navy wreaked havoc. In 1941 the *Vita* was captured by the enemy, the *Blia* sank upon its return, and the *Nordsjon*, dashed against the shore, foundered. These mishaps explain why the results were mediocre. During the 1942–1943 season, twenty-three crossings out of forty succeeded (58 percent), a rate lower than the performance of airborne forces.[73] And, out of seventeen attempts between January and March 1943, nine—more than half—failed. It was not until winter 1944–1945 that the percentages began to improve: almost all the crossings (seventy-six out of eighty) ended in success, primarily because of a less aggressive Luftwaffe and Kriegsmarine.[74]

Norway remained the exception, though sea routes were sometimes used for the other countries as well. Patrol boats occasionally transported agents to the French coasts: seventy-seven missions originating in England delivered 88 agents and picked up 218. In addition, two feluccas, the *Sea Dog* and the *Sea Wolf*, operating from Gibraltar, served the Mediterranean coast, transporting 211 people and exfiltrating 655.[75] "These sardine fishing-boats were small, dirty-looking vessels, manned by strange crews, Spaniards, Poles, Greeks, who combined night fishing with the more remunerative business of smuggling."[76] Likewise, the Danes frequently crossed the North Sea to exfiltrate or deliver members of the resistance.

On the whole, however, the great majority of men were transported by air. Some parachuted in blindly, others were met by reception committees. But some people could not be dropped because of their physical condition.

They were then set down by airplane. As a general rule, SOE relied on its fleet of Lysanders, counting six aircraft in 1943, ten in January 1944, and thirteen in May of the same year.[77] These reconnaissance planes, each of which had only a pilot and no crew, had the advantage of being able to land and take off on short runways (about 1,300 to 2,100 feet long and 500 feet wide) with fairly low requirements.

> The ground surface must be firm. A plowed field can NEVER be used; stubble is possible but not recommended. Grass or stubble must NOT be more than 12 inches high. Snow must NOT be more than 4 inches thick.
>
> The field must be entirely free of obstacles such as ditches, ruts, molehills, fences, and animals. The plane may land at about 75 miles an hour, and even a very small obstacle can make a tire burst. Most accidents are caused by a bad surface.
>
> The runway lights are composed of three electric lanterns, each attached to a stake three feet high. They are designated A, B, and C.[78]

The flip side to the Lysander's advantages was that it had only a modest range, less than seven hundred miles, and could carry only two to four passengers. Consequently, the number of operations increased: one mission in 1941, nine in 1942, thirty-eight in 1943. That made it possible not only to transport agents but to deliver to England some of the mail composed by the internal resistance, whether in the form of maps, reports, or photographs.[79]

Sometimes, but less often, SOE mobilized its three, and later six, Hudsons, which had the capacity to transport ten passengers per flight. That small bomber required a larger runway (3,300 feet long and 650 feet wide),[80] and its weight, nearly nine tons, limited its maneuverability. On February 8, 1944, for example, the aircraft assigned to bring back to England a couple pursued by the Gestapo got stuck in the mud on Orion airfield, near Bletterans, in Jura. "It was only after three hours of effort, and by appealing to the entire population of the neighboring village, that the plane managed to take off, carrying only part of the mail and three of the nine expected passengers: Sergent Brough of the RAF and M. and Mme Aubrac of the Resistance."[81] In all, Hudsons conducted only sixteen flights on behalf of SOE in 1943,[82] but they transported a large portion of the personalities invited to sit on the Consultative Assembly in Algiers beginning in September 1943.

Air power, the RAF in the first place, thus provided the support—in men and materiel— that the United Kingdom and the United States offered the internal resistance in Western Europe. Prior to the major maneuvers of 1944, as has often been said, that support was moderate to say the least.

A Balance Sheet

Between 1940 and 1945, SOE delivered by air 47,139 tons of weapons and materiel to the internal resistance in Western Europe. It also sent in 3,352 people by parachute and transported 3,337 others via Hudson or Lysander.[83] But that respectable balance sheet must not obscure two essential facts.

In the first place, until 1944 the movements, networks, and maquis were given short shrift. France received a total of 71,240 shipping containers and 20,220 packages between 1941 and 1944. But only 6.5 percent of the containers and 5 percent of the packages were dropped in the first three years of the conflict.[84] Similarly, the Netherlands—whose misfortunes the SOE leaders were unaware of at the time—received only 544 containers and 74 packages in 1942 and 1943: respectively, 10 percent and 9.5 percent of the overall volume delivered during the dark years.[85] Denmark did not deviate from that norm. Its underground received 26 1/2 tons of materiel between 1941 and 1943, barely 4 percent of the 683 1/2 tons allocated to the kingdom between 1941 and 1945.[86] Nor was Norway an exception. Although more than 165 tons were transported via the Shetland Bus between 1941 and 1943, compared to 174 tons between 1943 and 1945, the contribution made by parachute drops, negligible until 1943 (244 containers), began to grow in 1944, reaching a total of 9,486 shipping containers in the last eighteen months of the conflict.[87]

Second, some countries fared better than others. Over the course of the war, Yugoslavia claimed the lion's share, obtaining 18,154 tons of materiel, more than 38 percent of the total. France was in second place, receiving 12,492 tons (more than 26 percent of the whole). Italy followed with 6,510 tons (4 percent), with the "other countries" dividing up the rest (5,326 tons).[88]

These statistics confirm that, before 1944, the British authorities did not believe it useful to arm the internal resistance. They departed from that principle only in the Balkans, because they did not want to intervene militarily there, given that the Yugoslav partisans had already taken on the task of making life difficult for the Germans. France was relatively well served because of its twofold strategic interest: it was contributing significantly to the Nazi war effort, and it would no doubt provide the site for the coming invasion. On the whole, however, the Allies were stingy toward the underground forces, and they had no intention of making them privy to their secrets. "The Chiefs of Staff were naturally enough unwilling to allow us to know more than was essential of their long-term plans," confirmed Maurice Buckmaster.[89] From that standpoint, the complaints expressed by members of the resistance are valid, but with one qualification: the British position did not stem from political motives. In fact, Churchill did not hesitate to arm the Communist Josip Broz Tito; London supported the Front de l'Indépendance in Belgium and also delivered materiel to the Communists in France, despite the BCRA's reservations. SOE dismissed them, believing it was pursuing, "with but one objective, the ousting of the Hun from France."[90] In July 1942 the Communist organizations operating on French territory received more than thirteen tons sent by RF section.[91]

By contrast, Anglo-American strategists always believed that, in military terms, the partisans counted for little. They therefore avoided arming them, maintaining that the resistance would play a significant role only in synchrony with a landing. In the meantime, they supported only minimally the networks, maquis, and movements. They thus became entangled in a contradiction. As Bickham Sweet-Escott, a veteran of SOE, noted, "unless the Free French achieved spectacular results in the way of acts of sabotage or *coups de main*, we were unlikely to persuade Bomber Command to produce more sorties. Yet without more sorties spectacular action was improbable."[92] It is true that the chiefs of staff were attempting the impossible: to encourage sabotage and keep volunteers from getting discouraged but also to dissuade them from launching premature uprisings. That dilemma, however, did not prevent London and Washington from continuing, if not escalating, their propaganda campaign for Fortress Europe.

CHAPTER XII

Propaganda

I n the eyes of the Anglo-Americans, the war of words turned out to be less costly than the war of weapons and appeared just as decisive in the effort to win hearts and minds, in view of the imminent final struggle. They therefore devoted unflagging attention to it.

The Airwaves

The governments in exile obtained a substantial increase in the number of broadcasts for Fortress Europe. By the end of 1941 the BBC was producing a large volume of programs. The Dutch had an hour and twenty minutes on the air every day, the Belgians thirty minutes, the Norwegians an hour and ten,[1] and the French three hours and forty-three minutes.[2] The length of these slots grew considerably in the months that followed. In the case of France, they rose to more than five hours by September 1942[3] and reached a peak of six hours and thirty minutes in May 1944.[4] Similarly, the Belgians were granted fifty minutes in mid-1942 and an hour and a quarter in early 1943.[5] In March of the same year, the BBC was broadcasting thirty-one hours and thirty-one minutes of programs every day, in twenty-three languages, on its various wavelengths.[6] That was an impressive result, but it must not be overestimated.

"At the time, all the belligerent parties exaggerated the power of radio. It is effective to the extent that public opinion already has sentiments favorable to the Allies. . . . The contribution of radio is to give the events their meaning. It breaks open the prison, amplifies hope, and catalyzes public opinion," the eyewitness historian Jean-Louis Crémieux-Brilhac points out.[7] The BBC, in other words, revived the hope of the oppressed peoples and conferred a meaning on the ordeals they were going through. But it avoided pushing them to act: as we have seen, the British, like the Americans, feared the outbreak of insurrections unconnected to their military operations. The Political Warfare Executive, in charge of propaganda, was thus extremely cautious. In September 1943, for example, it ordered the populations under the jackboot "to avoid premature uprisings, to maintain their underground organizations and with disciplined patience to await the instructions of the Allied High Command."[8] It added in December of the same year: "We have to create and influence a situation in Europe which will at the right time ensure the maximum hindrance to the enemy and the maximum support to our own forces. Timing is therefore a vital consideration. It will be determined by highest Allied authorities with the most accurate appreciation of the morale of the German forces and people at their disposal."[9]

But the BBC was not the only means to influence public opinion in Fortress Europe.

Radio Units

The British authorities increased the number of Radio Units tasked with black propaganda. The use of that procedure may appear surprising, but it had a number of advantages. The British authorities, in suggesting that the unit would broadcast from within the country, escaped the dark suspicion that the propaganda they were sending out served their own interests first and foremost. They also avoided negotiating with the governments in exile, which demanded right of inspection over the contents transmitted to their countries. And, in making every RU the mouthpiece for a specific social or political group, they targeted not an undifferentiated mass audience but precise sectors of the public—Italian royalist officers, French Catholics— whom they hoped to win over. Because the Radio Units aired impassioned views but did not broadcast news, they offered a release, channeling the emotions of people under the jackboot.[10] Because of their status, these units also enjoyed a creative freedom that dismayed the BBC, which was inclined to prefer tradition and conformism. That challenge did not displease Sefton Delmer, who was in charge of black propaganda radio. "I longed to show the BBC the difference between the stodgy news presentation of the old-fashioned journalism to which the BBC bowed down, and the sharp and vivid style of my side of Fleet Street which I hoped to adapt to radio. I wanted to demonstrate the mass appeal of the significant 'human story' until now absent from the air, the technique of 'personalizing' the news," he confided in retrospect.[11] It should be added that the broadcasting costs were lower than those for transmitting over long- or medium-wave radio,[12] especially since, as of 1942, the broadcasts relied on a new transmitter.

The idea of acquiring a transmitting set of unmatched power from the United States was approved on May 17, 1941. Although the price was high—111,801 pounds, 4 shillings, and 10 pence[13]—its power was no less so: Apidistra, as it was called, had a 500-kilowatt capacity, compared to the standard at the time, which was 150 kilowatts. The transmitter was buried under thirty-three feet of dirt and concrete, on the edge of the forest of Crowborough in Sussex, south of London, and a decoy was built a mile away to fool the German air force.[14] The BBC fought tenaciously to gain control of that transmitting set. "That it should be transferred to those rough, vulgar fellows of the 'black' was unthinkable. But after almost four weeks of papers, meetings, and arguments the BBC had been made to give way. Ivone Kirkpatrick had been my chief antagonist. 'Black is all right on short wave' he said with the clipped dogmatic self-assurance of the military man turned diplomat, 'but if you get on the medium wave with all your lies and distortion, you will undermine the whole currency value of British propaganda as a purveyor of truth.'"[15] An agreement was reached on May 15, 1942. The BBC could use the Apidistra as an auxiliary transmitter when it was not in service for black propaganda. But that compromise did not put an end to the controversies, because Apidistra could not only jam enemy airwaves, it could also broadcast, while passing itself off as the enemy's own radio. Should that formidable weapon be used? Fearing that the Germans, in retaliation, might interfere even more with the BBC, the war cabinet ruled out that option but allowed for an exception. During the North African landing, the Allies used it twice in the course of fifteen minutes to suggest that Radio-Rabat had been seized by the Americans. Ever after, they refrained from repeating that glorious feat. In any event, the transmitter began operations on October 13, 1942, and conferred a decisive advantage on the British, augmenting their broadcasting power by 40 percent.[16]

The United Kingdom therefore increased the number of Radio Units. In late 1942 its network covered twelve countries.[17] In 1944 three stations (Radio-Heraus/Vrijschutter, Sambre-et-Meuse, and Blauwvoet) were broadcasting to Belgium and the Netherlands, one (Hjemmefrontens) was transmitting to Denmark,[18] three (La France Catholique, Honneur et Patrie, and Radio-Inconnue) to France, and one (Giustizia e Libertà) to Italy.[19] On March 1, 1942, the RU and PWE offices migrated to Bush House, the building occupied by the European services of the BBC, which fostered the coordination of propaganda by limiting the dispersal of headquarters that had prevailed until that time. "By going to Bush House," noted Bruce Lockhart, director general of the Political Warfare Executive at the time, "we were now able to exercise the policy control, granted to us by the governors of the BBC, over broadcasts to enemy and enemy-occupied countries."[20]

Every station was designated by a letter to indicate nationality: "F" for French, "B" for Belgian, and "W"—insultingly—for "Wops."[21] Each unit worked independently, to avoid conscious or unconscious plagiarism. Imitation would have destroyed the identity of each station and would therefore have undermined the intention presiding over its creation.[22] In addition, the broadcasts were usually recorded in advance, to facilitate the work of the censors but also of the technicians, who, before the advent of Aspidistra, sometimes had to manage simultaneously twenty-three programs broadcast by four transmitters.[23]

The Germans and their allies feared the effects of that radio propaganda, whether white or black. They too set up Radio Units, such as De Gil ("burst of laughter"), a supposedly Dutch unit. Above all, they jammed English broadcasts and severely punished listeners who persisted in their ways. On October 31, 1941, for example, the occupation authorities forbade the French, on pain of imprisonment, from tuning in "broadcasts from British units, foreign or not, engaged in antinational propaganda, in all public or private places."[24] In 1942 listening to foreign radio stations in Norway was a capital offense.[25] To complete that arsenal of repression, the occupation authorities also confiscated radio sets. In Norway in 1941 radios had to be turned over to the local police, "but the German appetite for

plunder could not be restrained and,. . . in August 1942 many of the surrendered sets were confiscated and removed to Germany."[26] France, like
the other countries, was not spared—though it suffered to a lesser degree.
On October 31, 1941, for example, 1,650 sets were taken away from the
residents of Evreux.[27] The enumeration of these sanctions makes it clear
why the Anglo-Americans wished at the same time to resort to leaflets
dropped by parachute.

Leaflets and Newspapers

The British and the Americans learned the hard way the effectiveness of
the decisions made by the occupier. In April 1942 PWE leaders noted that the
jamming of British airwaves, the confiscation of radio sets, the harsh sanctions against listeners to the BBC, and the high cost of radios and spare
parts all reduced the value of radio as a medium.[28] To be sure, the experts
did not overestimate the effects of these measures, which did not prevent
listeners from picking up the BBC. The true danger, they believed, was
that jamming would "break up the BBC's European audience into lonely,
half-informed, small groups or individuals, unprepared for resolute and
effective action," particularly since power outages "limit listening severely
in many places."[29] From that standpoint, parachute drops of leaflets and
newspapers were a particularly appealing option, given that, by 1942, the
RAF had the capacity to turn written texts into a propaganda weapon more
powerful than ever before in Western Europe.[30] Its bombers improved their
parachuting technique, but without mastering all its subtleties. In fact, the
dropping of leaflets had several disadvantages.

First, such missions were particularly unpopular with the RAF. As late
as 1943 the crew had to throw out the leaflets by hand through an opening
in the fuselage. The packages, frequently sucked into the aircraft's slip-
stream, sometimes struck and damaged its tail fins. In addition, the operation required the work of two men, who had to abandon their posts, thereby
threatening the safety of the flight.[31] Loose pages, blown about by the wind,
sometimes got into the cabin and disrupted navigation.[32] Printed matter
was often dropped during bombings. Since the pilots wanted to rid themselves of that chore before moving on to serious matters, they threw them
out at random, very often into deserted regions.[33] In addition, PWE did
not always take distances into account when it set its objectives for pilots.

Vichy was more than nine hundred miles away from Mildenhall air base, northeast of Cambridge, and, as the RAF noted, some regions in the free zone were "as difficult to reach as Czechoslovakia and Italy," though PWE strategists did not seem to realize it.[34] It should be added—though this goes without saying—that leaders in the Royal Air Force believed it was perfectly useless to allocate their precious bombers to such a futile task. In June 1942 A. T. Harris, commander in chief of Bomber Command, noted bluntly: "It seems that . . . the leaflet dropping which is being done will be paid for by a loss of bomb load."[35] Brendan Bracken and Bruce Lockhart did their best to sway him, but to no avail. Harris acknowledged the value of print propaganda, "but he objected strongly to exposing his bomber crews to danger in order to drop what he called 'pieces of bumph.'"[36]

An aggravating circumstance: the dropping of printed matter was imprecise. Packages were thrown out in the daytime from an altitude of about eight thousand feet, at night from twenty thousand.[37] During their long descent, the wind sometimes carried them far from their target.[38] In July 1942 PWE observed that many leaflets landed outside the (admittedly very small) territory of Belgium.[39] Finally, multiple difficulties hampered logistics. The leaflets, once printed, were sent to dozens of squadrons scattered throughout British territory, where they waited for the planes to take off. The wait was sometimes long, and the propaganda could abruptly become out-of-date. What was the point of announcing the landing in Sicily if the island was already captured? And ultimately, logistics took up precious time. For the single month of February 1942, the ad hoc services covered close to twenty thousand miles to deliver the Bomber Command aircraft, and that required substantial material and human resources.[40]

The situation improved over time, however. In the first place, PWE waged a campaign to popularize these missions with RAF crews. It sent letters and dispatched emissaries to sensitize squadron commanders and the managers of the sixty-two air bases to the importance of propaganda.[41] It noted in particular that these sorties did not encroach on strategic bombings, because, as a general rule, they were undertaken by crews who were completing their instruction in Operational Training Units (OTU) or who were just beginning their service in a squadron. Winston Churchill in person emphasized that point in spring 1942.[42] Denmark and Norway were special cases, however. In those countries, Coastal Command took advantage of its reconnaissance flights to drop leaflets and newspapers.[43]

In addition, Captain James Monroe of the U.S. Air Force invented a leaflet bomb that made the use of packages unnecessary. "This was a cylinder of laminated wax paper 60 inches long and 18 in diameter. At an altitude of one thousand feet a fuse destroyed the container and released the leaflets. Instead of drifting for hundreds of miles, as in the early days of RAF leaflet raids, when the leaflets were dropped any old how from doors and bomb bays, the leaflets—eighty thousand to each bomb—scattered over an area of about one square mile."[44] In July 1944 the paper cylinder was replaced by metal, which made it sturdier.[45] Over time, that procedure proved satisfactory, especially since the bombers had guidance systems that, in improving navigation, increased the precision of the drops, as the RAF general staff happily acknowledged in September 1944.[46]

The British also used the balloon system employed during World War I. Simple and cheap (five pounds sterling per balloon), it had the advantage of sparing the lives of RAF crews. The process was rudimentary. A wooden frame held half the cargo in its center, the other half being divided into eight packages hanging from the sides by strings, which were consumed by a slow-burning fuse. Every hour, a package fell. After eight to nine hours in flight, the central package dropped and a fast-burning cord set the balloon on fire. That system had a few drawbacks, however. In April 1942 the British had to suspend manufacture of the devices for lack of rubber. Production resumed in late 1943, when the rubber balloon was replaced by a fabric casing treated with nitrocellulose. In addition, the drops were imprecise. Although the unit responsible could send out two hundred balloons in a night, not all of them reached their objective. During the first half of 1941, 35 percent of the deliveries to France failed, a proportion that reached 75 percent for Belgium and 100 percent for the Netherlands. In April 1941 fifty thousand copies of the *Courrier de l'Air*, originally intended for France, landed in Bilbao, Spain.[47]

To improve the efficiency of that propaganda, PWE constantly demanded that a unit be specifically dedicated to dropping leaflets. In April 1942 it proposed that sixteen Wellington bombers (plus two reserve aircraft) take charge of them, which would have required the work of 120 flight crew members, and 200 to 300 personnel on the ground.[48] PWE renewed that request in 1943 and again in 1944. Bruce Lockhart explained to Arthur Tedder: "As you are well aware the present policy for leaflet dropping by Bomber Command is that, except in special cases, it is incidental to bombing operations. Consequently, our leaflets can only be disseminated when and where operational missions happen to have been planned which are by no means necessarily when and where they are likely to be most effective. In the present situation this policy does not meet the propaganda needs for which I am responsible."[49] Even though Eisenhower's coordinator of Allied air operations had assured PWE that he sympathized with its difficulties,[50] the RAF consistently opposed these requests. To assign a squadron to the task would in no way solve the problems raised by the inaccuracy of the drops or bad weather, he maintained,[51] while at the same time noting that bombing operations had and would continue to have priority.[52]

The Americans, by contrast, rejected these quibbles and devoted considerable resources to the propaganda operations. They assigned a fleet of Flying Fortresses to leaflet air drops. In addition, in each of the six operational squadrons of the Eighth Air Force, two aircraft loaded exclusively with printed matter would dump their cargo while their comrades were shelling Europe.[53]

A Balance Sheet

In any case, the balance sheet was on the whole satisfactory, despite the difficult beginnings. For the first four months of 1942, PWE planned to disseminate 6.5 million leaflets over France, Belgium, and the Netherlands. But the results fell short of expectations in the occupied zone (400,000 parcels out of the 2 million anticipated) and in the free zone (zero out of 2.5 million), in Belgium (76,000 out of a million), and in the Netherlands (51,000 out of a million).[54] In early 1943, by contrast, the Political Warfare Executive could take pride in the progress made. Whereas in winter 1939 the United Kingdom had published only three or four leaflets a month in a single language—German—it was now fielding fifty to sixty titles a month in some ten languages, if not more. In the early part of the war, the average piece of printed material ran half a page; in 1943 it often exceeded forty-eight pages, and its quality had improved substantially. The texts, reduced photographically, contained twenty to forty thousand words within a limited but legible space. Maps, photographs, and graphs made for livelier reading, especially since the black-and-white images were now complemented by five-color rotogravure printing.[55] The publications displayed great variety. A typical parcel dropped over France included, for example, *Le Courrier de l'Air* as well as the *Revue de la Presse libre*. Some leaflets were dedicated to an idea (the Atlantic Charter) or a subject (the landing in North Africa); and there were books as well. Behind the innocuous title *The Role of Vitamins in the Fight Against Malnutrition* was advice for avoiding the STO, while the tantalizing *What a Young Lady Needs to Know* gave a devastating assessment of the first year of German occupation.[56] Modern presses allowed for large and speedy print runs: 480,000 copies an hour for Odhams Press, 110,000 for Waterlow's, and 90,000 for the *Sun* newspaper,[57] whose facilities were occasionally used by PWE. That expansion came at a high price. The cost of the leaflets in 1943 reached the tidy sum of 900,000 pounds.[58]

That sudden improvement in quality was accompanied by a leap in quantity. In 1942, 312 million units were dropped over Europe as a whole.[59] In 1943 the total was 573 million.[60] In all, more than 1.5 billion pieces of printed matter were disseminated during World War II over the Old Continent. Although Germany received the lion's share (757 million, or 50 percent), France was close behind (676 million, or 44.5 percent), with the other countries (Belgium, Holland, and Italy) dividing up a modest 72 million printed items.[61] Although that imbalance generally reflected the priorities of the Allies, who were inclined to give precedence to France and Germany for strategic reasons, it sometimes stemmed from more mundane motives. For example, the might of the German fighter force and antiaircraft system discouraged the RAF from flying over Denmark,[62] which explains why that country received only 6 million leaflets.[63] On the whole, distribution by balloon, though not negligible, played only a marginal role: 95 million leaflets were dropped by that mode, a minimal number representing only 6 percent of the total volume.[64] By contrast, the role played by the Americans proved decisive. Between 1941 and 1945 every resident of Western Europe—man, woman, and child—received on average thirty leaflets. Three-quarters of them had been dropped by U.S. Air Force planes.[65]

The Allies thus allocated considerable resources to propaganda, whether written or broadcast over the radio, intended first and foremost to raise the morale of the captive populations and, secondarily, to impel them to act. Nothing guaranteed, however, that the watchwords conveyed would be heard or, a fortiori, acted on.

CHAPTER XIII

Cadres

A hasty but certainly comforting apprehension of things would suggest that the men engaged in subversive warfare set aside their differences out of respect for the struggle. Keeping their resentments to themselves and forgetting their former quarrels, they made a clean sweep of the past to fight as brothers against the Nazi Hydra. Yet that reassuring vision obscures the passions that inflame men. The struggles for power, the political fevers, the flood of emotions, and the weight of representations all shaped the shadow war as well.

Lofty Spheres

Although plunged into a terrible war and intent on hastening its end, the Allied leaders did not forget the sins of the past. Even as they avoided fanning the flames of discord, they remembered—not without bitterness—their allies' failings and their adversaries' turpitude. The cause of unity, to be sure, dictated that the rancor be cast aside, and this precept was generally followed. Nevertheless, it would return unexpectedly from time to time, no doubt a tribute paid by the superego to the unconscious.

Winston Churchill found it hard to swallow the neutrality policy followed by Belgium, the Netherlands, Denmark, and Norway before the storm. Even while concealing his anger, he could not resist a few jabs at his partners from time to time. For example, in a speech broadcast over the radio on February 9, 1941, he declared: "We saw what happened last May in the Low Countries [i.e., Belgium and the Netherlands]—how they hoped for the best, how they clung to their neutrality, how awfully they were deceived, overwhelmed, plundered, enslaved and, since, starved. We know how we and the French suffered when at the last moment, at the urgent, belated appeal of the King of the Belgians, we went to his aid."[1] Hubert Pierlot immediately leapt to his king's rescue: "That policy has often been attributed to the king of the Belgians, and it is as such that you evoked it. It was, in any case, that of the government, approved almost unanimously by the nation as a whole. It is therefore up to the government to take responsibility for it, and the government could not fail to do so without neglecting an essential duty. It is not my intention to revisit the reasons that led Belgium to follow that policy; but I cannot refrain from telling you that we found it a touchy subject to raise before public opinion in the present circumstances."[2] Churchill tried to placate him: "I cannot conceal from you my own personal belief that if Belgium had adhered to the Allied cause at the outbreak of the war, the whole movement of the French Armies and the whole course of events might have taken an entirely different turn. But as you know, my policy is to look forward and not to look back, and I am sure that any British Government which emerges successfully from this war will do its utmost to right the wrongs which Belgium has suffered."[3]

That quarrel concealed a fundamental conflict: the Belgian exiles were defending the right to exist of the smaller nations, whereas many of the personalities "had a tendency to accuse them of being responsible for the war due to their inability to defend themselves, or of being an obstacle to Europe organising itself in the aftermath of the war."[4]

Similarly, the British placed within a broader perspective the complaints that the Norwegians formulated about the neutrality of Sweden, which was intent on treading lightly when it came to mighty Germany: "Circumstances indeed alter cases, for I suspect that if Norway had been allowed by Hitler to remain neutral she would now be interpreting her own neutrality in favour of Germany in very much the same way as are the Swedes. Indeed, the Norwegians were already doing so in 1939–40 and the fact that they allowed the Germans to use Norwegian territorial waters as a means of getting their ships past the British blockade was what eventually occasioned the 'Altmark' case."[5] The *Altmark*, a German oil tanker supposedly engaged in commercial ventures, was actually transporting 299 captive English sailors. It had found refuge in Norwegian waters, which led the Royal Navy to attack the ship on February 16, 1941, an incident that showed that Norwegian neutrality was a pretense and left a few scars.

In a completely different context, many Whitehall leaders—beginning with the foreign secretary—had little appreciation for the Italians. "Eden was violently anti-Italian. His unpleasant, even humiliating experiences at Mussolini's hands had obviously left very bad memories."[6] Winston Churchill also proved particularly inflexible toward Rome, but not because of the ferocity of Mussolini's regime. In the prime minister's eyes, "Fascism's only crime was the attack on Britain."[7]

The conflict opened the Allies' eyes about the limits of their splendid isolation. Rex Leeper of PWE noted:

The historian who will one day record the events of our time will . . . observe that the British people, one of the most politically mature peoples in the world, failed to understand that they were an integral part of Europe, members of one family who had lived either in peace or at war with one another for centuries past. He will observe that those twenty miles of water which separate us from the Continent created not only a barrier to the invading enemy, but also a barrier to a full understanding of our European responsibilities. He will likewise observe that this lack of a full understanding brought us to the very verge of ruin and destruction in the summer of 1940.[8]

The leaders of the "minor allies" were not to be outdone. To the surprise of the British ambassador to the Netherlands, the Dutch prime minister declared during a luncheon that "the Germans had learned the concentration camp technique from the British habits in the South African War."[9] That caustic remark, invoking the still-raw memory of the Boer War, stunned Neville Bland. On a completely different level, the Dutch authorities refused to recognize the Soviet Union because of the murder of the Romanovs. It was not until July 1942 that they finally dispatched a representative to Moscow.[10] These trivialities were rarely of consequence. But they point to a climate that sometimes turned chilly.

From that perspective, Charles de Gaulle was most certainly the champion of rigidity. Many British criticized his intransigence. The diplomat Herbert Somerville-Smith, for example, reminded Churchill's adviser that the Man of June 18 had "anti-British views" and a "complete lack of discretion in stating them."[11] And it is true that the Rebel did not back down from extreme positions. On September 29, 1942, during a particularly stormy conversation with de Gaulle, one that also included Anthony Eden and René Pleven, commissioner at Foreign Affairs, the British prime minister exploded: "'You claim to be France! You are not France! I do not recognize you as France!' Then, still as vehemently: 'France! Where is France now? Of course I don't deny that General de Gaulle and his followers are an important and honorable part of the French people, but certainly another authority besides his could be found which would also have its value.' [De Gaulle] interrupted him. 'If, in your eyes, I am not the representative of France, why and with what right are you dealing with me concerning her world-wide interests?'"[12]

In the face of such inflexibility, London used the strongest pressure possible to curb wrong-headed thinking. De Gaulle reported:

Without having experienced it oneself, it is impossible to imagine what a concentration of effort, what a variety of procedures, what insistence, by turns gracious, pressing, and threatening, the English were capable of deploying in order to obtain satisfaction. . . . After these manifold influences had been given full play, suddenly silence spread. A sort of void was created around us by the British. No more interviews or correspondence; no more visits or lunches. Questions remained pending. Telephones no longer rang. Those of the British with whom chance brought us nonetheless in contact were sombre and impenetrable. We were ignored, as if for us the page of the alliance, and even that of life, had henceforth been turned. In the heart of concentrated and resolute England, an icy coldness enveloped us.[13]

The defense of sometimes antagonistic interests accounts for these clashes. The "minor allies," even while desiring the defeat of the Reich and the liberation of their countries, also wanted to protect their fellow citizens from the rigors of war, even at the risk of contradicting the Anglo-American strategy. In addition, all parties were thinking of their countries' future, which sometimes led them to privilege political considerations over strategic imperatives, and as a result to dissociate themselves from the positions of London or Washington. For that very reason, the Pierlot government proved to be less inflexible toward the king of the Belgians than did the

British government. "We . . . were convinced of the need to avoid, if possible, the likely dangerous post-war consequences of the conflict with Léopold," Paul-Henri Spaak commented in retrospect. "All four of us were monarchists, albeit for different reasons, and we thought that a constitutional crisis following the liberation could have grave repercussions in Belgium. We thus resolved not to make political capital out of our disagreement with the King."[14] Conversely, de Gaulle always manifested a stony intransigence toward Philippe Pétain, whom he would have liked to see disappear politically. It was a hope that neither Franklin Roosevelt nor Winston Churchill shared (though Churchill was somewhat less adamant). In essence, the historian Martin Conway concludes, "The Allies were trying to win a war; the exile regimes were on the whole much more concerned to win the peace."[15]

Psychological factors played just as great a role as such political considerations. Prominent leaders, once lords in their own countries, had witnessed the defeat and then the occupation of their homelands. As guests of the United Kingdom, they had to bow to censorship before expressing their views on the BBC. Destitute, they begged their mentors for the right to use planes for travel or to be granted materiel to arm their poor legions. In short, they lived in a state of subjection, which constantly reminded them of their misfortunes and of the downfall of their ill-fated homelands, as de Gaulle understood. "Certainly these governments, still deploying the ceremony of authority, made a brave show of serenity. But deep among the anxieties and sorrows in which they were all plunged, each one in shadow lived through his own heart-rending tragedy."[16] That was especially true inasmuch as exile often entailed a painful separation from loved ones.

The tragedy was all the more difficult to bear, given that these men had a front-row seat on the greatness of England at war. Endowed with a charismatic leader, the country had stood firm in 1940 and had pursued its lonely battle against the titan Hitler for a full year. Its population displayed an exemplary public-mindedness, and its vibrant democracy functioned under the falling bombs. The press remained free, and Churchill himself bowed to the exigencies of a Parliament that exerted its rights without compromise. Great Britain stood in striking contrast to a continent where Pétain, Quisling, and the Dutch Nazi Anton Mussert were wreaking havoc. That could only distress and aggrieve the émigré leaders.

These quarrels very often interfered with the development of subversive warfare. SOE's anti-Gaullism led it to support the Carte network, for which it pointlessly sacrificed considerable resources. In addition, it developed a policy of going it alone that limited the efficiency of the French and British secret services, which were more inclined to compete than to cooperate. The watch-and-wait attitude of the Belgian authorities, supported by the British Intelligence Service, handicapped the actions of the Special Operations Executive, at least until 1943. In short, the conflicts reigning within the state apparatus of the various nations and the rivalries between them were more a brake on the resistance than a driving force.

The case should not be overstated, however. Even while making a display of their opposition at times, the powers in exile never broke ranks with London or Washington. All ardently wished for the defeat of Nazi Germany, which prompted them to make the necessary compromises. Moreover, the balance of power prevailed. The "minor allies" had no means to hold out against the British or the Americans, on whom they were materially dependent. The Anglo-Americans were fully cognizant of that advantage. Maurice Buckmaster, head of F section at SOE, recalled, for example: "While we could respect [de Gaulle's] *amour-propre national*, in practice his attitude caused us great inconvenience and disillusionment, for, after all, the means to carry out any operations in occupied France had to be found by the British."[17] De Gaulle himself lucidly assessed his own powerlessness. Before moving to Algiers in 1943, he had considered going into exile in Brazzaville, to flee the banks of the Thames, but he gave up on the idea immediately: "How, from the depths of Africa, communicate with our country, make myself heard by it, influence the resistance? In Great Britain, on the contrary, there are the means required for liaison and information. Again, our diplomatic action upon the Allied governments implies relations and an atmosphere which the English capital offers us and of which, quite obviously, we would be deprived on the bank of the Congo. Lastly, I must keep contact with those of our forces which can be based only in the British Isles."[18]

The marriage between allies, whether of love or convenience, thus withstood the storms.

Public Schools and the Ivy League

Although these ordeals spared the leaders of the special services (SOE and OSS) as well as the architects of propaganda (PWE and OWI), other perils lay in wait for them.

In the first place, they did not all have the same political opinions. The Office of War Information, for example, tended to be composed of proponents of the New Deal, while the Office of Strategic Services was "a stronghold of Republicans."[19] According to the historian Bradley Smith, OSS was not "an organization of doubters or nay-sayers but something more akin to a cross between a Rotary Club and Moral Rearmament."[20] Similarly, the Political Warfare Executive leaned somewhat to the left,[21] SOE to the right.

In the United Kingdom, that political coloring was not a problem a priori, given that Labour and the Tories governed in concert. But it sometimes complicated the operations of the services, when two leaders on opposing sides had to work together. Hence, the "cohabitation" between the Labour Party's Hugh Dalton and the Conservative leaders of SOE was sometimes stormy. As might be suspected, labor relations sometimes suffered as a result of these cleavages. As Robert Bruce Lockhart pointed out: "My Socialist colleagues insisted that, more and more, we were fighting for a better world. I tried to believe them and, when I drove through [the London working-class neighborhood of] Camden Town . . . and saw the long drab rows of wretched houses, my sense of justice was outraged by the inequalities of our social system. But very soon I saw clearly that my friends, whether they realised it or not, were as totalitarian in their hearts as the Germans or the Russians."[22] In the United Kingdom, finally, the organizers of subversive warfare demonstrated a supreme disdain for politicians. "One curious feature of this Woburn organization (which includes many freaks, some genuine antiques, several fakes and a few geniuses) is the almost universal contempt for the professional politician including the ministers," Bruce Lockhart noted in December 1940.[23]

In the United States, political life followed its own course, punctuated by elections—presidential and midterm—during which Republicans and Democrats faced off. OWI prided itself on "not having a Republican on its list of members." Naturally, it was accused "of (i) being semi-Communist and (ii) of existing merely to 'boost' Mr Roosevelt for a fourth term of office."[24] The State Department reproached the service for its indulgence toward Moscow, while OWI had a tendency to call all diplomats "reactionary."[25] These differences undermined both cooperation between the American services and collaboration with the British services. In January 1943 David Bowes Lyon, head of the PWE mission to Washington at the time, noted: "Powerful reactionary elements [exist] in OSS—business and military—which means that on many occasions we shall come into head-on collisions between British and American private interests in trying to work out common efforts at political warfare."[26]

Less anecdotally, ideological biases were suspected of influencing the discourse the Allies addressed to Fortress Europe. At PWE and at the European service of the BBC, many thought that "propaganda had an important contribution to make to victory by raising revolution in the occupied countries." As Bruce Lockhart recalled, "The revolution which the British official envisaged was a pale-pink affair of the British Socialist type. . . . Their instinct told them that Europe was going Left. They saw no reason why it should not go the British way."[27]

That progressivism originated in the first place in individual political preferences. But it resulted as well from the conditions for action, since subversive warfare sometimes led to a reliance on Socialist and even Communist groups. "Like SOE, OSS also had discovered that to produce change in an enemy-occupied territory, one had to depend on people who desired change which meant that Donovan's organization would lean more frequently toward the political left than toward the conservative right."[28] Agents in the field therefore tended to be fairly open-minded. Shying away from sectarianism, they relied on any assistance from the left and right that could help fight Nazism. But the ruling cadres, by virtue of their training and their prejudices, were not always inclined toward ecumenicism.

Such was the case for OSS. The Research and Analysis (R&A) branch, responsible, as its name indicates, for processing data, included a large number of people who had not obtained their positions through family connections but "had received a generous measure of Ivy League education stressing modern scientific research techniques and a belief that elitist higher education harmonized with the interests of the social and political groups who ran the country."[29]

Likewise, the upper echelons of SOE were packed with "senior businessmen and bankers or others aspiring to be such when the war was over." Even so, as Basil Davidson, a veteran of the service pointed out, "SOE's chief aim and job, more and more after 1940, was promoting armed resistance, a work which took SOE straight into the middle of politics: and politics of a special kind. This was the politics of upheaval and protest, of the subversion of conservative order, even of revolution: the kind of politics, in short, that was rightly held in horror by senior businessmen and bankers. They knew absolutely nothing of such matters, having previously regarded them as the business of the police."[30] In fact, many of the cadres had passed through the United Kingdom's elite institutions of learning, Eton or Harrow first, then Oxford or Cambridge—beginning with the two ministers, Dalton and Selborne. They therefore cultivated a kind of chumminess that did not always lead them to embrace with enthusiasm the revolutionary prospects delineated by certain prophets, even those as moderate as Lord Beveridge, who in 1941 was given the task of drawing up a report, *Social Insurance and Allied Services*, that would become the blueprint for the welfare state.

Their culture, moreover, predisposed them to engage in interminable and pointless discussions, which one (anonymous) agent made fun of:

The Chairman apologized for calling the meeting at such short notice but said that the matter was one of urgency, the building was on fire. It appeared that some confidential waste in the basement had been smouldering for some days and had now burst into flames.

Mr. Peewit (SO What) said it was quite clear that the first thing to do was to get a general directive. The charter laid down that . . . it was the business of SO2 to put out fires. It was unfortunate that the Director was in the country but he would be back in a few days.

Mr HS (SO2) said the fire was a large one and he felt very strongly that something ought to be done at once.

Mr Peewit said that there was no doubt that nothing could be done until a general directive had been obtained, no useful purpose would be served by attempting to put out the fire too soon; it might well be that the fire was a large one, but it was necessary to look at these things in their proper perspective. The building was also a large one; he had no doubt that the matter had to be dealt with on a VERY HIGH PLANE, in fact the higher the flame, the higher the plane.

Mr AP (SO2) said he was willing to put out the fire himself without any directive.

Mr Abbey (SO what) said he felt the Committee could not agree to Mr AP assuming this responsibility, there appeared to be some confusion of thought. SO2 seemed to think that the most important thing to do was to put out the fire; this of course was not so; if everybody started putting out fires as soon as they broke out, nothing but chaos and confusion would arise. The most important thing was not to put out the fire but to put it out in the right way; after all, the fire had been burning for several days and he could not see that the loss of a day or two would do any harm.

Mr Peewit said he did not wish to be unreasonable under the charter SO. What was empowered to direct operations on the ground floor, the first, the second and fourth floors, if and when the fire reached the third floor, SO2 could do what they liked. The roof raised a very delicate problem; if, however, the flames did reach the roof—a possibility that he personally did not envisage—he did not think there would be any objection to SO2 taking discreet action.

At this point, the floor collapsed and the Committee, very properly, was precipitated into the flames.[31]

At PWE, by contrast, cadres such as Noel Newsome were eager to welcome the winds of change. His positions, often labeled leftist, earned him reprimands from his superiors. In March 1944 Selborne complained to Anthony Eden about the radio program "The Man in the Street," claiming it engaged in "continuous left-wing propaganda to all Europe, frequently not in line with His Majesty's Government's foreign policy."[32] The broadcast was suspended,[33] but Bruce Lockhart stepped forward to defend it. "If Lord Selborne's contention were right, we should have received complaints from many other sources and, in particular, from the Allied Governments who listen in assiduously to our foreign broadcasts. Such complaints have been remarkably few."[34] On April 30, 1944, the head of the European service of the BBC recommended that his services celebrate May Day with enthusiasm: "Those who for one reason or another are dismayed, or discouraged by apparent indications that, on the eve of victory, reactionary forces are increasing their power and influence among the victors-to-be can and must be reassured by our projection of the vast progressive forces of organized labour inside and outside the Continent, and of liberal and forward looking people in other spheres both here and in the underground liberation movements that we are going forward indeed and not back or standing still after victory."[35]

The Conservative Brendan Bracken, minister of information, was startled. He wrote to Bruce Lockhart: "I have often warned you of the dangers of Mr Newsome's Left mania. And as often I have been promised that a strict control is kept over all his official activities. I ask you to read this directive carefully. It provides all the evidence that FO or Tory MPs could wish for in confirmation of their belief that PWE plans a Left autocracy for Europe after the war."[36]

Bruce Lockhart took up the defense of his subordinate. "Mr Newsome . . . informed me that, if he had any left wing tendencies, he would feel it is his duty to resign. He told me that he had none, that he is, in fact, a traditionalist, and that the Prime Minister had no greater admirer than himself. You may think this strange but I am satisfied that what he says is true and that, whereas you receive evidence of his left-wing tendencies, you are never shown the Russian complaints about his ultra-nationalistic attitude."[37]

In other words, political differences sometimes troubled the working relationship of the leading cadres and influenced propaganda destined for Fortress Europe, though the impact of ideological orientations should not be overestimated. Within OSS, for example, a fairly large minority of officers had no strong commitment to the right or the left. "These men agreed with Donovan that their primary objective should be victory."[38] Political cleavages were thus at work along the fringes, as were essentialist representations of the different peoples described by the secret services.

Representations

To succeed at subversive warfare or develop effective propaganda, the Allied services had to possess a proven knowledge of Western Europe. From that standpoint, the presence within OSS and SOE of cadres who had long lived in the countries for which they were responsible provided a guarantee. Ralph Hollingworth, head of the Danish section, had worked in bicycle sales in Denmark and later served at the British Embassy in Copenhagen. Maurice Buckmaster, head of F Section, had resided in France before the war, first as a journalist for *Le Matin*, then as head of the country's Ford subsidiary. In addition, these men were in regular contact with the foreign employees of the governments in exile, which made them familiar with their culture. Experts from all over Europe, finally, placed themselves in the service of the Allies, favoring the intermingling of cultures. The case must not be overstated, however. Many agents and leaders had only a rough knowledge of the countries where they were operating, which explains the persistence of antiquated stereotypes.

"The national character of the Danes must be taken into consideration. They are by no means revolutionary and their distaste for confusion and disorder is a natural consequence of the pride which they take in the efficiency of their agriculture, industry and education," noted SOE.[39] "The courage of the individual Dane is not impressive, but marching in a flock they can display great qualities," added PWE.[40] In the Netherlands, attention focused on women, because "quite apart from what the women can do themselves as active protagonists, their capacity to influence their menfolk is exceptional. Although the average Dutchman would deny it, Holland is to a large extent matriarchal."[41] In 1942 the British propaganda services lamented the low number of resistance demonstrations, which they attributed to the Dutch character, said to be "conservative and lacking in initiative."[42] In Norway, by contrast, "the people themselves are hardy and independent, strong and individualistic," to a degree not seen elsewhere.[43] "The Norwegians are a proud and frequently a stubborn people. They have an intense and somewhat touchy patriotism," the Americans added.[44]

But the British singled out the Italians for particular attention.

ALWAYS BEAR IN MIND

That Italians have a keen sense of humour
That they are logical
That they are jealous
That they are vain
That they are theatrical
Therefore exploit these faculties in the . . . propaganda.

So advised the Ministry of Information in September 1940.[45] Similarly, the manual prepared under SOE auspices in 1943 was not shy about piling on the stereotypes:

[The Italians] are on the whole sober, hard-working and strong, skilled with their hands . . . and very ingenious at "making things do." . . . Discipline is generally slack, Italians being traditionally "against the Government" and authority. . . . The people are no milk-sops but hot-blooded and quick-tempered, proud of their country and its history and touchy on questions of "honour." They have long been familiar with conspiracy and secret societies, believe in revenge, can be ruthlessly cruel, and use guns and knives instead of fists to settle a quarrel. . . .

As to women, the less you have to do with her [sic], the better. The men are jealous, the code of morals exceedingly strict and "loose women" almost unknown, except in the cities.[46]

These clichés rarely had serious consequences, with two exceptions. First, they reinforced the sense of superiority that some British felt on occasion, which interfered with the relations they maintained with their foreign counterparts. Lord Selborne asserted—quite seriously—that, upon the liberation of the Isle of Beauty in September 1943, British prestige there increased to a baffling degree, and many Corsicans asked that their country be attached to the British Commonwealth.[47] Along the same lines, the subjects of His Most Gracious Majesty manifested a certain paternalism toward their American cousins, as has already been noted. And in the Norwegian sections of SOE established in London and Stockholm, the staff adopted a condescending attitude, a "kindly—but none the less galling—superiority to foreigners." Its members doubted Milorg's capacity to take simple precautionary measures and did not cooperate fully with the movement when collaboration was required: "Norway had the men; Great Britain had the facilities for training, transport and supply and experience drawn from a wider field; united they stood; divided they would have fallen."[48] Second, stereotypes impaired judgment. The harsh view of the Italians, for example, did not facilitate the dialogue that London established with Brindisi, the provisional headquarters of the Italian government, after the fall of Mussolini and the conclusion of the armistice in September 1943.

Grinds for Glory

On a more modest scale, SOE and OSS dispatched agents to the Continent to set up networks, support the underground groups, or disseminate propaganda.

In late May 1944 the Special Operations Executive employed nearly 10,000 people—including 1,847 officers, 471 noncommissioned officers and enlisted men, and a female auxiliary staff of 1,558. Agents were a relatively small percentage—1,951 individuals, or some 20 percent—the overwhelming majority of whom were deployed to Europe (1,599), with the rest (352) serving in the Far East.[49] The Political Warfare Executive, for its part, enlisted 1,200 people in 1944.[50] The Office of Strategic Services, a late-comer on the scene, fielded a team of more modest size. In late August 1943 it had 1,284 members, not counting the staff based in Washington. Of that group, 537 worked in North Africa and 239 in Europe, with the remainder dispersed throughout the world, especially in Asia.[51] A slight but significant difference distinguished London from Washington: among the British, the civilian workforce was dominant, while on the American side, military personnel prevailed, constituting 80 percent of the staff.[52]

The geographical distribution of missions was uneven. Of 4,223 agents dispatched to Europe during World War II, 1,770—that is, 42 percent—went to France. Norway (542) and Italy (540) came next, with Belgium (198), the Netherlands (120), and Denmark bringing up the rear.[53] The men were primarily deployed beginning in 1944. SOE sent 86 agents to the Netherlands in 1944 and 1945, compared to 55 the three previous years.[54] And though the numbers were evenly balanced in Denmark (29 agents sent out between 1941 and 1943, compared to 28 for 1944–1945), they were clearly lopsided in Norway (66 arrived by parachute in 1941–1943, compared to 109 between 1944 and 1945).[55]

These differences reflected, in the first place, the Allies' strategic priorities. Because the Anglo-Americans believed that the resistance would play an important role in connection with the landing, they gave precedence to France, while intensifying their efforts for Europe as a whole from 1944 on. From that point of view, the surge in the deliveries of weapons and in the dropping of agents logically went hand in hand.

Other factors came into play. In relative terms, Belgium, the Netherlands, and Denmark were poorly served, since the small size of their territories and the aggressiveness of the German defense system complicated the task of Allied airpower. Conversely, the proximity of the Swedish border to Norway, the expanse of Norwegian territory, and the length of its coast made that country relatively accessible to SOE and OSS, which explains the relatively high proportion of agents deployed there.

Although OSS and SOE fielded a respectable number of personnel, recruitment remained a nagging problem from the beginning to the end of the war. By preference, Baker Street enlisted foreign nationals, who, because they spoke the language of the country and knew its customs, blended more easily into life underground. But the pool was small. In 1941 the British services estimated that some 5,000 French were serving in the Free French Naval Forces, about 1,000 in the army, and 600 in the RAF; added to this total were 10,213 civilians, two-thirds of whom had not declared any allegiance to de Gaulle.[56] Two years later, Great Britain was home to only 5,349 Danes (including 1,775 women)[57] and 14,781 Belgian refugees, 63 percent of them women and children.[58] And not all émigrés intended to volunteer for subversive warfare. Some wanted to fight openly; others wished to serve their country, not Uncle Sam or the British Crown—a tendency encouraged by their governments, which were anxious to hold onto their best people.[59] Finally, even supposing they had opted for SOE or OSS, nothing indicated that the volunteers would be accepted.

The selection criteria targeted a combination of physical and intellectual attributes. For agents sent out on missions, OSS privileged the qualities of a secret agent, and secondarily, skills in radio communications.[60] It turned to the best academics in the country to analyze the data. The different profiles were easily distinguishable. "If one could spot the Research and Analysis staffer by the thick glasses and library pallor so common to the group, one could spot the Special Intelligence staffer by the Ivy look."[61] SOE, for its part, verified the language skills of the volunteers and delved into their motives and character, to avoid impulsive temperaments. If the test results were positive, an investigation was done by MI 5. The candidate was again interviewed; then, at a third meeting, either accepted or rejected.[62]

As a general rule, an ardent patriotism and the desire to combat the Nazi plague motivated the candidates to apply. Nancy Wake, a young Australian, had gone to Austria before the war to observe the misdeeds of Nazism with her own eyes. "It was in Vienna that I saw several groups of Jews being persecuted. I was horrified and revolted by the public scenes. People have often asked me how I came to work against the Germans. It was easy. It was in Vienna that I formed my own opinion of the Nazis. I resolved there and then that if I ever had the chance I would do anything, however big or small, stupid or dangerous, to try to make things more difficult for their rotten party. When war came to France, followed by the Occupation, I found it quite natural to take the stand I did."[63] Other motivations could also come into play, especially a taste for risk taking and adventure. As a result, SOE and OSS often recruited free spirits with strong wills. On the flip side, obedience to the chain of command was not necessarily their foremost quality. As Noreen Riols points out, "They were not military geniuses, who fitted neatly into the British forces' organization charts. They were individualists, self-reliant people who preferred to operate singly rather than in large groups, happy to be their own master and make their own decisions, rather than being obliged to obey orders made by others, which they often considered futile."[64]

Idealism was sometimes combined with more mundane concerns. In 1944 the Norwegian authorities decided that the Shetland Bus, under civilian control until that time, would henceforth be entrusted to the Royal Navy, which would deprive crew members of the bonuses they had been receiving. Before the operating season began, the junior officers and the men who served on its three boats signed a petition demanding that one pound sterling for every day of navigation be paid to them; otherwise they would submit their resignations. The administration flatly refused. The sailors, recognizing that they had been led astray, put to sea once more "with as much energy and courage as previously."[65]

The agents, once recruited by the special services, were sent to receive training. SOE did not skimp on resources. It ran forty-one training schools in England and Scotland during the war and trained 5,766 men and women in them.[66] During a first two- to four-week session, the recruit might receive basic physical training in Wanborough Manor, near Guilford, or in Inchmery, not far from Southampton, combined, beginning in June 1943, with psychological tests and interviews.[67] "I remember that some questions were so indiscreet that one day I sent my examiner packing, even though he was a colonel," related Jacques Poirier, a member of F section.[68] These sessions toughened up the novices and also eliminated the least promising recruits. Those selected then left for Arisaig, Scotland, for even more demanding paramilitary training. "We learned to manage on our own and to fight, even with hand weapons. I learned 'silent killing,' how to sabotage train tracks, trains, the whole panoply of the saboteur," commented Poirier.[69] Among the instructors at the Hertfordshire school were "Captain Fairbairn and Sykes, two ex-officials of the Shanghai Police, whose subject was Silent Killing. Sykes had many methods to impart. They were all long, complicated, and hard to remember, but each of them ended with the phrase: 'and then kick him in the testicles.'"[70] Parachute training later took place at Ringway, the Manchester airfield. There volunteers did four or five jumps, one of them at night. A final session was held in a manor in Beaulieu, not far from Southampton. It taught exclusively the rules of underground life: how to conceal one's identity, elude a tail, withstand an interrogation. "None of it was easy, because the instructors readily got caught up in it, and, sometimes disguised as Nazis, did not hesitate to give us a very realistic idea of what awaited us."[71] Ordeals and tests, however, did not guarantee that the agent would hold out if arrested. "Patriotism and loyalty? Of course. But who is to say that these will not fade under torture and turn the most steadfast operative into the most dreaded of all espionage weapons, the double agent?"[72]

Taking the Plunge

After a few days or a few weeks, the newly trained agents were taken to their departure airfield. Aircraft were loaded an hour and a half before take-off, so that, in case of emergency, the freight could be modified. During that time, the agents were dressed for their mission.

> Their ankles were bandaged to cushion the shock on landing, and they were helped into their cumbersome flying suits. They were like an enormous eider-down, because inside the planes it was not only dreadfully noisy, but also terribly cold. The suit was very heavy since there were about twenty pockets containing a trowel with which to bury their parachute and flying suit on arrival, a small compass, maps of the area for which they were destined, a first aid kit, emergency rations and, for the men, a hand gun and a dagger. Women agents rarely carried guns, though, like the men, they were given a sharp double-edged knife—for silent killing, in case their grip on an enemy throat was not strong enough.[73]

Every "Joe," since that was their nickname at the airfields, also received an L tablet of cyanide for committing suicide, six B tablets of Benzedrine to keep them awake, and six K tablets as a sleep aid.[74]

U.S. Army medical services, alarmed by how freely the cyanide tablets were distributed, cracked down on the practice. If they were misused or if the fact that OSS was issuing them came to be known, Lieutenant-Colonel Sylvester Missal warned, "the resulting publicity would be a serious violation of security. It would make a good newspaper story, but it would be poor advertising for the OSS. Consequently, only those individuals who are judged responsible and capable of handling such dangerous drugs are permitted to draw them and even they are cautioned as to the use they are to be put."[75] That said, several agents refused to accept the poison, believing they risked committing suicide needlessly;[76] others declined the ration of rum generously offered. Were the services doping their men unbeknownst to them? "Frankly, I have often thought that some dope must have been put in my food for, never before, was I so eager to jump. Of course, I do not expect anyone to answer this question," noted Lieutenant Maurice Basset (Ludovic), who was sent over Nangis, France, on the night of April 10, 1944.[77]

The agents tended to be dropped in small groups rather than solo. Every group brought along a radio operator, a transmitter, a code, a table indicating frequencies, and the schedule for liaisons with London. "Each set had its own code name. The names of rodents seemed to be chosen for the sets in Norway, of vegetables for the Dutch sets, and so on. By the beginning of 1942 there was a large filing cabinet in Frank Nelson's office containing these messages. It was labelled 'Birds and Rabbits.'"[78] Then the plane took off. From the B-24s, the agents were dropped at a speed of 125 miles per hour, at an altitude between 500 and 1,000 feet, 800 feet being considered the ideal.[79] The novice jumped first, experience having shown that the best-trained recruits were the least reluctant to leap into the void.[80] Once they had landed, the agents shed their parachutes, which they buried. Then they began their missions.

Things sometimes went awry. Agents under stress might take the wrong plane and land at a site where they were not expected. If their luggage had been put on the right aircraft, their mission could turn catastrophic. In addition, the traffic controllers on the bases were sometimes ineffective or indifferent. Finally, parachute drops did not always take place at the proper altitude; the plane might be too high or too low.[81] But though several agents died or broke bones, safety rapidly improved, and accidents became increasingly rare over time. The greatest perils loomed when the mission in hostile territory began.

In theory, the agents had a cover story, false papers, and clothes that were sufficiently threadbare to suggest that, like their fellow citizens, they were subject to the harsh discipline of rationing. But the proper precautions were not always taken. For example, the quality of the civilian clothes manufactured in Great Britain was too high, which led SOE to demand that the tailors, rather than give them a Continental cut, make sure they looked worn.[82] The false papers were also sometimes defective. The identity cards issued to Lauwers and Taconis, for example, included in their watermark two royal lions following each other instead of facing each other; and the coins given to the two men, who were parachuted into the Netherlands, had just been withdrawn on the order of the Nazi authorities.[83]

The secret services made sure to familiarize their agents with local customs and practices. "As Americans operating on the continent one of the first things we had to teach our operatives was how to 'eat continental' without shifting the knife and fork from hand to hand with each mouthful of food."[84] But not all customs could be taught. A team sent into Sardinia in December 1942 was promptly uncovered. One detail did them in. Pisano and Gabriel had accosted a shepherd to ask him their way. "In that region nobody would approach a shepherd in charge of his flock and the shepherd consequently reported having been accosted by strangers—and the hunt was up."[85] The greatest perils, however, rarely arose from such errors: it was the infiltrated agents who dealt the harshest blows to the clandestine agents, occasioning an arrest that too often led to torture, the concentration camp, or death.

The Great Game?

Some agents went through these ordeals with an indomitable courage, if not good cheer. For these young adults, life continued to assert its claims. The agents Pessac, Forman, Le Tac, Varnier, and Cabard, after dynamiting the Pessac power plant, "set out for Spain at their leisure; they got through a quarter of a million francs . . . in two months, and left a trail of broken glass if not broken hearts behind them."[86] With money plentiful, SOE and OSS envoys lived it up, even while accomplishing their missions with determination.

Others, by contrast, could not withstand the terrible pressure they were enduring. One agent, Steeno, having returned from the Borzoi mission in Belgium via Geneva, struggled to recover from the ordeal he had been through and, at the Brixham clinic in 1943, displayed

> symptoms of a nervous disorder. He is highly anxious, especially in the evening, and cannot be alone; he is very voluble, talking a great deal about his expedition. . . . Above all, he is haunted by the idea of the Gestapo and tells of his incessant fear of being followed and of

the difficulty of crossing the borders. He explains Gestapo methods and some tortures; says that it is impossible for him to speak of the others; that those who are subjected to them go mad or die as a result. . . . Steeno's remarks are characteristically incoherent. All his accounts are extremely disjointed. He is very excitable, declaring he wants to go back and will return in three months. He has very morbid ideas and also often repeats that he cannot forget those who have been killed, he wants to join them, takes out photos, etc. The friends who knew him before he left have found him unrecognizable.[87]

Likewise, two men were parachuted into France in April 1944, but one of them, Cyril, could not endure the demands of life underground. Placed on a farm, he refused to come out from under his bed. "That's where he is, all the time," the farmer lodging him told Roger Landes of SOE. "Just like a dog. I have been tempted to give him the dog's bowl under there for his meals. He seems to be out of his mind." The agent was later hidden in a bistro. "But the sight of the German uniforms entering the café beneath his window was enough to drive Cyril under the bed for several hours each day. He locked himself in his room, never came out, and refused to open the door when Roland or 'Luc' came to visit him." Cyril was ultimately exfiltrated via Spain.[88]

Agents, subjected to the pressures of underground action, were often afflicted by such pathologies. "Most agents when they return from the Field seem to show some degree of emotional disturbance, some of it normal and some of it pathological in nature. Mild cases complain of sudden and inexplicable fatigue and a sense of aimlessness. A severe case shows gross tremor, tension, marked egocentricity and irritability with varying degrees of failing memory." The anonymous author, a true expert on the secret services, continued: "I have furthermore been impressed in the past by the compensatory over-talkativeness of the agent when he returns from the Field. This has, in some cases, even led to security problems. . . . This over-talkativeness is but an expression of a disturbance of emotional balance—a disturbance which is to be expected in view of the considerable strain they have undergone." He added that many of the returning agents had an exaggerated sense of their own importance and that problems had arisen in the past when that symptom had been overlooked. In conclusion, he noted that nothing had been done to treat these agents: the BCRA's system, which had allowed them "to rest and worry at their own discretion until their condition deteriorates," was, he said, deplorable.[89]

The leaders, for their part, tended to succumb to burnout, which sometimes occasioned depressive episodes. Winston Churchill, for example, was frequently overcome by discouragement. "I am an old and weary man. I feel exhausted," he confided to Harold Macmillan in June 1944, even as victory was on the horizon. "Mrs. Churchill said, 'But think what Hitler and Mussolini feel like!' To which Winston replied, 'Ah, but at least Mussolini has had the satisfaction of murdering his son-in-law.'"[90] Frank Nelson, also exhausted, opted for retirement. Illnesses with a psychosomatic component were not unusual: Robert Bruce Lockhart's eczema was so severe that he had to take a month's leave in April 1943.[91] Many men drowned their troubles in alcohol, beginning with the crews that parachuted men over occupied Europe. At the end of a difficult mission lasting between five and eight hours, they would go to the mess, where a doctor administered "a two ounce medicinal ration of whiskey."[92] Bruce Lockhart also noted in his diary in September 1940: "I am drinking far too much—like most people in Whitehall these days. The ministers are no better; Dalton . . . drinks hard and has a particular liking for brandy; Brendan is rarely completely sober after 11 p.m., and even Eden takes a man's full share in the evening. War effect on nerves, I suppose."[93]

Although subversive warfare was sometimes exhilarating, most often it was a terrible ordeal, especially for the agents sent to Western Europe, where they risked their lives. "Many went into enemy territory not once, but several times, and lived to slip quietly back into the everyday world of peace. Some served with high distinction only to end in a twilight zone of insanity. Some never came back."[94]

CHAPTER XIV

Minor Maneuvers, Major Policies

B ritish and American leaders often swore that they had not intervened in the internal affairs of the Western European countries.
"The British Government cannot propose to Italy a different form
of government, since that would be regarded as interference and resented,"
wrote Duff Cooper, minister of information at the time, to Anthony Eden.[1]
General Henry Maitland Wilson, supreme Allied commander at the Italian front, claimed that the policy of the Allies "is to guarantee to the Italian people the free choice of their own Government and Institutions and
to maintain strict neutrality in all internal Italian Political matters."[2]

These assertions do not stand up to analysis, however, as the case of Italy
demonstrates. The historian Norman Kogan sums things up: "From the
time in the late summer or early autumn of 1943 when King George of
England sent a letter to Victor Emmanuel of Italy promising support for
his shaky throne, to February 1946 when the referendum was suggested as
the best way to settle the institutional question, the British government
intervened in what were supposedly internal Italian issues."[3]

In effect, London and Washington meddled in national politics in the
name of three imperatives. First, they set out to have at their disposal
authorities whose legitimacy would be strong enough to ensure that the
internal resistance would obey their instructions and align themselves with
their strategies. Second, they wanted these authorities to take control immediately upon liberation, to avoid chaos and maintain law and order. They

preferred, finally, that the governments emerging from the storm of war respect and even serve their interests rather than opposing them. These imperatives prompted the United States and Great Britain to keep a close watch. Three countries—France, Denmark, and Italy—held their attention, though for different reasons.

The Algiers Conflagration

France had been living under Philippe Pétain's iron rule since July 1940. For a long time, London and Washington believed that the Vichy regime would ultimately come over to their side. Winston Churchill gradually came to see this was a vain fantasy; still, he did not ask that British propaganda attack the Victor of Verdun. As late as July 1942 SOE believed that such a strategy would be a mistake. "There is evidence of widespread feeling in France that the Marshal, whatever lip services he has found it necessary to give the collaborationist adepts, has in fact been unwavering in his refusal to give up the important assets at his disposal: the fleet and the North African ports."[4] Franklin Roosevelt shared that opinion. He was persuaded that the French troops stationed in the Maghreb would greet the arrival of their liberators with cheers.

The question of who should be in charge remained theoretical until 1942. But on November 8 the Anglo-Americans landed on the banks of the Maghreb, an action that reshuffled the cards. To whom should they hand over the keys to power? Washington opted for General Henri Giraud, who, in the dark hours of 1940, had not proven unworthy. In 1942 he had made a stunning escape from the Königstein Fortress in East Prussia, where he had been held prisoner; even while assuring the marshal of his profound respect, he clearly rejected the collaboration in which the French State had been entangled since the meeting with Hitler at Montoire. Courtesy of Marie-Madeleine Fourcade's Alliance network, Giraud was therefore transported by submarine to Gibraltar, before being taken to Algeria. The situation looked extremely promising, but the unexpected presence of Admiral François Darlan suddenly turned the situation on its head.

Darlan, the Vichy regime's number 2 man, had supported collaboration. He even led France to the banks of the Rubicon, by undertaking negotiations on military accords with the Reich in spring 1941. Domestically, he had supported the regime's choices, toughening the Statut des Juifs (anti-Jewish legislation) in June 1941, persecuting republicans and Communists, and hunting down resistance fighters and Gaullists without fail. On November 5, 1942, he crossed the Mediterranean to keep watch at the bedside of his ailing son Alain. After wavering for a long time, he rallied behind the Anglo-Americans, who, on November 13, appointed him high commissioner in Africa.

The Americans' calculations were not without foundation. Powerless to induce the French fleet to cast off from Toulon—it scuttled all its craft, except for five submarines—Darlan ordered a cease-fire in Morocco and Algeria, which limited Anglo-American losses. But he did so only on November 10, which is to say, after three days of battles. On the 23rd, he also won the allegiance of Admiral Pierre Boisson, governor general of French West Africa, who brought with him his piece of the empire. Giraud also organized a government, forming an imperial council that included—in addition to the governors and colonial residents—General Giraud, General Jean Bergeret, and Henri d'Astier de la Vigerie, a royalist resistance fighter. On November 22 the American authorities spelled out the terms of their recognition in the Clark-Darlan accords, guaranteeing the integrity of the empire. The police, the administration, and the laws would remain French; in return, the tricolor forces would support the Allied troops.[5]

That "Darlan deal" immediately caused an outcry. Although the American press supported its president, the British newspapers went on the attack. They were followed by the Foreign Office, SOE, and PWE.[6] In addition, during a trip to the United States, Trygve Lie, the Norwegian minister of foreign affairs, expressed his dismay that personalities as discredited as the admiral were supported in that country, an objection received coolly by Cordell Hull, head of the State Department. Hull seemed to consider "any objection to his government's policy as a personal attack on himself; and a reference by Mr. Lie to the services which General De Gaulle had rendered to the Allied cause by his attitude in the year 1940 had provoked a tremendous harangue from Mr. Hull on the services which the US Government had rendered at the same time—which was of course quite beside the point."[7]

The agreement was shocking in moral terms because it rewarded the most shameless opportunism. It also created a troubling precedent. In choosing to deal with an officially recognized Vichyist, the Allies might be led in the future to negotiate with figures who were just as despicable, beginning with the Italian Fascists. The example set was a source of confusion for the populations in Fortress Europe and demoralized the resistance fighters, who were outraged by that immoral realpolitik. Darlan's rise to power, warned Selborne, had led to "violent reactions on all our subterranean organizations in enemy occupied territories, particularly in France where it has had a blasting and withering effect."[8] Meanwhile, experts at PWE scoffed at the inexperience of their American allies: "How green are our Allies," they snickered, a sly allusion to the best seller *How Green Was My Valley*, which Richard Llewellyn had published in 1939.[9] On November 17 Roosevelt reassured everyone that the admiral was only a "temporary expedient," but to no avail: the damage was already done.

The situation reached an unexpected denouement. On December 24, 1942, a young royalist, Fernand Bonnier de la Chapelle, executed the admiral. Had he been activated by the Gaullist services? Nothing in the sources suggests so. "The least improbable hypothesis would be that of a plot of Algiers activists led by monarchists."[10] In any event, Darlan left the stage, and Giraud made his entrance.

Giraud Versus de Gaulle

On December 26, 1942, the army general succeeded the admiral of the fleet. Assuming the title of civilian and military commander in chief, Giraud retained his predecessor's political staff and the Vichyist laws in the liberated empire. The French State's anti-Semitic measures were not abrogated; the interned Communists remained in their jails; and the Gaullists guilty of having supported the Allies during the landing were thrown into them. Indeed, though opposed to collaboration, Giraud remained a dyed-in-the-wool Vichyist who endeavored to combine "a vigorously anti-German position and a continued allegiance to the values of National Revolution."[11] Giraud, "a general with long training in desert affairs, and inclined to simplification," as Jean Monnet, his political adviser of the time, coyly noted,[12] did not exactly distinguish himself by his progressivism or his political savvy. As the British diplomat Harold Macmillan summed it up, "he was stupid and vacillating, always 'preferring the discomforts of a fence to the horrors of a decision.'"[13]

Because the absence of democratization upset the Americans, Giraud had to make concessions. He ultimately released the twelve Gaullists who had been imprisoned in December 1942, then the twenty-seven Communist legislators interned at the Maison-Carrée prison. On March 14, 1943, Giraud, duly chaperoned by Jean Monnet, whom the Americans had sent as a mentor, would even deliver what he called—not without naïveté— the "first democratic speech of [his] life."[14] His remarks dismayed his most reactionary collaborators. Three of them—Lemaigre-Dubreuil, Bergeret, and Rigault—immediately resigned. Giraud also translated words into acts. He reestablished the municipal councils dissolved by the Pétainist regime and abrogated several Vichyist laws—the Charte du Travail (Work Charter), for example. But he refused to restore French citizenship to the Jews, which the Crémieux decree, declared invalid by Pétain, had granted them in 1870.[15] Public opinion, both French and international, judged his concessions inadequate, and Giraud had to agree to negotiate with de Gaulle, a prospect that the Anglo-Americans contemplated without enthusiasm.

Although Winston Churchill had supported Charles de Gaulle in 1940, he had no intention of sacrificing the American-British alliance to defend him. And Franklin Roosevelt was always hostile to the Man of June 18. In his eyes, realpolitik required remaining on good terms with Pétain. To that end, he had dispatched to Vichy an ambassador, a close friend of his, William Leahy, whose admiral's stars were supposed to win over François Darlan. The U.S. president then supported Henri Giraud, quite simply because the general's docility served American interests and guaranteed that their strategy would not be contested.[16] In addition, Roosevelt believed that de Gaulle, unanointed by any democratic process, was a dictator in training.

For French people living today, fascinated as they are by de Gaulle's legend, it can only be disappointing or disturbing that the Anglo-Americans haggled over recognition of the great man. But the situation seemed less brilliant when viewed from London or Washington. Despite the valor and zeal of the Free French troops, the modesty of their contribution to the Allied war effort was at odds with the excesses of Gaullist propaganda. The British writer H. G. Wells found it annoying:

[De Gaulle's] boats patrolled the oceans and sank hostile submarines. "Ses avions protègent les convois britanniques" [His planes protected the British convoys] and bombarded German towns. Finally we see the de Gaullists in North Africa "déjouant complètement les plans de Rommel" [completely thwarting Rommel's plans] with no acknowledgment to any British or American cooperation—and with that the picture book concludes.

This is the nationalist bunkum upon which a new generation of French children are to be trained for the great day of the de Gaullist plebiscite.[17]

An aggravating circumstance: de Gaulle had been unable to rally the empire as a whole between 1940 and 1942. Worse, some of his initiatives had damaged American-British relations. In December 1941, for example, the Gaullists had regained control of the archipelago of Saint Pierre and Miquelon, previously under Vichyist authority, with the support of London but the disapproval of Washington. In fact, the United States had made a pledge to the Latin American countries to discourage any transfer of sovereignty or of possessions, any control of territory in the Western Hemisphere, a promise that was undercut by de Gaulle's feat.[18] The Rebel, moreover, did not look like a paragon of progressivism, at least in 1940–1942. "I see an uncomfortable parallel between our backing of General De Gaulle and our support of [the reactionary generals] Korniloff, Denikin and Wrangel [during the Russian Revolution] in 1918," Bruce Lockhart noted in January 1942.[19] In the eyes of many Britons, the liabilities far outweighed the assets, as Macmillan remarked. "We could not understand why the Free French had been greeted with bullets and shells instead of with cheers wherever they had gone, as at Dakar or Syria. Why was de Gaulle thought a traitor and not a saviour?" wondered the British resident in North Africa.[20]

Churchill, speaking before the House of Commons, which met in secret committee on December 10, 1942, gave free rein to his anger. "The House must not be led to believe that General de Gaulle is an unflattering friend of Britain. . . . I cannot feel that de Gaulle is France, still less that Darlan and Vichy are France. France is something greater, more complex, more formidable than any of these sectional manifestations." And he concluded: "I could not recommend you to base all your hopes and confidence upon him, and still less to assume at this stage that it is our duty to place, so far as we have the power, the destiny of France in his hands."[21] The historian Jean-Louis Crémieux-Brilhac notes: "That tirade would be kept secret for twenty years. Churchill omitted it from all the editions of his speeches published during his lifetime. The text was accessible after de Gaulle's death, but, fifty years after he delivered it, it still does not appear in the folder of the British archives where it is referenced."[22]

In short, mistrust dominated, particularly since some French clouded the issue, whether consciously or unconsciously. Granted, several eminent personalities—beginning with Léon Blum—publicly supported de Gaulle. But others shamelessly criticized him. Some, motivated by a fanatical anti-Gaullism, spewed their venom. The diplomat Alexis Léger, better known by his pen name, Saint-John Perse, explained to Winston Churchill in December 1942 that Charles de Gaulle was hostile to both Great Britain and the United States. Even while feigning Communist sympathies, Léger added, de Gaulle had Fascist tendencies. These words were music to the prime minister's ears. Once again, they corresponded to his own feelings, as he admitted to Anthony Eden. "I am increasingly convinced that I ought to write de Gaulle a letter telling him that in consequence of his behavior we cannot any longer recognize the validity of the letters exchanged between us."[23]

More surprisingly, proven Gaullists sometimes betrayed both the letter and the spirit of their mentor's law. For example, in April 1942 Raoul Aglion, though a delegate for the general and Free France in the United States, recommended that his American contacts maintain their ties to Philippe Pétain. "He thought that our position would be much stronger with the people of France, and the cleavage between the Vichy Government and the French people much greater, if we stayed on until Vichy forced the break. He felt that the collaborationist French would have a much freer hand if we were out of the way and that our presence there, even with Laval in, would be a serious deterrent."[24] The delegate repeated himself in January 1943: "If it could only be made clear to De Gaulle, said M. Aglion, that there was no longer any chance of his becoming 'Chief of State' [sic] and if at about the same time an opportunity were offered for him to resume a high military command in the French forces and regain therewith the recognition and esteem of the French military leadership, it was entirely possible that, after some further mental struggle, he would accept such a solution, first with a feeling of relief and then of satisfaction."[25]

The hostility that some of the Allies felt for General de Gaulle did not stem, therefore, from an irrational attitude, blind as it may appear in retrospect. But the blinkered policy Giraud pursued led to an impasse, as the Allies realized before long.

Negotiations

Although de Gaulle had no intention of negotiating with Darlan, he agreed to compromise with Giraud—but on his own conditions. In January 1943 the two men met in Anfa, in the suburbs of Casablanca, at the instigation of the Anglo-Americans. But their chilly discussion did not bear fruit; the two generals confined themselves to signing a vague joint declaration. True, they were opposites in every way. Giraud was pursuing "a single aim, victory," and pretended to take no interest in political questions. De Gaulle, by contrast, intended to restore France's prestige, so that it could sit at the table of the victors. Political cleavages intensified that fundamental opposition. The Königstein escapee, who was close to Action Française, remained a steadfast Vichyist; the Man of June 18, intrinsically democratic, was more open to the winds of change.[26] After long bargaining sessions adroitly conducted by General Catroux, a compromise was hammered out. On May 30, 1943, de Gaulle landed in Algiers, and on June 3 he assumed the cochairmanship of the Comité Français de Libération Nationale (CFLN), alongside his rival. In addition to the two generals, five men sat on the committee: the diplomat René Massigli and the Socialist André Philip for the Gaullist camp; Jean Monnet and General Alphonse Georges for the Giraudist camp; and General Georges Catroux, who was approved by both sides.

That tortuous route to the obvious confirms that the Anglo-Americans intervened over and over again in French domestic affairs. Granted, they had powerful means at their disposal with which to impose their views. De Gaulle was banned from the BBC airwaves on November 21 and censored on December 3.[27] He could not move about freely—go to Algiers, for example. Yet the material assets brandished by the Allies proved ineffectual. General Giraud's mediocrity and the Vichyist measures he took quickly alienated his supporters, while the French internal resistance inveighed against the persistence of Pétainism in the liberated territories. In addition, the Anglo-American leaders, living within a democratic system, had to take public opinion into account. The populations disputed their leaders' choices and noisily let them know it, through the press and through legislators. Finally, part of the state apparatus rebelled, for moral as well as pragmatic reasons. The supposedly realist policy followed in Algiers proved counterproductive: it demoralized the resistance fighters, who were disgusted and outraged by such maneuvers. It also put the Allies in an awkward position: How could they preach the crusade against evil and at the same time have dealings with cynical opportunists or military reactionaries? In the end, the second-rate, morally shocking schemes hatched in the Maghreb sun failed. Far from favoring union, they sowed discord and undermined the joint war effort. All in all, that experience offered valuable lessons. Nothing suggested, however, that these lessons would be remembered and that the Allies would refrain elsewhere from repeating the same mistakes.

Neutrality Danish Style

Unlike the confusion in Algiers, the situation prevailing in Denmark was notable for its simplicity. It should be remembered that, though the kingdom was defeated by the Reich in under four hours in 1940, it retained both its government and its king. For many long months, Great Britain and the United States put up with that situation and refrained, for the time being, from fanning the flames. As the Foreign Office explained in August 1941: "The time has not yet come when it would be to our advantage that a situation should be produced where the Germans would be compelled to take over the direct administration of Denmark, but it should be our object ultimately to produce this result, and the exact time when it would be desirable that this climax should be reached would necessarily depend on the strategic plans of the General Staff."[28] In other words, the Allies envisioned compelling Germany to rule Denmark directly, but indefinitely put off taking action. They thus avoided inciting a rebellion. In August 1942 the founding principle of the Political Warfare Executive's propaganda was that military considerations required the maintenance of the status quo. In practical terms this meant:

1. Giving a certain limited support for the present Coalition Government and accepting their argument that their motives are, in principle, well-intentioned
2. Making no reference whatsoever to existing secret activist organizations and no appeal to form new ones
3. Not inciting the Danes to active resistance against either Danish Nazis or Germans on the grounds that if this resistance became substantial it

would force the Germans to strengthen their forces in Denmark, thereby upsetting the status quo

4. Not issuing direct exhortations to Danes to try to escape to Great Britain.[29]

The Foreign Office as a whole agreed "that it was undesirable for the BBC to propagandize the Danes to commit acts of sabotage. The Danes were quite able to look after this matter for themselves without outside prompting." So noted the United Kingdom's ambassador to Sweden in December 1942.[30] The diplomats provided reassurances in April 1943[31] and confirmed that line to the Americans the same month: "It is agreed with SOE and the Chiefs of Staff that it would be premature to go in for a policy of stirring up the maximum possible trouble in Denmark." To the State Department, Great Britain's embassy declared: "We are not convinced that there would at this stage be any advantage in an attempt on our part to upset the Government and to work for a state of affairs approximating more to that of other occupied countries."[32]

But London and Washington bent that rule somewhat. For example, the U.S. authorities recognized the Danish ambassador to Washington, Henrik Kauffmann, even though he had broken with Copenhagen on April 9, 1941.[33] Granted, the diplomat did not arrive empty-handed. The same day, he signed a treaty on his own initiative granting the United States the right to establish bases in Greenland,[34] which gave the Americans a considerable strategic advantage. His counterpart in London, Count Ernst zu Reventlow, followed suit. Arguing that his government had joined the Anti-Comintern Pact on November 25, 1941, he resigned the same month. On a different level, the Danish Council had been formed in London in 1940. These were not strong cards, however, and the Allies hesitated to play them.

They refused to rely on the Danish Council, which might have developed into, if not a provisional government, then at least a National Committee, were it not for several obstacles that had hindered that process. The Americans rejected the council on principle, claiming, on December 10, 1941, that the experience "of the past year has shown that the theoretical advantage of 'free movements' has been difficult to transform into practical utility."[35] They added that, in dealing with Kauffmann, they were unable to recognize "unofficial Danish bodies."[36] The Free Danes, moreover, had no preeminent personalities. Although Møller's presence gave them real political weight, it also pulled them to the right, awakening the Americans' suspicion. Roderick Gallop, in charge of Danish affairs at the Foreign Office, reported: "In the United States I found a widespread impression (disapproving) that we had definitely put our shirt on the conservatives and Mr. Christmas Møller. This impression does us no good, partly owing to the feeling in the United States that Mr. Christmas Møller is not representative of Danish public opinion, and partly owing to the prevailing suspicion of British Conservatism generally."[37]

It is true that the British, who had the upper hand in the matter, might have reinforced the council's legitimacy by adding diplomats to it. Count Reventlow, having broken with Copenhagen, agreed to be its honorary chair on December 4, 1941,[38] but he backed down at the end of the same month, fearing it would look like he was forming the embryo of a dissident government.[39]

Any expansion of the Danish Council also ran up against the suppressed hostility that Møller and Kauffmann felt for each other. While showing mutual respect in public, they did not refrain from denigrating each other. During a trip to the United States in December 1942, the Conservative leader confided that he did not really think "that any Dane at this distance from Denmark could really be qualified to know the best way in which Danish affairs should be handled." The ambassador responded in kind, calling his rival "politically immature, parochial and quite unable to understand the international politics which had to be considered in dealing with the Denmark situation."[40] In September 1943 Kauffmann pointed out that there was "no political body outside Denmark which held a mandate from the people. Since, unlike Norway, no King and Government existed in exile, the only responsible people outside Denmark were diplomats, including himself and Reventlow. . . . Kauffmann envisages the creation of a 'National Committee' composed of diplomatic representatives with himself in the chair. He suggested by inference that Danish Council had no place in his scheme."[41] The British gave that idea a cool welcome. "Setting up a body of diplomats, most of whom have no popular appeal, seems in any case quite inappropriate in the case of an essentially parliamentary country."[42] On an even more serious note, "if we allow Mr. Kauffmann to get away with the initiative, the voice of Britain will lose some of its effect."[43] Beyond personal animosities, the conflict "symbolized the contrast between a more tolerant attitude to Danish collaboration, represented by Kauffmann and Washington, and a more critical attitude, represented by Møller and London."[44] In short, political dissensions, personal rivalries, and diverging national interests prevented the Danish Council from broadening its base.

Above all, London was afraid to break ranks with the Danish king, who enjoyed great popularity. Supporting the council would have meant portraying it as an alternative to the government in Copenhagen, an option the British authorities ruled out for the years 1941 to 1943. As the Foreign Office noted in 1941, "The Danish Government in Copenhagen is a collaborationist Government. We cannot be entirely hostile to it because we do not want to attack the King and because there is no alternative to it; the only alternative to it would be a Danish Movement with a recognized and legalized status. It is the absence of this legalized status that makes it difficult for us to play it up too much."[45] That line still prevailed in April 1943. "It would be the wrong tactics for the Free Danish Movement [i.e., the Danish Council] to do anything which would savour of setting themselves up as an alternative Danish Government or opposition movement, since the King of Denmark continues to cooperate with the Danish Government, the Government itself maintains its democratic basis and the popularity of the King and expediency of the Government would make it extremely inept for the Free Danish Movement to do so."[46] As a result, the Danish Council obtained only minimal recognition: although "enjoying the support of His Majesty's Government,. . . it has no official status and is not on the level of a Government or even of a National Committee."[47]

Tensions

That strategy divided the British state apparatus, for reasons both moral and pragmatic. Although the Council of the Chiefs of Staff and the Foreign Office overall advocated maintaining the status quo, PWE, SOE, and the Political Intelligence Department (PID) within the Foreign Office rejected it. "The Danes should be told that the better their conduct from the Allied point of view now the better will be their treatment after the war, when Great Britain and her friends plan and organize the new political and economic order in the world," warned Thomas Barman of PID in March 1941.[48] And he added in June of the same year: "The time has come to stiffen the tone of our broadcasts to Denmark. All the evidence available in this country tends to show that the Danes are well satisfied with the reputation they believe they have established for themselves as 'cold shoulderers' of the Germans. They should be told, discreetly, that this is not enough. There is a chair waiting for Denmark at the Allied Council table in London, but it has to be earned. It can be earned only by deeds."[49] PWE shared that view:

> At a time when the greatest struggle in history is being fought . . . it seems bad psychology, to say the least, to beg the Danes to maintain the status quo and not to risk their skins. . . . Have we no other message to the youth of Denmark . . . than a vague appeal to order?
>
> . . . How can we hope for any Danish contribution to the war effort if the impression is left in Danish minds—as it is now—that Denmark is unimportant and that therefore the existence of a German puppet Government in Copenhagen is not viewed with disfavor by the leaders of the United Nations?[50]

In other words, if Denmark wanted to enjoy privileged status on the day of victory, PWE and SOE believed, it had to participate more actively in the great crusade.

In addition, the support that propaganda and the British secret services provided to the Danish internal resistance contradicted the United Kingdom's diplomacy, as Brinley Thomas, responsible for propaganda for the northern countries, noted in May 1943:

> The object of our political warfare in the last six months can be summed up as follows: to promote the growth of the small active front at the expense of the large passive front but without going as far as to drive a wedge between the National Government on the one hand and the people on the other. . . . But it is clear that the active front can only reach maturity by competing with the passive front; and so at some point, a rift must appear between the collaborationist Government and the militant element among the people.

Brinley Thomas thus called on the authorities to stay the course. "We need to know from a high level whether it is desirable on operational grounds that Denmark should become more troublesome to the Germans now. Would it be a good thing to have the Germans forced to use more troops and administrative personnel in that country at a time when their resources are being seriously thinned out?"[51] The question, already raised in October 1942, had remained unanswered.[52] But time was of the essence, because, beginning in 1943, the Reich carried out a particularly devious strategy.

The German Strategy and the English Response

Werner Best, appointed "plenipotentiary of the Reich" in Denmark on November 5, 1942, attempted to be subtle in his approach. A cultivated jurist and fanatical Nazi, that SS officer, stationed in Paris between 1940 and 1942, did not want to treat the Danes harshly. Rather, he sought to charm them, both to facilitate German domination and to present an appealing showcase for Nazism. "He would thereby establish a counter-model to the policy of occupation implemented in the countries administered by the Wehrmacht and in the territories within the ambit of the party and its Reichskommissars, a policy whose arbitrariness and lack of coherence he so sharply criticized."[53] When Ribbentrop and Hitler called for the formation of a government with a strong Nazi coloring, Best maneuvered, setting in place the Scavenius cabinet. Erik Scavenius, former head of Danish diplomacy during World War I, was no Nazi, as Roderick Gallop observed: "He regards Nazism as merely a passing phenomenon, a cloud-shadow temporarily darkening the face of that eternal Germany which he admires."[54] Best achieved what he set out to do. He administered a country of 4 million with a staff of only two hundred, whereas Josef Terboven, his counterpart in Norway, employed three thousand agents to bring to heel 2.8 million Norwegians.[55]

On March 23, 1943, Best sent a strong signal. He allowed legislative elections to be held in Denmark and to proceed freely, with only one sour note: the Communists were excluded. The British, far from blocking that surprising process—by calling on voters to abstain, for example— set only limited objectives: "To secure the rejection by the voters of as many collaborationists as possible [and] to encourage the election of strong national-minded personalities, irrespective of party."[56] That modest wager paid off. The Nazis had an absurdly poor showing, receiving only about 2 percent of the votes. But the elections were also "a remarkable success for the German side politically and in terms of propaganda; and, for Best, quite simply a triumph," notes the historian Ulrich Herbert.[57] The plenipotentiary's strategy confirmed the judgment of Victor Mallet, His Majesty's ambassador to Sweden. "Contrary to expectations, von Best [*sic*] has turned out to be a man of surprisingly sensible views and is believed to have reported that it would be idiotic to stir up Denmark to behave like another Norway."[58]

That perilous situation obviously called for action, particularly since some Danes could no longer put up with the status quo.

Attacks

In 1943 Denmark saw a sudden flare-up of violence. There were 2 attacks in 1940, 12 in 1941, and 59 in 1942, but they jumped to 816 in 1943. That increase occurred unevenly over the course of the year. Remaining in the low range between January (24) and June (47), the number skyrocketed in August (213). A strike movement was launched alongside the attacks, first to demand wage increases, then to protest the armed guards the Germans had posted to avert sabotage[59] and to respond to the marked increase in the occupier's security checks. Rankled by these humiliations, 390,000 Danes—which is to say, a tenth of the population—engaged in a work stoppage.[60] The movement was obviously large in scope, attesting to the exasperation of a large part of the population.

Several factors combined to push the Danes toward action. After the Battle of Stalingrad, the defeat of the Reich appeared on the horizon, and Copenhagen undoubtedly realized the need to abandon the pro-German line Erik Scavenius was following. In addition, civilians were suffering from the German presence; daily frictions were growing.[61] Finally, and perhaps above all, the resistance in general and SOE in particular wanted to provoke a break with Berlin. In intensifying the struggle against the occupier, they developed a strategy of tension that placed the Scavenius government before a Cornelian dilemma: either agree to go after the resistance fighters, at the risk of getting caught up in a cycle of repressive actions; or refuse, and expose itself to the wrath of the Germans.

Is it possible that the British special services deliberately pushed the Danish resistance to act? That complex question requires a response that is no less so.

Baker Street—and this is obvious—greatly increased its parachuting activity over Denmark. Between March 11 and May 17, 1943, eleven men and forty-seven shipping containers were dropped, and at least seven drops followed between July 15 and August 15 of the same year.[62] Granted, these deliveries were still minimal, compared to the quantities that would be sent in 1944 and 1945, for example. They were enough, however, to spread unrest, especially since there were far more explosives than weapons in the containers, a sign that London favored sabotage over guerilla warfare. In the same vein, the leaders exerted mounting pressure on The Princes to finally take action.[63]

It should be noted, however, that in July 1943 SOE leaders had assigned their chief agent, Flemming Muus, modest objectives: "to reduce the Germans' ability to wage war and not to cause the breakdown of political co-operation. . . . Muus was clearly instructed to pursue the former and to take no interest in the latter."[64] That directive corresponded in every particular to the wishes of military personnel, who, in July 1943, had finally answered the questions that SOE leaders had addressed to them. The general staff demanded that the resistance be intensified in the kingdom, but at a slow pace: an interim peak was supposed to be reached in October 1943, with the final push occurring in spring 1944.[65] Police investigations revealed that, of 336 sabotage operations, 121 had been committed using British materiel, a significant proportion to be sure, but still in the minority.[66]

These factors invite us to draw certain conclusions. SOE, while it wanted the resistance to proceed apace, did not want to cross the Rubicon in the summer of 1943. The escalation in actions thus stemmed in the first place from the Danish people's exasperation, as the scope of the strikes suggests, and from the anger of the internal resistance, as confirmed by the marked increase in the number of sabotage operations. Flemming Muus likely encouraged that upsurge. Eager to "support a political upheaval in Denmark, by intensifying sabotage activities, he repeatedly ignored urgent appeals to keep a low profile until the storm had blown over."[67] Granted, not all sabotage operations were the work of his teams. But the parachute drops, beyond the material assistance they provided, gave many resistance fighters the sense that they were now in contact with the free world; as a result, their battle came into sharper focus.[68] It should be repeated, however, that the movement was primarily homegrown, a sign that some Danes, without seeking to undermine the government's authority, intended above all to seize what they no doubt considered their final opportunity to show their opposition to the Germans.[69]

Clearly, times had changed. On September 2, 1942, Erik Scavenius's predecessor, Prime Minister Vilhelm Buhl, had condemned the attacks and the men whose "goal is to subvert the existing good relations with Germany,"[70] even calling on people to denounce the perpetrators. Four days later, however, Christmas Møller launched a diametrically opposed appeal: "Action is required of us all, of each one of us. . . . Denmark and you at home must take your share of the burden."[71] The underground press, following suit, had made the shift in winter 1942–1943 from reticence to an "unconditional and unvarnished support" of sabotage.[72] The BBC, finally, continually publicized the glorious deeds of the resistance and urged the Danes to take things into their own hands. Its broadcasts, in and of themselves, did not occasion the German ultimatum and the resulting collapse of the government. But "they had helped to bring the Danish population to such a pitch that the failure of the government and of its policy was the logical conclusion to Danish unrest."[73]

The Germans did not waste any time on speculation. On August 24, 1943, Best was summoned to Berlin. He returned four days later and issued an ultimatum. The Danish authorities were to impose the death penalty on saboteurs and institute martial law. Strikes and demonstrations were henceforth forbidden, and the Germans arrogated to themselves the right to censor the press. The Copenhagen authorities rejected that diktat on the 29th and immediately resigned. The German army then seized the executive power, arrested hostages, and disarmed the troops. The fleet preferred to scuttle itself.[74]

The Danish exception had breathed its last; the kingdom fell into line with all the other countries.

Epilogues

All things considered, the crisis of August 1943 removed a major stumbling block. The survival of the political system depended on the Danish government's ability to guarantee the safety and interests of the German troops and therefore to avoid the development of the internal resistance,[75] which was incapacitated by that strategy because the authorities were themselves the embodiment of the opposition to Nazism: in contrast to Philippe Pétain, the Danish government never sought to create a new order. The end of that government therefore brought relief to a large portion of the population. "Despite the certainty that one could now expect harsh repression from the occupying power, that decision [of the government to resign] came as a liberating shock for Danish politicians. It was finally necessary to emerge from the shadow of collaboration, and they resolved to establish unequivocal relations with the occupier."[76] In the same vein, The Princes revealed themselves for what they were. They had always refused to take action in order not to "compromise their plan for military resistance on the day the Germans assumed complete control. When that day came, as on 9th April 1940, there was no resistance of any kind." As one leader noted, because The Princes "failed in 1940 and again in 1943, there is every reason for [them] to desire to take a prominent place in the liberation of Denmark in 1944. SOE personnel, while recognizing their value, have no high opinion of their importance."[77] The British, in short, faced the facts: rather than wager in vain on the military, they had to keep alive the flame of the civilian resistance.

Had the Germans cynically provoked the showdown? Ronald Turnbull, the head of the SOE subbranch in Stockholm, believed so. The occupation authorities, he judged, "set about *deliberately* to provoke a crisis which, it was hoped, would break Danish resistance and bring to light underground organizations which, according to Hanneken [the head of the military administration], were planning in collaboration with the Danish army and navy to give assistance to a theoretically imminent Allied invasion of Denmark."[78] Even more than sabotage, the strikes alarmed the occupier. Because they occurred throughout the territory, they showed that the Danes were now refusing to cooperate.[79] They also proved that the government's authority had eroded: it had lost control of the situation. The Germans therefore had to take the bull by the horns, which explains the deliberately provocative attitude of the occupation troops. In Aarhus during the strike, the military commander notified the civic authorities that the troops placed under its command, as an exercise, would march through the streets of the city with brass bands and regimental banners. "The civic authorities protested and pointed out that, in view of the tense atmosphere such a proceeding could scarcely fail to create trouble. The commander then telephoned to Copenhagen but was told that General von Hanneken personally had ordered the march and that it must take place."[80] The military also took advantage of the crisis to sideline Best: his policy of charming the Danes hardly met with enthusiasm from the Wehrmacht.

Politically, the shadows had not entirely dissipated, since Denmark's legal status remained ambiguous. The country could not be considered a cobelligerent, because no state of war had been declared between Berlin and Copenhagen. A fortiori, London, Moscow, and Washington could not view it as an ally—at least without resorting to legal contortions.[81] Eden admitted his perplexity: "It has not proved possible to find any way out of the difficulties which arise from the fact that Denmark has no Government, is not formally at war with Germany and maintains a Legation in Berlin."[82] Furthermore, Scavenius's resignation by no means opened the way for the Danish Council of Freedom. The king and its government, having grown in stature by their act of refusal, conserved a legitimacy to which the council could not claim. By contrast, the internal resistance, by virtue of its courage, would grow stronger as a result of the ordeal. That was both an asset and a risk. Having become a rallying point, it could gather all Danes under its banner. But the purity of its intentions and the ardor of its actions could just as easily be used to form a stark contrast with the attitudes of the émigrés in London and of political has-beens. By presenting itself as a counterpower, it could thereby become a factor of divisiveness. All things considered, the crisis of August 1943 cleared up many ambiguities, but it did not shift Denmark into the Allied camp—a major difference that distinguished that country from Italy.

CHAPTER XV

Italian Complexities

B y 1943 the situation in Italy had significantly deteriorated. On May 13 the Italo-German forces had surrendered at Cap Bon in Tunisia. The Axis powers had definitively lost North Africa; the imperial dream Mussolini had nurtured vanished in the desert sands. More worrying for Il Duce, on July 10 of the same year, the Anglo-Americans landed in Sicily, not far from the Apennine Peninsula. The regime was holding on, to be sure, but it continued to weaken over time. In the wake of the Second Italo-Ethiopian War (1935–1936), a portion of the elites, criticizing the state's growing influence in the economic sphere, fearing the breakdown in ties with the Western democracies, and dreading Il Duce's military adventurism, had turned their back on him.[1] In the winter of 1942–1943, the disaffection grew. The king, taking note of the growing disrepute in which Fascism was held, feared for his crown; and, in view of the military setbacks, the generals were in dread of a crushing defeat. In 1943, therefore, disaster seemed ineluctable, an eventuality that some Italian leaders immediately took to heart. A handful of men close to the king and to military circles, along with a few senior-level Fascists, decided to take things into their own hands. After convening the Grand Council of Fascism, they voted at dawn on July 25 to depose Il Duce, with nineteen in favor, seven opposed, and one abstention. At the same time, the king appointed Marshal Badoglio, former chief of staff of the armies, who had been relieved of his duties in 1940, to be head of the government.[2] Mussolini was taken under guard to the island of Ponza, then to La Maddalena, an island located not far from Sardinia, before being transferred in late August to Abruzzo. An SS commando led by Otto Skorzeny freed him on September 12 and put him in charge of the Republic of Salò.[3]

Badoglio, the head of the Italian government, faced a difficult situation. He wanted to get Italy out of the war and attract the good graces of the Anglo-Americans, but without unleashing Germany's fury. His margin for maneuvering was slight. If he threw himself at the Anglo-Americans, he would receive only a hypothetical benefit—they refused to compromise—which might come at a high cost: more than a million and a half Italian soldiers were fighting outside the borders. Furthermore, the government could not count on the German command's leniency. The Oberkommando der Wehrmacht (OKW), banking on the foreseeable defection of its ally, had by May 1943 made plans that included, among other things, disarming the Italian forces in the Balkans (Operation Konstantin), invading the peninsula (Operation Alaric), and taking over the Italian-occupied zones of France (Operation Siegfried). By mid-May units had been sent to the peninsula, and, once Il Duce was deposed, they were assisted by reinforcements. On July 26 eight divisions crossed Brenner Pass, while the 305th Division left France for Italy. London and Washington, for their part, were preparing to accept the surrender of Rome. As a result, the policy tightrope Badoglio was walking only showed how little latitude he had.

To be sure, the Italian about-face did not come as a surprise. Since 1942 several emissaries had discreetly sounded out the Allies and, among the myriad potential coconspirators, Badoglio's name had been put forward many times. In October 1941, for example, the U.S. Embassy in Rome indicated that a group had proposed he attempt a coup d'état, in order to conclude a separate peace. Badoglio had replied that he would act only on the king's orders.[4] In addition, the SOE subbranch in Bern had maintained contact with the marshal since May 1942,[5] and he quickly came to seem the only card to play. "If the Army were to make a move Badoglio would be the most natural leader of it," the Foreign Office pointed out in March 1943. "It is not known what support in the Army Badoglio could command but if he were acting in the King's name it might be considerable. . . . Apart from Badoglio we know of no generals who might be expected to lead a revolt."[6]

The British diplomats, then, lucidly grasped the situation. But in January 1943 Anthony Eden refused to negotiate with General Pesenti, whom

Badoglio had proposed to dispatch to Cyrenaica. Eden offered only two alternatives, "sinking or surviving." "We hope that this tough line, supplemented by heavy raids and the threat of invasion, will suffice to frighten the Italians out of the war."[7] The Foreign Office proved intransigent, because it could promise Italy nothing: not the return of its colonies or the guarantee of its borders, which the Yugoslavs, wishing to recover Istria, had in their sights. Another argument also may have come into play: "The left-wing members," it was said, "could not agree to negotiations with effete Italian aristocrats."[8] By the time the War Cabinet changed its mind, on March 18, the contact established with SOE's assistance had already been broken.[9]

If, in addition to these measures, one considers the fact that the Italian legation in Lisbon had met with a Romanian intermediary in late 1942 to propose a separate peace, even as the consul general of Italy in Geneva was trying to create a channel of communication between the British government and the duke of Aosta,[10] a cousin to Victor Emmanuel III, it becomes clear that the request for an Italian armistice did not come out of thin air. The Anglo-Americans had planned it and had decided on their strategy during the Quebec Conference: Italy would have to surrender unconditionally. That was the reply that the U.S. general Bedell Smith gave on August 19, 1943, to General Castellano, who had been sent by his prime minister to negotiate in Lisbon.

These talks, opened by the Badoglio government in the greatest secrecy, were rife with ambiguities. The Italian authorities were "apparently nursing the hope that Italy would be allowed to lay down her arms with the consent of both sides."[11] But the Germans did not intend to let their former ally sign a separate peace, whereas the Anglo-Americans wished to cause "such disorder as would necessitate a German occupation."[12] In turning the land of Dante into a battlefield, Allied strategists expected to relieve the pressure on the Russian front and pare down the number of German garrisons stationed in France, at a time when the Normandy landing was already in the planning stage.

Although the wish to force Italy to accept unconditional surrender met with approval, the terms of the armistice were open to discussion. "Should it be brief and practical, enabling Eisenhower to declare hostilities immediately ended—and thus also Italy's role as an Axis partner—or should it attempt to deliver total control of the Italian nation and people, defining every aspect of their external and internal condition, yet without formally ending the war with Italy?"[13] The partners dealt with the most urgent matters first. On September 3, 1943, they signed in the greatest secrecy an accord at Cassibile, a Sicilian village not far from Syracuse. Known as the "short armistice," it dealt solely with military matters.

On September 8, 1943, the Anglo-American forces landed in Taranto, Reggio Calabria, and above all Salerno, south of Naples, dashing the Italian authorities' hopes that the intervention would take Rome as its target. An air operation was considered for a time, but General Maxwell Taylor, commander of the 82nd Airborne Division, canceled it.[14] As a result, Badoglio had second thoughts. In a message transmitted to Eisenhower, he explained: "Due to changes in the situation brought about by the disposition and strength of the German forces in the Rome area, it is no longer possible to accept an immediate armistice as this could provoke the occupation of the Capital and the violent assumption of the government by the Germans. Operation Giant Two (airborne operation) is no longer possible because of lack of forces to guarantee the airfields." The supreme Allied commander replied sharply: "Any failure on your part to conduct to the finish all the obligations of the signed agreement can have very grave consequences for your country. No future action on your part can then restore any confidence in your good faith and consequently will be followed by the dissolution of your government and of your nation."[15] Immediately thereafter, Ike announced over the radio the news of the armistice, which had been kept secret until that time.

The revelation caused chaos. On September 8 the Italian fleet cast off for Malta, suffering a few losses—including the battleship *Roma*, which was sunk by the Luftwaffe. The Germans seized the capital, which was declared an open city on September 10. Above all, three million soldiers were left to fend for themselves. Some let themselves be captured, others deserted, and some went over to the Allied side. The outcome was sometimes tragic. On the Greek island of Cephalonia, more than three thousand men were massacred after surrendering to the Germans.[16] Meanwhile, the king and his government fled the Eternal City. On September 9 seven vehicles transporting Victor Emmanuel III, Pietro Badoglio, and other officials headed for Pescara, where they boarded the corvette *La Baionetta* for Brindisi.[17] The king refused to stay in Rome, fearing he would "meet the fate of the regent Horthy, whom the Germans forced to say on the radio the opposite of what he had expressed spontaneously a few days earlier." He added, "I do not wish to run the risk of ending up like the king of the Belgians." That flight to Varennes was unglamorous. On the ship, "the royal couple bedded down on deckchairs, with a blanket over their knees, while the others settled in anyplace they could find on the deck."[18] Above all, their escape was judged harshly: the Italian population believed, not without reason, that they had been abandoned to their fate.

As might be guessed, the "short armistice" of September 3 left many questions hanging. These were partly resolved with the signing of the "long armistice" in Malta on September 29, 1943. Spelling out the political, economic, and financial conditions to be applied to the defeated nations, it gave the Allies control over the Italian armed forces, permitted the country's exploitation, and proclaimed the desire to destroy Fascism. A few of the terms were modified on November 9, a way of treading lightly on sensitive issues. The name of the "Long Armistice was changed from 'Instrument of Surrender to Italy' to 'Additional Conditions of Armistice with Italy.' In Article I the last word 'unconditionally' was deleted so that it read, 'The Italian Land, Sea, and Air Forces wherever located hereby surrender.'"[19] The details of that agreement were kept secret because the British War Office believed that "their publication would give the enemy an excellent propaganda opportunity and would provide material for ill-intentioned journalists both here and in America."[20]

The long armistice did not solve two crucial issues: the status of Italy and the question of who would rule.

Allied Strategies

In reality, the various Allies followed different strategies. It is true that the Moscow declaration, made public on November 1, 1943, argued for the eradication of Fascism and "its diabolical influence." It also demanded that the Italian government be democratized through "the introduction of representatives of those sections of the Italian people who have always opposed Fascism."[21] But such irenics did little to conceal the divergent interests of London and Washington, not to mention Moscow.

The United Kingdom considered the Mediterranean a crucial zone of influence controlling the Suez route and therefore communications with a large part of the British Empire. It also showed no indulgence toward Italy, which had had the effrontery to declare war on Great Britain and had forced it to wage battle to hold on to its African colonies. The United States was more easy-going. Franklin Roosevelt had little interest in the Apennine

Peninsula, at least until 1944: the presidential election held that year suddenly made him more attentive to the votes of Italian Americans.[22] As a result, the Anglo-American strategy lacked clarity, wavering between the desire to punish the former enemies and the wish to consider them a new ally. "You will be guided in your attitude towards the local population by the memory of years of war in which the Italians fought against your people and your Allies" were the instructions given to the officers in charge of administering the country.[23] But in March 1943 Pierson Dixon of the Foreign Office noted that "a benevolent policy should be adopted towards the civilian population of the occupied territory."[24] On the eve of the landing in Sicily, the Political Warfare Executive ordered that the propaganda should specify that "the Allied forces are attacking Italian territory not as enemies of the Italian people but because it is a necessary step towards the destruction of the German war-machine and of German domination."[25] In a sign of that confusion, PWE recommended focusing in the propaganda on Italians who were cooperating with their liberators, but without using the term "friends"—and even less, "allies"—to designate them.[26]

On October 13, 1943, Italy declared war on Germany: the declaration was signed by the king on October 11 and transmitted to Berlin through the Italian Embassy in Madrid. Eisenhower had insisted that the sovereign make that gesture, to sweep aside the claims of Il Duce, who, as head of the Republic of Salò, said he represented his country and was waging a ruthless civil war against the resistance. The supreme commander of the Allied force was also hoping to galvanize the populations of Mezzogiorno[27] and to kindle a flickering flame in the army's ranks. Indeed, the Italians were fighting "with singularly little energy and enthusiasm . . . to expel the Germans." Now that Italy was a cobelligerent, "the determination with which they set about this task may be fortified," while the resistance in the northern part of the country would be invigorated.[28]

Victor Emmanuel III had shown some reluctance. Not without reason, he wanted an alliance and not cobelligerence,[29] an imprecise concept: "While guaranteeing some form of assistance to the Allied war effort, the term marked the fact, as British legal experts pointed out, that Italy had not acquired Allied status. . . . The declaration contained no commitment to practical support of any war effort Italians might make, nor did it guarantee the personal positions of Badoglio or Victor Emmanuel." In essence, the Foreign Office noted, the Italians were being treated "as friends and foes at the same time."[30] That no man's land satisfied the Anglo-Americans, who held a trump card: they could put pressure on the Italian authorities by dangling a change of status before them. As a result, a great deal of water flowed under the bridges of the Tiber before that thorny question was settled.

A Contested Power

The question of power was a second problem. It consisted of two distinct, albeit connected, questions. Should support be given to the king? And was it appropriate to strengthen Badoglio? True, the two men were confederates, having long been fellow travelers with Fascism. Victor Emmanuel III had favored Benito Mussolini's accession to power, and Pietro Badoglio, despite his dismissal in 1940, had not only covered up the war crimes committed during the Italo-Ethiopian War—especially the use of gas—but also faithfully supported the regime until late 1940.

That burdensome past did not prevent the British, with Churchill in the lead, from actively working to have them kept on. The king's presence guaranteed the obedience of the armed forces,[31] while the compromised principles of the two men guaranteed their docility, making them "unable to protect and assert Italian interests effectively."[32] The British prime minister admitted it outright: the Badoglio government, he wrote to Roosevelt in February 1944, "is tame and completely in our hands. It will obey our directions far more than any other that we may laboriously constitute."[33] He then confided to Harold Macmillan, minister resident with the Allied general staff in North Africa at the time: "When I want to lift a pot of hot coffee, I prefer to keep the handle."[34] In short, as the historian Claudio Pavone puts it, the king and his prime minister "appeared at the very least as useful weathervanes, who seemed to be reviving the age-old habit the Savoys had of never concluding a war on the same side they had begun it on—unless, as was also said, they had changed front twice."[35] Propaganda was enlisted to popularize that view. In early October 1943, for example, the effort was made to depict the government as the rallying point for the entire Italian resistance, because it had obtained the support of the leftist parties and was becoming a vast "anti-Fascist coalition including patriotic, liberal and left-wing elements."[36] The question arose, however: Would the Italian resistance agree to cooperate with personalities compromised by the fallen regime?

Other solutions presented themselves. Count Carlo Sforza, an émigré to the United States at the time, had composed a manifesto that was unanimously approved at a meeting of a Pan-American Congress of Free Italians in Montevideo in August 1942.[37] As minister of foreign affairs in 1920–1921 and later ambassador to Paris, he had resigned dramatically when Benito Mussolini was named prime minister in 1922. Although he had an impeccable antifascist pedigree, he came up against the hostility of the British. According to Gladwyn Jebb, "In the first place we believe him entirely discredited in Italy, representing indeed the very type of man of the prefascist regime that the Italians would not wish to have foisted back on them. Moreover I have always heard myself that he is immensely vain and now bordering on the ga-ga!"[38] In February 1943 the Labour MP Ivor Thomas asked the British authorities to meet with Sforza. Eden opposed the request, arguing that a visit would signify that Sforza had their "official support."[39] These fallacious arguments concealed the real reasons for Churchill's animosity. A proponent before the war of an agreement with Il Duce, the resident of Downing Street never forgave the scathing criticisms Sforza had formulated at the time. By contrast, the count enjoyed Roosevelt's strong support—a base tactic designed to win the election. "What perhaps was insufficiently realised was that New York State was the key state in the coming Presidential elections, and Sforza claimed to swing many thousand of votes," Harold Macmillan recalled, not without lucidity.[40]

At first, the Anglo-Americans played their cards well. Liberated Italy was divided into two zones. One was under a military government (the Allied Military Government in Occupied Territory, or AMGOT) which, to avoid the brutality of that designation, was renamed the Allied Military Government (AMG) on October 18, 1943. Often composed of elderly officers, it was promptly nicknamed "Ancient Military Gentlemen on Tour."[41] The other zone—the provinces of Taranto, Brindisi, Lecce, and Bari—was under the control of the Badoglio government but subject to the oversight of the Allied Control Commission. Intent on exercising its powers fully,[42] the commission was headed by Noel Mason-MacFarlane, former governor of Gibraltar, whose incompetence greatly annoyed Churchill.[43] Anxious to spare the Italians' feelings, Eisenhower wanted to rename it the "Allied Commission," a concession the British found irritating. "We should not abandon the view that Italy is a defeated enemy country, and such apparently trivial matters as the name of the Commission may assume considerable significance, particularly in the eyes of the minor Allies like the

Greeks and the Yugoslavs. An 'Allied Com' might very easily become an 'Allied Mission.'" The Foreign Office was not heeded, and the new designation was imposed on October 24, 1943.[44] On February 11, 1944, the entire liberated territory was returned to the Italian authorities,[45] but under the aegis of the Allied Commission. By contrast, the AMG administered the combat zones and the region of Naples, whose port was vital for the logistics of the military campaign. It should be noted that the Anglo-American administration was under the control of the military. The Allied Commission thus reported to the Civil Affairs Division of the War Office, not to a civilian ministry.[46] In any case, the resistance had no voice in the matter, a situation that incensed it.

Rebellions

It was not long before the organization chart prompted criticisms on two different fronts. Without disputing the principle of monarchy, some critics called for Victor Emmanuel's departure; without demanding Badoglio's resignation, others wanted a broader base for his government. Still others demanded both.

On September 9, 1943, a Comitato di Liberazione Nazionale (CLN; National Liberation Committee) had secretly formed in Rome. Chaired by the Socialist Ivanoe Bonomi, it assembled the six principal political parties (Communist Party, Socialist Party, Action Party, Christian Democrats, Liberals, and Progressive Democrats) and was modeled explicitly on the Conseil National de la Résistance founded by Jean Moulin the previous May.[47] That structure was something of a miracle. In a relatively short span of time, the six major groups on the peninsula, persecuted for more than twenty years by Mussolini's regime, had managed to come back to life and to reach an agreement on a simple but essential program: to call for resistance, "restore the place that Italy deserves among free nations,"[48] and launch a political *aggiornamento*.

To make their views known, these political groups met in Bari on January 28 and 29, 1944. They formed a council and demanded the king's departure and the establishment of a regency, but they did not make Badoglio's departure a precondition. The philosopher and historian Benedetto Croce, albeit a monarchist at heart, summed up the feelings of many participants: "As long as the present King remains head of the state, we feel that Fascism is not finished, that it remains attached to us, that it continues to corrode us and to weaken us, that it will resurge more or less camouflaged; and to sum up, this way we cannot breathe and live."[49] The philosopher remained true to the line he had advanced in November 1943: "None of us thought to open, while the war lasts and we have the Germans on our territory, a discussion on monarchy or republic, and we were agreed to postpone this problem to the end of the war; but . . . the *institutional* question was one thing and the *personal* question another." He therefore suggested making the prince of Naples head of the regency.[50]

Nevertheless, Churchill stayed the course. Although he agreed to expand the government to include a few liberal elements, in order to strengthen Victor Emmanuel and Badoglio, he put off any major change until the fall of Rome.[51] Furthermore, the king refused to abdicate, which according to him would have amounted to acknowledging responsibility for the advent of Fascism and the declaration of war, something he refused to do.[52] He also feared entrusting the reins to his son Umberto, for fear that the rumors about the younger man's homosexuality would rattle him; Victor Emmanuel also had doubts about his son's personality and abilities.[53] A sign of that embarrassment: PWE recommended avoiding in its propaganda "ALL DISCUSSIONS OF THE ITALIAN GOVERNMENT AND KING."[54]

Political pressure mounted, however. In Algiers, Harold Macmillan took the measure of the growing disfavor in which the Italian authorities were held: "The King is discredited and his abdication at some stage may well be the best solution if it can be effected by the Italians themselves without damage to the body politic or to our interests."[55] In February 1944 the resident minister thus suggested the formation of a broader-based government, "ranging from the Right to the extreme Left," as a result of which, he added, "we shall have the satisfaction of adopting a policy in accordance with the deeper spiritual purposes for which we are at war."[56] The Americans, suffering from "an inverted Darlan complex," lent their support.[57]

London reluctantly gave in. On February 16, 1944, Harold Caccia and Samuel Reber (respectively, the British and American leader of the political section of the Allied Commission) approached the council, hoping it would propose a plan. Following the suggestion of the Liberal Enrico de Nicola,[58] they decided that Umberto would be named lieutenant general of the kingdom and that a broader-based government would be formed, a plan that was approved by the Combined Chiefs of Staff.[59]

Badoglio, sensing the threat, attempted to maneuver. On March 8 he persuaded the Soviet Union to recognize his government. It was a clever move. In fact, the USSR had been completely pushed aside during the negotiations; in giving its approval to the Brindisi government, it once again became a player in the Italian game. At the same time, the Soviets did little to disrupt the situation, since they merely acknowledged the existence of a power that the Anglo-Americans officially supported. London and Washington nevertheless felt the impact. The intervention of the Soviets ran the risk of shoring up the leftist parties, by showing the Italians there would be "more plums in the Russian cake."[60] In addition, Moscow was able to promise an alliance, as well as guarantee the eastern borders. The Anglo-Americans, furious, issued a sharp call to order. "The Italian Government are not entitled to enter into any arrangement with any foreign power whether Allied or neutral, without the consent of the Supreme Allied Commander, which should be sought through the Control Commission."[61] But the damage was done, and the Anglo-Americans had to make a gesture. On April 5 they announced that they would send in high commissioners— Noel Charles for the British, Alexander Kirk for the Americans—but without conceding Italy's full sovereignty. The two men would not be officially recognized by the Italian government, and Brindisi would not be allowed to send representatives to London and Washington.[62]

But something good came out of this bad situation. Kirk and Charles were able to deal with the political questions—an area beyond MacFarlane's purview—and defend the interests of their respective countries. Whereas MacFarlane, an agent of the supreme commander, was looking out for Allied interests, the high commissioners were in the service of their own nations.[63]

The Badoglio government also enjoyed the unexpected support of Palmiro Togliatti. In an unanticipated speech in Salerno (March 31, 1944), the general secretary of the Italian Communist Party, having just returned from Russia, called for the formation of a national union government, without demanding the king's departure as a precondition. That shift reshuffled the cards and placed liberals and moderates in an awkward position: "On the one hand, they long to enter the Government and would hate to see the Communists and Socialists collar all the best jobs and all the power; on the other hand, they have made so many speeches and uttered such brave words, that a lot of the latter would need to be eaten if they were to come along and join Badoglio."[64]

Such support was not enough to save Victor Emmanuel III, who was obliged to bow out. "The King with his record of collaboration with Mussolini and at least partial responsibility for Italy's entry into the war is anathema to the opposition," MacFarlane warned.[65] If the situation did not change, Macmillan added, the Russians would enjoy a greater margin for maneuvering.[66] There was therefore a risk that the Allies would see an extremist government installed in Rome once the capital was liberated.[67] On April 9, 1944, three emissaries—MacFarlane, the American Murphy, and Macmillan—showed up at the Villa Episcopio in Ravello. "Having arrived in shirtsleeves and shorts—the maid even specified that their chest hair was peeking out from their open shirts—they were sent away by the king, who invited them to return the next day."[68] The three men demanded either a regency or abdication. The king gave in and agreed to create a lieutenancy for the kingdom,[69] which would be entrusted to his son after the fall of Rome. The news was confirmed on the radio on April 12. The king sighed: "It cannot be said that, ever since Italy was formed, things have been good for my house."[70]

Although the sovereign did not keep his crown, Badoglio saved his own neck. On April 22, 1944, he formed a new government that included representatives from the six main parties and thus embodied a kind of national unity. Churchill opposed that scenario to the end and by every means possible. He told Roosevelt that the British War Cabinet had doubts that the six parties were "representative in any true sense of the Italian democracy or Italian nation or that they could at the present time replace the existing Italian Government which has loyalty and effectively worked in our interests."[71] He claimed that the United States was in agreement about maintaining the status quo before the capture of Rome, an inaccurate assertion that Cordell Hull sharply corrected: "You are instructed to have placed on the agenda for the next meeting of the Council a general discussion of the solutions which the various Italian groups have presented," the U.S. secretary of state prescribed to the diplomats from London and Algiers.[72] Churchill made a personal appeal to Roosevelt's feelings, reminding him of the "strong support" the British prime minister had granted during the Darlan deal[73]—which he did not regret. "Several thousand British and American soldiers are alive today because of it and it got us Dakar at a time when we could ill have spared the large forces needed for its capture."[74] In the end, he ferociously criticized Sforza and Croce. "Macmillan tells me Croce is a dwarf Professor about 75 years old who wrote good books about aesthetics and philosophy. Vyshinsky [Moscow's representative in Italy] who has tried to read the books says they are even duller than Karl Marx."[75] These arguments left Roosevelt unmoved, and the process played out to its conclusion.

That process, however, did not comfort a deeply embittered Badoglio. In submitting to the humiliating conditions, the marshal had hoped to obtain the status of ally for his country—but to no avail, despite the concessions to which he had consented. Italy had agreed to declare war on Germany, triggering a bloody repression in the northern part of the country. "Italian soldiers are co-belligerent when fighting in the line but [are still] prisoners of war twenty miles behind it. . . . How was it possible to reconcile the solemn assurances that the Allies had landed in Italy as liberators; that they were fighting Mussolini and Fascism but not the Italian people, if things proceeded exactly as they did eight months ago, notwithstanding the obvious good faith of Italian co-operation?" If no gesture was made, Badoglio threatened, the government "would not last more than a few weeks." The Allies therefore needed to be magnanimous and recognize Italy as their ally.[76] Neither London nor Washington was ready to take that step, especially since, in granting that status, they would have provoked the anger of the British public, not to mention the French, the Greeks, and the Yugoslavs, "who bitterly resent Italians being placed on the same footing as themselves."[77] As a result, Italy did not acquire the distinction of being considered an ally, and Badoglio wallowed in his bitterness.

The Allies, then, did not hesitate to intervene in the domestic affairs of France and Italy, and even of Denmark, where they encouraged the status quo. But they failed to impose their views in the Brindisi heat and in the Algiers sunshine and had to go along with the Danish rebellion without managing to control it. The diverging interests of London and Washington, the pluralism prevailing within the state apparatus of each, and the force of public opinion prevented the most cynical scenarios from coming to pass. In the historical arena, the skill of one side and the missteps of the other also had decisive weight, which confirms the preeminent role that individuals sometimes assume in the march of history. In these three countries especially, the resistance managed to make its voice heard, to see that discredited men were pushed aside, and to steer away—albeit only partially—from the ambiguities. At a time when the liberation of the Old Continent was in the planning stage, all these factors surely deserved to be pondered.

CHAPTER XVI

Planning for Liberation

As of 1943 the war took a new course. The Allies inflicted two major defeats on the Germans, first in the Egyptian sands of El Alamein in October-November 1942, then in the frozen ruins of Stalingrad, where Marshal Friedrich Paulus's troops surrendered on February 2, 1943. These victories were a prelude to a much more complex challenge: the liberation of Western Europe, which the Anglo-Americans took up without delay. In July 1943 they seized Sicily (Operation Husky); in September they landed on the southern peninsula of Italy (Operation Avalanche), then undertook an interminable march up the Boot, ending with the capture of Rome on June 4, 1944. Finally, on June 6, 1944, some 130,000 men rushed onto the beaches of Normandy (Operation Overlord), the prelude to the deliverance of France, Belgium, and the Netherlands, which promised the ineluctable collapse of the Third Reich.

In that modern war, the regular forces, whether of land, air, or sea, waged most of the battles. The strategists, however, did not underestimate the role that the internal resistance would play. Underground groups would be able to contribute to the support of the newly landed troops. But they also had to be assigned duties and given the necessary resources to carry them out.

Striking the Enemy Before D-Day

In making plans for the landing, the Allied general staff distinguished between two phases. Before the launch of Operation Overlord, the internal resistance would strike the occupier from time to time; then, when the invasion began, the army of shadows would attack enemy positions.

In 1943, then, the time for action had come. In the western theater of operations, the Allies set four principal objectives: demoralize the German troops, prevent the deportation of workers to the Reich, exacerbate the occupier's administrative problems, and, above all, engage in a series of sabotage operations primarily targeting the enemy's communications networks.[1]

In large measure, that program was achieved. In France, the railroads were the object of the vigilant attention of the resistance. Between June 1943 and May 1944, 1,822 locomotives were sabotaged.[2] For the year 1943, the Danes claimed responsibility for the disruption of three hundred railroad networks in Jutland and Zealand and for seven derailments. In the same vein, the Belgians announced they had derailed a train carrying troops between Brussels and Liège, causing many fatalities in the Wehrmacht's ranks.[3] On the night of July 22, 1943, Jean-Marie Pellay was dropped by parachute to destroy the Gigny Dam and thereby prevent transport by German barges, which were traveling on the river en route to Italy. On July 27 the dam blew up. It took the Germans three months to reestablish river traffic; on November 11 a new team blew it up again.[4]

But the Allies also targeted some industrial sites, particularly aeronautics firms. On January 19, 1944, a specially trained British officer struck the Ratier factories in Figeac, which were manufacturing variable-pitch propellers. In Tarbes, raids were launched on March 29 and April 13, 1944, against the Hispano-Suiza factories, which specialized in airplane engines. Manufacturers of ball bearings were not overlooked. For example, Malicet et Blin was attacked on May 19, 1944, Timken on April 6, 1944, and SKF on May 17, 1944.[5] Along the same lines, Danish resistance fighters attacked the Madsen factory, which made machine guns, while the Norwegians destroyed the Eydehavn smelting works southwest of Oslo, which every month processed 440 tons of carborundum, an abrasive said to be hard as diamonds.[6] The saboteurs also acted against targets they simply happened on: for example, four ships were sunk in the Port of Aarhus. Finally, certain apparently odd objectives assumed real importance. The Danes struck factories manufacturing ice because it was used to preserve all food products—from butter to fish—that left the kingdom to fill German bellies.[7]

Other initiatives had a less happy outcome. In autumn 1943 SOE planned a "Week of the Rat," intended to eliminate collaborators and other quislings. But that campaign ended in failure. "Lettuce," the head of a Dutch resistance organization, cabled that "their best men had decided that they could not carry out London's proposals for dealing with dangerous traitors. They were willing to do any work which would contribute to the winning of the war but they declined on principle to undertake murderous assaults."[8] Because the Norwegian resistance fighters felt the same reluctance, a commando that parachuted into the Oslo region in April 1944 took on that grim task. In late 1944 it claimed responsibility for forty-five executions, including, on December 11, that of Ivar Grande, a collaborating agent who had wreaked havoc by infiltrating the underground groups.[9]

In any event, until 1943 subversive warfare appeared to be in competition with regular warfare. Assigning aircraft to support the clandestine war always meant taking away resources from the air offensive being conducted by Arthur Harris's Bomber Command. After 1943, however, the underground struggle was an *alternative* to operations conducted in the light of day. The resistance replaced the Royal Air Force or the U.S. Air Force when one of these forces could not or would not strike certain targets. The heavy water factory at Vemork was attacked by the underground because planes could not destroy it. In addition, the emotional reaction to the killing caused by Allied bombs led the high command to suspend its bombing campaigns against the French railroad network in autumn 1943, to avoid further losses. As SOE pointed out in November 1943, "The persistent attack by RAF fighter aircraft is having the opposite effect of that intended. The damage to personnel is considerably greater than the effective damage to locomotives, and is having disastrous results on our relations with the cheminots who are, in fact, our most precious and important contacts."[10] The service did not hesitate to use that argument when proposing that sympathetic industrialists allow their installations to be sabotaged rather than have them annihilated in a deluge of fire. Peugeot accepted that agreement, but Michelin rejected it,[11] which led the RAF to bomb the Clermont plant on March 16, 1944.[12]

That said, the sabotage campaign did little to threaten enemy operations, despite the courage and ardor of the resistance fighters. Harry Sporborg, deputy head of SOE, acknowledged: "Our activities in this direction are not in any sense an alternative to the bombing plan but have been most carefully worked out to be complementary of it. . . . Further, we always have to remember the comparative uncertainty of our work. We can *guarantee* nothing and have always made it clear to SHAEF [Supreme Headquarters, Allied Expeditionary Force, the general staff under Eisenhower] that our railway contribution must be regarded by them as in the nature of a 'bonus.'"[13] In other words, though subversive warfare became the complement of regular warfare, nothing guaranteed its success, which explains why strategists gave their full attention to the Italian theater.

Italian Lessons

The Sicily campaign, then the Italy campaign, offered many lessons.

From the start, SOE was involved in the Allied landings. Beginning in July 1943 Major Malcolm Munthe and his group, attached to the Eighth Army, would establish contacts in Sicily with resistance elements able to harass the enemy behind the lines. Munthe embarked with the troops who landed in Salerno on September 8, 1943.[14] Here again, his assignment was to promote an intensification of the resistance behind enemy lines.

Until spring 1944 the results were disappointing. To be sure, SOE leaders celebrated the results of that detachment, which according to them performed many glorious deeds, "ranging from the collection of enemy arms and the infiltration behind the German lines of Italian saboteurs with plastic-filled melons to personal incursions by British members of the party in enemy-held territory." Between September 1943 and January 1944 Munthe's men claimed responsibility for about seventy missions conducted in the Naples region.[15]

In actuality, however, the balance sheet was less complimentary. In July 1943 neither OSS nor SOE was capable of offering "much assistance" to the resistance or the regular armies,[16] for lack of personnel and resources. The organization charts added to the confusion. For the Italian theater, SOE at first reported to its head office in London, hence J section, run by Lieutenant-Colonel Cecil Roseberry. Some political questions, however, were treated from Bern by Jock McCaffery for SOE or by Allen Dulles for OSS. But subversive warfare in the strict sense was also part of the North African theater of operations (Allied Force Headquarters, AFHQ), hence the so-called Massingham branch, which exercised operational control over OSS and SOE from the Club des Pins in Algiers, under the leadership of Colonel Douglas Dodds-Parker. In addition, on September 29, 1943, an SOE subbranch was set up in the city of Monopoli on the Adriatic coast, which added yet another echelon.

Clarification was obviously called for. It came in autumn 1943: subversive warfare was attached to the "operations" branch (G3) of the Fifteenth Army Group (GA) and therefore to the British general Cecil Sugden. The boundaries of each command were more sharply delineated in November 1943: the resistance north of the La Spezia/Ravenna line would report to the Fifteenth Army Group; to the south, it would remain under the orders of the AFHQ.[17]

That reshuffling turned out to be of critical importance. Subversive warfare was, as a result, entrusted to military personnel—and no longer to civilians—and its leadership was placed as close as possible to the front, whereas operations had previously been directed from London or Washington. From then on, the resistance was fully integrated into the conduct of operations, since generals determined its use on the ground. Correlatively, OSS and SOE leaders lost a share of their power: "Henceforward Baker Street's influence on operations in Italy was remote and its involvement mainly confined to logistics."[18]

That shift complicated the articulation between the political and the military, two closely correlated spheres. "Now the Chiefs of Staff and the Commanders-in-Chief under them were responsible for strategy and the Foreign Office for policy."[19] Risks of conflict were very real if the generals, to hasten the victory, relied on underground groups—Communists, for example—that the diplomats were fighting against for geopolitical reasons.

Support for the resistance in Italy thus proved perilous, especially since it differed from the underground in other countries. In the first place, the Italian resistance did not stem "from a popular revolt against Fascism or the traditional State . . . [but was] a rebellion against a foreign invader and his local puppets. This had the effect of limiting the potential political impact of the movement: would it then be simply a minority force for national freedom or a mass movement for national renovation?"[20] From the first, the resistance in Italy was politicized. It constantly swung back and forth between the desire to drive the Germans from the peninsula and the wish to proceed to a political *aggiornamento*. If that peculiarity linked it to France, it clearly distinguished Italy from Denmark and Norway.

The Italian resistance developed first in the civilian realm and only later envisioned military possibilities. Elsewhere in Western Europe, by contrast, these two components were combined from the start. Labor strikes multiplied in the industrial north of Italy in March 1943, then in March 1944, when more than a million workers staged a work stoppage for more than a week.[21] These movements reflected both the exasperation of the workers, who were subjected to difficult living conditions, and the rejection of the Fascist regime. They also manifested the combativeness of laborers and the strength of the Italian Communist Party, which, despite twenty years of persecution, was capable of waging powerful collective struggles. Viewed from elsewhere in Europe, such mobilizations were hardly surprising—they had made a mark in both Belgium and France. Compared to the situation in Germany or Japan, however, they were the exception, a point that deserves to be emphasized. But it was not until September 8, 1943, that the Communist Party launched its Garibaldi Battalion, and only on October 10 did the CLN call for creating "Gruppi Combattimenti in Italia" (Combat Groups in Italy).

Although OSS intended to support these armed groups, SOE was more circumspect. The British feared that liberationist "governments" would be created behind the front lines and would defy the authority of Badoglio and Victor Emmanuel.[22] In addition, the *partigiani* and the Allied powers did not have the same objectives. The partisans wanted to repel the invaders as quickly as possible, while the Allies, as we have seen, counted on drawing the maximum number of German divisions into Italy, to prevent them from reinforcing "either the eastern front against the Russians or the western front in France."[23] That was a significant difference.

These debates remained largely academic until spring 1944: neither SOE nor OSS had the resources to arm the Italian resistance, which did, however, possess weapons abandoned by the regular army after September 8. It was not until December 23, 1943, that a first parachute drop (modestly) equipped the shadow fighters.[24] They therefore carried out only rare sabotage operations: the destruction of the Sette Luci Bridge, west of Foggia, on the night of December 20, 1943; or an attack on the Rome–Cassino rail line that destroyed two trains.[25]

The situation began to evolve in 1944. In the first place, the political situation became more settled: the "Salerno turn," initiated by Palmiro Togliatti, head of the Italian Communist Party, in March of that year, provided reassurances about the loyalty of the Communist elements, while the Badoglio government, in embracing the full spectrum of parties, stabilized the executive branch without placing it in the line of fire of anti-fascist groups. In addition, General Harold Alexander, the supreme Allied commander, boasted in May 1944 that the resistance had immobilized six of the twenty-five German divisions fighting at the time on the northern part of the peninsula,[26] which confirmed the strategic interest the army of shadows had assumed. At a time when the Anglo-Americans were preparing to conquer the Eternal City, the partisans were therefore called on to play an important role in Operation Diadem, which began on May 11, 1944.

The Anglo-Americans hoped that the partisans would harry the enemy or commit multiple sabotage operations against the railroads or telephone lines. In April 1944 they sent in fifty tons of weapons by parachute drop, even while fine-tuning their plans. In the North, an Italian officer, Edgardo Sogno, a veteran of the Spanish Civil War on the Francoist side, set to work in early May to form reception committees and prepare a mass action, while at the same time encouraging the resistance groups to refrain from any premature assault. In the South that same month, Gerry Holdsworth of SOE activated his contacts in the northern and central parts of the country, to launch a sabotage campaign in support of the offensive that was sweeping the kingdom's capital.[27] There was no question, however, of promoting large-scale guerilla warfare, or a fortiori of encouraging insurrectional movements.

The Four Days of Naples

From that standpoint, the Four Days of Naples were an alarming precedent. Exasperated by Italy's about-turn in September 1943 and by the Salerno landing, the Germans reacted with brutality. In the first of a long series of provocations, on September 23 they proceeded to a first roundup of men born between 1910 and 1925, which constrained some eighteen thousand men in Latium and Campania to forced labor. A second roundup followed three days later in the city of Naples. Immediately afterward the Germans ordered the evacuation of a strip of coast a thousand feet long and imposed martial law. These iniquitous measures provoked unrest. On the night of September 27 the Neapolitan population revolted. In the morning it erected barricades, then attacked the Germans in multiple coups de main. The Nazis ultimately withdrew, but not before murdering dozens of civilians. On October 1, 1943, the Allies finally entered the city.

That spontaneous insurrection was no urban convulsion expressing the rage of a blind and unbridled mob. It mobilized the common people from the neighborhoods, who were anxious to protect and liberate their own space.[28] For the Allies, that insurrection augured ill. It confirmed the barbarism of an occupier who had not hesitated to fire on the city with cannons and who for a time even considered bombing it. The toll was devastating: 663 Neapolitans died during the "Glorious Four," and the number might have been even higher if the maze of streets, the courage of the Neapolitan population, and the proximity of the Allied troops had not prompted the Wehrmacht to beat a retreat.

All in all, that tragedy hardly led the Anglo-Americans to promote insurrectional movements. When their forces approached Rome, the city did not make a move. An attack mounted on via Rasella on March 23, 1944, had resulted in the death of thirty-two SS officers, but it had been followed by bloody reprisals. In any event, the Germans had decided to conduct a terrorism policy to cut the resistance off from its civilian supporters.[29] They therefore seized on the pretext of that attack to shoot 335 hostages in the Fosse Ardeatine—an antecedent whose brutality had a dampening effect. In withdrawing, meanwhile, the Germans rendered any plans of insurrection for the Eternal City null and void. In the end, the Allies preferred to count on sabotage and harassment of the enemy rather than wager on revolt. During Operation Diadem, they parachuted in twelve detachments, four of them composed of SOE saboteurs. That option was a prelude to a new modus operandi: to send liaison officers assigned to support the underground groups in their sabotage activities but also to engage in guerilla warfare[30] in conjunction with regular operations—a Copernican revolution destined for a great future in the months that followed.

The Corsican Affair

In addition to the Italy campaign, the liberation of Corsica in September 1943 fueled the reflections of war strategists.

Indeed, the Anglo-Americans were interested in the Island of Beauty for strategic reasons. In invading it, they hoped to force the Germans to disperse their forces,[31] pushing them to withdraw from Naples and even to retreat from Rome. That would favor the Allied offensive at the time of the Salerno landing. They all believed that the Wehrmacht, in the highly likely scenario of an Italian armistice, would abandon Sardinia and move back to Corsica—which impelled them to use the island to siphon off enemy forces.[32] In short, reconquering Corsica was far from an exclusively French concern.

Neither the British nor the Americans, however, had the ships and troops necessary to launch the offensive. They therefore assigned SOE the responsibility for planning it[33] and counted on the local resistance to carry it out. On April 4, 1943, Paulin Colonna d'Istria, a French officer, was set down by a British submarine on the eastern coast of the island, with the task of organizing the underground troops. At the same time, the RAF began to drop weapons by parachute. Only one air mission took place in May and another in June, but the pace accelerated in July (11), August (25), and September (30), supplying in all 8,000 submachine guns, 1,000 rifles, 150 machine guns, 98 Bren automatic rifles, and several mortars. Not all the operations were crowned with success, however. The uneven terrain did not make things any easier; reception committees were not always at the dropping zone; parachute drops often occurred at too high an altitude (over 1,000 feet); many of the shipping containers, having been hastily prepared, burst; and finally, parachutes failed to open—in 15 percent of cases for the single month of September.[34] Despite these setbacks, the Allies agreed to a fairly substantial effort to ensure the success of the insurrection.

Certainly, the French participated in the planning. The submarine *Casabianca*, having escaped from Toulon in November 1942 to join the Allies, went back and forth multiple times between Corsica and North Africa and transported in all sixty-seven tons of weapons. But that contribution represented only a third of the volume delivered by air. In addition, sea transport did not guarantee success: the failure rate ranged between 25 and 50 percent, compared to the some 22 percent loss rate occurring during parachute drops.[35] That said, the ten thousand Corsican partisans enlisted on the eve of the big day (perhaps a high estimate) were in possession of a relatively decent arsenal.

The news of the Italian armistice, made public on September 8, lit the match. The same day, the Corsican Liberation Committee, dominated by

Communists, called for insurrection. In response, twelve thousand Germans were deployed to the Bastia region. To support the resistance fighters, who were at risk of being overrun by these experienced warriors, General Giraud immediately dispatched 109 men from the Third Shock Company, who disembarked from the *Casabianca* in Ajaccio on the night of September 12. Five hundred men transported by the destroyers *Fantasque* and *Terrible* followed. In early October the partisans and the regular troops seized Bastia; the German forces then evacuated both Corsica and Sardinia.

Politically, the episode profoundly affected French internal affairs. Henri Giraud had not informed Charles de Gaulle of the operation beforehand, and the reply was not long in coming. On October 2 the Man of June 18 ordered the Königstein escapee to choose between command of the French forces and political responsibilities. On November 9 Giraud took the first option, leaving his rival to exercise power on his own. The Corsican insurrection thus settled the debts remaining from the Algiers imbroglio. At the same time, it opened the Communist Pandora's box. The Parti Communiste Français, via the Front National, had in fact controlled the insurrectional process. In the liberated communes, it had immediately seized power: the populations entrusted their town halls to its representatives by a show of hands. The Gaullist prefect Charles Luizet, dispatched in haste, strove for two months to return to more canonical forms of democracy, even while declining to organize municipal elections, which appeared risky in that situation. These methods raised questions about the objectives being pursued by the French Communists: Did they want to take power upon liberation? Or were they playing the patriotic card of national union? That question, unanswered for the time being, gnawed away at French political leaders. Paradoxically, it did not trouble the Allied authorities. "Political differences there were; but they became manifest only when the campaign was nearly over, and the fighting itself was marked by an exceptional solidarity of resistance and a fusion of political parties in the fervor of action."[36]

Those in charge of subversive warfare looked less kindly on the military capacities of the resistance. They noted that the German retreat had been planned before the maquis went on the attack, that it had unfolded in an orderly fashion,[37] and that the enemy had left the island when it chose to do so.[38] "Corsica," noted OSS envoys, "was 'conquered by default'— the Germans evacuated it as quickly they could."[39] In the same vein, the Wehrmacht had defeated the partisans on its own schedule and "could have taken Ajaccio at any time had they so pleased."[40] Observers were also aston-ished by the behavior of the patriots, "swaggering about Ajaccio's cafes armed with Sten guns over each shoulder and revolvers and daggers every-where."[41] Finally, they pointed out that the partisans had seemed more concerned to "settle scores with Vichy officials instead of performing their assigned invasion-support tasks. A number of observers therefore concluded that the resistance would behave similarly on D Day, inclining Eisenhow-er's command to doubt the value of resistance activity prior to the Nor-mandy invasion."[42] Conversely, the resistance fighters, in view of their detailed knowledge of the terrain, had been useful in delivering informa-tion to the regular units[43] and in acting as guides or scouts.[44]

All things considered, the Allies saw firsthand that they could count on the partisans to carry out sabotage but not to commit large-scale acts of war, since the underground was not "sufficiently armed to offer serious and sustained resistance to organized enemy troops."[45] In addition, they ruled out the possibility of calling for insurrection, fearing that the Germans would use bloody violence to repress an uprising—the Neapolitan exam-ple was a grim portent. Finally, the SOE and OSS men on the ground, unlike their leaders (who were often haunted by the Red Peril), did not overestimate the danger of the Communists, believing not without reason that their ardent desire to liberate their country prevailed over their wish for a new October Revolution.

On the basis of these observations, strategists defined the role they intended to assign to the resistance within the framework of Operation Overlord.

CHAPTER XVII

Plans and Instructions

The Allied general staff, fresh from the Italian experience and basing themselves on the example of Corsica, contemplated the missions they would entrust to the internal resistance. In light of the recent events, they asked the resistance to make paralyzing the enemy's communications its top priority. As PWE noted, "If the Germans are able to switch troops rapidly it will make the battle infinitely more costly and will add to the land hazards which lie behind the beaches. The greatest contribution which general resistance in occupied Europe can make is by undetectable methods, immobilizing or heavily retarding the movement of these forces in and towards the areas involved."[1] In France, the three principal objectives were to sabotage railroads and transportation hubs, to interfere with the reinforcements—especially armored vehicles—moving from the north and west, and to disrupt telecommunications and highway traffic systems. French resistance fighters were also instructed to strike targets of opportunity (oil and munitions depots or airbases, for example).[2] Identical directives were given in Belgium. "It was a matter of disrupting every mode of transport, paralyzing their vital work, keeping the enemy from using radio, telegraph, telephone etc., inasmuch as these various public and private services are controlled by the civilian Belgian population." As much as possible, the patriots were also to work against the occupier's scorched-earth policy and protect their country's vital installations.[3]

At the same time, strategists had no illusions about the capacities of the underground forces, which they judged incapable of acting "without active military support from outside."[4] They also doubted that these forces could avoid the enemy's depredations, since the resistance fighters would not only have to capture the objectives, they would also have to hold them. Because of the high strategic value of these objectives, the Germans "would certainly stage counter-attacks against which the lightly armed patriots could not be expected to defend a small fixed point,"[5] a view the secret services ratified. Major Knight, head of SOE's Belgian section, confided in December 1943: "I would expect major demolitions to be carried out by the enemy because no effective armed opposition could be counted on from SOE Resistance Groups."

The Allies also doubted that the resistance could intervene effectively in the landing zone, "owing to the density of enemy troops and special security measures. For the same reason they could not be relied on to function a short distance behind the enemy lines and must be used for strategic rather than tactical roles." The general staffs, finally, did not believe in the possibility of guerrilla warfare. "Resistance Groups lacked mobility and could not normally operate outside a radius of 10 or 20 miles from their centre. They had no transport, and movement on foot must be undertaken normally cross-country and clandestinely. . . . Their lack of heavy equipment and regular training made it impossible for them to seize and hold a strategic point for any length of time against an organized attack by regular formation."[6] Modern warfare, based on speed and firepower, therefore gave the underground forces only a modest role, ruling out any spectacular military action.

Insurrection?

Should a national insurrection be encouraged despite the Neapolitan precedent, in the nonviolent form of a general strike, for example? Charles de Gaulle had proclaimed on April 18, 1942, that "the duty of every Frenchman, of every Frenchwoman, is to fight actively by every means in his or her power, both against the enemy himself and against the people of Vichy, who are the enemy's accomplices. To those people, as to the enemy, the French owe nothing, except to drive them out and, in the meantime, sabotage their orders and despise their faces. National liberation is inseparable from national insurrection."[7] In fact, the Free France leader believed that his countrymen, far from standing passively by during their liberation, had to take an active part. In his mind, however, that insurrection was to be as brief as possible and to occur in close correlation with the progress of the Allied forces. The Communists did not see things the same way. They were counting on a general insurrection, preceded by a vast movement of strikes that, they hoped, would allow them to accelerate the pace of liberation, to celebrate the role of the underground forces, and to welcome in the capacity of victors the Anglo-American liberators. "For de Gaulle," the historian Philippe Buton concludes, "insurrection belonged to the symbolic realm; for the PCF, to the strategic realm."[8] The Belgian Communists pleaded in unison for a national uprising, but they ran up against both the government in London, which they claimed to recognize, and the resistance organizations, with which, they said, they were collaborating.[9]

The Anglo-American leaders feared that scenario, as we have seen. To be sure, they realized the advantages of a vast strike movement, believing that, in the days following the landing—a "vitally important" period— "strikes will assist in seriously obstructing communications and supplies in the enemy's tactical and strategic back areas and will impose a new and unrehearsed, and therefore incalculable, strain upon his manpower and organizations at the moment most likely to assist our military operations."[10] As a result, they were inclined to believe "that mass disobedience by the ordinary civilian population, including active sabotage of communications and telecommunications and disruption of enemy administrative control, etc., can render the maximum assistance to Overlord if called for on D Day or a few days after."[11] "Even should we adopt a policy of trying to prevent them," they averred, "spontaneous and unorganized strikes are likely to occur in many areas. This is in itself an argument for directing and coordinating them in order to inflict the maximum strain upon the enemy."[12]

At the same time, the Anglo-Americans feared that the Germans, in a bloody repression, would engage in massacres. SHAEF, the Allied staff in charge of Operation Overlord, pointed out that "a small guard armed with automatic weapons need have little fear of a crowd."[13] Authorized voices from the resistance and from the governments in exile voiced their agreement. "The Belgian Government is anxious to avoid any instructions which would incite a 'mass rising' in the occupied territory as it considers that the loss of life and destruction caused would be out of proportion with the expected results," Hubert Pierlot explained to Lord Selborne in

March 1944.[14] The resistance fighter Michel Brault (Jérôme), originally from the Combat movement, was sent to London to plead the cause of the maquis, and he agreed with that approach. Believing that France had between thirty-five and forty thousand armed men, he pointed out that, of that group, "about ten thousand, those in the maquis, would have at their disposal the ammunition sufficient to do battle for twenty-four hours. It does not seem to me, therefore, that the strategic and tactical interest of an immediate insurrection is high. In conclusion, I am absolutely opposed to a call for general insurrection at the time of the landing. It would almost certainly end in failure."[15]

The Allies rallied behind that point of view[16] and refrained from issuing instructions,[17] preferring to wash their hands of the whole affair. "From the humanitarian point of view, we would prefer the mass rising never to take place," concluded SHAEF in April 1944. If de Gaulle were to proceed regardless, "we should make it clear that the decision is entirely his own and not the result of any pressure from us, but that we will assist him as far as practicable in widening the scope of the rising, increasing its strength and prolonging its duration."[18]

All in all, the Anglo-Americans did not overestimate the importance of the internal resistance, as General Frederick Morgan, in charge of planning Operation Overlord, explained.

These groups are concentrated in centers of population and thus could not operate in effective numbers in the coastal defended areas. Moreover, leaders of groups on the Continent could not be warned in advance of the date and time of the operation. Consequently, no assistance from resistance groups can be expected during the initial assault. After the assault has taken place, however, pre-arranged plans could be put into effect for the demolition of railway communications in certain specific areas and for guerilla activities on the German lines of communication. . . . At a later stage in the invasion local uprisings in the rear of the enemy lines could be organized with a view to immobilizing enemy troops in the protection of rearward installations. General uprisings should be limited to the areas to be occupied by our forces, as otherwise the functioning of organized groups will be disrupted.

And he concluded: "The assistance of the groups should therefore be treated as a bonus rather than an essential part of the plan."[19] It was still necessary to make sure that the resistance groups would obey instructions—something that was uncertain at the very least.

Differences Among Allies

To entrust a role to the underground forces in the liberation of Western Europe required that the Anglo-Americans speak with one voice. They had to define a joint strategy, issue identical instructions, and coordinate their propaganda so that the resistance would follow without deviation the prescribed line. These imperatives seemed to constitute an impossible mission, given the rivalry playing out on opposite shores of the Atlantic.

On the basis of their long experience, the British aspired to educate their American cousins by revealing to them the arcana of subversive warfare. These pedagogical ambitions veiled more mundane concerns: the British were seeking to exert control over the Americans, while reserving for themselves the bulk of the operations. Quite logically, OSS rebelled. While contributing to the defeat of the Reich, General Donovan's services had to defend the interests of their country and impose their existence on a military hierarchy doubtful of their utility. They were therefore inclined to go it alone. On January 6, 1943, Lieutenant-Colonel Huntington was sent to London to implant a subbranch of the OSS action service there. His instructions were clear: "You must collaborate fully with our good friends. At the same time grow and mature as rapidly as possible. SOE will 'baby' us for a time, but at some point we must be fully prepared to shift for ourselves."[20] The historian William Langer, head of the R&A branch in Washington, made the same argument: "No one esteems or respects our British Allies more than I do, but it appears to me to be most dangerous for us to depend upon them in the intelligence field or to accept their control over our intelligence activities."[21]

In addition to differences relating to the defense of respective national interests, strategic variables also came into play. OSS tended to defend a military notion of subversive warfare, which entrusted to the general staffs the task of defining the targets of the underground groups. SOE, by contrast, preferred "to go out into enemy territory deliberately and then to search for objectives," an approach that caused perplexity in its ally.[22]

The Americans, finally, were worried about the monopoly the British exerted over the delivery of weapons to the resistance, especially the French resistance. "Unwillingness or inability of the United States to make an effective contribution to airlift might constitute one more confirmation in the mind of the French that the United States are not favorably disposed to Resistance at large, and might thereby create a lasting resentment in the mind of those most-likely to control affairs in post-war France," Colonel Haskell of the Action branch pointed out.[23]

Donovan's men tried to make things right. For example, they mounted solo operations, which were sometimes favored by technical factors. In the Italian theater, the SOE base was in Monopoli, on the Adriatic coast; OSS, operating from the Mediterranean coast, could conceal some of its actions from its ally.[24] Beginning in 1943, therefore, OSS increased the number of parachute drops for the French resistance, which was no simple matter. Eisenhower's chief of staff, General Bedell Smith, realizing the extent of Franklin Roosevelt's hostility toward Charles de Gaulle, suggested that the requests for parachute drops be made directly to his superior and not submitted to the president, a point on which, in March 1944, he proved "most emphatic."[25] In the United States, then, the dictum *cedant arma togae* did not always hold sway: military power was not necessarily subject to civil authority.

The British were angered by these secessionist tendencies. "Almost each time Walter or I meet an OSS man," David Bowes Lyon of the Political Warfare Executive warned in January 1943, "we hear of some plan or project in progress about which OSS has not informed or consulted us. . . . In no sense do I mean that we must expect hostility from OSS; every contact we have implies cordial cooperation. . . . In relations with OWI we could expect 'ideological differences' (eg on imperialism) but now we can expect to meet in OSS the products of crude commercial competition."[26] At the same time, His Majesty's services, themselves expert in the art of dissimulation, could not openly inveigh against these maneuvers. They therefore used roundabout means. "There has been a tendency to consider that since physical operations have to start from the United Kingdom, nothing can be done without the approval of the British," explained Whitney Shepardson, who naturally feared that coordination would become subordination. "The issue is not expressed as clearly as this. It is suggested that it is necessary to 'coordinate' intelligence activities with the British or to conduct such activities only with their knowledge and with their agreement."[27]

Yet the Allies avoided adding fuel to the fire. The Americans did indeed remain dependent on the British, for both their expertise and their logistics—liaisons, for example. Major Maddox observed: "Our inability to obtain necessary facilities from American authorities makes a certain dependence on the British inevitable."[28] On the other side, SOE's aspiration to monopolize the aid given to the underground forces was grounded in reality. Between February and April 1944 the Americans oversaw 253 missions from England or North Africa, which supplied more than 240 tons of materiel to the French; at the same time, the Royal Air Force's 1,586 sorties provided 1,350 tons. "If the British had tried to 'monopolize the credit' for aid to the French resistance," the State Department noted, "they had also done most of the work."[29]

William Donovan was fully aware of these realities, as he explained to David London, head of OSS in London, in April 1943:

> I am prepared to accept their leadership and experience and it is needless to add am more than grateful for the help so generously given. If however you mean by "complete integration of SO [the Special Operations branch of the OSS] and SOE" that we should merge and our identity thus lost, then I think it would be better to have no participation. If by "complete integration" you mean to accept a position of authority under British leadership by maintaining our organization in that secondary position, although subject to British orders, I have no objection whatever, because certainly at this time this should properly be done. . . . Obviously we are far behind SOE in recruiting and training but now have full approval [of] our Army for organization [of] our forces and consequently can make promises with confidence.[30]

The competition between the services did not degenerate into open warfare, therefore, and for a time OSS accepted the preeminence of SOE. But that situation sometimes spurred members of the resistance to play one side against the other, as the Swiss affair confirms.

The Swiss Affair

In November 1942 Philippe Monod, head of Combat for the Alpes-Maritimes, met in Cannes with Max Shoop, a lawyer with whom he had previously worked. Through him, Allen Dulles, head of the Swiss subbranch of OSS, proposed a deal: Combat would supply intelligence to the Americans, who in return would fund the movement. The agreement was concluded in April 1943, and a delegation headed by General Davet, representing Combat and other movements in the southern zone, took up residence in Bern.

General de Gaulle's representative, Jean Moulin, had not been informed of these talks. When he learned of them in late April, he flew into a rage. "We know how you've stabbed De Gaulle in the back!" he told Henry Frenay.[31] At a time when the Man of June 18 was attempting to assert his claim on North Africa, the agreement between Combat and OSS weakened him, since it deprived the Gaullist camp of a major advantage: a monopoly on the intelligence transmitted to the Allies. Such, at least, is the dark view adopted by many historians, such as Daniel Cordier, Moulin's former secretary. "To what extent did Donnavan [sic] and Dulles implement the US president's policy against de Gaulle? It is difficult to give an accurate assessment, since the documents in that affair are not yet available for consultation. But the American agents' intentions matter less than the possibility they offered Frenay and the other movements to emancipate themselves from de Gaulle's oversight and to finally deal with him as equals in the international game under way."[32]

Did Frenay want to stab de Gaulle in the back? That accusation seems at the very least exaggerated. The head of Combat felt no inclination to side with General Giraud; at the height of the Algiers wrangling, he had always loyally supported the Man of June 18.[33] In any case, in dealing with the Americans, he did not mean to strike a blow against Fighting France. He was hoping, however, to recalibrate a balance of power that worked against him, by obliging the Gaullists to treat the movements as equals rather than subordinates—a radically different approach from that followed by Jean Moulin. In addition, Frenay's maneuver implicitly targeted General de Gaulle's representative. In confining him "to the role of observer or ambassador, [the leaders of Combat] seized hold of his position as financier, arms supplier, and liaison agent with the Allies. Henceforth, [they] would be in charge of external liaisons with the Resistance and would supply weapons and money to the movements."[34] Moulin was lucid in his assessment of the peril. In his reports, he cast outrageous aspersions, claiming, in what was a reckless ellision, that Frenay was negotiating "with the Americans and, by force of circumstance, with Giraud."[35] That barb could only exacerbate the hostility between the two generals.

Should we concede, then, that the Americans, in dealing with Frenay, were seeking to weaken the Cross of Lorraine camp? That interpretation seems risky at least, especially since it obscures an important fact: Roosevelt, unlike Churchill, allowed his services a great deal of independence. The Swiss affair was not dealt with in the Oval Office; it remained confined within OSS's sphere. And relations between the Gaullists and the American secret services were excellent. In July 1942 Charles de Gaulle had even asked that OSS "deal exclusively with him," but General Donovan put him off, replying "that he was not in a position to do this, but he would support all French resistance through any proper channel."[36] Subsequently, a relation of trust was established between the Gaullist and the U.S. secret services. OSS leaders acknowledged: "The larger contribution to the September [1943] total was made by the Free French Intelligence, which accounted for nearly a third of all the reports received."[37] They also noted that, between April 1, 1943, and April 1, 1944, they had handled "61,000 documents (BCRA 18,000 / SIS 10,000 / SI OSS 12 000)."[38] In short, OSS did not by any means intend to weaken the Gaullist camp. Its position diverged from the underhanded maneuvers of SOE, which, it will be recalled, had blindly supported the anti-Gaullists in the pathetic Carte affair. From that standpoint, the Office of Strategic Services deviated from the line that both the White House and 10 Downing Street were pursuing.

OSS did hope, in dealing directly with the French resistance, to gain independence from the Special Operations Executive and the Intelligence Service. The British were not taken in, and OSS was prompted to hedge. Anticipating London's protests, David Bruce reminded his agents that he had the greatest confidence in Allen Dulles's talents. He added nonetheless that "any negotiations with French Resistance Groups in Switzerland must be coordinated with British-American plans here." And he added: "You will understand probably what we are facing, namely that there must be a complete coordination in dealing with the French, so far as SO-SOE activities are concerned in London, and that no financial advances or other commitments should be made to them, without clearing from London."[39]

Two weeks later, Charles Hambro, the head of SOE, spelled things out. He refused to allow the French resistance movements to have any representatives in Switzerland. "The resultant situation must be utterly confusing and the security position deplorable. It can only lead sooner or later to a disaster inside France. . . . We have consistently tried to weld these resistance groups into a coordinated movement, in order to forge a single weapon for use in conjunction with the military liberation of France. . . . It is essential therefore to have a strongly consolidated movement, which will be capable of receiving and executing the directives they will receive from London for action."[40] He added: "The control of the French resistance movements comes within the sphere of British influence as outlined in the agreement between OSS and SOE of last January. . . . Thus coordination must be carried out in London between you and us, and no independent instructions sent from elsewhere."[41]

To drive the point home, in June and July the BCRA refused to provide OSS with intelligence, an embargo "attributable to the allegedly unsympathetic attitude of the American Government towards de Gaulle." That sanction caused Donovan's men no end of suffering. Lieutenant-Colonel Maddox reminded the U.S. Embassy in London "that the State Department's policy toward the French political situation should give weight to the fact that the Fighting French Intelligence Service was then producing more and better information from the Continent than any other service.[42] He also courted Passy, head of the BCRA, emphasizing his "strong desire" to see their relations "re-established on the basis of which they have operated so agreeably during the past year."[43]

These exchanges confirm that Allen Dulles, far from implementing an anti-Gaullist line, had attempted—in conjunction with his leaders—to develop contacts with the French resistance "in anticipation of the day when they might be useful." Although the home office approved the first developments in the Switzerland situation, it had no intention of falling out with the British, especially since, in the spring of 1943, OSS did not have the means to engage in a test of strength.[44] In any event, an accord was reached in summer of 1943.[45] Davet's delegation would receive 4 million francs a month to support the maquis, a million of which would be held in reserve to draw on in case of emergency.[46] Inasmuch as, in June, the CFLN recognized General Davet as its representative,[47] the Gaullists exerted—albeit only nominally—control over the distribution of the funds that mighty America was paying the French resistance. That support was not merely symbolic. In November 1944 Lieutenant-Colonel Van den Stricht noted that a total of 65,750,000 francs had been paid by the Swiss OSS between March 29, 1943, and November 20, 1944,[48] a sign that, in Donovan's view, support for the French partisans took precedence over the battle against the Gaullist clan.

That said, the temptation to bank on the Americans was not confined to the Swiss affair. In April 1944 Sûreté de l'État, the state security service in Belgium, opened negotiations with OSS to sponsor a mission in that country. Once again, that strategy did not meet with unanimous approval. Although Fernand Lepage, the head of Sûreté, stubbornly defended reliance on the British, his assistant, William Ugeux, recommended "more closely working with the Americans."[49] These maneuvers were doomed to failure: over time, OSS and SOE fell into step.

Integration

Indeed, the two secret services gradually came to cooperate more closely. In early 1943 an American-British committee—SOE/SO—took on the task of coordinating them. In late October 1943 an OSS/SOE mission, known as Westfield, was established in Stockholm to coordinate the aid being provided to the Norwegian resistance.[50] But the decisive shift came about in Italy, because subversive warfare was now controlled by the commanders on the ground. The same system was adopted for Operation Overlord. Underground operations were at first overseen by the provisional chief of staff, COSSAC (Chief of Staff to Supreme Allied Commander), then came under the authority of SHAEF on January 31, 1944.[51] The following March, therefore, General Eisenhower's services were in charge of sabotage and the organization of the resistance forces for Western Europe, with the notable exception of Italy and Southern France, which were under the Mediterranean command[52] until May 10 of the same year.[53]

A new phase began on May 1, 1944. A Special Forces Headquarters (SFHQ) was formed, succeeding SOE/SO. Directly incorporated into SHAEF and reporting to its operations branch (G3), it oversaw all operations, apart from those related to intelligence, an area that the Intelligence Service intended to hold on to. The OSS leaders noted this progress with satisfaction. "Our relations with SOE have been clarified in London and Algiers. Specifically in London our relationship with SOE has resolved itself into a more perfect union with both allies occupying a combined headquarters in a separate building. Parity is the objective of the merger, and all efforts are being made to achieve it both in personnel and supplies."[54] Moreover, the Special Project Operations Center, established on May 23, 1944, coordinated the resistance in southern France and transmitted SHAEF's orders to it.[55] In actuality, SHAEF retained control of the underground forces until the landing in Provence on August 15, 1944.

Yet nothing guaranteed that the French resistance fighters would obey the Allies. On May 24, 1944, General Pierre-Marie Koenig suggested forming a tripartite general staff to solve that problem. On the 30th of the same month, SHAEF gave its consent and, on June 17, Koenig obtained the same status as all Allied commanders serving under Eisenhower's orders. But according to Jean-Louis Crémieux-Brilhac, that promotion also satisfied General de Gaulle, since "his right to formulate his own political and strategic ideas and to assert them vis-à-vis the 'Supreme Commander' through one of his generals was now recognized."[56] That statement is open to dispute, however: in actuality, SHAEF was not concerned with defending "political ideas"; its mission was to secure victory. In incorporating Koenig into its organization chart, it ensured itself first and foremost of the obedience of the French underground forces, which otherwise would have escaped its control.

The coordination of propaganda met a less happy fate. True, the Allied command created a Psychological Warfare Division (PWD), which it entrusted to General Robert MacClure. But the British Political Warfare Executive and its American counterpart, the Office of War Information, retained their independence. "The efforts of PWD to absorb them have completely failed," noted Rae Smith of PWE in May 1944. "At the present time PWD-SHAEF can only issue *requests* to PWE and OWI. . . . PWD-SHAEF is merely a coordinating agency, and all actual psychological warfare from Britain is done by the separate organizations."[57]

Apart from that sour note, the integration of the secret services into Allied military operations guaranteed that the resistance would participate in the liberation. But it was still necessary to see that the orders would be carried out.

Decentralization

As a general rule, the resistance in the countries of Western Europe had adopted a centralized structure, which gave orders to its regional components from the top. The British questioned that system, arguing that, if the leaders were to fall, the entire organization would collapse. "For security reasons de-centralisation is absolutely essential," noted Lieutenant-Colonel Hollingworth, head of the Danish section of SOE, expressing the prevailing view.[58] But decentralization also allowed the British to submit the internal resistance to their power. Orders would be transmitted directly from London to the regional level, without going through a national general staff.

The exiled powers and the internal resistance in the various countries yielded to these positions with more or less good grace. Milorg divided Norway into twenty-two independent districts. In 1944 Denmark was split up into six regions; on March 22 of the same year, six officers in charge of liaisons between them and the SOE arrived in London.[59] The six zones were completely independent and received their instructions from England.[60] The same system was set in place in Belgium, which was divided into five parts, both for sabotage activities and for the Secret Army.[61]

Only France refused to comply. Charles de Gaulle, true to the Jacobin heritage and anxious to defend the national interest, entrusted to a delegate, Jean Moulin, the task of representing him in metropolitan France and of exercising a right of inspection over the underground forces, in his role as chair of the Conseil National de la Résistance. As we have seen, Moulin named General Charles Delestraint head of the Secret Army.

But on June 9, 1943, Delestraint was arrested, and Moulin met the same fate on the 21st of that month. Disastrous in the short term, these events clearly showed that the Germans had infiltrated the Gaullist organizations. SOE made the most of these catastrophes.[62]

> The only workable system would seem to be for SOE and the reorganised French services under the COMITE FRANÇAIS DE LA LIBERA-TION NATIONALE in ALGIERS and LONDON to make contact with the groups of resisters at the lowest echelon. . . . Arms and materials . . . must be delivered to them direct and not through the intermediary or central control. . . . In other words, the military activities of the resisters must be decentralized to the utmost, kept in separate cells entirely controlled from LONDON headquarters if we are to ask the Chiefs of Staff to place reliance on the execution on D-day of the plans that are being or have been made.[63]

It is true that advances in radio transmission allowed for that reorganization, which would have been impossible in 1942.

The French compromised—in their own way. On August 25, 1943, a directive created the regional military delegates (*délégués militaires régionaux*, DMR), who, on one hand, were supposed to "organize and coordinate the paramilitary resistance of the movements on that new scale and, on the other, set in place sabotage plans, made by the BCRA and approved by the Allies, in view of facilitating a hypothetical landing on the French coasts. Their directive thus defined them as both ambassadors and technicians." A national military delegate (*délegué militaire national*, DMN) and two delegates in charge of inspections, one for the northern zone, the other for the southern, completed that setup, which restored the chain of command de Gaulle held dear. Despite difficult beginnings, the Gaullists managed to give each of the eleven French regions a delegate, accompanied by his assistants. These duties were performed by about a hundred officers at one moment or another.[64]

These men had extensive resources available to them. In the first place, they brought substantial funds along with them. In September 1943 the two zone military delegates, Louis-Eugène Mangin for the South, Pierre Marchal for the North, each had at his disposal 5 million francs, and in November each DMR received 500,000 francs. In June 1944 the ambassadors from London had an overall budget of 140 million francs. They also enjoyed good liaisons with England, thanks to miniaturized receivers called Midgets. On March 30, 1944, Rhônes-Alpes and Provence-Côte d'Azur received 106 of these devices.[65] As a result, delegates were able to receive the general staff's instructions. Because they were in communication with London, they could also ask for parachute drops of weapons—a considerable power that worried some resistance leaders. Maurice Chevance-Bertin, a veteran of the Combat movement who was in Algiers at the time, observed:

> The DMRs, in fact, have the transmission capabilities, the funding, the weapons. They have often played the role of arbiter between organizations. For that reason, they have often become regional leaders. The powers they are given in these plans tend to strengthen them in their command.
>
> *That is a mistake.*
>
> The sensibility of the Resistance suffers as a result. *By virtue of the position he holds, a DMR, even a very mediocre one, carries more weight than even a more important regional chief.*[66]

The question of who should command the internal resistance, present from the beginning, was now clearly articulated. Theoretically, SHAEF had control of actions, which it exerted through Koenig and the DMRs, but some underground leaders demanded that they be put in charge. They asserted that, since they were on the ground and therefore in a better position than London, they could set priorities and seize the opportunities that arose. The debate, whose terms were laid out well before the landing, would be revived with burning urgency in summer 1944. For the moment, other pressing matters held sway.

Preparations

The Allies now had to translate their principles into concrete plans.

Before Eisenhower assumed leadership of SHAEF in January 1944, COSSAC had developed a scenario that, in broad terms, established the framework for Operation Overlord. SOE and OSS learned of it on August 11, 1943, and in their turn, in a plan presented on December 11, summed up the contribution expected from the underground forces.[67] But the French were not in on the secret. The Allies feared they would talk too much and also did not want to link the Gaullist services with the liberation of France. Eric Mockler-Ferryman, the director of SOE for London, stated the case with the utmost firmness: his men should in no case tip off the French. "We must not hazard lives in this most decisive Operation. Any leakage will lead to the most vigorous investigation, and any offender, be it you or I, will deserve any punishment that may be given."[68] These drastic instructions posed a major risk, however, since they excluded the French resistance from Allied operations.

To obviate that risk, SOE and the BCRA formed a planning committee. Their attention focused on three sets of objectives. Plan Vert (Green Plan), developed from April 19, 1943, onward, targeted the railroad network. Plan Violet (Violet Plan), elaborated beginning on April 29, set its sights on striking the enemy's telephone and telegraph communications. Plan Tortue (Tortoise Plan), finally, envisioned as of May 10, had the ambition of slowing the Panzer divisions on their way to the Normandy front. In June 1943 an envoy from London, Claude Bouchinet-Serreulles, brought to France microphotographs of these three plans, which it was up to the DMRs to adapt to their respective regions.[69]

On the eve of D-Day, the system was in place: 1,188 railway targets had been identified. Of these, 571 were ready to be attacked; 275 had been compromised by arrests; and the rest could be destroyed if resistance fighters received the necessary materiel. The resistance had the capability to move immediately, in unison, to cut off 30 highways, and, if the underground fighters were armed, to attack an additional 103 targets. Thirty-two communications objectives could be demolished, 38 of them being already reconnoitered.[70] In December 1943 and January 1944 a dress rehearsal of Plan Vert was launched in the Rhône-Alpes region (R1); its results were relatively satisfactory.[71]

Other countries, while belonging to SHAEF's sphere of influence, were too far from the Norman theater of operations to launch a mass action on D-Day. Still, the Allies strove to place the internal resistance in order of battle everywhere in Western Europe, urging it to set up paramilitary groups and assigning it sabotage targets. Back from London on December 7, 1943, Flemming Muus, the chief organizer for SOE, devoted the first quarter of 1944 to that task, asking that, in return, the Danish resistance curtail its activities.[72]

Eisenhower's services were led to exercise restraint because of the distance of the resistance from the beachhead. Eric Mockler-Ferryman of SOE noted in May 1944: "As the Allied assault will not approach Belgium for some time and as the temperament of the Belgians is more inclined to caution, it has been found preferable to withhold the implementation of the Belgian railway and road sabotage plan until there is evidence that major enemy reinforcing movements are taking place through Belgium. The Belgian Government has agreed, however, that general harassing action and intensified general sabotage is to take place as from D-Day."[73] That was also the case in the Netherlands: "The remoteness of Holland from the lodgment area, combined with the lethargy of the people, makes continuation (but, if possible extension) of passive resistance the only possible line."[74] Norway and Denmark were to confine themselves to supporting roles, since their liberation would not come in the immediate future. "As Overlord involves no military operations in Scandinavia, no detailed planning of post D Day resistance has been possible. Both in Denmark and Norway, however, plans have been prepared to interrupt rail, road and telecommunications to delay any withdrawal of German troops for use against the Allied bridgehead in the West."[75] In all, SHAEF had modest ambitions. It doubted, for example, that "action by Resistance Groups in Denmark is likely to contribute much to the general plan."[76]

The Allied general staff focused its attention on France, where the battle would get under way. Dubious about the combat potential of its resistance, it sought to strengthen it by parachuting in war professionals (or so-called professionals).

Reinforcements

The idea was not really new. As of May 1943 the British chiefs of staff had, at Colin Gubbins's initiative,[77] considered sending small teams composed of French-speaking personnel into the Western European theater of operations. They were to bring weapons and establish liaisons with SOE. In July 1942 the teams were given the name "Jedburgh," after a Scottish village for which, it was said, Lord Mountbatten had a fondness. On July 22 a plan laid out the main positions. The seventy anticipated teams would be American-British; launched behind the German lines, they would press the local resistance to engage in guerilla warfare[78] but would not attempt to collect intelligence. On January 1, 1944, a special school—Milton Hall, located in Peterborough, not far from Cambridge—opened its doors and trained its first volunteers. The teams would ultimately comprise two officers and a radio operator; two of the men would be British or American, the third a citizen of the host country—France, Belgium, or the Netherlands, as the case might be.

That plan, though attractive, was difficult to implement because of the diversity of team members. Some were infantry officers who had been through a baptism of fire, in the Middle East, for example. Others had no combat experience or came from branches of the armed forces where training in the harsh discipline of the infantry was virtually nonexistent.[79] In addition, the French were unable to supply a sufficient number of volunteers. Above all, the clashes between different nationalities were difficult to overcome. The British held forth about the "Yankees," who had been so slow to enter the war. The Americans, in turn, complained about the horrible food being served them. As an aggravating circumstance, the leaders were not always up to the task. The first director of Milton Hall, Lieutenant-Colonel Frank Spooner, was more interested in morning parades and shoe polish than in subversive warfare.[80] He imposed a fastidious discipline, forbidding the "Jed" from visiting the nearby village, for example. The Americans who had volunteered to be radio transmitters complained that they had not been promoted to sergeants as they had been promised,[81] a slight that affected their concentration. "To date, the W/T [wireless transmitter] group has proved to be a most difficult detachment. The men are inattentive and fail to apply themselves to the work. Morale is low and complaints about broken promises in regard to promotions and parachute pay are numerous. There is a general complaint from the men that they are unable to work their wireless sets satisfactorily. The chief instructor is most discouraged and doubts whether the men will progress to the point of perfection necessary to operate in the field."[82]

Not long after, however, the situation improved. The French fulfilled their pledges by appealing to officers from the Army of Africa. The promised promotions were forthcoming. And Frank Spooner was replaced by Lieutenant-Colonel George Musgrave, a veteran of the Somaliland campaign (1941). He was popular for his jet-black mustache, for his decision to abandon the pesky rules and allow the men to go into town, and for his recruitment of new cooks. By May 1944 ninety-seven teams had been formed: eighty-eight for France, five for Belgium, four for the Netherlands.[83] Their level of competence had improved significantly: 60 percent of the teams were considered excellent, 25 percent satisfactory, and only 15 percent poor.[84] The three-person teams could be expected to get along, because the men chose one another. In March 1944 "a furious and occasionally embarrassing bout of political maneuvering" got under way. "Men would get 'engaged' only to have the engagement broken in a fit of pique the next day. Some fickle and flirtatious souls would get themselves engaged secretly to two or three others, just to be on the safe side."[85]

The principal mission of the Jedburghs was to establish liaisons with the resistance groups. "It is NOT the intention that JEDBURGH teams will necessarily usurp the authority of local leaders, but it is felt that the arrival of Allied soldiers, in uniform, behind the enemy lines, will have a marked effect on patriotic morale and that these teams, representing as they do the Allied High Command, will act as a focus for local resistance." The three men were thus responsible for equipping the underground groups, teaching them how to handle weapons and use the materiel, and eventually leading a group already in operation.[86] Deployed far from the bridgehead to disrupt the enemy's rear lines, they were to offer support and liaison services to the resistance groups, not take charge of commando operations.

The latter task was assigned to the operational groups (OG). Composed of four officers and thirty men, the OGs were to carry out coups de main against precise objectives—oil or munition depots, for example. Unlike the Jedburghs, they operated not only in the zones where a resistance group existed but throughout the theater of operations, and they did not assume liaison missions.[87]

The Allies, it should be clear, did not place inordinate hopes in the assistance the resistance could lend to Operation Overlord. But they were intent on giving it every chance by backing it militarily, especially by sending in Jedburgh teams. To attack, however, the resistance had to be able to receive the orders it was supposed to carry out.

Messages

Caution was exercised in the propaganda, so as not to give away the secret of D-Day: no allusion was made to the gigantic operation under way. "No broadcast must suggest that invasion is imminent," PWE prescribed to its Belgian announcers,[88] an instruction applicable to all of Western Europe. Beyond that imperative for discretion, the Political Warfare Executive feared awakening unreasonable hopes, especially since expectations had already been dashed many times. "We have no need to insist on the preparations for the attack on Europe. Our audience is inclined, by the very force of circumstance, to interpret all signs of military activity as indicative of an Allied landing," it explained to the French section of the BBC.[89]

The Allied general staff was nonetheless supposed to order the resistance to take action. To do so, it anticipated disseminating messages over the radio. A first series, transmitted on June 1 and repeated the next day, would place the underground fighters on alert; a second, sent out on June 5 at nine o'clock P.M., would launch the battle.[90] Because France comprised many regions, SOE intended to take over the airwaves completely to send its instructions. That idea sparked the fury of the BBC.

Its management used every means possible to avoid that uncalled-for intrusion. If listeners tuned in too assiduously to English radio, they claimed, the Germans would be prompted to confiscate radio sets, which would keep the resistance fighters from receiving their instructions. "A sudden increase in the volume of secret messages will impair the security of all operations, including those of SOE and will make it impossible for PWE to carry out its responsibilities of directing and controlling the reactions of the masses of the French people up to and during Overlord."[91] Ritchie Calder, director of plans and campaigns at PWE, explained that, all things considered,

> PWE is strongly opposed to any substantial diversion of the BBC European Service's broadcasting time from its legitimate function of providing overt news information and instructions for the benefit of the European public at large.
>
> . . . On or around D Day, the period at which such a mass appeal for disciplined co-operation will be of the greatest Military value, it is proposed that all the main transmissions to France should be diverted to carrying special SOE messages to a restricted group.
>
> Overt broadcasting is not the proper channel for messages of this type because . . . [it] derives its authority almost entirely from the fact that it is what it purports to be and carries genuine news information and instruction for all to hear. If it is diverted to covert uses of the type proposed its normal output is likely to be discredited in the mind of the ordinary listener. . . .
>
> In short, the relations of the BBC European Service with its many thousands of listeners would be jeopardized, just at the very time when it should be at its most effective, for the sake of passing messages to an infinitesimal fraction of the potential audience.[92]

A compromise was ultimately reached. SOE agreed to "reduce its demands" on the European BBC Services by using short-wave transmissions.[93] In return, beginning on April 8, 1944, it was allotted four minutes during the broadcasts of 1:30 P.M. and 2:30 P.M., and six minutes for those of 7:30 P.M. and 9:15 P.M.[94]

Based on their experience in Corsica and Italy, the Allies thus possessed, on the eve of the landing, guidelines that assigned a sabotage mission to the resistance before and after D-Day but ruled out—except in special cases—guerilla warfare and insurrection. Having overcome their differences, they succeeded in organizing an integrated chain of command that guaranteed, or at least they hoped it did, that their orders would be executed. A major problem persisted, however: What would be the status of the liberated countries?

CHAPTER XVIII

Political Liberation

The military liberation of Western Europe was an essential issue, but the political future of the liberated countries also preoccupied both the general staffs and Allied political circles. The Anglo-Americans and the authorities in exile feared that the partisans would demand the right to rule upon the Germans' departure, by putting forward their legitimacy—acquired at great cost in the underground darkness—to oppose the sovereignty that the émigré governments on the banks of the Thames claimed to embody. In addition, London and Washington pondered what legal status they ought to assign to the liberated countries. Should they administer them directly, by imposing a military government, or should they allow authorities within each country to govern them freely? That question was by no means settled in 1944.

The Specter of Dual Power

The resistance fighters who had stood up to Nazism dreamed above all of contributing to the expulsion of an occupier as brutal as he was despised. But though patriotism was their primary motivation, they were also attuned to the political issues, whether that concern had been a mobilizing factor from the first or had gradually taken root.

The interest shown in these questions stemmed in the first place from past wounds, which the ordeals of the war had done nothing to heal. In Belgium and the Netherlands, in Norway and Denmark, the shadow warriors often contested the neutralist line that their leaders had followed before the war, a choice, they believed, that had led to ruin. And the defeat had not eliminated proponents of that line, such as Paul-Henri Spaak, the Belgian minister of foreign affairs, or Dirk Jan de Geer, the Dutch prime minister, who in 1940 argued in favor of entente with the Reich. These aberrations were even more blatant in Italy, where many of the ministers, such as Alcide De Gasperi, had for a time supported Mussolini. In France, finally, several pioneers of the resistance cultivated an intense antiparliamentarianism and denounced the bankruptcy of the ruling elites, whose incompetence, the resistance fighters believed, had led to the defeat. Alban Vistel, a member of the Libération-Sud movement, summed it up this way: "No one disputed the fact that the deal-making among parties, having become an end in itself, now provided only a caricature of parliamentarianism, and that the political world of the past had ultimately lost touch with reality. Bitter experience was delivering a lesson that ought not to be forgotten."[1]

Far from abolishing these conflicts, the occupation exacerbated them, because the parties—with the exception of the Communists, who became fully engaged in the struggle on June 22, 1941—rarely placed themselves in the forefront of the battle. Rather than cooperate with one another, resistance movements and political groups tended to split apart. The movements, pointing to the absence of politicians in their ranks and arguing for their own clear-sightedness and courage, demanded a share of power upon liberation. For example, they called for provisional local authorities to be appointed in anticipation of the elections. More broadly, they sometimes asked for an *aggiornamento* that would reconstruct the institutional, economic, and social order of the prewar period, which they considered out-of-date. The parties, conversely, invoked the legitimacy bestowed by the ballot box, in order to deny the resistance fighters the right to assume responsibilities without democratic approval. That split created many tensions throughout Western Europe; it was particularly marked in Denmark, France, and Italy.

Tensions in Denmark

Following the crisis of August 1943, the Danish resistance fighters decided to form the Frihedsråd (Council of Freedom), the first meeting of which took place on September 16. According to Frode Jakobsen, a resistance fighter close to the Social Democrats who had founded the Ringen, the Frihedsråd had no objectives in the strict sense. But it set the goal of coordinating underground activities and even assuming command of them. It also aspired to form a sort of outlaw government—both within and outside its borders—which Denmark did not have at the time. The political parties did not sit on the council in an official capacity, and they mistrusted it. Doubting the effectiveness of the resistance, they feared that its activism during the occupation would result in a complete takeover by the Nazis and, upon liberation, would open the corridors of power to the Communist elements.[2] By contrast, in December 1943 the military agreed to subordinate itself to the council. There was some duplicity involved: they were hoping thereby to gain control of the resistance and were secretly acting on behalf of the traditional parties, to which they remained loyal.[3] To lead the underground struggle, the Frihedsråd then created an ad hoc entity called the M Committee, which met for the first time on January 18, 1944.

The emergence of the Council of Freedom radically changed the situation, since the council aspired to take charge of the underground forces. Although the career officers accepted that oversight, they did so reluctantly, refusing, for example, to train the army of shadows and to hand weapons over to it. Their cooperation was more like an "arranged marriage" than a passionate love affair.[4] The Allies too balked: they demanded control of the Secret Army, so that it would obey their orders on the day of the invasion. Naturally, they had no intention of denying themselves that right.

To clarify the situation, emissaries from the council went to Stockholm in March 1944 to negotiate with the SOE representatives. An Allied directive, submitted on April 27, prescribed that strategic coordination be assigned to London and the supreme commander. The very next day, the council sharply rejected it, arguing that the Anglo-Americans were attempting to bypass its authority and to impose an unrealistic solution, since they were entrusting the keys of action to an authority too far from the field. A modus vivendi was ultimately reached. Until the invasion of the kingdom, operations would be conducted by the internal resistance, which would then pass the torch to SHAEF. Immediately thereafter, the M Committee was dissolved and replaced by a K Committee, which, though emanating from the Council of Freedom, also named two general staff officers, Viggo Hjalf and Kaj Lundsteen—a way to attract the army's good graces.[5] As Lieutenant-Colonel Hollingworth, head of the Danish section of SOE, put it on June 16, 1944, the resistance groups would nevertheless receive "their orders for action direct from SHAEF only, and . . . work on Directives issued from time to time from their respective Regional Headquarters, acting on the authority of SHAEF."[6]

The Council of Freedom, while demanding control of the underground forces, also sought to bring their influence to bear in a diplomatic capacity. In particular, it wished to reestablish ties with Moscow. That move was expected to be difficult, since in November 1941 Denmark had joined the Anti-Comintern Pact, a hostile gesture Stalin had not forgotten. But in spring 1944, Thomas Døssing accepted a goodwill mission. He certainly had solid resistance credentials. A Social Democrat and former director of the Kongelige Bibliotek (Royal Library), Døssing had played a role in publishing the underground newspaper *Frit Danmark* and had twice been sent to prison. The Soviets, sounded out by the British legation to Stockholm, gave their agreement on April 12, 1944; Døssing left Denmark on June 9 and, after lengthy peregrinations, reached Baku on July 30. His status remained at the very least vague. As the historian Jørgen Hæstrup points out with humor: "A minister was delegated who was not a minister, from an ally who was not an ally, by a government which was not a government."[7]

Finally, the Frihedsråd contested the leadership of the Danish population that the traditional parties had arrogated to themselves. The council was particularly adamant because elements favorable to the Danish Communist Party were influencing it. In fact, there was a gulf between the "old politicians," as they were sometimes nicknamed, and the resistance, which burned with greater ardor. Ronald Turnbull, SOE representative to Stockholm, noted—not impartially—in March 1944: "These politicians have been aiming, not at providing a basis for active resistance, but at preserving their political and Trade Unions organisations in order to regain Denmark's previous standard of living and also her export trade after the war. . . . Against this gloomy materialistic background the magnificent and sustained work of the small but determined body of activists of the resistance movement shines brightly."[8] "They only know the word 'to save' and that at any cost—where we know the expression 'to sacrifice' where this can create a spiritual or material advantage," commented Mogens Fog, a Communist resistance leader, in August of the same year. And he added: "The idea of fighting for spiritual values, that is to say of real fighting in practice, seems to be completely unknown to the majority of old politicians."[9]

The latent crisis between the two camps finally erupted in summer 1944. On June 22 the resistance launched an attack against an arms depot that put ammunition and dozens of machine guns in its hands. In retaliation, the Germans executed eight partisans and imposed a curfew. On June 26 the employees at the Burmeister & Wain shipyard stopped work to tend to their own affairs. They were imitated by thousands of Danes. Taking the Germans at their word, they went home very early, to comply with Teutonic instructions. Werner Best made concessions, relaxing the terms of the curfew, but to no avail: the mob did not lay down its arms. In rage, it attacked the tramways and, on June 30, launched a general strike. The plenipotentiary of the Reich responded by imposing a state of siege on Copenhagen and the surrounding region, while local Nazis—the Schalburg Korps—randomly shot passersby. The toll on July 1 was high: 23 dead and 203 wounded.[10] A week later it had risen to 97 dead and 600 wounded.

That movement, largely spontaneous, had not been ordered by the Council of Freedom. But it gave rise to bitter conflict. The traditional authorities—trade unions, representatives of the administration and of the business world—were alarmed by the spiraling violence and called for a return to work on June 30. The previous day, by contrast, the Frihedsråd had encouraged the workers to continue the fight and had laid out its conditions to the occupier. The Schalburg Korps had to be withdrawn and the repressive measures suspended, with no reprisals against the strikers. Best finally agreed to the terms of this compromise, and public services were back in operation on July 2; the Council of Freedom called for the resumption of work two days later.[11] After another week, the same council encouraged the Danes to observe two minutes of silence to commemorate the end of the movement. The display of force, widely observed, confirmed that the government parties had lost their touch: the population preferred to follow the instructions of the internal resistance rather than obey the orders of a discredited political class. The Council of Freedom had achieved the leadership role to which it had continually laid claim.[12]

The Art of Compromise

The importance suddenly acquired by the Frihedsråd caused perplexity and anxiety.

The British wondered whether they ought to support it. They feared creating "grounds for conflict between the political parties and the Council of Freedom"[13] or even of confusing matters upon liberation by superimposing a new organization on the traditional parliamentary government system. The Foreign Office observed in spring 1944: "If we were to give the Council the sort of recognition which it asks for, we might alienate the party leaders (perhaps the King), the Trade Unions and various unofficial circles which have not hitherto been closely associated with active resistance. It might be argued that at this stage we should lose little by alienating them, but the risk of causing disunity in the country is a grave one which we should not want to run unless we are assured that substantial advantage would result."[14] London was also worried about the frictions that might arise between the Council of Freedom and the Free Danish Movement (formerly the Danish Council), chaired by Christmas Møller in London. At the same time, the British prided themselves on possessing a channel, thanks to the Council of Freedom, that allowed them to activate the underground forces. They also hoped that that council would bridge the gap between the internal resistance and the traditional politicians.[15]

With the exception of the Communists, the parties considered the new council "a foreign body, which had made its sudden entry on the political stage without mandate."[16] They had to face the facts, however. Their star had faded, and the public was now heeding the resistance more than their voices. That realization obliged them to come to terms with the Frihedsråd, certainly a painful ordeal. The negotiations led them not only to share power but also to acknowledge their mistakes. In conceding the full legitimacy of the internal resistance, the parties were also admitting that it had made the right choice, whereas the watch-and-wait attitude advocated by the old parties had been an error. That mea culpa was all the more painful in that it served the Communist Party, which had been cast aside by the national union government in 1940, had been forbidden from participating in the elections of 1943, and was the militant wing of the resistance.

Nevertheless, the necessary compromises were finally reached. For military matters, SHAEF agreed that leadership of the resistance would be in the hands of the Council of Freedom, which would exercise it through the K Committee. October 6, 1944, marked a new phase: the council asked General Ebbe Gørtz to assume command of the underground forces. That decision was far from satisfactory to the British. Burned by their previous experience with the Danes, they distrusted the Danish militants and feared that the resistance would reconnect with its old centralizing demons.[17] The aim of that measure was primarily to reassure military circles, in order to obtain their full cooperation. The military had every reason to be satisfied. In late 1944–early 1945, they controlled all the regional commands of the resistance[18]—which, in their eyes, neutralized the risk of a Communist takeover.

In the political arena, negotiations opened in Copenhagen in October 1944. The Social Democrats accepted the Council of Freedom's line and agreed to have two Communists—the resistance fighter Mogens Fog and an individual to be designated later—participate in the government, which would be run by one of their own, Vilhelm Buhl.[19] In the same vein, the council demanded in September 1944 that Christmas Møller come back "at once" to Denmark,[20] to help heal the fracture between the two councils. Despite the risks, the Conservative leader acquiesced. Although fifty years old, he immediately agreed to be parachuted in,[21] but he broke his ankle during training at Ringway.[22] The proposal therefore went nowhere.

In December 1944, finally, the Frihedsråd sent a letter to the four largest parties—Agrarian-Liberal (Venstre), Conservative (Det Konservative Folkeparti), Social Democratic (Socialdemokratitet), and Social Liberal (Det Radikale Venstre). Although agreeing to bow to consensus, the council set its conditions. In the first place, it demanded that Denmark acknowledge "that the Resistance policy was right, 'the Scavenius policy' wrong." It also required that small groups—the Communist Party, the Danish Unity Party—as well as the principal resistance organizations be represented in the corridors of power. In May 1945 an agreement was reached: the government headed by Buhl would have eighteen members: nine would come from traditional groups, nine from the resistance. Christmas Møller would head Foreign Affairs.[23]

Entente had therefore prevailed, albeit belatedly. To obtain it, the internal resistance fighters had capitalized on their courage and determination, leading the Danish people to recognize the Council of Freedom as the inspiration for their actions and the symbol of their aspirations. The traditional parties, whose policy of accommodation had been rejected, found themselves deprived of the monopoly they had sought. But, through their support for the council, they obtained resistance credentials.[24] That said, those in the underground had not been overly exigent. While demanding that they participate in the exercise of power—a recognition justified by the sacrifices they had agreed to make in the struggle—their program simply called for the reestablishment of democracy, the punishment of traitors, the naming of a constitutional government by the king, and the holding of elections within six months.[25]

To be sure, a few leaders embraced more extreme positions. Thomas Døssing, for example, having returned from Russia in January 1945, pleaded for the resistance to eliminate the old politicians—whom he despised—and obtained, in addition to the top position in the cabinet, the portfolios of Justice and Foreign Affairs.[26] But he was alone in his quest. Several leaders, including the Communist Mogens Fog and Erling Foss, a moderate member of the resistance, advocated restraint. As Fog explained to Christmas Møller, his position was that, "to avoid the Freedom Council becoming revolutionary,. . . it should refrain from attacking the old politicians." Moreover, he was working "always for the sake of the struggle not to come in conflict with the Social Democrats." And he added: "I think if I had not been in prison and subsequently partially out of the game I could have solved the problem by getting politicians on to the Council. It very nearly came off in January–February this year."[27] Likewise, the internal resistance fighters did not wish to perpetuate their hold on power. They declared loud and clear that the Frihedsråd "will cease to exist when it is possible for the normal constitutional authorities to resume their functions"[28]—even though, as we have seen, the Communists were hoping that the council would become the nexus of the Popular Front they so ardently wanted. Flemming Muus, finally, made the case for an accord, fearing that the institutions would falter if the traditional parties collapsed.

In short, the extremist elements on both the left and the right remained in the minority from start to finish, to SOE's great satisfaction. Indeed, with victory on the horizon, London feared the dreamy idealists more than the time-tested politicians. The British authorities also endeavored to reduce the ambitions of the internal resistance to "a more realistic level—a level that did not threaten the established political order but which gave some promise of political renewal." Such a renewal would serve the interests of Great Britain by solidly binding Denmark to the West.[29] That result was reached by consensus, but one that marked the victory of the internal resistance. The movements had succeeded in imposing both their interpretation of the events—the condemnation of the Scavenius experiment—and their men, who were invited to participate in the exercise of power. Finally, the agreement had been obtained without any institutional upheaval: with the exception of the Council of Freedom, no new structure had been invented to build compromise. That was assuredly not the case in France.

Rough Weather for France

In spite of the Scavenius government, Denmark had always been considered, if not an ally, then at least a friend. France did not enjoy that privileged status. Having long treated Philippe Pétain with kid gloves, Winston Churchill and Franklin Roosevelt, burned by the welcome the Vichyist regime had reserved for the troops landing in North Africa, now considered the French State an enemy. But they also refused to recognize de Gaulle. The Man of June 18, to get a foothold among the Anglo-Americans, therefore had to win the battle of legitimacy, at any cost. He also had to demonstrate in the eyes of the world that he bore within himself the lifeblood of the entire country.

To do so, he charged his delegate, Jean Moulin, with the task of setting in place an original organization, the Conseil National de la Résistance (CNR). Founded on May 27, 1943, it brought together the eight principal resistance movements and the two major trade unions: the Confédération Générale du Travail (CGT; General Confederation of Labor) and the Confédération Française des Travailleurs Chrétiens (CFTC; French Confederation of Christian Workers). It also included the major parties, on both the left (the PCF, the Section Française de l'Internationale Ouvrière [SFIO; French Section of the Workers' International], and the Radical Socialists) and the right (the Popular Democrats, the Democratic Alliance, and the Republican Federation).

The CNR, chaired by Jean Moulin, had the advantage of binding the internal resistance to Fighting France, which prevented the underground from emancipating itself from de Gaulle's control. It also facilitated the unification of the army of shadows, now gathered in a common structure speaking with a single voice. Finally, it allowed General de Gaulle to demonstrate his capacity to assemble the French people as a whole under his banner. During the conflict between him and General Giraud, that gave him a weighty advantage. De Gaulle commented: "The voice of this crushed yet rumbling and reassured France suddenly drowned out the whispers of intrigue and the palavers of compromise. I was at once the stronger for it, while Washington and London measured without pleasure, but not without lucidity, the significance of the event."[30] In fact, the support of the Conseil National de la Résistance allowed him to prevail over his rival.

To bring that plan to fruition, in September 1943 de Gaulle convened an Assemblée Consultative (Consultative Assembly) in Algiers. With no real power—as its name indicates—it assembled all the political colors of France, with the exception, of course, of the Pétainists and collaborationists. Its 103 members included envoys from the internal and external resistance, delegates of the political parties, and representatives of the colonies and of the general councils. The chair of the Comité Français de Libération Nationale also took care to broaden the base of his government over time: in November 1943 he incorporated members of the resistance (Henri Frenay, Emmanuel d'Astier de la Vigerie) and politicians (Pierre Mendès France, Louis Jacquinot); then, on April 4, 1944, he opened his government to the Communists (François Billoux and Fernand Grenier).

Unlike many of the Western European countries, then, Free France had invented the integrative mechanisms that favored national unity and the unification of the underground forces, even while bridging the gap between the two branches of the resistance, internal and external. Even so, the game was not won, because certain movements disputed that process.

Some denounced the resistance credentials that the Conseil National de la Résistance was conferring on discredited political parties. "The movements that set up the resistance and are in charge of the executive branch cannot admit that, to slake the thirst for consideration and future power on the part of the parties' former cadres, a Superexecutive is being created in which Resistance militants will be in the minority, and thanks to which the partisan groups will once again take the helm," warned Emmanuel d'Astier de la Vigerie, head of Libération-Sud, in April 1943.[31] "Upon learning that General de Gaulle was preparing to place the movements,. . . the parties, and the trade unions on equal footing, we had the sense of a real betrayal," relates Claude Bourdet, the number 2 man of Combat. "The Radical Party? The Democratic Alliance?. . . The Republican Federation?. . . What are we to do with these revenants that no one had heard of since 1940?"[32] That debate anticipated the conflict between the Council of Freedom and the Danish political groups.

Others, as we have seen, refused to place themselves under the command of General de Gaulle and his delegate, Jean Moulin. Many resistance fighters, finally, believed that it was their calling to conduct underground action, a mandate General de Gaulle and the Allies were claiming for themselves.

Moulin's arrest in Caluire on June 21, 1943, offered the antiestablishment camp the opportunity to retake control. General de Gaulle's delegate had imagined creating, in addition to the CNR—which he likened to an underground Parliament—an Interzones Committee, which would assume the actual leadership of the resistance in metropolitan France. In spite of his disappearance, the leaders of the movements proceeded with the constitutive meeting planned for June 25. They founded a Comité Central des Mouvements (Central Committee of Movements), which aspired to lead the underground forces and exert "power in France in anticipation of a provisional government being installed. In that capacity, it will have authority over state employees and public administrations."[33] That demand was of course unacceptable to General de Gaulle.

The interim delegate, Claude Bouchinet-Serreulles, maneuvered skillfully. He arranged to be elected chair of said committee and then limited its powers. Above all, the committee's proponents made multiple strategic errors. They restricted the influence of the Communists, who were limited to one representative and who, in retaliation, practiced the "empty chair" policy. They excluded the movements that had been shunted aside by the CNR—Défense de la France, for example—which deprived them of important assistance. Finally, the CNR had acquired so much weight that the committee could not compete with such a prestigious rival. It quickly fizzled and was soon forgotten.

The irredentism of the internal resistance did not totally disappear, however. Without Jean Moulin, the CNR fell into the hands of the movements, which elected one of their own to head it, the Christian Democrat resistance fighter Georges Bidault. The Communists pressed their advantage. On July 14, 1943, the Front National passed a motion that entrusted the council with "the mission to inspire, coordinate, and lead the struggle of the French people on its own soil."[34] The CNR thus arrogated to itself command of the underground forces, which it claimed to exert via COMAC (the Comité d'Action), initially formed by the Comité Central des Mouvements but attached to the Conseil National de la Résistance on May 24, 1944. The Communists dominated COMAC: of the three "Vs" who composed it in 1944, only Jean de Vogüé of the Organisation Civile et Militaire, a northern conservative movement, did not belong to the PCF. By contrast, Pierre Villon was part of the Front National and Maurice Kriegel-Valrimont was in Libération-Sud.

Before the landing, then, a dual threat weighed on General de Gaulle. The internal resistance, assembled in the CNR, which it dominated, could in the first place defy him by invoking a legitimacy on the basis of its resistance credentials. This legitimacy was particularly strong, in that it was grounded in a plan. On March 15, 1944, the council had defined the major measures that, in its view, were required upon liberation. In particular, it set out a program of large-scale nationalization, central planning, a social security system, and the reestablishment of the freedoms trampled by the Vichyist regime and the German occupier. Furthermore, COMAC was able to exert control over underground action, denying the powers entrusted in General Koenig. The risk of a dual power could not be averted, especially since the Communists were seizing many of the leadership positions of the French resistance.

Italian Antagonism

The situation was comparable in Italy. In the South, a government, first headed by Pietro Badoglio, then by Ivanoe Bonomi, a moderate Socialist, administered the liberated territories on a conditional basis. The North, by contrast, remained subject to the *lex germanica*, as well as the bloody Republic of Salò headed by Benito Mussolini. On September 11, 1943, the major parties there had nevertheless created a Comitato di Liberazione Nazionale Alta Italia (CLNAI; Liberation Committee of Northern Italy), dedicated to leading the underground forces. That ambition awakened suspicion. The Anglo-Americans feared that the CLNAI would present itself as an alternative to the Italian government, a hypothesis that roused particular dread in that, on June 9, 1944, the committee created military groups—the Volontari per la Libertà (Freedom Volunteers)—and because local underground liberation committees were thriving. "In Mr Eden's view the situation is reminiscent of that of Greece and there is a danger of our creating, as in that unfortunate country, not only a rival to the legitimate Government in Rome but also a rival to the Italian army now fighting on the Allied front, thus creating the essential elements for a civil war in which British troops when they come to occupy Northern Italy would inevitably become involved."[35] The Anglo-Americans were also afraid that the military authority, with the Allied Military Government behind it, would be unable to take root in that forward area.[36] The Allies hesitated, therefore, fearing the risk of a dual power but tempted by the military support the partisans were promising them,[37] the value of which the general staffs had learned to appreciate. "Resistance in northern Italy is a serious factor. In its active form of sabotage and armed hostility, it constitutes a constant irritant of enemy and has reached a stage of organization where the withdrawal of enemy forces from the north and north-west will be seriously menaced. . . . In its passive form it ensures the deprivation of Italian war factories of many thousands of workers and makes it possible for workers to avoid transportation to Germany. It provided the Allied Intelligence with military and political information." So judged Lieutenant-Colonel Roseberry in October 1944. Quite logically, he pleaded for recognition of the CLNAI.[38]

Other advantages were factored in. Granting legitimacy to the CLNAI would favor the coordination of action between the partisans and the regular troops; the committee could thereby be entrusted with the burden of disarming the resistance and maintaining order upon liberation.[39] Above all, by taking that action, the Allies would avoid creating an antagonism between North and South that would have "disastrous results to the future unity of this country."[40] The Bonomi cabinet and General William Stawell, in charge of special operations in the Mediterranean theater, therefore recommended that the committee be recognized, which would facilitate control over the local liberation committees. Recognition would also increase the influence of the resistance on the industrialists who were supposed to help protect vital installations from the enemy's destruction. And it would shield the partisans from the reprisals launched by the Fascists, "whom they feared more than the Germans,"[41] because they knew the terrain better than their allies and were proving to be ruthlessly cruel in that civil war.

But the committee also had to control its troops. "It is essential that we should not once again create a Frankenstein monster as in the case of [the Communist] EAM in Greece," warned Sir Orme Sargent of the Foreign

Office in October 1944. "Therefore we must establish a firm control over the CLNAI so as to prevent its being captured by the Communists."[42]

That problem, though seemingly impossible, was in fact solved. First, in August 1944 the Allies succeeded in getting General Raffaele Cadorna, former commander of the elite Ariete Armored Division, to assist the Freedom Volunteers as military adviser. In December 1944 the CLNAI even proposed that he command them—a measure that met one of the conditions set by the Allies.[43] Second, in November 1944 the committee dispatched a delegation to Caserta, then to Rome, to negotiate with the Anglo-American command. "On the one side, imposing and majestic as a pro-consul, Sir H. Maitland Wilson, on the other the four of us," related Ferruccio Parri, a member of the delegation. "A glass of something, a word or two, a hand-shake, and then the signing. I ask myself if whenever the British pro-consuls sign agreements with some sultan of Baluchistan or the Hadramut it is not a little the same."[44] The Rome Protocols, concluded with the Anglo-Americans—but not with the Italian authorities—on December 7, sealed a compromise agreement. The CLNAI pledged to implement the Allies' instructions, to recognize the authority of the Italian government, and to ensure the maintenance of order until the Allied Military Government was established.[45] It received in exchange a monthly subsidy of 160 million lire and was considered the legal representative in captive Italy of the Rome authorities.[46] A comparable accord was signed with the Bonomi government on December 26, 1944. The committee received the right to represent the government in the occupied territories and exercised its delegated authority there.[47] Two days later the Italian cabinet pledged to take over the funding of the northern resistance.[48] In short, a regular authority and the internal resistance were finally backing each other, which averted the risk of a northern secession.

Honeymoons

In Belgium, the Netherlands, and Norway, the situation proved less perilous. In fact, the internal resistance in those countries manifested few irredentist tendencies: in Norway, it cooperated loyally with the powers in exile; in Belgium and the Netherlands, it was too weak to impose its views.

A few tensions did come to light, however. As a general rule, they concerned the appointment of the authorities who would be running the country between the occupier's departure and the installation of a regular government. In Norway, the internal resistance laid claim to that prerogative and obtained satisfaction. The government promised that elections would take place very quickly. During the interim period, the Nederlandse Binnenlandse Strijdkrachten (NBS; Dutch Forces of the Interior) could appoint officials in a temporary capacity, "subject to the over-riding powers of the Allied military authorities." The internal resistance agreed.[49] Likewise, the Front de l'Indépendance in Belgium asked that liberation committees be allowed to replace the legal authorities at the local level. It later changed its mind: the committees would place themselves "at the disposal of the legal representative instead of supplanting him."[50] The Dutch government followed the dictum that it was better to be safe than sorry. In May 1944 it formed a Greater Consultative Council that was supposed to advise it regarding the measures to be adopted during the transitional period. The College van Vertrouwensmannen (Council of Trustworthy Men) was also created to assume the powers of the authorities in exile should a power vacuum occur.[51]

The question of who should lead the underground forces was sometimes resolved by an artifice. In Norway and the Netherlands, crown princes received the command of the Forces of the Interior, while being incorporated into SHAEF, a move that combined respect for national sovereignty and military effectiveness. Prince Bernhard received such an assignment on August 31, 1944,[52] and the Gerbrandy government solicited the approval of the movements in the internal resistance for that appointment.[53]

The British authorities prided themselves on the cooperation existing between the Norwegian government and the Dutch Forces of the Interior, "the former constantly consulting the latter on all questions affecting the present and the future of Norway. (In fact the Government have at times appeared to pay overmuch attention to the views of the Home Front [i.e., the NBS] and to be rather too nervous of doing anything with which the latter do not agree)."[54] The absence of political demands strengthened that entente. In Norway, Belgium, and the Netherlands, the resistance organizations refrained from elaborating a program, instead favoring a political truce to ensure that the struggle against the occupier be given top priority.

That irenics did not prevent the authorities in exile from keeping a close eye on things. For example, the Pierlot government confirmed in a telegram of January 1944 that "formal government instructions prescribe that all civilian and military groups refrain from all political concerns. Stop. Legal authorities only ones competent maintain order upon liberation. Stop. They may also proceed to requisitions in conformance with the law."[55] Other leaders, such as Queen Wilhelmina, attempted to instrumentalize the internal resistance groups.

The queen hoped that the war would allow her to consolidate her power. In her mind, the liberation Parliament, appointed rather than elected, should include a majority of representatives from the resistance. In urging her son-in-law, Prince Bernhard, to take command of the Dutch armies, she also expected he would be placed at the head of the military administration that was to manage the country upon liberation. Eisenhower undercut that calculation by naming Bernhard head of the underground forces only. Wilhelmina persevered nonetheless. In late September 1944 she asked the Dutch resistance to dispatch a delegation to discuss postwar reforms with her. The movements turned a deaf ear. Too divided to speak with a single voice, too weak to make a difference, they intended in the first place to respect constitutional legality.[56] As PWE noted, "The fear that Parliament may not be recalled at the moment of liberation has caused the Dutch clandestine press to give complete priority to discussions of reconstruction problems. But this state of political consciousness is due to a desire to preserve the constitutional liberties which were enjoyed by the Dutch in the past, and not to any aims of a revolutionary character."[57]

In short, the governments placed themselves within a strictly legal framework, an approach that, as a general rule, the men of shadow also adopted. Some leaders, such as Hubert Pierlot, made public pledges to that effect.

As soon as it is possible to reestablish the embryo of a central organization on Belgian soil, the government will be moved to the liberated zone. . . .

The time will come when the majority, if not the totality, of the territory will be liberated and the capital will be free.

The king will resume the exercise of his constitutional prerogatives.

The Chambers will meet once more. A legislative decree has extended parliamentary terms of office, as was done during the last war, so that the country will not find itself without national representation, even during a transitional period.

The government will be obliged to report to the head of state and to the Chambers. . . .

The government would consider it impossible that its oversight should end without being subjected to the country's judgment through regular procedures.

On July 21, 1943, the head of the Belgian government promised that, after that final discharge of responsibilities, a new government would be formed.[58]

The Dutch authorities were just as clear. Pieter Gerbrandy explained on December 8, 1943: "The Government requires at the moment of liberation an organization for the transition period between the occupation and the return of normal administrative machinery. Our country, when free or any part of it as it becomes free, will immediately and legally come under a special state of siege. During this state of siege the Government makes use of a so-called military authority."[59]

Toward Social Democracy?

Some authorities in exile realized that the return to the status quo prevailing before the war would be impossible. The harsh ordeals that had left their mark on the populations during the dark years came to be added to the torments of the interwar period, characterized, as is well known, by an economic crisis that had ravaged the Old and New Worlds. The people, in other words, were expecting not merely a return to business as usual upon liberation. They were hoping for some sort of New Deal, which, in the United Kingdom, for example, was outlined in the Beveridge Report. Granted, that hope was less ardent in the Scandinavian countries, inasmuch as their governments had already undertaken far-reaching economic and social reforms. By contrast, it was keen in France, Belgium, and the Netherlands, as well as in Italy, and quite obviously paved the way for reforms that would include the state's intervention in the economy, the formation of a social security system, broader access to education, and the expansion of individual and collective freedoms.

Sometimes the internal resistance shouldered the responsibility for reform, as expressed, for example, in the CNR's program. Furthermore, negotiations to define the new rules of the game got under way as early as October 1941 between some employers, trade union organizations, and Belgian high officials. In April 1944 these talks culminated in a "social pact" that put forward a social security plan and a collective bargaining system between management and the trade unions.[60] Nevertheless, "the real significance of the Pact lay not in the vision it presented of a new era of social welfare but rather in the way in which its preparation demonstrated the degree of common ground that had emerged during the Occupation between an influential cadre of reform-minded employers and many of the principal Socialist and, to a lesser extent, Catholic trade-union leaders."[61] The émigré powers, far from simply defining the norms of institutional transition, also sought to lay the foundations for reform. In France, the Comité Général d'Études (General Studies Committee) surveyed the internal resistance about its wishes and transmitted them to Fighting France. In Algiers, the CFLN also contemplated several reforms—especially of the press—and de Gaulle proclaimed loud and clear his desire for a break with the past. "The good people who imagine that, after so much blood spilled, so many tears shed, so many humiliations suffered, our country will agree, when victory comes, either simply to return to the regime that abdicated even as its armies were surrendering, or to hold onto the system of oppression and delation built on disaster, these good people, I say, will do well to rid themselves of their illusions."[62]

The same ambition motivated the Dutch leaders, who in London created the Van Rhijn Commission, which was tasked with setting out the main lines of a social security system in anticipation of the postwar period. As of 1941, moreover, the Commission pour l'Étude des Problèmes d'Après-Guerre (CEPAG; Commission for the Study of Postwar Problems), chaired by the Catholic Paul Van Zeeland, had the mission of considering both the transitional period and long-term reforms in Belgium. It recommended free trade but also stipulated "welfare for all," an objective that entailed developing a social security system and creating commissions on which management and unions would be equally represented. The economy would be subject to state intervention and central planning.[63] These ideas were not new, having been inspired by the plans set in place and the experiments attempted in Belgium before the war.[64] Political motives also lay behind the venture. "It is not unthinkable that P.-H. Spaak and the other ministers created CEPAG to channel the energies of the idle Belgian politicians in London and thus to avoid the formation of open political opposition to a government with very poor credibility in the eyes of the Allies."[65] In spite of everything, the ideas that had been debated prior to the 1940 conflagration were no longer simply utopian schemes but now entered the realm of possibility.

All things considered, the exiled authorities were not fearful that the internal resistance would secede, especially since it had signed solemn pledges addressed to the public, which it would find difficult to break.

Red Perils?

During the war, the Communist groups enjoyed great prestige in Western Europe, by virtue of the courage of their resistance fighters and the heroism of the Red Army. They were also the bearers of great political and social hopes. In contrast to the political parties, discredited both by their impotence during the crisis of the 1930s and by their conduct under the occupation, the Communists embodied the promise of a political and social renewal that met with enthusiasm from a portion of the societies under the jackboot.

Many Anglo-American leaders at the highest echelons of the state worried about that popularity. On the ground, however, SOE and OSS agents were less concerned. For example, the agent called Tybalt noted in December 1943: "There is nothing that would lead us to assume that the Communist Party will seek at any moment to use the [Belgian] Front de l'Indépendance in view of an antinational subversive action."[66] Drawing up a retrospective balance sheet of its actions, the Belgian section of SOE noted that the national Communist Party "had no intention of making a 'putsch' when the question of Belgium's future Government came to be considered, provided that it was given official recognition as one of the National Parties and not persecuted and regarded as outside the pale as it had been in 1940."[67]

In reality, two observations contributed to that state of calm. The British and the Americans noted in the first place that the fight against the Nazis was the top priority of the Communist parties, whatever their calculations. That assessment was valid for the Netherlands[68] and for Norway, where the political forces, obsessed with the desire to drive out the Germans, did not have any "intention of wasting their energies on a political showdown which they well know would only serve to defeat the ends they can gain by unity."[69] The urgency of the war also imposed its law in Italy, as Mauro Scoccimarro, an Italian Communist Party leader, explained in December 1943: "For the time being we'll start publishing articles about reconstruction in *L'Unità*, but a genuine programme might even be inopportune at this moment. Our fundamental programme now is war against the Germans and the destruction of Fascism and we wouldn't like to formulate programmes of economic and social reforms that might upset the unity of the national front."[70] The Salerno turn only made that strategy more visible.

The balance of power shored up the Anglo-Americans' optimism. In some countries, the Communists were strong enough not to bother with a putsch. In Denmark, observed SOE, they had "such a big chance of being successful at the post-war election that it would be stupid if they hazarded this chance by attempting a coup."[71] And it concluded: "It is not considered that the Communist Party in its present form constitutes any danger to Post-war democratic Denmark."[72]

That view was not altogether accurate. The Danish Communists hoped to take power, by creating a Popular Front that included both the Social Democrats and conservatives, Christmas Møller especially. The attraction they exerted over certain Social Democrats, sickened by the policy of presence long advocated by their leaders, increased their optimism and fed their adversaries' fears. In fact, the traditional politicians were afraid of two scenarios: the constitution of a Popular Front based in the resistance, one that would eliminate the former elites on grounds of collaboration, and a brutal seizure of power facilitated by the weapons concealed in the underground darkness.[73]

In February 1945 the Communists tried to press their advantage, demanding that the Council of Freedom—the nexus of the Popular Front they ardently wished for[74]—put together a political program for the postwar period. That effort fell short. Frode Jakobsen flatly refused, pointing out that the resistance was not supposed to engage in politics. In addition, the Social Democrats rejected their rival's advances. Above all, these maneuvers had no chance of coming to fruition because the Danish Communists were laboring under a misapprehension. They foolishly believed that the prestige acquired in the underground struggle indicated the public's adherence to their ideology, when in fact it accounted only for a sympathy mixed with admiration for their clandestine actions.

In Norway as well, though the Red resistance fighters proved "extremely energetic in organizing units, publishing underground papers, promoting sabotage etc.," the publicity that their glorious deeds earned them was "out of proportion to their actual strength."[75] They made the case for sabotage operations and assassinations and recommended starting a war of partisans on the Yugoslav model. But, PWE pointed out in February 1945, "They do not take up an openly hostile attitude towards the Norwegian government in London, nor are they disloyal to the King."[76]

In the Netherlands, finally, Gerbrandy, deeply affected by the memory of World War I, feared that the liberation would lead to a period of insurrection comparable to that which had struck Germany in 1918. But the Dutch Communist Party, decimated by the repression, was too weak to attempt a seizure of power—supposing it had even wanted to do so.

These reassuring observations suggested that the eventuality of a coup was a fantasy. But that did not rule out the need for caution. Although the Anglo-Americans supplied the Danish Communists with explosives, they refrained from handing weapons over to them.[77] In Belgium, they gave precedence to the Secret Army rather than the Front de l'Indépendance, which was given short shrift. Peeved by the Norwegian Communists' activism, they decided that no support, "either directly or indirectly" via Sweden, would be given them.[78] In Italy, finally, the Anglo-Americans proved circumspect. "When the Allied armies have expelled the Germans, they [the Communists] will come out in their true colours. On the convocation of the Constituent Assembly they may no doubt try to overthrow the Monarchy and eliminate all political parties which do not accept their dictate." So declared Noel Charles, the British high commissioner, in April 1944.[79] The Foreign Office deemed the attitude of Palmiro Togliatti, leader of the Italian Communist Party, troubling, in that he was making every effort to undermine Badoglio and torpedo the constitutional accord. His ultimate aim was "to secure predominant position of Communist Party by breaking down every alternative structure," the Foreign Office concluded in June 1944.[80] In Italy, warned William Donovan in October 1944, Communism was without a doubt "a real danger. . . . If the Communists should obtain a majority and dominate the Government, there is serious fear that they will introduce dictatorship."[81] The special services noted in January 1945: "Many reports have reached this HQ from British missions in Northern Italy during the last few months which leave no doubt that those who control Communist bands are preparing to seize power by force when the Germans are expelled by the Allies."[82] Here again, the Allies threatened to suspend deliveries of materiel if the leaders of the resistance did not ensure that weapons and money would not be used in revolutionary actions.[83] But that threat remained hypothetical. In addition to the fact that it was difficult to separate the (moderate) grain from the (Communist) chaff, the Anglo-Americans feared giving rise to "hostile reactions" that would poison the situation.[84]

All in all, on the eve of Operation Overlord, the resistance was considered an asset more than a threat. The movements were conciliatory, more inclined to cooperate with the Allies than to take their chances alone. Realizing what was at stake, the partners proved to be responsible and, in Denmark, Norway, Belgium, and the Netherlands, intent on respecting the institutional rules. In France and Belgium, moreover, the army of shadows received assurances that a new order would rise up from the rubble. To be sure, the compromises reached had often been hard-won. They had sometimes caused tensions and controversies and, in France, for example, had even required the invention of integrative mechanisms—the CNR and the Consultative Assembly of Algiers. In addition, in France and Italy, the Allied authorities were not unaware of the influence of the Communists, though they refrained from overestimating it. Politically, the Allies thus displayed little anxiety before launching their assault on Fortress Europe. But they still had to define the status to be reserved for the liberated territories, certainly a complex matter.

Principles

The British and the Americans followed a cardinal principle. Because the countries concerned were considered "friendly" territories, they were to be "liberated" and not "occupied," which ruled out any military regime. At the Quebec Conference in August 1943, J. G. Ward at the Foreign Office addressed Cordell Hull at the State Department, stressing "the importance of making it plain that there was no intention on the part of our two Governments to use AMGOT on the Sicilian model as the pattern for the liberated countries. Mr Hull agreed and later put forward a draft for a joint Anglo-American declaration intended to reassure the minor Allied Governments and their peoples as to our intentions."[85] The liberators thus expected to hand over, as soon as possible, "responsibility for civil administration in liberated friendly territory at an early date to a restored national government or provisional authority." That transfer would not be immediate, however. At the request of the general staffs, power would be entrusted, in "a 'first' or 'military' phase," to the supreme commander.[86] The generals were supposed to cooperate with and count on "loyal local authorities,"[87] which would facilitate both operations and the maintenance of law and order.

The Americans, however, displayed "evasiveness and reluctance" regarding that line.[88] The War Department, for example, balked at committing itself, favoring "a much more direct form of military administration in Allied territory and France, extending over a longer period than we contemplate," as the Foreign Office pointed out. "They do not have the close relations and ties which we have with the Allied Governments in exile and they evidently prefer not to be committed in any way to their restoration and to leave the question of the eventual national regimes in Allied territory, and in France, to be dealt with empirically."[89] Likewise, some "minor allies" grumbled. The Dutch would have preferred that their country be "brought under Dutch military government from the outset," an option that concealed, as we have seen, Queen Wilhelmina's shrewd calculations. Conversely, the Belgian authorities were relieved that their return would be preceded by "a period during which the Commander in Chief will be responsible for the maintenance of law and order. This no doubt reflects the weaker position of the Belgian Government, who are deprived of the constitutional support of their sovereign."[90]

The obstacles were gradually removed: Washington came around to London's position, and the governments in exile accepted "the need for a short initial period of military control on the basis that it is essential to the successful progress of military operations."[91] Although the principle was accepted, its implementation was sometimes a delicate matter.

Good Pupils

Three countries presented only minor problems. Norway and the Netherlands, on the strength of the legitimacy conferred on them by the presence of their sovereign and their government on British soil, were relatively simple cases to settle. It was a different matter for Belgium, which had lost its king. There was a risk that "the loyalty and affections of the Belgians" would turn toward Léopold, which could cause a conflict between the ministers and their monarch. As a result, the supreme commander could be faced with a sensitive situation, if the exiled authorities were managing the civil administration, reorganizing and reestablishing administrative and legal services, and appointing the leaders, "when the Belgian people . . . expect King Léopold to exercise these prerogatives." The British War Office therefore found it inadvisable to commit itself to the Pierlot cabinet and suggested entrusting the keys to a Belgian government "acceptable to the Belgian people."[92] The Foreign Office refused to take that path.[93] Having always considered the exiled authorities legitimate, it was not inclined to change its opinion, especially since it believed that Léopold and the émigré ministers would ultimately reach an agreement. "The best solution for all concerned is that King and Government should resume their respective functions under the Constitution and that the breach between them be healed."[94] The British had no doubts on that point: both parties "realize[d] the importance of preserving the authority of the other."[95] Pierlot himself, in a speech of July 21, 1943, had promised that Léopold would "resume the exercise of his constitutional prerogatives."

These obstacles having been removed, a series of bilateral accords was concluded with Norway, the Netherlands, and Belgium on May 16, 1944. Committing the Soviet Union as well as the United States and the United Kingdom, the accords stipulated that "supreme responsibility and authority" would fall to the supreme commander in the military phase, before being handed over, as soon as possible, to the national authorities.[96] The term "supreme authority" had been given much thought: it meant that sovereignty still belonged to the regular government of the countries concerned.[97] France and Denmark, however, were exceptions to that common framework.

Danish Complexity

Denmark, occupied by the Germans since 1940 and without a government since 1943, was assuredly a special case. It could not be considered a "minor ally," inasmuch as the Free Danish Movement, though supported by London, did not enjoy recognition from Washington. The country was nonetheless not considered an enemy because of the importance of its internal resistance. The British thus envisioned treating it with "benevolence," a position supported by SOE[98] but rejected by Anthony Eden.[99] Christian

Warner of the Foreign Office, who was in charge of the Nordic countries, proposed in November 1943 that it be treated as an "associated nation," a suggestion that was declined by Washington. The White House had no intention of falling out with the Kremlin, which still had not forgiven Copenhagen for signing the Anti-Comintern Pact.[100] True, on August 2, 1944, Vyacheslav Molotov, Soviet minister of foreign affairs, had agreed to meet with Thomas Døssing. But Molotov, condemning Danish policy, played his hand skillfully.[101] His aim was to recognize the internal resistance via the emissary of the Council of Freedom, but only to better discredit the traditional parties,[102] which had been unwilling to engage in immediate action.[103] It was to counter that strategy that the British supported the efforts aimed, as we have seen, at mitigating the disagreements between the internal resistance and the traditional forces.[104]

To escape that impasse, Anthony Eden, responding to a question opportunely raised by an MP, declared before the House of Commons on July 12, 1944, that Denmark was an ally but did not legally enjoy that status, because the USSR was opposed to it.[105] That announcement was ill-conceived. The British had sounded out King Christian X without consulting the Soviets beforehand and without really conferring with the Americans. That infuriated PWE, which had also been excluded from these maneuvers. Brinley Thomas, in charge of propaganda for the Nordic countries, howled: "If we could be convinced that there resided in the Northern Department of the Foreign Office such a superiority of mind, judgment or information, we might be content to regard their attitude with due humility. The record, however, speaks for itself."[106] That bungling led the Allied chiefs of staff to give General Eisenhower extremely vague instructions. "Denmark should be treated for the purposes of the planning and execution of civil affairs so far as possible as an Allied state. . . . It will, however, be your general aim to facilitate the establishment, by the constitutional action of the King of Denmark, at the earliest possible moment after the arrival of your forces in Denmark of a Danish Government pledged to support the Allied cause."[107] In early September of the same year, a SHAEF mission was formed and entrusted to the British general Richard Dewing. It symbolized de facto—but not de jure—recognition of Denmark,[108] which Moscow still rejected. It was only in the wake of the German surrender on May 5, 1945, that the country became the beneficiary of the framework stipulated in May 1944 for the "minor allies."[109]

De Gaulle, Adversary or Ally?

France, finally, was most certainly a special case. The Anglo-Americans agreed to a minimal recognition of the CFLN. The United States considered it "the leading organization governing the French overseas territories, which recognize its authority," a formulation that the United Kingdom, albeit with a few sour notes, also adopted.[110] But the British refused to commit themselves for the future. In 1943 they proposed that power be entrusted to the supreme commander, who was responsible for keeping "the scales even between all French political groups sympathetic to the Allied cause." He was not to do business with the Vichy regime, "except for the purpose of liquidating it."[111]

De Gaulle fought with all his might against that obstructionist strategy. His diplomats—René Massigli, Pierre Viénot, and Henri Hoppenot—tried multiple approaches with the British and Americans, but to no avail. Churchill dug in his heels. "We ought not to quarrel with the President for fear of offending de Gaulle. De Gaulle, for all his magnitude, is the sole obstacle to harmonious relations between Great Britain and America on the one hand, and the skeleton and ghost of France on the other. . . . He will be the bitterest foe we and the United States have ever had in France."[112] The CFLN then turned to Moscow, hoping that a Soviet intervention would alter the situation. But that hope fizzled. The Soviet ambassador declared in London on May 23, 1944, in perfect bureaucratese: "Inasmuch as the governments of Great Britain and the United States are of the opinion that it is at present inappropriate to recognize the CFLN as the provisional government of France, the Soviet government declares itself ready to support the position of its Allies and to act jointly in that affair with the governments of Great Britain and the United States."[113] In short, neither Joseph Stalin nor Winston Churchill wished to fall out with Franklin Roosevelt for the sake of Charles de Gaulle.

That head-in-the-sand policy caused astonishment, if not anger, among some leaders. The Foreign Office, under the Francophile Anthony Eden, sought to escape the impasse. "All the British authorities concerned now consider that it is urgent to decide the basis upon which liberated Metropolitan French territory occupied by an Allied Expeditionary Force should be administered, and that if only for practical reasons we must collaborate in this matter with the French Committee at Algiers." The British Foreign

Office asked that their American counterparts follow that line and send a delegation to London to discuss the practicalities.[114]

Other voices rose up to lament the Allied leaders' blindness. A high official from the Political Intelligence Department pointed out: "It will be very difficult to explain to the poor benighted Frenchman that De Gaulle represents his country to a lesser degree than His Excellency M. Pierlot. Frankly speaking, I was waiting for a . . . document [similar to the agreement of May 16, 1944]. We are confronting a most dangerous situation and now an effort is being made—I am sure on many levels—to share the responsibility and put the blame on the French Authorities and what ultimately amounts to the French nation."[115] SOE leaders expressed astonishment, saying it was strange that, "having created De Gaulle, the British Government never ceased to desire his downfall, to believe all those who prophesied it, and to encourage every possible revolt against him."[116]

Nevertheless, the Anglo-Americans had no intention of placing France under the AMGOT regime, whose name was objectionable enough for Churchill to have considered rebaptizing it "Solomon," to recognize "the wisdom of our Civil Administrators."[117] That suggestion caused perplexity. "I cannot believe that the Prime Minister meant this suggestion to be taken seriously," said J. G. Ward in surprise,[118] and Gladwyn Jebb wondered whether it was genuine.[119] These surrealistic exchanges confirm that AMGOT did not have a very good image. Reserved for the defeated countries, it did not apply to the liberated territories, and therefore to France, an obvious fact that U.S. Secretary of State Cordell Hull drove home in April 1944: "The United States had neither the intention nor the desire to govern France or to administer its affairs, except insofar as it might be necessary for the purpose of conducting military operations against the enemy. 'It is of the highest importance,' he emphasized, 'that civil authority in France be exercised by a Frenchman.'"[120] SHAEF also indicated that a "Military Government will not be established in liberated France. Civil administration in all areas will normally be controlled by the French themselves."[121] The Third Army's general staff went even further in June 1944: "It is not intended that Military Government be established in liberated France. Local civil administration will, as the rule, be conducted and controlled by the French themselves. Only when the French Civil Authorities fail to carry out a required action of the military commander, and the success of the military operations is jeopardized and/or allied security is threatened as a result, may direct controls be initiated."[122] Contrary to a persistent legend, AMGOT was thus not prescribed for France and, in fact, had not been implemented in Corsica in autumn 1943.

Roosevelt still had to make up his mind to state his views clearly. On March 15, 1944, he signed the draft of a directive. Eisenhower would determine "where, when and how civil administration in France shall be exercised by French citizens remembering always that the military situation must govern" the decision. He could also "consult with French Committee of National Liberation and . . . authorize them . . . to select and install the personnel necessary for such administration." The president added: "You are, however, not limited to dealing exclusively with said Committee for such purpose in case at any time in your best judgment you determine that some other course is preferable."[123] In short, Roosevelt handed off the decision to the head of SHAEF, but not without lecturing him: "No existing group outside of France can be given the kind of domination over the French people in France which would dominate the free expression of a choice."[124] The services in charge of propaganda elaborated an extensive interpretation of these instructions. "The soldiers must be free to fight the Germans; Civil Affairs must be able to administer; the French Committee and De Gaulle must be able to assume some legitimate authority, at least during the early phases; and the French people must be given the feeling that their country is liberated *for them*."[125] In short, SHAEF was headed toward a surreptitious recognition of de Gaulle's authority. By June 2, 1944, "it was clear that General Eisenhower wished General Koenig to take the lead in administering liberated French territory, particularly from the political angle."[126] But that de facto recognition was not officially sanctioned.

With the notable exception of France, then, the Anglo-Americans developed a precise idea of the political future of the friendly countries. Fearing neither the irredentism of the internal resistance nor a Communist coup, they were preparing to entrust the keys of power to the authorities in exile, who had loyally supported them in the darkest hours. But an enormous challenge awaited them: to liberate Western Europe militarily.

CHAPTER XIX

Action!

Two days after taking Rome on June 4, the Anglo-American forces rushed onto the beaches of Normandy, beginning the liberation of Western Europe. Then, on June 22, the Soviets launched Operation Bagration, the prelude to the liberation of Eastern Europe. The resistance, having feverishly awaited the landing for months, had every intention of having its rendezvous with history on D-Day. The time for action had finally come.

Instructions for Action

At 9:15 p.m. on June 5 the BBC broadcast the two hundred or so messages ordering the French resistance to take action.[1] But though the overall scheme was to have the regions apply the plans gradually, Eisenhower decided to launch them in France as a whole. He counted on achieving a massive effect and on fooling the Germans about the importance of Overlord, which was portrayed as a mere diversion operation: the services in charge of confounding the enemy claimed that the Allies would actually land in Pas-de-Calais. As Walter Bedell Smith, Dwight D. Eisenhower's chief of staff, explained, it was "indispensable to secure the maximum effort in France on the very night before D-day," to ensure the success of the landing, on which everything depended.[2]

The top priorities of the army of shadows, as we have seen, were to strike the railroads (Plan Vert) and communications (Plan Violet), and to slow the movements of the German forces on the highways (Plan Tortue). On the whole, the resistance acquitted itself brilliantly in these missions. On D-Day there were more than a thousand disruptions of rail service,[3] and that number jumped to three thousand between June 6 and 27.[4] The resistance fighters destroyed 217 locomotives in June, 253 in July, and 188 in August[5]—2,500 in all between April 1943 and August 1944.[6] In short, SOE estimated, 50 percent of the identified targets had been destroyed, a low estimate, no doubt, given the shortage of confirmation reports.[7] Lieutenant Maurice Basset, who was in charge of SOE's Beggar network, participated directly in these raids. "Between 8 June and 31 August, our 13 railroad objectives were attacked altogether approximately 70 times. About 50 of these attacks were successful," he noted, claiming responsibility for six derailments, for example.[8]

In addition, the French resistance provided tactical and strategic intelligence to the Allies. Even before June 6 it had greatly contributed to informing the general staffs about enemy operations. William Donovan estimated that the BCRA had supplied 80 percent of the intelligence useful for the preparation of Overlord.[9] For the month of June alone, OSS received five thousand reports from the Gaullist services.[10] After the invasion, the underground fighters carried on in the same vein, to the great surprise of the Anglo-Americans. "Although passing of intelligence is not a normal part of the activity of the FFI, much up-to-date intelligence has been received from Resistance Groups and passed to the authorities concerned. This intelligence has covered, not only information relating to the enemy's movements and dispositions, but also . . . the indication of targets of value to the Allied Air Forces."[11]

For example, the resistance responded to the requests of the general staff, which on August 18 inquired about the number of German military depots in the Paris region: it received an answer within thirty-six hours. The local resistance also pointed out targets that could not be spotted in aerial photographs. The air force was all the more delighted, inasmuch as it was also informed of the consequences of its missions. One agent, for instance, reported that Luftwaffe aircraft were being concealed in the Bois de Jouarre, east of Paris. The base was attacked a few days later: fifteen planes were destroyed and ten others damaged, according to the agent who reported the results of the raid.[12]

Finally, the progress of the Allied armies was greatly facilitated by resistance fighters, who had the distinct advantage of knowing the terrain thoroughly. From that perspective, Brittany was a textbook case. The Americans, having succeeded in breaking through into Avranches in late July 1944, decided on August 3 to launch an appeal for generalized guerilla warfare. Some thirty thousand Forces Françaises de l'Intérieur (FFI; French Forces of the Interior) enthusiastically responded. The next day, by way of support, the Americans parachuted in a general staff headed by Colonels Éon and Passy. The resistance went on to seize Saint-Brieuc on August 6, took control of the Brest-Rennes railroad line, and saved several engineering structures, including the viaducts of Morlaix and Plougastel. Working in perfect harmony, it liberated several cities, including Loudéac, Josselin, Malestroit, and Quimper. Finally, and perhaps above all, the resistance fighters guided the U.S. troops and relieved them of lesser but labor-intensive missions— the guarding of prisoners and of certain installations. In short, they played the role of an infantry, and the motorized units saw them rising up "everywhere they arrived," when, that is, the resistance forces "had not already cleared the terrain."[13] Along the same lines, Colonel Zeller, head of the FFI in southeastern France, exhorted the Allied forces, who had landed in Provence on August 15, 1944, to pick up the pace so that they could seize the poorly defended French Alps as quickly as possible. General Alexander Patch's troops complied. A motorized brigade sped over the Alps as the FFI sprang into action. They forced the Annecy garrison to surrender and hastened the liberation of Grenoble.

Such successes were also recorded in other regions. In the Massif Central, resistance fighters hindered the enemy's movements and sometimes obliged the Germans to surrender—in Brive and Limoges, for example. In the Southwest, they secured the capitulation of the occupying forces and captured thirteen thousand men in the Midi-Pyrénées region. Finally, when several tens of thousands of German combatants attempted to flee the Atlantic coast, the FFI relentlessly harried about twenty thousand stragglers, Elster's Column. They laid down their arms in the city of Issoudun on September 10.

Kudos

These remarkable results elicited the praise of the Allied commanders. George Patton, commander of the Third U.S. Army, acknowledged that, in Brittany, "the support of Resistance has been invaluable."[14] The ruling circles admitted their surprise. "The Resistance has so far done a far better job than I expected they would," confided Desmond Morton, Winston Churchill's assistant, to his boss. "The danger is that their enthusiasm may cool rapidly if they meet with misfortune."[15] A SHAEF report noted: "The results achieved by the Forces Françaises of the Interior have far surpassed the results generally expected. Wherever armament is sufficient, they have displayed unity in action and a high fighting spirit."[16] General Frederick Butler, commander of the task force that landed in Provence, estimated that the contribution of the resistance to his operation was equivalent to that of four or five divisions.[17] In short, the Allies pointed out,

> The achievements of resistance groups during the first ten days of the battle have been greater than could reasonably have been expected. Full reports have not yet come in, but evidence so far received shows that the railway system of France has been so dislocated as to make the movement of both troops and supplies by rail, if not impossible at any rate subject to delays of unpredictable length. This railway sabotage was particularly successful in southeastern France and in the area of the Rhone valley, where, apart from one or two local trains, movements were at standstill for some days. . . . The combined result of rails and telecommunications sabotage has been to make it increasingly difficult for the Germans to coordinate or in some cases to effect in any reasonable time the moves of their reserve formations. . . . 21 Army Group have stated that, in their opinion, the over-all action of French Resistance has resulted in an average delay of 48 hours being imposed on movements of German formations to the bridgehead area.

A report of 1944 concluded that actions carried out by the maquis had created "chaotic conditions in large parts of France, generally hampering the German military machine. In limited areas, Resistance is in complete control."[18]

Shadows

These laudatory reports should not be allowed to conceal less flattering truths. The reports sometimes came from French sources, which were naturally inclined to overestimate the distinguished service the resistance had rendered to the Allied troops. For example, one report stated that, because of the ambushes laid by the FFI, the bloody Das Reich division required two weeks to get from Toulouse to the Normandy front "at a crucial time."[19] The truth was harder to swallow. General Lammerding's unit, "during a forced march to the front, was not delayed or harried and thereby impelled to carry out reprisals. On the contrary, it had the express mission of fighting against the bands, which is why it had taken a detour. In fact, and this confirms the assertion, in the first days after the landing, because of ignorance about the adversary's intentions, the German high command's plans by no means entailed throwing all the available divisions onto the front."[20] That explains why the ascent was so slow and left death in its bloody wake: in the city of Tulle, 99 hostages were hanged, and in the village of Oradour-sur-Glane, 642 civilians were massacred. SOE and OSS leaders, moreover, were intent on showing sometimes skeptical political and military leaders that they had not wagered on subversive warfare in vain. The aim of the favorable balance sheet they drew up was not only to extol their actions but to protect the future of their services, which some authorities—the U.S. military, for example—advocated eliminating upon victory.

On a completely different level, it was sometimes difficult to "render unto Caesar." Was the disruption of the enemy network in France, for example, attributable to the underground forces or to Allied airpower? SHAEF leaned toward the second hypothesis. "Any consideration of this subject must be prefaced by an emphatic statement that the major cause of delay to enemy troop movements was action by the Allied strategic and tactical air forces. Resistance action was only a secondary element in causing delay."[21] The statistics confirm that assessment. Until March 1944 the locomotives damaged by the resistance (748) outnumbered those destroyed by air attacks (387). But beginning in April the air force took the lead, damaging 324 in June (compared to 217 by the resistance), 301 in July (compared to 253), and 195 in August (compared to 188). The underground fighters claimed responsibility for 2,504 sabotage operations, but the air force had done more than half the total damage: it destroyed 3,315 train engines, which is to say, 57 percent.[22] Such dry statistics cannot conceal two realities, however. On its own, Allied airpower could not have paralyzed railroad traffic, unless it had devoted all its missions to the task; and, until the landing in Provence, the South of France was not subject to bombings, so that, in that region, the responsibility for blocking the enemy's movements fell solely to the underground forces.[23]

Plan Violet, however, was begun too late—it was launched by the Allies on June 12—to achieve its full potential.[24] And intelligence collection suffered from the amateurism of the resistance fighters, who, for lack of training, did not always assess the information at its true value. As a result, American units coming up the Rhone Valley "were sent out into places that were not supposed to be defended. The men did not return."[25] All in all, concluded Major Crosby of OSS, "the effectiveness of the FFI was quite variable. In some of the mountain regions they were magnificent. In other places their value was nil."[26]

The shift from subversive to open warfare also worried the Allies. As we have seen, they doubted the military capacities of the resistance. SHAEF therefore recommended against developing regular military operations, particularly since the discipline of the underground groups sometimes left something to be desired—as Lieutenant MacCarthy, sent to the Le Blanc region, observed. After a man was placed in detention for having gone AWOL, the maquisards went on strike until the prisoner was released. "Each night there was a dance in town the whole group dropped everything and attended, leaving the barracks, chateau and road block unmanned and nothing was ever done to remedy the situation."[27]

Nevertheless, on May 29, 1944, General Maitland Wilson, supreme commander in the Mediterranean, ordered "guerilla" actions to be conducted in the South, in conjunction with General Béthouart, chief of staff of Défense Nationale. "But, whatever the reason was—failure to communicate, deliberate intent or misunderstanding—the fact remains that, at this moment, just days away from D-Day, the orders being sent to the Resistance in southern France by London and Algiers were fatally muddled and contradictory."[28] The speech General de Gaulle delivered on June 6 may have added to the confusion: "For the sons of France, wherever they are, whoever they are, the simple and sacred duty is to fight by every means at their disposal."[29] Yet on the same day, Dwight D. Eisenhower warned: "A premature uprising of all Frenchmen may prevent you from being of maximum help to your country in the critical hour. Be patient, prepare."[30] As Paddy Ashdown remarks, "With messages so ill thought out and so contradictory as those they heard on 6 and 7 June, it is scarcely surprising that French men and women followed their instinct, which, whether wise or not, was to stand up and fight."[31]

Consequently, the French resistance sometimes engaged in open warfare when it did not have the means to do so. It suffered large-scale losses when it faced regular troops.[32] It also built up large maquis, which as a general rule died in bloodbaths. For example, thousands of volunteers had gathered at Mont Mouchet in the Massif Central, to cut off the German forces who would be retreating from the Atlantic coast. On June 10, 1944, General Kurt von Jesser's troops decided to destroy the maquis, which within a week was forced to disperse, suffering high losses: 125 maquisards and 50 civilians for the first assault alone.[33] Although the maquisards sometimes blamed the Allies, members of the missions set the record straight. René Dussaq, an envoy from London, noted that resistance fighters tended "to justify their defeat at Monmoucher [sic] and St. Martial and later at Le Bourguet by blaming London for not equipping them with the proper weapons." He was very blunt in his assessment: "Our efforts had been to discourage the massing of large bodies of men in any given spot. We had insisted on keeping away from towns but rather on placing small guerilla groups to ambush German convoys along roads, blowing up bridges and generally harassing the enemy. As for the weapons, they were excellent, and it was certainly not our fault if the men did not apply themselves more seriously to the task of learning all about them."[34] It should be pointed out, however, that the formation of large maquis was consistent with a notion developed by the Gaullists and/or by the military, which the resistance movements had never approved.

For example, one plan, called Montagnards (Mountaineers), foresaw turning the Vercors Massif into an impregnable citadel, which, from its peaks, would block the Wehrmacht if it passed through the Rhone Valley while fleeing the Mediterranean coasts. On the night of June 8 Colonel Marcel Descour, on the assurances of the Gaullist services, undertook to block access routes to the plateau. More than four thousand volunteers poured in, and the Allies dispatched a few missions to support them. The Germans had no intention of tolerating that trouble spot. On July 21 they launched an offensive and did not skimp on resources: they deployed ten thousand men as well as airborne troops.[35] Within three days, the maquis was annihilated. The losses were appalling: 326 resistance fighters and 130 civilians were massacred by General Pflaum's men,[36] and 35 wounded, sheltered in the Grotte de La Luire, were savagely finished off. An OSS leader concluded, not without reason: "The fall of the Vercors is a major reverse for French resistance which has always aspired towards the conception of liberated areas deep within non-liberated France. However, it demonstrates conclusively the age old principle that Resistance Forces *cannot* hold territory, but must be fluid and adhere strictly to basic guerilla tactics. The Vercors Plateau 'reduit' was something that arose spontaneously and it is sincerely believed that no amount of material or French Airborne cadres could have aided them in holding out for long against units such as the 9th Panzer Division [*sic*]."[37]

On a completely different level, the resistance sometimes set out willy-nilly to liberate cities. On June 6, 1944, it occupied Saint-Amand-Montrond, a subprefecture of Cher. The next day the Francs-Tireurs et Partisans (FTP) captured Tulle, but only briefly. On June 9 the Germans, enraged at the sight of some forty corpses belonging to their ranks lined up in the hospital, retook the prefecture of Corrèze, hanged 99 residents by the city's lampposts, and deported another 149.[38] Guéret, the capital of the Creuse department, was also briefly held on June 7, before being reoccupied by the Germans, who in this case refrained from engaging in their usual atrocities.

As a general rule, the Allies disapproved of these operations, pointing out that in "very rare instances were such liberations of tactical value. . . . The Germans held what they wanted to as long as they wanted to. . . . The FFI had neither the arms, discipline, training or sufficient leadership to organize a large scale operation against a determined enemy."[39] An aggravating factor was that the resistance fighters had never been trained in street combat. "The Maquis has been prepared for fighting in the open country only, and were at great disadvantage when assisting in the liberation of towns."[40] Several leaders of the internal resistance kept a cool head, restraining enthusiasm of their troops. Henri Romans-Petit, head of the Ain maquis, dissuaded his men from occupying Bourg-en-Bresse: "We can, of course, besiege the city, enter it, take many prisoners. But we will have heavy losses and will probably be unable to hold on there, because what can a few heavy weapons do against armored tanks? The city will probably be retaken and will face terrible reprisal measures. That operation, spectacular to be sure, has too many risks to be attempted." He concluded afterward: "I demonstrated its impossibility to the advocates—sometimes unexpected—of that grandstanding, which was not at all important militarily."[41] Georges Guingouin too opted for caution, waiting until August 12 to surround Limoges and until the 21st to enter the city, even though his FTP superiors had ordered him to seize the prefecture of Haute-Vienne as quickly as possible.

In short, SHAEF and the special services entreated the underground to give precedence to sabotage and guerilla warfare rather than engage in spectacular military operations, for which they were obviously not prepared. "The most effective and successful work that has been performed by the Partisans, has been the harassing of the Germans by acts of sabotage, disrupting lines of communications, destroying bridges. . . . It should not be thought that the Partisans can carry out large scale operations against the Germans, since they do not have the required military materials."[42] And OSS lamented: "Especially in the last months, many targets of very good opportunity for guerilla attack were neglected in favor of more spectacular projects."[43]

That observation coincided with the analysis of General Koenig, who was alarmed by the influx of volunteers. In January 1944 France counted (subject to verification) fifty thousand FFI. That number jumped to one hundred thousand in June and reached five hundred thousand by liberation.[44] But the head of the internal resistance feared that these men, poorly armed and largely untrained, would be massacred by the German forces. On June 10 he therefore ordered a stop to guerilla warfare. The message, repeated on June 14 and 16, concluded: "Impossible at present to supply you with arms and ammunition in sufficient quantity. Stop. Break off contact everywhere to degree possible to allow reorganization phase stop Avoid large gatherings. Form small isolated groups."[45] These instructions sowed confusion. Some believed they were fake. Others, such as Charles Tillon, commander of the FTP, judged them inappropriate and refused to implement them.[46]

Finally, the Allies hoped that the resistance would protect installations, making it possible both to continue the war and to help restart the French economy. They used every means possible to achieve that objective. For instance, every detachment of the Special Forces brought with it 1.5 million francs "for bribing of French officials and officers enrolled under the Germans."[47] In the Port of Sète, some guards agreed to disconnect the charges placed at strategic points in exchange for "packets of cigarettes." The thermal power station of Chantenay, on the outskirts of Nantes, was saved when the resistance approached the German inspector. An electrical engineer in civilian life, he agreed—out of professional pride—to suspend the destruction of the turbines.[48] But the overall results were less brilliant. The resistance proved incapable of protecting several power stations and some commutators, which led to a partial paralysis of the transmission of current, "with disastrous results on economy and industry." Likewise, the Germans were able to sabotage most of the shipyards and some crucial industrial sites. It took only three hundred men to destroy the Schneider plant in Le Creusot. "In spite of the fact that some 15,000 workmen were still employed in the plant the relatively small body of German saboteurs was able to operate unhampered and was also able to overpower the small bodies of FFI who had been stationed in the factory to protect it."[49] All in all, the "counterscorching" policy was disappointing. Despite these mixed results, the balance sheet for the French underground forces was generally positive, which induced the Allies to arm them.

Manna from Heaven

The Anglo-Americans, as we have seen, had hesitated to increase the number of weapon drops, especially since the complex parachuting operations ran into many obstacles. The successes achieved by the army of shadows overcame these objections, and, in summer 1944, shipping containers rained down on France.

In 1943, 4,498 containers and 937 packages had been released over metropolitan France. In 1944 the change of scale was obvious. A total of 66,532 containers, as well as 19,208 packages, were dropped into the country, which is to say, more than 90 percent of the materiel delivered during the entire war to the French resistance fighters. That number, moreover, does not include the 7,572 containers dropped by the U.S. Air Force.[50] The Allies also innovated, overseeing four daylight operations. On June 25, 180 Flying Fortresses released 2,019 containers over Ain, Jura, Haute-Vienne, and Vercors (Operation Zebra). On July 14, 349 aircraft did the same (Operation Cadillac, 3,791 containers),[51] followed on August 1 by a new raid, Operation Buick (2,286 containers, primarily over Savoie). On September 9 Operation Grassy brought the proceedings to a close (809 containers over Franche-Comté).[52] In all, 7,013 sorties departed from the United Kingdom (that is, 83 percent of the missions conducted between 1941 and 1945), 65 percent of which succeeded,[53] a sign that the Allied crews had now mastered the art of dropping containers, while also benefiting from the slowdown of the Luftwaffe, which was in dire straits.

That manna from heaven was unevenly distributed. Precedence was given to western France and the Massif Central, which were easier to reach and less well defended. Of the 86 sorties requested for those regions, 85 percent were executed. Neglected, by contrast, were the Northeast (13 percent of the 278 missions requested were honored), the East (9 percent of 268 requests), and the North (only 1 mission of the 11 requested).[54] As a result, the weapons intended for some 100,000 men did not necessarily land in the regions where they would have been useful.[55] The mass parachute drops also required complex logistics. During Operation Zebra, the 420 containers for Vercors entailed the mobilization of four hundred volunteers and all the vehicles—"carts and lorries"—in the surrounding area.[56] In a pernicious effect, the more weapons the maquis received, the more volunteers it attracted, which, Bedell Smith feared, risked increasing the demand "to arm and feed them. Such a continued process would rapidly result in an unjustifiable dispersion of effort from the main battle."[57] But the speed of the Allied advance, after the breakthrough into Avranches in late July, and the landing in Provence on August 15 dispelled these alarms.

The Allies also dispatched Jedburgh teams to the resistance groups. Fewer than three hundred men in all were deployed,[58] but their role was indisputably more important than the modesty of their numbers suggests. The Bruce mission, for example, was composed of an American, William Colby (future head of the CIA), and two Frenchmen, Jacques Favel and Louis Giry. Dropped by parachute on August 15 into the area surrounding Montargis in Loiret, the team was supposed to assist SOE's Donkeyman network, which had taken over the tasks of the Carte organization. It trained the FFI in the Loiret department, received a dozen parachute drops over Yonne, and then, during the American advance, guided General Patton's troops.[59] Likewise, the Desmond team, accompanied by Davout d'Auerstaedt, deputy military delegate, delivered intelligence to the 106th Cavalry Regiment of the Third U.S. Army, which allowed it to coordinate the capture of Châtillon-sur-Seine, thanks to a joint attack of the FFI and the U.S. forces.

With money and transmission capabilities at their disposal, the Allied agents assisted the local resistance by training it, teaching it to handle weapons, and providing it with materiel. By virtue of the prestige conferred on them by their status and uniforms, they also reduced political tensions by practicing a sort of arbitration. The Hugh mission, for example, deployed in Indre in the first days of June 1944, improved relations between Surcouf from the Secret Army, Martel from the Organisation de Résistance de l'Armée (Army Resistance Organization), and Rolland from Francs-Tireurs et Partisans. "As the ultimate conclusion to any argument, these three good Frenchmen . . . could always be convinced by our pleas for French unity in the war effort."[60]

But sometimes the results were less impressive. For example, the Bugatti mission, parachuted into the Pyrenees from Algiers on June 28, did not manage to obtain weapons, which led to its being discredited. "The resistance groups began to doubt our capacity to furnish anything but promises. . . . Sabotage activities stopped because we lacked plastic explosives."[61] Above all, the chain of command hindered action. SFHQ, given command of metropolitan France as a whole, was swamped by the scope of the task and therefore slow to send out the three-man teams. Of ninety-three teams, only fourteen were deployed in June, a delay aggravated by "the absence of an overall plan."[62]

Yet the balance sheet was positive, especially since, at least at the local level, the Jeds contributed to implementing the orders from London, a mission that was no simple matter.

The Chain of Command

An underlying conflict pitted the Allies and Gaullists, on one hand, against the internal resistance, on the other. Through its action committee, COMAC, the internal resistance claimed to be in charge of the underground forces. While conceding that "the FFI must execute the prescribed plans and missions entrusted by the Allies," it asked for "the ability to undertake and carry out operations it has planned, designed to liberate all national territory possible by its own action. To do so, the FFI must be commanded from here, from Paris, and not from London."[63]

Three disagreements fueled the dispute: COMAC was demanding leadership of underground action, to which SHAEF also laid claim; the committee advocated national insurrection, whereas the Allies recommended acting in correlation with the progress of their troops; and it pleaded for the masses to participate in the liberation process, calling for strikes, for example. That scenario worried both General Eisenhower and General de Gaulle, who were anxious to obtain military rather than political support from the FFI and to avoid bloody reprisals. In addition, Eisenhower was preoccupied with the risk of a Communist putsch.

In June and July COMAC strove to impose its views. For example, it rejected the order given by General Koenig on June 10, 1944. On June 14 it instead prescribed that the FFI prepare to collaborate

> with the masses, in view of national insurrection: the reinforcement of *guerilla action* against the enemy is one of the elements paving the way for national insurrection; it galvanizes the will of the people in their struggle. . . . Everywhere the balance of power allows, the aim of insurrection must be to rid the country of the invader, to depose the representatives of Vichy and replace them with provisional authorities established and controlled by the liberation committees and, wherever they exist, by those designated by the Provisional Government of the French Republic, and to mobilize all the forces of the liberated region, in order to drive the enemy from the rest of the territory.[64]

During the meetings held in June, July, and August, COMAC stubbornly renewed its efforts to be entrusted with the command of the FFI. But the national military delegate (DMN), Jacques Chaban-Delmas, avoided the showdown with consummate skill.

Born in 1915, that young inspector of finances had joined the Hector network in late December 1940, before becoming, in October 1943, the unofficial assistant to André Boulloche, regional military delegate for Greater Paris (region P). In early May Chaban, despite his youth, was accepted by the BCRA as an interim national military delegate.[65] The choice proved judicious: despite his lack of experience, Chaban deftly practiced the art of the dodge, taking refuge behind vague formulations in order not to antagonize his interlocutors, while firmly defending the rights of SHAEF and the CFLN. The members of COMAC were not fooled: "The DMN, whom we have known for a long time, has often been mistaken and, rather than recognize his errors, has always attempted to mask them by using a brilliant dialectic: that is not the act of a leader."[66] These delaying tactics proved effective, however: on August 7, when the Americans had already broken through the German lines, COMAC was still exploring avenues for an accord with London. In the end, on August 14 it received "the supreme command of the FFI over metropolitan territory . . . by delegation of General Koenig."[67] But the die was cast: in view of the speed of the Allied advance, that compromise remained without effect.

In fact, COMAC did not have a direct liaison with SHAEF, which prevented it from cooperating with the Anglo-American troops. In addition, the FFI command was decentralized, a tendency exacerbated by the powers of the regional military delegates, dispensers of weapons, money, and liaisons. COMAC realized the danger. It attempted—in vain—to obtain control over the DMRs and tried to relieve them of their duties at the local level. In northern Seine-et-Oise, the dispute between the Communist Henri Rol-Tanguy, head of the FFI, and the DMR, Pierre Sonneville, was brought before COMAC on July 3, 1944. It ended in a victory for Rol. Sonneville agreed to submit his budget to the Communist and to give the weapons to the FFI leaders. Always cautious, Jacques Chaban-Delmas hastened to explain that "the role the DMR establishes for himself is not binding on the Military Delegation's opinion regarding the role of the DMRs in general."[68] In the Morvan, by contrast, the outcome turned to the advantage of the London representative. Colonel Dupin, named head of the mobilization maquis of the region, was encroaching on Nièvre, a department organized by the military delegate Rondenay. He refused to cede power and, supported by London and Chaban, prevailed.[69]

On the whole, however, internal resistance fighters and regional military delegates cooperated harmoniously. Claude Monod, regional leader of the FFI in Franche-Comté, noted that his relations "with Colonel Hanneton have always been perfect, almost friendly. The DMR has never sought to overstep his authority and override the FFI regional command, despite the opportunities that the privileges of age and his actual rank in the army might have given him. Colonel Hanneton's uprightness and loyalty, the word of that senior officer, was for me a sufficient guarantee."[70] Even the Communist Georges Beaufils, the FTP representative for COMAC in western France, could not praise enough Valentin Abeille and Guy Chaumet, military delegates for the Greater West and the North of France, respectively. "They applied themselves very sincerely," he noted, "in aiding the movements with which they were in contact, including the FTP,"[71] the armed group of the Communist Party. The historian Philippe André concludes:

Perceived upon their arrival as emissaries of London charged with taking control of the French Resistance, [the military delegates] quickly proved by their actions that they were simply following the instructions of their dual mission. As distinguished and important ambassadors to the internal resistance, they were able to establish a modus vivendi with every regional resistance group. With the possible exception of COMAC and its envoys, neither the archives analyzed nor the memoirs of former resistance fighters mention the slightest blackmail using money or weapons: that absence confirms the exemplary behavior of the military delegates, who did not use their financial resources and materiel to seize the command of the regional resistance.[72]

Through the DMRs, then, the resistance followed Allied instructions, even though several voices had raised the fear that the underground would go it alone. "French Resistance, whether technically commanded by the Algiers Committee [sic] or SOE [sic], has so far unanimously obeyed SHAEF's orders as conveyed through SOE [sic], without any attempt to make political difficulties," pointed out Desmond Morton, adviser to Winston Churchill, with due satisfaction.[73]

COMAC therefore did not manage to impose it law, which dispelled fears of a Communist coup. In fact, neither the Allied representatives nor the Gaullist delegates believed one was in the offing. During the short trip to London he took from August 8 to 16, Jacques Chaban-Delmas confided to the leaders of the Ministry for the Interior that he absolutely did not fear "any FTP danger. They know they do not constitute all the forces of the FFI or of the Resistance."[74] "The reality," observes Jean-Louis Crémieux-Brilhac, "was that they did not have the means to launch and even less to lead an insurrection on a national scale: lacking transmission capabilities, which were in the hands of the General Delegation and the regional military delegates, locked away in the artificial atmosphere of Paris, having become suspect to the Socialists and the northern zone movements, they had no reliable forces except those of the Party and the Francs-Tireurs et Partisans, and their capacity to mobilize the masses was limited to the Paris region."[75]

Nonetheless, the prominence of the Communists in the insurrection of Paris caused anxiety among the London authorities.

The Paris Insurgency

After the breakthrough into Avranches, the British and the Canadians sped due north, while the Americans rushed eastward. General Patton's troops, having captured Mantes-la-Jolie on August 19, crossed the Seine the next day, but without attempting to take Paris. Eisenhower feared waging a street battle, which would have been deadly, and was hardly eager to take over the provision of supplies for a city with a population of more than 2.5 million at the time. The supreme commander therefore planned to bypass the capital, so that, after being surrounded, it would fall without a fight. That plan satisfied the secret services, which, as we have seen, ruled out any call for insurrection.

The events decided otherwise. At the initiative of the Communist leaders of the Paris region, an insurrectional movement got under way in early August. On the 10th, railroad workers called a strike, which was immediately joined by postal employees, then by the police, who stopped work on the 15th. On August 18 the Communist Henri Rol-Tanguy, head of the FFI for the Paris region, drew up a mobilization order, which was posted during the night. The next day the principle of insurrection received the approval of Alexandre Parodi, general delegate of the provisional government, and the insurrection immediately erupted.

At the time the FFI had between twenty and twenty-five thousand men, not all of them armed—far from it. By contrast, the forces of law and order (police, gendarmerie, Republican Guard) had about twenty thousand weapons. The Germans counted approximately twenty thousand soldiers and some fifty tanks.[76] But they had no intention of fighting to the bitter end. Dietrich von Choltitz, commander of *Gross Paris*, had been newly assigned to the City of Lights on August 9, 1944. He believed it was impossible to hold the city, which Hitler was ordering him to do at all cost.[77] The general engaged in a complicated game with his superiors, apparently respecting orders while making every effort to circumvent them.

Tensions continued to mount in the capital. On August 19 a small committee, composed, notably, of Léo Hamon (Comité Parisien de Libération), Roland Pré (Délégation), and Henri Ribière (Conseil National de la Résistance), decided to negotiate a truce through the consul of Sweden, Raoul Nordling. That initiative was vehemently contested by the advocates of insurrection, who denounced "those who still feared, as they had always feared, that insurrection would be unable to withstand the enemy forces, that the Allied forces would not arrive in time, that Paris would be reduced to ashes, and that the social order would be disrupted."[78] Rol ordered the battles to continue. But he had a lucid assessment of his weakness and resolved to ask for the assistance of the Allies.[79] On August 20 he sent his chief of staff, Major Gallois, to request the aid of the regular troops. De Gaulle voiced his agreement: in a letter composed on the 21st and transmitted the next day by Juin and Koenig, he implored Eisenhower to move ahead. Ike complied. On August 23 General Leclerc's Second Armored Division set out; its first tanks took their positions on the square outside city hall the next day. Finally, on August 25, the city fell. Leclerc and Rol-Tanguy accepted Choltitz's surrender at the Gare Montparnasse, while de Gaulle meticulously prepared for his return. After he too stopped at the Gare Montparnasse, he proceeded to the Ministry of War, which he had left on June 10, 1940, along with Paul Reynaud. After these long detours, and having greeted the men at the prefecture of police, he ultimately reached city hall to meet with the members of the resistance. In a memorable speech, he extolled "Paris! Paris outraged! Paris broken! Paris martyred! But Paris liberated! Liberated by itself, liberated by its people with the help of the French armies, with the support and the help of all France, of the France that fights, of the only France, of the real France, of the eternal France!"[80] But he had meager praise for the Anglo-American forces, simply expressing the wish to drive out the enemy "with the support and the help of our dear and admirable allies," which was in reality a spectacular inversion of the balance of power.

The apotheosis came the next day, when Charles de Gaulle walked down the Champs-Élysées, acclaimed by hundreds of thousands of Frenchmen, overjoyed to celebrate the liberation and their liberators. He would later write:

> I went on, then, touched and yet tranquil, amid the inexpressible exultation of the crowd, beneath the storm of voices echoing my name, trying, as I advanced, to look at every person in all that multitude in order that every eye might register my presence, raising and lowering my arms to reply to the acclamations: this was one of those miracles of national consciousness, one of those gestures which, sometimes, in the course of centuries, illuminate the history of France. In this community, with only a single thought, a single enthusiasm, a single cry, all differences vanished, all individuals disappeared.[81]

The insurrection of Paris thus culminated in a brilliant success. It marked the triumph of the internal resistance, which had succeeded in mobilizing the population and involving it in the struggle. The Communists, under the leadership of Henri Rol-Tanguy, had played a central role, but without having achieved their ends, namely, to welcome Charles de Gaulle in a city that had liberated itself.

The Communists had a few advantages. On the regional level, the FFI answered to Henri Rol-Tanguy, and the Comité Parisien de Libération was chaired by André Tollet. Both were steadfast Communists. But they did not succeed in controlling the insurgent masses. Of the some twenty thousand Parisian combatants, the Communist apparatus was in charge of only four thousand men—at most a fifth of the total.[82] Rol made every effort to enlist volunteers. "All able-bodied Frenchmen and Frenchwomen must consider themselves mobilized. They must immediately join the FFI groups or the patriotic militias in their neighborhood or factory," he prescribed in his order of August 18, 1944.[83] He repeated himself on the 24th: "The commanders of departments must immediately organize the enlistment centers to gather together all the volunteers determined to participate in the struggle against the Boche."[84] But these directives—which were rarely followed—arrived too late to reverse the trend.

The Gaullist authority had just as much trouble controlling the course of events. The BBC, far from setting the dynamic in motion, fell silent on August 18 and gave no instructions for action to the Parisians. Granted, the faulty communications between the two shores of the Channel prevented the London authorities from getting a clear picture of the situation. The telegrams sent by Jacques Chaban-Delmas were decoded with a delay of three, four, even six days.[85] But the strike movement also plunged the Allied authorities into confusion. If they supported the strikes, they would run the risk of paralyzing production vital for the capital (especially in the energy sector) and of facing an insurrection. By that measure, the tragic precedent of 1871—the massacre that the Versailles government perpetrated on the Communards—had left such a lasting mark that de Gaulle exclaimed to Leclerc on August 23, 1944: "Go quickly . . . we cannot have another Commune."[86]

At the same time, de Gaulle could not cut himself off from such a popular mass movement. The BBC's silence reflected the uneasiness with which the men in London assessed its impact. "The absence of instructions for Paris is a serious shortcoming, given that these instructions are most urgent and the only ones that pose real difficulties," observed Georges Boris, head of the London subbranch of the Ministry for the Interior on August 11.[87] Three days later, an anonymous report (no doubt from the same ministry), noted:

"It is to be feared that if the [Provisional Government of the French Republic; GPRF] does not give directions and instructions to Paris, the movement will be launched without the GPRF's authorization."[88] Two factors allowed General de Gaulle to take things in hand: the dispatching of the Second Armored Division and the announcement—deliberately made in advance—of the liberation of Paris, which the BBC broadcast on August 23, 1944.

It has been said that the Allies were wary of the insurrectional movements, and not without reason: for though Paris jubilantly celebrated its liberation, Warsaw, during the same month, was subjected to horrible massacres and all-out destruction. The capital of France escaped that tragic fate. Losses were relatively low. Depending on the estimates, the Armored Division lost between 76 and 130 men, the FFI 900 to 1,000; among the Paris population, there were 582 dead and 2,000 wounded.[89] By contrast, the toll recorded in Warsaw was grim: 18,000 dead within the ranks of the resistance, 160,000 to 180,000 dead among the population at large. It is true that, in Paris, the external and the internal resistance had cooperated with each other, whereas the Soviet forces stationed on the right bank of the Vistula had refused to assist the Polish patriots. In France, therefore, order reigned: the Communists had not taken power, and General de Gaulle imposed his authority, thanks to the anointing he had received during the parade of August 26, 1944.

All things considered, the liberation of Paris was a comforting spectacle that confirmed the Allies' belief that the resistance, responding to their orders and cooperating with them, understood the weight of its responsibilities and did not strike out on its own. The offensive to follow in the Western European theater of operations looked all the more auspicious and encouraging in that victory now seemed within reach.

CHAPTER XX

Peripheries

Although France was the principal theater of operations, the Allies meant to keep up the pace and liberate all of Western Europe as quickly as possible. In view of their progress—they reached Brussels to the north and Lyon to the south in early September—that prospect seemed relatively imminent for Belgium and the Netherlands, but more remote for Denmark, Norway, and Italy. Aware of that discrepancy, the general staffs tailored the instructions they sent to the peoples under the jackboot, taking into account their very different situations.

Belgium: A Lightning-fast Liberation

In Belgium, the coded alert signal ("the foliage is concealing the old mill from you") was broadcast on June 1, 1944, and the action was launched on the evening of June 8 through a message of confirmation ("King Solomon has put on his big sabots").[1] The orders were to sabotage telecommunications as well as highways and railways, but to refrain from any general guerilla action.[2] On June 6 London also recommended that the intelligence networks concentrate on the collection of information: "Movements troops materiel parachutists and planes with identification and marks lines of defense and all military and civilian measures taken by the Germans."[3] Such caution met with the satisfaction of the Pierlot cabinet, which feared a bloodbath. Using the "lack of arms supplied as an excuse," the ministers repeated again and again that a "great slaughter" would occur if the resistance groups were called on to show themselves before the Allies had entered their countries.[4]

The resistance was particularly cautious in following these instructions, given that Eisenhower did not manage to break through into Normandy until late July 1944. But action intensified after the breakthrough into Avranches got under way on July 25. Between August 3 and 24, 415 sabotage operations struck Belgian railroads, 18 bridges were destroyed or damaged, and 88 locomotives sabotaged.[5] During the liberation phase, the resistance claimed responsibility for 600 disruptions of railroad service, 63 derailments, and the destruction of 9 highway bridges, 50 railroad bridges, and 140 locomotives.[6] True, it benefited from parachute drops of weapons—40.2 tons were released over Belgium in the third quarter of 1944[7]—but, though they helped it fulfill its mission, they remained inadequate. "It cannot be said that the desired objective, the total blockage of communications, was achieved, primarily because of the lack of explosives. Nevertheless, the displacement of troops and the transportation of fresh supplies will be seriously disrupted."[8] Above all, the advance of the Allied armies was so rapid that it took the partisans by surprise. The order to attack the German forces, issued on September 2, proved pointless and limited the harrying action to two or three days.[9] Many volunteers never picked up their weapons.

The underground forces did succeed in protecting from destruction the installations judged to be vital, beginning with the Port of Antwerp. Thanks to the complicity of some of its employees, they were able to occupy the quays, protect the locks, and keep the Germans from sinking ships in the docks. The occupiers inflicted only minor damage on the large port.[10] The Anglo American special services hailed that success, attributing it largely to the intervention of the resistance.[11] But though Antwerp fell on September 4, the first Allied convoy did not enter its waters until November 26: Field Marshal Bernard Montgomery, in his exuberance, had neglected to sweep the banks of the Scheldt to rid them of their German defenders and had to wage costly battles to retake them.

In perfect harmony, the Belgian partisans assisted the Anglo-American troops in their advance, serving as "guides and flank guards for US and

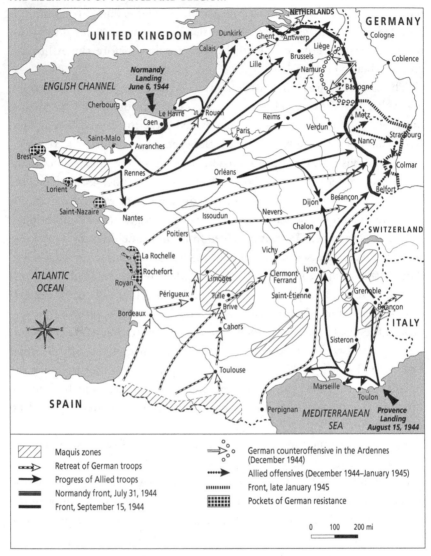

British columns." They also participated in mopping up "overrun areas such as Mons, Namur and Charleroi."[12] The Allied authorities expressed their satisfaction. General Brian Horrocks, head of the Thirtieth Corps of the British Army, deemed the contribution of the Belgian resistance "invaluable" and pointed out that the rapid advance of his troops "would have been impossible without its help."[13]

The Dutch Tragedy

Things went less well in the Netherlands. Although the Allies had progressed rapidly north, they eventually ran into the resistance of the German forces and by early September had captured only twenty miles of terrain, at a crawl. Marshal Montgomery, head of the Twenty-first Army Group, decided to strike a major blow. On September 17, 1944, he launched Operation Market Garden. An assault waged by airborne units would capture several bridges over a series of waterways before crossing the Rhine; at the same time, General Horrocks would move forward to join the parachutists. The offensive was disastrous. The Thirtieth Corps failed to meet up with the First Airborne Division, whose men, exhausted, surrendered on September 27.[14]

Until then, the resistance had been only moderately involved, having barely recovered from the *Englandspiel* disaster. The instructions sent to the Dutch in June recommended refraining from any mass uprising and specified that "even localized overt resistance is [not] desirable at present."[15] In fact, the military resistance as such did not exist.[16] In September, therefore, rather then inciting action, the Allies placed the emphasis on counterscorching. Eisenhower instructed: "Your orders are to protect, not to sabotage factories, mines or other industrial installations. Safeguard these, especially stores of petrol oil and lubricants, against destruction by the enemy. All these facilities will soon be needed by the people of Netherlands and their Allies."[17]

The Dutch resistance had only limited manpower (twenty thousand men, according to SOE)[18] and were still sorely lacking in weapons. For all of 1944, it received only 2,759 containers and 365 packages,[19] a very low number, equivalent to the deliveries dropped over Savoie during Operation Buick alone. The Bomber Command refused to allow the aircraft based in Tempsford to take off except during full-moon phases.[20] In addition, the Germans had a vigorous antiaircraft defense system: the concentration of enemy troops prevented the teams on the ground from acting, and a fortiori from moving away if the dropping zone was suddenly changed.[21] Finally, the underground movements were divided; the Allies called for unification, but it occurred belatedly. It was not until September 1944 that the underground forces joined together in the Nederlandse Binnenlandse Strijdkrachten (NBS), placed under Prince Bernhard's command. Despite these weaknesses, the Dutch government ordered the railway workers to launch a strike. The railroad management, eager to erase the memory of the compromises the company had made with the Reich, agreed without hesitation to that order, but the rank-and-file were less enthusiastic: the repression of the movements in April and May 1943 had left an indelible mark.[22] Railway traffic was nevertheless suspended, but to no purpose, since Operation Market Garden had failed.

The Netherlands were then cut in two. Whereas the Allies held the South, the Germans occupied the North, which they submitted to an iron law. Above all, the railroad strikes dragged on and on, almost all the railway workers having fled to the underground. Consequently, merchandise could not be transported anywhere in the country. The population suffered through the *Hongerwinter* (winter of famine), a terrible ordeal resulting in fifteen thousand deaths.

At this point, the resistance entered a dormant phase, from which it did not emerge until March 1945. Benefiting from more substantial parachute drops—5,337 containers and 775 packages delivered in 1945[23]—it backed the general offensive launched by the Anglo-Canadian troops on March 23 and 24. At the same time, the Dutch partisans organized the sabotage of telecommunications, as well as attacks on the highways and the railway in Overijssel. As the Allies advanced, the same scenario was played out in Frisia, Groningen, Drenthe, and Gelderland—"with considerable success," according to SOE.[24] Electrical outages made it difficult to send out instructions, however, requiring the use of leaflets dropped from planes to alert the population.[25]

Scandinavia, a Minor Theater

Although the resistance in the Netherlands held on to the hope of hastening the liberation of that country, such hope was dashed in Denmark and Norway. Because Scandinavia was remote from the theater of ground operations, the partisans were condemned to relative inaction. SHAEF's only wish was that they take action against the railways, to keep the enemy from reinforcing the defense of the western front by transferring its troops.

The army of shadows fulfilled that expectation. Of 723 railway sabotage operations carried out in Denmark, 328 occurred in 1944, and 245 in January and February 1945.[26] There were several surges. In August, September, and October the Danish partisans performed 300 sabotage missions.[27]

On December 5, 1944, the high command asked the Norwegian partisans to intensify their attacks against the roads and the railway, "with the object of preventing and delaying the enemy from reaching the Continent." The partisans complied, to the Allies' great satisfaction.[28] In early 1945, as the defeat of the Reich was coming into view, the resistance fighters multiplied the number of raids. OSS claimed that, in Denmark, their actions had been so effective that traffic was paralyzed and it took a month for the Germans to evacuate two divisions that they needed.[29] Yet the success seems to have been less brilliant. A careful examination has revealed that the railroad sabotage carried out in Jutland had no effect "on the German troop movements to the front. The wrong trains were sabotaged and the coordination between the individual groups was too bad to obtain the accumulating effect of delays which was necessary to impede the very quick and effective repairwork."[30] In Norway, the railroad lines leaving from Oslo were sabotaged on the night of March 14, 1945,[31] in response to a suggestion made by Milorg on March 6 and approved by SHAEF.[32] In authorizing that sort of action, the Allied staff hardly expected tactical gains; above all, it meant to keep up the morale of the resistance, at a time when idleness risked extinguishing its flame.[33]

With that aim in view, twenty-five Mosquito fighter-bombers attacked the Gestapo's headquarters for Jutland in Aarhus on October 31, 1944, at the request of Lieutenant-Colonel Bennike, a Danish resistance fighter. Some 165 Gestapo agents and 20 to 40 Danish informers were killed, while many resistance fighters managed to flee. On March 21, 1945, eighteen Mosquitos and twenty-two Mustangs from the Second Tactical Air Force repeated the maneuver, this time attacking Copenhagen, but the result was less successful. Although several prisoners got away, others, like Admiral Hammerich, a resistance fighter, were killed instantly; four Mosquitos and two Mustangs were shot down; and a school next to the Shellhus that held the Nazi torturers was hit.[34]

On a completely different level, the Allies and Milorg considered creating bases to welcome the Norwegians fleeing the compulsory labor service imposed in May 1944. The idea was both to protect a few hundred men and to lead them to launch a guerilla attack in the event of a German retreat. Four sites were identified: one northwest of Oslo (Elg), another north of Kristiansand (Vag), plus Bjorn East and Bjorn West in the Bergen region. The results were inconclusive. Two men were parachuted into Elg on August 31, 1944; in November, an advance force to Vag followed; and a small group was dropped in December over Bjorn West.[35] Although the first phase in Elg was completed—110 men were assembled and weapons as well as food were stockpiled[36]—the rigors of the climate doomed the enterprise, which never went beyond the preparatory stage.[37]

To support the partisans, the Allies did not hesitate to parachute weapons into the two kingdoms, though in modest proportions. In the third quarter of 1944 Denmark received 5.79 tons, while Norway was more fortunate, receiving 52.64 tons.[38] And 484 tons were released over Denmark in 1945—which is to say, more than 70 percent of the tonnage dropped onto its soil by the Allies over the entire course of the war.[39] It was almost too much, and undoubtedly far too late.

But the Allies knew perfectly well that they would not be taking action in Scandinavia. They therefore avoided sending out the resistance on pointless missions. In what was known as the "September Directive,"[40] they asked that the shadow fighters practice self-discipline, in view of the 350,000 Germans stationed in Norway. But they also suggested that the resistance make life as difficult as possible for the Germans, by using "go slow" and "ice-front" tactics—that is, that the population turn a cold shoulder to the occupiers.[41] SHAEF stayed the course in October and ordered the underground not to harry the German forces that were retreating from Norway, preferring that it concentrate on protecting vital installations.[42] "The fact that no Allied offensive land operations were contemplated [on D-Day] implied that no outside assistance could be given in support of large scale overt action by Resistance. The decreased likelihood of a German withdrawal nullified the principal role hitherto allotted to Resistance, that of hindering such a withdrawal or of forcing it to be made by sea."[43] The underground forces thus had to focus their attention on the counterscorching policy, a priority affirmed for Norway in December 1944,[44] and on the maintenance of order.[45]

The tragedy that unfolded in Finnmark, in the northern part of the country, did not radically change these priorities. Moscow and Helsinki had concluded an armistice on September 25, 1944, and the 225,000 Germans who had fought alongside the Finns tried to flee the country at that time. They beat a retreat to Norway, because since August 1943 Sweden had refused to allow troops to travel through its territory. The Red Army, in pursuit, crossed the border into Norway on October 18 and entered Kirkenes a week later. The Norwegian authorities, worried about the situation, dispatched a small contingent from the United Kingdom to secure liberated Finnmark (Operation Crofter). It landed in Murmansk on October 31, 1944. Two corvettes and three minehunters were also sent to the Kola Peninsula on December 7, 1944. But the resistance refrained from engaging in battle, even though the German troops had wreaked devastation, conducting a ruthless scorched-earth policy. The underground fighters simply strove to protect the vital installations as much as possible. Despite the lobbying of the Norwegian government, the Allies refused to send in troops. At a time when the Germans were launching their counteroffensive in the Ardennes, the priority was assuredly not Scandinavia.[46]

In other words, the Anglo-Americans were anxious to spare the lives of Danish and Norwegian resistance fighters, knowing that their engagement in a premature action risked ending in a bloodbath. Conversely, they were resolutely counting on the Italian partisans to fight.

The Italian Offensive

After the fall of Rome on June 4, 1944, the Allies resumed the offensive, first in early June, then beginning on August 25, counting on a quick victory. Ancona and Livorno fell on July 18 and 19, followed by Rimini on September 21, but the advance ended with the onset of autumn. Well served by the terrain, the Germans had managed to withdraw in orderly fashion, using the Apennines and the many waterways to shore up and hold a solid defensive line—pompously called the Gothic Line—from Pisa to Rimini. The British general Harold Alexander had hoped to reach Po Plain quickly, but he had to lower his sights. By September 17, 1944, he still had thirteen rivers to cross before reaching that promised land. He therefore suspended his operations in late summer, postponing by nearly a year the definitive confrontation with the Wehrmacht.

In that gloomy situation, the Italian partisans were encouraged to support the regular forces. Time was truly of the essence. To ensure the success of the landing in Provence, on August 15, 1944, seven divisions—three American, four French—had been withdrawn from the Italian theater in summer 1944; in winter, five new divisions were pulled out, to reinforce the Allied troops preparing to surge against the Reich in spring 1945.[47] In that context, with between eighty and a hundred thousand volunteers in

August 1944,[48] according to SOE, the Italian resistance was supposed to provide Alexander's forces with the men he lacked. The French experience served as a precedent: the Allies no longer underestimated the potential of the army of shadows. "The patriot bands in Northern Italy could, if sufficiently well armed, give as much aid to the Allied Armies in Italy as the French Maquis has done to the Allied armies in France." But, SOE warned in August 1944, "the inadequate airlift available prevents this."[49]

As a result, Alexander's services assigned three major missions to the partisans. In the center and northwest of the peninsula especially, they were to attack communications to interfere with the enemy's movements.[50] They were also responsible for immobilizing the German units, in Piedmont for example, to prevent them from moving off toward the front.[51] Already in May 1944 the British general estimated that the partisans in the North had their sights on six of the twenty-five German divisions fighting in the Boot.[52] Finally, the resistance would support regular operations to facilitate the Allies' progress, working closely with the general staffs. In September 1944, for example, the attacks by the resistance were coordinated with the Fifth Army's command. "A system has been worked out where any of our 12 team radios in the zone will report traffic tieups with warrant night bombing by Tactical Airforces. Road blocks are planned and executed by our Partisan groups with the purpose of causing concentrations on the road net which Germans must use for retreat from the Gothic Line. Our radios arrange to transmit on the emergency channel merely using a designating code word and the coordinates of the point where traffic has piled up."[53] These activities increased in the final phase of the campaign, to the point of becoming "actual guerilla warfare—through the hope of early liberation, the early arrival of spring, and the increase of supplies available to them."[54]

Conversely, and following France's example, the Allies recommended against open attacks against enemy troops, inasmuch as the resistance fighters were "inadequately equipped."[55] In addition, a climate of civil war prevailed. Lieutenant-Colonel J. M. Stevens wrote: "At present, the Partisans are not capable of taking even small [Fascist] Republican garrisons of 30 or 40 men. This is not because of lack of equipment or shortage of men, but because they are afraid of them. As the Republicans are equally petrified of the Partisans, the results have been a not very edifying series of actions, mostly with machine-guns fired at or above extreme range."[56] A report estimated that 60 percent of the ammunition was wasted because

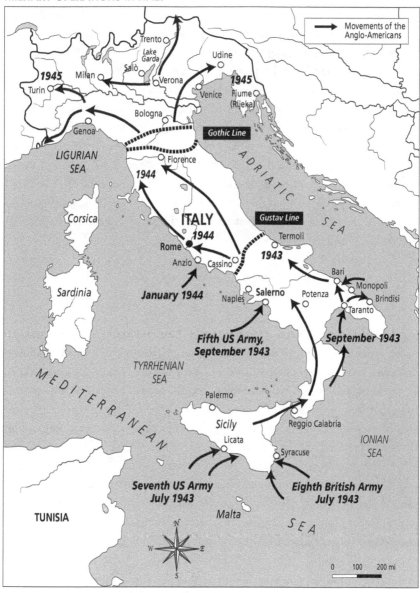

the volunteers avoided close-range fighting[57]—and for good reason. The Fascists of the Republic of Salò proved to be of an extraordinary savagery, committing multiple atrocities against resistance fighters and the civilian populations. "The Fascists shot partisans who gave themselves up after promising them that their lives would be spared. . . . They flaunted their joy at having killed three other outlaws with the weapon they had taken off the first partisan to be killed. They simulated executions to terrorise the prisoners (though it needs recalling that simulations of this sort occurred at times at the hands of the partisans as well). They took pleasure in the sufferings they inflicted."[58] The Germans were not to be outdone, engaging in a bloody repression to cut the resistance off from its local support. Between September 29 and October 5, 1944, they massacred more than nine hundred civilians in the village of Marzabotto, not far from Bologna, a crime recalling the one that had afflicted Oradour-sur-Glane in June of the same year. That act of infamy was by no means an exception, and other cities experienced comparable atrocities. For example, in Sant'Anna di Stazzema, near Lucca, on August 12, 1944, the SS murdered about 560 villagers, including 130 children.

Arming the Partisans

To defend their compatriots and assume their missions, the partisans had to be properly armed, which was easier said than done. The British delivered 244 tons of materiel in June, 310 tons in July, 174 in August, 204 in September, and 80 in October—low figures, to say the least,[59] which confirm that Italy, unlike France, remained in SHAEF's eyes a secondary theater of operations. True, the abysmal weather prevented parachute drops. Between January and late April 1945, 856 sorties were to take place, but 551 failed, 146 because of climate conditions. In addition, reception was problematic. Thirty containers borne by two aircraft required a hundred men in the dropping zone; it is easy to imagine the difficulties raised by a raid of twenty bombers. During the same period, in fact, 121 missions were aborted because of inadequate reception teams.[60] When the two problems occurred in combination, many bombers turned back with their holds full.[61] To complete that depressing picture, it should be noted that, too often, weapons fell into the hands of the Germans or the Italian Fascists;[62] Dakotas, the planes used for a time, proved to be unfit for their missions;[63] and in September 1944 the air support provided to the insurgents of Warsaw occurred at the expense of the partisans on the peninsula.[64]

The choice of equipment was also a delicate matter. At first the Allies parachuted in Italian weapons with which the resistance fighters, having been in their country's army, were familiar. As of July 1944 British materiel was dropped; but it was not until early 1945 that heavy weapons—machine guns and 88 mm mortars—which were difficult to handle, were sent in.[65] The Anglo-Americans were sometimes parsimonious, fearing that their containers would fall into the hands of Communists, too Red in their eyes to be honest. They therefore refrained from resupplying the Italian resistance with individual weapons in February and March 1945,[66] to avoid providing the partisans with "a potential weapon of disorder" by overequipping them.[67] "In restricting the flow of weapons to the Italian resistance, the British and American military leaders were consciously sacrificing a tactical advantage to an obsession for law and order. Such politically tainted decisions had been extremely rare during the full fury of the campaign, but as V.E. Day neared, they became more common."[68]

That policy triggered anger among the Allied leaders in charge of subversive warfare. "Winter will be hard time for the Partisans and if we cannot send them the reinforcements and supplies they need we shall be depriving ourselves of a valuable weapon, crippling our existing Missions and laying numbers of Italian communities open to fearful German reprisals," wrote Lord Selborne on October 24, 1944.[69] To make himself quite clear, the minister repeated his view the next day.

> Acting on instructions I called the Italian Maquis out and they have done a magnificent job, far better than I ever expected; in fact, just as good as the French did. The decision now is that supplies to Northern Italy "be restricted to minimum tonnage necessary for the maintenance of existing commitments." I plead that this will be liberally interpreted. When you have called a Maquis out into open warfare it is not fair to let it drop like a hot potato. These men have burned their boats and have no retreat. If we fail them with ammunition, death by torture awaits them.[70]

Even so, on November 13, 1944, the failure of his offensive led Alexander to ask the Italian resistance to take a break from their operations and return home. That order caused consternation. Many fighters were former conscripts who had deserted and could not go back to a normal life. Others, having left their jobs, were unable to provide for their needs. In short, the supreme commander's decision proved traumatic, "a cold shower in a season which was already itself physically and morally icy enough," commented one Italian political leader, Ferruccio Parri.[71] The order was contested all the more in that it came on top of the discrimination practiced against Communist groups, which the American leaders denounced. "It has been apparent for some time that the AFHQ policy in regard to resistance is guided largely by the British experience in Greece, and that they fear some form of armed revolution in the immediate post-combat period."[72] That policy, added Lieutenant-Colonel Hughes, risked shattering the unity of the resistance and causing "party strife." "If the British wish to avoid a repetition of the experience in Greece, they should pursue a diametrically opposite course. . . . Giving the Communists equal treatment with other parties might not infallibly avoid such strife, but an opposite policy would almost certainly bring it on."[73]

Moral considerations shored up these political arguments, as Colonel Riepe of the AFHQ pointed out. "In the beginning the Partisan movement in Italy was spontaneous but since that time 15th Army Group has supplied them, furnished some 14 missions in North Western Italy, exhorted them to do this and to do that and he felt that a clear cut moral responsibility to do what they could to maintain them lay with 15th Army Group."[74] In short, all factors converged to arm the Italian partisans. In March 1945 Colonel Oster noted:

On the one hand it is known that Anglo-American stock is not very high in Northern Italy. The cessation of all deliveries of supplies to the Partisans would be politically disastrous. Nor would the exclusive delivery of nonwarlike stores prove much more happy. Even when cold and hunger were most severe the Partisans' first request has always been for arms and ammunition. On the other hand is the danger of factional strife after the enemy has been ejected from Northern Italy. To reduce this danger every precaution must be taken to prevent Allied arms from finding their way into the hands of undesirables. Between the rock and the whirlpool must be found a navigable channel.[75]

The high command ultimately yielded to these pressures. In January 482 tons were dropped by parachute,[76] followed in February by 992 tons, thanks to unusually mild weather.[77] About two hundred Allied missions were dispatched to the underground groups,[78] to train and even lead them. The

Ruina mission, headed by Major John Wilkinson, parachuted in on the night of August 12, 1944, and established itself in Asiago, Veneto. Bringing along two million lire, it was welcomed by about thirty partisans and was supposed to unify the command of the local resistance, sabotage highways and railroads, and assist General Alexander's offensive.[79] As a general rule, these teams increased the Allies' prestige, lifted the partisans' morale, and facilitated the coordination of efforts. "In some cases the parachuted missions too were a vehicle of mutual esteem and understanding, all the stronger for the fact that both parties were risking their lives."[80] Above all, they guaranteed that orders would be obeyed,[81] at a time when such obedience was slacking off. Indeed, if at first the Allies assigned precise targets to the resistance fighters, they gradually gave them free rein, letting them choose objectives as opportunities arose, even when these targets did not coincide with strategic priorities.[82]

The Allies hailed the contribution of the Italian resistance. The partisans had liberated more than a hundred cities, facilitating the progress of Allied troops.[83] During the taking of Florence, for example, they had harried the enemies' rear lines, transmitted intelligence, and then conducted search and sweep operations, by virtue of "their detailed knowledge of the terrain."[84] Above all, the antifascist forces had established "a nearly complete administrative organization" in the capital of Tuscany, to the astonishment of OSS officers.[85]

In April 1945 the resistance prepared to launch an insurrection in the principal cities of occupied Italy. In Milan, a railway workers' strike that began on April 23 was the prelude to insurrection; on the 26th the city was almost entirely in the hands of the resistance, which, however, suffered thirty losses, with another hundred wounded.[86] The same process unfolded in Genoa. The CNL called for a work stoppage on April 24, and General Meinhold's troops surrendered the next day. Six thousand German and Italian Fascist soldiers were captured in the city at the time—in addition to the twelve thousand taken in the surrounding mountains—but the resistance suffered heavy losses: 187 to 400 dead, depending on the source.[87] The counterscorching policy was a stunning success. The Italian resistance strove to preserve the power stations and to safeguard the port installations of Genoa.[88] "Partisan contribution to the saving of the economic structure of their country may be regarded as the most far-reaching aspect of the part they played in the whole Italian campaign."[89] In short, the special forces concluded, "the Partisan contribution to Allied victory in Italy was a distinguished one which far exceeded the most sanguine expectations."[90]

All in all, the military contribution of the internal resistance to the victory was real, though it must not be overestimated. With or without the underground forces, the Allies would have succeeded in liberating Western Europe, as the Scandinavian example proves a contrario: in the absence of an Allied invasion, the Danes and the Norwegians were unable to liberate themselves on their own, which is what SHAEF had wished. They therefore endured the torments of the German occupation until May 1945. It is nonetheless true that, without the assistance of the resistance, liberation in the other countries would have taken a different course. It would have lasted longer and been more costly and painful. It is therefore clear why the Anglo-Americans, initially skeptical, had greeted the aid offered by the armies of shadows with all the more enthusiasm in that they had long doubted the possibilities of subversive warfare. The resistance had participated in the military victory, and not without glory. It contributed equally to stabilizing the political situation, keeping Western Europe from sinking into chaos.

CHAPTER XXI

Order or Chaos?

The military liberation of Western Europe met with various fortunes and occurred at different rates—rapid for France and Belgium, slower for the Netherlands, interminable for Denmark, Norway, and Italy. It turned out to be just as complex on the political level. The status reserved for the friendly states had been settled by the accords concluded in May 1944, but the fate of France and Italy remained uncertain. The Allies balked at the idea of recognizing Charles de Gaulle and haggled over the degree of independence to grant Ivanoe Bonomi. London, and especially Washington, doubted the capacity of the émigré governments to prevail. They feared that the resistance, on the strength of the weapons it possessed, would impose its rule, engage in barbarous settlings of accounts, and fan the flames of conflict. They also questioned the intentions of the Communist groups: Would they attempt to storm the Winter Palace?

We now know, of course, that Stalin was maneuvering cautiously. In Italy, he recommended against starting a civil war, preferring to avoid tensions with the Anglo-Americans, in order to win the war and stabilize Eastern Europe in his manner. The Italian Communist Party had to restrain its zeal, play the national union game, while proposing reforms that might ensure its victory in the elections to come.[1] In France, the Kremlin conducted a more subtle strategy, urging the PCF to come to an agreement with de Gaulle, even while hoping that the party's influence on liberation would win it more far-reaching control. It was a vain hope. "The failure of national insurrection, de Gaulle's intelligent policy, and international constraints prevented [the French Communist Party] from crossing the Rubicon and, after some hesitation, it abandoned its claims in late 1944."[2] In short, "the objective of building Socialism in the two countries was not abandoned, but in Moscow it was not considered realizable in the immediate future."[3] And yet the political emancipation of Western Europe, fraught with peril, caused anxiety within the ruling Allied circles and their general staffs.

The Gaullist Conundrum

Until the eve of the landing, Roosevelt and Churchill had refused to recognize Charles de Gaulle as a legitimate authority. But as the Allied fleet was preparing to cast off in the assault against Fortress Europe, that head-in-the-sand policy was no longer tenable. The Anglo-Americans had to make sure that the French authorities and the population would obey their orders, so as to avoid a disorder prejudicial to the progress of their troops. Clearly, it was imperative to negotiate with the Gouvernement Provisoire de la République Française (GPRF), which had succeeded the CFLN on June 3, 1944.

On May 31, 1944, the British prime minister took the plunge: he invited the head of the GPRF to join him in England. De Gaulle landed near London on June 4 and immediately went to Portsmouth, where the special train belonging to his host awaited. Although the initial discussions were relatively cordial, it was not long before the storm was brewing. Over lunch, Churchill asked de Gaulle to negotiate with both the British and the Americans, which roused the anger of the Man of June 18.

> That battle is about to begin, and I will speak on the radio. Fine. But as regards discussing the question of [civil] administration, it is clear that the President has never wanted to see me, and yet now suddenly I am being told I must go and talk to the President. . . . Why do you seem to think that I need to submit my candidacy for [exercising] authority in France to Roosevelt? The French government exists. I have nothing to ask of the United States in this respect, nor of Great Britain. This being said, it is important for all the Allies that the

relations between the French administration and the military command should be organized. Nine months ago we proposed as much. Since the armies are about to land in France, I understand your haste to see the question settled. We ourselves are ready to do so. But where is the American representative? Without him, as you well know, nothing can be decided. Furthermore, I note that the Washington and London governments have made arrangements to do without an agreement with us. I have just learned, for example, that despite our warnings the troops and services about to land are provided with so-called French currency, issued by foreign powers, which the government of the republic absolutely refuses to recognize and which, according to the orders of the inter-Allied command, will have compulsory circulation on French territory. I expect that tomorrow General Eisenhower, acting on the instructions of the President of the United States and in agreement with you, will proclaim that he is placing France under his authority. How do you expect to come to terms on this basis? *Allez, faites la guerre, avec votre fausse monnaie* [Well then, make war, with your counterfeit money].[4]

De Gaulle was then taken to Eisenhower's headquarters, where the main lines of the plan were laid out for him. The supreme commander handed him the speech he intended to deliver on the BBC. In the eyes of the Constable of Free France, it was unacceptable: Ike was calling on the French to "carry out his orders" and declared that "in the administration, everyone will continue to fulfill his functions unless contrary instructions are received." In short, de Gaulle would write, he "appeared to be taking control of our country even though he was merely an Allied general entitled to command troops but not in the least qualified to intervene in the country's government."[5] The proclamation was already printed up, so Eisenhower could not modify it—even supposing he had shown any desire to do so.

De Gaulle then went head to head with the supreme commander, refusing to address the French people over the airwaves immediately after him. "By speaking immediately after Eisenhower I should appear to sanction what he said—of which I disapproved—and assume a place in the succession unsuitable to the dignity of France."[6] It was only on his own time, in the late afternoon, that he delivered a speech, which was preceded by a new heated exchange.

The Man of June 18, "frigidity itself,"[7] having entered the BBC studios at Bush House at about 12:30 p.m., demanded to speak live, rousing great fear in the British authorities. A leery Foreign Office was afraid that de Gaulle would say whatever came into his head. It therefore wanted the text to be recorded, to verify that its content corresponded to Allied watchwords. But de Gaulle said he had no script: "He had had no time to prepare more than a few notes." Robert H. Bruce Lockhart later reported:

> I thought that we were lost. If we said that the script must be "vetted," he would refuse to broadcast. Then Ivone Kirkpatrick [head of the BBC] had a flash of genius. "General," he said with eloquent conviction, "your broadcast today is the most momentous that you have ever made, perhaps that you ever will make. Its effect will reach far beyond the limits of France. All the oppressed countries are waiting for your lead. We have made arrangements to put your talk out in twenty-four languages. We must have a record for our translations." The General gave way, and in a deathly silence we grouped ourselves round the glass walls of the recording room. Without a trace of nervousness he delivered a superb broadcast. . . . Tears came into my eyes and, self-conscious in my lack of control, I looked at my neighbours and found comfort. They, too were deeply moved.[8]

In his memoirs, the Man of June 18 preferred to pass over this episode in silence. "After several harsh confrontations in the wings, the London radio was in fact put at my disposal under the conditions I had requested," he reported soberly, not without taking a few liberties with the truth.[9] But his speech was equal to the task: "The final battle is now joined. After so much fighting, fury and suffering, the decisive clash is now upon us, the clash that has so long been hoped for. This is of course the battle of France—it is also France's battle!. . . In the nation, in the empire, and in the armies there is but a single will, a single hope. From behind the heavy clouds of our blood and tears now reappears the sun of our grandeur." That speech was all the more remarkable, as Churchill sourly pointed out, in that France had not yet thrown one soldier into the fight.[10]

De Gaulle's fiery rhetoric concealed two poisoned arrows. First, de Gaulle refrained from mentioning the Americans. Second, he asked that "the instructions given by the French government and by the leaders qualified to make them be followed exactly."[11] But because that "government" had not been recognized by the Allies, it would have been preferable to use the expression "provisional government." Anthony Eden, hastily consulted, found that misrepresentation tolerable. "'I'll have trouble with the Prime Minister about this' he said 'but we'll let it go.' He was smiling."[12] The speech was therefore broadcast at 6:15 p.m. on June 6.

To keep the pressure on, de Gaulle canceled the departure of the Mission Militaire de Liaison Administrative (Military Administrative Liaison Mission), which, under the leadership of Pierre Laroque, had trained 160 officers and more than 50 female volunteers to administer the liberated territories, in accordance with modalities that remained to be specified. Finally, and perhaps above all, the head of the provisional government announced that he did not recognize the currency that the Allies intended to use. That "invasion franc" was unacceptable. Symbolically, it flouted French sovereignty, inasmuch as the right to mint money is a regalian prerogative. And it deprived France of control over the money supply, which posed a risk: the Allies could print as many bills as they wished, without having to guarantee them. And who would pay in the end? If the provisional government were to recognize that currency, the French Republic would be obliged to fund Allied expenses without right of inspection; failing which, London and Washington would settle the bill.

Churchill and Roosevelt, surprised by de Gaulle's resistance, initially held firm. The resident of Downing Street pretended to believe that the French would accept that currency without a fight.[13] He tactlessly noted that the United States was holding on to a portion of French gold—a total of 500 million pounds—which provided "some means of arguing later on."[14] For his part, Roosevelt judged that de Gaulle's obstructionism would cause the franc to fall precipitously in relation to the dollar and pound, a luxury France could ill afford.[15]

But it was not long before the two men began to express a few doubts. Upon looking at specimens of the bills, Churchill told Roosevelt, "They do not strike us as very reassuring. They look very easy to forge. Nothing is said on whose responsibility they are issued and who is responsible for redeeming them. Surely there must be some authority behind them. . . . Please my dear friend, look at them yourself and say what we ought to do. Should we let de Gaulle obtain new status as his price for backing these notes or should we take the burden on ourselves for the time being and improve the issue later on and settle up at the Peace Table where there will be many accounts to be presented?"[16] The British chancellor of the exchequer was more direct. In the absence of an accord, he said, "the whole of the burden of financing the conduct of operations inside France might fall on us and not on the French authorities,"[17] since the debt would ultimately be honored by the British or U.S. Treasury.

On June 21 Churchill faced the facts.

> The notes give no indication of the authority by whom they are issued. Unless we reach an understanding with the French Committee, we shall be morally responsible for seeing that they are honoured. Under the mutual aid arrangements which we are making with the other European Allies, they will bear the cost of civil administration and of supplies and services to our troops in their countries. But if we should become responsible for the whole of the military notes issued in France, the French would contribute no mutual aid to the American and British Armies of Liberation.[18]

In threatening to classify the invasion francs as counterfeit money, de Gaulle had played his hand shrewdly, placing the Anglo-Americans before a Cornelian dilemma: pay or negotiate.

London and Washington ultimately gave in. To circumvent Roosevelt's declared hostility, the British agreed to begin the talks on their own. A Franco-British committee met on June 19 to work out the bases for an accord, which would subsequently be presented to the United States. But the question of recognition was not resolved.

To calm matters, Roosevelt requested that de Gaulle be allowed to return to France.[19] Churchill grudgingly complied and asked Montgomery to perform a minimal service: "I must inflict on you a visit from General de Gaulle tomorrow. This is, on no account, to be a burden to you in any duties you have to discharge. . . . Our relations with him are formal, but we are nonetheless his host. I do not think that you should receive him at the beach." Montgomery need only meet de Gaulle at headquarters. And, Churchill added, "It will be much better he shall make any discourses he wishes after he returns to England. It would surely be undesirable to gather large crowds in Bayeux and have anything in the nature of a political demonstration. If however the people are anxious to welcome him on his way through, it is not for us to deny him."[20]

Taking Power

General de Gaulle, having embarked on the destroyer *La Combattante* on June 14, reached Montgomery's headquarters in Creully, before proceeding to Bayeux, where he delivered a brief speech. After going to Isigny and then to Grandcamp, he set off for Courseulles that very evening. The welcome the Normans gave him, without having the appearance of a referendum, was friendly and sometimes warm, as the officers from Civil Affairs noted.

> The Norman is not a demonstrative person and as this part of Normandy has suffered very little, physically or morally, no white-hot enthusiasm could be expected. However, the people were undoubtedly pleased at seeing French officers who were not under the German boot and there was a natural curiosity to see de Gaulle, the symbol of the Resistance. His visit did give the effect to the inhabitants that they had their sovereignty back. His reception was much more fervent in the devastated areas such as Isigny and other places. In some there were scenes of emotion.[21]

But de Gaulle did not intend to be merely a symbolic figure, however moving. A shrewd politician, he had brought on board *La Combattante* François Coulet, general commissioner of the Republic, as well as the military delegate Pierre de Chevigné, whom he expected to place at the helm of the liberated French departments. During his meeting with Montgomery, he had casually mentioned that Commissioner Coulet would take care of administrative questions, but Monty remained in the dark: "He has left behind in Bayeux one civilian administrative officer and three colonels but I have no idea what is their function."[22] De Gaulle's trusted men immediately seized local power. On June 15 the Vichyist subprefect of Bayeux, Pierre Rochat, had to cede his position to Raymond Triboulet, a local figure and resistance fighter on the Liberation Committee.

Unlike their superiors, the officers at Civil Affairs instantly grasped the meaning of the maneuver. On June 16, 1944, the senior civil affairs officer (SCAO) noted, not without melancholy:

> De Gaulle has staged a very clever coup d'état, with or without the connivance of London. I feel very sore that I got no notice whatever

of the visit beforehand, as I would of course have stuck to the man like a leech. I also feel that I should have received some guidance beforehand as to the line I was to take in case of any attempt such as has been made. . . . I have of course kept my commander informed. His attitude is that he will have absolutely nothing to do with politics in any shape or form and has no intention of issuing any instructions, or making any comment whatever. That of course leaves me to use my "common sense"; a phrase I am getting rather acclimatized to.[23]

In the absence of instructions from London or Washington, therefore, the Allied leaders dealt with the Gaullist authorities on the local level. If the French accepted these men, the Anglo-Americans would bow out. But if the French rebelled, the Allies would intervene. "The next days will show whether Coulet and Triboulet can establish themselves and win the people's confidence as the de facto government. Meanwhile we are treating them as such; the high question of 'recognition' has now left the stratosphere of diplomatic exchange and [is] being decided on the ground," concluded the British general Lewis, head of Civil Affairs.[24]

Churchill and Roosevelt, then, washing their hands of the whole affair, let their officers decide. In fact, the provisional government authorities administered the liberated territories in an optimal manner. As Colonel Durbin pointed out:

It is quite apparent that the French administrative authorities appointed by de Gaulle are doing everything in their power to advance the status of the General. This, of course, is understandable, and need not constitute grounds for too great worry so long as they at the same time continue to afford cooperation as has been the case to date. . . . To summarize it would appear that if we accept the administration now functioning in France, and furnish them a reasonable degree of assistance, both administrative and in a material sense, there is no need to particularly worry about ability or desire of the people to do a good job.[25]

The American lieutenant-colonel Copp agreed:

Generally the people appear disinterested in politics but the leadership of de Gaulle through his appointees and liaison officers is unchallenged.

His representatives in the higher echelons lose no opportunity to press the political advantage given them by the position we have permitted them to assume. They wear the cross of Lorraine, appear prominently with resistance leaders and encourage display of the resistance armband which is being worn by those claiming membership in the resistance. In these circumstances the public cannot help but feel that we are supporting de Gaulle, whatever we may say in White House press conferences. De Gaulle's instructions seem to be for his agents to cooperate completely in everything that concerns the military necessity, reserving to themselves the right to control those matters not of military concern. . . . [They] are proving invaluable. . . . Though [the French liaison officers] are patently de Gaullist and clearly pushing the cause of the Provisional Government, there has been no case brought to my attention in which they have failed to comply with any request of the military authorities.[26]

In addition, Normandy remained calm and refrained from punishing acknowledged or presumed collaborators during the battles. Granted, a handful of individuals claiming to belong to the resistance caused some unrest. Composed of young, unemployed thugs who had grown up during the war, "they find in the Resistance (with the danger passed) a vent for the spirit which in our country go[es] into college fraternity initiations and football rallies," wrote Lieutenant-Colonel Copp of the First U.S. Army. "If there is to be trouble in France it will arise as leadership in the Resistance is assumed by these small fry who respect no rights. In one community they have armed themselves, ignored orders of the mayor, appropriated his car, and without authority placed under house arrest persons they suspect of collaboration. . . . In another they have cut off the hair of young girls suspected of affairs with Germans. These incidents are not widespread, but promise trouble if not suppressed."[27]

All things considered, the disturbances remained limited. Although a few women had their hair sheared off, the spontaneous purge was relatively benign in Normandy. In total, the department of Manche recorded only 1 summary execution upon liberation; Calvados, 12; and Orne, 43—compared to 275 for Dordogne (in southwest France) alone.[28] That observation is valid for many regions, and, as a general rule, the French authorities guaranteed the rule of law. France did see eight to nine thousand extrajudicial executions, but 80 percent of these occurred before the liberation of the territory and can therefore be considered acts of war, with only one to two thousand taking place while the legal purge was under way.[29] Whatever the view taken of that balance sheet, it must be said that France did not sink into a bloodbath, and the Allies took pride in that fact. In June they ordered their propaganda services to celebrate the provisional government's ability to maintain order. "Liberated France—run by Frenchmen" was the slogan the Political Warfare Division imposed on the media, breaking with the official position of the White House.[30]

Law and Order

De Gaulle, taking advantage of the foot-dragging of the Allied leaders and the discreet indulgence of Eisenhower, who, after the Algiers experience, had absolutely no intention of assuming administrative or political responsibilities for liberated France, succeeded in imposing his authority. From that standpoint, Normandy served as a precedent. Anthony Eden noted in June 1944: "Our estimate of General De Gaulle's position in France has been confirmed in Normandy and his representative has been accepted here. If the same attitude is adopted by the people of, say Brittany and other parts of France which may shortly be liberated continued refusal to recognize the Committee would be unwise."[31] The Allied services maintained that neither de Gaulle nor the leaders of the army of shadows really dreamed of seizing power by force. "All our evidence goes to show that the resistance leaders in France are determined to re-establish democratic forms of government; and the same has been true of the Consultative Assembly in Algiers. If De Gaulle tried to override that desire, the probability is that the forces of the resistance would turn against him, but there is no reason to believe that he will try to override it."[32]

In the same vein, the liberators feared neither the Communists nor the armed resistance fighters. In their view, the thirty thousand FTP that OSS identified in July 1944 represented no danger. "There is no evidence that they are planning a putsch, in opposition to the other resistance forces, or that they would be successful if they did."[33] Even the region of Toulouse, though shrouded in a sulfurous reputation, maintained calm, as the Allied officers pointed out. "I wish to report my own conclusion that, considering the times, there is a high degree of order here and that there are no valid grounds for rumors of violent struggles," noted the civil affairs officer.[34]

And SHAEF affirmed that "neither the FFI nor the FTP constitute a move-ment for preparing for imminent violence to overthrow the regime. They are not even, in themselves, active factors in French politics in the sense of pressure groups working for certain general political ends."[35]

The Allied agents in the field confirmed that judgment, but with a few sour notes. In Oise, Lieutenant Maurice Basset was unable to cooperate with the FTP, whose leaders informed him that, "after ampler consider-ation their organization was not prepared to receive instructions from our London headquarters. They wished to keep absolute military autonomy and a complete liberty of action. In other words," he reported, "my posi-tion towards them would have merely been that of a weapons distributor. I decided that I had not come to the field for that simple purpose and I brought my relations with the FTP to an end."[36] Conversely, Roger Hen-quet had a good working relationship with the FTP leader of Loir-et-Cher. "Marcel[37] was to remain the chief of his men. I was to work with him more as an advisor and a liaison with headquarters than a superior. We would discuss problems of organization with him, but he would be the one to pass the orders in the field. He would obey orders from headquarters trans-mitted by me, but he would continue to furnish activity reports to his 'responsibles' [leaders]."[38]

As a general rule, then, the situation caused no anxiety, especially since national insurrection, on which the Communist Party had counted as a possible means to take power, had failed. Of 212 large French cities, only 5 saw insurgencies, and that situation restrained considerably "the strate-gic space offered the PCF."[39] Granted, Paris was one of the five, but it was more the exception than the rule. Furthermore, on October 28, 1944, the provisional government dissolved the Milices Patriotiques, the military arm of the Communist Party, and London and Washington recognized the GPRF the same month. Stalin lucidly drew the unavoidable conclusions. The head of the Soviet government scolded Maurice Thorez upon meet-ing with him on November 19, 1944. The French Communists had not understood that the situation had changed; it was necessary to move on. "The CP is not strong enough to strike the government at the top. It must build up forces and seek allies."[40] In short, revolution was not the order of the day.

The French general secretary, having returned from Moscow on Novem-ber 27, 1944, immediately implemented that line, and Eisenhower's ser-vices took due note. Thorez was "apparently determined to support or, at any rate not to impede, the war effort and it seems unlikely that the Communist Party will break with the Government so long as Germany remains undefeated."[41] And SHAEF concluded in January 1945: "We believe that in France little danger exists of any major political disturbance occurring such as would seriously affect Allied military operations during this winter."[42] Paradoxically, the risk now lay with the Anglo-Americans. "There will be a grave danger of civil war if the Allies, ignoring De Gaulle and the National Committee, attempt to set up a puppet government in opposition to the wishes of the resistance and the majority of the French people."[43]

Toward Recognition

Between June 8 and 20 the Czechs, Poles, Belgians, Luxembourgers, and Norwegians granted recognition to the GPRF, "despite the immediate American and British appeals that they abstain." Only the Dutch held off, hoping that "by deferring in this matter to Washington's desires they would obtain greater American sympathy in regard to Indonesia."[44] The British and the Americans, by contrast, stood firm. Roosevelt did take a first step by receiving de Gaulle in the United States in the summer of 1944, but his motives were basely political: on the eve of the presidential election, he hoped to win over public opinion, which was favorable to Free France. Charles de Gaulle handled the situation with good grace. He arrived in Washington on July 6, making only a brief but triumphant stop in New York, "in order not to furnish occasions for popular manifestations which, three months away from the Presidential election, might seem to be directed against what had hitherto been the President's policy. . . . All the more so since Dewey, the candidate opposing Roosevelt, was the governor of New York State."[45] Upon his return to Algiers, de Gaulle saw the first dividends of his strategy: he found a copy of a declaration published on July 13 by the U.S. government, conceding the right of the CFLN to oversee the administration of France and thus granting de facto recognition.

The talks undertaken between the French and the British accelerated at that time. In late July the Americans agreed to participate in the discussions. The negotiations, nearly completed on August 8, concluded on the 25th with a formulation that echoed the accords reached with the friendly countries in May 1944. The Allies legitimized the GPRF, which, in return, pledged to entrust the supreme commander with the powers necessary to conduct military operations. The provisional government would mint money to supply the Allies with cash, in exchange for payment in dollars, while France would be a beneficiary of the American lend-lease program and of British mutual aid.[46] After long months of impasse, the situation was settling down, though the Allies had still not recognized de jure the GPRF.

Several factors eventually led them to make that move. The victory in Paris that August showed that de Gaulle enjoyed enormous popularity. On September 9, moreover, the head of the GPRF took care to reshuffle his government, in order to include party officials and members of the resistance, the old elites and up-and-coming figures, from both Algiers and the French metropolis. "The two branches of the resistance were merged, the generations brought together, and technocrats coexisted with former parliamentarians: the amalgam was made at the highest level."[47] In the same vein, the Consultative Assembly of Algiers, having been transferred to Paris, was expanded, and it held its first session on November 7, 1944.

In the provinces, the Gaullist authority set about disarming the underground forces. On August 28, 1944, the GPRF dissolved COMAC and the regional FFI general staffs in the liberated zones. On October 28 of the same year, as we have seen, the Milices Patriotiques were abolished. The authorities encouraged the shadow fighters to enlist in the regular army, a way for them to again take up arms but at the same time channel their ardor. The provisional government thereby demonstrated its capacity to maintain order, while offering the democratic guarantees Franklin Roosevelt was calling for.

At the same time, de Gaulle avoided upping the ante: he did not fruitlessly oppose the Allied authorities. Fearing the Communists' intentions, real or fantasized, in August 1944 he even appealed to General Eisenhower for "the temporary loan of two American divisions to use . . . as a show of force and to establish his position firmly. . . . Here there seemed a touch of the sardonic in the picture of France's symbol of liberation having to ask for Allied forces to establish and maintain a similar position in the heart of the freed capital."[48] The head of the GPRF, moreover, seemed in no great hurry to take total control of the country, preferring, in the words of Desmond Morton, "to leave the great responsibility of government to SHAEF for some time longer, so that in the event of disorders he could disclaim responsibility and shelter behind SHAEF."[49] In short, de Gaulle, far from rushing things, advanced cautiously.

On the strength of these guarantees, the military command campaigned vehemently for recognition.

> The present trend and the general acceptance of De Gaulle by the liberated French people indicate that a cabinet under his leadership together with the consultative assembly reconstituted to include at least fifty percent resistance membership, seem likely to remain in control of the situation until such a time as elections can be held. In these circumstances should recognition by the Allied Governments be withheld pending the technical expression of popular will through the lengthy process of elections, the prestige of any interim French administration will suffer and consequently it will be in a less favorable position to assure that measure of stability in France required not only for the further prosecution of the war but for the difficult early period of reconstruction. . . . From a military point of view there is no reason to delay a further degree of recognition.[50]

The Allies bowed to its reasoning and recognized the GPRF de jure on October 23, 1944.

Even so, London and Washington had taken a very long time to accept the obvious, which caused anger among several OSS and SOE leaders. "Recognition of De Gaulle: this is perhaps the most serious failing of the section, even more unfortunate since the rank and file of the section from very early on took the position that the De Gaulle movement was more representative, more democratic and more able to contribute to the Allied war effort than any alternative group," OSS admitted. That paragraph, however, was struck before the postliberation report in which it appeared was published, and a handwritten comment affirmed that this was a "non-realistic statement."[51] The heads of the Office of Strategic Services found it difficult to disavow President Roosevelt in an official document.

In any event, General de Gaulle had prevailed, despite the many obstacles that the Allies had strewn in his path. The power of the Man of June 18 was recognized and his authority accepted—an outcome that the head of the Belgian government would certainly have preferred.

Belgian Complexities

Although Belgium posed no problems a priori, the Allies had worried during the dark years about the lack of popularity of Hubert Pierlot and his ministers. Subsequent events confirmed their alarm. On September 8, 1944, the Belgian government landed at Evere Airfield "amidst complete indifference."[52] "We disembarked on a deserted aerodrome from planes which had been put at our disposal by the British Government," recalls Paul-Henri Spaak. "Nobody had been warned of our arrival. The cars which took us into town were preceded by a jeep. One of our colleagues stood in it, shouting to the few citizens we passed: 'Here is your Government.' I must confess that this produced no reaction at all, neither hostility nor enthusiasm, just total indifference."[53] The minister speaks of "cars," but other sources are crueler, saying that the return occurred in a big rig and a mail van.[54] In any event, the Belgian government's "comeback" took place without ceremony, in stark contrast to the fervor that had surrounded Charles de Gaulle in Paris two weeks earlier. On September 10 General George Erskine, head of the SHAEF mission for Belgium, also returned to that country; four days later he entrusted the civil government to the regular authorities. That rapid devolution of power spared the kingdom the torments of a power vacuum where everything would have been up for grabs. But appearances were deceiving, because Léopold's antagonism, the rancor of members of the resistance, and the Parti Communiste Belge's strategy undermined the authority of the Pierlot cabinet.

The government in exile, it should be recalled, had never sought a confrontation with the king. Léopold conducted a personal policy and, unlike Pétain, did not dream of installing a new order. But he had never forgiven his ministers for what he considered treachery. He was taken to Germany in June 1944, having composed a political testament in a particularly acerbic tone in March of the same year.[55]

Military honor, the dignity of the Crown, and the good of the country converged to prevent me from following the government out of Belgium. . . .

The essential task of the government will be to ensure once and for all good relations between Flemings and Walloons; the continuation of an independent Belgium will depend on that being achieved.

I consider broad social reforms an urgent matter, because the scandalous contrast between the poverty to which some have been condemned on account of war on two different occasions, and the exorbitant profits that others have procured, proclaims the iniquity of a self-serving and unhealthy system and the duty to put an end to it. . . .

There is not one patriot who is not tormented by the memory of certain speeches delivered before the entire world, in which Belgian ministers took the liberty, in extraordinarily critical times—when the safeguarding of national dignity called for extreme circumspection—of hastily making charges of the greatest gravity against the conduct of our army and the acts of its leader. . . .

It goes against the prestige and honor of the Crown and the honor of the country for the authors of these speeches to exercise any authority whatever in liberated Belgium, so long as they have not repudiated their error and made formal and complete reparations. The nation would not understand or allow the dynasty to agree to associate its actions with men who have committed such an affront, which the world witnessed with astonishment.[56]

Far from seeking concord, the monarch denounced the attitude of his ministers, even though they had contributed to preserving Belgium's honor throughout the ordeal. That manifesto, commented Winston Churchill, "suggests that King Leopold, like the Bourbons, has learned nothing and forgotten nothing."[57] Hubert Pierlot, informed of its substance in June 1944 but not officially briefed until September 9, took the blow hard[58] but reacted without delay. While saying nothing about the document, which for a long time remained secret, he named the king's brother, Charles, to the regency, a choice endorsed by Parliament on September 20. The prince took an oath the next day. For the time being, then, the monarchy was saved and the king posed no danger, particularly since the United Kingdom displayed strict neutrality—unlike the strategy it was pursuing toward Victor Emmanuel III. "In our view the essential thing is that if the King returns to Belgium he should not arrive in the country in a SHAEF vehicle or aircraft or be escorted or accompanied on his drive into Brussels by any military officers or personnel. His journey and arrival should be a purely Belgian affair and Belgian authorities must be responsible for taking whatever security measures they think necessary."[59] The "Royal Question" was still unresolved, however. It poisoned the kingdom's political life until Léopold's return in 1950, and, because of the controversies to which his presence gave rise, he ultimately abdicated in 1951.

In the meantime, other matters were more pressing. Some seventy thousand members of the resistance (twenty-five thousand of them belonging to the Front de l'Indépendance) held on to their weapons until late October 1944,[60] certainly a worrying situation in terms of the kingdom's stability.

Belgium was experiencing a relatively high level of violence, owing more to the climate of anomie than to the resistance. Political, and especially financially motivated, murders had increased from 200 a year before the war to 700 in 1943, reaching a peak of 1,852 in 1944.[61] In addition, arbitrary arrests made within the context of the purge multiplied upon liberation, generating an often "blind and uncontrolled" violence.[62] The attitude of the resistance fighters, frustrated at not having participated militarily in their own liberation, was alarming. "Far from being seen as the new elite of the liberated nation, they were widely distrusted as a disruptive presence, driving around in requisitioned jeeps and vehicles, flaunting their weapons, and becoming engaged in illegal if not outright criminal actions."[63]

Granted, the situation was less dramatic than the actors perceived it to be. The presence of the Allied troops confined the violence within narrow limits. And though the resistance sometimes threw oil on the fire, it much more often played a pacifying role, reducing the number of flare-ups. The historian José Gotovitch notes: "The government could clear itself of all responsibility for the blunders, repeat the mantra that it was returning the country to a legal framework, grant itself a certificate of purity. But without the spontaneous intervention of the resistance forces, nothing would have been possible except direct revenge and the settling of accounts."[64]

And yet the government felt threatened, and not without reason. On September 5 the Catholic, Liberal, and Socialist parties demanded that a new cabinet be formed. The London émigrés would play a minor role in it, pending new elections. "The large majority of the political elite who had remained within Occupied Belgium were determined that power should now return to the parliament, based, until elections could be held, on its pre-war membership."[65] "There was a fear that we had returned as judges, ignorant of what had happened under the occupation and anxious to dominate," Paul-Henri Spaak commented in retrospect.[66] The population, moreover, held the Pierlot government in low esteem, "not because it represented an illegitimate political regime, but because its members for the most part personified the legalistic caution and political compromises which much of the population held responsible for the failures of the 1930s."[67] Nonetheless, a new Pierlot government incorporating the three major prewar parties (Catholic, Liberal, Socialist) and adding two Communist ministers was formed on September 25. But that response did not fulfill the society's anxious expectations.

Above all, the authorities did not have sufficient manpower to maintain order. In autumn 1944 they had to rely on only eight thousand poorly armed gendarmes. Weakened politically, lacking the means to repress the population, the Belgian authorities were presented with an equation composed of simple terms but complicated to solve: disarm the resistance and arm the forces of law and order. As General Erskine summed it up in September 1944: "The Belgian Government feel that they might find themselves much embarrassed with large numbers of the various resistance movements under arms but their own Gendarmerie unarmed."[68]

Disarming

The disarmament of the resistance encountered two distinct but related obstacles. First, the partisans balked, not caring to lose the real or symbolic attributes of their power. Pierlot's attempts to deal with the situation were clumsy. SHAEF pointed out in September 1944: "The resistance representatives have complained that the Government, instead of being appreciative of the part played by resistance in the liberation of the country is only concerned in suppressing and disarming resistance groups. There appears to be some truth in this complaint."[69] Second, the Communists looked on that operation with a baleful eye. Did they wish to take power? "No red flags flew over Brussels and, far from challenging the nascent political order, the Communists promptly declared their readiness to work within it." At the same time, they had pushed the case for a national uprising. "In this way, a dual power structure would be created, whereby the government would be obliged to accept the de facto power of the Resistance and more especially of the Communist-directed Resistance coalition, the *Front de l'Indépendance*."[70] The Allied advance had foiled that calculation, but the strategy of the Parti Communiste Belge was worrying.

In any event, the disarmament of the resistance was an especially urgent obligation in that Belgium served as the Allies' logistical base and, in December 1944, would be dramatically threatened by the counteroffensive in the Ardennes. SHAEF did not intend to tolerate the slightest disorder in its rear lines.

On October 2, 1944, Eisenhower demanded that the weapons be handed over. Two days later, the resistance groups agreed, on the condition that the new Belgian army incorporate former partisans. But the government could not honor its promise, made on October 31, 1944, because the British refused to equip new units.[71] On November 10 Pierlot leapt into the fray, prompting the resignation of the two Communist ministers on the 16th. On the 25th of the same month, the Front de l'Indépendance held a major demonstration, to show that the prime minister had lost the people's confidence. Demonstrators invaded the "neutral zone" in the heart of Brussels, where access to government buildings was barred. The aim of that breach was not to seize power but to show the anger of the mob. It was nevertheless harshly repressed. The forces of law and order fired on the demonstrators: thirty-four of them were wounded, as were fifteen in the ranks of the police and the gendarmerie. During the night, George Erskine summoned Fernand Demany, head of the Front de l'Indépendance, and Jean Terfve, the number two man in the Parti Communiste Belge. Over a bottle of whiskey, the British general told them that he would no longer tolerate any disturbances. Nevertheless, the Communist labor unions called for a protest strike on November 28. Apart from the fact that few observed it, the British mounted a show of force, deploying tanks and arresting a few armed resisters. Ten days later, twelve thousand weapons had been turned in.[72] Eleven thousand volunteers were absorbed by the army in February 1945,[73] and 41,727 weapons had been collected by July.[74]

On December 12 Erskine drew the lesson from these tragic events: "The political situation after a sharp rise in temperature has settled down and reached a degree of stability which it has not had since the liberation of Belgium. But it must be made absolutely clear to all concerned that political ambitions cannot be fought out in the streets across our lines of communication. If this happens, or there is a serious treat, the military forces become involved."[75] In that sense, he was conforming to the directives received. "The sole concern of the military authorities is to ensure that the Allied war effort is not impeded by internal dissension in Belgium. We have no desire to interfere in Belgian internal affairs, but it is our duty adequately to secure our installations and lines of communications, and full precautions must, therefore, be taken."[76]

The situation calmed down subsequently. Order reigned, and the Pierlot cabinet, under pressure from the parties and public opinion—which had little appreciation for it—resigned on February 7, 1945. That action inspired few regrets in the Allies. The government, SHAEF had pointed out in January of the same year, "is not only weak and unenergetic in dealing with the difficult problems of distribution of coal and food . . . but it is also unrepresentative of the political complexion of the nation. It is mildly right wing whereas Belgium is predominantly left wing and it has not recognized the claims of the resistance movement to be adequately represented in the government." In addition, the strikes that swept through the ranks of the miners and dock workers in winter 1945 did not cause much alarm. "We do not believe . . . that the Communists would resort to violence or are likely to cause a major upheaval, while the war with Germany continues. So long as the Belgians believe the Allies have their well-being at heart, we do not think that a state of affairs will occur in which Allied military operations would be in jeopardy."[77]

The Pierlot government, despite its ardent patriotism, had not succeeded in maintaining order or in federating all Belgian political forces under its banner. Yet its achievements cannot be reduced to that disappointing balance sheet. The prime minister had managed, in a difficult situation, to keep Belgium in the war. And from London, he had prepared for the liberation with a seriousness of purpose, planning bold programs with Camille Gutt, his minister of finance. The two men, by imposing an exchange of banknotes, taking deflationist measures, and instituting large-scale tax reform, curbed inflation in their country and allowed reconstruction on solid foundations to begin. De Gaulle, by contrast, rejected a comparable plan submitted to him by Pierre Mendès France, minister of national economy, preferring to yield to the laxity recommended by his minister of finance, René Pleven, who was reluctant to make the population swallow such a bitter pill after the trauma of the occupation. Let us add, for good measure, that beginning on December 28, 1944, Pierlot created a social security system and formed a Conseil National de la Résistance (National Council of the Resistance), which would be consulted on questions relating to the army of shadows. Conversely, he roused little of the enthusiasm sparked by the Cross of Lorraine. Too closely linked to the prewar period to personify renewal, scrupulously respecting the letter of the constitution, that mediocre orator was unable to fire the imagination of his people, a shortcoming he paid for with an enduring unpopularity: to this day, no street in Brussels is named after Pierlot.

Starvation

The Allies loyally supported the Pierlot government but without success, whereas the strategy they followed in the Netherlands attracted the wrath of the Dutch authorities. The country, as we have seen, was facing a tragic situation: because of the paralysis of the railroads, it was suffering the torments of starvation. On September 28, 1944, Pieter Gerbrandy requested deliveries of food from Winston Churchill to relieve civilians' distress. The British prime minister refused, claiming that "any food admitted to Holland would directly or indirectly nourish the Germans, who were themselves short of food and ammunition." Conversely, Eisenhower was open to an agreement, but negotiations hit a stumbling block. The Nazis proposed using the Rhine to transport food aid, which awakened suspicion: the Allies suspected their enemies of wanting to take advantage of that windfall so that the river, spared by the bombings, would serve their logistics. Implementation of the plan was thus put off. In late January 1945, however, two Swedish ships, the *Noreg* and the *Dagmar Bratt*, delivered 3,330 tons of flour, margarine, and cod liver. In late April some 2,200 tons sent courtesy of Stockholm helped the population to hold on, though the amount was absurdly small, given the soaring mortality rate. In mid-January 1945 Queen Wilhelmina wrote in person to Roosevelt and Churchill, beseeching them to avert "a major catastrophe the like of which has not been seen since the Middle Ages." In early February an equally alarmist Montgomery demanded that aid finally be provided to the Dutch. Eisenhower heard these appeals and ordered the delivery of 120,000 tons, which improved the situation by early March.[78] By contrast, and despite the urgent request of the Netherlands government,[79] he refused to modify his plans and liberate the occupied part of the country, preferring to focus his efforts on the offensive to destroy the Reich.

The British and the Americans ultimately negotiated, however. On April 28, 1945, General Freddy de Guingand, Montgomery's delegate, met with Ernst Schwebel, representative of Reichskommissar Arthur Seyss-Inquart. Dropping zones were designated and, on April 29, B-17s dropped their first containers, a prelude, Eisenhower hoped, to daily parachute drops of 1,650 tons.[80] The next day Seyss-Inquart validated the terms of a truce with Bedell Smith, Prince Bernhard, and General Ivan Susloparov, the Soviet representative, leading on May 5 to the surrender of General Blaskowitz, commander of the Twenty-fifth Army. The war in the Netherlands was finally ending, after five interminable years of suffering.

These drawn-out discussions did not fail to damage relations between the Allies and the Dutch government. The Anglo-Americans had refused to sacrifice their military objectives to humanitarian imperatives, a line they had followed consistently since 1940. That position roused the anger of Pieter Gerbrandy and Queen Wilhelmina, who were sensitive to the hellish conditions their fellow citizens were enduring. "We have handed over to the Allies everything we had," the Dutch prime minister recalled.

> Our ships, our men, our navy, even our supplies, are no longer at our disposal and we are obliged to take a passive role and wait until SHAEF acts. Nevertheless, while millions are starving, the question will sooner or later be asked: has the Netherland Government done everything that it could to help. If it appears that more could have been done and that a large number of loyal Dutchmen . . . met their deaths because we were insufficiently prepared or our plans too clumsy for rapid operation, such a revelation will come not only as a shock to public opinion, but as a scandal, the responsibility for which will be laid at the door not only of the Dutch Government, but also, I fear, of the British Government.[81]

Royal Games

Apart from that humanitarian crisis, the Allies had to manage a complicated political situation. Queen Wilhelmina, it should be recalled, dreamed of extending her power when liberation came. To serve that design, she had one asset: Prince Bernhard, her son-in-law, commanded both the Forces of the Interior and the modest Dutch Brigade, which had two thousand men.[82] The two royals therefore endeavored to postpone the government's return. "Meanwhile Prince Bernhard . . . indicated that he and his personal advisers as well as the Queen did not view the proposed move to Brussels of the Prime Minister and his party with any enthusiasm and in his view they would be better advised to remain in London until they were able to return to the Netherlands direct. This has put the Supreme Commander in an awkward position for whatever decision he gives must be unwelcome to one or other of the party."[83] Espousing the government's cause, the Anglo-Americans were leery. "There is nothing new in the reference to the autocratic tendencies of HM Queen Wilhelmina: it has long been known that the bed of Her Ministers is beset with thorns of Her strewing."[84] They were therefore vigilant, knowing that the queen, who had the use of a private plane, could fly out and land in Holland "without any previous arrangement either with SHAEF of with the Dutch Government."[85]

To avert such a power grab, they decided to repatriate the Gerbrandy cabinet as quickly as possible. On November 25 part of the cabinet took off aboard *The Balmoral Castle*. Johannes Van den Broek, minister of finance, energetically refused to wear a life jacket, "explaining . . . that, if he had the misfortune to fall into the sea at this time of the year, he would prefer to drown out of hand." As a sign of her royal wrath, the queen refrained from greeting her ministers on the departure runway.[86]

That advance party quickly installed itself in the liberated portion of the country, in Oisterwijk, before returning to the capital. Accused of conducting the purge too half-heartedly, the government, reshuffled in February 1945, had to be expanded to include men who enjoyed the confidence of the resistance. The Allies worried, however, about the unpopularity of the Gerbrandy cabinet. SHAEF noted in March 1945: "There is a danger that the resistance groups, seeing the grave dangers in accepting office in any government immediately after liberation, may prefer to stay outside and leave the government to the émigré and big business elements and to the Netherlands Military Administration neither of which is popular. Unless the government is prepared to take strong measures against those who have collaborated with the Germans, there may well be disorders."[87] In fact, Gerbrandy resigned on May 5, 1945, giving up his seat to the Socialist Willem Schermerhorn, before elections called in May 1946 turned the page once and for all. The queen for her part made a brief trip to Breda in March 1945, only to return on May 2; she was fêted by her fellow citizens in The Hague and Amsterdam.

All things considered, the political situation seemed to have stabilized, though the internal resistance had sometimes appointed mayors and local authorities. In addition, they did not wish to comply with the instructions of the government in exile, which, via the Dutch Militair Gezag (MG;

Military Authority), set out to impose its law. In Nijmegen, for example, when the collaborationist town councillor was dismissed, the Militair Gezag, the local resistance, and the Allied force each appointed its own mayor. In addition, the resistance set about arresting collaborators or presumed collaborators, arguing that the police had been compromised during the dark years. By the summer of 1945 some 120,000 people—perhaps even 150,000—had been detained and were waiting to learn their fate.[88]

Despite these snags, the Gerbrandy government ultimately imposed its authority. The Allies promoted a "restatification" of the country, to borrow the historian Peter Romijn's expression.[89] On the local level, society compensated for the deficiencies of the state, forming spontaneous committees that, for example, oversaw resupply operations and medical care,[90] as they waited for the public authorities to take over. Furthermore, the internal resistance was gradually neutralized, either incorporated into the Allied armies as auxiliary troops or absorbed by state or para-state structures: municipal councils, the army, the police. Finally, the queen's prestige remained unchanged, particularly since, for many years, the Dutch did not know of her maneuvers to extend the specter of her scepter. The Dutch government was thus able to guarantee law and order, a key imperative in the eyes of the Allied rulers.

Limited Sovereignty

Whereas relative calm reigned to the west, Italy looked like a land on fire. The tensions resulted in the first place from hesitations in London and Washington, which were considering what fate they should reserve for the kingdom. Should Italy be considered an ally, a status befitting its role as a cobelligerent, or as a defeated state, a sanction called for by its past alignment with the Reich? The United States leaned toward the first option, the United Kingdom toward the second. Churchill had a long memory and was still holding a grudge. "British interest was overwhelmingly concerned with the past, specifically with Mussolini's unprecedented violation of the highways and equilibrium of empire."[91] But since the balance of power tilted toward Washington over the course of time, London had to come to terms. By means of the declaration issued from President Roosevelt's residence in Hyde Park on September 26, 1944, and made public the next day, the control exerted over the Italian government was eased. Rome received the right to designate diplomatic representatives, to issue decrees, and to make appointments to civilian jobs without consulting the occupying authorities.[92] The Anglo-Americans thus moved from the principle of exerting control to that of giving counsel, a shift that Macmillan's promotion to acting president of the Allied Commission in December 1944 finalized[93] and that a directive from the Allied Combined Chiefs of Staff ratified on January 30, 1945.[94]

On October 26, 1944, the White House reestablished diplomatic relations with the Quirinal Palace—Downing Street did not follow suit—and Italy was conditionally granted the benefit of humanitarian aid dispensed through the United Nations Relief and Rehabilitation Administration (UNRRA).[95] Furthermore, the Allies in concert increasingly relinquished Italian territories. On July 20, 1944, the provinces of Naples, Benevento, Avellino, Foggia, and Campobasso came under the control of the Bonomi government; on the following August 15 the provinces of Rome, Littoria, and Frosinone were added to that list,[96] accompanied, on October 16, by Aquila, Teramo, Viterbo, Chieti, Pescara, and Rieti.[97]

Despite these advances, Italian sovereignty remained limited. The Americans wished to negotiate a preliminary peace treaty, but the British refused.[98] Above all, they continually intervened in the country's internal affairs. For example, the Socialist Ivanoe Bonomi, named prime minister on June 18, 1944, had consulted Noel Charles, His Majesty's representative to the Italian authorities, on June 9. Charles noted:

He asked me whether I thought Sforza would be a good choice for Foreign Minister. I told him that I thought the appointment would not meet much approval on the part of Allied Governments. I suggested to him that unless he had some other candidate in view there was much to be said for him reserving this appointment for himself. Bonomi asked if the Allies would have any objection to civilians being appointed to [military] Service Ministries. I said we were most anxious that Admiral de Courten should remain Minister of Marine and Bonomi promised in this case he would make no change.[99]

The ambassador also saw to it that Raimondi [sic][100] and Fano, undersecretaries at the Ministry of Communications, who "had proved of great value to us by reason of their technical qualifications," were given a second chance. Having been "omitted from Bonomi's Government," they were "immediately reinstated" at Charles's request.[101] In short, the British had no intention of abdicating their right of inspection, to which Churchill openly laid claim: "Since when have we admitted the right of the Italians to form any Government they please? They are a conquered country administering assigned territory under strict Allied control," he reminded his representative on June 10, 1944.[102] Consequently, after Badoglio's fall, the British general Noel Mason-MacFarlane, inexperienced and too indulgent with the Italian authorities, was replaced by Rear Admiral Ellery Stone as head of the Allied Commission. "He has made various gross mistakes or breaches of duty," Churchill said of MacFarlane. "The major one is in not insisting upon the proceedings being adjourned until, at least, he could communicate with the Ambassador when he saw they involved the fall of Badoglio's Government, about which he has received many instructions."[103]

Maintaining Order

Apart from these political concerns, the Allies were preoccupied with the maintenance of law and order, and not without reason. The country's dismal economic situation had led to a worrisome increase in violence. On October 19, 1944, the carabinieri opened fire on the Palermo labor strike committee, which was demanding wage increases; 30 people were killed and 150 wounded. The conscription imposed in September 1944 also gave rise to anger. Between January 4 and 9, 1945, protests erupted in Ragusa, Sicily: confrontations there resulted in at least 37 dead and 86 wounded.[104]

The overly lenient purge conducted by Pietro Badoglio and Ivanoe Bonomi also prompted the ire of Italians, exasperated to see that major and minor figures in the fallen regime enjoyed an impunity felt to be scandalous. "More than a year after their liberation, many communities in southern Italy were still being run by the same mayors, police chiefs and landowners, who used the same violent and repressive measures to oppress them as they had done during the Fascist years."[105] Because the state apparatus was failing them, many Italians decided to take the law into their own hands. On September 18, 1944, Pietro Caruso, chief of the Roman police, was put on trial. He had ordered the roundups of Jews and had provided the Germans with the 335 prisoners designated for execution in the Fosse Ardeatine in reprisal for the attack on via Rasella. The judge canceled the hearing, arguing that there were too many spectators. But in the audience, the crowd recognized Donato Carretta, director of Regina Coeli prison. He was lynched, dragged to the Tiber, and thrown into the waves.[106] Mario Roatta, former chief of staff of the imperial army, managed to elude his judges by leaving the Eternal City and taking refuge in Francoist Spain. The news of his escape prompted a large demonstration on March 6, 1945. After fiery speeches, thousands of demonstrators rushed to the Quirinal Palace and attempted to enter. A launched grenade killed one Italian and wounded two Allied soldiers and a Roman police officer. The carabinieri responded by opening fire.[107]

The Anglo-Americans feared such protean violence. In particular, the North was still in the hands of the Germans and under the rule of the Republic of Salò; with the coming of liberation, it risked becoming the theater of even greater fury, especially if the Communists seized power.

Revolution?

Some Allied leaders at the highest echelons of the state, and sometimes on the ground as well, feared that the Communists would engage in a coup d'état. Lieutenant-Colonel Hewitt pointed out in January 1945: "In many areas the Communist bands are well organized and have fought well. They are led by fanatical commanders and political commissars and are numerically strong. They therefore constitute a powerful force either against the Germans and Fascists or against the Allies."[108] Even more worrying, it appeared that the Soviets were financing them. For example, the British Liaison Mission was asked to negotiate a check for nine million lire drawn on the Mantrust of New York, the agency of the Bank of Moscow.[109] Finally, the Communist Mauro Scoccimarro's appointment as a minister in occupied Italy in the third Bonomi government was hardly reassuring, since he was overseeing the potentially revolutionary regions, the industrial North especially.

To ward off these dangers, in winter 1945 the Allies oversaw more closely their deliveries of materiel to the partisans, "to reduce the risk of armed insurrection or revolution against the existing Italian Government, or armed resistance against the Allies after the enemy has been ejected from that part of Italy at present occupied by him, while still sustaining resistance by those groups which agencies believe will restrict their fighting to that against the Germans and Italian Republicans and Fascists."[110] In the same vein, they supported the CLNAI, wagering that it would be successful in federating all the underground forces, while ardently praying it would not become "a rival to the Rome Government."[111] They also paid particular attention to the fifteen or so "liberated zones" that sprang up.[112]

In the regions controlled by the partisans, in fact, they founded short-lived republics, which, before the Germans destroyed them, engaged in political and social experiments,[113] while at the same time conducting guerilla actions.

In Friuli, eighty thousand people lived in the Republic of Carnia, an area of about a thousand square miles, between August and October 1944. In August, elections filled the positions on the local council. Professors who could not guarantee "the teaching of democratic lessons" were dismissed; previous taxes were eliminated and replaced by a 2 to 8 percent tax on goods; jury trials were reinstated; and on October 10 capital punishment was abolished.[114]

In Ossola, not far from Ticino, Switzerland, sixty to eighty thousand residents lived a brief interlude of freedom between September 10 and October 10, 1944, until the Fascist troops entered Domodossola. The republic enjoyed the real but skeptical support of the Allies. Jock McCaffery, a representative of SOE in Bern, did not believe in the possibility of an Italian uprising but thought that, if there was a chance, it should be seized. The Republic of Ossola, he added, would cut off the supply lines of the enemy forces, which would hasten their collapse; it would also show whether the Italians would govern through union or civil war. On September 7 Lieutenant George Patterson, a Canadian, arrived in Ossola as an observer and adviser. Although he poured twenty million lire into the republic, he could not impose a unified command because of the political disputes between the Communists and the moderates.[115]

The Partisan Republic of Montefiorino, between Modena and La Spezia, lasted about forty days, from June to early August 1944. It was relatively well received by the peasants, to whom it offered manpower for summer farm work. The republic experimented with a form of direct democracy: the partisans asked heads of households to designate their representatives in the villages, and mass meetings were held in the public squares. A new tax system was adopted, and the prices of essential foodstuffs were put to a vote. Rich farmers were compelled to hand over part of their harvests to the partisans. On July 30 a German attack suspended the experiment, which the Allied envoys judged harshly. Sergeant Richard Isenberg of OSS noted in December 1944: "The division counted as many as 8,000 Partisans, attracted by the easy life, the rich food and the authority they had over the civilian population. The population . . . was often unduly taxed, and suffered much from this domination. [The Communist] Armando, acting as a dictator, governed over the zone by means of his two general commissars 'Ercole' and 'Davide' who robbed and extorted the population without pity."[116]

All in all, the results achieved in the liberated zones must be considered mixed. "Many of the economic measures enacted were fundamentally demagogic and aimed to gain the approval of a generally diffident population," the historian Gustavo Corni argues.[117] Basil Davidson, inclined to praise the courage and sacrifice that motivated the *partigiani*, qualifies that view: "The true epic of those years lay in the courage and determination with which countless men and women followed the hope and vision of a radical democracy. Vaguely perceived, perhaps: sometimes utopian, this too: and yet so real and so worthwhile, in the grim conditions of that time, as to be worth everything you had to give."[118]

In any event, the Italian resistance, far from confining its action to the struggle against the enemy, dreamed of a new political and social order on the local level. It shared that ambition with the Greek Communist resistance, which "organised economic activity, reshaped the judicial and educational system, and introduced social reforms for women,"[119] defining in practice a "laocracy" in the territories subject to its control.

By contrast, that aspiration for a new order differentiated the Italian resistance from the French, though a few maquis did attempt to establish new rules. Two realms were generally privileged. In the first place, the maquis imposed a system for prices and requisitions that was believed to be more equitable. In Limousin, for example, the Communist Guingouin's men set the prices for farm goods and threatened black market traffickers.[120] In Vercors on July 15, 1944, the resistance subprefect of Die also established maximum retail prices.[121] The maquis sought to purge the zones it controlled by relieving compromised authorities of their duties and punishing traitors or presumed traitors. In Limousin as well, Guingouin exerted strong pressure to force out some special delegations appointed by Vichy in the communes. Their efforts were not without effect: on December 16, 1943, M. Lebrun, who had been placed at the head of the small village of Cheissoux, resigned.[122] The Comité de Libération Nationale in Vercors, in theory exercising the prerogatives of civil authority, dismissed the mayor of Saint-Julien-en-Vercors in late June, for having delivered supplies to members of the Milice; and, on July 18, it relieved the chief magistrate of Vassieux of his duties, for having abandoned his town council.[123] The Republic of Vercors, as it was baptized, set in place a military tribunal on June 14, which, after sentencing three members of the Milice to death, was replaced by a simple board of inquiry. A temporary camp lodged about a hundred suspects, primarily prominent individuals. But one should not picture a new version of the 1793 Reign of Terror, blindly unleashing its thunderbolts. "In general," the historian Gilles Vergnon points out, "the 'justice' of the maquis looks rather lenient and intent on respecting the rule of law: in the forty-three days of the 'Republic of Vercors,' there were only five death sentences."[124]

The partisan republics and the masses of armed resistance fighters, regardless of their revolutionary potential, alarmed the Anglo-Americans, who feared a replay in Italy of the Greek scenario. In December 1944 the repression of a demonstration in Athens had set the country ablaze, pitting the royalists against the Communists, inciting the British to intervene militarily, and acting as the prelude to a horrible civil war that did not end until 1949. "Unless we are very careful, we shall get another . . . [Greek] situation in northern Italy," wrote a worried Harold Macmillan.[125] From that standpoint, the liberation of northern Italy was an unknown that posed major risks: Would the liberation committees play along, or would they take things into their own hands?

Cooperation?

On the whole, the local liberation committees turned out to be cooperative. SOE summed things up after liberation: "One of the most remarkable features of the campaign was the cooperation and good sense of the partisans under the guidance of CNL's and Allied Missions in maintaining law and order."[126] At the same time, the resistance had no intention of having its victory stolen away. It therefore sought to put in place its own men, sometimes entering into open or latent conflict with the Allied authorities. In Florence, the committee wanted an old Socialist, Gaetano Pieraccini, to become mayor; the Allies initially refused but ultimately rallied behind his candidacy.[127] In addition, the AMG accepted the partisans' choice for the Livorno region but rejected those for Arezzo, Sienna, and Viareggio.[128] In short, the Allied authorities played it by ear and avoided showdowns. "In practically all instances, for example, the CNL had . . . designated Prefects. These men had taken possession of their offices by the time AMG officers arrived. AMG could remove them if they were considered unsatisfactory. But it may be doubted that it was legally necessary for AMG to 'appoint' them, if it desired to continue to use their services, as they had already been appointed by bodies recognized by Rome as having the right to govern the regions."[129] The Allies acknowledged that, inasmuch as the CLNAI presented itself as the legitimate representative of the Rome government, its appointments rested on a legal foundation. They were all the more accommodating in that these administrators—like their Gaullist counterparts—were up to the task. As the services of the Fifth Army pointed out in April 1945: "The Committees of National Liberation were conducting Provincial and Communal administration with efficiency, and AMG was therefore faced with the entirely novel problem of tactfully taking over the reins from an existing organization, in contrast to its experience further South where no such organization was functioning at the time of Liberation."[130]

The CLNAI, doubting—not without reason—the stability of the Bonomi government, also set out to conduct a vigorous purge. It created courts of the people, which practiced a kind of "frontier justice"—they sometimes convicted innocents, the loved ones of Fascist dignitaries, for example. In addition, an extrajudicial purge was unleashed on April 25, 1945, the date on which the liberation committees had called for insurrection. That order sometimes gave rise to violence. Colonel John Stevens, head of the Allied mission, is said to have declared to Franco Antonicelli, president of the Liberation Committee in Turin: "Listen, president, clear things up in two, three days, but on the third day, I no longer want to see dead on the streets."[131] In the capital of Piedmont alone, that bloody vendetta led to 1,138 deaths. Giuseppe Solari, head of the Fascist Party in Turin, reputed for his fanaticism and cruelty, was sentenced to death by a tribunal of partisans. He was forced to pass through the streets of the city while spectators booed, before he was hanged at the very site where four resistance fighters had been killed on his orders a few days earlier. The strongest moment symbolically was, of course, the execution of Mussolini and his lover on April 28, 1945, and the display of their bodies, hung by their feet, on the very plaza in Milan where the Fascist regime hanged resistance fighters.[132] In all, that purge is said to have caused the death of twelve to twenty thousand Fascists—or presumed Fascists.[133] That may seem a high toll. It can be explained by the tensions caused by twenty years of Fascist rule, intensified by the de facto impunity that Mussolini's henchmen enjoyed.

Finally, the intentions of the Italian Communist Party caused perplexity, because its line seemed so muddled. In fact, Palmiro Togliatti was walking a tightrope: fearing that his ideology would put off the moderate elements, he carefully weighed his revolutionary language and strove to reassure his partners, as a means to ensure union within the Bonomi government. But he also had to compromise with the militants, many of whom displayed a vehement anticlericalism, for example.[134] Cino Moscatelli, political commissar in the Sesia Valley, north of Piedmont, explained to his local federation in August 1944 the dilemma he was facing: "Many times have I had to intervene to remove red trimmings from uniforms, red flags from lorries; I have had to ban little red flags from machine-guns and rifles. . . . And the more I intervene the worse it gets. Many of our officers have asked to join the party. I've banned them from singing [the revolutionary] Bandiera Rossa when they march; they sing and sing yet they always end up with that song."[135]

These deviations remained within limits, however. The first priority of the Communist partisans was to hasten the liberation of their country, especially since their contribution supported the Soviet war effort. In addition, "the party's unitary line, which deferred the revolution sine die, was accepted in the meantime insofar as it felt guaranteed by the country of the Revolution . . . whose force would, come what may, safeguard Italy from relapsing into a new Fascism and from the seduction of reformism."[136] In short, the future demanded that the promises of revolution be renounced, at least temporarily.

Consequently, Italy avoided the apocalyptic scenarios—chaos or Communist putsch—that obsessed the Allied leaders. To be sure, many questions remained hanging. The form of the regime (monarchy or republic) was settled, by referendum, only in June 1946, and the peace treaty was not signed until 1947. Likewise, the purge, imperfect to say the least, allowed big and small fish to prosper for years. To paraphrase Goethe, the Allies and the Italian authorities had preferred injustice to disorder. For many long years, that choice fueled a deep-seated bitterness in the ranks of the resistance, which, in the fury of the battles and the blood of its sacrifices, had hoped that the liberation would open brighter futures, that it would punish the Fascist officials who had imposed their barbarous law during the *ventennio* and who had led Italy into the abyss of a deadly war.

Idyllic Transitions

By contrast, Denmark and Norway, the last bastions of German Europe, experienced an idyllic democratic transition. The accords concluded in May 1944 were implemented and the questions left hanging settled in short order.

In Norway, the situation caused no anxiety. The good relations between the government and the internal resistance were reassuring, and the Foreign Office hoped that the situation would "not resemble that with which we are now faced in Greece."[137] The payment of military expenses was settled without any difficulties on November 4, 1944. London would refrain from asking for reimbursements of the materiel supplied during the war to the Norwegian forces, while Oslo promised in return not to demand compensation for the British troops who would use that infrastructure while participating in the liberation of the country.[138] Yet the occupation continued until May 1945: 350,000 German soldiers were still stationed in Norway. The surrender did not take place until May 8. The political transition went smoothly: on May 13 Prince Olav returned to the capital, accompanied by three members of the cabinet. On the 31st the other ministers landed in Oslo, and, on June 7, King Haakon returned to his country aboard the *Devonshire*—the same ship that had taken him to England five years earlier—to be fêted by a jubilant crowd. Two days later, fifteen thousand men from Milorg proudly paraded past their king, celebrating the union of the internal resistance and the government in exile.

Once again, the army of shadows struggled to make its voice heard. Paal Berg, the leader of the internal resistance, attempted to form a government before the elections, but he encountered the hostility of Parliament, which preferred to entrust the keys of power to Einar Gerhardson, mayor of the capital city and leader of the Social Democratic Party. The machinery of power nevertheless returned to working order, so much so that the military commander, General Andrew Thorne, suspended the transitional phase of the military government on June 7, 1945,[139] handing over full powers to the civil authorities.

A somewhat sour note marred that harmony. The Norwegian general Wilhelm von Tangen Hansteen proposed to equip his forces by helping himself to the German booty. General John Bond, director of liaisons and ammunition at the War Office, refused, "to avoid future dependence on German production."[140] This was a sign that London now intended to include Norway within its zone of influence. Apart from that minor episode, the transition from an oppressive regime to the rule of democracy came off without a hitch, which, noted Lieutenant-Colonel John Henrietto, was a phenomenon unprecedented in the history of the world: "The change-over from a regime, viewed with implacable hatred for five years, to an *ad hoc* government by a resistance group was smooth, controlled, restrained and thoroughly effective."[141] Tore Gjelsvik, a historian and former member of the resistance, adds: "The transfer of power went like a dream: instead of shots and cannon fire, we heard church bells all over the country ringing in the peace."[142]

Denmark, which in spring 1945 was still coping with the presence of 200,000 German soldiers, was characterized by the same state of calm. The Nazi forces gave up on May 5, after capitulating in Lüneburg. The day before, a government headed by the Social Democrat Buhl had been formed. Half its members were resistance fighters, half traditional politicians, and the portfolio for Foreign Affairs went to Christmas Møller. The only dark spot in the picture: on May 7 the Soviets had attacked the island of Bornholm, which the Germans were refusing to give up. The Soviets occupied the island and did not return it until a year later, on April 5, 1946. Apart from that snag, the democratic transition took place in orderly fashion, to the great satisfaction of the Allies. "The political rivalry which developed during the occupation between the resistance leaders of the Freedom Council and the established political parties was submerged in the successful joint effort to establish and operate the present provisional government," concluded OSS.[143] The Danes, moreover, reimbursed cash on the nail some 341,161 pounds, the cost of support for their underground forces. "To be slightly cynical," the historian Knud Jespersen comments, "one could say that the direct cost to Denmark of achieving inclusion in the ranks of the Allies was about 6 million kroner if one just looks at the figures."[144]

The installation of regular powers did not mean that Scandinavia avoided a violent purge. Some women had their hair sheared off, and, as soon as the guns fell silent, the resistance strove to lock up the presumed collaborators. More than twenty thousand Danes were interned in the first week following liberation.[145] In addition, about fifty individuals were condemned to death in Denmark (thirteen death sentences per million residents) and about thirty in Norway (ten per million residents), figures to be compared to those for France (thirty-nine per million residents).[146] The major difference between these two countries and the rest of Western Europe was that their governments were installed concurrently with the cessation of hostilities, eliminating the transitional phase that marked France, the Netherlands, and Belgium.

The political liberation of Western Europe, then, belied the pessimistic scenarios that the Allied leaders had drawn up in the fever of war. The western part of the Old Continent escaped revolutionary convulsions, and democracy was restored. True, the presence of the Anglo-American troops contributed toward averting the Communist regimes that were inflicted on the eastern countries. But that necessary condition was by no means sufficient: the Allied contingents did not prevent Greece from becoming caught up in a horrible civil war, its flames fanned by Churchill's partisan policy. Other factors therefore played a role. In the first place, the Communist parties were not eager to venture into the unknown. Although these societies were seeking renewal, they had no intention of giving up the guarantees of democracy. Finally and perhaps above all, the internal resistance groups in Western Europe had only a low revolutionary potential. While including radical elements, they also had in their ranks both moderate and conservative forces, who were in no case dreaming of a new October Revolution.

In certain respects, the resistance was a disruptive element that sometimes launched an extrajudicial purge and imposed on the local level men who had not been duly elected. Often it refused to lay down its arms. But these shadows hardly loom large when compared to the contributions of the resistance, since in great part it ensured the peaceful and orderly transition of power. By virtue of its prestige, it aided the regular powers to reestablish democracy, limited settlings of accounts, and agreed to step back in favor of the legitimate authorities. On the whole, it demonstrated a keen sense of responsibility and, as a general rule, helped avert the torments of a civil war in countries marked by a grueling occupation. By that measure, the shadow fighters were very often valiant militants of democracy as well.

Epilogue

I n July 1940 Hugh Dalton and Winston Churchill were hoping to "set Europe ablaze." Because of the power of the Reich and its bloody brutality, that dream was condemned from the start to sink in the icy waters of reality. The United Kingdom, soon backed by the United States, had to rethink the terms of subversive warfare, which relied at the time on intelligence, sabotage, and propaganda. Later the Anglo-Americans supported through military actions the operations conducted in Western Europe by the regular troops.

The Debate on Effectiveness

Are we to concede, therefore, that the resistance in general and the Anglo-American secret services in particular succeeded in striking the German war machine in significant ways, before and after the landings of 1943 and 1944? As a general rule, the historians express their skepticism.

As a matter of fact, the army of shadows, even with the backing of SOE and OSS, did not manage to make a significant impact on the production intended for the enemy. For example, the value of Dutch exports to Germany rose from 313 million guilders in 1940 to 525 million guilders in 1943 and remained at a high level during the first half of 1944: 311 million guilders. In the first three years of German occupation, there were rarely "spectacular delays in the production process or cases of industrial sabotage. Instead, the [German services] . . . repeatedly stressed the high quality of the work done by Dutch employees and their 'impressive ability to keep to deadlines.'"[1] The case of France confirms that observation. "Everything indicates that sabotage did not substantially diminish the French industrial potential placed in the service of the German war machine," notes the historian Sébastien Albertelli. He adds: "Even if we assume a disproportionate effect, how are we to imagine that, with fifty-seven sabotage operations leading to serious damage in the Paris region, the production delivered to the Germans could have been greatly slowed?"[2] The historian Alan Milward draws up what is overall an irrefutable balance sheet. The sabotage operations, he says, were, "from a German standpoint, economically insignificant, no more disturbing than the high accident rate caused by longer hours, worse food, a less expert labour force, and depreciating capital equipment." And, he concludes, "For all its heroism the evidence seems to point to the conclusion that resistance was one of the least successful, and in terms of opportunity one of the most costly, of all wartime strategies."[3]

The question of propaganda requires a balanced judgment. The BBC did play a major role in keeping the captive populations informed, reviving their hopes, and inciting them to take action. Although it contributed to delegitimizing the collaborating forces and to encouraging certain forms of civil disobedience—against compulsory labor in the first place—it did not manage to set in motion a process of insurrection or to transform the resistance into a mass movement. The Paris insurrection confirms that observation a contrario. The movement was launched by the Communist resistance, and the British airwaves, as we have seen, refrained from giving the Parisians instructions for action. The actors themselves minimized the impact of propaganda, whether white or black. Richard Crossman, head of the German section of PWE and future Labour leader, confided in retrospect: "Although we found the left-hand activities enormous fun, although a vast amount of talent went into them, although I am sure they entertained the Gestapo, I have grave doubts whether black propaganda had an effect in any way commensurate with that of straightforward propaganda from the enemy to the enemy."[4] And Ellic Howe, in charge of black propaganda, remarks: "In any case the Germans were ultimately defeated by the Allied and Russian armed forces and not by propaganda."[5]

That balance sheet, however, must not obscure the successes of the internal resistance. The underground forces made an invaluable contribution in the area of intelligence. They played a not insignificant role in the liberation of Western Europe. They often delivered information useful to the Anglo-American troops, helped to locate the enemy forces, disrupted their movements, and, during the retreat, played a role in protecting vital installations from the Germans' avenging fury. In more isolated cases, the resistance assisted Allied airpower through the repatriation of crews downed in Europe—3,500 pilots in all were exfiltrated from France, Belgium, and the Netherlands.[6] On October 20, 1944, OSS listed 3,870 crews rescued from the Mediterranean, which entailed the repatriation of 23 percent of the 11,695 pilots lost on their missions.[7] That success, the American service stated, was to be credited to the resistance. Once "close contact had been developed between the Air Forces and OSS the rescue of downed air men had gone up from 10% to 17% in Italy, and five out of every nine attributed their escape directly to OSS and its Partisan contacts."[8]

That said, the resistance was able to intervene only marginally in Western Europe. From the moment modern warfare rested on firepower and mobility, the partisans, for lack of transportation, armored vehicles, artillery, and training, were condemned to play supporting roles. "Norwegian Resistance did not 'win the war.' The final victory over the Axis came through the massive military effort of the Allied great power—an effort in which Norway, including its military Resistance, could only play a minor part."[9] That observation applies to all the countries of Western Europe, including Italy and France.

But such dry statistics cannot mask the essential thing. Actors and historians often evaluate the effectiveness of the resistance on the basis of moral criteria, asking what the people subject to the *lex germanica* ought to have done. The question can be understood differently: we may ask what the societies in question *could* do, as the sociologist Claire de Galembert points out.[10] The margin for maneuvering available to individuals was narrow: they faced a powerful occupying force that did not recoil from any atrocity in imposing its law. In that regard, the homegrown resistance groups and the Anglo-American services played a preeminent role, by opening avenues for action to men and women who, in reality, were in no way predestined to become involved. In response to the appeals of the BBC, Allied special services, and underground organizations, citizens could show their anger by drawing Vs in chalk, without taking unreasonable risks; some developed "insaisissable" sabotage; others, finally, became more radically engaged by blowing up trains or joining the maquis. The resistance, in other words, allowed a minority to become actors in their own history, abandoning the sullen shores of *attentisme* or resignation. Underground newspapers, demonstrations, and attacks only marginally modified the course of the conflict, which was won in the snows of Stalingrad or the wet pastures of the Norman bocage; but they showed to the eyes of the world that the societies under the jackboot refused to bow down and meekly accept servitude. The resistance fighters succeeded in "extracting hope and human value from the misery of war. They cleared a space for civic decency and even progress in all the brutish squalor of those years. They held that space and they used it."[11] In that respect, "the historical role of the resistance movement became psychological, moral and political rather than military."[12] But that role must in no case be underestimated, especially since these men and women risked their lives to ensure the triumph of democratic ideals over the grim realities promised by the brownshirt order.

With or without the resistance, Western Europe would have been liberated by the Anglo-American forces. But it would not have been liberated in the same terms—a significant nuance. The underground fighters facilitated the advance of the Allied troops and limited the human cost of a horrible conflict. They also prevented a perilous power vacuum from emerging, by taking up the baton from the German authorities and the collaborating minorities that supported them, and passing it on to the new governments. That transition was at times accompanied by a few excesses, including, throughout Europe, the sad spectacle of women whose hair had been shorn. On the whole, however, the devolution of power occurred without major incident, and the underground forces demonstrated a keen sense of responsibility. In a notable paradox, "in Denmark, the greatest achievement of the organization that was formed in order to set Europe ablaze was in the role of a fire-fighter."[13] The resistance became a guarantor of law and order, a role that Hugh Dalton and Winston Churchill had certainly not anticipated in the dark hours of 1940. That balance sheet is even more striking when it is linked—at the risk of anachronism—to the situation that prevailed, and which still prevails, in Iraq and Afghanistan after Western intervention. The resistance contributed to guaranteeing order and freedom in Western Europe, whereas chaos now reigns in those two countries—not to mention Libya.

In that overall scheme, the Anglo-American services—SOE, OSS, PWE, and OWI—played a major role. "Without the organization, communications, material, training and leadership provided by SOE (with the help of OSS from November 1943), resistance [in Scandinavia] would have been of no military value."[14] That rule is valid for the six countries considered in this book. Deprived of the means made available to them by London and then Washington, the underground fighters could not have fought or communicated. In addition, the Allies were able to incorporate them into an overall strategy, which kept their efforts from becoming dispersed and also reinforced their belief that the risks were worth taking, since they were contributing to the victory.

Even so, could London and Washington have been less stingy? Could they have been stronger in their support of the European resistance? From Oslo to Milan and from Brussels to Bordeaux, all resistance fighters complained of the meager resources available to them, suspecting their mentors of dark ulterior motives of a political nature. A few Allied leaders echoed their complaints. In June 1944 Lord Selborne, minister of economic warfare, "privately" lamented to Winston Churchill that SHAEF "has not sufficiently planned what can be done to help the resistance movement, which is bigger than anything *they* anticipated."[15] In addition, internecine struggles prevented the Allied services from reaching their full potential. In Scandinavia, propaganda and psychological warfare were "seriously impaired, especially in the early years of the war, by organization and management that could hardly have been worse."[16] The underground fight, finally, suffered from the ideological blind spots of the top leaders. Franklin Roosevelt's narrow-minded anti-Gaullism compromised the effectiveness of the French resistance, and Winston Churchill's conservatism handicapped its Italian counterpart, which was ordered to submit to a discredited king and a marshal with heavy liabilities. "It is difficult to understand how an intelligent statesman could hope to build a political policy in the middle of the twentieth century based on the King and those around him," writes Norman Kogan.[17]

These criticisms are assuredly well founded, especially since the Allies' decisions often corresponded to strategic choices—the precedence given to bombing over support of the resistance, for example. But they must not overshadow the considerable obstacles that stood in the way of the Allies offering the underground forces the material support they requested. Parachuting in weapons and sending instructors and organizers were tricky matters, and the shadow fighters underestimated the complexity of these tasks, both during and after the war. Despite a few rare precedents, the Allied leaders had no experience with subversive warfare. The failures about which so many resistance fighters complained stemmed in part from that lack of experience, which SOE or OSS leaders made up for in the course of a long and sometimes painful learning process. The reverse is equally true. The partisans had to learn on the job the demands of secret warfare, whose basic rules they mastered only over time. In other words, it was pointless to hope that, in 1940, the Allies and the resistance could have known how to forge a perfect military tool of which they would have complete mastery from the start, especially since the governments in exile were temporizing. Even while supporting the United Kingdom and the United States in order to ensure victory, they did not always make the Allied powers' job easier. Defending their sovereignty tooth and nail, anxious to treat with consideration the civilian populations they claimed to protect, they were sometimes a constraint more than a stimulus to underground action.

Typology?

Should the resistance in Western Europe be considered a homogeneous whole, or did the differences outweigh the resemblances? At the risk of simplification, I would have to say that the underground forces as a whole confronted identical problems. All of them set out to participate militarily in the liberation of their country and strove to pursue their actions in conjunction with the Allied grand strategy; all attempted to mobilize their fellow citizens in the struggle and maintained complicated relations with the political parties and legal authorities who claimed to be in charge of them; all undertook a painful unification process. Along the same lines, the governments in exile faced the same storms, seeking to preserve their independence while bowing to the demands of the common fight, and to spare their population while asking it to agree to the necessary sacrifices.

Yet the underground forces, in diverse situations governed by a variety of factors, solved these equations with several unknowns. The presence in London of legal and legitimate authorities indisputably favored their struggle, which, conversely, was hampered by the maintenance in Denmark, France, and Italy of governments under the jackboot. Furthermore, societies that were united during the prewar period—Denmark and

Norway, for example—faced the squall resolutely, while following what were certainly different time frames, as these two countries illustrate. The divided nations—France, Belgium, and, to a lesser degree, the Netherlands— had a harder time choosing the path of dissidence.

In addition, the role played by individuals, contingencies, and context proved to have a decisive weight. Charles de Gaulle's political genius gave him a presence on the national scene and in the international arena, while Hubert Pierlot's lack of charisma weakened his government's position. Monarchs were sometimes a unifying factor—as the examples of Haakon VII, Christian X, and Wilhelmina show—but they could just as easily be factors of division, as attested by the cases of Léopold III and Victor Emmanuel III.

On a completely different level, the shadow cast by the prewar period exerted a determining influence. The social progress achieved in Scandinavia before the great storm hardly impelled the shadow fighters to demand a New Deal, which had been accomplished in large part by the Danish and Norwegian Social Democrats. By contrast, it was still a dream for their French, Belgian, and Italian comrades. Other factors also played a role. Geographical location sometimes favored the resistance, as in Norway, which was well served by the porousness of its border with Sweden; conversely, the lowlands of Belgium and the Netherlands precluded the creation of maquis. Last but not least, the location of the theaters of operations had varying impacts. The landing in Normandy fanned the flame of the French and then the Belgian resistance, while the distance from the front discouraged the Scandinavian fighters.

In Norway, Denmark, and the Netherlands, the resistance was more military than political, while in France, Belgium, and Italy, ideological considerations colored the battle. The unification of the underground forces was well served by the low intensity of ideological differences (Norway) and the ingenuity of integrative mechanisms, designed or agreed to by the legal or legitimate authorities (the Danish Council of Freedom, the CLNAI in Italy, the French CNR). By contrast, it was hindered by political conflicts (Belgium) or the weakness of the resistance (the Netherlands). Dependence on London or Washington was just as variable. The absence of representatives in London (Denmark) or the good relations between the Allies and the governments in exile (Norway, the Netherlands) favored the subordination of the partisans to the Allied services; conversely, disputes between the Allies and the official governments (France and Italy) opened a space of autonomy that favored the irredentism of national resistance movements, both toward the authorities that claimed to be in control and toward SOE or OSS.

Although it is impossible to construct a comprehensive typology of the resistance in these six European countries, the overall results lead us to revise downward the level of exceptionalism in which each nation likes to drape itself. The unification of the French resistance, due largely to Jean Moulin, may have served as a model; but it cannot be taken for an exception, if we compare the French to the Danes or Italians. Charles de Gaulle certainly encountered the hostility of the Anglo-Americans; but Hubert Pierlot, Pietro Badoglio, and Ivanoe Bonomi had to fight just as hard to preserve the independence of their countries. The BCRA complained about the underhanded procedures of SOE; but Sûreté de l'État was just as critical of Gubbins's service. In short, every country and every national resistance confronted similar problems, which ultimately blunts the particularity of each one, especially since the policy conducted by the Anglo-Americans contributed toward homogenizing national resistance in the various countries.

Even while taking due note of local specificities, the authorities in London and Washington followed common procedures vis-à-vis their "minor allies." They addressed identical instructions to each national resistance movement, urging them all to scrawl Vs, to work sluggishly, and to conduct "insaisissable" sabotage, rather than undertaking guerilla operations or insurrections, the risks of which they were well aware. Along the same lines, models—or antimodels—circulated and aided the Anglo-Americans to hone their doctrine. The disastrous Darlan deal, the perfect foil, led the British and the Americans to avoid repeating that regrettable precedent, which ultimately impelled them to drop Badoglio and Victor Emmanuel III. In a more positive vein, the French BBC broadcasts served as an example from which their counterparts in other countries could take inspiration. The Man of June 18 may have irritated Churchill and Roosevelt, but the two men sought in vain an Italian de Gaulle. By that measure, the resistance in Western Europe, seen from London or Washington, was truly a European resistance.

Legacy

In the end, the experiences of World War II marked with their seal the second half of the twentieth century, though their effects were uneven.

Subversive warfare sputtered before 1940, but it met with remarkable fortunes from 1945 on. Propaganda, widely used during World War I, expanded considerably afterward, first under the totalitarian regimes, then during the dark years, and finally over the course of the Cold War. The secret services, having grown from infancy to maturity, mounted multiple attacks and undertook many crooked schemes as soon as the weapons fell silent. But neither OSS nor SOE was there to promote them. Despite Donovan's entreaties, OSS was abolished in December 1945, yielding to the combined opposition of the army and the FBI, which had always looked on that rival with a baleful eye. SOE too disappeared in February 1946, the victim of the vendetta of IS, which assumed the bulk of its activities. Nevertheless, brainwashing campaigns, sabotage, secret maneuvers, and guerrilla warfare punctuated the decades following the collapse of the Reich. From that standpoint, the Bay of Pigs invasion, the "lovely little war" fought by the Viet Minh in Indochina, and the assaults exchanged between the pro-independence Algerian forces and the activists in the Organisation de l'Armée Secrète (OAS; Secret Army Organization)—the list is far from exhaustive—confirm that many actors took to heart the lessons of World War II.

International relations changed just as radically in light of the experience of the dark years. Several countries that had firmly embraced a neutralist line until that time repudiated it, understanding that their naïveté had served Hitler's designs. In 1941 Norway pleaded for the installation of Anglo-American bases on its soil[18] and for a "defensive plan for the North Atlantic"—with the British, the Norwegians, and, if possible, the Americans as partners—to protect Norway from the appetites of the Soviet Bear.[19] Likewise, the Belgians agreed that henceforth "Belgium had to collaborate with its neighbours under the leadership of Britain."[20] That shift in orientation occurred on two levels: Denmark, Norway, Belgium, and the Netherlands repudiated their neutrality, and they also placed themselves under the protection of Great Britain and the United States.

Furthermore, the contact established among exiles, as well as the relations developed through daily contact between the British authorities and the governments in exile, favored the emergence of a European, if not a universalist, consciousness. True, the creation of the United Nations Organization and the formation of the Common Market were based on principles other than simply the brotherhood of the war years. Nonetheless, the fact that Paul-Henri Spaak, André Philip, and even Winston Churchill became ardent promoters of the "European idea" suggests that their London years influenced their choices and their aspiration for a better world. It is also not insignificant that, for example, Trygve Lie, the first secretary general of the United Nations, a former Norwegian minister of foreign affairs, had spent the war in the English capital, which at the very least broadened his horizons.

Ingratitude

I began this book, as the reader may recall, by pointing out that the assistance provided by the British was forgotten both by the actors and by historians. This observation, valid for all six countries under study, was anticipated by the leaders of subversive warfare in the days just after liberation. The British Embassy in Paris, for example, asked that a publication mention London's support of the French underground forces, "as memories were short and the French would very soon forget what had been done for them and might be more inclined to remember things that had not been done."[21] The OSS envoy to Norway lamented as well that "here, as elsewhere in Europe, there is a very strong tendency to exaggerate the importance of their own efforts at the expense of their great Allies. . . . We are endeavouring to combat this by presenting the story of the Allied war effort as strongly as possible, and this will no doubt help to set people thinking about the war as a whole and not as a special Norwegian affair."[22] These efforts met with ingratitude from the nations and clashed with their desire to reconstruct themselves by portraying the resistance as a homegrown process. It was therefore not surprising that "Italians preferred to believe that their resistance was spontaneous and owed little or nothing to allied support . . . given the urgent need—after more than twenty years of Fascist dictatorship, foreign occupation and a devastating war waged on its soil—to see the birth of a new, democratic and self-made Italy."[23] Is it necessary to point this out? Belgium, the Netherlands, Denmark, and France subscribed to that agreed-upon, if not exactly accurate, view. They sometimes enjoyed unexpected support. For instance, for four decades the British Foreign Office blocked the French translation of Michael R. D. Foot's *SOE in France*, fearing it would attract Charles de Gaulle's wrath, at a time—now very remote—when the United Kingdom was begging to be let into the Common Market.[24]

That tendency to forget the aid provided by the United Kingdom and the United States, though understandable given the context, is troubling nonetheless. It prevents us from truly grasping the principles that governed underground action in Western Europe and, by that measure, makes the army of shadows unintelligible. Contrary to the prevailing view, the Western resistance would have been powerless without Anglo-American aid; but the Allied secret services would have been blind without the cooperation of national resistance movements. To destroy Fascist Italy and Nazi Germany, unity was imperative. It was certainly a battle, but it was also a real force.

Acknowledgments

Having come to the end of this project, I should like to thank all the relatives, friends, colleagues, and institutions that made it possible.

In the first place, I am grateful to the Institut Universitaire de France, which, in accepting me as a member, allowed this book to come into existence: first, by discharging me of a large share of my obligations; second, by granting me a comfortable research budget; and third, by giving me total freedom.

The principal archive centers also greatly aided my research. In addition to the National Archives and Records Administration (NARA) in College Park, Maryland, I would especially like to acknowledge the assistance provided by the National Archives in Kew—a paradise for the historian—and by Jeff Walden of the BBC Written Archives' Center at Caversham, who, with a great deal of kindness, guided my path in the arcana of the Beeb. The librarians of the Bibliothèque Nationale de France, their colleagues at the Institut d'Histoire du Temps Présent—Valérie Hugonnard and Nicolas Schmidt—and Nathalie Barnault of the École Normale Supérieure de Cachan greatly facilitated the bibliographical work, for which I express my profound gratitude.

Several good angels pored over the manuscript, agreeing to proofread it and devoting their precious time to it. I hope I have made the best use of their always-pertinent remarks. The book owes a real debt to their sharp eyes, always tempered by their friendship and kindness. My thanks, therefore, to Sébastien Albertelli, Raphaëlle Branche (Université de Rouen), Emmanuel Debruyne (Université de Louvain-la-Neuve), Alain Geismar, Gabriella Gribaudi (Università degli Studi di Napoli Federico II), Stéphane Hardin, Nicola Labanca (Università degli Studi di Siena), Pieter Lagrou (Université Libre de Bruxelles), Peter Romijn (University of Amsterdam), Raphaël Spina (Institut d'Études Politiques d'Aix-en-Provence), Fabrice Virgili (Centre National de la Recherche Scientifique–Sorbonne, Identités, Relations Internationales, et Civilisations de l'Europe), and Niels Wium Olesen (Aarhus Universitet). In addition, Raphaële Balu referred me to files that, without her assistance, I would have overlooked.

All my gratitude as well to Éditions Perrin and their editors, Benoît Yvert first and then Nicolas Gras-Payen, whose suggestions greatly contributed to improving this book.

I must not forget, for this U.S. edition that I am honored to see published, the confidence of Jennifer Crewe, director of Columbia University Press, and the decisive role played by Philip Nord and Robert Paxton. My thanks as well to Jane Marie Todd, for her talents as a translator.

May they all find here the expression of my deep gratitude.

Notes

Foreword

1. *Eisenhower's Own Story of the War: The Complete Report of the Supreme Commander, General Dwight D. Eisenhower, on the War in Europe from the Day of Invasion to the Day of Victory* (New York: ARCO, 1946), 8.
2. John Steinbeck, *Nuits noires* (Paris: Minuit, 1944).
3. John A. Armstrong, *Soviet Partisans in World War II* (Madison: University of Wisconsin Press, 1964), 35, 389–90.
4. Andrew Knapp, with Claudia Baldoli, *Forgotten Blitzes: France and Italy Under Allied Air Attack, 1940–1945* (London: Continuum, 2012); Stephen Alan Bourque, *Beyond the Beach: The Allied War Against France* (Annapolis, Md.: Naval Institute Press, 2018).

Prelude

1. Charles de Gaulle, speech of August 25, 1944, quoted in Michael Neiberg, *The Blood of Free Men: The Liberation of Paris 1944* (New York: Basic Books, 2012), 237.
2. Pieter Lagrou, *The Legacy of Nazi Occupation: Patriotic Memory and National Recovery in Western Europe, 1945–1965* (Cambridge: Cambridge University Press, 2000), 26.
3. Knud J. V. Jespersen, *No Small Achievement: Special Operations Executive and the Danish Resistance, 1940–1945* (Odense: University Press of Southern Denmark, 2002), 15.
4. For the exception, see Henri Bernard, *Histoire de la résistance européenne. La "quatrième force" de la guerre 39–45* (Brussels: Marabout, 1968).

5. David Stafford, *Britain and European Resistance, 1940–1945: A Survey of the Special Operations Executive* (London: Macmillan, 1980), 63.

1. Reinventing a Coalition

1. Jean Stengers, *Léopold III et le gouvernement. Les deux politiques belges de 1940*, 2nd ed. (Brussels: Racine, 2002), 48.

2. David Reynolds, *From World War to Cold War: Churchill, Roosevelt, and the International History of the 1940s* (Oxford: Oxford University Press, 2006), 26.

3. Llewellyn Woodward, *British Foreign Policy in the Second World War*, vol. 1 (London: Her Majesty's Stationery Office, 1970), 326.

4. Eberhard Jäckel, *La France dans l'Europe de Hitler* (Paris: Fayard, 1986; German ed. 1966), 57.

5. Yves Durand, *Le Nouvel Ordre européen nazi. 1938–1945* (Brussels: Complexe, 1990), 15ff, 29.

6. Tore Gjelsvik, *Norwegian Resistance, 1940–1945* (Montreal: McGill/Queen's University Press, 1979; Norwegian ed. 1977), 1ff.

7. Norwegian Legation in Stockholm to the Norwegian Legation to London, June 29, 1940, quoted in *British Documents on Foreign Affairs: Reports and Papers from the Foreign Office Confidential Print, from 1940 Through 1945*, vol. 9: *Scandinavia, January 1940– December 1941*, ed. Patrick Salmon (Frederick, Md.: University Publications of America, 1998), 323.

8. Olav Riste and Berit Nökleby, *Norway 1940–1945: The Resistance Movement* (Oslo: Johan Grundt Tanum Forlag, 1970), 12.

9. Speech by Haakon VII, August 26, 1940, quoted in Salmon, *British Documents on Foreign Affairs*, 9:330.

10. Gjelsvik, *Norwegian Resistance*, 9.

11. Military Commander in Norway, September 28, 1940, in secret German documents seized during the raid on the Lofoten Islands on March 4, 1941, The National Archives, Kew (hereafter cited as TNA) FO 371/29 416.

12. Woodward, *British Foreign Policy*, 1:131.

13. Gjelsvik, *Norwegian Resistance*, 13.

14. Louis de Jong, *The Netherlands and Nazi Germany* (Cambridge, Mass.: Harvard University Press, 1990), 54ff, 61, 67–68, 65–66.

15. Gerhard Hirschfeld, *Nazi Rule and Dutch Collaboration: The Netherlands Under German Occupation, 1940–1945* (Oxford: Berg, 1988; German ed. 1984), 57ff, 59–60, 66–86.

16. De Jong, *The Netherlands*, 59.

17. Michael R. D. Foot, *SOE in the Low Countries* (London: St. Ermin's, 2001), 78.

18. Neville Bland to Anthony Eden, summary of events for the year 1940, June 18, 1941, quoted in Salmon, *British Documents on Foreign Affairs*, 9:546.

19. Stengers, *Léopold III*, 37, 33.

20. Woodward, *British Foreign Policy*, 1:185.

21. Stengers, *Léopold III*, 34, 16.

22. Thierry Grosbois, *Pierlot. 1930–1950* (Brussels: Racine, 2007), 136–37.

23. Stengers, *Léopold III*, 67.
24. Quoted in Stengers, *Léopold III*, 68.
25. Quoted in Stengers, *Léopold III*, 75.
26. Quoted in Stengers, *Léopold III*, 76.
27. Letter from the Belgian minister of foreign affairs to the French minister of foreign affairs, June 24, 1940, quoted in Stengers, *Léopold III*, 77–78.
28. Paul-Henri Spaak, *The Continuing Battle: Memoirs of a European, 1936–1966* (London: Weidenfeld and Nicolson, 1971; French ed. 1969), 50.
29. Quoted in Stengers, *Léopold III*, 89.
30. Quoted in Stengers, *Léopold III*, 82.
31. Quoted in Marcel-Henri Jaspar, *Souvenirs sans retouche* (Paris: Fayard, 1968), 430.
32. Stengers, *Léopold III*, 86.
33. Winston Churchill to Alexander Cadogan, June 18, 1940, TNA PREM 3 69/A.
34. Quoted in Stengers, *Léopold III*, 117.
35. Quoted in Stengers, *Léopold III*, 117.
36. Spaak, *The Continuing Battle*, 63, 64.
37. Grosbois, *Pierlot*, 158.
38. Halifax, note to prime minister, November 30, TNA PREM 3/69-A.
39. Charles de Gaulle, *The Complete War Memoirs*, 3 vols., trans. J. Griffin and R. Howard, vol. 1: *The Call to Honour* (New York: Simon and Schuster, 1967; 1st French ed. 1954), 80.
40. Woodward, *British Foreign Policy*, 1:321–22.
41. De Gaulle, *The Call to Honour*, 71.
42. Meeting between Charles Corbin and Lord Halifax, quoted in Woodward, *British Foreign Policy*, 1:326.
43. Quoted in Woodward, *British Foreign Policy*, 330.
44. Jean-Louis Crémieux-Brilhac, *La France libre. De l'appel du 18 Juin à la Libération* (Paris: Gallimard, 1996), 66–71.
45. Durand, *Le Nouvel Ordre*, 85–86.
46. Jeremy Bennett, *British Broadcasting and the Danish Resistance Movement, 1940–1945: A Study of the Wartime Broadcasts of the BBC Danish Service* (Cambridge: Cambridge University Press, 1966), 10.
47. Quoted in Woodward, *British Foreign Policy*, 1:181.

2. Set Europe Ablaze!

1. Hugh Dalton to Lord Halifax, July 2, 1940, quoted in Michael R. D. Foot, *An Outline History of the Special Operations Executive, 1940–1946* (London: Bodley Head, 2014 [1984]), 15.
2. Sébastien Albertelli, *Histoire du sabotage. De la CGT à la Résistance* (Paris: Perrin, 2016), 197.
3. David Stafford, *Britain and European Resistance, 1940–1945: A Survey of the Special Operations Executive* (London: Macmillan, 1980), 12, 11.

4. Stafford, *Britain and European Resistance*, 22.

5. Stafford, *Britain and European Resistance*, 16, 17.

6. Peter Wilkinson and Joan Astley Bright, *Gubbins and SOE* (London: Barnsley, Pen and Sword, 2010 [1993]), 26.

7. Foot, *An Outline History*, 7.

8. Wilkinson and Astley Bright, *Gubbins*, 36.

9. Nigel West, *Secret War: The Story of SOE Britain's Wartime Sabotage Organisation* (London: Hodder and Stoughton, 1992), 16.

10. David Stafford, "Churchill and SOE," in *Special Operations Executive: A New Instrument of War*, ed. Mark Seaman (London: Routledge, 2006), 48.

11. Foot, *An Outline History*, 17, 16.

12. Foot, *An Outline History*, 3.

13. Foot, *An Outline History*, 6ff.

14. Alan J. P. Taylor, *English History, 1914–1945* (Oxford: Oxford University Press, 1975 [1965]), 219ff, 225–26.

15. Foot, *An Outline History*, 15.

16. Stafford, *Britain and European Resistance*, 25.

17. Foot, *An Outline History*, 16.

18. Mark Seaman, "A New Instrument of War: The Origins of the Special OE," in *Special Operations Executive: A New Instrument of War*, ed. Mark Seaman (London: Routledge, 2006), 16.

19. Stafford, *Britain and European Resistance*, 29, 24, 25.

20. Hugh Dalton to Clement Attlee, July 6, 1940, quoted in Knud J. V. Jespersen, *No Small Achievement: Special Operations Executive and the Danish Resistance, 1940–1945* (Odense: University Press of Southern Denmark, 2002), 29.

21. Michael Balfour, *Propaganda in War, 1939–1945: Organisations, Policies and Publics in Britain and Germany* (London: Routledge and Kegan Paul, 1979), 91.

22. Gladwyn Jebb, *The Memoirs of Lord Gladwyn* (London: Weidenfeld and Nicolson, 1972), 101, 104.

23. Robert Hamilton Bruce Lockhart, *Comes the Reckoning* (London: Putnam, 1947), 136.

24. F. T. Davies, February 19, 1941, TNA HS 8/272.

25. Bickham Sweet-Escott, *Baker Street Irregulars* (London: Methuen, 1965), 41.

26. Sweet-Escott, *Baker Street Irregulars*, 48.

27. David Garnett, *The Secret History of PWE, 1939–1945* (London: St. Ermin's, 2002), xiii.

28. Symposium on Revolution in Europe, October 19, 1940, TNA HS8/268.

29. Hugh Dalton, "Propaganda Policy," December 6, 1941, TNA FO 898/12.

30. Hugh Dalton to the prime minister, July 16, 1941, TNA, FO 898/9.

31. TNA, FO 898/9.

32. D. E. Ritchie, "Broadcasting as a New Weapon of War," May 4, 1941, TNA FO 371/26 583.

33. Jeremy Bennett, *British Broadcasting and the Danish Resistance Movement, 1940–1945: A Study of the Wartime Broadcasts of the BBC Danish Service* (Cambridge: Cambridge University Press, 1966), 4.

34. Aurélie Luneau, *Radio-Londres. Les voix de la liberté* (Paris: Perrin, 2005), 17–18.

35. Charles Cruickshank, *The Fourth Arm: Psychological Warfare, 1938–1945* (London: David-Poynter, 1977), 48.

36. Gladwyn Jebb, "Subversion," October 5, 1940, TNA HS8/251.

37. M, "The Prospects of Subversion," April 21, 1941, TNA HS 8/272.

38. Comments by AD/Z [Colonel F. T. Davies] on paper by M, June 5, 1941, TNA HS 8/272.

39. Olim X, program for SO 2, June 9, 1941, TNA HS 8/272.

40. PWE, unsigned note, "The Importance of Leaflet Dissemination," April 24, 1942, FO 898/458.

41. PWE, "Britain Serves Europe: II. The Written Word," March 31, 1943, FO 898/458.

42. Rex Leeper, "Black Propaganda," December 17, 1942, TNA FO 898/61.

43. Sefton Delmer, *Black Boomerang* (New York: Viking, 1962), 85.

44. Cruickshank, *The Fourth Arm*, 108.

45. Balfour, *Propaganda in War*, 98.

46. Ritchie, "Broadcasting as a New Weapon of War."

47. PWE, "Monthly Report on Propaganda for December 1941," TNA FO 898/50.

48. PWE, Propaganda to Denmark, March 15, 1941, TNA FO 898/240.

49. From T.G.M. Harman to Colonel Chambers, notes, Holland and Belgium, June 17, 1941, TNA FO 898/71.

50. PID, French Intelligence Section, "Analysis of BBC Propaganda to France," May 21–June 9, 1941, TNA FO 371/ 28 431.

51. X, "Long Term Plan of Propaganda to Belgium," September 25, 1941, TNA FO 898/231.

52. PID, French Intelligence Section, "Analysis of BBC Propaganda to France," May 21–June 9, 1941, TNA FO 371/ 28 431.

53. Ritchie, "Broadcasting as a New Weapon of War."

54. PWE, "Progress Report for the Week Ending 16th May 1941," TNA FO 898/50.

55. D. E. Ritchie, "The V Committee," May 16, 1941, TNA FO 371/26 583.

56. PWE, "Progress Report for the Week Ending 18th July 1941," TNA FO 898/50.

57. Bennett, *British Broadcasting*, 40.

58. Nathaniel Hong, *Sparks of Resistance: The Illegal Press in German-Occupied Denmark: April 1940–August 1943* (Odense: Odense University Press, 1996), 99.

59. Weekly Bulletin of the BBC broadcast to Europe, Belgium, July 31, 1941, BBC Written Archives' Center, Caversham (hereafter cited as BBC WAC) E 2/57.

60. Luneau, *Radio-Londres*, 103.

61. Captain Ivor Thomas, "Radio Italia: The First Year's Work," November 17, 1941, TNA FO 898/60.

62. Colonel Stevens, "Black Activities," May 18, 1942, TNA FO 898/60.

63. France, RU F4, "Report no. 1," August 25–October 11, 1941, TNA FO 898/60.

64. X, "Proposal of a Belgian RU, Meeting Held on 6th May 1941," TNA FO 898/51.

65. Radio Heraus, August 15, 1941, TNA FO 898/57.

66. Michael R. D. Foot, *SOE in the Low Countries* (London: St. Ermin's, 2001), 101.

67. The Flitspuit, September 11, 1941, TNA FO 898/57.

68. PWE, "Rumours," February 7, 1942, TNA FO 898/69.

69. From Colonel W. Sinclair to R. Murray, January 29, 1941, TNA FO 898/70.

70. From Colonel Sinclair to R. Murray, January 16, 1941, TNA FO 898/70.

71. Olim X, SO2 programme, June 9, 1941, TNA HS 8/272.

72. SOE, September 16, 1941, TNA HS8/273.

73. Foot, *SOE in the Low Countries*, 103–6.

74. CD, letter of October 1, 1941, to SO, TNA HS7/58.

75. "An Outline of SOE in Italy (1941–1945), September to October 1945," TNA HS 7/58.

76. Jørgen Hæstrup, *Le mouvement de la résistance danoise* (Copenhagen: Direction Générale de Presse et d'Information du Ministère Danois des Affaires Étrangères, 1970), 23.

77. Jørgen Hæstrup, *Secret Alliance: A Study of the Danish Resistance Movement, 1940–45,* vol. 1 (Odense: Odense University Press, 1976), 47.

78. Jespersen, *No Small Achievement*, 85.

79. Hæstrup, *Secret Alliance*, 1:87–88.

80. Frank Nelson to Gladwyn Jebb, n.d. (September 1940?), TNA HS 8/2 71.

81. Foot, *SOE in the Low Countries*, 246.

82. T section history (Lieutenant Colonel Hardy Amies?), "Report," June 14, 1945, TNA HS 7/100.

83. Foot, *SOE in the Low Countries*, 249.

84. T section history (Lieutenant Colonel Hardy Amies?), "Report," June 14, 1945.

85. Étienne Verhoeyen, *La Belgique occupée. De l'an 40 à la Libération* (Louvain-la-Neuve: De Boeck, 1994), 447.

86. Foot, *SOE in France*, 153–54, 157–59.

87. Foot, *SOE in France*, 163–65, 195, 197.

88. Stafford, *Britain and European Resistance*, 70.

89. Major R. A. Bourne-Patterson, "British Circuits in France. 1941–1944," June 30, 1946, TNA H7/122.

90. Charles Cruickshank, *SOE in Scandinavia* (Oxford: Oxford University Press, 1986), 92–93, 277.

91. SOE Norwegian section, "History," n.d., TNA HS 7/174.

92. Christopher Mann, *British Policy and Strategy Towards Norway, 1941–1945* (London: Palgrave Macmillan, 2012), 44.

93. Mann, *British Policy*, 45–46, 47.

94. SOE Norwegian section, "History."

3. Internecine Struggles

1. Michael R. D. Foot, *An Outline History of the Special Operations Executive, 1940–1946* (London: Bodley Head, 2014 [1984]), 21.

2. Gladwyn Jebb, "The Technique of Subversion," May 6, 1942, TNA HS 8/251.

3. Entry of November 25, 1940, quoted in Kenneth Young, *The Diaries of Sir Robert Bruce Lockhart*, vol. 2: *1939–1965* (London: Macmillan, 1980), 84.

4. On this episode, cf. Gunter Peis, *Naujocks: The Man Who Started the War* (London: Odhams, 1960), 132–48.

5. David Stafford, *Britain and European Resistance, 1940–1945: A Survey of the Special Operations Executive* (London: Macmillan, 1980), 20.

6. Nigel West, *Secret War: The Story of SOE, Britain's Wartime Sabotage Organization* (London: Hodder and Stoughton, 1992), 22, 37.

7. Stafford, *Britain and European Resistance*, 38.

8. David Stafford, "Churchill and SOE," in *Special Operations Executive: A New Instrument of War*, ed. Mark Seaman (London: Routledge, 2006), 53, 58.

9. Stafford, *Britain and European Resistance*, 20.

10. Foot, *An Outline History*, 37.

11. Hugh Dalton, *The Fateful Years: Memoirs 1931–1945* (London: Frederick Muller, 1957), 366.

12. Charles Cruickshank, *SOE in Scandinavia* (Oxford: Oxford University Press, 1986), 123.

13. Henry Hopkinson to Victor Mallet, March 21, 1941, TNA FO 371/29 408.

14. Jebb, "The Technique of Subversion."

15. Diary of Hugh Dalton, quoted in Bradley F. Smith, *The Shadow Warriors: OSS and the Origins of the CIA* (London: Andre Deutsche, 1983), 17.

16. Quoted in Michael R. D. Foot, *SOE in France: An Account of the Work of the British Special Operations Executive in France, 1940–1944* (London: Her Majesty's Stationery Office, 1966), 140.

17. Quoted in Foot, *SOE in France*, 15.

18. Sébastien Albertelli, *Histoire du sabotage, De la CGT à la Résistance* (Paris: Perrin, 2016), 248.

19. David Garnett, *The Secret History of PWE, 1939–1945* (London: St. Ermin's, 2002), 96.

20. N. F. Newsome, "General Guidance and Background," December 9, 1941, Archives of the BBC, bbc.co.uk/archives.

21. N. F. Newsome, "The European Service: Principles and Purposes. Problems and Policy Points," November 1942, TNA FO 898/41.

22. Jebb, "The Technique of Subversion."

23. Jebb, "The Technique of Subversion."

24. Robert Hamilton Bruce Lockhart, *Comes the Reckoning* (London: Putnam, 1947), 57.

25. Charles Cruickshank, *The Fourth Arm: Psychological Warfare 1938–1945* (London: David-Poynter, 1977), 33.

26. Thomas Barman, letter of 1968, quoted in Ellic Howe, *The Black Game: British Subversive Operations Against the Germans During the Second World War* (London: Queen Anne, 1988 [1982]), 49.

27. "Propaganda to Enemy Countries," May 19, 1941, TNA FO 898/9.

28. Garnett, *The Secret History of PWE*, xi.

29. Bruce Lockhart, *Comes the Reckoning*, 143.

30. R. H. Bruce Lockhart, "Progress Report for Week Ending August 11, 1941," TNA FO 898/9.

31. Dalton, *The Fateful Years*, 382.

32. Cruickshank, *The Fourth Arm*, 21.

33. Garnett, *The Secret History of PWE*, xiii.

34. Cruickshank, *The Fourth Arm*, 31.
35. Germany-Austria, France, Italy, Scandinavia, the Low Countries (i.e., the Netherlands and Belgium), the Balkans, Poland-Czechoslovakia.
36. Cruickshank, *The Fourth Arm*, 33.
37. Michael Balfour, *Propaganda in War, 1939–1945: Organisations, Policies, and Publics in Britain and Germany* (London: Routledge and Kegan Paul, 1979), 93.
38. Bruce Lockhart, *Comes the Reckoning*, 126.
39. Garnett, *The Secret History of PWE*, 95–96.
40. T. Barman, "Memorandum on the Regional Directors Meeting with Mr. Kirkpatrick Held 17th December 1941," December 22, 1941, TNA FO 898/41.
41. Garnett, *The Secret History of PWE*, 97.
42. Ivone Kirkpatrick, "Position of Regional Directors Submitted to Executive Committee of PWE," December 4, 1941, quoted in Garnett, *The Secret History of PWE*, 89.
43. Brendan Bracken to Winston Churchill, December 11, 1941, TNA PREM 3/365–68.
44. Bruce Lockhart, *Comes the Reckoning*, 127.
45. Bruce Lockhart, diary entry of December 2, 1940, quoted in Young, *Diaries*, 85.
46. Cruickshank, *The Fourth Arm*, 27.

4. Ententes Cordiales?

1. Charles de Gaulle to Winston Churchill, August 3, 1940, TNA PREM 3/69-A.
2. Hugh Dalton to Paul-Henri Spaak, December 21, 1940, TNA PREM 3/69-A.
3. Letter from Emile-Ernest Cartier de Marchienne to Winston Churchill, July 7, 1942; letter from W. Churchill to E. E. Cartier de Marchienne, August 31, 1942, TNA PREM 3/74/2.
4. Laurence Collier to Anthony Eden, November 10, 1941, TNA FO 371/29 417.
5. Leslie Hollis to Victor Mallet, November 28, 1941, TNA FO 371/29 422.
6. Orme Sargent, note, December 11, 1941, TNA FO 371/29 422.
7. SOE Norwegian section, "History," n.d., TNA HS 7/174.
8. Christopher Mann, "The Norwegian Armed Forces in Britain," in *Europe in Exile: European Exile Communities in Britain, 1940–1945*, ed. Martin Conway and José Gotovitch (New York: Berghahn, 2001), 156.
9. He was replaced in May 1942 by Colin Gubbins.
10. Sébastien Albertelli, *Les Services secrets du général de Gaulle. Le BCRA 1940–1944* (Paris: Perrin, 2009), 40.
11. Albertelli, *Les Services secrets*, 61.
12. Étienne Verhoeyen, *La Belgique occupée. De l'an 40 à la Libération* (Brussels: De Boeck, 1994), 430.
13. Emmanuel Debruyne, *La guerre secrète des espions belges, 1940–1944* (Brussels: Racine, 2008), 110–11, 121.
14. Debruyne, *La guerre secrète des espions belges*, 120.
15. T section history, "Report," June 14, 1945 (report undoubtedly compiled by Lieutenant-Colonel Hardy Amies), HS 7/100.

16. Verhoeyen, *La Belgique occupée*, 432, 369–70.

17. Michael R. D. Foot, *SOE in the Low Countries* (London: St. Ermin's, 2001), 78–80.

18. Two hundred, according to Dick van Galen Last, "The Netherlands," in *Resistance in Western Europe*, ed. Bob Moore (Oxford: Berg, 2000), 190; seventeen hundred in the view of Agnes Dessing, a detail kindly communicated to me by Peter Romijn.

19. Knud J. V. Jesperson, *No Small Achievement: Special Operations Executive and the Danish Resistance, 1940–1945* (Odense: University Press of Southern Denmark, 2002), 50.

20. Daniel Cordier, *Alias Caracalla* (Paris: Gallimard, 2009), 238–39.

21. Albertelli, *Les Services secrets*, 51–52.

22. "Memorandum for SO," January 28, 1941, TNA HS 7/128.

23. T section history, "Report," June 14, 1945.

24. Verhoeyen, *La Belgique occupée*, 430.

25. Albertelli, *Les Services secrets*, 50, 71–72.

26. Albertelli, *Les Services secrets*, 88.

27. Verhoeyen, *La Belgique occupée*, 444, 445.

28. Debruyne, *La guerre secrète des espions belges*, 61.

29. T section history, "Report," June 14, 1945.

30. Claude d'Abzac-Epezy, *L'Armée de l'Air des années noires. Vichy 1940–1944* (Paris: Economica, 1998), 220ff.

31. Simon Kitson, *The Hunt for Nazi Spies: Fighting Espionage in Vichy France* (Chicago: University of Chicago Press, 2008; French ed. 2005), 82.

32. "Policy to France," meeting of November 17, 1940, TNA FO 898/9.

33. William Strang to Bruce Lockhart, August 25, 1941, TNA FO 898/11.

34. Henry H. A. Thackthwaite, RF section history, n.d., TNA HS 7/128.

35. Committee on Foreign (Allied) Resistance, meeting of January 30, 1941, TNA FO 371/28 419.

36. PWE, Propaganda to Denmark, March 15, 1941, TNA FO 898/240.

37. Christopher Warner (FO) to Charles Hambro (MEW), May 15, 1941, TNA FO 371/29 301.

38. Edward Spears, "The Free French, Vichy and Ourselves," n.d. (February 1941), TNA FO 371/28 419.

39. José Gotovitch, *Du rouge au tricolore. Les communistes belges de 1939 à 1944. Un aspect de l'histoire de la Résistance en Belgique* (Brussels: Labor, 1992), 111.

40. Jacques Sémelin, *Unarmed Against Hitler: Civilian Resistance in Europe, 1939–1943*, trans. Suzan Husserl-Kapit (Westport, Conn.: Praeger, 1993; French ed. 1989), 149–50.

41. On these points, cf. Tore Gjelsvik, *Norwegian Resistance, 1940–1945*, trans. Thomas Kingston Derry (Montreal: McGill/Queen's University Press, 1979; Norwegian ed. 1977), 30ff; and Olav Riste and Berit Nökleby, *Norway 1940–1945: The Resistance Movement* (Oslo: Johan Grundt Tanum Forlag, 1970), 24ff.

42. Gjelsvik, *Norwegian Resistance*, 45ff.

43. Low Countries, March 7, 1941, TNA FO 898/64.

44. Minutes of meeting of the Scandinavian Section, August 1, 1941, TNA FO 898/240.

45. Low Countries, March 7, 1941.

46. Anthony Eden to Brendan Bracken, July 31, 1941, TNA FO 371/26 583.

47. Charles Cruickshank, *The Fourth Arm: Psychological Warfare, 1938–1945* (London: David-Poynter, 1977), 128.

48. PWE, Propaganda to Norway, March 15, 1941, TNA FO 898/240.

49. X, Long-term plan for propaganda to Belgium, September 28, 1941, FO 898/231.

5. Legitimacy at Stake

1. X, "Propaganda to Belgium," January 28, 1941, TNA FO 898/231.

2. Thierry Grosbois, *Pierlot. 1930–1950* (Brussels: Racine, 2007), 176.

3. Halifax, note to the prime minister, November 30, 1940, TNA PREM 3/69-A.

4. Grosbois, *Pierlot*, 165–74.

5. Minutes of the Council of Ministers, February 16, 1943, quoted in Grosbois, *Pierlot*, 171.

6. Winston Churchill, note for the Foreign Office, December 13, 1940, TNA PREM 3/69-A.

7. Halifax, note to the prime minister, November 30, 1940.

8. Joassart resigned in July 1943, to be replaced in September by the Socialist Joseph Bondas; Raoul Richard, a technical expert, become undersecretary of resupply services on the same day.

9. Grosbois, *Pierlot*, 181.

10. Laurence Collier to Anthony Eden, August 27, 1941, TNA FO 371/29 422.

11. My thanks to M. François Alabrune, general counsel at the Ministry of Foreign Affairs, for these particulars.

12. Jacques Sémelin, *Unarmed Against Hitler: Civilian Resistance in Europe, 1939–1943,* trans. Suzan Husserl-Kapit (Westport, Conn.: Praeger, 1993; French ed. 1989), 49, 54.

13. Darsie Gillie, "How to Provoke Demonstration," June 11, 1941, TNA FO 371/28 431.

14. Churchill to the Foreign Office, February 17, 1941, TNA PREM 3/69-A.

15. Jean-Louis Crémieux-Brilhac, *La France libre. De l'appel du 18 juin à la libération* (Paris: Gallimard, 1996), 133.

16. "Record of a Meeting between the Prime Minister and General de Gaulle," September 12, 1941, TNA PREM 3/120/2."

17. W. Churchill to A. Eden, September 26, 1941, TNA, PREM 3/120/4.

18. Jørgen Hæstrup, *Secret Alliance: A Study of the Danish Resistance Movement, 1940–45,* trans. Alison Borch-Johansen (Odense: Odense University Press, 1976), 1:29.

19. Hæstrup, *Secret Alliance*, 41.

20. Roderick A. Gallop, note of November 14, 1941, TNA FO 371 29303.

21. X, "The History of the Danish Country Section," n.d. [1945], TNA HS 7/109.

22. Foreign Office, "Policy of HM's Government Towards Denmark," March 5, 1942, TNA HS 2/43.

23. Hæstrup, *Secret Alliance*, 1:77.

24. X, "The History of the Danish Section."

25. Hæstrup, *Secret Alliance*, 1:77–78.

26. Letter drafted by Turnbull, British Legation, Stockholm, to Møller, October 29, 1941, TNA FO 371/36 782.

27. Knud J. V. Jespersen, *No Small Achievement: Special Operations Executive and the Danish Resistance, 1940–1945*. (Odense: University Press of Southern Denmark, 2002), 135.

28. X, Foreign Office, "Pros and Cons of Launching a Free Italy Movement and of Sponsoring a Free Italy Committee," December 18, 1940, TNA FO 898/161.

29. Duff Cooper to Anthony Eden, Free Italy Committee, January 15, 1941, TNA FO 371/29 935.

30. P. Dixon, note, January 17, 1941, TNA FO 371/29 935.

31. X, Foreign Office, "Pros and Cons of Launching a Free Italy Movement and of Sponsoring a Free Italy Committee."

32. O. Sargent, note, March 6, 1941, TNA FO 371/29 935.

33. G. A. Martelli, "Memorandum on the Free Italy Movement," March 24, 1941, TNA FO 371/29 936.

34. P. Dixon, comment on a note from Knight, July 22, 1941, TNA FO 371/29 937.

35. P. Dixon, August 12, 1941, TNA FO 371/29 937.

36. C. Petrone to P. Dixon, November 8, 1941, TNA FO 371/29 938.

37. P. Dixon to Kirkpatrick, December 4, 1941, TNA FO 371/29 938.

38. F.W.D. Deakin, "SOE and Italy," n.d. [1945], TNA HS 7/59.

39. Winston Churchill to General Ismay, February 11, 1941, TNA PREM 3/242/8.

40. War Cabinet, "The Formation of a Free Italian Movement," February 1941, TNA PREM 3/342/8.

41. War Cabinet, "The Formation of a Free Italian Movement in the Italian Colonies," March 3, 1941, TNA FO 371/29 935.

42. Head of SOE to SO, October 15, 1941, TN AHS 7/58.

43. David Garnett, *The Secret History of PWE, 1939–1945* (London: St. Ermin's, 2002), 137–41.

44. From the commander in chief in the Middle East to the War Office, March 21, 1941, TNA FO 371/29 936.

45. From the commander in chief in the Middle East to the War Office, April 9, 1941, TNA FO 371/29 936.

46. General F. H. N. Davidson to V. F. W. Cavendish-Bentick, April 18, 1941, TNA FO 371/29 936.

47. F. W. D. Deakin, "SOE in Italy," n.d. [1945], TNA HS 7/59.

48. Charles Cruickshank, *The Fourth Arm: Psychological Warfare 1938–1945* (London: David-Poynter, 1977), 53.

49. T. H. Harman (?), "Relationship with Allies Governments and with the Minister of Information," October 1, 1941, TNA FO 898/23.

50. Garnett, *The Secret History of PWE*, 11–13.

51. Michael Stenton, *Radio London and Resistance in Occupied Europe: British Political Warfare, 1939–1943* (Oxford: Oxford University Press, 2000), 50.

52. Minutes of a meeting, Dutch Government Broadcasts, July 19, 1940, BBC WAC E2/12/1.

53. D.O.I. to C.O., "Free Time for Refugee Governments," July 9, 1940, BBC WAC E2/12/1.

54. Aurélie Luneau, *Radio Londres, 1940–1944. Les voix de la liberté* (Paris: Perrin, 2005), 58.

55. Winston Churchill to the foreign secretary and to the secretary at Information, February 11, 1941, TNA FO 898/9.

56. Winston Churchill to Duff Cooper, February 11, 1941, quoted in Stenton, *Radio London*, 53.

57. Italian forces programme enquiry committee, September 18, 1941, BBC WAC E1/1003.

58. "Minutes of a Meeting Held at Broadcasting House," July 19, 1940, BBC WAC EI/830.

59. Nigel Law (Ministry of Information) to Ivone Kirkpatrick (BBC), August 11, 1941, BBC WAC E2/12/1.

60. PWE, "Directive for French Service, Week 39, 1941," September 29, 1941, BBC WAC R 34/654/1.

61. Winston Churchill to Frederick Ogilvie, July 28, 1940, BBC WAC E2/14/1.

62. From Barman to Bruce Lockhart, November 1, 1941, TNA FO 898/241.

63. From Barman to Bruce Lockhart, September 23, 1941, TNA FO 898/241.

64. Victor de Laveley was in charge of broadcasts in French, Fernand Geersens (alias Jan Moedwill) of programs in Dutch.

65. Letter from P.-H. Spaak to the minister of the interior, April 1941, BBC WAC E 2/7/1 [in French in the British archives, my translation—JMT].

66. Oliver Harvey to J.S.A. Salt, June 6, 1941, BBC WAC E 2/57.

67. Crémieux-Brilhac, *La France libre*, 229.

68. Stenton, *Radio London*, 50.

69. W. R. Elston to the Office of New Editor, Newsome and Salt, "Radio Orange," September 4, 1940, BBC WAC E 2/12/1, Foreign General Allied Governments Broadcasts, Holland 1940–1941.

70. Oliver Harvey to William Strang, April 25, 1941, quoted in Stenton, *Radio London*, 53–54.

71. For example, in "Minutes of Dutch Weekly Programme Meeting," February 6, 1941, BBC WAC E I/830.

72. Garnett, *The Secret History of PWE*, 49.

73. PWE, "Black Report, Week Ending 7th August 1942," TNA FO 898/64.

74. Some notes on the Dutch Service, n.d. (1950), BBC WAC, E I/289.

75. "Minutes of Dutch Weekly Programme Meeting," April 9, 1941, BBC WAC E I/830.

76. "Minutes of Dutch Weekly Programme Meeting," February 13, 1941, BBC WAC E I/830.

77. "Minutes of Dutch Weekly Programme Meeting," February 19, 1941, BBC WAC E I/830.

78. SOE, report on clandestine activity in Holland, n.d., TNA HS 7/161.

79. SOE, report on clandestine activity in Holland, n.d., TNA HS 7/161.

80. Garnett, *The Secret History of PWE*, 186.

81. Minutes of BBC Italian weekly service meeting, May 1, 1941, BBC WAC E 1/1003.

82. Minutes of BBC Italian weekly service meeting, September 11, 1941, BBC WAC E 1/1003.

83. Camille Huysmans to Cecil de Sausmarez, November 4, 1941, TNA FO 989/232.

84. Sir J. Dashwood (FO), March 7, 1941, TNA FO 371/29 440.

85. Ivone Kirkpatrick, *The Inner Circle Memoirs* (London: Macmillan, 1959), 160–61.

86. D. E. Ritchie, "Britain's Right to Speak," May 10, 1942, TNA FO 898/41.

87. Stenton, *Radio London*, 60.

88. N. F. Newsome, "The European Service. Principles and Purposes. Problems and Policy Points," November 1942, TNA FO 898/41.

6. The Dual Shock of 1941 and Its Consequences

1. T. Barman, "Draft Directive for Danish Broadcast, June 18th–June 24th 1941," TNA FO 371/29 276.

2. Ohto Manninen, "Operation Barbarossa and the Nordic Countries," in *Scandinavia During the Second World War*, ed. Henrik S. Nissen, trans. Thomas Munch-Petersen (Minneapolis: University of Minnesota Press, 1983), 174.

3. Manninen, "Operation Barbarossa," 176.

4. José Gotovitch, *Du rouge au tricolore. Les Communistes belges de 1939 à 1944, un aspect de l'histoire de la Résistance en Belgique* (Brussels: Labor, 1992), 104.

5. Quoted in Stéphane Courtois, *Le PCF dans la guerre. De Gaulle, la Résistance, Staline . . .* (Paris: Ramsay, 1980), 162.

6. Ministry of Information, "Intelligence Report no. 40 for French Section," June 24, 1941, TNA FO 371/28 431.

7. From Stafford Cripps to Anthony Eden, July 6, 1941, TNA PREM 3/184/9.

8. Gotovitch, *Du rouge au tricolore*, 144.

9. Henrik S. Nissen, "The Nordic Societies," in *Scandinavia During the Second World War*, ed. Henrik S. Nissen, trans. Thomas Munch-Petersen (Minneapolis: University of Minnesota Press, 1983), 25.

10. Gotovitch, *Du rouge au tricolore*, 143.

11. David Stafford, *Britain and European Resistance, 1940–1945: A Survey of the Special Operations Executive* (London: Macmillan, 1980), 70.

12. X, Pickaxe operations in France, June 10, 1943, TNA HS 8/199.

13. Denis Peschanski, "21 août 1941: Attentat du métro Barbès," in *Dictionnaire historique de la Résistance*, ed. François Marcot (Paris: Robert Laffont, 2006), 607–8.

14. Quoted in Henri Noguères, Marcel Degliame-Fouche, and Jean-Louis Vigier, *Histoire de la Résistance en France de 1940 à 1945*, 5 vols. (Paris: Robert Laffont, 1967–1981), 2:73.

15. Ole Kristian Grimnes, "The Beginnings of the Resistance Movement," in *Scandinavia During the Second World War*, ed. Henrik S. Nissen, trans. Thomas Munch-Petersen (Minneapolis: University of Minnesota Press, 1983), 213, 214.

16. Denis Peschanski, "Attentats individuels contre les Allemands," in Marcot, *Dictionnaire historique*, 703.

17. Grimnes, "The Beginnings of the Resistance Movement," 213.

18. Charles de Gaulle, speech of October 23, 1941, in Charles de Gaulle, *Discours et messages* (hereafter cited as *DM*), vol. 1: *Pendant la guerre, 1940–1946* (Paris: Plon, 1970), 122–23.

19. From Sporborg to Coote (FO), September 23, 1942, TNA FO 898/241.

20. Norwegian government, "Aide-mémoire" (in French), September 5, 1942, TNA FO 371/32 825.

21. Anthony Eden to the ambassadors of Poland and Belgium, to the Norwegian, Dutch, Greek, Luxemburger, Yugoslav, and Czech ministers, and to General de Gaulle, November 12, 1941, TNA FO 898/12.

22. PWE, "Weekly Directive for BBC French Service, 11th–18th January 1942," January 9, 1942, TNA FO 371/28 431.

23. France, RU F4, "Report no. 1," August 25–October 11, 1941, TNA FO 898/60.

24. From Sporborg to Coote (FO), September 23, 1942, TNA FO 898/241.

25. PWE, "Progress Report," January 1942, TNA FO 898/64.

26. Robert Hamilton Bruce Lockhart, *Comes the Reckoning* (London: Putnam, 1947), 151.

27. Bradley F. Smith, *The Shadow Warriors: OSS and the Origins of CIA* (London: Andre Deutsche, 1983), 26.

28. Bickham Sweet-Escott, *Services Secrets* (London: Methuen, 1965), 134.

29. Robert Hayden Alcorn, *No Bugles for Spies: Tales of the OSS* (New York: David McKay, 1962), 42.

30. "Memorandum of Establishment of Service of Strategic Information."

31. Smith, *The Shadow Warriors*, 64–65.

32. Quoted in Richard Harris Smith, *OSS: The Secret History of America's First Central Intelligence Agency* (Berkeley: University of California Press, 1972), 2.

33. Smith, *OSS*, 20, 68.

34. Smith, *OSS*, 69–78.

35. Quoted in Smith, *OSS*, 115.

36. Smith, *OSS*, 120–21, 161.

37. Smith, *OSS*, 103.

38. Nelson MacPherson, *American Intelligence in War-Time London: The Story of the OSS* (London: Frank Cass, 2003), 50–52.

39. Alcorn, *No Bugles for Spies*, 60.

40. MacPherson, *American Intelligence*, 54.

41. MacPherson, *American Intelligence*, 60.

42. Smith, *The Shadow Warriors*, 172.

43. Quoted in MacPherson, *American Intelligence*, 45.

44. Sweet-Escott, *Services Secrets*, 154, 153.

45. Peter Loxley and Orme Sargent, minutes, September 1, 1942, TNA HS 8/10.

46. From CD to all the regional directors, January 19, 1943, TNA HS 8/13.

47. X (C?), SOE, "Negotiations with the American SOE," June 18, 1942, TNA HS 8/13.

48. From Wheeler-Bennett to Bruce Lockhart, August 3, 1942, TNA FO 898/102.

49. Reginald Campbell to Stephens, August 11, 1942, TNA FO 898/102.

50. From David (?), British Political Warfare Mission, to Bruce Lockhart, January 3, 1943, TNA FO 898/102.

51. Smith, *OSS*, 163.

52. Sweet-Escott, *Services Secrets*, 137.

53. Rex Leeper to Richard Law, April 30, 1942, TNA FO 898/13.

54. Peter Murphy to David Stephens, March 19, 1942, TNA FO 989/50.

55. Regional directors of PWE, reports, January 1942 (?), TNA FO 898/11.

56. D. Stephens (PWE), Propaganda policy, January 19, 1942, TNA FO 898/11.

57. Regional directors of PWE, reports, January 1942 (?), TNA FO 898/11.

58. Political Warfare Executive Committee, "The Importance of Political Warfare Now," March 4, 1942, TNA FO 898/12.

59. Stafford, *Britain and European Resistance*, 66, 58, 81.

60. From M to D/R, Directive from the COS, May 15, 1942, TNA HS 8/274.

7. Coming of Age

1. Claude Bourdet, *L'aventure incertaine. De la Résistance à la Restauration* (Paris: Stock, 1975), 95–96.

2. Tore Gjelsvik, *The Norwegian Resistance, 1940–1945*, trans. Thomas Kingston Derry (Montreal: McGill/Queen's University Press, 1979; Norwegian ed. 1977), 45ff.

3. José Gotovitch, *Du rouge au tricolore. Les Communistes belges de 1939 à 1944, un aspect de l'histoire de la Résistance en Belgique* (Brussels: Labor, 1992), 215.

4. Jørgen Hæstrup, *Secret Alliance: A Study of the Danish Resistance Movement, 1940–45*, trans. Alison Borch-Johansen, 3 vols. (Odense: Odense University Press, 1976–1977), 1:93–94.

5. Hæstrup, *Secret Alliance*, 1:95.

6. Hæstrup, *Secret Alliance*, 1:99.

7. Nathaniel Hong, *Sparks of Resistance: The Illegal Press in German-Occupied Denmark, April 1940–August 1943* (Odense: Odense University Press, 1996), 139–40.

8. Fabrice Maerten, "Presse clandestine," in *Dictionnaire de la Seconde Guerre mondiale en Belgique*, ed. Paul Aron and José Gotovitch (Brussels: André Versaille, 2008), 343–44.

9. Hans Kirchoff, "Denmark," in *Resistance in Western Europe*, ed. Bob Moore (Oxford: Berg, 2000), 101.

10. Ole Kristian Grimnes, "The Beginnings of the Resistance Movement," in *Scandinavia During the Second World War*, ed. Henrik S. Nissen (Minneapolis: University of Minnesota Press, 1983), 215–16.

11. Étienne Verhoeyen, *La Belgique occupée. De l'an 40 à la Libération* (Brussels: De Boeck, 1994), 384 86.

12. Bourdet, *L'aventure incertaine*, 99–100.

13. Philippe Viannay, *Du bon usage de la France. Résistance. Journalisme. Glénans* (Paris: Ramsay, 1988), 34.

14. Henri Noguères, Marcel Degliame-Fouché, and Jean-Louis Vigier, *Histoire de la Résistance en France de 1940 à 1945*, 5 vols. (Paris: Robert Laffont, 1967–1981), 1:236.

15. SOE Cabinet Papers, Denmark, final draft, n.d. (after November 1944, before May 1945), TNA HS 8/242. See also Hæstrup, *Secret Alliance*, 1:122.

16. This analysis was developed at length in Robert Paxton, *Vichy France: Old Guard and New Order* (New York: Knopf, 1972).

17. Claude d'Abzac-Epezy, *L'Armée de l'Air des années noires. Vichy 1940–1944* (Paris: Economica, 1998), 224.

18. Hæstrup, *Secret Alliance*, 1:122.

19. Hæstrup, *Secret Alliance*, 1:122.

20. SOE Cabinet Papers, Denmark, final draft.

21. X, "The History of the Danish Country Section," n.d., 1945, TNA HS 7/109.

22. Hæstrup, *Secret Alliance*, 1:124–25.

23. X, "The History of the Danish Country Section."

24. Jeremy Bennett, *British Broadcasting and the Danish Resistance Movement, 1940–1945: A Study of the Wartime Broadcasts of the BBC Danish Service* (Cambridge: Cambridge University Press, 1966), 68.

25. SOE Cabinet Papers, Denmark, final draft, n.d. (after November 1944, before May 1945).

26. Interview quoted in Noguères et al., *Histoire de la Résistance en France*, 3:38.

27. Paul Paillole, *Services spéciaux (1935–1945)* (Paris: Robert Laffont, 1975), 399.

28. X, "The History of the Danish Country Section," n.d. 1945.

29. Verhoeyen, *La Belgique occupée*, 344.

30. Dick van Galen Last, "The Netherlands," in *Resistance in Western Europe*, ed. Bob Moore (Oxford: Berg, 2000), 195.

31. Bernard, *Histoire de la résistance européenne*, 219.

32. Grimnes, "The Beginnings of the Resistance Movement," 200–201.

33. Ivar Kraglund, "SOE and Milorg: Thieves on the Same Market," in *Special Operations Executive: A New Instrument of War*, ed. Mark Seaman (London: Routledge, 2006), 72.

34. Olav Riste and Berit Nökleby, *Norway 1940–1945: The Resistance Movement* (Oslo: Johan Grundt Tanum Forlag, 1970), 32.

35. Emmanuel Debruyne, *La guerre secrète des espions belges, 1940–1944* (Brussels: Racine, 2008), 21.

36. See Debruyne, *La guerre secrète*.

37. Gjelsvik, *Norwegian Resistance*, 52–53.

38. Jean-Marc Binoit and Bertrand Boyer, *L'argent de la Résistance* (Paris: Larousse, 2010), 23.

39. Hæstrup, *Secret Alliance*, 2:90.

40. Henrik S. Nissen, "Adjusting to German Domination," in *Scandinavia During the Second World War*, ed. Henrik S. Nissen (Minneapolis: University of Minnesota Press, 1983), 116.

41. Gjelsvik, *Norwegian Resistance*, 74–75.

42. Grimnes, "The Beginnings of the Resistance Movement," 202–3.

43. Jean-Louis Crémieux-Brilhac, *La France libre. De l'appel du 18 juin à la libération* (Paris: Gallimard, 1996), 241.

44. Henri Frenay, *The Night Will End*, trans. Dan Hofstadter (London: Abelard, 1976), 190.

45. Joint Report by the Committee of His Majesty's Government with the Allies Movements in the UK, September 19, 1941, TNA FO 898/23.

46. Christian Pineau, *La simple vérité* (Paris: Phalanx, 1983 [1960]), 159.

47. Declaration of General de Gaulle, second version, quoted in Pineau, *La simple vérité*, 608.

48. Verhoeyen, *La Belgique occupée*, 463, 470–71.

49. Verhoeyen, *La Belgique occupée*, 469.

50. Debruyne, *La guerre secrète*, 109.

51. Lieutenant-Colonel Hardy Amies (?), T Section History, Report, June 14, 1945, TNA HS 7/100.

52. As Pierlot declared to Gubbins, note from Keswick, September 10, 1942, TNA HS 7/241.

53. Note from Keswick, September 10, 1942, quoted in Belgian section, Report, n.d., TNA HS 7/241.

54. Belgian section, October 1940–June 1942, TNA HS 7/241.

55. From Harman to Bruce Lockhart, August 29, 1942, TNA FO 898/68.

56. X (no doubt Rex Leeper), "Black Report, Week Ending 21st August 1942," TNA FO 898/64.

57. Verhoeyen, *La Belgique occupée*, 463–79.

58. Verhoeyen, *La Belgique occupée*, 115, 123.

8. Developments

1. Ellic Howe, *The Black Game: British Subversive Operations Against the Germans During the Second World War* (London: Queen Anne, 1988 [1982]), 51.

2. Michael R. D. Foot, *An Outline History of the Special Operations Executive, 1940–1946* (London: Bodley Head, 2014 [1984]), 31.

3. Peter Wilkinson and Joan Bright Astley, *Gubbins and SOE* (Barnsley: Pen and Sword, 2010 [1993]), 100.

4. Gladwyn Jebb, *The Memoirs of Lord Gladwyn* (London: Weidenfeld and Nicolson, 1972), 107.

5. Wilkinson and Astley, *Gubbins and SOE*, 101.

6. Hugh Dalton, *The Fateful Years: Memoirs 1931–1945* (London: Frederick Muller, 1957), 369.

7. Nigel West, *Secret War: The Story of SOE, Britain's Wartime Sabotage Organization* (London: Hodder and Stoughton, 1992), 59.

8. Quoted in Wilkinson and Astley, *Gubbins and SOE*, iv.

9. Brooke to Selborne, July 8, 1942, TNA HS 8/919.

10. Lord Selborne, "SOE Activities for the Prime Minister. Quarter: March June 1942," July 15, 1942, TNA PREM 3/409/5.

11. SOE Norwegian Section, History, n.d., TNA HS 7/174.

12. Lord Selborne, "SOE Activities for the Prime Minister," February 5, 1943, TNA PREM 3/409/5.

13. SOE Norwegian Section, History, n.d. TNA HS 7/174.

14. Lord Selborne, "SOE Activities for the Prime Minister," April 6, 1943, TNA PREM 3/409/5.

15. SOE Norwegian Section, History, n.d. TNA HS 7/174.

16. From the Senior Naval Officer to the Commander in Chief, "Operation Biting," February 28, 1942, TNA PREM 3/73.

17. Michael R. D. Foot, *SOE in France: An Account of the Work of the British Special Operations Executive in France, 1940–1944* (London: Her Majesty's Stationery Office, 1966), 184.

18. Foot, *SOE in France*, 184.

19. Olav Riste and Berit Nöklebyit, *Norway 1940–1945: The Resistance Movement* (Oslo: Johan Grundt Tanum Forlag, 1970), 53.

20. SOE Norwegian Section, History, 1940–1945, n.d., TNA HS 7/174.

21. SOE Norwegian Section, History, 1940–1945.

22. Nigel Sutton (PWE), "Note on the Position in Regard to Operational Propaganda in Norway," quoted in General Report, TNA HS 7/281.

23. SN/I (Norwegian section of SOE), note, March 10, 1943, TNA FO 898/73.

24. "SOE Long-Term Policy in Norway," September 21, 1942, TNA HS 7/175.

25. Charles Cruickshank, *SOE in Scandinavia* (Oxford: Oxford University Press, 1986), 177.

26. Tore Gjelsvik, *Norwegian Resistance, 1940–1945*, trans. Thomas Kingston Derry (Montreal: McGill/Queen's University Press, 1979; Norwegian ed. 1977), 126.

27. Quoted in Belgian Section, October 1940–June 1942, TNA HS 7/241.

28. Belgian Section, October 1940–June 1942.

29. Lieutenant-Colonel Hardy Amies (?), T Section, History, Report, June 14, 1945, TNA HS 7/100.

30. Belgian Section, General Report, TNA HS 7/242.

31. Belgian Section, October 1940–June 1942.

32. For an overview, see Thomas Rabino, *Le réseau Carte. Histoire d'un réseau de la Résistance antiallemand, antigaulliste, anticommuniste et anticollaborationniste* (Paris: Perrin, 2008).

33. Rabino, *Le réseau Carte*, 151.

34. Rabino, *Le réseau Carte*, 195.

35. Rabino, *Le réseau Carte*, 301.

36. Rabino, *Le réseau Carte*, 207.

37. Rabino, *Le réseau Carte*, 217.

38. De Gaulle to Eden, December 30, 1942, TNA FO 898/60.

39. Sutton to Leeper, January 8, 1943, TNA FO 898/60.

40. Rabino, *Le réseau Carte*, 247.

41. Charvet (H. Frenay), "Rapport de Combat sur l'organisation Radio-Patrie," February 15, 1943, TNA FO 898/60.

42. Rabino, *Le réseau Carte*, 151–52.

43. Jørgen Hæstrup, *Secret Alliance: A Study of the Danish Resistance Movement, 1940–45*, trans. Alison Borch-Johansen, 3 vols. (Odense: Odense University Press, 1976–1977), 1:150.

44. X, History of the Danish Section, n.d., 1945, TNA HS 7/109.

45. Cf. Hæstrup, *Secret Alliance*, 1:159.

46. Hæstrup, *Secret Alliance*, 1:160.

47. Hæstrup, *Secret Alliance*, 1:165.

48. Cruickshank, *SOE in Scandinavia*, 152–53.

49. Colin Gubbins, memorandum of July 30, 1043, quoted in Knud J. V. Jespersen, *No Small Achievement: Special Operations Executive and the Danish Resistance, 1940–1945* (Odense: University Press of Southern Denmark, 2002), 151.

50. Hæstrup, *Secret Alliance*, 1:177.
51. From SD (director of the Danish section) to AD/E (director of the London group), January 19, 1944, TNA HS 2/43.
52. SOE Cabinet Papers, Denmark, final draft, n.d., TNA HS 8/242.
53. X, History of the Danish Section.
54. Hæstrup, *Secret Alliance*, 1:178.
55. X, History of the Danish Section.
56. Étienne Verhoeyen, *La Belgique occupée. De l'an 40 à la Libération* (Brussels: De Boeck, 1994), 400, 402, 404.
57. Verhoeyen, *La Belgique occupée*, 356.
58. Lieutenant-Colonel Hardy Amies (?), T Section History, Report, June 15, 1945, TNA HS 7/100.
59. Foot, *SOE in France*, 231.
60. Foot, *SOE in France*, 197.
61. Foot, *SOE in France*, 203, 212–13.
62. Sébastien Albertelli, *Les Services secrets du général de Gaulle. Le BCRA 1940–1944* (Paris: Perrin, 2009), 88.
63. H.H.A. Thackthwaite, RF Section History, Report, n.d., TNA HS 7/128.
64. Thackthwaite, RF Section History, Report, n.d. TNA HS 7/128.
65. Albertelli, *Les Services secrets*, 227.
66. From M to D/R, COS directive for SOE, May 15, 1942, TNA HS 8/274.
67. SOE Belgium October/December 1943, TNA HS 7/243.
68. M (Gubbins) to CD (Nelson), April 18, 1942, TNA HS 8/274.
69. Lieutenant-Colonel Hardy Amies (?), T Section History, Report, June 14, 1945, TNA HS 7/100.
70. Verhoeyen, *La Belgique occupée*, 418.
71. Lieutenant-Colonel Hardy Amies (?), T Section History, Report, June 14, 1945.
72. Verhoeyen, *La Belgique occupée*, 419–21.
73. Belgian Section, general report, TNA HS 7/242.
74. Verhoeyen, *La Belgique occupée*, 418.
75. Lieutenant-Colonel Hardy Amies (?), T Section History, Report, June 14, 1945.
76. Riste and Nöklebyit, *Norway 1940–1945*, 50, 64–67.
77. SOE Norwegian Section, History, 1940–1945, n.d., TNA HS 7/174.
78. Joint Planning Section, Operations in Norway, May 4, 1943, TNA PREM 3/254/2.
79. Thackthwaite, RF Section History, Report, n.d., TNA HS 7/128.
80. Charvet (H. Frenay), "Rapport de Combat sur l'organisation Radio-Patrie," February 15, 1943, TNA FO 898/60.

9. Compulsory Labor

1. Adam Tooze, *The Wages of Destruction: The Making and Breaking of the Nazi Economy* (London: Penguin, 2007 [2006]), 513.
2. Tooze, *The Wages of Destruction*, 517.

3. Detlev Korte, "The Recruitment of Civilian Workers for the German Reich During World War II," Documentatiaegroep '40–45, https://www.documentatiegroep40–45.nl, consulted January 27, 2016.

4. Dominique Barjot, "Emploi et travail forcé aux Pays-Bas, 1940–1945," in *La main-d'oeuvre française exploitée par le IIIe Reich*, ed. Bernard Garnier and Jean Quellien (Caen: Centre de Recherche d'Histoire Quantitative, 2003), 362; and Pieter Lagrou, *The Legacy of Nazi Occupation: Patriotic Memory and National Recovery in Western Europe, 1945–1965* (Cambridge: Cambridge University Press, 2000), 132–33.

5. Gerhard Hirschfeld, *Nazi Rule and Dutch Collaboration: The Netherlands Under German Occupation, 1940–1945*, trans. Louise Wilmot (Oxford: Berg, 1988; German ed. 1984), 221.

6. Lagrou, *The Legacy of Nazi Occupation*, 132–34.

7. Frans Selleslagh, "Les réquisitions de main d'oeuvre en Belgique," in *La main-d'oeuvre française exploitée*, ed. Bernard Garnier and Jean Quellien (Caen: Centre de Recherche d'Histoire Quantitative, 2003), 371.

8. Patrice Arnaud, "Les travailleurs civils français en Allemagne pendant la Seconde Guerre mondiale," Ph.D. thesis, Université Paris-I, 2006, 1:58.

9. Jean Quellien, "Les travailleurs forcés en Allemagne: Essai d'approche statistique," in *La main-d'oeuvre française exploitée*, ed. Bernard Garnier and Jean Quellien (Caen: Centre de Recherche d'Histoire Quantitative, 2003), 75.

10. Harry Paape, "How Dutch Resistance Was Organized," in *Holland at War Against Hitler: Anglo Dutch Relations, 1940–1945*, ed. Michael R. D. Foot (London: Frank Cass, 1990), 88.

11. Belgian Section, general report, TNA HS 7/242.

12. José Gotovitch, *Du rouge au tricolore. Les Communistes belges de 1939 à 1944, un aspect de l'histoire de la Résistance en Belgique* (Brussels: Labor, 199), 236–37.

13. Belgian Section, general report, TNA HS 7/242.

14. X, Mission Lena, May 27, 1944, TNA FO 898/89.

15. Tybalt Report, December 23, 1943, TNA FO 898/80.

16. SOE Belgium October/December 1943, TNA HS 7/243.

17. SOE Belgium October/December 1943..

18. Étienne Verhoeyen, *La Belgique occupée. De l'an 40 à la Libération* (Brussels: De Boeck, 1994), 499–500.

19. Note for Hector II, December 1, 1943, TNA FO 898/88.

20. Socrate telegram, March 13, 1944, TNA FO 898/88.

21. Socrate telegram, September 4, 1944, TNA FO 898/88.

22. Eleven, Twelve, Thirteen, Report on the Dingo organization, January 5, 1944, TNA FO 898/78.

23. Verhoeyen, *La Belgique occupée*, 502.

24. Verhoeyen, *La Belgique occupée*, 504; Gotovitch, *Du rouge au tricolore*, 236.

25. Korte, "The Recruitment of Civilian Workers."

26. Gotovitch, *Du rouge au tricolore*, 241.

27. Georges Guingouin, *Quatre ans de lutte sur le sol limousin* (Limoges: Lucien Souny, 1991), 75.

28. Henri Frenay, *The Night Will End*, trans. Dan Hofstadter (London: Abelard, 1976; French ed. 1973), 238.

29. François Marcot, "Maquis," in *Dictionnaire historique de la Résistance*, ed. François Marcot (Paris: Robert Laffont, 2006), 675–76.

30. Frenay, *The Night Will End*, 262.

31. Telegram from the MUR to General de Gaulle, March 3, 1943, received March 20, 1943, quoted in Daniel Cordier, *Jean Moulin. La République des catacombes* (Paris: Gallimard, 1999), 322.

32. Cordier, *Jean Moulin*, 352.

33. Jean Moulin, report of June 4, 1943, quoted in Colonel Passy, *Missions secrètes en France* (Paris: Plon, 1951), 196.

34. Frenay, *The Night Will End*, 248–49.

35. Raphaël Spina, "La France et les Français devant le Service du Travail obligatoire, 1942–1945," Ph.D. thesis, École Normale Supérieure de Cachan, 2012, 881.

36. Claude Bourdet, *L'aventure incertaine: De la Résistance à la Restauration* (Paris: Stock, 1975), 192.

37. Gilles Vergnon, *Le Vercors. Histoire et mémoire d'un maquis* (Paris: Éditions de l'Atelier, 2002), 44–45.

38. Harry Kedward, *In Search of the Maquis: Rural Resistance in Southern France, 1942–1944* (Oxford: Clarendon Press, 1993), 29.

39. Bourdet, *L'aventure incertaine*, 225.

40. Spina, "La France," 937, 939.

41. Spina, "La France," 953.

42. Plan quoted in Vergnon, *Le Vercors*, 47.

43. Vergnon, *Le Vercors*, 49.

44. De Gaulle, letter to Churchill, March 10, 1943, TNA HS 8/963.

45. Selborne (?), note, June 21, 1943, TNA HS 8/924.

46. Quoted (in French) in Cordier, *Jean Moulin*, 333.

47. Cordier, *Jean Moulin*, 334.

48. Passy, *Missions*, 73.

49. Spina, "La France," 500.

50. Quellien, "Les travailleurs forcés en Allemagne," 71.

51. Spina, "La France," 307–8.

52. Spina, "La France," 420, 938, 23.

53. Spina, "La France," 906–10, 913–17.

54. OS, SOE Directive for 1943, quoted in Miscellaneous Section, general report, n.d., TNA HS 7/286.

55. Tore Gjelsvik, *Norwegian Resistance, 1940–1945*, trans. Thomas Kingston Derry (Montreal: McGill/Queen's University Press, 1979; Norwegian ed. 1977), 95–96.

56. Gjelsvik, *Norwegian Resistance*, 155–57.

57. Olav Riste and Berit Nöklebyit, *Norway 1940–1945: The Resistance Movement* (Oslo: Johan Grundt Tanum Forlag, 1970), 74–75.

58. "Gunnar Sønsteby Obituary," *Guardian*, May 22, 2012, https://www.theguardian.com/world/2012/may/22/gunnar-sonsteby.

59. Gjelsvik, *Norwegian Resistance*, 161.
60. SOE Norwegian Section, History, 1940–1945, n.d., TNA HS 7/174.
61. Tooze, *The Wages of Destruction*, 517, 537.

10. Mixed Results

1. Gubbins to Seymour Blizard, August 26, 1942, TNA HS 7/274.
2. Directive from Gubbins to Bingham, May 8, 1943, in general report, n.d., TNA HS 7/274.
3. Lieutenant-Colonel Michael Alan Wethered Rowlandson, communication, February 5, 1943, quoted in general report, TNA HS 7/274.
4. Meeting of April 30, 1943, quoted in general report, n.d., TNA HS 7/274.
5. Directive from Gubbins to Bingham, May 8, 1943, in general report, n.d., TNA HS 7/274.
6. General report, n.d., TNA HS 7/274.
7. Telegram quoted in general report, n.d., TNA HS 7/274.
8. Michael R. D. Foot, *SOE in the Low Countries* (London: St. Ermin's, 2001), 197.
9. David Stafford, *Britain and European Resistance, 1940–1945: A Survey of the Special Operations Executive* (London: Macmillan, 1980), 94.
10. Michael R. D. Foot, *SOE in the Low Countries*, 188–89.
11. SOE, general report, n.d., TNA HS 7/276.
12. SOE, general report, n.d., TNA HS 7/276.
13. Foot, *SOE in the Low Countries*, 96.
14. Jo Wolters, *Dossier Nordpol: Het Englandspiel onder de Loep* (Amsterdam: Boom, 2003), 291–97 (summary in English).
15. Wolters, *Dossier Nordpol*, 154.
16. SOE, report of 1945, TNA HS 7/58.
17. David Stafford, *Mission Accomplished: SOE and Italy, 1943–1945* (London: Bodley Head, 2011), 94.
18. F. W. D. Deakin, "History of the Italian Sector," n.d., TNA HS 7/59.
19. Stafford, *Mission Accomplished*, 99–100.
20. Deakin, "History of the Italian Sector."
21. For an overview, see Giuseppe Fiori, *Il cavaliere dei rossomori* (Milan: Einaudi, 2000).
22. SOE, Cabinet Papers, Italy, n.d. (1945–?), TNA HS 8/242.
23. SOE, report of 1945, TNA HS 7/58.
24. SOE, report of 1945.
25. SOE, Cabinet Papers, Italy, n.d. (1945?), TNA HS 8/242.
26. Anthony Eden, Memorandum, November 20, 1942, quoted in F. W. D. Deakin, "SOE and the Italian Resistance (1941–1945)," n.d., TNA HS 7/59.
27. A. Eden to W. Churchill, February 17, 1943, TNA PREM 3/242/9.
28. Deakin, "SOE and the Italian Resistance (1941–1945)."
29. Major Roseberry, "Comments on CD report," October 11, 1942, in general report, n.d., TNA HS 7/262.

30. Italy, general report, n.d., TNA HS 7/262.
31. Stafford, *Britain and European Resistance*, 83.
32. From Gubbins to Major Card, Joint Planning Staff, April 21, 1942, TNA HS 8/274.
33. From CD to CEO, February 9, 1942, TNA HS 8/23.
34. Stafford, *Britain and European Resistance*, 86–87.
35. John Hanbury W. and E. W. Playfair, "Report on SOE," June 18, 1942, TNA HS 8/252.
36. Lord Selborne to Churchill, January 12, 1944, TNA PREM 3/408/4.
37. I have adapted here the analysis developed by Stafford, *Britain and European Resistance*, 137–42.
38. Jacques Sémelin, *Unarmed Against Hitler: Civilian Resistance in Europe, 1939–1943*, trans. Suzan Husserl-Kapit (Westport, Conn.: Praeger, 1993; French ed. 1989), 76.
39. Sémelin, *Unarmed Against Hitler*, 83.
40. From Desmond Morton to Winston Churchill, May 3, 1943, TNA PREM 3/221/13 A.
41. From Selborne to Morton, May 6, 1943, TNA HS 8/924.
42. Gerhard Hirschfeld, *Nazi Rule and Dutch Collaboration: The Netherlands Under German Occupation, 1940–1945*, trans. Louise Wilmot (Oxford: Berg, 1988; German ed. 1984), 54.
43. Sémelin, *Unarmed Against Hitler*, 83.
44. R. H. Bruce Lockhart, entry of May 29, 1942, in *The Diaries of Sir Robert Bruce Lockhart*, ed. Kenneth Young (London: Macmillan, 1980), 169.
45. Sémelin, *Unarmed Against Hitler*, 76.
46. Charles Hambro to Alan Brooke, March 16, 1943, TNA HS 8/963.
47. Selborne, "SOE Activities for the PM. Quarter: March–June 42," July 14, 1942, TNA PREM 3/409/5.
48. Selborne, "SOE Activities for the PM. Quarter: July–September 42," October 15, 1942, TNA PREM 3/409/5.
49. Selborne, "SOE Activities for the PM. Quarter: October–December 42," February 5, 1943, TNA PREM 3/409/5.
50. Selborne, "SOE Activities for the PM. Quarter: April to June 1943," July 6, 1943, TNA PREM 3/409/5.
51. Selborne, "SOE Activities for the PM. Quarter: July–September 42."
52. Selborne, "SOE Activities for the PM. Quarter: April to June 43."
53. Selborne to Churchill, June 24, 1943, TNA PREM 3/184/6.
54. Summary for the PM, January to March 1943, n.d., TNA HS 8/250.
55. Selborne, "SOE Activities for the PM. Quarter: April to June 43."

11. Taking Up Arms

1. Serge Ravanel, *L'esprit de résistance* (Paris: Le Seuil, 1995), 227.
2. Henri Frenay, *The Night Will End*, trans. Dan Hofstadter (London: Abelard, 1976; French ed. 1973), 190.
3. Lord Selborne to Winston Churchill, April 10, 1942, TNA HS 8/251.

4. General L. W. Rooks, Allied Force Headquarters (AFHQ), to General Deane, "OSS Activities from North Africa," August 14, 1943, National Archives and Records Administration, Washington, D.C. (hereafter cited as NARA), MI 1642/reel 6.

5. SOE History, "Participation of the FFI in the Liberation of France, 1944," n.d., TNA HS 7/133.

6. Chief of Staff of the Army Air Force, "Aircraft for SOE Purposes," July 24, 1943, TNA PREM 3/408/3.

7. Noreen Riols, *The Secret Ministry of Ag. and Fish: My Life in Churchill's School of Spies* (London: Macmillan, 2013), 57.

8. Selborne, note to the prime minister, January 26, 1944, TNA PREM 3/408/3.

9. SOE History, "Participation of the FFI in the Liberation of France, 1944."

10. Knud V. Jespersen, *No Small Achievement: Special Operations Executive and the Danish Resistance, 1940–1945* (Odense: University Press of Southern Denmark, 2002), 33.

11. Bickham Sweet-Escott, *Baker Street Irregulars* (London: Methuen, 1965), 102.

12. Nigel West, *Secret War: The Story of SOE, Britain's Wartime Sabotage Organization* (London: Hodder and Stoughton, 1992), 45.

13. Richard Overy, *The Bombing War: Europe 1939–1945* (London: Allen Lane, 2013), n.p.

14. X to the general command, "Requirements for a Storage, Packing and Departure Center," October 12, 1943, NARA RG 226/E 190/box 231.

15. OSS (David Bruce?), "Aircraft for the Secret Army in France," May 10, 1943, NARA RG 226/E 190/box 230.

16. Chief of Staff of the Army Air Force, "Aircraft for SOE Purposes,"July 24, 1943.

17. X to the general command, "Requirement for a Storage, Packing, and Departure Center."

18. "Comparison of Total RAF Bomber Command Sorties from UK and Those Carried Out for SOE," n.d., TNA HS 8/382.

19. SOE History, "Participation of the FFI in the Liberation of France, 1944."

20. Note, May 24, 1944 TNA HS 7/287.

21. Michael R. D. Foot, *An Outline History of the Special Operations Executive, 1940–1946* (London: Bodley Head, 2014 [1984]), 107.

22. SO Branch, Air Operations, n.d., vol. 6, NARA RG 226 MC 1623/reel 9.

23. SOE History, "Participation of the FFI in the Liberation of France, 1944."

24. "Annex V Dated 31st January 1944 Submitted by the Minister of Economic Warfare to the Prime Minister," TNA PREM 3/185/1.

25. X to the general command, "Requirements for a Storage, Packing and Departure Center."

26. SO Branch, Air Operations, n.d., vol. 6.

27. From Glavin to Bruce for Donovan, February 7 (?), 1944, NARA MC 1642/reel 104.

28. From Selborne to Sinclair, August 20, 1943, TNA HS 8/277.

29. From CD Plans to CD, July 15, 1943, TNA HS 8/277.

30. From F. Bayard Rives to Carl O. Hoffmann, May 29, 1944, NARA RG 226/E 99/box 112.

31. D/RO to D/R, "Operational Developments in the Six Months April–September 1943," September 22, 1943, TNA HS 8/143.

32. Colonel Edward J. Glavin to W. Donovan, February 21, 1944, NARA MC 1642/reel 80.
33. D/RO to D/R, "Operational Developments in the Six Months April–September 1943."
34. War Diary, "Special Operation Branch, London, March 1945," NARA RG 226 OSS MC 1623/reel 6.
35. SO Branch, Air Operations, n.d., vol. 6.
36. SOE, "Beaconry in Norway and Denmark," July 31, 1946, TNA HS 7/182.
37. SO Branch, Air Operations, n.d., vol. 6.
38. SOE History, "Participation of the FFI in the Liberation of France, 1944."
39. SOE, Report on clandestine activity in Holland, TNA HS 7/161.
40. Evaluation of SOE activities in France, n.d., TNA HS 7/135.
41. Evaluation of SOE activities in Norway, n.d., TNA HS 7/178.
42. Paddy Ashdown, *The Cruel Victory: The French Resistance, D-Day and the Battle for the Vercors 1944* (London: William Collins, 2014), 235.
43. Evaluation of SOE activities in France, n.d.
44. Maurice Buckmaster, *Specially Employed: The Story of British Aid to French Patriots of the Resistance* (London: Batchworth, 1952), 41.
45. Foot, *An Outline History*, 110.
46. SOE History, "Participation of the FFI in the Liberation of France, 1944."
47. From DR/OPD to MG and AL, n.d. (first quarter of 1944), TNA HS 8/143.
48. SOE, "Beaconry in Norway and Denmark," July 31, 1946.
49. Michael R.D. Foot, *SOE in France: An Account of the Work of the British Special Operations Executive in France, 1940–1944* (London: Her Majesty's Stationery Office, 1966), 80.
50. From DR/OPD to MG and AL, n.d.
51. SOE, "Beaconry in Norway and Denmark," July 31, 1946.
52. From Muus to Hollingworth, quoted in Jørgen Hæstrup, *Secret Alliance: A Study of the Danish Resistance Movement, 1940–45*, trans. Alison Borch-Johansen (Odense: Odense University Press, 1976–1977), 1:230.
53. Conversation with Francis J. Reardon, May 29, 1944, NARA RG 226/E 99/box 112.
54. SOE, "Beaconry in Norway and Denmark," July 31, 1946.
55. Foot, *SOE in France*, 85.
56. David Stafford, *Britain and European Resistance, 1940–1945: A Survey of the Special Operations Executive* (London: Macmillan, 1980), 140.
57. Overy, *The Bombing War: Europe 1939–1945*, n.p.
58. SOE, Report on Clandestine Activity in Holland, n.d., TNA, HS 7/161.
59. From D. Morton to the prime minister, "Arming French Resistance," April 12, 1944, TNA PREM 3/185/1.
60. SOE, "Statistics for 1940–1945 UK and Mediterranean," n.d., TNA HS 8/382.
61. X to the general command, "Requirements for a Storage, Packing and Departure Center."
62. Selborne, "Assistance to French Resistance. Report on May Moon Operations," May 25, 1944, TNA PREM 3/185/1.
63. Selborne, "Assistance to French Resistance," May 25, 1944.
64. Selborne, "Assistance to French Resistance," May 25, 1944.
65. Charles Cruickshank, *SOE in Scandinavia* (Oxford: Oxford University Press, 1986), 279.

66. SOE, "The History of the Danish Country Section," n.d., 1945, TNA HS 7/109.

67. SOE, "Beaconry in Norway and Denmark." July 31, 1946.

68. Foot, *SOE in France*, 88.

69. Sébastien Albertelli, "Les services secrets de la France libre: Le Bureau central de renseignement et d'action," Ph.D. thesis, Instituts d'Études Politiques (IEP)-Paris, 2006, 1035.

70. Cruickshank, *SOE in Scandinavia*, 277.

71. Sir Brooks Richards, "SOE and SEA Communications," in *Special Operations Executive: A New Instrument of War*, ed. Mark Seaman (London: Routledge, 2006), 39.

72. SOE, Evaluation of SOE Activities in Norway, n.d., TNA HS 7/178.

73. SOE Norwegian Section, History, 1940–1945, n.d., TNA HS 7/174.

74. Cruickshank, *SOE in Scandinavia*, 97.

75. Foot, *An Outline History*, 127.

76. Edward H. Cookridge, *They Came from the Sky* (London: Heinemann, 1965), 10.

77. Foot, *An Outline History*, 115.

78. X, "Life in the Underground," TNA HS 7/131.

79. SOE, "Statistics for 1940–1945 UK and Mediterranean."

80. X, "Life in the Underground," TNA HS 7/131.

81. D'Astier to Selborne, February 21, 1944, TNA HS 8/935.

82. SOE, "Statistics for 1940–1945 UK and Mediterranean."

83. SOE, "Statistics for 1940–1945 UK and Mediterranean."

84. Evaluation of SOE Activities in France, n.d., TNA HS 7/135.

85. Evaluation of SOE Operations in Holland, n.d., TNA HS 8/419.

86. SOE, "The History of the Danish Country Section," n.d., 1945, TNA HS 7/109.

87. Cruickshank, *SOE in Scandinavia*, 278.

88. SOE, "Statistics for 1940–1945 UK and Mediterranean."

89. Buckmaster, *Specially Employed*, 85.

90. Major R. A. Bourne-Patterson, "British Circuits in France, 1941–1944," June 30, 1946, TNA HS 7/122.

91. Michael Stenton, *Radio London and Resistance in Occupied Europe: British Political Warfare, 1939–1943* (Oxford: Oxford University Press, 2000), 193.

92. Sweet-Escott, *Baker Street Irregulars*, 109.

12. Propaganda

1. M. Hubert to Cecil Graves and Ivone Kirkpatrick, December 22, 1941, BBC WAC E 2/7/1.

2. M. Hubert to I. Kirkpatrick, January 24, 1942, BBC WAC E 2/7/1.

3. Jean-Louis Crémieux-Brilhac, *La France libre. De l'appel du 18 juin à la libération* (Paris: Gallimard, 1996), 213.

4. Aurélie Luneau, *Radio Londres, 1940–1944. Les voix de la liberté* (Paris: Perrin, 2005), 234.

5. X, "Development of Service to Belgium," n.d., BBC WAC E 2/57.

6. PWE Central Directive, Annex 1, "Britain Serves Europe. The Spoken Word," March 18, 1943, BBC WAC E 2/128/2.

7. Crémieux-Brilhac, *La France libre*, 705.

8. PWE Central Directive (week beginning Thursday 23rd September 1943), September 22, 1943, BBC WAC E 2/128/2.

9. PWE Central Directive (week beginning Thursday 30th December 1943), December 29, 1943, BB WAC E 2/128/2.

10. David Garnett, "The Uses of RUs to Occupied Europe. Preliminary Considerations," March 21, 1943, TNA FO 898/65.

11. Sefton Delmer, *Black Boomerang* (New York: Viking, 1962), 83.

12. Garnett, "The Uses of RUs to Occupied Europe."

13. David Garnett, *The Secret Story of PWE, 1939–1945* (London: St. Ermin's, 2002), 115.

14. Charles Cruickshank, *The Fourth Arm: Psychological Warfare, 1938–1945* (London: David-Poynter, 1977), 106.

15. Delmer, *Black Boomerang*, 124.

16. Ellic Howe, *The Black Game: British Subversive Operations Against the Germans During the Second World War* (London: Queen Anne, 1988 [1982]), 159–60, 164.

17. Cruickshank, *The Fourth Arm*, 105.

18. List of RUs (about May 1944), TNA FO 898/51.

19. Garnett, *The Secret Story of PWE*, 210–11.

20. Robert Hamilton Bruce Lockhart, *Comes the Reckoning* (London: Putnam, 1947), 153.

21. Cruickshank, *The Fourth Arm*, 103.

22. Edward I. Halliday, "Note on the Operation of PID Research Unit," October 4, 1945, TNA FO 898/51.

23. Halliday, "Note on the Operation of PID Research Unit."

24. Luneau, *Radio Londres*, 137.

25. PWE, "Report on Norwegian and Danish RUs for the Week Ending 12th November 1942," TNA FO 898/57.

26. PWE, Central Directive, Annex 1, "Confiscation of Radios," May 27, 1943, BBC WAC E 2/128/2.

27. Luneau, *Radio Londres*, 114.

28. X, "The Importance of Leaflet Dissemination," April 24, 1942, TNA FO 898/458.

29. PWE, "Monthly Report on Propaganda for April 1942," TNA FO 898/50.

30. PWE, "Monthly Report on Propaganda for August 1942," TNA FO 898/50.

31. R. T. Morison, RAF, Central Mediterranean Force, "Dropping of Propaganda Leaflets from Aircraft," December 31, 1943, TNA FO 898/458.

32. Cruickshank, *The Fourth Arm*, 87.

33. Garnett, *The Secret Story of PWE*, 189.

34. "Leaflet Dissemination, Minutes of a Meeting Held in Air Ministry," June 4, 1942, TNA FO 898/458.

35. A. T. Harris, Bomber Command, to Brendan Bracken, June 3, 1942, TNA FO 898/458.

36. Bruce Lockhart, *Comes the Reckoning*, 171.

37. Cruickshank, *The Fourth Arm*, p. 87.

38. R. T. Morison, RAF, Central Mediterranean Force, "Dropping of Propaganda Leaflets from Aircraft," December 31, 1943, TNA FO 898/458.

39. T.F.D. Rose to Brooks, July 3, 1942, TNA FO 898/458.

40. X (PWE), Leaflet Dissemination, May 7, 1942, TNA FO 898/458.

41. Cruickshank, *The Fourth Arm*, 88.

42. From R. S. Greenfow to T. L. Rowan, 10 Downing Street, April 11, 1942, TNA PREM 3/365/11.

43. Cruickshank, *The Fourth Arm*, 89.

44. Delmer, *Black Boomerang*, 167–68.

45. Cruickshank, *The Fourth Arm*, 92.

46. R. B. Hodglinson, squadron leader, to Brooks, November 27, 1944, TNA FO 898/458.

47. Cruickshank, *The Fourth Arm*, 93, 94–95.

48. Taylor, note, April 2, 1942, TNA FO 898/458.

49. RHBL (Bruce Lockhart) to Tedder, July 19, 1944, TNA FO 898/458.

50. From Tedder to Brooks, July 25, 1944, TNA FO 898/458.

51. "Leaflet Dissemination, Minutes of a Meeting Held in Air Ministry," June 4, 1942, TNA FO 898/458.

52. From Tedder to Brooks, July 25, 1944.

53. Cruickshank, *The Fourth Arm*, 91.

54. Cruickshank, *The Fourth Arm*, 90.

55. PWE, "Britain Serves Europe: II The Written Word," March 31, 1943, TNA FO 898/458.

56. Cruickshank, *The Fourth Arm*, 98–99.

57. Note from R. Leeper, November 15, 1942, TNA FO 898/63.

58. Garnett, *The Secret Story of PWE*, 378.

59. PWE, "Britain Serves Europe: II The Written Word."

60. Michael Balfour, *Propaganda in War, 1939–1945: Organisations, Policies, and Publics in Britain and Germany* (London: Routledge and Kegan Paul, 1979), 96.

61. Cruickshank, *The Fourth Arm*, 96.

62. Garnett, *The Secret Story of PWE*, 177.

63. Cruickshank, *The Fourth Arm*, 96.

64. Cruickshank, *The Fourth Arm*, 96.

65. Balfour, *Propaganda in War*, 96.

13. Cadres

1. Winston Churchill, speech broadcast on February 9, 1941, https://www.ibiblio.org/pha/timeline/410209awp.html.

2. Hubert Pierlot to Winston Churchill, February 14, 1941, TNA PREM 3/69/A.

3. Winston Churchill to Hubert Pierlot, February 21, 1941, TNA PREM 3/69/A.

4. Pascal Deloge, "Belgian Military Plans for the Post-War Period," in *Europe in Exile: European Exile Communities in Britain, 1940–1945*, ed. Martin Conway and José Gotovitch (New York: Berghann, 2001), 99.

5. O. Sargent, comments, February 23, 1943, TNA FO 371/36 874.

6. David F. Ellwood, *Italy 1943–1945* (Leicester, U.K.: Leicester University Press, 1985), 9.

7. Norman Kogan, *Italy and the Allies* (Cambridge, Mass.: Harvard University Press, 1956), 175.

8. Rex Leeper, "Never Again," February 3, 1942, TNA FO 898/11.

9. From Neville Bland to Anthony Eden, August 20, 1943, TNA FO 371/34 532.

10. N. David J. Barnouw, "Dutch Exiles in London," in *Europe in Exile: European Exile Communities in Britain, 1940–1945*, ed. Martin Conway and José Gotovitch (New York: Berghann, 2001), 230.

11. H. Somerville-Smith to D. Morton, August 30, 1941, FO 371/28 545.

12. Charles de Gaulle, *The Complete War Memoirs*, vol. 2: *Unity*, trans. J. Griffin and R. Howard, (New York: Simon and Schuster, 1967; 1st French ed. 1956), 341–42.

13. Charles de Gaulle, *The Complete War Memoirs*, vol. 1: *The Call to Honour*, trans. J. Griffin and R. Howard (New York: Simon and Schuster, 1967; 1st French ed. 1954), 164.

14. Paul-Henri Spaak, *The Continuing Battle: Memoirs of a European, 1936–1966*, trans. Henry Fox (London: Weidenfeld and Nicolson, 1971 [French ed. 1969]), 74.

15. Martin Conway, "Legacies of Exile: The Exile Governments in London during the Second World War and the Politics of Post-War Europe," in *Europe in Exile: European Exile Communities in Britain, 1940–1945*, ed. Martin Conway and José Gotovitch (New York: Berghann, 2001), 259.

16. De Gaulle, *The Call to Honour*, 244.

17. Maurice J. Buckmaster, *Specially Employed: The Story of British Aid to French Patriots of the Resistance* (London: Batchworth, 1952), 61.

18. De Gaulle, *The Call to Honour*, 276.

19. Robert Hamilton Bruce Lockhart, *Comes the Reckoning* (London: Putnam, 1947), 182.

20. Bradley F. Smith, *The Shadow Warriors: OSS and the Origins of CIA* (London: Andre Deutsche, 1983), 215.

21. Bruce Lockhart, *Comes the Reckoning*, 215.

22. Bruce Lockhart, *Comes the Reckoning*, 164.

23. Kenneth Young, ed., *The Diaries of Sir Robert Bruce Lockhart* (London: Macmillan, 1980), entry of December 29, 1940, 87.

24. Young, ed., *The Diaries of Sir Robert Bruce Lockhart*, entry of May 31, 1943, 238.

25. From Dewitt Poole to William Donovan, April 6, 1943, NARA MI 1642/reel 112.

26. D. Bowes Lyon to R. Bruce Lockhart, January 13, 1943, TNA FO 898/102.

27. Bruce Lockhart, *Comes the Reckoning*, 291–92.

28. Smith, *The Shadow Warriors*, 333.

29. Smith, *The Shadow Warriors*, 361.

30. Basil Davidson, *Special Operations Europe: Scenes from the Anti-Nazi War* (Newton Abbot, U.K.: Readers Union, 1981 [1980]), 71.

31. Minutes of a meeting held between representatives of SO2 and SO What (undated), TNA HS8/383.

32. From Selborne to Eden, March 6, 1944, TNA FO 898/41.

33. From I. Kirkpatrick to R. H. Bruce Lockhart, April 17, 1944, TNA FO 898/41.

34. From R. H. Bruce Lockhart to O. Sargent, April 8, 1944, TNA FO 898/41.

35. N. Newsome, "General Directive," April 30, 1944, TNA FO 898/41.

36. B. Bracken to R. H. Bruce Lockhart, May 2, 1944, TNA FO 898/41.

37. R. H. Bruce Lockhart to B. Bracken, May 4, 1944, TNA FO 898/41.

38. Richard Harris Smith, *OSS: The Secret History of America's First Central Intelligence Agency* (Berkeley: University of California Press, 1972), 19.

39. "Evaluation of SOE Activities in Denmark," n.d., TNA HS7/110.

40. TMT (?), Propaganda in Denmark, January 11, 1941, TNA FO 898/245.

41. PWE Holland, "Basic Regional Considerations Regarding the Application of Political Warfare to Holland," November 11, 1941, TNA FO 898/234.

42. From Press Reading Bureau, Stockholm, to PID, March 2, 1942, TNA FO 371/31 029.

43. SOE Norwegian Section, History, 1940–1945, n.d., TNA HS 7/174.

44. OWI (?), "Draft Plan for Dion Phase in Norway," January 4, 1944, TNA FO 898/381.

45. Ministry of Information, Italian section, September 20, 1940, TNA FO 898/161.

46. Policy and Planning Committee, "Draft for Booklet on Italy," April 24, 1943, TNA FO 898/304.

47. Lord Selborne, "SOE Assistance to Overlord, October 1944," TNA HS 8/300.

48. SOE Norwegian Section, History, 1940–1945, n.d., TNA HS 7/174.

49. SOE, "Home and Overseas Establishment as of 29 May 1944: Personnel Employed by SOE," TNA HS 8/382.

50. X, War Diary, R&A Branch, OSS London, February 1, 1946, NARA MC 1623/reel 3.

51. Washington Office Report, "OSS Order of Battle," August 31, 1943, NARA RG 226/E 99/box 109.

52. Washington Office Report, "OSS Order of Battle."

53. SOE, "1940–1945 Statistics for 1940–1945 UK and Mediterranean," n.d., TNA HS 8/382.

54. SOE, "Evaluation of SOE Operations in Holland," n.d., TNA HS 8/419.

55. Charles Cruickshank, *SOE in Scandinavia* (Oxford: Oxford University Press, 1986), 278.

56. Security Executive, "Suspected Fifth Column Activities among Frenchmen in the UK," November 24, 1941, TNA FO 371/28 368.

57. From Verena in Harsfall Home Office, to E. O. Coote, Foreign Office, November 2, 1943, FO 371/36 783.

58. Luis Angel Bernardo y Garcia and Matthew Buck, "Belgian Society in Exile: An Attempt at a Synthesis," in *Europe in Exile: European Exile Communities in Britain, 1940–1945*, ed. Martin Conway and José Gotovitch (New York: Berghann, 2001), 55.

59. SOE, "Brief History of SOE," n.d., TNA HS 7/1.

60. G. Edward Brixton, "Memorandum for the Joint Staff Planners," June 29, 1943, NARA MI 1642/reel 6.

61. Robert Hayden Alcorn, *No Bugles for Spies: Tales of the OSS* (New York: David McKay, 1962), 80.

62. Michael R. D. Foot, *An Outline History of the Special Operations Executive, 1940–1946* (London: Bodley Head, 2014 [1984]), 57–58.

63. Nancy Wake, *The Autobiography of the Woman the Gestapo Called the White Mouse* (Melbourne: Macmillan Australia, 1985), 4.

64. Noreen Riols, *The Secret Ministry of Ag. and Fish: My Life in Churchill's School of Spies* (London: Macmillan, 2013), 73.

65. SOE Norwegian Section, History 1940–1945, n.d., TNA HS 7/174.

66. "Brief History of SOE," n.d., TNA HS 7/1.

67. Michael R. D. Foot, *SOE in France: An Account of the Work of the British Special Operations Executive in France, 1940–1944* (London: Her Majesty's Stationery Office, 1966), 54.

68. Jacques R. E. Poirier, *La girafe a un long cou* (Paris: Éditions du Félin, 2003), 83.

69. Poirier, *La girafe a un long cou*, 84.

70. Bickham Sweet-Escott, *Baker Street Irregulars* (London: Methuen, 1965), 37.

71. Poirier, *La girafe a un long cou*, 89.

72. Alcorn, *No Bugles for Spies*, 1–2.

73. Riols, *The Secret Ministry of Ag. and Fish*, 75–76.

74. SO Branch, Air Operations, vol. 6, n.d., NARA RG 226 MC 1623/reel 9.

75. Lieutenant-Colonel Sylvester Missal to the director of OSS, May 31, 1944, NARA MI 1642/reel 113.

76. SOE, "Evaluation of SOE Activities in France," TNA HS 7/135.

77. "Activity Report of 1st Lieutenant Maurice R. Basset (Ludovic), Beggar Circuit," n.d., 1945, NARA MC 1623/reel 6.

78. Sweet-Escott, *Baker Street Irregulars*, 104.

79. Colonel Monro MacCloskey, to the general commander, "Standard Operations Procedure, Dropping of Agents B 24," April 14, 1945, NARA RG 226/E 190/box 94.

80. Colonel Monro MacCloskey, to the general commander, "Standard Operations Procedure."

81. SOE, "Report on Clandestine Activity in Holland," n.d., TNA HS 7/161.

82. SOE, "Evaluation of SOE Activities in France."

83. Michael R. D. Foot, *SOE in the Low Countries* (London: St. Ermin's, 2001), 108, 110.

84. Alcorn, *No Bugles for Spies*, 2.

85. X, "An Outline of SOE Activity in Italy (1941–1945)," TNA HS 7/58.

86. Foot, *SOE in France*, 158–59.

87. Secret, unsigned, September 30, 1943, TNA FO 898/76.

88. Edward H. Cookridge, *They Came from the Sky* (London: Heinemann, 1965), 217–18.

89. R 2073, "Post-Day Psychiatric Work," May 11, 1944, TNA HS 8/299.

90. Harold Macmillan, *The Blast of War, 1939–1945* (London: Macmillan, 1967), 507.

91. Bruce Lockhart, *Comes the Reckoning*, 241.

92. SO Branch, Air Operations, vol. 6, n.d., NARA RG 226 MC 1623/reel 9.

93. Young, ed., *The Diaries of Sir Robert Bruce Lockhart*, entry of December 4, 1941, 130.

94. Alcorn, *No Bugles for Spies*, vii.

14. Minor Maneuvers, Major Policies

1. From Duff Cooper to Anthony Eden, "Free Italy Committee," January 15, 1941, TNA FO 371/29 935.

2. From General Wilson to General Marshall, SHAEF et al., February 19, 1944, TNA PREM 3/243/8.

3. Norman Kogan, *Italy and the Allies* (Cambridge: Mass.: Harvard University Press, 1956), 172.

4. Major Buckmaster, Major Neame, Squadron Leader Sprinks, meeting, July 22, 1942, TNA FO 898/26.

5. Jean-Pierre Azéma, "L'énigme Darlan," *L'Histoire* (September 2012): 57–59.

6. Jean-Louis Crémieux-Brilhac, *La France libre. De l'appel du 18 juin à la libération* (Paris: Gallimard, 1996), 443, 436.

7. From L. Collier to A. Eden, May 6, 1943, TNA FO 371/36 888.

8. Lord Selborne to Eden, November 20, 1942, quoted in Michael R. D. Foot, *SOE in France: An Account of the Work of the British Special Operations Executive in France, 1940–1944* (London: Her Majesty's Stationery Office, 1966), 221.

9. Robert Hamilton Bruce Lockhart, *Comes the Reckoning* (London: Putnam, 1947), 217.

10. Azéma, "L'énigme Darlan," 59.

11. Jacques Cantier, *L'Algérie sous le régime de Vichy* (Paris: Odile Jacob, 2002), 376.

12. Quoted in Crémieux-Brilhac, *La France libre*, 455.

13. Harold Macmillan, *The Blast of War* (London: Macmillan, 1967), 396.

14. Henri-Honoré Giraud, *Un seul but, la victoire, Alger, 1942–1944* (Paris: Julliard, 1949), quoted in Cantier, *L'Algérie sous le régime de Vichy*, 378.

15. Cantier, *L'Algérie sous le régime de Vichy*, 378–79.

16. Crémieux-Brilhac, *La France libre*, 460.

17. H. G. Wells, "The Truth about de Gaulle," n.d. (probably second half of 1942), NARA RG 226/E 190/box 230.

18. Llewellyn Woodward, *British Policy in the Second World War,* vol. 2 (London: Her Majesty's Stationery Office, 1971), 82.

19. Bruce Lockhart, note, January 8, 1942, TNA FO 898/13.

20. Macmillan, *The Blast of War*, 396.

21. W. Churchill, speech of December 10, 1942, quoted in Winton Churchill, *The Power of Words: His Remarkable Life Recounted Through His Writings and Speeches*, ed. Martin Gilbert (London: Bantam, 2012), 323–24.

22. Crémieux-Brilhac, *La France libre*, 438.

23. From Winston Churchill to Anthony Eden, May 21, 1943, TNA PREM 3/184/9.

24. W. Donovan, "Memorandum for the President," April 17, 1942, NARA MI 1642/reel 23.

25. Dewitt Poole, Foreign Nationalities Branch, note, January 13, 1943, NARA MI 1642/reel 15.

26. Crémieux-Brilhac, *La France libre*, 460–62.

27. Crémieux-Brilhac, *La France libre*, 434–35.

28. "11th Meeting for the Danish Interdepartmental Committee," August 21, 1941, TNA FO 371/29 302.

29. PWE, note, August 10, 1942, TNA FO 898/245.

30. From Mallet to Eden, December 16, 1942, TNA FO 371/32 760.

31. Comment of Warner, April 4, 1943, TNA FO 371/36 782.

32. British Embassy to the State Department, April 8, 1943, quoted in *Foreign Relations of the United States: Diplomatic Papers, 1943*, vol. 2: *Europe* (Washington, D.C.: Government Printing Office, 1964), 6–7.

33. C. Hull to Kauffmann, April 14, 1941, quoted in *Foreign Relations of the United States: Diplomatic Papers, 1943*, 2:51.

34. C. Møller, "Report on Mr. Christmas Møller's Visit to the USA," December 31, 1942, TNA FO 371/36 782.

35. A. Berle, State Department to all diplomatic and consular officers in the other American republics, Canada, Egypt, Algeria, and England, March 23, 1943, NARA RG 59/ entry 2599A/box 265.

36. From the State Department to the British Embassy in Washington, "Aide-mémoire," October 1, 1943, in *Foreign Relations of the United States: Diplomatic Papers, 1943*, 2:21.

37. R. Gallop, comments, April 5, 1944, TNA FO 371/43 108.

38. Foreign Office to Washington, December 1, 1941, TNA FO 371/29 327.

39. M. Warner, note, December 24, 1941, TNA FO 371/29 327.

40. SO London Report no. 669, December 29, 1942, TNA FO 371/36 780.

41. From R. Campbell to the Foreign Office, September 4, 1943, TNA FO 371/36 780.

42. From the FO to the British Embassy in Washington, September 14, 1943, TNA FO 898/245.

43. From the director of the Northern Region to M. Scarlett, September 11, 1943, TNA FO 898/245.

44. Hans Kirchoff, "Denmark," in *Resistance in Western Europe*, ed. Bob Moore (Oxford: Berg, 2000), 102.

45. From David Stephens to T. Barman, February 4, 1942, TNA FO 898/240.

46. C. Warner, Comments, April 4, 1943, TNA FO 371/36 782.

47. Ward to Peake, December 28, 1943, TNA FO 371/35 223.

48. T. Barman, "Propaganda to Denmark," March 15, 1941, TNA FO 371/29 276.

49. T. Barman, "Directive for Danish BBC Broadcast June 18th June 24th 1941," TNA FO 371/29 276.

50. PWE, note, August 10, 1942, TNA FO 898/245.

51. Brinley Thomas, director for the Nordic countries, "Political Warfare to Denmark: The Next Phase," May 12, 1943, TNA FO 371/36 789.

52. "Meeting of the Danish Committee," October 6, 1942, TNA HS 2/79.

53. Ulrich Herbert, *Werner Best: Un nazi de l'ombre*, trans. Dominique Viollet (Paris: Tallandier, 2010; German ed. 2006), 326.

54. R. A. Gallop, "Political Review of Denmark for 1942," January 25, 1943, TNA FO 371/36 787.

55. Nathaniel Hong, *Sparks of Resistance: The Illegal Press in German-Occupied Denmark, April 1940–August 1943* (Odense: Odense University Press, 1996), 46.

56. PID, Northern Region, note, March 12, 1943, TNA FO 371/36 788.

57. Herbert, *Werner Best*, 340.

58. From Mallet to Eden, November 21, 1942, TNA FO 371/32 760.

59. PWE, "Northern Intelligence Review no. 1, Denmark for Week Ending 2nd September 1943," n.d., TNA FO 371/36 790.

60. Hong, *Sparks of Resistance*, 49.

61. Hong, *Sparks of Resistance*, 49–50.

62. Jørgen Hæstrup, *Secret Alliance: A Study of the Danish Resistance Movement, 1940–45*, trans. Alison Borch-Johansen (Odense: Odense University Press, 1976–1977), 1:235.

63. Hæstrup, *Secret Alliance*, 1:238, 175.

64. Knud J. V., Jespersen, *No Small Achievement: Special Operations Executive and the Danish Resistance, 1940–1945* (Odense: University Press of Southern Denmark, 2002), 191.

65. "Report on Meeting Held at FO 9th July 1943 to discuss the Intensification of Resistance to the Enemy in Denmark," TNA HS 2/43.

66. Jespersen, *No Small Achievement*, 211.

67. Jespersen, *No Small Achievement*, 211.

68. Hæstrup, *Secret Alliance*, 1:241, 254.

69. Niels Wium Olesen, "The Obsession with Sovereignty: Cohabitation and Resistance in Denmark, 1940–45," in *Hitler's Scandinavian Legacy*, ed. John Gilmour and Jill Stephenson (London: Bloomsbury, 2013), 66.

70. Hong, *Sparks of Resistance*, p. 51.

71. Jeremy Bennet, *British Broadcasting and the Danish Resistance Movement, 1940–1945: A Study of the Wartime Broadcasts of the BBC Danish Service* (Cambridge: Cambridge University Press, 1966), 80.

72. Hæstrup, *Secret Alliance*, 1:173.

73. Bennet, *British Broadcasting and the Danish Resistance Movement*, 80.

74. Jørgen Hæstrup, *Le mouvement de la résistance danoise*, trans. Françoise Schade-Poulsen (Copenhagen: Direction Générale de Presse et d'Information du Ministère Danois des Affaires Étrangères, 1970), 30.

75. Wium Olesen, "The Obsession with Sovereignty," 49.

76. Herbert, *Werner Best*, 352.

77. X (?), "The Resistance Movement in Denmark," December 1943, TNA HS 2/91.

78. R. Turnbull, "Recent Events in Denmark," September 21, 1943, TNA HS 2/23.

79. Bannock (SOE Stockholm), report, September 15, 1943, TNA HS 2/23.

80. R. Turnbull, "Recent Events in Denmark."

81. Karen Gram-Skjoldager, "The Law of the Jungle? Denmark's International Legal Status During the Second World War," *International History Review* 33, no. 2 (2011): 235–56.

82. From Eden to Selborne, January 14, 1944, TNA HS 2/43.

15. Italian Complexities

1. Renzo de Felice, *Le Fascisme, un totalitarisme à l'italienne* (Paris: Presses de Sciences Po, 1988; Italian ed. 1981), esp. 210ff.

2. Pierre Milza, *Mussolini* (Paris: Fayard, 1999), 826–35.

3. Milza, *Mussolini*, 818–25.

4. MCA Foster, note, October 28, 1941, TNA FO 371/29 931.

5. SOE to the chief of staff, January 7, 1943, TNA FO 371/37 260A.

6. Foreign Office, "Internal Situation in Italy," March 8, 1943, TNA FO 371/37 260A.

7. From Eden to Churchill, February 17, 1943, TNA PREM 3/242/9.

8. X (Lieutenant-Colonel Keswick?), "An Outline History of SOE Activity in Italy (1941–1945)," 1945, TNA HS 7/58.

9. F.W.D. Deakin, "SO and the Italian Resistance," n.d. (after 1980), TNA HS 7/59.

10. Foreign Office, note of January 7, 1943, TNA FO 371/37 260 A.

11. Roberto Battaglia, *The Story of the Italian Resistance* (London: Odhams, 1958; Italian ed. 1953), 43.

12. Llewellyn Woodward, *British Foreign Policy in the Second World War* (London: Her Majesty's Stationery Office, 1970–1971), 2:463.

13. David W. Ellwood, *Italy 1943–1945* (Leicester, U.K.: Leicester University Press, 1985), 36.

14. Tom Behan, *The Italian Resistance: Fascists, Guerillas and the Allies* (London: Pluto, 2009), 29.

15. Norman Kogan, *Italy and the Allies* (Cambridge: Mass.: Harvard University Press, 1956), 38, 39.

16. Henri Michel, *La Seconde Guerre mondiale* (Paris: Omnibus, 2001 [1969]), 554.

17. Behan, *The Italian Resistance*, 29.

18. Frédéric Le Moal, *Victor-Emmanuel III. Un roi face à Mussolini* (Paris: Perrin, 2015), 459, 444, 457.

19. Kogan, *Italy and the Allies*, 47.

20. Ellwood, *Italy 1943–1945*, 40.

21. Moscow Conference, Three Power Declaration, November 1, 1943, TNA PREM 3/243/8.

22. Ellwood, *Italy 1943–1945*, 7.

23. Ellwood, *Italy 1943–1945*, 52.

24. P. Dixon (FO), "Policy Towards Italy," March 6, 1943, TNA FO 371/37 260A.

25. PWE, "Special Directive on Assault on Sicily," July 10, 1943, BBC WAC E 2/128/2.

26. PWE, "Central Directive (Week Beginning 16th September 1943)," September 15, 1943, BBC WAC E 2/128/2.

27. Kogan, *Italy and the Allies*, 43.

28. R. Law, "Advantages Gained by the United Nations from the Co-Belligerent Status of Italy," October 15, 1943, TNA PREM 3/243/8.

29. Kogan, *Italy and the Allies*, 44.

30. Ellwood, *Italy 1943–1945*, 43, 2.

31. From Macmillan to FO, transmitted to Churchill, November 3, 1943, TNA PREM 3/243/8.

32. Kogan, *Italy and the Allies*, 62.

33 From W. Churchill to F. Roosevelt, February 13, 1944, TNA FO 371/43 909.

34. Harold Macmillan, *The Blast of War, 1939–1945* (London: Macmillan, 1967), 476.

35. Claudio Pavone, *A Civil War: A History of the Italian Resistance* (London: Verso, 2013; Italian ed. 1991), 54.

36. PWE, "Central Directive (Week Beginning 30th September 1943)," September 29, 1943, BBC WAC E 2/128/2.

37. Michel, *La Seconde Guerre mondiale*, 545–46.

38. Gladwyn Jebb to David Scott, March 7, 1942, TNA FO 371/33 222.

39. A. Eden to I. Thomas, February 26, 1943, TNA FO 371/37 256.

40. Macmillan, *The Blast of War*, 501.

41. Ellwood, *Italy 1943–1945*, 50.
42. A. Eden to W. Churchill, January 25, 1944, TNA PREM 3/241/7.
43. From Churchill to Macmillan, March 18, 1944, TNA PREM 3/248/8.
44. D. Laskey, Comments, October 19, 1943, TNA FO 371/37 310.
45. "Terms of Restoration of Italian Territory," n.d., TNA PREM 3/243/8.
46. P. J. Dixon (Southern Department, FO), "Control Commission and Arrangements in Italy," September 29, 1943, TNA FO 371/37 309.
47. Ellwood, *Italy 1943–1945*, 74.
48. Behan, *The Italian Resistance*, 52.
49. B. Croce, speech of Bari, January 28, 1944, quoted in Kogan, *Italy and the Allies*, 50.
50. From Croce to Lipman, November 18, 1943, TNA FO 371/37 258.
51. Ellwood, *Italy 1943–1945*, 73.
52. Kogan, *Italy and the Allies*, 53.
53. Le Moal, *Victor-Emmanuel III*, 474.
54. PWE, "Central Directive (Week Beginning 16th September 1943)," September 15, 1943, BBC WAC E 2/128/2.
55. From the resident minister to the Foreign Office, October 31, 1943, TNA FO 371/37 312.
56. H. Macmillan, note, February 7, 1944, TNA FO 371/43 909.
57. From the resident minister to the Foreign Office, October 31, 1943.
58. From Maitland Wilson to the Allied chiefs of staff, February 29, 1944, TNA FO 31/43 910.
59. Kogan, *Italy and the Allies*, 56–57.
60. H. Macmillan to W. Churchill, "Note on the Italian Situation," March 21, 1944, TNA PREM 3/248/8.
61. From H. Macmillan to the Foreign Office, March 26, 1944, TNA FO 371/43 910.
62. Kogan, *Italy and the Allies*, 59.
63. Foreign Office to Macmillan, March 7, 1944, TNA PREM 3/243/8.
64. Macmillan, *The Blast of War*, 490.
65. N. MacFarlane, "The Political Situation in Italy," February 11, 1944, TNA PREM 3/243/8.
66. H. Macmillan to W. Churchill, "Note on the Italian Situation," March 21, 1944.
67. MacFarlane, "The Political Situation in Italy," February 11, 1944.
68. Le Moal, *Victor-Emmanuel III*, 476.
69. From Noel Charles to the Foreign Office, April 11, 1944, TNA FO 371/43 910.
70. Le Moal, *Victor-Emmanuel III*, 477.
71. W. Churchill to F. Roosevelt, March 15, 1944, TNA PREM 3/243/8.
72. C. Hull to Algiers and London, March 25, 1944, NARA RG 59/E 2599 A/box 288.
73. W. Churchill to F. Roosevelt, telegram of March 8, 1944, quoted in W. Churchill to General Wilson, March 15, 1944, TNA PREM 3/248/8.
74. From W. Churchill to F. Roosevelt, February 13, 1944, TNA FO 371/43 909.
75. W. Churchill to F. Roosevelt, telegram of March 8, 1944.
76. From Noel Charles to the Foreign Office, May 5, 1944, TNA FO 371/43 911.
77. Orme Sargent, Comments, May 11, 1944, TNA FO 371/43 911.

16. Planning for Liberation

1. PWE, "Weekly Directive for Dutch Talks," December 23, 1943, BBC WAC R 34/644.
2. HQs Files, "Industrial Sabotage," n.d., TNA HS 8/415.
3. SOE, "Sabotage, Guerrilla, Clandestine and Other Activities in 1943," n.d., transmitted on January 11, 1943, TNA PREM 3/408/4.
4. Sébastien Albertelli, *Les Services secrets du général de Gaulle. Le BCRA 1940–1944* (Paris: Perrin, 2009), 453–54.
5. SOE, "SOE in Europe," May 1946, TNA HS 7/1.
6. SOE, "Sabotage, Guerilla, Clandestine and Other Activities in 1943."
7. SOE Danish Section, report, n.d., TNA HS 7/282.
8. Low Country Section, report, n.d., TNA HS 7/275.
9. SOE Norwegian Section, "History 1940–1945," TNA HS 7/174.
10. SOE Council, "Minutes of a Meeting Held on November 16th 1943," TNA HS 8/200.
11. SOE, "Sabotage, Guerilla, Clandestine and Other Activities in 1943."
12. Sébastien Albertelli, *Histoire du sabotage. De la CGT à la Résistance* (Paris: Perrin, 2016), 241.
13. From V/CD (H. Sporborg) to SO (OSS), May 8, 1944, TNA HS 8/278.
14. David Stafford, *Mission Accomplished: SOE and Italy, 1943–1945* (London: Bodley Head, 2011), 2–4.
15. SOE Cabinet Papers, Italy, n.d. (no doubt 1945), TNA HS 8/242.
16. Bradley F. Smith, *The Shadow Warriors: OSS and the Origins of CIA* (London: Andre Deutsche, 1983), 229.
17. Smith, *The Shadow Warriors*, 231, 233.
18. Peter Wilkinson and Joan Bright Astley, *Gubbins and SOE* (Barnsley, U.K.: Pen and Sword, 2010 [1993]), 152.
19. Bickham Sweet-Escott, *Baker Street Irregulars* (London: Methuen, 1965), 159.
20. David W. Ellwood, *Italy 1943–1945* (Leicester, U.K.: Leicester University Press, 1985), 76.
21. Roberto Battaglia, *The Story of the Italian Resistance*, trans. P. D. Cummins (London: Odhams, 1958; Italian ed. 1953), 92.
22. David Stafford, *Britain and European Resistance, 1940–1945: A Survey of the Special Operations Executive* (London: Macmillan, 1980), 192.
23. Stafford, *Mission Accomplished*, 23.
24. Stafford, *Mission Accomplished*, 101.
25. Battaglia, *The Story of the Italian Resistance*, 84.
26. Tom Behan, *The Italian Resistance: Fascists, Guerillas and the Allies* (London: Pluto, 2009), 1.
27. Stafford, *Mission Accomplished*, 117, 105–6, 119–20.
28. On this episode, cf. Gabriella Gribaudi, "Naples 1943. Espaces urbains et insurrection," *Annales. Histoire, Sciences sociales* 5 (2003): 1079–1104.
29. On this point, cf. Alessandro Portelli, *L'ordine è già stato eseguito. Roma, le Fosse Ardeatine, la memoria* (Rome: Donzelli, 1999).
30. Stafford, *Mission Accomplished*, 119–20.
31. Arthur Funk, "Les Américains et les Britanniques dans la libération de la Corse," *Guerres mondiales et conflits contemporains* 174 (1994): 12.

32. SOE, "Report on Corsica Campaign," n.d. (January 1944), TNA HS 7/168.

33. Selborne, "SOE Assistance to Overlord," October 1944, TNA HS 8/300.

34. SOE, "Report on Corsica Campaign."

35. SOE, "Report on Corsica Campaign."

36. SOE, "Report on Corsica Campaign."

37. SOE, "Report on Corsica Campaign."

38. Major C. S. Coon, "OSS Activities in Corsica. September 12th to October 5th 1943," n.d. (late 1943), NARA MC 1642/reel 80.

39. Lieutenant S. P. Karlow, OSS, "Notes on Corsica," November 15, 1943, NARA MC 1642/reel 80.

40. Coon, "OSS Activities in Corsica. September 12th to October 5th 1943."

41. Karlow, "Notes on Corsica," November 15, 1943.

42. Smith, *The Shadow Warriors*, 232.

43. Karlow, "Notes on Corsica," November 15, 1943.

44. SOE, "Report on Corsica Campaign," n.d. (January 1944).

45. SOE, "Report on Corsica Campaign," n.d. (January 1944).

17. Plans and Instructions

1. PWE, "Special Directives on Operation Against Western Europe," June 6, 1944, BBC WAC E 2/137.

2. From D/RP to RF/P, February 10, 1944, TNA HS 8/287.

3. Claudius/Tybalt FIL Mission, June 29, 1943, TNA FO 898/79.

4. Joint SOE/PWE, "Survey of Resistance in Occupied Europe," April 1, 1943, TNA WO 898/97.

5. E. Mockler-Ferryman to G3 SHAEF, "Preservation of Railway Engineering Work," April 19, 1944, TNA HS 8/289.

6. From T to D/RP, Port Counter-Scorching, Belgium, December 27, 1943, TNA HS8/289.

7. Charles de Gaulle, speech of April 18, 1942, *DM*, 182.

8. Philippe Buton, *Les lendemains qui déchantent. Le Parti communiste français à la Libération* (Paris: Presses de Sciences Po, 1993), 99.

9. José Gotovitch, *Du rouge au tricolore. Les Communistes belges de 1939 à 1944, un aspect de l'histoire de la Résistance en Belgique* (Brussels: Labor, 1992), 389.

10. "Proposal for Joint PWE and SOE Action in Support of a Military Invasion of Occupied Europe," n.d. (late 1943?), TNA FO 898/376.

11. SHAEF, Political Warfare Division, "Psychological Warfare Working Plan for Occupied Countries in Support of Overlord," April 24, 1944, TNA FO 898/382.

12. "Proposal for Joint PWE and SOE Action in Support of a Military Invasion of Occupied Europe."

13. SHAEF, "Resistance by the General Public in France," April 29, 1944, NARA RG 331/entry 2/box 109.

14. From H. Pierlot to Lord Selborne, March 14, 1944, TNA HS 8/933.

15. Jérôme, "Rapport sur l'opportunité d'un appel à l'insurrection générale en France au jour 'J,'" n.d., spring 1944, TNA HS 8/287.
16. From Lord Selborne, March 14, 1944, TNA HS 8/933.
17. "Proposal for Joint PWE and SOE Action in Support of a Military Invasion of Occupied Europe."
18. SHAEF, "Resistance by the General Public in France," April 29, 1944.
19. General F. Morgan, Operation Overlord, report and evaluation, July 15, 1943, NARA RG 331/E 35/B226.
20. War Diary, Special Operations Branch, March 1945, NARA MC 1623/reel 6.
21. W. Langer to W. Donovan, November 3, 1943, NARA MC 1642/reel 80.
22. First Lieutenant R. Crosby to Colonel Eddy, "Report on Activities with British SOE Group," March 15, 1944, NARA RG 226/entry 90/box 90.
23. Colonel J. Haskell, SO Branch, "Request for Additional American Aircraft for the Purpose of Arming Resistance Groups in Support of Operation Overlord," February 22, 1944, NARA MC1642/reel 104.
24. SOE, "OSS/SOE Activities from Mediterranean Bases Into Central and Eastern Europe," April 13, 1944, TNA HS 8/2.
25. From J. Haskell to W. Donovan, March 4, 1944, NARA MC 1642/reel 104.
26. From Bowes Lyon to R. Bruce Lockhart, January 13, 1943, TNA FO 898/102.
27. W. Shepardson to W. Donovan, October 8, 1943, NARA MC 1642/reel 80.
28. From Major Maddox to Lieutenant-Colonel D. Bruce, SI Branch, "Monthly Report," July 15, 1943, NARA RG 226 E 99/box 1.
29. Bradley F. Smith, *The Shadow Warriors: OSS and the Origins of CIA* (London: Andre Deutsche, 1983), 250.
30. From W. Donovan to D. Bruce, April 13, 1943, NARA RG 226/entry 90/box 231.
31. Henri Frenay, *The Night Will End*, trans. Dan Hofstadter (London: Abelard, 1976; French ed. 1973), 256.
32. Daniel Cordier, *Jean Moulin. La République des Catacombes* (Paris: Gallimard, 1999), 351.
33. Robert Belot and Gilles Karpman, *L'Affaire suisse. La Résistance a-t-elle trahi de Gaulle? (1943–1944)* (Paris: Armand Colin, 2009), 153–60.
34. Daniel Cordier, *Jean Moulin. L'inconnu du Panthéon*, vol. 1: *Une ambition pour la République* (Paris: JC Lattès, 1989), 214.
35. Jean Moulin, letter to General de Gaulle, May 7, 1943, quoted in Belot and Karpman, *L'Affaire suisse*, 130.
36. "Note on a Meeting Held on July 26th 1942," TNA HS 8/199.
37. OSS Historical Reports, "Description of Operations Carried Out by National Sections of SI/ETO until the End of 1944," NARA MC 1623/reel 5.
38. OSS Historical Reports, "Description of Operations."
39. From OSS-London (D. Bruce?) to W. Shepardson (Washington), May 5, 1943, NARA RG 226/entry 90/box 232.
40. From CD (C. Hambro) to D. Bruce, May 19, 1943, NARA RG 226/entry 190/box 230.
41. From CD (C. Hambro) to D. Bruce, May 19, 1943, TNA HS 8/9.
42. OSS Historical Reports, "Description of Operations Carried Out by National Sections of SI/ETO until the End of 1944," NARA MC 1623/reel 5.

43. From Maddox to Passy, July 22, 1943, NARA RG 226/entry 190/box 320.

44. Belot and Karpman, *L'Affaire suisse*, 161, 168.

45. OSS, War Diary, Special Operations Branch, London, "Planning," February 1945, NARA MC 1623/reel 6.

46. Belot and Karpman, *L'Affaire suisse*, 201.

47. Robert Belot, *Henri Frenay. De la Résistance à l'Europe* (Paris: Seuil, 2003), 394.

48. OSS, War Diary, Special Operations Branch, London, "Planning," February 1945.

49. OSS Historical Reports. "Description of Operations Carried Out by National Sections of SI/ETO until the End of 1944," NARA MC 1623/reel 5.

50. SOE Norwegian Section, report, n.d., TNA HS 7/174.

51. General H. Bull, "SHAEF Order," January 31, 1944, NARA RG 226/entry 190/box 211.

52. OSS, War Diary, Special Operations Branch, London, March 1945, NARA MC 1623/reel 6.

53. OSS, War Diary, Special Operations Branch, London, "Planning," February 1945.

54. From C. Hoffman to W. Carey, June 1, 1944, NARA RG 226/entry 99/box 112.

55. OSS, War Diary, Special Operations Branch, London, March 1945.

56. Jean-Lous Crémieux-Brilhac, *La France libre. De l'appel du 18 juin à la libération* (Paris: Gallimard, 1996), 862–63.

57. R. Smith, "The Present Position and Future Prospect of MO Branch-London," May 1944, NARA RG 226/entry 190/box 230.

58. From SD (Hollingworth) to Golsen and Tolstrup, August 1, 1944, TNA HS 2/93.

59. SOE, "History of the Danish Section," n.d., TNA HS 7/109.

60. X to Gort, December 27, 1944, NARA RG 226/entry 190/box 283.

61. SOE Belgian section, general report, n.d., TNA HS 7/242.

62. Sébastien Albertelli, *Les Services secrets du général de Gaulle. Le BCRA 1940–1944* (Paris: Perrin, 2009), 340.

63. SOE, Memorandum no. 1, October 23, 1943, quoted in Albertelli, *Les Services secrets*, 340.

64. Philippe André, "Les ambassadeurs de Londres. Les délégués militaires régionaux (DMR) du général de Gaulle. Septembre 1943–septembre 1944," Master's thesis, Paris-I, 2011, 5, 6.

65. André, "Les ambassadeurs de Londres," 432, 249.

66. M. Chevance-Bertin, "Note relative au plan de mise en oeuvre des FFL Observations," May 20, 1944, quoted in André, "Les ambassadeurs de Londres," 259.

67. OSS, War Diary, Special Operations Branch, London, "Planning," February 1945.

68. From AD/E (E. Mockler-Ferryman) to all members of the HQ of SOE/SO, April 20, 1944, TNA HS 8/296.

69. Albertelli, *Les Services secrets*, 330.

70. OSS, War Diary, Special Operations Branch, London, "Planning," February 1945.

71. X, report, 1945?, HS 7/124.

72. SOE, "History of the Danish Section"; and SOE, "Sabotage, Guerilla, Clandestine and Other Activities in 1943," n.d., transmitted January 11, 1944, TNA PREM 3/408/4.

73. From ADE/SAC to AD/ME, May 25, 1944, TNA HS 8/290.

74. SHAEF, Political Warfare Division, "Psychological Warfare Working Plan for Occupied Countries in Support of Overlord."

75. From ADE/SAC to AD/ME, May 25, 1944.

76. From Mockler-Ferryman to G3, SHAEF, February 4, 1944, TNA HS 2/91.

77. O. Arthur Brown and Marianne Walle, "Les Jedburghs: Un coup de maître ou une occasion manquée?" *Guerres mondiales et conflits contemporains* 174 (April 1994): 128.

78. SOE, "History of Jedburghs in Europe," n.d. (undoubtedly 1945), TNA HS 7/17.

79. SOE, "History of Jedburghs in Europe," n.d. (undoubtedly 1945).

80. Douglas C. Waller, *Disciples: The World War II Missions of the CIA Directors Who Fought for Wild Bill Donovan* (New York: Simon and Schuster, 2015), 173.

81. OSS, War Diary, Special Operations Branch, London, "Planning," February 1945.

82. OSS, European Theater of Operations, "Report for the Month of January 1944," NARA RG 226/entry 99/box 21.

83. From ADE/SAC to AD/ME, May 25, 1944.

84. SOE, "History of Jedburghs in Europe," n.d. (undoubtedly 1945).

85. Stewart Alsop and Thomas Braden, "Operation Jedburgh," in their *Sub Rosa: The OSS and American Espionage* (New York: Reynal & Hitchcock, 1946; reprinted New York: Open Road Media, 2016), n.p.

86. AD/E/203, "Jedburghs," December 20, 1943, TNA HS 8/288.

87. X, "Employment of Operational Groups in the European Theater of Operations," June 6, 1944, NARA RG 226/entry 190/box 231.

88. PWE, "Weekly Directive for BBC Belgian Talks," March 9, 1944, BBC WAC R 34/644.

89. PWE, "Directive for BBC French Services," January 23, 1944, BBC WAC R 34/654/3.

90. X, report, 1945? TNA HS 7/124.

91. From B. Bracken to Lord Selborne, March 1, 1944, TNA FO 898/24.

92. R. Calder to the assistant to the director general, "Draft Minutes on Use of BBC European Service for SOE Messages," March 9, 1944, TNA FO 898/24.

93. PSE/SOE Co-ordinating Committee, May 5, 1944, TNA FO 898/25.

94. From H. Sporborg to I. Kirkpatrick, April 3, 1944, TNA HS 7 287.

18. Political Liberation

1. Alban Vistel, *La nuit sans ombre. Histoire des mouvements unis de résistance, leur rôle dans la libération du Sud-Est* (Paris: Fayard, 1970), 81.

2. Jørgen Hæstrup, *Secret Alliance: A Study of the Danish Resistance Movement, 1940–45,* trans. Alison Borch-Johansen (Odense: Odense University Press, 1976–1977), 2:42–44, 54.

3. Niels Wium Olesen, "Change or Continuity in the Danish Elites? Social Movements and the Transition from War to Peace in Denmark, 1945–1947" (forthcoming), 6.

4. Hæstrup, *Secret Alliance,* 2:159.

5. Hæstrup, *Secret Alliance,* 2:170ff, 194–95.

6. From SD (Hollingworth) to the Council of Freedom, June 16, 1944, TNA HS 2/92.

7. Hæstrup, *Secret Alliance*, 2:224.

8. R. Turnbull, March 31, 1944, TNA HS 2/24.

9. From M. Fog to C. Møller, August 19, 1944, TNA FO 371/43 102.

10. Hæstrup, *Secret Alliance*, 2:343.

11. X, "Review of Events in Denmark June–July 1944," n.d., TNA HS 2/24.

12. Hæstrup, *Secret Alliance*, 2:339–43, 27.

13. PID, Northern Region, "Propaganda note 12. Denmark's Council of Freedom," November 19, 1943, TNA FO 371/36 792.

14. Clarke, "Comments," n.d. (April or May 1944), TNA FO 371/43 095.

15. Knud J. V. Jespersen, *No Small Achievement: Special Operations Executive and the Danish Resistance, 1940–1945* (Odense: University Press of Southern Denmark, 2002), 225.

16. Hæstrup, *Secret Alliance*, 3:26.

17. Hæstrup, *Secret Alliance*, 3:132.

18. Niels Wium Olesen, "The Obsession with Sovereignty: Cohabitation and Resistance in Denmark, 1940–45," in *Hitler's Scandinavian Legacy*, ed. John Gilmour and Jill Stephenson (London: Bloomsbury, 2013), 67.

19. Hæstrup, *Secret Alliance*, 3:91–95.

20. From Lieutenant-Colonel Wilson to A.A.F. Haig (FO), September 19, 1944, TNA FO 371/43 102.

21. C. Warner, note, November 2, 1944, TNA FO 371/43 102.

22. Hæstrup, *Secret Alliance*, 3:266.

23. Hæstrup, *Secret Alliance*, 3:289, 349–50.

24. Wium Olesen, "The Obsession with Sovereignty," 67.

25. R. A. Gallop, "Political Review of Denmark in 1943," January 15, 1944, TNA HS 2/24.

26. Hæstrup, *Secret Alliance*, 3:330.

27. From E. Foss to C. Møller, May 1, 1944, TNA FO 371/32 095.

28. From Turnbull to the Northern Department of the Foreign Office, April 27, 1944, TNA FO 371/43 095. Same observation in PID Northern Region Intelligence, "Northern Region Intelligence Review no. 72 Denmark for Week Ending 2nd March 1944," TNA FO 898/38.

29. Jespersen, *No Small Achievement*, 375.

30. Charles de Gaulle, *The Complete War Memoirs*, vol. 2: *Unity*, trans. J. Griffin and R. Howard (New York: Simon and Schuster, 1967; 1st French ed. 1956), 417.

31. E. d'Astier de la Vigerie, Memorandum, April 1943, quoted in Jean-Pierre Azéma, *Jean Moulin. Le rebelle, le patriote, le résistant* (Paris: Perrin, 2003), 331.

32. Claude Bourdet, *L'aventure incertaine. De la Résistance à la Restauration* (Paris: Stock, 1975), 216–17.

33. Jean de Vogüé, plan for June 28, 1943, quoted in Olivier Wieviorka, *Une certaine idée de la Résistance. Défense de la France (1940–1949)* (Paris: Le Seuil, 1995), 235–36.

34. Appeal to the Nation, August 2, 1943, quoted in Daniel Cordier, *Jean Moulin, l'inconnu du Panthéon*, vol. 1: *Une ambition pour la République* (Paris: JC Lattès, 1989), 270.

35. A. Cadogan, note, January 8, 1945, TNA PREM 3/241/7.

36. H. L. d'A. Hopkinson, "Draft Statement Prepared for the Chief Commissioner," December 18, 1944, TNA WO 204/9810.

37. David W. Ellwood, *Italy 1943–1945* (Leicester, U.K.: Leicester University Press, 1985), 162.

38. "Report from Lt-Cl. C. L. Roseberry on the CLNAI," October 31, 1944, TNA FO 371/43 878.

39. Major Biago M. Corvo, "What Can Be Gained by Our Recognition of CLNAI?" n.d. (November 1944?) NARA RG 226, entry 190/box 92.

40. "Notes on a Meeting with Major General Stawell and Commander Holdsworth, Commanding Officer no. 1 Special Force," November 18, 1944, TNA WO 204/9810.

41. Sacmed, Political Commission, November 22, 1944, quoted in Harry L. Coles and Albert K. Weinberg, *Civil Affairs: Soldiers Become Governors* (Washington, D.C.: Office of the Chief of Military History, 1964), 540.

42. Orme Sargent, Comments, November 27, 1944, TNA FO 371/43 878.

43. From the Foreign Office to the resident minister in Caserta, November 28, 1944, TNA FO 371/43 878.

44. Quoted in F.W.D. Deakin, "SOE and the Italian Resistance (1941–1945)," n.d., TNA HS 7/59.

45. Memorandum of Agreement between the Supreme Allied Commander Mediterranean Theater of Operations and the CLNAI, n.d. (December 7, 1944), TNA WO 204/9810.

46. Coles and Weinberg, *Civil Affairs*, 541.

47. Colonel J. H. Lascelles, note, December 27, 1944, TNA WO 204/9810.

48. B. Pleydell-Bouverie, "CLNAI Finance," March 15, 1945, NARA RG 226/entry 99/box 33.

49. From L. Collier to A. Eden, July 27, 1943, TNA FO 371/36 891.

50. Report of Scipio, February 28, 1944, quoted in SOE Belgian section, report, n.d., TNA HS 7/243.

51. Peter Romijn, "Liberators and Patriots: Military Interim Rule and the Politics of Transition in the Netherlands, 1944–1945," in *Seeking Peace in the Wake of War: Europe, 1943–1947*, ed. Stefan-Ludwig Hoffmann, Sandrine Kott, Peter Romijn, and Olivier Wieviorka (Amsterdam: Amsterdam University Press, 2015), 124.

52. Letter from General W. Bedell Smith to Prince Bernhard, August 31, 1944, quoted in SOE, general report, n.d., TNA HS 7/275.

53. From London to Rummy, September 1, 1944, quoted in SOE, general report, n.d., TNA HS 7/275.

54. Ward, "Norway and the Norwegian Government," December 28, 1943, TNA FO 371/36 891.

55. Telegram from the Belgian government to Hector, January 31, 1944, quoted in Ganshof, note for Captain Aronstein, February 17, 1944, TNA FO 898/79.

56. Louis de Jong, *The Netherlands and Nazi Germany* (Cambridge, Mass.: Harvard University Press, 1990), 69, 70.

57. PWE Intelligence series, "Evolution in the Aims of Resistance Movements," n.d. (1944), TNA FO 898/39.

58. H. Pierlot, speech of July 21, 1943, TNA FO 371/34 321.

59. P. Gerbrandy, speech of December 8, 1943, TNA FO 371/34 525.

60. Dirk Luyten, "Social Security and the End of the Second World War in France, the Netherlands and Belgium," in *Seeking Peace in the Wake of War*, ed. Stefan-Ludwig Hoffmann, Sandrine Kott, Peter Romijn, and Olivier Wieviorka (Amsterdam: Amsterdam University Press, 2015), 260–61.

61. Martin Conway, *The Sorrows of Belgium: Liberation and Political Reconstruction, 1944–1947* (Oxford: Oxford University Press, 2012), 25.

62. C. de Gaulle, speech in Algiers, July 14, 1943, *DM*, 311–12.

63. Diane de Bellefroid, "The CEPAG," in *Europe in Exile: European Exile Communities in Britain, 1940–1945*, ed. Martin Conway and José Gotovitch (New York: Berghann, 2001), 128.

64. De Bellefroid, "The CEPAG," 129.

65. Thierry Grosbois, *Pierlot. 1930–1950* (Brussels: Racine, 2007), 231.

66. Tybalt report, December 23, 1943, TNA FO 898/80.

67. Belgian Section, report, n.d., TNA HS 7/242.

68. Joint Intelligence Subcommittee, "French Resistance," April 19, 1944, NARA RG 331/entry 2/box 109.

69. Lieutenant L. Fossel to Major W. Maddox, January 19, 1944, NARA RG 226/entry 190/box 303.

70. Mauro Scoccimarro, December 20, 1943, quoted in Claudio Pavone, *A Civil War: A History of the Italian Resistance*, trans. Peter Levy with the assistance of David Broder (London: Verso, 2013; Italian ed. 1991), 431.

71. From D/S to A/CD, "Communists in Denmark," April 27, 1944, TNA HS 2/41.

72. From L/IS to A/CD, "Communist Activities in Denmark," October 30, 1943, TNA HS 2/42.

73. Wium Olesen, "Change or Continuity in the Danish Elites?" 7.

74. Wium Olesen, "Change or Continuity in the Danish Elites?" 9.

75. Lieutenant L. Fossel to Major W. Maddox, January 19, 1944.

76. PWE, "The Norwegian Clandestine Press," note, n.d. (about February 1945), TNA FO 898/244.

77. The L/IS to A/CD, "Communist Activities in Denmark," October 30, 1943, TNA HS 2/42.

78. SOE Norwegian section, report, n.d., TNA HS 7/174.

79. From Noel Charles to the Foreign Office, April 19, 1944, TNA FO 371/43 911.

80. Foreign Office to the High Commissioner, June 2, 1944, TNA PREM 3/243/15.

81. W. Donovan, "Memorandum for the President," October 23, 1944, NARA MC 1642/reel 24.

82. Special Force no. 1 to AFHQ, report of January 1945, quoted in Ellwood, *Italy 1943–1945*, 176.

83. Ellwood, *Italy 1943–1945*, 177.

84. Lt-Cl R. T. Hewitt, HQ no. 1 Special Force to the G3, 15th AG, January 15, 1945, NARA RG 226/entry 190/box 131.

85. From J. G. Ward (FO) to C. Kerr (Moscow), September 19, 1943, TNA FO 371/25 218.

86. J. G. Ward (FO), "Title of Temporary Allied Military Administration to Be Set Up in Friendly Liberated Territory by Combined Anglo-American Operations," September 20, 1943, TNA FO 371/35.

87. Foreign Office, "Civil Administration of Friendly European Territory Liberated by Allied Expeditionary Forces," August 12, 1943, FO 371/35 217.

88. From O. Sargent to A. Cadogan, August 20, 1943, TNA FO 371/25 217.

89. Foreign Office, "Civil Administration of Friendly European Territory."

90. J. G. Ward (FO), "Foreign Ministers' Conference," October 6, 1943, TNA FO 71/35 219.

91. Ward (FO), "Title of Temporary Allied Military Administration."

92. From Lieutenant-Colonel X (?), War Office, to J. G. Ward, FO, September 13, 1943, TNA FO 371/35 234.

93. J. G. Ward to S. W. Kirby, September 22, 1943, TNA FO 371/35 234.

94. PWE, "Working Plan in Belgium," March 31, 1944, TNA FO 898/238.

95. J. G. Ward, Comments, September 9, 1943, TNA FO 371/35 234.

96. "Memorandum of Agreement Regarding Civil Administration and Jurisdiction in Norwegian Territory Liberated by an Allied Expeditionary Force," May 16, 1944, TNA FO 898/241. The accords are also published in *Foreign Relations of the United States* (1944), vol. 3.

97. F.S.V. Donnison, *Civil Affairs and Military Government Central Organization and Planning* (London: Her Majesty's Stationery Office, 1966), 122.

98. Jespersen, *No Small Achievement*, 397.

99. J. G. Ward, Comment on the Problem of Committee, December 11, 1943, TNA FO 371/35 221.

100. Jespersen, *No Small Achievement*, 399.

101. Hæstrup, *Secret Alliance*, 3:78–79.

102. R. Turnbull, Memorandum, n.d. (November 1944), TNA FO 371/43 101.

103. X, note, April 21, 1945, TNA HS 2/41.

104. R. Turnbull, Memorandum, n.d. (November 1944).

105. Jespersen, *No Small Achievement*, 401–2.

106. From B. Thomas and K. J. Varley to I. Kirkpatrick, May 26, 1944, TNA FO 898/245.

107. CCS to SCAEF, "Basic Civil Affairs Directive for Denmark," n.d. (June 1944), TNA FO 371/40 414.

108. Jespersen, *No Small Achievement*, 423.

109. Donnison, *Civil Affairs and Military Government Central Organization and Planning*, 122.

110. Jean-Baptiste Duroselle, *L'abîme, 1939–1945* (Paris: Imprimerie Nationale, 1982), 477–78.

111. "Draft Basic Scheme for Administration of Liberated France as Approved by President Roosevelt and Prime Minister Churchill," n.d., 1943, TNA FO 371/35 221.

112. W. Churchill to the secretary of foreign affairs, May 10, 1944, TNA CAB 101/244.

113. Quoted in François Lévêque, "Les relations franco-soviétiques pendant la Seconde Guerre mondiale. De la défaite à l'Alliance (1939–1945)," Ph.D. thesis, Paris-I, 1992, 909.

114. Foreign Office, "Civil Administration of Friendly European Territory Liberated by Allied Expeditionary Forces," August 12, 1943, TNA FO 371/35 217.

115. From Paniguian to Calder, May 30, 1944, TNA FO 898/379.

116. X, report, 1945? TNA HS 7/124.

117. From Bovenschen to O. Sargent, October 26, 1943, TNA FO 371/35 220.

118. J. G. Wood, Comments, n.d., TNA FO 371/35 220.

119. Comment of Gladwyn Jebb, TNA FO 371/35 220.

120. Cordell Hull, April 9, 1944, quoted in Olivier Wieviorka, *Normandy: The Landings to the Liberation of Paris*, trans. M. B. DeBevoise (Cambridge, Mass.: Belknap Press of Harvard University Press, 2008), 313.

121. SHAEF to the Supreme Allied Commander, Mediterranean Theater of Operations, May 14, 1944, quoted in Coles et Weinberg, *Civil Affairs*, 148.

122. U.S. Third Army, plan for G5, June 10, 1944, NARA RG 331/entry 35/box 228.

123. F. Roosevelt, Instructions of March 15, 1944, NARA RG 331/entry 12/box 108.

124. F. Roosevelt to D. Eisenhower, May 14, 1944, Eisenhower Library Pre-Presidential Papers/box 133.

125. SHAEF, Psychological Warfare Division, "Guidance for PWD staff in the Field Covering Attitudes and Actions with Respect to the French," May 29, 1944, TNA FO 898/379.

126. SOE Council, "Minutes of a Meeting Held on June 2nd 1944," TNA HS 8/201.

19. Action!

1. Lord Selborne, "SOE Assistance to Overlord," October 1944, TNA HS 8/300.

2. Michael R. D. Foot, *SOE in France: An Account of the Work of the British Special Operations Executive in France, 1940–1944* (London: Her Majesty's Stationery Office, 1966), 388.

3. SOE, "Summary for the PM, April to June 1944," n.d., TNA HS 8/250.

4. SHAEF, "The Value of SOE Operations in the Supreme Commander's Sphere," July 13, 1945, TNA HS 8/378.

5. X, "French Resistance," March 24, 1945, NARA RG 226/entry 190/box 283.

6. "French Resistance, Railway Sabotage," March 24, 1945, TNA HS 7/125.

7. SOE Evaluations, "French Resistance. Delays to German Build-up in the Northern Battle Area from 6 June 1944," n.d., TNA HS 8/423.

8. "Activity Report of 1st Lieutenant Maurice R. Basset (Ludovic), Beggar Circuit," n.d., 1945, NARA MC 1623/reel 6.

9. W. Donovan, "Memorandum for the President," April 6, 1945, NARA MC 1642/reel 25.

10. SI Branch, OSS London, "War Diary. Report Division," n.d. (July 1945?), NARA MC 1623/reel 5.

11. X, "Tenth Monthly Progress Report to SHAEF from SFHQ London. June 1944," June 20, 1944, NARA RG 266/entry 190/box 132.

12. SI Branch, OSS London, "War Diary. Report Division," n.d. (July 1945?), NARA MC 1623/reel 5.

13. National general staff of the FFI, "6e synthèse," August 12, 1944, TNA CAB 106/989.
14. G3, report on the resistance operations in Brittany, no. 6, August 8–9, 1944, NARA RG 331/entry 30/box 145.
15. From D. Morton to the prime minister, June 17, 1944, TNA PREM 3/185/1.
16. X, "Tenth Monthly Progress Report to SHAEF from SFHQ London. June 1944," June 20, 1944.
17. SOE, general report on France, n.d., TNA HS 7/18.
18. "La résistance française pendant les dix premiers jours des opérations en Normandie," undated, unsigned report, NARA OSS MI 1642/reel 103.
19. "SOE in Europe, Prepared for VCSS Lecture," May 1946, TNA HS 7/1.
20. Eberhard Jäckel, La France dans l'Europe de Hitler, trans. Denise Meunier (Paris: Fayard, 1968; German ed. 1966), 460.
21. SHAEF, "The Value of SOE Operations in the Supreme Commander's Sphere," July 13, 1945.
22. X, "French Resistance," March 24, 1945.
23. SHAEF, "The Value of SOE Operations in the Supreme Commander's Sphere," July 13, 1945.
24. Sébastien Albertelli, "Les services secrets de la France libre. Le Bureau Central de Renseignement et d'Action," Ph.D. thesis, Institut d'Études Politiques-Paris, 2006, 498.
25. Major Richard Crosby to Colonel Edward W. Gamble for W. Donovan, "Report of OSS Activities with 7th Army," October 14, 1944, NARA MC 1642/reel 80.
26. Crosby to Gamble for Donovan, "Report of OSS Activities with 7th Army."
27. "Activity Report of 2nd Lieutenant Robert J. MacCarthy (Miguel) (Shipwright)," n.d., 1945, NARA MC 1623/reel 6.
28. Paddy Ashdown, The Cruel Victory: The French Resistance, D-Day and the Battle for the Vercors 1944 (London: William Collins, 2014), 158.
29. Charles de Gaulle, speech of June 6, 1944, DM, 407.
30. D. Eisenhower, speech of June 6, 1944, quoted in Ashdown, The Cruel Victory, 177–78.
31. Ashdown, The Cruel Victory, 179.
32. SFHQ, "10th Monthly Report to SHAEF," July 10, 1944, NARA RG 226/entry 99/box 23.
33. Eugène Martres, "Mont-Mouchet (maquis du)," in Dictionnaire de la Résistance, ed. François Marcot (Paris: Robert Laffont, 2006), 740.
34. "Activity Report of 1st Lieutenant René A. Dussaq (Anselme) (Freelance Circuit)," n.d., 1945, NARA MC 1623/reel 6.
35. Gilles Vergnon, Le Vercors. Histoire et mémoire d'un maquis (Paris: Éditions de l'Atelier, 2002), 90, 106.
36. Gilles Vergnon, "Vercors (maquis du)," in Dictionnaire de la Résistance, ed. François Marcot (Paris: Robert Laffont, 2006), 767.
37. Lieutenant-Colonel William P. Davis and Lieutenant-Colonel J. Anstey, "Semi-monthly Report," August 1, 1944, NARA RG 226/entry 190/box 133.

38. Henri Noguères, Marcel Degliame-Fouché, and Jean-Louis Vigier, *Histoire de la Résistance en France de 1940 à 1945* (Paris: Robert Laffont, 1967–1981), 5:124–25.

39. Commanding officers report, operational report, Company B., n.d., NARA RG 226/ entry 99/box 98.

40. SOE Evaluations, "French Resistance. Delays to German Build-up in the Northern Battle Area from 6 June 1944," supplement of March 24, 1945, TNA HS 8/423.

41. Henri Romans-Petit, *Les maquis de l'Ain* (Paris: Hachette, 1974), 138.

42. Captain Se. J. Passaseni, report for Major B. M. Corvo, "Patriot Situation. November 1–December 1 1944," n.d., NARA MC 1642/reel 60.

43. Commanding officers report, operational report, Company B, n.d., NARA RG 226/ entry 99/box 98.

44. Philippe Buton, "La France atomisée," in *La France des années noires*, ed. Jean-Pierre Azéma and François Bédarida, vol. 2: *De l'Occupation à la Libération* (Paris: Seuil, 1993), 429.

45. Quoted in Jean-Louis Crémieux-Brilhac, *La France libre. De l'appel du 18 juin à la libération* (Paris: Gallimard, 1996), 860.

46. Charles Tillon, *On chantait rouge. Mémoires pour l'histoire d'un ouvrier breton devenu révolutionnaire professionnel, chef de guerre et ministre* (Paris: Robert Laffont, 1977), 375.

47. OSS, War Diary, Special Operations Branch, vol. 2, Planning, February 1945, NARA MC 1623/reel 6.

48. R. 3205, "Report on Counter-Scorching—France and Belgium," n.d. (1944), TNA HS 8/416.

49. R. 3205, "Report on Counter-Scorching."

50. "Evaluation of SOE Activities in France," n.d., TNA HS 7/135.

51. "A Short Story of EMFFI," September 21, 1944, TNA HS 7/126.

52. SO Branch, Air operations, n.d., NARA MC 1623/reel 9.

53. "Evaluation of SOE Activities in France,"n.d., TNA HS 7/135.

54. "A Short Story of EMFFI."

55. From D. Morton to the prime minister, June 20, 1944, TNA PREM 3/185/1.

56. Ashdown, *The Cruel Victory*, 240.

57. Major Morton to Winston Churchill, report, June 20, 1944, TNA PREM 3/185/1.

58. Will Irwin, *The Jedburghs: The Secret History of the Secred Allied Forces, France 1944* (New York: Public Affairs, 2006), xvii.

59. Irwin, *The Jedburghs*, 139–40, 145–46.

60. Report of Hugh mission, quoted in Robert Frank, "Les missions interalliées et les enjeux de la lutte armée en France," in *Lutte armée et maquis*, ed. François Marcot (Besançon: Annales littéraires de l'université de Franche-Comté, 1996), 359–60.

61. Quoted in Philippe André, *La Résistance confisquée? Les Délégués militaires du général de Gaulle. De Londres à la Libération* (Paris: Perrin, 2013), 212.

62. O. Arthur Brown and Marianne Walle, "Les Jedburghs: Un coup de maître ou une occasion manquée?" *Guerres mondiales et conflits contemporains* 174 (April 1994): 137.

63. Maurice Kriegel-Valrimont, *La Libération. Les archives du COMAC (mai–août 1944)* (Paris: Éditions de Minuit, 1964), 16.

64. COMAC, order of operation, June [14] 1944, quoted in Kriegel-Valrimont, *La Libéra-tion*, 45–47.

65. Report of the telegrams received on May 11 from the civilian mission, London, quoted in Philippe André, "Les ambassadeurs de l'ombre. Les délégués militaires régionaux (DMR) du général de Gaulle. Septembre 1943–septembre 1944," Master's thesis (M2), Paris I, 2011, published as *La Résistance confisquée? Les Délégués militaires du général de Gaulle. De Londres à la Libération* (Paris: Perrin, 2013), 154.

66. Minutes of the session of June 26, 1944, quoted in André, *La Résistance confisquée?*, 205.

67. Accord of August 14, 1944, quoted in Kriegel-Valrimont, *La Libération*, 45–47.

68. COMAC, session of July 3, 1944, AN 72 AJ 3.

69. André, *La Résistance confisquée?*, 203–4.

70. Quoted in André, *La Résistance confisquée?*, 278.

71. Quoted in André, *La Résistance confisquée?*, 278–79.

72. André, *La Résistance confisquée?*, 280.

73. From D. Morton to the prime minister, June 17, 1944, TNA PREM 3/185/1.

74. "Résumé de l'entretien avec Chaban," telegram from the Ministry for the Interior (London) to the Ministry for the Interior (Algiers), August 11, 1944 (date of arrival), AN 72 AJ 1901.

75. Crémieux-Brilhac, *La France libre*, 873.

76. Colonel Rol-Tanguy and Roger Bourderon, *Libération de Paris. Les cent documents* (Paris: Hachette, 1994), 189, 186.

77. Quoted in Hans Umbreit, "La libération de Paris et la grande stratégic du IIIe Reich," in *Paris 1944. Les enjeux de la Libération*, ed. Christine Levisse-Touzé (Paris: Albin Michel, 1994), 102.

78. Rol-Tanguy and Bourderon, *Libération de Paris*, 222.

79. Rol-Tanguy and Bourderon, *Libération de Paris*, 229.

80. Charles de Gaulle, speech of August 25, 1944, quoted in Michael Neiberg, *The Blood of Free Men: The Liberation of Paris 1944* (New York, Basic Books, 2012), 237.

81. Charles de Gaulle, *The Complete War Memoirs*, vol. 2: *Unity*, trans. J. Griffin and R. Howard (New York: Simon and Schuster, 1967; 1st French ed. 1956), 654.3.

82. Olivier Wieviorka, "La résistance intérieure et la libération de Paris," in *Paris 1944. Les enjeux de la Libération*, ed. C. Levisse-Touzé (Paris: Albin Michel, 1994), 146.

83. Quoted in Rol-Tanguy and Bourderon, *La Libération de Paris*, 158a.

84. Rol-Tanguy, directive of August 24, 1944, SHD 13 P 42.

85. Jean-Louis Crémieux-Brilhac, "Ici Londres, l'arme radiophonique," in *Paris 1944. Les enjeux de la Libération*, ed. C. Levisse-Touzé (Paris: Albin Michel, 1994), 161.

86. Quoted in John Keegan, *Six Armies in Normandy: From D-Day to the Liberation of Paris* (London: Penguin, 1994 [1982]), 306.

87. Georges Boris, telegram to d'Astier, August 11, 1944, AN F1A 3717.

88. "Idées sur le soulèvement national à Paris," August 14, 1944, AN 72 AJ 1901.

89. The sources disagree. In his "Le général de Gaulle et la libération de Paris," in *Paris 1944. Les enjeux de la Libération*, ed. C. Levisse-Touzé (Paris: Albin Michel, 1994), p. 171, André Martel reports 130 dead for the Second Armored Division, 1,000 dead for the

FFI (included those who were executed), and 582 dead among civilians; the Fondation Charles-de-Gaulle counts 76 dead for the Second Armored Division and 901 in the ranks of the FFI, figures comparable to those given by the Fondation de la France Libre.

20. Peripheries

1. Henri Bernard, *L'Armée secrète 1940–1944* (Gembloux, Belgium: Duculot, 1986), 77.
2. From Colonel Haskell to General J.F.M. Whiteley, "Action Messages to Belgian Resistance Groups," June 9, 1944, TNA HS 8/293.
3. Emmanuel Debruyne, *La guerre secrète des espions belges, 1940–1944* (Brussels: Racine, 2008), 73.
4. SOE, T Section history, Report, June 14, 1945, TNA HS 7/100.
5. "Review of SOE Activity for August 1944," n.d., TNA HS 8/246.
6. "Note on the Assistance Given to the 21st AG by the Forces of the Belgian Armée Secrète," May 1946, TNA HS 7/1.
7. OSS Special Operations Branch, London, "War Diary. Western Europe," vol. 3, 1945, NARA MC 1623/reel 6.
8. Bernard, *L'Armée secrète*, 82.
9. Bernard, *L'Armée secrète*, 82.
10. MUS/1602/224, "Preservation of the Port of Antwerp," December 10, 1944, TNA HS 8/416.
11. SFHQ, "Monthly Report to SHAEF for September 1944," October 10, 1944, NARA RG 226/entry 99/box 23.
12. W. Donovan, "Memorandum for the President," October 1944, NARA MC 1642/reel 24.
13. SFHQ, "Monthly Report to SHAEF for September 1944."
14. Anthony Beevor, *The Second World War*, audiobook (Solon, Ohio: Findaway World, 2010), n.p.
15. PWE, "Weekly Directive for BBC Dutch Talks, 9–15th June 1944," June 8, 1944, TNA FO 371/39 328.
16. D. van Galen Last, "The Netherlands," in *Resistance in Western Europe*, ed. Bob Moore (Oxford: Berg, 2000), 190.
17. Supreme commander, Appeal, September 17, 1944, TNA FO 371/39 328.
18. "Summary for the Prime Minister, October to December 1944," January 9, 1945, TNA HS 8/250.
19. SOE, "Evaluation of SOE Operations in Holland," n.d., TNA HS 8/419.
20. SOE, Holland general report, TNA HS 7/275.
21. SFHQ, "Monthly Report to SHAEF for September 1944."
22. H. Paape, "How Dutch Resistance Was Organized," in *Holland at War Against Hitler: Anglo Dutch Relations, 1940–1945*, ed. Michael R. D. Foot (London: Frank Cass, 1990), 82–83.
23. SOE, "Evaluation of SOE Operations in Holland."

24. Review of SOE activities for period April 1945, TNA HS 8/247.

25. W.H.A. Bishop to Air Marshall Peck, March 23, 1945, TNA FO 898/383.

26. PID Northern Region Intelligence, "Northern Region Intelligence Review no. 79 for Week Ending March 2, 1945," n.d., TNA FO 898/38.

27. Charles Cruickshank, *SOE in Scandinavia* (Oxford: Oxford University Press, 1986), 230.

28. From Colonel J. H. Aims to SHAEF G3, April 16, 1945, NARA RG 226/entry 190/box 283.

29. G. Edward Buxton, "Memorandum for the President, June 1945," NARA MC 1642/reel 25.

30. Hans Kirchoff, "Denmark," in *Resistance in Western Europe*, ed. Bob Moore (Oxford: Berg, 2000), 108.

31. G. Edward Buxton, May 16, 1945, NARA MC 1642/reel 80.

32. OSS Headquarters ETO, "Report on Railway Sabotage in the Oslo Fjord Area 14–15 March 1945," March 26, 1945, NARA MC 1642/reel 80.

33. Christopher Mann, *British Policy and Strategy Towards Norway, 1941–45* (London: Palgrave Macmillan, 2012), 192.

34. SOE, History of the Danish Section, 1945, TNA HS 7/109.

35. SOE, Report, n.d., TNA HS 7/175.

36. Norwegian High Command, supplement to Milorg Survey per 15th March 1945, TNA HS 7/180.

37. SOE, Report, n.d., TNA HS 7/175.

38. OSS Special Operations Branch, London, "War Diary. Western Europe," vol. 3, 1945, NARA MC 1623/reel 6.

39. SOE, "The History of the Danish Country Section," n.d. (1945), TNA HS 7/109.

40. Jens C. Hauge, *The Liberation of Norway* (Oslo: Gylendal Norsk Forlag, 1995; Norwegian ed. 1950), 23.

41. From FO to Washington, September 15, 1944, TNA FO 371/43 232.

42. From General Andrew Thorne to Brinley Thomas, October 8, 1944, TNA FO 898/243.

43. SOE Norwegian Section, History, 1940–1945 (undated), TNA HS 7/174.

44. Cruickshank, *SOE in Scandinavia*, 241.

45. SOE Norwegian Section, History, 1940–1945.

46. Mann, *British Policy and Strategy Towards Norway*, 179.

47. Basil Henry Liddell Hart, *The History of the Second World War* (New York: Putnam, 1970), 539 40, 542.

48. X, "An Outline of SOE Activity in Italy (1941–1945)," 1945, TNA HS 7/58.

49. "Review of SOE Activity for August 1944," n.d., TNA HS 8/246.

50. X, "An Outline of SOE Activity in Italy (1941–1945)."

51. Major C. Martin Wood to Assistant Chief of Staff, G3, AFHQ, November 23, 1944, NARA RG 226/entry 190/box 91.

52. Tom Behan, *The Italian Resistance: Fascists, Guerillas, and the Allies* (London: Pluto, 2009), 1.

53. Gifford M. Proctor, "Bi-Weekly Report, 15–30 September 1944," October 1, 1944, NARA RG 226/entry 190/box 110.

54. Major Arthur R. Borden, "Semi-monthly Report 1–15 March," March 18, 1945, NARA RG 226/entry 190/box 108.

55. SOE Cabinet Papers Italy, n.d. (after April 1945), TNA HS 8/242.

56. Lieutenant-Colonel J. M. Stevens, "Report on Conditions in Piedmont, Period 18 November–4 March 1945," n.d., NARA RG 226/entry 190/box 131.

57. Captain A. Clarke, Report, 1945, TNA HS 7/63.

58. Claudio Pavone, *A Civil War: A History of the Italian Resistance*, trans. Peter Levy with the assistance of David Broder (London: Verso, 2013; Italian ed. 1991), 520–21.

59. David Stafford, *Mission Accomplished: SOE and Italy, 1943–1945* (London: Bodley Head, 2011), 225.

60. "Air Operations to Northern Italy from January to April 45," TNA HS 7/60.

61. First Lieutenant Jack Daniels, "Semi-monthly Report on MO Operations 16 April–2 May 1945," NARA RG 226/entry 190/box 108.

62. Captain Se. J. Passaseni, report for Major B. M. Corvo, "Patriot Situation. November 1–December 1 1944," NARA MC 1642/reel 60.

63. General Ismay to W. Churchill, November 7, 1944, TNA PREM 3/408/3.

64. Stafford, *Mission Accomplished*, 225.

65. Captain A. Clark, Report, 1945, TNA HS 7/63.

66. Captain A. Clark, Report, 1945, TNA HS 7/63.

67. X, "An Outline of SOE Activity in Italy (1941–1945)," 1945, TNA HS 7/58.

68. Bradley F. Smith, *The Shadow Warriors: OSS and the Origins of CIA* (London: Andre Deutsche, 1983), 305.

69. Lord Selborne to W. Churchill, October 24, 1944, TNA PREM 3/408/3.

70. Lord Selborne to W. Churchill, October 25, 1944, TNA PREM 3/408/3.

71. Quoted in Stafford, *Mission Accomplished*, 232.

72. Major William G. Suhling to the Commanding Officer, 2677th Regiment, March 29, 1945, NARA RG 226/entry 190/box 91.

73. Lieutenant-Colonel Stuart Hughes to Colonel Glavin, April 7, 1945, NARA RG 226/entry 190/box 91.

74. X, "Notes Taken at Meeting on Supplies to Partisans in North Italy Held at HQs 6th Army Group," January 17, 1945, NARA RG 226/entry 190/box 111.

75. Colonel H. H. Oster to the Allied Forces HQs, March 24, 1945, NARA RG 226/entry 190/box 112.

76. Stafford, *Mission Accomplished*, 227.

77. SOE Cabinet Papers Italy, n.d. (after April 1945), TNA HS 8/242.

78. Behan, *The Italian Resistance*, 210.

79. Stafford, *Mission Accomplished*, 183–93.

80. Pavone, *A Civil War*, 240–41.

81. X, "An Outline of SOE Activity in Italy" (1941–1945), 1945, TNA HS 7/58.

82. Lieutenant-Colonel J. G. Beevor to G3, January 26, 1945, NARA RG 226/entry 190/box 131.

83. "Report on no. 1 Special Forces Activities During April 1945," June 3, 1945, NARA MC 1642/reel 59.

84. MAAF Plan section, "The Italian Resistance Movement in Relation to Allied Air Aid," January 23, 1945, NARA RG 226/entry 190/box 131.

85. David W. Ellwood, *Italy 1943–1945* (Leicester, U.K.: Leicester University Press, 1985), 152.

86. Behan, *The Italian Resistance*, 101.

87. Behan, *The Italian Resistance*, 104–5.

88. Roberto Battaglia, *The Story of the Italian Resistance*, trans. P. D. Cummins (London: Odhams, 1958; Italian ed. 1953), 256.

89. Lieutenant-Colonel Hewitt, "Report on Special Forces Activities During April 1945," 1945, TNA HS 7/60.

90. "Report on no. 1 Special Forces Activities During April 1945."

21. Order or Chaos?

1. Georges-Henri Soutou, *La Guerre de cinquante ans. Les relations Est-Ouest, 1943–1990* (Paris: Fayard, 2001), 62.

2. Philippe Buton, *Les lendemains qui déchantent. Le Parti communiste français à la Libération* (Paris: Presses de Sciences Po, 1993), 13.

3. Soutou, *La Guerre de cinquante ans*, 62.

4. Quoted in François Kersaudy, *Churchill and de Gaulle* (London: Collins, 1981), 336, translation slightly revised by Malcolm DeBevoise.

5. Charles de Gaulle, *The Complete War Memoirs*, vol. 2: *Unity* 3, trans. J. Griffin and R. Howard (New York: Simon and Schuster, 1967; 1st French ed. 1956), 559.

6. De Gaulle, *Unity*, 560.

7. Kenneth Young, ed., *The Diaries of Sir Robert Bruce Lockhart*, vol. 2: *1939–1965* (London: Macmillan, 1980), entry of June 6, 1944, 2:319.

8. Robert Hamilton Bruce Lockhart, *Comes the Reckoning* (London: Putnam, 1947), 303–4.

9. De Gaulle, *Unity*, 560.

10. Winston Churchill to Franklin D. Roosevelt, June 8, 1944, TNA CAB 101/25.

11. De Gaulle, speech of June 6, 1944, *DM*, 1:407–8.

12. Bruce Lockhart, *Comes the Reckoning*, 304.

13. Winston Churchill to Franklin D. Roosevelt, June 9, 1944, TNA CAB 66/51.

14. Winston Churchill to the foreign secretary and the chancellor of the exchequer, June 9, 1944, TNA CAB 101/244.

15. Franklin D. Roosevelt to Winston Churchill, June 13, 1944, TNA CAB 66/51.

16. Winston Churchill to Franklin D. Roosevelt, June 10, 1944, TNA CAB 101/250.

17. Appended notes to the cabinet council, June 13, 1944, TNA CAB 65/46.

18. Winston Churchill to Franklin D. Roosevelt, June 21, 1944, TNA CAB 101/250.

19. Franklin D. Roosevelt to Winston Churchill, June 13, 1944.

20. Winston Churchill to General Montgomery, June 13, 1944, TNA CAB 120/867.

21. Captain de Pury, Report on Civil Affairs, Reconnaissance of the Area by the Second Army, June 19, 1944, NARA RG 331/entry 54/box 290.

22. General Montgomery to Winston Churchill, June 15, 1944, TNA CAB 120/867.

23. SCAO, letter to the DCCAO, June 16, 1944, NARA RG 331/entry 54/box 292.

24. General DCCAO (Civil Affairs), political developments in Normandy, June 19, 1944, NARA RG 331/entry 54/box 290.

25. Colonel Durbin, report on a trip to the field from July 1 to July 10, July 18, 1944, NARA RG 331/E 54/B 282.

26. Lieutenant-Colonel Copp, First U.S. Army, G2, *Special Intelligence Bulletin* 4 (July 10, 1944), NARA RG 331/entry 54/box 282.

27. Copp, *Special Intelligence Bulletin* 4.

28. Jean Quellien, "Les Normands au coeur de la guerre," in *Les populations civiles face au débarquement et à la bataille de Normandie*, ed. Bernard Garnier, Jean-Luc Leleu, Françoise Passera, and Jean Quellien (Caen: Mémorial de Caen, 2005), 16.

29. Henry Rousso, "L'épuration en France. Une histoire inachevée," in his *Vichy, l'événement, la mémoire, l'histoire* (Paris: Gallimard, 2001 [1992]), 543.

30. Political Warfare Division, Directive no. 3 (for the week beginning June 29, 1944), NARA RG 331/entry 3/box 51.

31. A. Eden, "Some Arguments in Favour of Recognition of FNCL as the PGFR," June 26, 1944, TNA FO 371/42 024.

32. Western European Section, SO Branch, July 7, 1944, NARA RG 226/entry 99/box 17.

33. Western European Section, SO Branch, July 7, 1944.

34. CA Liaison Officer, Sixth Army Group, report to Commanding Officer, 2678 CA Regiment, November 1, 1944, quoted in Harry L. Coles and Albert K. Weinberg, *Civil Affairs: Soldiers Become Governors* (Washington, D.C.: Office of the Chief of Military History, 1964), 765.

35. SHAEF Mission, G2 Division, "FFI and FTP Political Aspects," November 27, 1944, NARA RG 331/entry 2/box 110.

36. "Activity Report of 1st Lieutenant Maurice R. Basset (Ludovic), Beggar Circuit," n.d., 1945, NARA MC 1623/reel 6.

37. No doubt Marcel Bisault, who was given major responsibilities on the regional level. My thanks to Franck Liaigre and Gilbert Moreux for this detail.

38. Activity Report of 2nd Lieutenant Roger B. Henquet (Robert)," n.d., 1945, NARA MC 1623/reel 7.

39. Buton, *Les lendemains qui déchantent*, 106.

40. For a complete version, cf. Philippe Buton, "L'entretien entre Maurice Thorez et Joseph Staline du 19 novembre 1944," *Communisme* 45–46 (1996): 7ff.

41. SHAEF, Joint Intelligence Committee, "Political Developments in France and Belgium and Their Effect on Military Operations," January 1, 1945, NARA MC 1642/reel 15.

42. SHAEF, Joint Intelligence Committee, "Political Developments in France and Belgium," January 1, 1945.

43. Western European Section, SO Branch, July 7, 1944, NARA RG 226/entry 99/box 17.

44. De Gaulle, *Unity*, 562–63.

45. De Gaulle, *Unity*, 576.

46. Instructions retracing the main lines of the accords that went into effect on August 25, 1944, Ministry of Foreign Affairs, Political and commercial correspondence, PM/1466.

47. Jean-Pierre Rioux, *La France et la Quatrième République*, vol. 1: *L'Ardeur et la nécessité, 1944–1952* (Paris: Seuil, 1980), 73.

48. Dwight Eisenhower, *Crusade in Europe* (Garden City, N.Y.: Doubleday, 1948), 297–98.

49. D. Morton, "Conditions in France and Belgium," October 3, 1944, TNA CAB 66/56.

50. From SHAEF Forward to Agwar (General Marshall) for J. C. Dunn, September 13, 1944, NARA RG 331/entry 2/box 109.

51. X, "History of the Research and Analysis Branch in the OS. June 1941–September 1944," n.d., NARA RG 226/entry 99/box 98.

52. Luis Angel Bernardo y Garcia and Matthew Buck, "Belgian Society in Exile: An Attempt at a Synthesis," in *Europe in Exile: European Exile Communities in Britain, 1940–1945*, ed. Martin Conway and José Gotovitch (New York: Berghann, 2001), 61.

53. Paul-Henri Spaak, *The Continuing Battle: Memoirs of a European, 1936–1966*, trans. Henry Fox (London: Weidenfeld and Nicolson, 1971; French ed. 1969), 91.

54. Martin Conway, *The Sorrows of Belgium: Liberation and Political Reconstruction, 1944–1947* (Oxford: Oxford University Press, 2012), 63.

55. Conway, *The Sorrows of Belgium*, 43.

56. Léopold III, Testament, June 7, 1944, TNA PREM 3/69/B.

57. W. Churchill, October 4, 1944, TNA PREM 3/69/B.

58. Conway, *The Sorrows of Belgium*, 65.

59. FO to Brussels, June 18, 1945, TNA PREM 3/69/B.

60. Peter Schrijvers, *Liberators: The Allies and Belgian Society. 1944–1945* (Cambridge: Cambridge University Press, 2009), 101.

61. Conway, *The Sorrows of Belgium*, 50.

62. Schrijvers, *Liberators*, 73.

63. Conway, *The Sorrows of Belgium*, 90–91.

64. José Gotovitch, *Du rouge au tricolore. Les Communistes belges de 1939 à 1944, un aspect de l'histoire de la Résistance en Belgique* (Brussels: Labor, 1992), 409.

65. Conway, *The Sorrows of Belgium*, 63.

66. Spaak, *The Continuing Battle*, 91.

67. Conway, *The Sorrows of Belgium*, 89.

68. G. Erskine to F. Morgan, September 15, 1944, NARA RG 331/entry 1/box 41.

69. SFHQ, G3, "Periodic Report for 26 September 1944," NARA RG 226/entry 99/box 18.

70. Conway, *The Sorrows of Belgium*, 73, 74.

71. Conway, *The Sorrows of Belgium*, 95.

72. Conway, *The Sorrows of Belgium*, 106, 107, 108.

73. Pieter Lagrou, "Belgium," in *Resistance in Europe*, ed. Bob Moore (Oxford: Berg, 2000), 54.

74. Schrijvers, *Liberators*, 102.

75. Schrijvers, *Liberators*, 102.

76. SHAEF, "Directive to Commander in Chief, 21 AG, 12 AG, SHAEF Mission," November 18, 1944, quoted in Coles and Weinberg, *Civil Affairs*, p. 807.

77. SHAEF, Joint Intelligence Committee, "Political Developments in France and Belgium," January 1, 1945.

78. William Hitchcock, *The Bitter Road to Freedom: A New History of the Liberation of Europe* (New York: Free Press, 2008), 102, 103, 105, 106, 107.

79. From W. Churchill to Eden and Halifax, April 19, 1945, TNA PREM 3/221/12.

80. From SHAEF to Agwar (General Marshall), May 1, 1945, TNA PREM 3/221/12.

81. From P. Gerbrandy to W. Churchill, March 7, 1945, TNA PREM 3/221/12.

82. Peter Romijn, "Liberators and Patriots: Military Interim Rule and the Politics of Transition in the Netherlands," in *Seeking Peace in the Wake of War: Europe, 1943–1947,* ed. Stefan-Ludwig Hoffmann, Sandrine Kott, Peter Romijn, and Olivier Wieviorka (Amsterdam: Amsterdam University Press, 2015), 123.

83. From Duff Cooper, to FO, October 16, 1944, TNA FO 371/39 331.

84. From N. Bland to A. Eden, November 28, 1944, TNA FO 371/39 331.

85. Roberts (FO), note, September 18, 1944, TNA FO 371/39 351.

86. From N. Bland to A. Eden, November 25, 1944, TNA FO 371/39 351..

87. SHAEF, Joint Intelligence Committee, "Conditions in Holland and Their Effect on the Military Situation," March 20, 1945, NARA MI 142/reel 15.

88. Romijn, "Liberators and Patriots," 127, 129.

89. Romijn, "Liberators and Patriots," 140.

90. Romijn, "Liberators and Patriots," 129–32.

91. David W. Ellwood, *Italy 1943–1945* (Leicester, U.K.: Leicester University Press, 1985), 240.

92. CCS to Alexander, Directive, January 31, 1945, TNA PREM 3/241/7.

93. Coles and Weinberg, *Civil Affairs,* 493.

94. Directive from CCS to AFHQ, January 30, 1945, quoted in Coles and Weinberg, *Civil Affairs,* 515.

95. From J. M. Case Beale to Bromley (Treasury), October 21, 1944, TNA FO 371/43 914.

96. FO, "Handing over to the Italian Government of Further Territory," August 10, 1944, TNA FO 371/43 838.

97. Civil Affairs Report Italy no. 15, October 15, 1944, TNA FO 371/43 838.

98. From A. Cadogan to the British Embassy in Washington, draft, October 5, 1944, TNA FO 371/43 913.

99. From N. Charles to the Foreign Office, June 10, 1944, TNA PREM 3/243/12.

100. Actually Giovanni di Raimondo, in charge of the railroads.

101. N. Charles to the Foreign Office, June 22, 1944, TNA PREM 3/243/15.

102. From W. Churchill to N. Charles, June 10, 1944, TNA PREM 3/243/12.

103. From W. Churchill to A. Eden, June 14, 1944, TNA PREM 3/243/12.

104. Tom Behan, *The Italian Resistance: Fascists, Guerillas and the Allies* (London: Pluto, 2009), 113, 24–25.

105. Keith Lowe, *Savage Continent: Europe in the Aftermath of World War II* (New York: St. Martin's, 2012), 180.

106. Behan, *The Italian Resistance,* 109–10.

107. Coles and Weinberg, *Civil Affairs,* 479.

108. Lieutenant-Colonel R. T. Hewitt to G3, Fifteenth AG, January 15, 1945, NARA RG 226/entry 190/box 131.

109. From Bari to the Office of the Minister Resident, Caserta, November 17, 1944, TNA FO 371/43 878.
110. General A. M. Gruenther, "Support of Italian Resistance in North Italy," February 12, 1945, NARA RG 226/entry 190/box 131.
111. From J. (Lieutenant-Colonel Roseberry) to G. 400 (OSS), April 10, 1945, TNA HS 8/45
112. Behan, *The Italian Resistance*, 176.
113. Behan, *The Italian Resistance*, 176ff.
114. Behan, *The Italian Resistance*, 179–80.
115. David Stafford, *Mission Accomplished: SOE and Italy, 1943–1945* (London: Bodley Head, 2011), 212–13; Behan, *The Italian Resistance*, 180–89.
116. Sergeant Richard M. Isenberg to Major Vincent A. Abrigangi, December 17, 1944, NARA RG 226/entry 190/box 93.
117. Gustavo Corni, "Italy," in *Resistance in Western Europe*, ed. Bob Moore (Oxford: Berg, 2000),176.
118. Basil Davidson, *Special Operations Europe: Scenes from the Anti-Nazi War* (Newton Abbot, U.K.: Readers Union, 1981 [1980]), 152.
119. Mark Mazower, *Inside Hitler's Greece: The Experience of Occupation, 1941–44* (New Haven: Yale University Press, 1993), 265.
120. Georges Guingouin, *Quatre ans de lutte sur le sol limousin* (Limoges: Lucien Souny, 1991), 107.
121. Gilles Vergnon, *Le Vercors. Histoire et mémoire d'un maquis* (Paris: Éditions de l'Atelier, 2002), 98.
122. Guingouin, *Quatre ans de lutte*, 108.
123. Vergnon, *Le Vercors*, 98.
124. Vergnon, *Le Vercors*, 101.
125. Harold Macmillan, *The Blast of War, 1939–1945* (London: Macmillan, 1967), 677.
126. SOE Cabinet Papers, Italy, n.d. (after April 1945), TNA HS 8/242.
127. Behan, *The Italian Resistance*, 91.
128. Ellwood, *Italy 1943–1945*, 155–56.
129. G5, Fifth Army, "Report for April 1945," quoted in Coles and Weinberg, *Civil Affairs*, 560.
130. HQ Allied Commission, "Report for May 1945," quoted in Coles and Weinberg, *Civil Affairs*, 561.
131. Lowe, *Savage Continent*, 150.
132. Gabriella Gribaudi, Olivier Wieviorka, and Julie Le Gac, "Two Paths to the Same End? The Challenges of the Liberation in France and Italy," in *Seeking Peace in the Wake of War: Europe, 1943–1947*, ed. Stefan-Ludwig Hoffmann, Sandrine Kott, Peter Romijn, and Olivier Wieviorka (Amsterdam: Amsterdam University Press, 2015), 106–7.
133. Lowe, *Savage Continent*, 150.
134. Behan, *The Italian Resistance*, 75.
135. Behan, *The Italian Resistance*, 74.
136. Claudio Pavone, *A Civil War: A History of the Italian Resistance*, trans. Peter Levy with the assistance of David Broder (London: Verso, 2013; Italian ed. 1991), 484.
137. O. Sargent to Hollis (War Cabinet Office), December 22, 1944, TNA FO 371/43 254.

138. J. E. Galsworthy (FO), note, September 27, 1944, TNA FO 371/43 242.

139. Christopher Mann, *British Policy and Strategy Towards Norway* (London: Palgrave Macmillan, 2012), 225.

140. Mann, *British Policy and Strategy Towards Norway*, 222.

141. Lieutenant-Colonel John Enrietto, Allied Land Forces Norway, May 1–31, quoted in Coles and Weinberg, *Civil Affairs*, 844.

142. Tore Gjelsvik, *Norwegian Resistance, 1940–1945*, trans. Thomas Kingston Derry (Montreal: McGill/Queen's University Press, 1979; Norwegian ed. 1977), 212–13.

143. OSS Research and Analysis Branch, "Denmark After Liberation," August 3, 1945, NARA MC 1642/reel 29.

144. Knud J. V. Jespersen, *No Small Achievement: Special Operations Executive and the Danish Resistance, 1940–1945* (Odense: University Press of Southern Denmark, 2002), 96.

145. Niels Wium Olesen, "Change or Continuity in the Danish Elites? Social Movements and the Transition from War to Peace in Denmark, 1945–1947," forthcoming, 14.

146. Rousso, "L'épuration en France," 545–46.

Epilogue

1. Gerhard Hirschfeld, *Nazi Rule and Dutch Collaboration: The Netherlands Under German Occupation, 1940–1945*, trans. Louise Wilmot (Oxford: Berg, 1988; German ed. 1984), 198, 191.

2. Sébastien Albertelli, *Histoire du sabotage. De la CGT à la Résistance* (Paris: Perrin, 2016), 381, 382.

3. Alan S. Milward, "The Economic and Strategic Effectiveness of Resistance," in *Resistance in Europe*, ed. Stephen Hawes and Ralph White (London: Allen Lane, 1975), 196, 202.

4. Charles Cruickshank, *The Fourth Arm: Psychological Warfare, 1938–1945* (London: David-Poynter, 1977), 186.

5. Ellic Howe, *The Black Game: British Subversive Operations Against the Germans During the Second World War* (London: Queen Anne, 1988 [1982]), 265.

6. M.R.D. Foot, "What Good Did Resistance Do?" in *Resistance in Europe*, ed. Stephen Hawes and Ralph White (London: Allen Lane, 1975), 208.

7. Charles A. Bane, "Staff Meeting of 30 November 1944," NARA MC 1642/reel 112.

8. X, "Outline of Material for 1946 Budget Presentation. Europe-Africa Theaters," n.d., NARA RG 226/entry 99/box 59.

9. Olav Riste and Berit Nökleby, *Norway, 1940–1945: The Resistance Movement* (Oslo: Johan Grundt Tanum Forlag, 1970), 90.

10. My thanks to my colleague Claire de Galembert for these exchanges and the avenue they opened up.

11. Basil Davidson, *Special Operations Europe: Scenes from the Anti-Nazi War* (Newton Abbot, U.K.: Readers Union, 1981 [1980]), 278.

12. Kirchoff, "Denmark," in *Resistance in Europe*, ed. Bob Moore (Oxford: Berg, 2000), 114.

13. Knud J. V. Jespersen, *No Small Achievement: Special Operations Executive and the Danish Resistance, 1940–1945* (Odense: University Press of Southern Denmark, 2002), 514.

14. Charles Cruickshank, *SOE in Scandinavia* (Oxford: Oxford University Press, 1986), 265.

15. From Lord Selborne to W. Churchill, June 22, 1944, TNA PREM 3/185/1.

16. Cruickshank, *The Fourth Arm*, 176.

17. Norman Kogan, *Italy and the Allies* (Cambridge, Mass.: Harvard University Press, 1956), 174.

18. Sargent, note, April 8, 1941, TNA FO 371/29 421.

19. Eden to Collier, December 2, 1941, TNA FO 371/29 422.

20. Pascale Deloge, "Belgian Military Plans for the Post-War Period," in *Europe in Exile: European Exile Communities in Britain, 1940–1945*, ed. Martin Conway and José Gotovitch (New York: Berghann, 2001), 106.

21. SOE Council, "Minutes of a Meeting Held on June 5th 1945," TNA HS 8/202.

22. Lieutenant-Colonel A. J. Petch, report, June 10, 1945, NARA RG 331/entry 161/box 271.

23. David Stafford, *Mission Accomplished: SOE and Italy, 1943–1945* (London: Bodley Head, 2011), 334.

24. Jean-Louis Crémieux-Brilhac, preface to the French translation of Michael R. D. Foot, *SOE in France: An Account of the Work of the British Special Operations Executive in France, 1940–1944* (London: Her Majesty's Stationery Office, 1966): M. R. D. Foot, *Des Anglais dans la Résistance* (Paris: Tallandier, 2011), 11.

Bibliography

Primary Sources

Only the boxes containing documents used in this book are listed here.

National Archives (TNA), Kew, United Kingdom

PREM 3 (Prime Minister) 69/A, 69/B, 70, 73, 74/2, 74/4, 74/6, 74/8, 74/9, 74/10, 123/1,
    123/2, 184/6, 184/9, 185/1, 221/6, 221/10, 221/11, 221/12, 221/13 A, 221/13/A, 221/13
    B, 241/3, 241/7, 241/1, 241/3, 241/7, 242/1, 242/3, 242/5, 242/8, 242/9, 243/8, 243/9,
    243/12, 243/13, 243/14, 243/15, 245/7, 250/1, 254/2, 257/1, 257/2, 257/4, 257/5, 328/8,
    328/9, 328 A/8, 328 A/9, 365/8, 365/9, 365/11,408/3, 408/4, 408/5, 408/7, 409/5
CAB 65 (War Cabinet and Cabinet: Minutes) 46
CAB 66 (War Cabinet and Cabinet: Memoranda) 51, 56
CAB 84 (Joint Planning Committee) 45
CAB 101 (War Cabinet and Cabinet: Historical Section) 244, 250
CAB 118 (War Cabinet and Cabinet: Private Officials Files) 42
CAB 120 (Minister of Defence: Records) 867
Foreign Office: Political Departments, General Correspondence, 1906–1966 (FO 371) 26583,
    28368, 28419, 28420, 28431, 28519, 28545, 28546, 29276, 29301, 29302, 29303, 29327,
    29408, 29416, 29417, 29421, 29422, 29435, 29440, 29921, 29925, 29931, 29935, 29936,
    29937, 29938, 29943, 29960, 29967, 31029 31032, 31040, 31976, 32757, 32758, 32759, 32760,
    32825, 32826, 32827, 32829, 33222, 33240, 34302, 34303, 34310, 34317, 34318, 34321, 34399,
    34525, 34532 35217, 35218, 35219, 35220, 35221, 35223, 35234, 35236, 36032, 36780, 36782,
    36783, 36787, 36788, 36789, 36790, 36792, 36828, 36874, 36876, 36880, 36886, 36887,

36888, 36891, 37256, 37257, 37258, 37260A, 37307, 37308, 37309, 37310, 37311, 37312, 39923, 39324, 39325, 39328, 39330, 39331, 39351, 40413, 40414, 42024, 42096, 43064, 43101, 43095, 43102, 43108, 43149, 43232, 43242, 43250, 43253, 43254, 43829, , 43838, 43878, 43909, 43910, 43911, 43912, 43913, 43914, 43929

Political Warfare Executive (FO 898) 9, 11, 12, 13, 14, 16, 17, 22, 23, 24, 25, 26, 27, 28, 41, 50, 51, 52, 57, 60, 61, 62, 63, 64, 65, 69, 70, 71, 73, 74, 75, 76, 77, 78, 79, 80, 81, 82, 83, 85, 86, 87, 88, 89, 90, 91, 92, 93, 97, 98, 102, 161, 230, 231, 232, 233, 234, 235, 236, 238, 239, 240, 241, 242, 243, 244, 245, 303, 304, 376, 379, 380, 381, 382, 383, 420, 458

HS/2 (SOE, Group C: Scandinavia, Registered Files) 13, 23, 24, 41, 43, 79, 91, 92, 219

HS/7 (SOE, Histories and War Diaries) 1, 16, 17, 18, 19, 58, 59, 60, 62, 63, 64, 100, 101, 109, 110, 122, 124, 125, 126, 127, 128, 129, 130, 131, 133, 134, 135, 160, 161, 168, 174, 175, 178, 179, 180, 181, 182, 199, 241, 242, 243, 262, 263, 264, 265, 274, 275, 276, 279, 280, 281, 282, 286, 287

HS/8 (SOE, Headquarters, Records) 2, 9, 10, 11, 13,20, 38, 42, 44, 45, 88, 143, 144, 198, 199, 200, 201, 202, 204, 242, 243, 244, 245, 246, 247, 248, 250, 251, 252, 266, 267, 268, 271,272, 273, 274, 275, 276, 277, 278, 287, 288, 289, 290, 291, 292, 293, 294, 295, 296, 297, 298, 299, 300, 323, 376, 378, 382, 383, 414, 415, 416, 417, 419, 423, 436, 811, 825,919, 924, 926, 933, 934, 935, 937, 939, 962, 963

WO 204 (War Office) 9810

WO 898 (War Office) 97

BBC Written Archives Center, Caversham

E I 458, 702/1, 702/2, 702/3, 704, 705, 706, 829, 830, 1003
E 2 7/1, 7/2, 12/1, 14/1, 57, 128/2, 131/1, 132/2, 134, 135, 137
R 34 644, 647, 648, 654/1, 654/2, 654/3, 662/1, 662/2

National Archives and Records Administration (NARA), College Park, Maryland

RG 59 (STATE DEPARTMENT, FOREIGN SERVICES POSTS OF THE UNITED STATES)

Entry 2599 A (U.S. Embassy in Great Britain) 221, 222, 262, 263, 265, 288, 289, 291, 325, 328

RG 226: OSS COLLECTION

MC 1642 (Director's Office) 3, 5, 6, 14, 15, 23, 24, 25, 29, 59, 60, 61, 80, 104, 111, 112, 113
MC 1623 London Station 2, 5, 6, 7, 9
Entry 99 (History Office) 1, 2, 3, 4, 5, 13, 17, 18, 22, 23, 33, 34, 35, 59, 60, 97, 98, 107, 108, 109, 110, 111, 112, 114, 115, 116, 118, 119, 120, 122, 123, 124, 125, 126

Entry 190 (Director's Office Records, Field Stations) 30, 90, 92, 93, 94, 96, 97, 108,110,111, 112, 131,132, 133, 211, 230, 231, 232, 272, 273, 283, 302, 303, 304, 320, 321, 322

RG 331: SHAEF ARCHIVES

Entry 1 (Chief of Staff, Secretary, General Staff) 41
Entry 2 (Geographic Correspondence) 109, 110
Entry 27 (G3, Post Hostilities Planning Section) 86, 92
Entry 54 (Numeric Subject Operations File 1943–July 1945) 282, 290, 292
Entry 90 B (Special Staff, Psychological Warfare Division, Executive Section) 82, 83, 86, 87
Entry 99 (Special Staff, European Allied Contact Section) 1
Entry 110 (SHAEF Mission Denmark) 4
Entry 161, Psychological Warfare Group (Norway) 271

Memoirs and Journals

Alcorn, Robert Hayden. *No Bugles for Spies: Tales of the OSS.* New York: David McKay, 1962.

Bruce Lockhart, Robert Hamilton. *Comes the Reckoning.* London: Putnam, 1947.

Buckmaster, Maurice J. *Specially Employed: The Story of British Aid to French Patriots of the Resistance.* London: Batchworth, 1952.

Dalton, Hugh. *The Fateful Years: Memoirs 1931–1945.* London: Frederick Muller, 1957.

Davidson, Basil. *Special Operations Europe: Scenes from the Anti-Nazi War.* Newton Abbot, U.K.: Readers Union, 1981 [1980].

Delmer, Sefton. *Black Boomerang.* New York: Viking, 1962.

Dilks, David, ed. *The Diaries of Sir Alexander Cadogan, 1938–1945.* London: Cassel, 1971.

Dodds-Parker, Douglas. *Setting Europe Ablaze: Some Account of Ungentlemanly Warfare.* Southampton, U.K.: Springwood, 1983.

Frenay, Henri. *The Night Will End,* translated by Dan Hofstadter. London: Abelard, 1976; French ed. 1973.

Gaulle, Charles de. *The Complete War Memoirs,* translated by J. Griffin and R. Howard. 3 vols. New York: Simon and Schuster, 1967; 1st French ed., 1954, 1956, 1959.

Howe, Ellic. *The Black Game: British Subversive Operations Against the Germans During the Second World War.* London: Queen Anne, 1988 [1982].

Jebb, Gladwyn. *The Memoirs of Lord Gladwyn.* London: Weidenfeld and Nicolson, 1972.

Kirkpatrick, Ivone. *The Inner Circle: Memoirs.* London: Macmillan, 1959.

Macmillan, Harold. *The Blast of War, 1939–1945.* London: Macmillan, 1967.

McLachlan, Donald. *Room 39: Naval Intelligence in Action, 1939–45.* London: Weidenfeld and Nicholson, 1968.

Norwich, John Julius, ed. *The Duff Cooper Diaries.* London: Phoenix, 2005.

Poirier, Jacques R. E. *La girafe a un long cou.* Paris: Éditions du Félin, 2003.

Riols, Noreen. *The Secret Ministry of Ag. and Fish: My Life in Churchill's School of Spies.* London: Macmillan, 2013.

Spaak, Paul-Henri. *The Continuing Battle: Memoirs of a European, 1936–1966*, translated by Henry Fox. London: Weidenfeld and Nicolson, 1971; French ed. 1969.

Sweet-Escott, Bickham. *Baker Street Irregulars*. London: Methuen, 1965.

Tillon, Charles. *On chantait rouge. Mémoires pour l'histoire d'un ouvrier breton devenu révolutionnaire professionnel, chef de guerre et ministre*. Paris: Robert Laffont, 1977.

Wake, Nancy. *The Autobiography of the Woman the Gestapo Called the White Mouse*. Melbourne: Macmillan Australia, 1985.

Young, Kenneth, ed. *The Diaries of Sir Robert Bruce Lockhart*. Vol. 2: *1939–1965*. London: Macmillan, 1980.

Published Sources

Documents

Foreign Relations of the United States: Diplomatic Papers, 1941. Vol. 2: *Europe*. Washington, D.C.: Government Printing Office, 1959.

Foreign Relations of the United States: Diplomatic Papers, 1942. Vol. 2: *Europe*. Washington, D.C.: Government Printing Office, 1962.

Foreign Relations of the United States: Diplomatic Papers, 1942. Vol. 3: *Europe*. Washington, D.C.: Government Printing Office, 1961.

Foreign Relations of the United States: Diplomatic Papers, 1943. Vol 2: *Europe*. Washington, D.C.: Government Printing Office, 1964.

Coles, Harry L., and Albert K. Weinberg. *Civil Affairs: Soldiers Become Governors*. Washington, D.C.: Office of the Chief of Military History, 1964.

Petersen, Neal H., ed. *From Hitler's Doorstep: The Wartime Intelligence Reports of Allen Dulles, 1942–1945*. University Park: Pennsylvania State University Press, 1966.

Salmon, Patrick, ed. *British Documents on Foreign Affairs: Reports and Papers from the Foreign Office Confidential Print*, part 3, *From 1940 Through 1945*. Vol. 9: *Scandinavia, January 1940–December 1941*. Frederick, Md.: University Publications of America, 1998.

Salmon, Patrick, ed. *British Documents on Foreign Affairs: Reports and Papers from the Foreign Office Confidential Print*, part 3, *From 1940 Through 1945*. Vol. 12: *France, Belgium and Luxembourg and the Netherlands. January 1940–December 1941*. Frederick, Md.: University Publications of America, 1998.

On Propaganda

Balfour, Michael. *Propaganda in War, 1939–1945: Organisations, Policies and Publics in Britain and Germany*. London: Routledge and Kegan Paul, 1979.

Cruickshank, Charles. *The Fourth Arm: Psychological Warfare 1938–1945*. London: David-Poynter, 1977.

Garnett, David. *The Secret Story of PWE, 1939–1945*. London: St. Ermin's, 2002.

Luneau, Aurélie. *Radio Londres, 1940–1944. Les voix de la liberté*. Paris: Perrin, 2005.

Stenton, Michael. *Radio London and Resistance in Occupied Europe: British Political Warfare, 1939–1943*. Oxford: Oxford University Press, 2000.

On the Governments in Exile and Foreign Policy

Conway, Martin, and José Gotovitch, eds. *Europe in Exile: European Exile Communities in Britain, 1940–1945*. New York: Berghann, 2001.

Hawes, Stephen, and Ralph White, eds. *Resistance in Europe*. London: Allen Lane, 1975.

Woodward, Llewellyn. *British Foreign Policy in the Second World War*. Vols. 1–3. London: Her Majesty's Stationery Office, 1970–1971.

On the Resistance (Including OSS and SOE)

Belot, Robert. *Henri Frenay. De la Résistance à l'Europe*. Paris: Seuil, 2003.

Belot, Robert, and Gilles Karpman. *L'Affaire suisse. La Résistance a-t-elle trahi de Gaulle? (1943–1944)*. Paris: Armand Colin, 2009.

Bernard, Henri. *Histoire de la résistance européenne. La "quatrième force" de la guerre 39–45*. Brussels: Marabout, 1968.

Bourdet, Claude. *L'aventure incertaine. De la Résistance à la Restauration*. Paris: Stock, 1975.

Cookridge, Edward H. (pseud. for Edward Spiro.) *They Came from the Sky*. London. Heinemann, 1965.

Cordier, Daniel. *Jean Moulin. La République des Catacombes*. Paris: Gallimard, 1999.

——. *Jean Moulin. L'inconnu du Panthéon*. Vol. 1: *Une ambition pour la République*. Paris: JC Lattès, 1989.

Foot, Michael R. D. *An Outline History of the Special Operations Executive, 1940–1946*. London: Bodley Head, 2014 [1984].

Irwin, Will. *The Jedburghs: The Secret History of the Secred Allied Forces, France 1944*. New York: Public Affairs, 2006.

MacPherson, Nelson. *American Intelligence in War-Time London: The Story of the OSS*. London: Frank Cass, 2003.

Marcot, François, ed. *Dictionnaire historique de la Résistance*. Paris: Robert Laffont, 2006.

Moore, Bob, ed. *Resistance in Western Europe*. Oxford: Berg, 2000.

Seaman, Mark, ed. *Special Operations Executive: A New Instrument of War*. London: Routledge, 2006.

Sémelin, Jacques. *Unarmed Against Hitler: Civilian Resistance in Europe, 1939–1943*, translated by Suzan Husserl-Kapit. Westport, Conn.: Praeger, 1993; French ed. 1989.

Smith, Bradley F. *The Shadow Warriors: OSS and the Origins of CIA*. London: Andre Deutsche, 1983.

Smith, Richard Harris. *OSS: The Secret History of America's First Central Intelligence Agency*. Berkeley: University of California Press, 1972.

Stafford, David. *Britain and European Resistance, 1940–1945: A Survey of the Special Operations Executive*. London: Macmillan, 1980.

Waller, Douglas C. *Disciples: The World War II Missions of the CIA Directors Who Fought for Wild Bill Donovan*. New York: Simon and Schuster, 2015.

West, Nigel. *Secret War: The Story of SOE, Britain's Wartime Sabotage Organization*. London: Hodder and Stoughton, 1992.

Wilkinson, Peter, and Joan Bright Astley. *Gubbins and SOE*. Barnsley, U.K.: Pen and Sword, 2010 [1993].

On the Liberation and the Postwar Period

Buton, Philippe. *Les lendemains qui déchantent. Le Parti communiste français à la Libération*. Paris: Presses de Sciences Po, 1993.

Donnison, F.S.V. *Civil Affairs and Military Government Central Organization and Planning*. London: Her Majesty's Stationery Office, 1966.

Douglas, Ray M. *Orderly and Humane: The Expulsion of the Germans after the Second World War*. New Haven: Yale University Press, 2012.

Ellwood, David W. *Rebuilding Europe: Western Europe, America and Postwar Reconstruction*. London: Longman, 1992.

Hitchcock, William I. *The Bitter Road to Freedom: A New History of the Liberation of Europe*. New York: Free Press, 2008.

Hoffmann, Stefan-Ludwig, Sandrine Kott, Peter Romijn, and Olivier Wieviorka, eds. *Seeking Peace in the Wake of War: Europe, 1943–1947*. Amsterdam: Amsterdam University Press, 2015.

Lagrou, Pieter. *The Legacy of Nazi Occupation: Patriotic Memory and National Recovery in Western Europe, 1945–1965*. Cambridge: Cambridge University Press, 2000.

Lowe, Keith. *Savage Continent: Europe in the Aftermath of World War II*. New York: Viking, 2012.

Soutou, Georges-Henri. *La Guerre de cinquante ans. Les relations Est-Ouest, 1943–1990*. Paris: Fayard, 2001.

Belgium

Bernard, Henri. *L'Armée secrète. 1940–1944*. Gembloux: Duculot, 1986.

Conway, Martin. *The Sorrows of Belgium: Liberation and Political Reconstruction, 1944–1947*. Oxford: Oxford University Press, 2012.

Debruyne, Emmanuel. *La guerre secrète des espions belges, 1940-1944*. Brussels: Éditions Racine, 2008.

Gotovitch, José. *Du rouge au tricolore. Les Communistes belges de 1939 à 1944, un aspect de l'histoire de la Résistance en Belgique*. Brussels: Labor, 1992.

Grosbois, Thierry. *Pierlot. 1930–1950*. Brussels: Racine, 2007.

Schrijvers, Peter. *Liberators: The Allies and Belgian Society, 1944–1945*. Cambridge: Cambridge University Press, 2009.

Stengers, Jean. *Léopold III et le gouvernement. Les deux politiques belges de 1940.* Brussels: Racine, 2002 [1980].

Verhoeyen, Étienne. *La Belgique occupée. De l'an 40 à la Libération.* Brussels: De Boeck, 1994.

Denmark

Bennett, Jeremy. *British Broadcasting and the Danish Resistance Movement, 1940–1945: A Study of the Wartime Broadcasts of the BBC Danish Service.* Cambridge: Cambridge University Press, 1966.

Hæstrup, Jørgen. *Le mouvement de la résistance danoise,* translated by Françoise Schade-Poulsen. Copenhagen: Direction Générale de Presse et d'Information du Ministère Danois des Affaires Étrangères, 1970.

——. *Secret Alliance: A Study of the Danish Resistance Movement, 1940–45,* translated by Alison Borch-Johansen. 3 vols. Odense: Odense University Press, 1976–1977.

Herbert, Ulrich. *Werner Best. Un nazi de l'ombre,* translated by Dominique Viollet. Paris: Tallandier, 2010; German ed. 2006.

Hong, Nathaniel. *Sparks of Resistance: The Illegal Press in German-Occupied Denmark, April 1940–August 1943.* Odense: Odense University Press, 1996.

Jespersen, Knud J. V. *No Small Achievement: Special Operations Executive and the Danish Resistance, 1940–1945.* Odense: University Press of Southern Denmark, 2002.

Wium Olesen, Niels. "Change or Continuity in the Danish Elites? Social Movements and the Transition from War to Peace in Denmark, 1945–1947." Forthcoming.

——. "The Obsession with Sovereignty: Cohabitation and Resistance in Denmark, 1940–45." In *Hitler's Scandinavian Legacy,* edited by John Gilmour and Jill Stephenson, 45–72. London: Bloomsbury, 2013.

France

Abzac-Epezy, Claude d'. *L'Armée de l'Air des années noires. Vichy 1940–1944.* Paris: Economica, 1998.

Albertelli, Sébastien. "Les services secrets de la France libre. Le Bureau Central de Renseignement et d'Action." Ph.D. thesis, Institut d'Études Politiques-Paris, 2006.

——. *Les Services secrets du général de Gaulle. Le BCRA 1940–1944.* Paris: Perrin, 2009.

——. *Histoire du sabotage. De la CGT à la Résistance.* Paris: Perrin, 2016.

André, Philippe. "Les ambassadeurs de l'ombre. Les délégués militaires régionaux (DMR) du général de Gaulle. Septembre 1943–septembre 1944." Master's thesis (M2), Paris I, 2011, published as *La Résistance confisquée? Les Délégués militaires du général de Gaulle. De Londres à la Libération.* Paris: Perrin, 2013.

Ashdown, Paddy. *The Cruel Victory: The French Resistance, D-Day and the Battle for the Vercors 1944.* London: William Collins, 2014.

Barasz, Johanna. "De Vichy à la Résistance. Les vichysto-résistants 1940–1944." 3 vols. Ph.D. thesis, Institut d'Études Politiques-Paris, 2010.

Crémieux-Brilhac, Jean-Louis. *La France libre. De l'appel du 18 juin à la libération.* Paris: Gallimard, 1996.

Foot, Michael R.D. *SOE in France: An Account of the Work of the British Special Operations Executive in France, 1940–1944.* London: Her Majesty's Stationery Office, 1966.

Garnier, Bernard, Jean-Luc Leleu, Françoise Passera, and Jean Quellien, eds. *Les populations civiles face au débarquement et à la bataille de Normandie.* Caen: Mémorial de Caen, 2005.

Guingouin, Georges. *Quatre ans de lutte sur le sol limousin.* Limoges: Lucien Souny, 1991.

Jäckel, Eberhard. *La France dans l'Europe de Hitler,* translated by Denise Meunier. Paris: Fayard, 1968; German ed. 1966.

Kitson, Simon. *The Hunt for Nazi Spies: Fighting Espionage in Vichy France,* translated by Catherine Tihanyi. Chicago: University of Chicago Press, 2008; French ed. 2005.

Muracciole, Jean-François. *Les Français libres. L'autre résistance.* Paris: Tallandier, 2009.

Noguères, Henri, Marcel Degliame-Fouché, and Jean-Louis Vigier. *Histoire de la Résistance en France de 1940 à 1945.* 5 vols. Paris: Robert Laffont, 1967–1981.

Rabino, Thomas. *Le Réseau Carte. Histoire d'un réseau de la Résistance antiallemand, antigaulliste, anticommuniste et anti-collaborationniste.* Paris: Perrin, 2008.

Romans-Petit, Henri. *Les maquis de l'Ain.* Paris: Hachette, 1974.

Vergez-Chaignon, Bénédicte. *Les vichysto-résistants de 1940 à nos jours.* Paris: Perrin, 2008.

Vergnon, Gilles. *Le Vercors. Histoire et mémoire d'un maquis.* Paris: Éditions de l'Atelier, 2002.

Vistel, Alban. *La nuit sans ombre. Histoire des mouvements unis de résistance, leur rôle dans la libération du Sud-Est.* Paris: Fayard, 1970.

Wieviorka, Olivier. *The French Resistance,* translated by Jane Marie Todd. Cambridge, Mass: Belknap Press of Harvard University Press, 2016; French ed. 2013.

Italy

Battaglia, Roberto. *The Story of the Italian Resistance,* translated by P. D. Cummins. London: Odhams, 1958; Italian ed. 1953.

Behan, Tom. *The Italian Resistance: Fascists, Guerillas, and the Allies.* London: Pluto, 2009.

Ellwood, David W. *Italy 1943–1945.* Leicester, U.K.: Leicester University Press, 1985.

Felice, Renzo de. *Le Fascisme, un totalitarisme à l'italienne.* Paris: Presses de Sciences Po, 1988; Italian ed. 1981.

Fiori, Giuseppe. *Il cavaliere dei rossomori.* Milan: Einaudi, 2000.

Kogan, Norman. *Italy and the Allies.* Cambridge: Mass.: Harvard University Press, 1956.

Le Moal, Frédéric. *Victor-Emmanuel III. Un roi face à Mussolini.* Paris: Perrin, 2015.

Milza, Pierre. *Mussolini.* Paris: Fayard, 1999.

Pavone, Claudio. *A Civil War: A History of the Italian Resistance,* translated by Peter Levy with the assistance of David Broder. London: Verso, 2013; Italian ed. 1991.

Portelli, Alessandro. *L'ordine è già stato eseguito. Roma, le Fosse Ardeatine, la memoria.* Rome: Donzelli, 1999.

Stafford, David. *Mission Accomplished: SOE and Italy, 1943–1945.* London: Bodley Head, 2011.

The Netherlands

Duke, A. C., and C. A. Tamse, eds. *Britain and the Netherlands: War and Society.* The Hague: Martinus Nijhoff, 1977.

Foot, Michael R. D. *SOE in the Low Countries.* London: St. Ermin's, 2001.

——, ed. *Holland at War Against Hitler: Anglo Dutch Relations, 1940–1945.* London: Frank Cass, 1990.

Hirschfeld, Gerhard. *Nazi Rule and Dutch Collaboration: The Netherlands Under German Occupation, 1940–1945,* translated by Louise Wilmot. Oxford: Berg, 1988; German ed. 1984.

Jong, Louis de. *The Netherlands and Nazi Germany.* Cambridge, Mass.: Harvard University Press, 1990.

Wolters, Jo. *Dossier Nordpol: Het Englandspiel onder de Loep.* Amsterdam: Boom, 2003.

Norway

Gjelsvik, Tore. *Norwegian Resistance, 1940–1945,* translated by Thomas Kingston Derry. Montreal: McGill/Queen's University Press, 1979; Norwegian ed. 1977.

Hauge, Jens C. *The Liberation of Norway.* Oslo: Gylendal Norsk Forlag, 1995; Norwegian ed. 1950.

Mann, Christopher. *British Policy and Strategy Towards Norway, 1941–45.* London: Palgrave Macmillan, 2012.

Riste, Olav, and Berit Nökleby. *Norway 1940–1945: The Resistance Movement.* Oslo: Johan Grundt Tanum Forlag, 1970.

Scandinavia

Cruickshank, Charles. *SOE in Scandinavia.* Oxford: Oxford University Press, 1986.

Gilmour, John, and Jill Stephenson, eds. *Hitler's Scandinavian Legacy.* London: Bloomsbury, 2013.

Nissen, Henrik S., ed. *Scandinavia During the Second World War,* translated by Thomas Munch-Petersen. Minneapolis: University of Minnesota Press, 1983.

Index

Aarhus, 241, 257

Abeille, Valentin, 328

Abwehr, 115; SOE and, 165–66

Action Française, 61–62, 133

Afghanistan, 387

AFHQ. *See* Allied Force Headquarters

Afrikakorps, 81

Agents, secret: courage of, 221–22; recruitment of, 216–17; training of, 219

Aglion, Raoul, 230

Aircraft, 180–82

Air drops, 184–86

Air Force (US), 200

Ajaccio, 266

Albermale, 182

Albertelli, Sébastien, 140; on sabotage, 385

Alcohol consumption, 223

Alcorn, Robert Hayden, 100

Alexander, Harold (General), 262, 341–42, 345–46

Algeria, 22

Algiers, 178, 208; conflagration, 225–27; Consultative Assembly, 308; de Gaulle and, 296

Allied Control Commission, 250

Allied Council, 236

Allied Expeditionary Force, 259, 312

Allied Force Headquarters (AFHQ), 260, 346

Allied High Command, 195

Allied Military Government (AMG), 250, 299

Allied Military Government in Occupied Territory (AMGOT), 308, 313

Allies, 5, 8–10; Conway on, 207; industrial targets of, 257–58; interventions of, 255, 356; in North Africa, 170; representation in, 213–15; in Scandinavia, 340; strategy of, 71–72; subversive warfare of, 345; victories of, 256

Alpes-Maritimes, 158

Altenhoff, Richard, 137

AMG. *See* Allied Military Government

AMGOT. *See* Allied Military Government in Occupied Territory

Amies, Hardy (Lieutenant-Colonel), 42

André, Philippe, 140

Anglo-Norwegian Collaboration Committee, 145

Anti-Comintern Pact, 92, 233, 310–11

Anti-Revolutionaire Partij, 13

Antonicelli, Franco, 379

Antwerp, 335

Apidistra, 196

Arabs, 81

Ardennes, 149

Argenlieu, Georges Thierry d' (Admiral), 76

Arkhangelsk, 27–28

Armored Division, 333

Aronstein, Georges, 62

Ashdown, Paddy, 320

Assassination attempts, 98

Astier, Henri d', 226

Atlantic Charter, 105

Attentisme (wait-and-watch attitude), 68, 387

Attlee, Clement, 29

Auerstaedt, Davout d', 325

Austria, 217

Avranches, 329–30

Axis Powers, 31, 36, 83, 245

B-17 Flying Fortress, 182, 369–70

B-24s, 184, 220

Baardshaug, 128

Baasten, Arnoldus, 165

Badoglio, Pietro (Marshal), 243–44, 252, 298, 391; authority of, 261; W. Churchill and, 249, 254; Eisenhower and, 246; fall of, 374; purges, 374; Soviet Union and, 253; Togliatti and, 307

Baers, Maria, 147

Baissac, Claude de, 139

Balfour, Harold, 126

Balmoral Castle, The, 371

Balthazar, August, 74

Bandiera Rossa, 380

Banque de Bruxelles, 63

Barman, Thomas, 53–54, 85, 235; on Kirkpatrick, 56

Barrents Sea, 92

Basin, Francis (Lieutenant), 132

Basset, Maurice (Lieutenant), 220, 316, 359

Bastille Day, 174

Bastin, Jules, 142

Battle of Britain, 235

Battle of Stalingrad, 92

Baxter, James P., III, 101

BBC. *See* British Broadcasting Corporation

BCRA. *See* Bureau Central de Renseignement et d'Action

Beagle network, 138

Bedell Smith, Walter (General), 245, 272, 315

Bégué, Georges, 139

Belgian Congo, 17, 84

Belgium, 7–8; cabinet in, 365–66; Communism in, 279, 305; complexities of, 363–66; compulsory labor in, 147–48; W. Churchill on, 204; Dingo mission in, 151; disarmament in, 366–69; Germany and, 14–22; Gotovitch on, 365; internal dissension in, 367–68; legitimacy in, 72–74; liberation of, 334–36; partisans in, 335–36; propaganda in, 36, 38–39; Resistance movement in, 336; SOE in, 42, 66, 131, 135–38; United Kingdom and, 86–87; violence in, 365

Bennike, Vagn (Lieutenant-Colonel), 339

Benzedrine, 219

Berg, Paal, 381

Bergeret, Jean (General), 226

Bergonzoli, Annibale (General), 82

Bernard, Henri, 124, 142

Bernhard (Prince), 301–2, 337–38, 370–71

Best, Sigismund Payne, 49, 240

Best, Werner, 237, 291

Béthouart, Antoine (General), 320

Beveridge, William (Lord), 211

Beveridge Report, 303

Bichelonne, Jean, 161

Bidault, Georges, 297

Billotte, Pierre, 140

Bissault, Marcel, 450n37

Bjorn East, 339

Bjorn West, 339

Black propaganda, 35, 38–40; Radio Units, 195–98

Bland, Neville, 205

Blaskowitz, Johannes von (General), 370

Bloch, Georges, 43

Bodington, Nicholas, 133

Boer War, 205

Boer War, Second, 26

Boisson, Pierre, 226

Bolshevists, 13; crusade against, 92–93

Bomber Command, 181; air offensives of, 258

Bond, John (General), 382

Bondas, Joseph, 406n8

Bonomi, Ivanoe, 251, 298, 349, 391; purges of, 374–75

Bordeaux, 21, 42

Boris, Georges, 332

Bouchinet-Serreulles, Claude, 281, 297

Boulloche, André, 327

Bourdet, Claude, 156; on de Gaulle, 296–97; on movements, 108; on networks, 108

Bourg-en-Bresse, 322

Bourne-Patterson, Robert Archibald, 43

Bracken, Brendan, 30, 70, 126; on Dalton, 56–57; Lockhart and, 212–13

Brault, Michel, 154; on maquis, 270

Brindisi, 253

British Broadcasting Corporation (BBC), 4, 38; Crémieux-Brilhac on, 195; de Gaulle on, 352; European Services of, 55; instructions for action from, 315–17; Kirkpatrick and, 196; programs of, 194–95; propaganda and, 52; SOE and, 285–86

British War Cabinet, 254

Brixham clinic, 221

Brooke, Alan (General), 140

Bruce, David, 102, 275

Bruhn, Carl-Johann, 41

Brun, Louis, 157

Brussels, 370–71

Buckinghamshire, 49

Buckmaster, Maurice, 185–86, 193, 208

Buhl, Vilhelm, 239, 293

Bulgaria, 9, 94

Bureau Central de Renseignement et d'Action (BCRA), 222–23; de Gaulle on, 61; in Operation Overlord, 316; OSS and, 276, SOE and, 281, 391

Burgard, Raymond, 118

Burgers, Jean, 137

Bussy-Varache, 154

Butler, Frederick (General), 318

Buton, Philippe, 269

Caccia, Harold, 252

Cadogan, Alexander, W. Churchill and, 17–18

Cadorna, Raffaele, 300
Calder, Ritchie, 286
Cambridge, 199, 211
Camouflage du Matériel, 112
Campbell, Stuart, 28
Cap Bon, 243
Carmille, René, 113
Carnia, Republic of, 376
Carretta, Donato, 375
Carte: disaster, 132–35; support for, 207–8
Cartier de Marchienne, Emile-Ernest, 18, 58–59
Caruso, Pietro, 374
Casablanca (vessel), 264–65
Cassin, René, 76
Castellano, Giuseppe (General), 245
Cauvin, André, 63
Central planning, 15
CEPAG. See Commission pour l'Étude des Problèmes d'Après-Guerre
Cephalonia, 246
Ceretti, Giuliano, 94–95
CFLN. See Comité Français de Libération Nationale
CFTC. See Confédération Française des Travailleurs Chrétiens
CGT. See Confédération Générale du Travail
Chaban-Delmas, Jacques, 327, 329, 332
Chain of command, 326–29
Chamberlain, Neville, 27, 83
Chantenay, 323
Chantiers de la Jeunesse, 113
Chapelle, Fernand Bonnier de la, 227
Charles, Noel, 253, 307, 373
Chaumet, Guy, 328
Chavant, Eugène, 159
Cheissoux, 377–78
Chevance-Bertin, Maurice, 280
Chevigné, Pierre de, 355

Chief of Staff to Supreme Allied Commander, 277, 281
Choltitz, Dietrich von (General), 330
Christian X (King), 23, 68, 311, 390
Christiansen, Friedrich (General), 174
Churchill, Peter, 132, 392–93
Churchill, Winston, 8, 81; Badoglio and, 249, 254; on Belgium, 204; Cadogan and, 17–18; on Communism, 93; Crémieux-Brilhac on, 229–30; Dalton and, 29–30, 54–55, 384; de Gaulle and, 58, 75–76, 159, 229, 312, 350–51; on discouragement, 223; Eden and, 170–71; on France, 9, 22; on Free France, 77; on guerrilla tactics, 28; on Italy, 205; Kogan on, 388; on Léopold III, 364; Macmillan and, 249; on neutrality, 203–4; Roosevelt and, 353; on SIS, 50; on SOE, 50
Civet mission, 149
Civil Affairs Division, 251
Civil disobedience, 147, 163
Claser, Charles, 116, 142
CLN. See Comitato di Liberazione Nazionale
CLNAI. See Comitato di Liberazione Nazionale Alta Italia
Club des Pins, 260
CNR. See Conseil National de la Résistance
Coastal Command, 199
Cobelligerence, 58, 241, 248, 372
Cohen, Kenneth, 65
COI. See Coordinator of information
Colby, William, 325
Colijn, Hendrikus, 13
College van Vertrouwensmannen, 301
Collier, Laurence, 59
Collins, Michael, 28
Colonna d'Istria, Paulin, 264

Colson, Louis, 112

COMAC. *See* Comité d'Action Militaire

Combat (organization), 117, 121, 134, 274; on Fighting France, 156

Combattante, La, 355

Comintern, 29, 94

Comitato di Liberazione Nazionale (CLN), 251, 377; Allied Missions and, 378

Comitato di Liberazione Nazionale Alta Italia (CLNAI), 298; legitimacy of, 299

Comité Central des Mouvements, 297

Comité d'Action Militaire (COMAC), 297–98, 328; Communists and, 329; dissolution of, 361; FFI and, 327; leadership of, 326

Comité Directeur des Mouvements Unis de Résistance, 154

Comité Français de Libération Nationale (CFLN), 159, 296; de Gaulle at, 231; Soviet Union and, 312

Comité Général d'Études, 304

Commission pour l'Étude des Problèmes d'Après-Guerre (CEPAG), 304

Committee of Liberation, 159

Common Market, 392–93

Communards, 332

Communism and Communists, 292; in Belgium, 279, 305; COMAC and, 329; Council of Freedom and, 293; Crémieux-Brilhac on, 278; W. Churchill on, 93; de Gaulle on, 332; in Denmark, 96, 306–7; discrimination against, 346; Donovan on, 307; in France, 93, 297, 329, 331–32, 359; in Greece, 377; on insurrection, 269; in Italy, 380; in Netherlands, 305–6; in Norway,

305–6; opposition to Nazis from, 305–6; OSS on, 266; PWE and, 98; Resistance movements and, 93; SOE on, 266; threat of, 91–96; trade unions and, 109; during war, 305–8; Western, 5–6

Compulsory labor: in Belgium, 147–48; in France, 148; in Netherlands, 146–47; in Norway, 162–63

Confédération Française des Travailleurs Chrétiens (CFTC), 295

Confédération Générale du Travail (CGT), 295

Conseil de Défense de l'Empire, 76

Conseil National de la Resistance (CNR), 251, 279; Moulin and, 295; political parties and, 296

Constituent Assembly, 307

Consultative Assembly of Algiers, 308

Conway, Martin, on Allies, 207

Cooper, Duff, 80, 94, 224

Coordinator of information (COI), 100

Copenhagen, 136

Copp, Charles (Lieutenant-Colonel), 356

Corbin, Charles, 21

Cordier, Daniel, 64, 155, 274

Cornet, Jules, 17

Corni, Gustavo, 377

Corsica, 263–66

Corsican Liberation Committee, 264–65

COSSAC. *See* Chief of Staff to Supreme Allied Commander

Coulet, Francis, 355

Council of Freedom: Communists and, 293; leadership role of, 289–91; recognition of, 293–94; SHAEF on, 292–93; SOE and, 289–90; Soviet Union and, 290

Counter-intelligence (X2), 101

Counterscorching, 324, 337, 340, 347

Cowburn, Benjamin, 43, 139

Crémieux-Brilhac, Jean-Louis: on BBC, 195; on Communists, 278; on W. Churchill, 229–30

Crete, 25

Croce, Benedetto, 251, 254–55

Crosby, Richard (Major), 320

Crossman, Richard, 385

Culture clashes, 208–13

Currency, mining of, 353–54, 361

Cyanide, 219

Cyrenaica, 25

Dagmar Bratt, 369

Daily Express (newspaper), 88

Daily Mail (newspaper), 29

Dallas Brooks, Reginald Alexander (General), 54, 55

Dalloz, Pierre, 158

Dalton, Hugh, 26, 53, 78, 95, 106, 120, 387; Bracken on, 56–57; W. Churchill and, 29–30, 54–55, 384; Jebb and, 33; on Nazism, 27; Netherlands and, 167; personality of, 30; promotion of, 126; on propaganda, 31–32, 47; on revolution, 31; at SOE, 51–52; Spaak and, 58–59

Dame Blanche, 63

Dandoy, Aimé, 117

Danish Council, 233, 242, 390

Danish Unity Party, 136, 293

Danmarks Kommunistiske Parti (DKP), 111, 136

Darlan, François, 225, 254, 391; Selborne on, 227

Dauphin, Claude, 132, 134

Davet, Jules (General), 276

Davidson, Basil, 210, 377

Davidson, Francis (General), 82

Davies, F. T., 34

Davis, Elmer, 101

D-Day, 34, 107, 113, 141, 156, 176; eve of, 281–82; instructions for action, 315–17; Mockler-Ferryman on, 282; propaganda and, 285; striking before, 257–59; system during, 281–82

Deakin, William, 170

Decentralization, 278–81

Defense Committee, 174, 181

Défense de la France, 110

De Gasperi, Alcide, 288

de Gaulle, Charles (General), 1–2, 42, 65, 81, 96, 174, 391; Algiers and, 296; as ally, 312–14; ambitions of, 20–21; authority of, 350–58; on BBC, 352; BCRA and, 61; Bourdet on, 296–97; at CFLN, 231; on Communists, 332; W. Churchill and, 58, 75–76, 159, 229, 312, 350–51; as divisive factor, 114; Eden and, 134, 230, 358; Eisenhower and, 351, 358; Fighting France and, 295–96; Frenay and, 274; Gaullist conundrum, 350–54; Giraud and, 227–30; Lockhart on, 229, 352; Moulin and, 279; obstructionism of, 353; PCF and, 349–50; Pétain and, 207; recognition of, 362; return to Paris of, 331; Roosevelt and, 228, 272, 360; SOE and, 43, 207–8; taking power, 355–58; on United Kingdom, 206, 350–51; Vichyist regime and, 312

De Gil, 197

Délégués militaires régionaux (DMR), 320–21, 328–29

Delestraint, Charles (General), 121; arrest of, 279; SA commanded by, 144

Delfosse, Antoine, 74, 131

Delmer, Sefton, 196

Delorme, Danièle, 132

de Man, Henri, 15

Demany, Fernand, 367

Democratization, 227–28; of Denmark, 381–83; of Norway, 381–83

Democrats, 100, 209–10

Denmark, 7, 77, 189; ambivalence of, 22–24; Communists in, 96, 306–7; complexity of, 310–14; democratic transition, 381–83; division of, 279; Eden and, 310–11; Germany and, 68, 237–38, 240, 291; Hitler and, 237; legal status of, 241–42; liberation of, 348; national character in, 214; Nazism in, 240; neutrality of, 232–35; propaganda in, 36, 236; PWE on, 214, 236; railway sabotage in, 338–39; Resistance movement in, 257–58, 282; SOE in, 135–38, 214, 239; tensions with, 235–37, 289–91; trade unions in, 290; United Kingdom and, 77–78, 234; violence in, 238

Department of Defense, 4

Deppé, Arnold, 63

Descour, Marcel (Colonel), 321

Dessing, Agnes, 405n18

Deuxième Bureau, 61, 65

Deuxième Section, 66, 123, 131, 142

De Vleeschauwer, Albert, 16–18, 72

Devonshire, 10, 381

Dewavrin, André. See Passy

Dewé, Walthère, 41, 63

Dewing, Richard (General), 311

Diamant-Berger, Maurice, 132

Diana, La, 82

Diepenrijckx, Pierre (Colonel), 62

Dingo mission, in Belgium, 151

disarmament, in Belgium, 366–69

Division of labor, 107

Dixon, Pierson, 248

DKP. See Danmarks Kommunistiske Parti

DMR. See Délégués militaires régionaux

Dodds-Parker, Douglas, 260

Donkeyman network, 325

Donovan, William J., 100, 213; on Communism, 307; on SOE, 273

Døssing, Thomas, 290, 294, 311

Dourlein, Pieter, 166

Druon, Maurice, 132

Dual power, 287–88

Duclos, Jacques, 93

Ducq, Jean, 62

Dulles, Allen, 260, 273–74, 275

du Puy, Jean-Paul Marie, 43

Durbin, W. F. (Colonel), 356

Dussaq, René, 321

Dutch Brigade, 370–71

Dutch Forces of the Interior, 301

Dutch Nazi Party, 13

Economic warfare, 27

Eden, Anthony, 51, 70, 80, 85, 126, 224; W. Churchill and, 170–71; de Gaulle and, 134, 230, 358; Denmark and, 310–11; on Italy, 170–71; on Mussolini, 205; Pesenti and, 244–45

EIAR. See Entre Italiano per le Audizioni Radiofoniche

Eisenhower, Dwight (General), 201; Badoglio and, 246; de Gaulle and, 351, 358; on France, 320; on Italy, 250; Koenig and, 314; at SHAEF, 281

Electra House, 28

Ellis, Dick, 102

Elster's Column, 317

Englandspiel, 165–66, 167, 173

Enigma machine, 49

Entente Cordiale, 8

Entre Italiano per le Audizioni Radiofoniche (EIAR), 38

Erskine, George (General), 363, 366

Eton, 211

Eureka, 186; transportation of, 187
Europe: Leeper on, 205; Newsome
    on, 89
Evere Airfield, 363
Evreux, 198
Exile, responses to, 207

Fabri, Octave, 42
Farge, Yves, 158
Fascism, 35, 94, 243; atrocities of,
    343–344; fight against, 169, 347; in
    Italy, 41, 169, 347; opposition to, 247;
    responsibility for, 252
Fascist Party (Italy), 82
Favel, Jacques, 325
Federal Bureau of Investigation (FBI),
    392
Felner, R. M. J., 102
FFI. See Forces Françaises de l'Intérieur
FI. See Front de l'Indépendance
Fifth Army, 379
Fighting France, 144, 161–62, 274, 304;
    Combat on, 156; de Gaulle and,
    295–96
Finnmark, 340–41
FIS. See Foreign Information Service
Flak (antiaircraft guns), 187
Fleuret, Jean, 62
Floor, Idesbald (Major), 152
Florence, 347, 378
Flying Fortresses, 201
Fog, Mogens, 291, 294
Food shortages, 162–63. See also
    Starvation
Foot, Michael, 48, 138, 393
Forces Françaises de l'Intérieur (FFI),
    316, 317, 319–22, 445n89; COMAC
    and, 327; SHAEF on, 359; size of,
    323, 330
Foreign Information Service (FIS), 101
Foreign Office, 4, 79–80

Fortress Europe, 9, 127, 179, 350;
    broadcasts for, 194–95; population of,
    227; radio in, 32–33
Foss, Erling, 294
Fosse Ardeatine, 263, 374
Fourcade, Marie-Madeleine, 225
Four Days of Naples, 262–63
Frager, Henri, 132–33, 135
France, 2; Communism in, 93, 297, 329,
    331–32, 359; compulsory labor in, 148;
    W. Churchill and, 9, 22; Eisenhower
    on, 320; Hambro on, 275–76;
    insurrection in, 268–71; liberation
    of, 336; national liberation in,
    268–69; OSS and, 275; PWE on, 97;
    relationships with, 295–98; Resistance
    movement in, 388; Roosevelt on, 354,
    388; sabotage in, 385; SOE in, 42–43,
    185–86, 279–80; sovereignty of, 353;
    on STO, 153–57; unconstitutionality
    in, 85; United Kingdom and, 160.
    See also Free France
Franco, Francisco (General), 8, 375
Franc-Tireur, 121, 157, 176
Francs-Tireurs et Partisans (FTP), 322,
    325–26, 329; SHAEF on, 359
Free Danes, 233–35, 292; support of, 310
Free France, 42, 65, 87, 119, 121;
    W. Churchill on, 77; Naval Forces,
    217; Sweet-Escott on, 193; on
    unification, 296; United Kingdom
    and, 68
Free Italy Committee, 168
Free Italy Movement, 80–81
Frenay, Henri, 117, 121; de Gaulle and,
    274; on redoubts, 154; on Resistance
    movements, 178
French Civil Authorities, 313
Frère, Aubert, 112
Frihedsråd. See Council of Freedom
Frihedsstøtten, 111

Frit Danmark, 111

Friuli, 376

Front de l'Indépendance (FI), 94, 109, 111, 149, 301, 365, 366

Front National, 109, 157, 265

Front Populaire, 94, 120–21, 153

F Section, 132

FTP. *See* Francs-Tireurs et Partisans

Gaessler, Alfred, 61

Galembert, Claire de, 386, 454n10

Galen Last, Dick van, 405n18

Gallop, Roderick, 77, 324

Gare Montparnasse, 331

Garibaldi Battalion, 261

Geer, Dirk Jan de, 13–14, 75, 288

Geersens, Fernand, 408n64

Gendarmerie, 366

Genoa, 347

Gensoul, Marcel (Admiral), 22

Georges, Alphonse (General), 231

Georges, Pierre, 95

Gérard, Ivan (Colonel), 142

Gerbrandy, Pieter Sjoerds, 14, 85, 125, 167, 369–70; on authority, 303; on RAF, 175

Gerhardson, Einar, 381

Germany: Belgium and, 14–22; Denmark and, 68, 237–38, 240, 291; in Italy, 263–64; Norway and, 10–11; Radio Units in, 197–98; sabotage and, 385; Scandinavia and, 92; Soviet Union and, 93

Gerson, Victor, 43

Gestapo, 65, 138, 221–22, 385

Gibraltar Farm, 181

Gigny Dam, 257

Gillois, André, 134

Girard, André, 132, 135, 225

Giraud, Henri (General), 225, 295–96; de Gaulle and, 227–30; Macmillan on, 227; Monnet on, 227–28; Roosevelt and, 228

Giry, Louis, 325

Giskes, Hermann, 165

Gjelsvik, Tore, 382

Goebbels, Joseph, 38

Gogl, Hans, 166

Goldsmith, John Gilbert, 133

Gørtz, Ebbe (General), 293

Gothic Line, 342

Gotovitch, José, 152; on Belgium, 365

Gouvernement Provisoire de la République Française (GPRF), 350, 361; recognition of, 362

Grand, Lawrence, 28

Grande, Ivar, 258

Graziani, Rodolfo (General), 25

Greater Consultative Council, 301

Greece, Communism in, 377

Grenoble, 317

Group G, 137

Gruppi Combattimenti in Italia, 261

Gubbins, Colin, 27–28, 33–34, 136, 140, 142; on SOE, 124, 172

Guélis, Jacques de, 43

Guerrilla warfare, 268

Guingand, Freddy de (General), 369–70

Guingouin, Georges, 154, 322, 377

Gundel, Leif, 38

Gutt, Camille, 16, 18, 72, 368

Guyot, Raymond, 93

Gyth, Volle (Captain), 113

Haakon VII (King), 10–12, 23, 59, 89, 120, 381, 390

Hæstrup, Jørgen, 290

Hagelin, Albert Vijam, 69

Halifax (aircraft), 182

Halifax, Edward Frederick Lindley Wood (Lord), 8, 19, 73

Hamar, 10–11

Hambro, Charles, 30–31, 60, 123, 127, 131, 142; on France, 275–76; on Italy, 171; on Switzerland, 275–76

Hammer, Mogens, 136

Hammerich, Carl (Admiral), 339

Hamon, Léo, 330

Hanbury-Williams, John, 173

Hanneken, Hermann von (General), 241

Hanneton, Pierre (Colonel), 328

Hansen, Hans Hedtoft, 78–79, 136

Hansteen, Wilhelm von Tangen (General), 60, 382

Harris, Arthur Travers, 181, 258; on propaganda, 199

Harrow, 211

Hartmann, Paul, 75

Harvey, Oliver, 87

Haskell, Joseph (Colonel), 272

Haukelid, Knut, 129

Hayden, Joseph, 101

Hazan, Victor, 139

Henquet, Roger, 359

Henrietto, John, 382

Herbert, Ulrich, 237

Heslop, Richard, 138

Hess, Rudolf, 38

Hessa, 190

Hewitt, Richard Thornton (Lieutenant-Colonel), 375

Himmler, Heinrich, 69

Hispano-Suiza factories, 257

Hitler, Adolf, 7, 16–17, 92, 146, 204; Denmark and, 237

Hitra, 190

Højland Christensen, Aage (Lieutenant-Colonel), 118

Holdsworth, Gerry, 272

Holland, John Charles, 29

Hollingworth, Ralph, 136, 213, 278–79

Homburg, Albert, 40, 165

Home Front, 301

Hongerwinter, 338

Hopkinson, Henry, 50

Hoppenot, Henri, 312

Horrocks, Brian (General), 336

Hoste, Julius, 74

Howe, Ellic, 385

Hudson, 182, 191

Hughes, Stuart (Lieutenant-Colonel), 346

Hugh mission, 325

Hull, Cordell, 226, 254, 308, 313

Huntington, Ellery (Lieutenant-Colonel), 271

Huysmans, Camille, 18, 73, 88

Idealism, 218

India, 82

Intelligence Service (IS), 48–50, 116, 172–73

Iraq, 387

Irish Republican Army, 26, 28

Ironside, Edmund, 27

IS. See Intelligence Service

Isenberg, Richard, 377

Ismay, Hastings, 50, 81

Issoudun, 317

Italian Communist Party, 253, 261, 306, 349, 380

Italy: antagonism from, 298–300; Communism in, 380; contested powers in, 249–51; W. Churchill on, 205; Eden on, 170–71; Eisenhower on, 250; Fascism in, 41, 169, 347; German forces in, 263–64; Hambro on, 171; lessons from, 259–62; Liberated Italy, 250; long armistice, 247; Macmillan on, 378; McCaffery on, 376; offensive, 341–44; Resistance movement in, 260–61, 347–48; short armistice, 246; SOE on, 41, 168–72, 214–15; sovereignty

in, 372–74; Stalin on, 349–50;
surrender of, 245–46; United
Kingdom and, 79–83, 214

Jacobins, 279
Jakobsen, Frode, 109, 289, 306
Janson, Paul-Émile, 19
Janssen, Albert-Édouard, 149
Jaspar, Marcel-Henri, 16–17, 18
Jebb, Gladwyn, 30, 48, 126; Dalton
    and, 33
Jedburghs, 283–84, 325–26
Jespersen, Knud, 382
Jesser, Kurt von (General), 321
Jewish people, 80, 81, 112
JIC. See Joint Intelligence Committee
Joassart, Gustave, 74, 406n8
Joint Intelligence Committee (JIC),
    173
Jong, Louis de, 12
Jongh, Andrée de, 63
Joset, Camille-Jean, 117
Josse Allard bank, 152
Jottard, Marc, 19
Jourdain, Robert (Abbé), 41

Kauffmann, Henrik, 233
K Committee, 293
Keeble, Harold, 88
Kenney, Rowland, 86
Kerkhofs, Fernand, 42, 63
Kerkhofs, Louis-Joseph (Monsignor),
    42, 63
Kessel, Joseph, 132
Keswick, David (Major), 140
Kirk, Alexander, 253, 352
Kirkenes, 340–41
Kirkpatrick, Ivone, 55, 84; Barman on,
    56; BBC and, 196; on PWE, 56; on
    radio, 89
Klop, Dirk, 49

Knight, Claude (Major), 123
Knox, Frank, 100
Koenig, Pierre-Marie (General), 278,
    281, 323; delegation of, 327;
    Eisenhower and, 314
Kogan, Norman, 224; on W. Churchill,
    388
Kola Peninsula, 341
Kommissariat, 11
Kommunist-Partisans (KO-PA), 109
Kongelige Bibliotek, 290
KO-PA. See Kommunist-Partisans
Kremlin, 349–50
Kriegel-Valrimont, Maurice, 298
Kriegsmarine, 190
Kristiansand, 339
Kroyer-Kielbert, Michael, 77, 78
Kuomintang, 26

Labour Party, 27, 29
Lagrou, Pieter, 2
Lammerding, Hans (General), 319
Landelijke Knokploegen, 147
Landelijke Organisatie voor Hulp aan
    Onderduikers, 147
Landes, Roger, 222
Langellan, George, 43
Langer, William, 101; on United
    Kingdom, 271
Laroque, Pierre, 353
Lauwers, Huub, 165, 166
Laveleye, Victor de, 37–38, 86, 408n64
Leaflets: Lockhart on, 200; PWE on,
    200; RAF missions, 198–99
Leahy, William, 40, 228
Leblicq, Armand, 41
Lebon, Marcel, 110
Lebrun, Albert, 20, 377–78
Leclerc (General Philippe de
    Hautecloque), 331
Le Creusot, 324

Leeper, Rex, 35, 53–54; on Europe, 205; on United Kingdom, 104

Léger, Alexis (pseud. Saint-John Perse), 230

Légion Belge, 116, 122–23, 131, 142

Lenin, Vladimir, 94

Lentz, Robert, 116

Léopold III (King), 7, 14, 15, 23, 390; W. Churchill on, 364

Lepage, Fernand, 62, 123, 277

Le Ray, Alain, 158

Levant, 85

Liaigre, Franck, 450n37

Liberated Italy, 250

Libération (newspaper), 110

Libération-Nord, 109

Libération-Sud, 118, 121, 144, 176, 178, 296

Libre Belgique, 111, 118

Libya, 387

Lie, Trygve, 59–60, 75, 85, 226, 393

Limoges, 15

Limousin, 377

Linge, Martin, 47

Linge Company, 60

Litlabø, 128

Livio, Louis Angelo, 142

Ljungberg, Birger, 75

Llewellyn, Richard, 227

Lockhart, Bruce, 48, 53, 70; Bracken and, 212–13; on de Gaulle, 229, 352; illness of, 223; on leaflets, 200; on PWE, 57; on Resistance movements, 175; Selborne and, 212; on Socialism, 209

Lofoten Islands, 46, 92

Logelain, Robert, 111

Loiret, 325

Loir-et-Cher, 359

Lombard Odier Darier Hentsch et Cie, 133

London, David, 273

London Committee, 77

Lord, C. J., 138

Lower Telemark, 162

Luftwaffe, 95, 141, 164, 187

Luizet, Charles, 265

Lunding, Hans (Major), 113, 115

Lussu, Emilio, 169

Lyon, 174

Lyon, David Bowes, 209–10; on OSS, 272

MacCarthy, Robert (Lieutenant), 320

MacClure, Robert, 278

Macmillan, Harold, 223; W. Churchill and, 249; on Giraud, 227; on Italy, 378

Maddox, William (Major), 273; Passy and, 276

Maghreb, 225, 232

Magri, Alessandro, 80

Maison-Carrée prison, 228

Mallet, Victor, 50–51, 237–38

Malta, 246

Manche, 357–58

Mandel, Georges, 21

Mangin, Louis-Eugène, 280

Mansion, Jacques, 61

Mantes-la-Jolie, 330

Maquis, 151, 154–62, 179–80; Brault on, 270

Marissal, Adelin (Captain), 142–43, 149

Marissal, Jean (Lieutenant-Colonel), 124

Marshall, George (General), 100

Martel, André, 445n89

Marty, André, 93

Marxism, 15

Mason, Edward, 101

Mason-MacFarlane, Noel, 250, 253, 254, 374

Massif Central, 317, 324–25

Massigli, René, 231, 312

Mauriac, François, 158
May Day, 174, 212
Mazzini Society, 82
McCaffery, Jock, 168, 260; on Italy, 376
M Committee, 289
Melkstaking, 147
Mendes, Aristides de Sousa, 17
Mendès France, Pierre, 368
Menzies, Stewart, 49, 65
Mers el-Kebir, 22, 84
MI 5, 29, 217
MI 6, 28, 49
Midgets (miniaturized receivers), 280
Mikkelsen, Max, 136
Milan, 347, 379
Milice, 185
Milices Patriotiques, 360, 361
Military mirages, 112–15, 120
Milorg, 116–17, 130, 141, 143, 163, 279;
    bases created by, 339–40
Milton Hall, 283
Milward, Alan, 385
Ministry of Defense, 4
Ministry of Economic Warfare, 54;
    Selborne at, 126–27, 159, 173
Ministry of Foreign Affairs, 450n46
Ministry of Information, 54, 80
Ministry of Justice (German), 11
Miranda de Ebro, 42
Missal, Sylvester, 219–20
Mission Militaire de Liaison
    Administrative, 353
Mockler-Ferryman, Eric, 281; on
    D-Day, 282
Moens, Jean, 63
Mollard, Amédée (Major), 112
Møller, Christmas, 78–79, 115, 234, 292,
    306; on attacks, 239–40
Molotov, Vyacheslav, 311
Monarchism, Spaak on, 207
Monnet, Jean, on Giraud, 227–28

Monod, Claude, 328
Monod, Philippe, 273–74
Monroe, James (Captain), 200
Montefiorino, Republic of, 376
Montevideo, 250
Montgomery, Bernard (General), 335,
    337, 369
Mont Mouchet, 321
Moonlight squadrons, 181–84
Morbihan, 51
Mordkovitch, Hélène, 110
Moreaux, Gilbert, 450n37
Morgan, Frederick, 270
Morton, Desmond, 188, 318, 329
Moscatelli, Cino, 380
Moscow, 5, 209
Moser, Alfons, 95
Moulin, Jean, 120–21, 155, 158, 251, 274,
    391; arrest of, 297; CNR and, 295; de
    Gaulle and, 279
Mountbatten, Louis (Admiral Lord), 283
Mouvement National Belge, 117, 138
Mouvements Unis de Résistance
    (MUR), 155
Mowinckel, Johan Ludwig, 74
Muggeridge, Malcolm, 103
Munck, Ebbe, 41, 136
Munthe, Malcolm, 259
MUR. *See* Mouvements Unis de
    Résistance
Muselier, Émile (Admiral), 76–77
Mussert, Anton, 207
Mussolini, Benito, 8, 35, 298, 372;
    authority of, 170; deposition of, 171;
    Eden on, 205; execution of, 379–80;
    fight against, 169; militarism of, 243
Muus, Flemming, 137, 187, 239, 294

Nantes, 323
Naples, Four Days of, 262–63
Nasjonal Samling (NS), 10, 11, 69

National Assembly, 122

Naujocks, Alfred, 49

Nazification, Resistance movements and, 4–5

Nazi Germany, 1, 8–9

Nazism, 107; Dalton on, 27; in Denmark, 240; destroying, 5; fighting, 287–88

Nederlandse Binnenlandse Strijdkrachten (NBS), 301, 337

Nelson, Frank, 30–31, 65, 142; resignation of, 126–27; retirement of, 223

Netherlands, 12–14; Communism in, 305–6; compulsory labor in, 146–47; Dalton and, 167; legitimacy in, 74–75, 309; manpower in, 337–38; in Operation Overlord, 282; Resistance movement in, 337–38; SHAEF and, 301; SOE in, 164–68

Networks: definition of, 108

Neuman, Henri, 137

Neutrality, 392; W. Churchill on, 203–4; of Denmark, 232–35; opposition to, 289; of United Kingdom, 364

New Deal, 122, 303

New Order, 110

Newsome, Noel F., 52, 55; on Europe, 89; on PWE, 56, 212

Newspapers, 198–201

Nicodème, Jean, 62

Nicola, Enrico de, 252

Nijmegen, 372

Nohain, Jean, 132

Nordentoft, Einar (Lieutenant-Colonel), 113

Nordling, Raoul, 330

Noreg, 379

Normandy, 266, 357, 390

North Africa, 81, 115, 182; Allies in, 170

Norway, 7, 393; Communism in, 305–6; compulsory labor in, 162–63; democratic transition of, 381–83; division of, 279; Germany and, 10–11; legitimacy in, 74–75, 309; liberation of, 348; national character in, 214; in Operation Overlord, 282; protests in, 59–60; Resistance movements in, 386; SHAEF and, 301, 339; trade unions in, 108–9; women in, 214

Norway Medical Association, 69

Norwegian Communist Party, 10–11

NS. See Nasjonal Samling

Nygaardsvold, Johan, 1, 11, 85

OAS. See Organisation de l'Armée Secrète

Oberkommando der Wehrmacht (OKW), 244

Occupied France, 64, 68

October Revolution, 92, 116, 383

Odhams Press, 202

Office of Strategic Services (OSS), 101–2, 184; air transport, 189–92; on arms, 179–80; BCRA and, 276; on Communism, 266; effectiveness of, 384–89; employment at, 216; France and, 275; D. B. Lyon on, 272; role of, 388; Roosevelt and, 362; Bradley Smith on, 209; SOE and, 273

Office of War Information (OWI), 101, 104, 209; role of, 388

Ogilvie, Frederick, 85

Øksnevad, Toralv, 85

OKW. See Oberkommando der Wehrmacht

Olav (Prince), 381

Operation Alaric, 244

Operational Training Units (OTU), 199

Operation Anklet, 44, 60

Operation Avalanche, 256

Operation Barbara, 44

Operation Barbarossa, 91, 93

Operation Biting, 129

Operation Buick, 324, 337

Operation Claymore, 44

Operation Crofter, 341

Operation Diadem, 262, 263

Operation Dynamo, 8

Operation Giant Two, 246

Operation Grassy, 324

Operation Grouse, 128

Operation Gunnerside, 129

Operation Husky, 256

Operation Konstantin, 244

Operation Market Garden, 337; failure of, 338

Operation North Pole, 165; victims of, 166. *See also Englandspiel*

Operation Overlord, 256, 266, 269–70, 277, 285; BCRA in, 316; broadcasts during, 286; Denmark in, 282; framework for, 281; Netherlands in, 282; Norway in, 282

Operation Siegfried, 244

Operation Zebra, 324, 325

Oradour-sur-Glane, 319

Orde Dienst, 116

Organisation Civile et Militaire, 298

Organisation de l'Armée Secrète (OAS), 392

Organisation de Résistance de l'Armée, 325

Organizzazione di Vigilanza e Repressione dell'Antifascismo (OVRA), 169

Orlando, Ruggero, 38

Oslo, 257

Oslo gang, 163

OSS. *See* Office of Strategic Services

Ossola, Republic of, 376

Oster, Hans (Colonel), 346

OTU. *See* Operational Training Units

Ouzoulias, Albert, 95

Over-optimism, 70

Overy, Richard, 181

OVRA. *See* Organizzazione di Vigilanza e Repressione dell'Antifascismo

OWI. *See* Office of War Information

Oxford, 211

Paillole, Paul (Colonel), 115

Palestine, 81

Pan-American Congress of Free Italians, 250

Pans, J. M., 142

Panzer Divisions, 322

Parachutes, 220, 388–89; supply of, 183; training in use of, 218; weapon drops, 264

Paris insurgency, 329–33

Parodi, Alexandre, 330

Parri, Ferruccio, 300, 346

Parti Communiste Belge, 96, 363, 367

Parti Communiste Français (PCF), 94, 96, 265; de Gaulle and, 349–50

Pas-de-Calais, 69, 315

Passy (Colonel André Dewavrin), 61, 64–65, 160; Maddox and, 276; Sporborg and, 140

Patch, Alexander, 317

Patriotic School, 64

Patterson, George, 376

Patton, George S. (General), 325, 329–30

Paulus, Friedrich, 256

Pavone, Claudio, 249

PCF. *See* Parti Communiste Français

Pearl Harbor, 100

Pellay, Jean-Marie, 257

Pellegrini, Piero, 169

People's Commissariat for Internal Affairs, 95

People's Liberation Army, 26
Perse, Saint-John pseud. (Alexis Léger), 230
Pesenti, Gustavo (General), Eden and, 244–45
Pétain, Philippe (Marshal), 4, 76, 113, 240; de Gaulle and, 207; as Prime Minister, 20, 67; resignation of, 20; Roosevelt and, 228; rule of, 225
Petersen, Vilfred, 136
Petrone, Carlo, 80–81
Philip, André, 140, 156, 231, 392–93
Philips, William, 102
Picquendar, Odilon, 112
PID. *See* Political Intelligence Department
Piedmont, 379
Pieraccini, Gaetano, 378
Pierlot, Hubert, 1, 123, 149, 204, 301–2, 363, 391; government of, 72–73, 366; leadership of, 14–15; Selborne and, 269–270; Spaak and, 18–19
Pineau, Christian, 109, 122
Piquet-Wicks, Eric, 66
Pire, Jules, 142
Plan Montagnards, 158, 321
Plan P, 113, 114
Plan Tortue, 184, 281, 316
Plan Vert, 281, 316
Plan Violet, 281, 316; launch of, 320
Playfair, Edward, 173
Pleven, René, 206, 368
Poirier, Jacques, 218
Poland, 172–73
Political Intelligence Department (PID), 35, 235, 313
Political Warfare Division, 358
Political Warfare Executive (PWE), 31, 48, 83, 302; birth of, 55–57; on Communists, 98; on Denmark, 214, 236; employment at, 216; on France,

97; Kirkpatrick on, 56; on leaflets, 200; Lockhart on, 57; Newsome on, 56, 212; objective setting, 198–99; principles of, 232; propaganda and, 195, 210; role of, 388; SOE and, 168–69
Po Plain, 341
Portal, Charles (RAF Marshal), 51
Pré, Roland, 330
Prévost, Jean, 159
Princes, The, 113–15, 136, 239, 241
Production levels, 384–85
Propaganda: BBC and, 52; in Belgium, 36, 38–39; black, 35, 38–40, 195–98; contradictions of, 69–71; Dalton and, 31–32, 47; D-Day and, 285; in Denmark, 36, 236; efficiency of, 200–1; Harris on, 199; at impasse, 104–5; PWE and, 195, 210; Ritchie on, 35–37; in Scandinavia, 388; in subversive warfare, 392; tense relations in, 52–55; United Kingdom and, 99; white, 34–36
Psychological disorders, 221–23
Psychological Warfare Division (PWD), 278
Purges, 374–75, 377–78, 379–80, 382–83
PWD. *See* Psychological Warfare Division
PWE. *See* Political Warfare Executive

Quebec Conference, 245, 308
Quirinal Palace, 375
Quisling, Vidkun, 4, 10, 69, 207

R&A. *See* Research and Analysis Branch
Radio: in Fortress Europe, 32–33; Kirkpatrick on, 89; Spaak on, 86–87
Radio Belgique, 86
Radio Brazzaville, 87

Radio-Heraus, 39

Radio Oranje, 84, 87

Radio-Patrie, 133

Radio-Rabat, 196–97

Radio Units, 35; black propaganda, 195–98; in Germany, 197–98; in United Kingdom, 197

RAF. See Royal Air Force

Railroads, 257; in Denmark, 338–39

Rake, Denis, 138

Rasella, via, attack on, 374–75

Rauscher, André (Lieutenant), 67

Rebecca radar, 186–87

Reber, Samuel, 252

Red Army, 5, 91, 104, 305; successes of, 99

Redoubts, Frenay on, 154

Red Peril, 266

Refusants, 161

Regina Coeli prison, 375

Reichkommisar, 11

Reign of Terror (1793), 378

Reimers, Hans Gottfried, 95

Remembrance, 2–3, 393–94

Rémy. See Renault, Gilbert

Renault, Gilbert (Rémy), 61–62

Renthe-Fink, Cecil von, 22–23

Republicans, 100, 209–10

Réquin, Édouard (General), 112

Research and Analysis Branch (R&A), 101; role of, 210

Resistance movements, 2; action of, 176–77; arming, 179–80; in Belgium, 336; Communists and, 93; definition of, 108; in Denmark, 257–58, 282; development of, 108; effectiveness of, 384–89; in France, 388; Frenay on, 178; growth of, 4; ingratitude toward, 393–94; internal, 267; in Italy, 260–61, 347–48; legacy of, 391–93; liberation and, 387–88;

Lockhart on, 175; moral victories of, 386–87; Nazification and, 4–5; in Netherlands, 337–38; in Norway, 386; Pan-European, 3–6; RAF and, 181; in Scandinavia, 338–41; STO and, 160–61; typology of, 389–91; Vernant on, 178

Restatification, 372

Revanche, 112

Reventlow, Ernst zu, 233

Revers, Georges (General), 112

Revue de la Presse libre, 201

Reynaud, Paul, 7; resignation of, 20

Rhone Valley, 320

Ribbentrop, Joachim von, 237

Ribière, Henri, 330

Richard, Raoul, 406n8

Ridderhof, George, 165

Riepe, John Held (Colonel), 346

Rimini, 341

Ringen, 109, 289

Riols, Noreen, 218

Risorgimento, 38

Ritchie, Douglas, 32, 70, 89; on propaganda, 35–37

Road blocks, 342

Roatta, Mario, 375

Rochat, Pierre, 355

Role of Vitamins in the Fight Against Malnutrition, The, 201

Rolin, Henri, 74, 122–23

Rol-Tanguy, Henri, 328, 332

Romania, 94

Romans-Petit, Henri, 322

Rome, 79, 246, 379; conquering, 262; fall of, 341

Rome Protocols, 300

Romijn, Peter, 372

Rommel, Erwin (Marshal), 25

Ronin, Georges (Colonel), 67

Rooks, Lowell (General), 179

Roosevelt, Franklin, 8–9, 100, 225, 361; W. Churchill and, 353; de Gaulle and, 228, 272, 360; on France, 354, 388; Giraud and, 228; OSS and, 362; Pétain and, 228; Wilhelmina and, 369–70

Roseberry, Cecil (Lieutenant-Colonel), 171, 259–60, 299

Rosselli, Carlo, 169

Rottbøll, Christian (Captain), 135

Royal Air Force (RAF), 8, 25, 38, 51, 98, 127, 166; air offensives of, 258; Gerbrandy on, 175; leaflet missions, 198–99; Resistance movements and, 181; SOE on, 258; weapon drops, 264

Royal Navy, 25, 218

Royal Question, 364–65

Ruanda-Urundi, 17

Russian Revolutions, 27

Russo-Finnish War, 92

SA. *See* Secret armies

Saint-Amand-Montrond, 322

Saint-Julien-en-Vercors, 378

Saint Pierre and Miquelon, 229

Salerno turn, 262

Salmon, Robert, 110

Salò, Republic of, 244, 298, 375; atrocities of, 343–44

Salvemini, Gaetano, 80, 82, 169

Samuel, Simon, 157

Sant, François van't, 63

Sant'Anna di Stazzema, 344

Sardian Action Party, 169

Sardinia, 221

Sargent, Orme, 299–300

Sauckel, Fritz, 146, 160

Scandinavia, 1, 50; Allies in, 340; Germany and, 92; liberation of, 348; propaganda in, 388; purges in, 382–83; Resistance movement in, 338–41

SCAO. *See* Senior civil affairs officer

Scavenius, Erik, 237, 295; resignation of, 242

Schalburg Korps, 291

Schellenberg, Walter, 49

Schermerhorn, Willem, 371

Scheyven, Raymond, 149–50

Schneider plant, 324

Schryver, August de, 74

Schumann, Maurice, 84, 87

Schwebel, Ernst, 369–70

Scoccimarro, Mauro, 306, 375

Sea Dog, 190

Sea Wolf, 190

Second Boer War, 26

Secret armies (SA), 143; Delestraint commanding, 144; establishment of, 141–42

Secret Intelligence (SI), 101

Secret Intelligence Service (SIS), 28, 41, 173; W. Churchill and, 50; SOE and, 49–50

Seine-et-Oise, 328

Selborne, Rounder Palmer (Lord), 182, 183, 188, 211, 215; on Darlan, 227; Lockhart and, 212; at Ministry of Economic Warfare, 126–27, 159, 173; on partisans, 345; Pierlot and, 269–70; on SHAEF, 388

Senior civil affairs officer (SCAO), 355

September Directive, 340

Service de Renseignements (SR), 61

Service des Opérations Aériennes et Maritimes, 156

Service du Travail Obligatoire (STO), 148; fight against, 161; France on, 153–157; Resistance movement and, 160–61

Service National Maquis, 156

Servizio Informazione Militare (SIM), 169

Sessia Valley, 380

Sette Luci Bridge, 261
Seyss-Inquart, Arthur, 13, 369–70
SFHQ. *See* Special Forces Headquarters
Sforza, Carlo, 250, 254–55, 373
SHAEF. *See* Supreme Headquarters, Allied Expeditionary Force
Shepardson, Whitney, 272
Sherwood, Robert E., 100
Shetland Bus, 44, 45, 192
Shoop, Max, 273
SI. *See* Secret Intelligence
Sicé, Adolphe, 76
Sicily, 243, 256
Sikorski, Wladyslaw, 172
Silent Killing, 218
SIM. *See* Servizio Informazione Militare
Sinn Fein, 26
SIS. *See* Secret Intelligence Service
Six, Pieter Jacob, 116
Skjønsberg, Tor, 118
Skorzeny, Otto, 244
Sluyser, Meyer, 39
Smith, Bradley, on OSS, 209
Smith, Rae, 278
SO 1, 53, 71
SO 2, 53, 64
Social Democrats, 78, 289, 303–5
Social Insurance and Allied Services, 211
Socialism, 94–95; Lockhart on, 209
Socialist Party, 157
Social reform, 303–5, 376–77
Social Welfare Office, 150
Socrate, 149–53, 163, 177
SOE. *See* Special Operations Executive
SOE in France (Foot), 393
Sogno, Edgardo, 262
Solari, Giuseppe, 379
Somer, Jan Marginus, 64
Somerville, James (Admiral), 22
Somerville-Smith, Herbert, 205–6
Sønsteby, Gunnar, 163

South Africa, 205
Soviet Union, 25; Badoglio and, 253; CFLN and, 312; Council of Freedom and, 290; war entry, 91–96, 105–6
Spaak, Paul-Henri, 16, 72, 124, 288, 392–93; Dalton and, 58–59; on monarchism, 207; Pierlot and, 18–19; on radio, 86–87
Spanish Civil War, 26, 119
Spanish Irregulars, 26
Spears, Edward, 68
Special Forces Headquarters (SFHQ), 277, 326
Special Operations Executive (SOE), 5, 40, 57–58, 123; Abwehr and, 165–66; action and organization, 175–77; air transport, 189–92; on arms, 179–80; BBC and, 285–86; BCRA and, 281, 391; Belgian, 42, 66, 131, 135–38; birth of, 28–30; branches of, 31; on Communism, 266; cooperation with, 65–66; Council of Freedom and, 289–90; W. Churchill and, 50; Dalton at, 51–52; de Gaulle and, 43, 207–8; in Denmark, 135–38, 214, 239; doctrine of action, 30–34; Donovan on, 273; effectiveness of, 384–89; employment at, 215–16; in France, 42–43, 185–86, 279–80; goals of, 210–11; Gubbins on, 124, 172; heads of, 30–31; infiltration of, 173; on Italy, 41, 168–72, 214–15, militarization of, 127; in Netherlands, 164–68; OSS and, 273; paths of action for, 40–47; policy of, 60–65; PWE and, 168–69; on RAF, 258; Resistance Groups, 268; RF Section, 139–41; role of, 388; scaling back of, 106; short-term goals of, 40; SIS and, 49–50; staff of, 210; support of, 129–32; threats to, 172–74; Week of the Rat, 258

Special Project Operations Center, 277

Speer, Albert, 161

S-Phone, 186–87

Spina, Raphaël, 161

Spooner, Frank (Lieutenant-Colonel), 283

Sporborg, Harry, 140

Sporre, Cornelis, 40, 165

SR. *See* Service de Renseignements

Stafford, David, 30

Stalin, Joseph, 92, 312; on Italy, 349–50

Stalingrad, 177, 238, 256, 387

Stalinism, 105

Standardization, 182–84

Starheim, Odd, 44

Starvation, 369–70

State Department, 4

Stauning, Thorvald, 78, 92

Stawell, William (General), 299

Stephenson, William, 102

Stereotypes, 213–15

Stevens, J. M. (Lieutenant-Colonel), 342

Stevens, John (Colonel), 379

Stevens, Richard (Major), 49

Stirlings, 182

STO. *See* Service du Travail Obligatoire

Stockholm, 289

Stone, Ellery (Admiral), 374

Strikes, labor, 69, 93; in Belgium, 367–68; in Denmark, 238–39, 241, 291; in France, 268–69, 330, 332; in Italy, 261, 347, 374; in Netherlands, 147, 174–75, 338

Struye, Paul, 111

Sturzo, Luigi, 80

Subversive warfare, 26–28; airborne missions, 188, 258; of Allies, 345; military capacity in, 265–66; propaganda in, 392

Sugden, Cecil (General), 260

Sun (newspaper), 202

Sunde, Arne, 75

Súñer, Ramón Serrano, 9

Supreme Headquarters, Allied Expeditionary Force (SHAEF), 259, 270; on Council of Freedom, 292–93; Eisenhower at, 281; on FFI, 359; on FTP, 359; influence of, 282; leadership of, 326; on liberation, 348; Netherlands and, 301; Norway and, 301, 339; Selborne on, 388

Sûreté de l'État, 63, 65–66, 123, 131, 276

Susloparov, Ivan (General), 370

Sutton, Nigel, 134

Sweden, 50, 204

Sweet-Escott, Bickham, 30–31, 103, 104; on Free France, 193

Switzerland, 273–77; Hambro on, 275–76

Taconis, Thijs, 165

Tactical Airforces, 342

Tangmere, 42–43

Taxes, 151

Taylor, Maxwell (General), 246

Tedder, Arthur (Marshal), 200

Tehran Conference, 160

Terboven, Josef, 10, 11, 237

Terfve, Jean, 367

Terrorism, 4, 98

Third Reich, 1

Third Republic, 119

Third Shock Company, 265

Thomas, Brinley, 236, 311

Thomas, Ivor, 250

Thompson, J. Walter, 55

Thorez, Maurice, 93, 359

Thorne, Andrew (General), 381

Ticino, 168

Tillon, Charles, 323

Tirpitz, 92

Tito, Josip Broz, 193

Togliatti, Palmiro, 253, 380; Badoglio and, 307
Torp, Oscar, 130
Toulouse, 319, 358
Tournai, 142
Toussaint, Albert, 137–38
Trade unions, 292; Communism and, 109; in Denmark, 290; in Norway, 108–9
Trellu, Daniel, 157
Triboulet, Raymond, 355
Tromme, Emile, 41
Tromsø, 10
Trondheim, 92
Trotobas, Michael, 43, 139
Tulle, 319
Turnbull, Ronald, 50, 114, 290
Tuscany, 347
Tybalt, 150, 305

Ubbink, Ben, 166
U-boats, 137, 177
Ugeux, William, 111, 124, 277
Ultra system, 49
Umberto II (Prince), 252–53
Underground press, 110–12
United Kingdom, 9, 96–99, 183; aid from, 394; de Gaulle on, 206, 350–51; Denmark and, 77–78, 234; emigration to, 217; France and, 160; Free France and, 68; grievances, 87–90; Italy and, 79–83, 214; Langer on, 271; Leeper on, 104; Mediterranean and, 247–48; neutrality of, 364; partisans armed by, 344; propaganda and, 99; Radio Units in, 197
United Nations, 392–93
United Nations Relief and Rehabilitation Administration (UNRRA), 373

United States: aid from, 394; Mediterranean and, 247–48; war entry, 100–2
UNRRA. See United Nations Relief and Rehabilitation Administration

Valmy, 118
Van den Broek, Johannes, 371
Van den Stricht, Paul Robert (Lieutenant-Colonel), 276
Van der Meersch, Walter Ganshof, 125
Vandermies, Pierre, 63
Van Kleffens, Eelco, 23
Van Rhijn Commission, 304
Van Roey, Joseph-Ernest (Archbishop), 42, 147
Van Zeeland, Paul, 74, 304
Vassieux, 378
V Campaign, 37–38; suspension of, 70
V.E. Day, 345
Vemork factories, 176–77, 258
Vercors, Republic of, 377–78
Vercors Massif, 321–22
Vergnon, Gilles, 378
Verhoeyen, Étienne, 152
Vernant, Jean-Pierre, 178
Verneau, Jean-Édouard, 113
Viannay, Philippe, 110, 112
Vichyist regime, 68, 148, 227–28, 295; de Gaulle and, 312
Victor Emmanuel III (King), 245–46, 248, 252, 254, 390, 391; authority of, 261
Viénot, Pierre, 312
Vigra, 190
Vilain, Jules, 117
Villon, Pierre, 298
Vistel, Alban, 288
Vita, 44, 190
Voix des Belges, La, 117
Volontari per la Libertà, 298
Vomécourt, Pierre de, 138

Wake, Nancy, 217
Warburg, James, 101
Ward, J. G., 308
Warsaw, 333
Waterlow's Press, 202
Week of the Rat, 258
Wehrmacht, 2, 8, 115
Wellington bombers, 200
Wells, H. G., 228
Wendelen, André, 137, 149
Weygand, Maxime (General), 22, 67
Whaddon Hall, 49
What a Young Lady Needs to Know, 201
Whitehall, 50–52, 68, 205
White propaganda, 34–35, 36
Wiesenthal, Simon, 166
Wilhelmina (Queen), 12, 14, 23, 84, 302, 309, 390; Roosevelt and, 369–70

Wilkinson, Edouard, 138
Wilkinson, John, 347
Wilson, Henry Maitland, 224, 300, 320
Winkel, P. (Captain), 113
Winkelman, Henri, 7
Winterbotham, Frederick, 67
Woburn Abbey, 53
Wolters, Jo, 167–68
World War I, 26–27, 34, 59, 157, 200, 307

X2. *See* Counter-intelligence
XU, 116

Yugoslavia, 192, 245

Zeller, André (Colonel), 112, 317
Zéro, 111, 124
Zinoviev, Grigory, 29

Sylviane Agacinski, *Parity of the Sexes*

Michel Pastoureau, *The Devil's Cloth: A History of Stripes and Striped Fabric*

Alain Cabantous, *Blasphemy: Impious Speech in the West from the Seventeenth to the Nineteenth Century*

Julia Kristeva, *The Sense and Non-Sense of Revolt: The Powers and Limits of Psychoanalysis*

Kelly Oliver, *The Portable Kristeva*

Gilles Deleuze, *Dialogues II*

Catherine Clément and Julia Kristeva, *The Feminine and the Sacred*

Sylviane Agacinski, *Time Passing: Modernity and Nostalgia*

Luce Irigaray, *Between East and West: From Singularity to Community*

Julia Kristeva, *Hannah Arendt*

Julia Kristeva, *Intimate Revolt: The Powers and Limits of Psychoanalysis*, vol. 2

Elisabeth Roudinesco, *Why Psychoanalysis?*

Régis Debray, *Transmitting Culture*

Steve Redhead, ed., *The Paul Virilio Reader*

Claudia Benthien, *Skin: On the Cultural Border Between Self and the World*

Julia Kristeva, *Melanie Klein*

Roland Barthes, *The Neutral: Lecture Course at the Collège de France (1977–1978)*

Hélène Cixous, *Portrait of Jacques Derrida as a Young Jewish Saint*

Theodor W. Adorno, *Critical Models: Interventions and Catchwords*

Julia Kristeva, *Colette*

Gianni Vattimo, *Dialogue with Nietzsche*

Emmanuel Todd, *After the Empire: The Breakdown of the American Order*

Gianni Vattimo, *Nihilism and Emancipation: Ethics, Politics, and Law*

Hélène Cixous, *Dream I Tell You*

Steve Redhead, *The Jean Baudrillard Reader*

Jean Starobinski, *Enchantment: The Seductress in Opera*

Jacques Derrida, *Geneses, Genealogies, Genres, and Genius: The Secrets of the Archive*

Hélène Cixous, *White Ink: Interviews on Sex, Text, and Politics*

Marta Segarra, ed., *The Portable Cixous*

François Dosse, *Gilles Deleuze and Félix Guattari: Intersecting Lives*

Julia Kristeva, *This Incredible Need to Believe*

François Noudelmann, *The Philosopher's Touch: Sartre, Nietzsche, and Barthes at the Piano*

Antoine de Baecque, *Camera Historica: The Century in Cinema*

Julia Kristeva, *Hatred and Forgiveness*

Roland Barthes, *How to Live Together: Novelistic Simulations of Some Everyday Spaces*

Jean-Louis Flandrin and Massimo Montanari, *Food: A Culinary History*

Georges Vigarello, *The Metamorphoses of Fat: A History of Obesity*

Julia Kristeva, *The Severed Head: Capital Visions*

Eelco Runia, *Moved by the Past: Discontinuity and Historical Mutation*

François Hartog, *Regimes of Historicity: Presentism and Experiences of Time*

Jacques Le Goff, *Must We Divide History Into Periods?*

Claude Lévi-Strauss, *We Are All Cannibals: And Other Essays*

Marc Augé, *Everyone Dies Young: Time Without Age*

Roland Barthes: *Album: Unpublished Correspondence and Texts*

Étienne Balibar, *Secularism and Cosmopolitanism: Critical Hypotheses on Religion and Politics*

Dominique Kalifa, *Vice, Crime, and Poverty: How the Western Imagination Invented the Underworld*